KU-567-760

SECOND EDITION

HEORY AND PRACTICE OF
EADERSHIP ROGER GILL

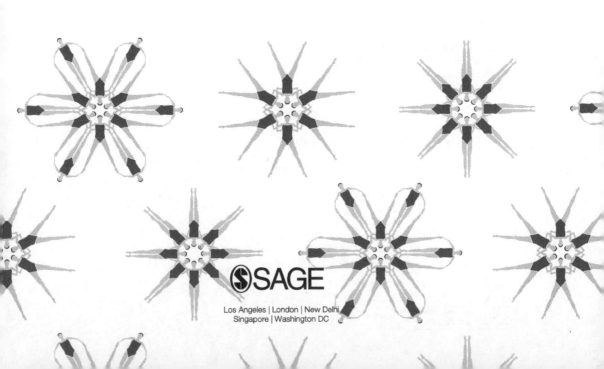

⑤SAGE

Los Angeles | London | New Delhi
Singapore | Washington DC

© Roger Gill 2011

First edition published 2006. Reprinted 2006, 2008 (twice), 2009, 2010

This edition published 2011

Reprinted 2013

Apart from any fair dealing for the purposes of research or private study, or criticism or review, as permitted under the Copyright, Designs and Patents Act, 1988, this publication may be reproduced, stored or transmitted in any form, or by any means, only with the prior permission in writing of the publishers, or in the case of reprographic reproduction, in accordance with the terms of licences issued by the Copyright Licensing Agency. Enquiries concerning reproduction outside those terms should be sent to the publishers.

All material on the accompanying website can be printed off and photocopied by the purchaser/user of the book. The web material itself may not be reproduced in its entirety for use by others without prior written permission from SAGE. The web material may not be distributed or sold separately from the book without the prior written permission of SAGE. Should anyone wish to use the materials from the website for conference purposes, they would require separate permission from us. All material is © Roger Gill, 2011

SAGE Publications Ltd
1 Oliver's Yard
55 City Road
London EC1Y 1SP

SAGE Publications Inc.
2455 Teller Road
Thousand Oaks, California 91320

SAGE Publications India Pvt Ltd
B 1/I 1 Mohan Cooperative Industrial Area
Mathura Road
New Delhi 110 044

SAGE Publications Asia-Pacific Pte Ltd
3 Church Street
#10-04 Samsung Hub
Singapore 049483

BLACKBURN COLLEGE LIBRARY	
BB 67115	
Askews & Holts	08-Nov-2017
UCL658.4092 GIL	

Library of Congress Control Number: 2011929091

British Library Cataloguing in Publication data

A catalogue record for this book is available from the British Library

ISBN 978-1-84920-023-3
ISBN 978-1-84920-024-0 (pbk)

Typeset by C&M Digitals (P) Ltd, Chennai, India
Printed and bound in Great Britain by CPI Group (UK) Ltd, Croydon, CR0 4YY
Printed on paper from sustainable resources

MIX
Paper from
responsible sources
FSC
www.fsc.org   FSC® C013604

Summary of Contents

Contents

List of Tables

List of Figures

List of Case Examples, Case Studies and Exercises

About the Author

Roger Gill is Visiting Professor of Leadership Studies at Durham Business School, Durham University in the UK, and an independent consultant on leadership and leadership development. He founded the Research Centre for Leadership Studies – the UK's first such centre – at the Leadership Trust in Ross-on-Wye, Herefordshire, England, and he was its Director for nine years. He is also founder and former Programme Director of the MBA in Leadership Studies – the UK's first such programme – run jointly by the Leadership Trust and the University of Strathclyde Business School.

Roger was formerly Professor of Business Administration and Director of Executive Development Programmes at Strathclyde, an assistant professor of OB & HRM at the State University of New York at Binghamton in the USA, and a lecturer in psychology at the University of Bradford School of Management in the UK. He has taught leadership courses on MBA programmes at several well-known business schools in the UK, Switzerland, Germany, Southeast Asia and the Gulf region. He also conducts leadership seminars and consultancy and leadership development programmes and gives talks and speeches on leadership for corporate clients and university business schools. He has held management positions in HRM in several industries in the UK and has many years' experience in management consulting, both full-time and part-time, in the UK, USA, Gulf region and Far East. He ran his own HRM consulting and management training consultancy for eight years in Singapore.

Roger is a Chartered Psychologist and a graduate of the Universities of Oxford, Liverpool and Bradford. In 2010 he was honoured with a Fellowship of the Leadership Trust Foundation in recognition of his contribution to the field of leadership and leadership development.

Preface

This book presents a review of the nature and importance of leadership and the major theories that attempt to explain it. In working for some seven years on the first edition published in 2006, I discovered several recurrent themes and associated practices of leadership in the extant literature that appeared to me to describe it well. My work since then has only confirmed this.

For this second edition, therefore, I have updated my review of the leadership literature and refined the model of core leadership themes and practices, incorporating input from many helpful colleagues and students. For example, I have split the original theme and practice of vision and mission/purpose into two separate ones as a result of recent literature on them, and they now each have a dedicated chapter. So there are now six core leadership themes and practices. I have also relabelled the theme and practice concerned with influence, motivation and inspiration as 'engagement' in line with current (and more economical) terminology, though its meaning and substance remain the same. The original chapter on leadership development has been greatly enlarged, with additional material on assessment of leadership competency and development needs. Some chapters have new material that replaces some that is dated. And I have replaced the original final chapter with a short one on leadership brand, which hopefully provides a fitting conclusion to the book. I have also restructured the book in order for it to be better organized and improved its readability by replacing in-text references with chapter endnotes.

Leadership has been very commonly perceived by scholars, students and practitioners alike as being largely about *influence*. The theories and practices that have resulted from this conception, I believe, have left us with piecemeal theories that each address only one specific aspect of leadership and wanting in our quest for a more general theory of leadership. I believe we need to go back to basics – to the original meaning of the word – in our thinking about leadership: that leadership is about *showing the way*. This definition underpins the model that is made up of six core leadership themes and practices.

These core themes and practices encompass: vision, purpose, values, strategy, empowerment and engagement. The model aims to make a useful contribution to leadership thought and practice by drawing on and integrating the several hitherto disparate strands of leadership thinking and research – the cognitive, emotional, social, cultural, spiritual, moral and behavioural aspects of leadership that I call 'multiple intelligences' of leadership. The model aims to be useful to three groups of people: those who serve in – or aspire to – leadership roles in organizations; those who work as specialists in leadership development; and those who study, research or 'teach' leadership.

The words of Michel de Montaigne, the sixteenth-century French essayist, aptly capture both my intentions and my feelings:

> **It could be said of me that in this book I have only made up a bunch of other men's flowers, providing of my own the string that ties them together.**[1]

I hope my model of six core themes and practices of leadership provides the string to tie together the disparate variety of leadership concepts, theories and practices that make up the flower arrangement. And I hope the book is also an engaging and enjoyable read.

Acknowledgements

Many people have helped, influenced and inspired me in researching and writing this book and I would like to acknowledge who they are and how they did so.

The Leadership Trust and its former CEO, Paul K. Winter, for kind permission to use proprietary leadership development models and material previously published by the Trust and for giving me the opportunity while I worked at the Trust from 1997 to 2005 to research my ideas and put them into practice in leadership development programmes with the Trust's client organizations.

Emeritus Professor Kees Van der Heijden, formerly at the University of Strathclyde and the University of Nijrenrode in the Netherlands, who first drew to my attention the limitations of current models of transformational leadership in respect of the importance of strategy and encouraged me to develop my new model.

Wilfred H. Gill, my father and honorary 'research assistant' for the first edition, for assiduously supplying me with a constant stream of corporate annual reports and newspaper and magazine articles on leadership.

For permission to use copyright material:

The Psychologist magazine, the British Psychological Society

The Chartered Institute of Personnel and Development (www.cipd.co.uk)

United Feature Syndicate Inc. (for the Scott Adams quotation)

Professor John Adair, formerly of the Royal Military Academy, Sandhurst, the University of Exeter and the University of Surrey

The Royal Navy and Rachel Tate, HR Research Manager, Directorate of Naval Personnel Strategy

Durham University and the Vice Chancellor, Professor Chris Higgins

Emeritus Professor Norman F. Dixon, University College London

Professor Beverly Alimo-Metcalfe, Chief Executive, Real World Group Limited, Leeds, and Professor of Leadership, University of Bradford School of Management

David Bosdet, Editor, *management-issues.com*

MT (Management Today) magazine

John Smythe of the consultancy Engage for Change and FT.com (*Financial Times*)

Jo Owen and BNET UK (CBS Interactive Inc.)

For helpful critical comments and suggestions:

Emeritus Professor Gerry Randell, University of Bradford School of Management

Professor Timothy Clark, Durham Business School, Durham University, who exercised 'shared leadership' with me in co-teaching the leadership module in Durham's MBA programme

Ian C. Buchanan, former Chairman, Asia-Pacific Region, Booz & Co., management consultants

Terry Deane, formerly a course director at the Leadership Trust

Tony Johnston, GreyRidge Software Ltd, Newcastle upon Tyne

My doctoral and MBA students at Durham University, the University of Strathclyde, the University of Bradford, TiasNimbas Business School, Cranfield University, and the Queen's University of Belfast for their ideas and frequent original insights into leadership; and participants in the management and leadership seminars and workshops I have conducted and in conferences on leadership over the years for their interesting and helpful ideas and material on leadership; in particular Lt Cdr Matthew Offord RN, my student first at the University of Strathclyde (MBA) and later at Durham University (DBA) for his help in obtaining material for the book.

Kiren Shoman, Alan Maloney, Natalie Aguilera, Rachel Eley, Kirsty Smy and Ruth Stitt at SAGE Publications for their enthusiasm for this book and for their constant encouragement, helpful suggestions and patience while I was writing it.

Pat, who became my wife during the preparation of this book and encouraged me to write it faster than might otherwise have been the case, and especially for reading and commenting very thoroughly and helpfully on the draft manuscript.

If any attributions in this book are wrong, or if I have inadvertently failed to acknowledge any sources, suggestions or help, I apologize.

Companion Website

Be sure to visit the companion website at **www.sagepub.co.uk/gill** to find a range of teaching and learning materials for both lecturers and students, including the following:

For lecturers:

- **Instructor's manual:** Contains overviews of every chapter, teaching notes and suggested examination questions for each chapter.
- **PowerPoint slides:** PowerPoint slides for each chapter for use in class are also provided. These slides can be edited by instructors to suit teaching styles and needs.
- **Links to additional case studies:** Links to relevant case studies for each chapter provide lecturers with additional resources.

For students:

- **Full-text journal articles:** Full access to selected SAGE journal articles related to each chapter, providing students with a deeper understanding of the topics in each chapter.
- **Links to relevant websites:** Direct links to websites for relevant key leadership journals and leadership centres.

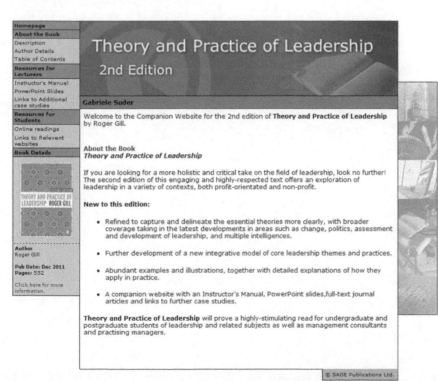

1 Introduction: The Nature and Importance of Leadership

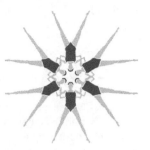

Everyone says there's a lack of leadership in the world these days. I think we should all be thankful, because the only reason for leadership is to convince people to do things that are either dangerous (like invading another country) or stupid ([like] working extra hard without extra pay).

Obviously you don't need any leadership to lead you to, for example, eat a warm cookie. But you need a lot of leadership to convince you to march through a desert and shoot strangers. Generally speaking, whenever there is leadership, there's lots of hollering and very few warm cookies. Let's enjoy the lack of leadership while we have it.

Scott Adams, *Don't Step in the Leadership*[1]

OVERVIEW

- In recent times the notion of leadership has increasingly met with cynicism and become a 'hot topic' for debate. Despite a burgeoning but fragmented literature, there is no agreed paradigm so far for the study and practice of leadership.
- This lack of consensus on what leadership is together with a spate of high-profile failures due to poor or absent 'leadership' have proven to be contributory factors towards the cynicism that has since developed.
- Yet 'good' leadership – that is both effective and moral – has nevertheless been long recognized as crucial to human achievement and well-being.
- This chapter considers the multiplicity of definitions of leadership and proposes an integrative and over-arching definition: *leadership is showing the way and helping or inducing others to pursue it.*
- Leadership is characterized by six core themes and their associated practices: envisioning a desirable future, promoting a clear purpose or mission, supportive values, intelligent strategies, and empowering and engaging all those concerned.
- Leadership effectiveness can be evaluated either in terms of behaviour – the extent to which a leader helps or induces others to pursue a given way and purpose or mission – or in terms of outcomes – the extent to which a given desired future becomes a reality as a result of a leader's behaviour. This means that there are many different possible measures of leadership according to the nature of the envisioned future, purpose and context in which leadership takes place.

(Continued)

(Continued)

- One fruitful approach to understanding leadership is to study followership: what followers expect of leaders and how leaders can satisfy these expectations.
- The chapter compares and contrasts concepts of management and leadership: we manage things and processes, but we lead people.
- Leadership is about showing the way – from where we are now to a desired place or state. Leadership, therefore, is about change and so we must explore the leadership of change.
- The past emphasis on individual leadership and command-and-control has been superseded by an emphasis today on shared and distributed leadership and collective leadership capacity. An organization's collective leadership capacity is the basis for a distinctive leadership 'brand' and its ability to change.

What is Leadership?[2]

Every week, probably even every day, we can read a fresh new article or book that says: 'Effective leadership is the key to success' – defined in terms of organizational and managerial effectiveness, financial results, or people's morale and happiness, or all of these. When I entered 'leadership' into Google on 24 February 2011, I was presented with 'about 176,000,000' entries. I then focused my curiosity and entered 'definition of leadership'. In 0.4 of a second I was presented with a mere 59,100,000 suggestions.

Now I cannot claim that this introductory section in Chapter 1 is a comprehensive summary of the extant literature on the question 'What is leadership?' But without reviewing all of it (to say the least), this is my humble attempt. After all, according to one Malaysian writer, theorizing about leadership is 'great fun, hugely indulgent and largely useless' (doing it instead, he says, is much more worthwhile).[3] Nevertheless, my aim in the first part of this chapter is unapologetically to indulge in what hopefully is an interesting – if not fun – account of how concepts and definitions of leadership agree and differ and the problems associated with this lack of consensus. I then attempt a synthesis that reflects the essence of the etymology of the term that I hope will be defensible to scholars and useful to practitioners.

How Concepts and Definitions of Leadership Agree and Differ: A Problem that Needs Resolving

Walter Friedman describes some of the earliest references to leadership in American newspapers and books. He says, 'The term "business leadership" appeared in U.S. newspapers only occasionally during [Andrew] Carnegie's heyday'[4] (b.1835, d.1919). Popular books on leadership started to appear from 1912 onwards. The British Academy of Management says: 'The subject of leadership has created a plethora of publications, research and debate and has become a key issue in both the public and private sectors'.[5] Today, leadership is a hot topic for debate.

The burgeoning leadership literature ranges from highly cerebral academic research studies and scholarly treatises that few if any actual leaders will read to idiosyncratic personal prescriptions by self-acclaimed paragons of virtuous leadership of how to be an outstanding leader at the 'popular' end of the spectrum. Some of the contributions to the leadership literature are both fictional and speculative:

> ... [divining] the dubious leadership acumen of either long-dead military leaders [e.g. Attila the Hun] of questionable reputation or fictional characters [such as Winnie the Pooh and Captain Picard of Star Trek] in order to proffer it to the masses as pearls of wisdom.[6]

John Roulet, a management consultant in the United States, feels that there is a surfeit of books, articles and discussion about leadership, with 'much competing and confusing information in the public domain' and that 'today's leaders seem to be getting worse instead of better'.[7] And Joel Kurtzman says that '... a consensus has so far failed to emerge with respect to what leadership is, how leaders develop, and – perhaps most important – how to become a more effective leader'.[8]

One of the problems with leadership studies, Robert Terry says, is that the subject has 'suffered from a lack of a common language'.[9] Victor Vroom of Yale University states, '... like many popular terms, [leadership] has been used in many different ways'.[10] Perhaps 'leadership' is a 'Humpty Dumpty' word:

> When I use a word, Humpty Dumpty said, in a rather scornful tone, it means just what I choose it to mean – neither more nor less. The question is, said Alice, whether you can make words mean so many different things. The question is, said Humpty Dumpty, which is to be master – that's all.[11]

Bruce Winston and Kathleen Patterson, addressing the problem of the lack of consensus on what leadership is, suggest, as I do, that the problem arises from studying the parts of leadership rather than the whole.[12] This is what I mean when I suggest that those theories which are well known to academics and practitioners alike – such as action-centred leadership, the managerial (leadership) grid, situational leadership and transformational/transactional leadership (which we discuss in Chapter 3 on leadership theories) – are each individual pieces in the jigsaw puzzle that is leadership. Winston and his team at Regent University carried out an extensive review of the leadership literature and produced 92 categories made up of over 1,000 constructs or statements relating to leadership. They distilled these into the following 'integrative definition of leadership':

> A leader is one or more people who selects, equips, trains, and influences one or more follower(s) who have diverse gifts, abilities, and skills and focuses the follower(s) to the organization's mission and objectives causing the follower(s) to willingly and enthusiastically expend spiritual, emotional, and physical energy in a concerted coordinated effort to achieve the organizational mission and objectives.

The definition then proceeds to describe *how* leaders do this. However this definition, while a heroic effort, is contentious in several ways. It has a top-down, directive tone that might be appropriate in some organizational and national cultures (see our discussion of culture in Chapter 6 on leadership and values), but not as a universal definition. For example, a leader might well 'focus' a follower – or somebody else who may not be a 'follower' as such – but the intention might be to *help* that person to identify, clarify, pursue or fulfil his or her personal 'mission' or objectives.

The definition also refers to 'gifts, abilities, and skills' – a confusing admixture. Elaborated in a later explanation, with a Christian biblical reference to Chapter 12 in *Romans*, it is still not made clear what these (seven) 'gifts' – 'driving characteristics of the individual' – are and how they are different from, and perhaps supplementary or complementary to, abilities or skills. Indeed their 'natural abilities', what people can do easily and well, that people are born with and which mature 'enough to be defined and measured' by the age of 14 years, and skills – 'function-related knowledge and physical skills that contribute to the success and efficiency in completing tasks' – are ill-defined, confusing and highly contentious.

How can one scientifically investigate something that is beset by its multiplicity of definitions? Indeed the very existence of 'leadership' as an observable phenomenon in daily life in organizations has been questioned by some scholars, such as Mats Alvesson and Stefan Sveningsson.[13] They say: 'Our general impression is that it is difficult to say anything of the possible existence of leadership in the great majority of organizations and management situations.' For example, they found the accounts that managers in a research-and-development company gave of leadership to be ambiguous, incoherent and often contradictory.

Simon Kelly, correctly in my opinion, questions whether the problem that Alvesson and Sveningsson see is 'a consequence of the research methods being used to make leadership visible and researchable in the first place'.[14] And one problem here is interpretation: the 'meaning of a word [in our case "leadership"]', Louis Pondy says, 'is the set of ways in which it is used'.[15] This requires further discussion that is beyond the scope of this book but which Kelly's article might assist.

Even the UK's Investors-in-People institution (IIP) does not explicitly define leadership. It says: 'Leadership and management are almost impossible to define because they mean different things to every organisation.'[16] Manfred Kets de Vries of INSEAD puts it more strongly:

> When we plunge into the organisational literature on leadership, we quickly become lost in a labyrinth: there are endless definitions, countless articles and never-ending polemics. As far as leadership studies go, it seems that more and more has been studied about less and less, to end up ironically with a group of researchers who studies everything about nothing. It prompted one wit to say recently that reading the current world literature on leadership is rather like going through the Parisian telephone directory while trying to read it in Chinese![17]

Warren Bennis, noted writer and leadership scholar, observes that: 'Leadership is what the French call a portmanteau field – a field with many different variables.'[18] He says there is no agreed paradigm for leadership or framework for studying it:

Researchers have so far failed to come up with a widely accepted framework for think-ing about leadership. There is no equivalent of Competitive Strategy, Michael Porter's 1980 classic, accorded near-biblical reverence by strategy experts ... I don't think [leadership] is yet a 'field' in the pure sense. There are something like 276 definitions of leadership. You can't say that there is a paradigm, any agreed-upon set of factors, that is generally accepted.

Gary Yukl criticizes the unhelpful way such variables have been classified:

Sometimes different terms have been used to refer to the same type of behaviour. At other times, the same term has been defined differently by various theorists. What is treated as a general behaviour category by one theorist is viewed as two or three distinct categories by another theorist. What is a key concept in one taxonomy is absent from another. Different taxonomies have emerged from different research disciplines, and it is difficult to translate from one set of concepts to another.[19]

Keith Grint of Warwick Business School in the UK in his 'constitutive approach' ques-tions whether we can be objective at all in defining the context of leadership and the leadership required. He suggests that when we do this we are merely constructing our own view of leadership behaviour and the situation in which it takes place:

We may never know ... the true essence of an identity, a leader, or a situation ... and must often base our actions and beliefs on the accounts of others from whom we can (re)con-stitute our version of events ... Leadership is an invention ... [it] is primarily rooted in, and a product of, the imagination.[20]

This view is misleading and unhelpful. Leadership may be 'created' or 'designed', for example as a process or a relationship, but it is hardly imagined, an invention – a 'fabricated story', 'made up, especially so as to deceive'.[21] In the 'real' world (whatever that is, Grint may say), we all experience and recognize leadership, 'good', 'bad' and inconsequential.

More reasonably David Collinson and Keith Grint do point out that, while there was still (in 2005) 'little consensus on what counts as leadership, whether it can be taught, or even how effective it might be', the recent plethora of publications of all kinds on leadership '[extols] the need for excellence in management and leadership ... in part fuelled by a breakdown in confidence in leadership'.[22] Our Scott Adams quota-tion on page 1 captures the confusion and cynicism that have grown rapidly around the idea of leadership since he wrote those words in 1999. This cynicism perhaps is a consequence of the unacceptable face of leadership in recent times that has so deeply pervaded politics, business and sport.

Top-level leaders are frequently criticized for being out of touch with employ-ees in their organizations. And this appears to have grown in recent years. In reporting research findings in January 2011 from Roffey Park, the management development institute in the UK, Carly Chynoweth notes that 'Many board direc-tors seem to be living in a rose-tinted bubble ... They feel more positive about everything … than their counterparts in executive management' as well as middle and junior managers.[23] This includes optimism about the future, the organization's sense of collective purpose, leadership in the organization, perceptions of the respect with which the organization is held by outsiders, and the extent to which leaders behave ethically towards stakeholders.

Almost as jaded a view of leadership as Scott Adams's, and perhaps reflecting the times,[24] is that from novelist and former journalist Robert Harris:

> **What [is] leadership, after all, but the blind choice of one route over another and the confident pretence that the decision [is] based on reason?[25]**

'The main goal of … leadership', according to Donald Krause, 'is to accomplish useful and desirable things that benefit the people being led'.[26] This is arguable. It certainly may be argued as desirable or ideal and may be part of a definition of good leadership. But on the other hand it may be argued as unrealistic. In reality many people are led by those who lead them not for their benefit but for the benefit of others elsewhere. Leaders in the business world may argue reasonably that in meeting shareholders' expectations, or even customers' needs and expectations, they are providing a benefit to employees – for example, employment and income. But this benefit is not necessarily their *raison d'être*. And, of course, some leaders will 'lead' (use) others to further their own interests.

Leadership has been variously defined in terms of traits, process, skill(s), competency, a relationship, and a construct. Sociologists frame leadership in terms of relationships among people rather than in terms of individual traits or characteristics, often focusing on power and dominance.[27] James MacGregor Burns argues that 'to understand the nature of leadership requires understanding of the nature of power'.[28] The two essentials of power, Burns states, are motives and resources. He explains that leadership is not just a top-down phenomenon with clear unidirectional causality between leaders' and followers' behaviour but also a series of complex, reciprocal relationships involving a use of power and the control of resources.

According to a 1920s' definition, leadership is 'the ability to impress the will of the leader on those led and induce obedience, respect, loyalty, and cooperation'.[29] By current standards this is a remarkably authoritarian viewpoint that has little currency today (at least in democratic countries and enlightened organizations). Donald Krause, drawing on the writings of Sun Tzu and Confucius, suggests that leadership comprises:

> **… the will to control events, the understanding to chart a course, and the power to get a job done, cooperatively using the skills and abilities of other people.[30]**

There are various levels at which one can define leadership. Jay Lorsch defines a leader straightforwardly and simply as 'an individual who influences others to follow him or her'.[31] Lorsch argues that leaders use influence gained from various sources of power (discussed in the chapter on leadership and engagement) such as charisma and knowledge (personal power) or the right to insist on action and the right to dispense rewards and punishments (position power or authority). He also argues that the definition applies equally to a senior executive and a first-level supervisor: both must get others to do their bidding. Lorsch's definition is appealing in its simplicity. But its brevity sacrifices clarity, scope and depth and begs many questions. For example, follow *where* (to what?) and *why*? And use influence *how*? It is also not true to the etymology of the word 'leader', namely 'one who shows the way'.

Underlying the leadership development programmes at the Leadership Trust is the following concept of leadership:

> **Leadership is using our personal power to win the hearts and minds of people to achieve a common purpose; the minds ... by giving people a clear understanding of what they have to do, why, and how it might be done; the hearts ... by generating feelings of challenge, involvement, ownership, commitment and excitement.**[32]

This otherwise useful working definition implies a directive style of leadership rather than a contextually more variable one. But it also implies three important principles of leadership:

1. There must be a common, shared mission or purpose, or at least one that a leader gets commitment to, and clear strategies for pursuing it.
2. Hearts and minds have to be won in the sense that the vision, mission and strategies must make sense intellectually and must also appeal to, or create, positive emotions, engagement and motivation or inspiration as a result.
3. The use of position power (authority) is abrogated in favour of gaining commitment through using one's personal power.

James MacGregor Burns defines leadership as a mobilization process undertaken by individuals who are using the power they draw from motives, values and access to resources in a context of competition and conflict in their pursuit of goals.[33] Another political scientist, Joseph S. Nye, Jr – former Dean of Harvard Kennedy School (the John F. Kennedy School of Government) – defines leadership as '[helping] a group create and achieve shared goals'.[34] Nannerl Keohane, a former president of both Wellesley College and Duke University and also a political scientist, says that leaders 'determine or clarify goals for a group of individuals and bring together the energies of members of that group to accomplish those goals'.[35] And an appealing definition of leadership comes from Charles Handy: 'To combine the aspirations and needs of the individuals with the purposes of the larger community to which they all belong.'[36]

Leadership is recognized in the well-known Business Excellence model promoted by the European Foundation for Quality Management (EFQM) and the British Quality Foundation (BQF). This model includes 'leadership' as an underpinning enabler in attaining key performance results. Leadership is defined as how:

> **... leaders develop and facilitate the achievement of the mission and vision, develop values required for long-term success and implement these via appropriate actions and behaviours ... [for example, strategies, management systems and operational plans].**[37]

Leadership is evaluated in the EFQM/BQF Excellence Model according to several sub-criteria:

✳ Leaders develop the mission, vision and values and are role models of a culture of excellence.
✳ Leaders are personally involved in ensuring the organization's management system is developed, implemented and continuously improved.
✳ Leaders are involved with customers, partners and representatives of society.
✳ Leaders motivate, support and recognize the organization's people.

In this model, leadership also includes:

✳ Stimulating and encouraging empowerment, innovation and creativity.
✳ Aligning organizational structure to support the delivery of policy and strategy.
✳ Supporting and engaging in activities that aim to improve the environment and the organization's contribution to society.
✳ Personally communicating the organization's mission, vision, values, policy and strategy, plans, objectives and targets to people.

This model identifies key themes or concepts in leadership: vision, mission, values, strategy, empowerment and motivation, but not all of these in a formal, composite way. We deal with this in later chapters as the basis for a formal model of leadership. The model also links leadership to management, implying rightly that both are necessary for organizational effectiveness.

All of these definitions share a common theme – the idea of facilitating the accomplishment of shared goals. Most definitions (the EFQM's excepted) say little or nothing about *how* this is done. Many are prescriptive (like the Leadership Trust's and the EFQM's) or aspirational (like Charles Handy's) rather than descriptive of the reality (like Nannerl Keohane's). And most stray from the etymological essence of the term 'leadership'. So how can we make sense of the multiplicity of definitions that exist for leadership?

Towards a General Definition of Leadership

I propose that one useful thing to do when exploring the meaning of leadership is to consult the etymology of the word and see how its meaning has developed.

The word 'lead' comes from the Old English *lædan*, corresponding to the Old Saxon *ledian* and Old High German *leiten*, meaning to 'take with one', to 'show the way'.[38] *Ledere* was the term for a person who shows other people the path to take and guides them safely along the journey.[39] The Old Icelandic derivative *leidha* means 'the person in front', referring to the person who guided ships through the pack-ice in spring. The word 'leader' appeared in the English language in the thirteenth century, but 'leadership' appeared only in the early nineteenth century. The terms *leadership* and *leader* are used today in ways that stray from their etymology and original meaning, which we will now discuss.

Showing the way is the essence of leadership. My definition of leadership, which underpins the model of the six core themes discussed in the following chapters, is this:

Leadership is showing the way and helping or inducing others to pursue it. This entails envisioning a desirable future, promoting a clear purpose or mission, supportive values and intelligent strategies, and empowering and engaging all those concerned.

The word 'induce' is used in preference to 'influence' because it has a wider meaning: 'to succeed in persuading or leading (someone) to do something',[40] 'prevail upon', 'bring about', 'cause' or 'attract' in addition to 'influence'. 'Influence' on the other hand has a more restricted meaning: 'to have an effect on the character or behaviour of someone'.[41] The wider meaning of 'induce' embraces leadership behaviour that employs position power or authority, such as directing or insisting on (even enforcing) particular actions by others in appropriate situations, as well as personal power – influence or persuasion – in more usual situations. This definition allows for the possibility of leading not only in the sense of 'being followed' but also in the sense of getting others to follow the way shown by the leader. It does not prescribe whether or not the leader should actually participate personally in that activity or whether or not others must necessarily (though desirably) be voluntarily willing.

'Showing the way' presupposes knowing, or at least believing in, that way. And 'the way' implies the route to a destination: a vision of a desirable future position – *what* we want to be or *where* we want to be. This may be a state of being or a position or place, even more specifically a goal, an objective or a target. Knowing or believing in the way also presupposes the desirability of this known or believed-in destination.

Desirability relates to *why* one wishes to promote and pursue a particular vision. One reason is that this vision relates to our purpose or mission. A purpose or mission is what we do and why we do it; a vision is a mental image of what the future will (or could) be like, based on imagination or wisdom,[42] which we discuss in Chapter 4 and Chapter 5 respectively. A related reason is that the vision relates to what we believe in, what we feel is meaningful, valuable and worthwhile in our work, and perhaps in our life in general. This spiritual dimension concerns our values and beliefs. So leadership is about promoting and pursuing a vision and a mission or purpose that reflect particular values. Effective leadership includes the creation and sustaining of a *shared* vision, mission or purpose and values.

But *how* do leaders and followers effectively pursue a vision, mission and values? They do so through *strategies* – 'ways and means' that involve the use of resources (as Burns says). Hence we have financial strategies, marketing strategies, product strategies, IT strategies, people strategies, and so on. Because leaders, like managers and indeed all of us, get things done with, by and through other people, we need to consider that special resource – people. What does it take for human beings to get things done? The answer is the ability (power) to do so and the desire to do so; in other words empowerment and motivation. Leadership therefore is about empowering people to be *able to* do what needs to be done and influencing, motivating or inspiring people to *want to do* what needs to be done. Influence, motivation and inspiration constitute what is now popularly known as *engagement*.

This definition provides the model of six themes and associated practices of leadership that this book proposes. This model is a synthesis of the extant themes, models and theories in the leadership literature. It prescribes the *practices* of effective leadership – *what effective leaders do*. The outcome of *effective leadership* is the achievement of what was intended – both the results (vision, goals, etc.) *and* appropriate behaviour – by a led person or group of people. We speak of effective leadership at a variety of levels: oneself, one-to-one (as in coaching or counselling, for example), team or group, organization-wide, national, regional or global. *'Good' leadership*, however, is defined by intentions (purpose, vision, goals), achievement (of what was intended) and behaviour (in achieving it) that are judged by those involved or affected to be ethical or moral (on the basis of their personal and shared values).

Good versus Bad Leadership

What is 'good' leadership as distinct from non-leadership and 'bad' leadership? Joanne Ciulla makes the point that 'good' has two senses that need to be interrelated: good in the moral sense and good in the sense of being effective (even if also morally 'bad').[43] Barbara Kellerman developed this distinction in her book *Bad Leadership*, with a model (Figure 1.1) and many case examples, acknowledging the 'dark side' of human nature and how this affects leaders and followers alike.[44] She identifies seven major forms of bad leadership: incompetent, rigid, intemperate, callous, corrupt, insular and evil. Her argument is that, if bad leadership is to be avoided, leadership must reflect a shared responsibility between leaders and followers. Birgit Schyns and Tiffany Hansbrough explain that leaders, followers and situational factors can make leadership go awry.[45]

	Unethical	**Ethical**
Effective	• Bad intentions • Change/goal accomplished	• Good intentions • Change/goal accomplished
Ineffective	• Bad intentions • Change/goal not accomplished	• Good intentions • Change/goal not accomplished

Figure 1.1   'Good' and 'Bad' Leadership (based on Barbara Kellerman, 2004, *Bad Leadership: What It Is, How It Happens, Why It Matters*. Boston, MA: Harvard Business School Press, 32–37)

So what is *good* leadership? Barbara Kellerman observes:

> Scholars should remind us that leadership is not a moral concept. Leaders are like the rest of us: trustworthy and deceitful, cowardly and brave, greedy and generous. To assume that all leaders are good people is to be wilfully blind to the reality of the human condition, and it severely limits our scope for becoming more effective at leadership.[46]

Most leadership textbooks – and indeed most leadership books for practising executives – constantly provide case studies or case examples of brilliant leadership. These are about what we might call 'heroic leaders', those people who turned around failing organizations apparently single-handedly (and inadvertently took the credit for doing so, which is why they would have agreed to the case study or example). There are occasional books on bad leadership, like Barbara Kellerman's. One notable case of bad leadership in 2010 illustrated Tony Hayward's rise and demise as a 'leader'; until that date he had been the CEO of BP. As Rosabeth Moss Kanter says, 'The case of Tony Hayward and the Gulf oil spill will be fodder for business school discussions for years to come, as a how-not-to-do-it guide for leadership when disaster strikes.'[47]

In an insightful psychological analysis, Jean Lipman-Blumen explains how 'toxic' leaders first charm and then manipulate, mistreat, weaken and eventually devastate their followers.[48] She explains how human beings are psychologically susceptible to toxic leadership and how we can reduce our dependency on 'strong' leadership, identify 'reluctant leaders' and nurture leadership within ourselves. Michael Maccoby believes this dependency is the result of what Sigmund Freud called 'transference' – the tendency to relate to a leader as some important person from the past, such as a father or mother, a brother or sister, or even a nanny.[49]

Those who suffer toxic leadership are, of course, primarily subordinates or followers. Leaders do not exist, of course, without followers. Leadership implies followership (oneself in the case of 'self-leadership'). As Manfred Kets de Vries and Elizabeth Laurent-Treacy say:

> Without followers, a leader's journey is solitary and unproductive. If the conductor of an orchestra lifts his or her baton and none of the musicians responds, there is no music.[50]

Followership is attracting increasing attention. For example, reflecting the trend, the term appears in the name of a leadership centre established in 2010 in Durham Business School at Durham University in the UK: the International Centre for Leadership and Followership.

Leadership and Followership

The desire to follow others is a basic human (indeed animal) instinct, Robert Ardrey suggests,[51] although it most certainly does not necessarily dominate human behaviour. While most theories of leadership focus on leaders, Stephen Covey suggests that: 'A more fruitful approach is to look at followers, rather than leaders, and to assess leadership by asking why followers follow.'[52] This question can be addressed by looking at the needs and aspirations that people have and how leaders use power in helping people to satisfy them.

Sometimes we will lead – in domains where we have expertise, for example – and sometimes we will follow, when we need direction or lack expertise. 'Followers also have the power to resist and to lead', says Joseph S. Nye, Jr, former Dean of the Kennedy School (the John F. Kennedy School of Government) at Harvard University.[53] As Stephen Fineman says, we talk a lot about our leaders – our bosses and politicians – and we also criticize them freely:[54] we can make intelligent judgements for ourselves. But our desire to follow has deep emotional roots, and interestingly the Bible emphasizes followership more than leadership.

While many writers have identified a 'crisis' in leadership, there is perhaps also a crisis in followership that has lasted some 20 years so far. Robert Kelley reports one study that indicated dissatisfaction among followers with their leaders:

※ Forty per cent questioned their ability to lead.
※ A minority (14 per cent) of leaders were regarded as role models.
※ Fewer than half were trusted.
※ Forty per cent were regarded as having ego problems: they were perceived to be threatened by talented subordinates, needing to act in a 'superior' way, and not sharing recognition.[55]

James MacGregor Burns points out that:

One talent all leaders must possess [is] the capacity to perceive needs of followers in relationship to their own, to help followers move toward fuller self-realization and self-actualization along with the leaders themselves.[56]

This is about empowerment. Followership, according to one leadership development practitioner, results from being empowered – through delegation, creating team values, coaching and mentoring, and building a high-performance team.[57]

In the political world, leaders appear to have fewer and fewer 'followers'. In democratic nations they are elected, but by whom? The 2001 general election in the UK was one example of a growing crisis in followership, where the lowest turnout for 80 years gave a large majority to the ruling Labour Party. Even so, only a small minority of the electorate actively supported the nation's political leadership – in effect they were 'followers'. And even within the Labour Party, there was some dissension from the policies the government was following, for example by the trade unions that supported it. Nor was the Conservative Party immune from dissension, which was part of the reason for its downfall from government in 1997 and its several subsequent leadership crises. And the proportion of the US electorate that 'followed' president George W. Bush was 51 per cent, according to the 2004 election.

The British government's report on *Strengthening Leadership* includes an interesting analysis of followership:

... the most successful organisations appear to be those where the errors which the leaders inevitably make are compensated for by their followers: responsible followers prevent irresponsible leaders. But where followers are unable or unwilling to constrain their leaders

the organisation itself may well suffer. This 'compensatory followership' operates right across the organisational and political spectrum such that, for example, the obsequient behaviour of most of Hitler's entourage (fortunately) failed to prevent him from making catastrophic strategic errors in the latter half of the Second World War.[58]

The report also gives a more contemporary example. In many hospitals, consultants are 'treated as "gods" and junior staff [are] afraid of "telling tales"'. While making mistakes is essential to learning and progress, examples of unnecessary tragic mistakes as a result of this culture in hospitals appear all too frequently. Institutionalizing the role of devil's advocate is one way of preventing leaders from making such mistakes.[59] Followers take turns to express dissent from the group's decisions with the purpose of focusing the attention of the group and the leader on potential problems.

Jonathan Swift, in *Gulliver's Travels*, provided a graphic account of how leaders may reflect the characteristics of their followers in an extreme way and how they may have a 'favourite' who is hated by everybody else:

> ... in most Herds there was a Sort of ruling Yahoo, (as among us there is generally some leading or principal Stag in a Park) who was always more *deformed* in Body, and *mischievous in Disposition*, than any of the rest. That, this *Leader* had usually a Favourite as *like himself* as he could get, whose Employment was to *lick his Master's Feet and Posteriors, and drive the Female* Yahoos *to his Kennel*; for which he was now and then rewarded with a Piece of Ass's Flesh. This *Favourite* is hated by the whole Herd; and therefore to protect himself, keeps always *near the Person of his Leader*. He usually continues in Office till a worse can be found; but the very Moment he is discarded, his Successor, at the Head of all *Yahoos* in that District, Young and Old, Male and Female, come in a Body, and discharge their Excrements upon him from Head to Foot. But how far this might be applicable to our *Courts* and *Favourites*, and *Ministers of State*, my Master said I could best determine.[60]

Whether Swift's analysis can be applied to business and political leadership today is self-evident. Political journalist and broadcaster Jeremy Paxman, describing former British prime minister Tony Blair's attempts to act 'normal', says: 'The successful leader would like to be as like his followers as possible.'[61] He quotes the political reporter, James Margach, who likens political parties, in the way they turn on their discarded leaders, to crabs, which devour their sick, wounded and dying.[62] Paxman describes how vulnerable political leaders are: cabinet ministers in particular, once discarded, will usually simply vanish from public view.[63] For prime ministers, losing an election or being sacked by their party, he says, can bring castigation and public humiliation – they become the 'excrement' of Jonathan Swift's yahoos. This is also true for prime ministers who resign over-tardily.

Added to this Paxman describes how power in (British) politics has come to be concentrated less in parliament and more in the prime minister, perhaps in a very small number of ministers (but not the Cabinet as a whole), and even in a coterie of special advisers who, controversially, will sometimes be given executive powers over the Civil Service. The media are quick to report the discarding of such special advisers – Swift's 'favourites' – and they usually suffer the same insalubrious fate.

Paxman suggests that loyalty, a characteristic of voluntary followership, is vacuous in politics: he comments, 'There is no room for either friendship or gratitude at the top.'[64] Witness the frequent Cabinet reshufflings, acrimonious ministerial sackings and resignations in government, and the subsequent sniping at the prime minister by those who are sacked. Add to this what Paxman says is an increasing tendency by prime ministers not only to make decisions without the consensus of, or even without consulting, their Cabinet but also to direct their ministers what to do, and we must call into question how effective prime ministers really are as *leaders*.

Followership in the literal sense has been evolving into collaboration and partnership. Even Admiral Lord Nelson, for example, saw his captains as a 'band of brothers'. And former US Secretary of State Colin Powell says that 'Leadership does not emerge from blind obedience to anyone.'[65] Leaders provide followers with protection and meaning. Followers identify with charismatic leaders, for better or worse, with pleasure and pride.

According to the respondents in Kelley's study of followership, the best followers are those who think for themselves, give constructive criticism, are 'their own person', and are innovative and creative.[66] Kelley's review of follower characteristics revealed an additional dimension, namely active engagement in the task: the best followers will take the initiative, participate actively, be self-starters, and do more than what is required.

Michael Maccoby, a noted psychologist, says that the definition of a leader is simple: 'A leader is someone whom people follow.'[67] And why do people follow leaders? Maccoby suggests one reason for this is fear, and he cites the example of people living in Iraq under the rule of Saddam Hussein. Another reason, he says, particularly in respect of religious leaders, is love, devotion or respect. However, this can be dangerous, and indeed sometimes lethal, as was the case for cult leader Jim Jones's 909 followers. And in addition, as Kurtzman says, 'followership is no excuse for wrongdoing, even when following the will of an elected leader', a principle established at the Nuremberg trials at the end of the Second Word War.[68]

Followership is dangerous when it entails surrendering one's judgement or one's will to a leader: being aligned to a common purpose does not entail surrendering the right to express an opinion, oppose a decision or withdraw from the group. Effective organizations and leaders respect dissidence. Followership also occurs, however, when one works with a leader whose purpose one shares, says Maccoby.[69] We discuss the place of purpose in leadership in Chapter 5.

Followers exert their influence on leaders in many ways. In democracies, Nanerl Keohane says, they hold the ultimate authority, and leaders are both formally and informally accountable to them.[70] A special report on global leaders by *The Economist* in January 2011 endorses this view:

> **Elections force politicians to take the public's wishes into account every few years. Competitive markets force business leaders to heed their customers' demands all the time. And the law applied to rich and poor alike ... in liberal democracies the powerful get on by pleasing others. In short, they work for us.**[71]

For a further discussion of followership, *The Art of Followership* by Ronald Riggio and colleagues is recommended.[72]

Leadership versus Management

The relationship between the concepts of management and leadership is the subject of continuing discussion among academics and consultants. For example, Marcus Buckingham, well known for his work on emphasizing strengths, writing in *Harvard Business Review*, says:

> [Great managers] discover what is unique about each person and then capitalize on it ... This is the exact opposite of what great leaders do. Great leaders discover what is universal and capitalize on it.[73]

This view is highly questionable: what Buckingham says is management is in fact equally a key aspect of effective leadership, posited specifically in one particular theory of transformational leadership that we discuss in the next chapter. If there is a real difference between what managers do and what leaders do, it is not this. Robert House and R.N. Aditya suggest that:

> Scholars of the traditional management and leadership literatures seldom take advantage of each other's contributions and, consequently, these two literatures are not adequately integrated.[74]

The term 'management' derives from *manus*, the Latin word for 'hand'. The term had to do with handling things, and it gained currency in its modern sense during the Industrial Revolution in the nineteenth century. The archaic French *ménager* meant to 'use sparingly'.

In the oft-quoted words of Warren Bennis and Bert Nanus, 'Managers are people who do things right; leaders are people who do the right things.'[75] For example, leaders ask the right questions about strategy and make sure the right answers are implemented.[76] And David Wills, training manager for the Motherwell Bridge Group in Scotland, says:

> Leadership is ... about vision and having the courage to do the right thing – different from management, which is all about doing the thing right – even if there is a risk.[77]

But this distinction is epistemologically unsound, according to Peter Gronn:

> ... it is an attempt to resurrect the traditional distinction between facts and values. Thus, 'things right' reduces to a competence or technical mastery [management], whereas 'the right thing' [leadership] implies desirable ends, purposes or values.[78]

The Work Foundation (formerly The Industrial Society) in the UK defines the differences between management and leadership simply. Managers plan, allocate resources, administer and control, whereas leaders innovate, communicate and motivate.[79] Vision is one of the key differences between a manager and a leader, according to Stanley Deetz and colleagues.[80] General Sir William Slim, the inspiring Second World War leader, saw the difference in the same way. In a speech in Adelaide as Governor-General of Australia in 1957, he said:

> ... we do not in the Army talk of 'management' but of leadership'. This is significant. There is a difference between leaders and management. [Leadership represents] one of the oldest, most natural and most effective of all human relationships. [Management is] a later product, with neither so romantic nor so inspiring a history. Leadership is of the spirit, compounded of personality and vision; its practice is an art. Management is of the mind, more a matter of accurate calculation of statistics, of methods, time tables, and routine; its practice is a science. Managers are necessary; leaders are essential.[81]

Amin Rajan contrasts management and leadership thus:

☀ Management is about path following; leadership is path finding.
☀ Management is about doing things right; leadership is about doing the right things.
☀ Management is about planning and budgeting; leadership is about establishing direction.
☀ Management is about controlling and problem solving; leadership is about motivating and inspiring.[82]

Warren Bennis suggests that the differences between leadership and management can be summed up as 'the differences between those who master the context and those who surrender to it' respectively.[83] These differences are detailed in Table 1.1 below.

John Kotter says that management produces orderly results that keep something working efficiently, whereas leadership creates useful change; neither is necessarily better or a replacement for the other; both are needed if organizations and nations are

Table 1.1 Differences between Managers and Leaders

The manager	The leader
Administers	Innovates
Is a 'copy'	Is an 'original'
Maintains	Develops
Focuses on systems and structure	Focuses on people
Focuses on control	Inspires trust
Takes a short-range view	Has a long-range perspective
Asks how and when	Asks what and why
Imitates	Originates
Accepts the *status quo*	Challenges the *status quo*
Is a classic 'good soldier'	Is his or her own person
Does things right	Does the right thing

to prosper.[84] A more useful suggestion is that we do not need both managers and leaders (i.e. people in separate roles) but managers who are leaders and leaders who are managers – people who can 'do the right thing right'? As Mitch McCrimmon says, 'It is vastly more empowering to define management as a type of activity than as a role.'[85] And with regard to organizational change, which is for some the preserve of a 'leader', he says:

> **Leadership sells tickets for the journey and, if resistance emerges en route, the tickets can be resold, but the bulk of the journey is a project requiring good management skills.**[86]

Warner Burke also agrees that both management and leadership are needed: 'For clarity of goals and direction, managers need leaders. For indispensable help in reaching goals, leaders need managers.'[87] We 'manage from the left, lead from the right', Stephen Covey says.[88] In terms of brain dominance theory, the manager's role is mainly left-brain dominated, whereas the leader's role is right-brain based. The left hemisphere of the brain deals more with words, specific elements, logic, analysis, sequential thinking and time. The right hemisphere deals more with emotions, aesthetics, pictures, relationships among elements and the *gestalt*, synthesis, and intuitive, simultaneous, holistic thinking, free of time constraints. An Eastern view is that leading involves the *yin* and managing involves the *yang*.

Managers may be good at *managing* and nominally regarded as leaders, but the most effective managers exercise *effective leadership*. John Nicholls says:

> **When we say that an organisation lacks leadership we mean that its managers are neglecting their leadership responsibility. It is leadership that is missing, not leaders. If every manager understood and fulfilled his or her leadership responsibilities, there would be no shortage of leadership. It is attention to their managerial leadership responsibilities that converts competent administrators into effective managers.**[89]

And Bernard Bass says:

> **Management is not only leadership, nor is leadership only management; however, those appointed to a position of responsibility as managers need to appreciate what leadership is expected of them.**[90]

People in management positions who have people reporting to them and avoid the leadership role may be perceived merely as administrators.[91] But while leadership is about innovation and change, Kouzes and Posner argue that it is not necessarily about entrepreneurship:

> **Leaders must be change agents and innovators. But they need not be entrepreneurs, if by that term we mean those who actually initiate and assume the risk for a new enterprise. Neither must they be 'intrapreneurs' – entrepreneurs within a corporation. In fact, we maintain that the majority of leadership in this world is neither entrepreneurial nor intrapreneurial.**[92]

United Technologies Corporation (UTC), the aerospace and defence company, published an arresting notice in the *Wall Street Journal* and several other newspapers and magazines in 1984:

> People don't want to be managed.
> They want to be led.
> Whoever heard of a 'world manager'?
> World leader, yes.
> Educational leader.
> Political leader.
> Religious leader.
> Scout leader.
> Community leader.
> Business leader.
> They lead.
> They don't manage.
> The carrot always wins over the stick.
> Ask your horse.
> You can lead your horse to water, but you can't manage him to drink.
> If you want to manage somebody, manage yourself.
> Do that well and you'll be ready to stop managing.
> And start leading.[93]

Eighteen years later, in 2002, UTC was ranked the world's most admired company in the aerospace and defence sector.[94] And in 2007 UTC was one of America's best-performing conglomerates and a darling of Wall Street, with shareholder returns that outstripped even GE's.[95] The point is that many of us over-manage people and under-lead them. The company's philosophy – and its practice – have evidently paid off, perhaps because its executives manage *things* and *processes* but *lead* people.

And this is the key point. Looking at the putative 'differences' between managers and leaders, nobody would ever want to be a manager, says psychologist Adrian Furnham: managers are dull; leaders 'fizz with electric creativity'.[96] Furnham also holds that neither stereotype exists: it is a 'false dichotomy'. But it is a helpful conceptual distinction if it is related to context. Good managers may be leaders too – they have to exercise leadership (with other people) in carrying out their managerial functions (with things and processes). And good leaders are poor managers. As Furnham says:

> The greatest of leaders are often forceful organisers as well as visionaries ... people who manage their own businesses know the importance of processes and procedures. A business with leaders and no managers would surely fail much faster than one full of managers and without leaders.[97]

Some companies have forsaken the title 'manager' for 'leader', for example W.L. Gore & Associates, one of the UK's best companies to work for (see Chapter 6). However, this may be symptomatic of what Julian Birkinshaw suggests is the demeaning of management over the past few decades in favour of leadership.[98] He says we need a fuller understanding of what management is really about, but unfortunately he muddies the water by defining it as 'the act of getting people together to accomplish desired goals'.

So far we have discussed the concept of leadership – in essence, showing the way; how leaders have followers; and how leadership relates to management. These discussions have brought up the issue of change. If leadership is about anything, it is about change. Leadership is showing the way from here to there, a way that may be unfamiliar or even unknown, to a place or state imagined but never before sought or reached. It is about a change from the present to a desired future.

Leadership and Change[99]

All things change, nothing is extinguished. There is nothing in the whole world which is permanent. Everything flows onward; all things are brought into being with a changing nature; the ages themselves glide by in constant movement.

So wrote the Roman poet Ovid, in *Metamorphoses*.[100] And in the graphic words of an African proverb, it is a journey that takes place every day:

Each morning a gazelle wakes up knowing that it must outrun the fastest lion or be eaten. And every morning the lion wakes up knowing that it must outrun the slowest gazelle or starve. Gazelle or lion, every morning you must run. That's what change is all about.[101]

The early 1980s saw a marked growth in interest in the leadership of change. Rosabeth Moss Kanter's concept of the 'change master' focused on entrepreneurship and innovation in organizations.[102] Bernard Bass's Full-Range Leadership model, which we discuss in Chapter 3, explained how leaders changed how people feel about themselves and could be inspired to achieve performance beyond their previous expectations – the concept of transformational leadership.[103]

The challenges ahead, more than ever before, require organizations, industries and societies to change and to keep changing. Change may be planned, proactive and about creating the future. Or it may be unplanned, reactive and about adaptation. In Warren Bennis's view, 'Leaders have to … create an environment that embraces change, not as a threat but as an opportunity.'[104] The change imperative itself has changed. The challenge used to be to respond positively to the need for change. Now it is the need to actively *create* change. This was expressed forcefully by the former chairman of British Leyland, Chloride and Dunlop, Sir Michael Edwardes:

And they [the new breed of top executives] have a particular drive, a desire to bring order out of chaos, or if something is too cosy, to create chaos in order to bring change.[105]

Change may be imposed, from a position of authority, or participative, generating ownership, commitment and creativity. Philip Sadler distinguishes between incremental and transformational change, in which incremental change concerns activities within a given culture and the latter changes the culture.[106] The most negative reaction that people display at work is not concerned with money, but with change. People will resist change for many reasons. Milan Kubr identified the following:

☀ A lack of conviction that change is needed.
☀ A dislike of *imposed* change.
☀ A dislike of surprises.
☀ A fear of the unknown.
☀ A reluctance to deal with unpopular issues.
☀ A fear of inadequacy and failure: a lack of know-how.
☀ Disturbed practices, habits and relationships: 'We've always done it this way.' Moving people from their 'comfort zone' means moving from the familiar, secure and controllable to the unfamiliar, insecure and uncontrollable.
☀ A lack of respect for and trust in the person promoting change.[107]

James O'Toole says that:

> ... to be effective, leaders must [set] aside that 'natural' instinct to lead by push, particularly when times are tough. Leaders must instead adopt the unnatural behavior of *always* leading by the pull of inspiring values.[108]

He says that any reversion to paternalistic behaviour will break trust with followers: the ultimate lack of respect for others is 'to impose one's will on them without regard for what they want or need and without consulting them'.[109] In fact, O'Toole in his analysis concludes: 'the major source of resistance to change is ... having the will of others imposed on us'.[110]

In addition, self-interest and shifts in power and influence will hinder change efforts. A loss or change of role is one example here. That change is difficult has been long recognized, for example by Machiavelli:

> ... there is no more delicate matter to take in hand, nor more dangerous to conduct, nor more doubtful in its success, than to set up as a leader in the introduction of changes. For he who innovates will have for his enemies all those who are well off under the existing order of things, and only lukewarm supporters in those who might be better off under the new.[111]

Andrew Mayo says, 'Our organisations are littered with the debris ... of yesterday's [change] initiatives.'[112] One reason for this may be the consequences of the tendency to introduce change when meeting any new situation. As Charlton Ogburn says:

> ... we tend to meet any new situation by reorganizing; and a wonderful method it can be for creating the illusion of progress while producing confusion, inefficiency, and demoralization.[113]

The ghosts of changes past can often return to haunt us. What effect does the history of change in an organization have on shaping employees' attitudes and behaviour, especially regarding change itself? With respect to change, 'once bitten, twice shy', one might imagine. But what exactly happens? And what leadership lessons can we learn from research into change?

Recent research investigated this question in two studies in the Philippines, one in a property development firm that was merging with another and the other in an educational institution that was undergoing extensive restructuring.[114] Based on theory deriving from previous research, cause-and-effect chains were hypothesized (see Figure 1.2).

In a questionnaire survey of 155 employees in the property development firm (a sample of just under 50 per cent of the total number), eight items measured aspects of poor change management (e.g. 'In my experience, past change initiatives have failed to achieve their intended purpose'). Trust was measured using seven items and cynicism was measured using eight items taken from previously validated questionnaires.[115] Inept change management was found to be inversely related to trust and directly related to cynicism, as had been predicted.

In the educational institution, the same procedure was followed with a sample of 124 employees (a response rate of 62 per cent), but with two additional aspects investigated. In the implementation of previous changes, staff had not been consulted and management had acted in an autocratic manner, leading to lawsuits being brought by some disaffected staff. Job satisfaction was measured using three items, turnover intentions were measured by four items and openness to change was measured using four items, again taken from validated instruments.[116] Data on employee turnover were collected two years later. The results for trust and cynicism were the same as in the first study. In addition, trust was found to be positively related to job satisfaction and inversely related to turnover intentions. And cynicism was found to be inversely related to openness to change. Actual employee turnover was predicted only marginally by intention to leave.

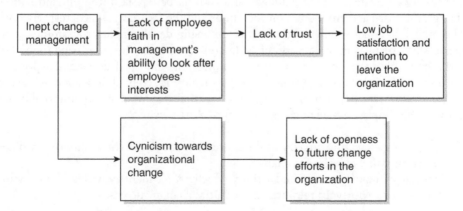

Figure 1.2 Cause and Effect in Organizational Change

Ineptly managed change clearly has dysfunctional consequences. It causes negative attitudes towards both change in general and the organization itself. A vicious cycle then results whereby employees will avoid participating in change initiatives, consequently prejudicing future changes and thereby reinforcing negative attitudes and behaviour.

In the words of Clarence Darrow, the American lawyer in the famous 'Scopes Monkey Trial' in 1925 defending the teaching of Darwinism by high school teacher John Scopes, 'It is not the strongest species that survive, nor the most intelligent, but rather the one most adaptable to change.'[117] There are many reasons why change efforts fail:

❊ A lack of communication or inconsistent messages.
❊ A lack of commitment to change due to a lack of compelling evidence for the benefits of change – and based on unrealistic expectations of the change effort. This lack of commitment shows itself in objections, an unwillingness to consider options or look at process issues and the use of 'hidden agendas' or delaying tactics.
❊ A lack of commitment by top-level management.
❊ A lack of dedicated effort.
❊ A lack of expertise in the organization.
❊ Poor planning and coordination.
❊ A lack of necessary resources, including training.
❊ Inconsistent human resource policies or systems, such as performance criteria used in performance appraisal and the way people are rewarded for their performance.
❊ Conflict between functional areas.
❊ An imposition of 'intellectual' solutions on emotional problems: a lack of emotional intelligence.
❊ A history of failed change initiatives leading to a 'culture' of change failures.

Traumatic change brings with it some well-known reactions: first, a denial that it has happened; then anger about its having happened, bargaining over what to do, depression, and finally acceptance.[118] John Mulligan and Paul Barber speak of the *yin* and *yang* of change: the social and emotional considerations and the technical aspects respectively.[119] The model of response to change used in leadership development programmes at the Leadership Trust has immobilization first (a non-response or 'freezing') and then minimization ('This doesn't concern or affect us'); after this come self-doubt and depression, the low point at which change either fails or its reality is accepted (in which case change is tested in a search for its meaning and benefits), followed up by internalization. Perhaps the simplest model of change is that of Kurt Lewin:[120]

❊ Unfreezing – creating anxiety or dissatisfaction about the *status quo* or a problem and stimulating a desire for change.
❊ Changing – new behaviour and activity which people identify with and internalize.
❊ Refreezing – positively reinforcing the initial change successes.

While the challenge of change requires effective management, even more does it require outstanding leadership. The challenges are to find new and better ways of motivating people, especially to make effective change happen, satisfy people's needs and expectations, and win their hearts and minds:[121]

* Responding positively to the need for change.
* Actively creating change.
* Making people comfortable with change.

John Kotter provides a model for creating effective change:[122]

1. Create a sense of urgency and importance to change
   Examine the market in which the organization operates and the competitive realities.
2. Create the guiding coalition
   Put together a group with enough power to lead the change and get it to work together as an effective team.
3. Develop a vision and strategy
   Create a vision for a desired future state as a basis for directing the change effort. Develop strategies for achieving the vision.
4. Communicate the change
   Use every method possible to constantly communicate and explain the new vision and strategy and ensure the guiding coalition models the behaviour expected of employees.
5. Empower people for action
   Get rid of obstacles to change, change systems or structures that undermine the vision, and encourage risk taking and new ideas and innovative activities.
6. Generate short-term wins
   Plan and create visible improvements in performance, or 'wins'. Visibly recognize and reward people who made the wins possible.
7. Consolidate gains and continue the change effort
   Use increased credibility to change all systems, structures and policies that do not fit together and do not fit the vision. Recruit, promote and develop people who can implement the change vision. Reinvigorate the change process with new projects, themes and change agents.
8. Embed the new approaches in the culture.
   Create better performance through customer-oriented and productivity-oriented behaviour and more effective management and leadership.

Kotter's model of change is criticized by Chris Argyris.[123] He says that it reflects 'Model 1' behaviour (command-and-control) that is aimed at getting compliance from people rather than Model 2 behaviour that is genuinely people-centred. Moreover, he questions whether creating a new sense of urgency would lead to desired outcomes and whether people in these circumstances would fully understand what they have to do and produce new ideas for overcoming obstacles.

Moreover, unrealistic expectations associated with a sense of urgency are very frequently dashed, with consequent demoralization and embarrassment. Leo Apotheker, who was appointed CEO of the Hewlett-Packard Company in November 2010, was asked by the *Wall Street Journal* why he wanted organizational change to happen so fast. He answered:

> There was a debate in the Swedish parliament in the 1960s about whether they should move from driving on the left side of the road to the right side of the road. True story. One member said jokingly we could do it gradually: on Monday the trucks, on Tuesday the bicycles, and Wednesday the cars. If a change has to happen why wait and do it gradually?[124]

Malcolm Higgs and Deborah Rowland report a study in seven organizations that found emergent change was more successful than master change or directive change.[125] The most effective change leadership behaviour was framing change rather than shaping behaviour or creating capacity. In fact a leader-centric shaping of behaviour impaired the implementation of change.

During strategic change a consensus appears to develop, but less through gaining strength and more through increasing scope, according to Livia Markoczy.[126] A consensus during the early stages of successful strategic change tends to appear mainly not in the top management team but in the key interest groups, such as product development or marketing.

Today change that is continuous or discontinuous and not stability is the order of the day. Alvin Toffler, in his disturbing and challenging book *Future Shock*, says: 'Change is essential to man ... Change is life itself' and that 'a strategy for capturing control of change' is essential to avoiding future trauma and to the future well-being of the human race.[127] As Warren Bennis says, 'Change is the only constant.'[128]

Change must be well managed. This entails planning; organization in terms of roles and responsibilities, procedures and adequate resources and know-how, monitoring and control; and compatible and supportive corporate policies, systems and practices. Raymond Caldwell, using a Delphi process with change agents, found that managing and leading changes were two distinct but complementary processes.[129] Effective leadership is necessary for change to be successfully introduced and sustained. Rosabeth Moss Kanter notes how there has been a shift of emphasis from managing change to leading change.[130]

Change requires not only good management but also good leadership.[131] What is our vision for change: what or where do we want to be? Why do we want or need to change anyway? What is important to us in the change process: what values and ethical principles will guide us? How are we going to change: what are our strategies for change? How will we empower people to *be able to do* what needs to be done? And how will we influence, motivate and even inspire them to *want to do* what needs to be done?

For the chief executive this means 'developing a vision of the future, crafting strategies to bring that vision into reality [and ensuring] that everybody in the organisation is mobilising their energies towards the same goals … the process we call "emotional alignment"', say Alan Hooper and John Potter.[132] Their model of leadership proposes seven competencies: setting the direction, making decisions, communicating effectively, creating alignment, setting an example, getting the best out of people, and acting as a change agent.[133] It can be argued that the most difficult challenges facing leaders today are making sure that people in the organization can adapt to change and that leaders can envisage where the organization is currently placed in the market and where it should be in the future.[134] Change is now driven by a global orientation and customer needs and demands. It requires, Manfred Kets de Vries says, an 'authoritative (or respect-based) leadership rather than authoritarian (position-based) leadership'.[135] Peter Drucker says:

> To survive and succeed, every organization will have to turn itself into a change agent. The most effective way to manage change successfully is to create it. But experience has shown that grafting innovation on to a traditional enterprise does not work. The enterprise has to become a change agent. This requires the organized abandonment of things that have been shown to be unsuccessful, and the organized and continuous improvement of every product, service, and process within the enterprise (which the Japanese call *kaizen*). It requires the exploitation of successes, especially unexpected and unplanned-for ones, and it requires systematic innovation. The point of becoming a change agent is that it changes the mind-set of the entire organization. Instead of seeing change as a threat, its people will come to consider it as an opportunity.[136]

The most frequently mentioned key to successful change, according to an American Management Association survey of 259 senior executives in *Fortune 500* companies in the United States, is leadership (see Table 1.2).[137]

Table 1.2 Keys to Successful Change

	% mentioning this as important
Leadership	92
Corporate values	84
Communication	75
Teambuilding	69
Education and training	64

Leadership for change requires competencies that can span the cognitive, emotional, cultural, spiritual, moral and behavioural domains of our being. And in the end, to change anything, perhaps we have to change ourselves in the process. In the words of an African proverb:

> When I was a young man, I thought I would change the world.
> When I was middle-aged, I thought I would change my village.
> Now that I am an old man, I think I will change myself.[138]

The Impact and Importance of Leadership

The rulers of ancient China studied leadership at great length. They were preoccupied with change and its associated chaos and uncertainty, as indeed we still are today. The writings on leadership of the general Sun Tzu in *The Art of War* and the philosopher Confucius in *The Analects* have endured over some two and a half millennia and are still quoted far and wide today. One lesson from Sun Tzu is that even the most brilliant strategy requires effective leadership to be successful.[139] This is a lesson that receives scant attention from strategy theorists and eludes many business school texts on business strategy, or is at best treated *en passant*. The importance of strategy to leadership is discussed in chapter 7.

Leadership is the crucial issue, Rosabeth Moss Kanter says, when a company is failing and its survival is at stake.[140] It matters most in respect of an openness and honesty in dialogue, mutual respect, collaborative problem solving, and the encouragement of initiative. She says that withholding information from employees and the public compounds a financial or strategic mess: the cover-up can be worse than the mistake. 'Leadership is the ultimate advantage', says Nikos Mourkogiannis. 'When it's present, it makes all other advantages possible. And poor leadership can turn even the best advantage into a disaster.'[141]

Mutual respect is not gained by punishing those responsible for mistakes. It is gained through recognizing what people have to offer and involving them in problem solving and decision making, for example in strategy formulation. And problem solving and a commitment to solutions in turnaround situations require collaboration across organizational boundaries. Moss Kanter quotes as an example how Greg Dyke, on taking over as Director-General of the BBC in 1999, used this approach in his 'One BBC: Making It Happen' strategy to rehabilitate a demoralized organization. Initiative can be encouraged by empowering employees to take action, again something that had been missing at the BBC and which Dyke introduced. Creating such a culture is key for leaders in turnaround situations. In the words of Moss Kanter: '... this is the true test of leadership: whether those being led out of the defeatism of decline gain the confidence that produces victories'.[142]

The Industrial Revolution, starting in the UK, shifted the emphasis from political and military leadership to business and economic leadership – building industrial enterprises, opening up markets, and innovation.[143] Such leadership, however, was ascribed to the relatively few ('born' leaders?) who were usually autocrats. As Douglas McGregor stated in his seminal book *The Human Side of Enterprise*:

Traditionally, leadership has tended to be equated with autocratic command and there are still many who see leadership mainly in terms of the issuing of orders which are eagerly obeyed by followers whose loyalty is largely determined by the charisma of the leader.[144]

Over half a century later, this is still true.

Research by the Council for Excellence in Management and Leadership, set up by the British government in April 2000, revealed a need to 'increase the commitment of organisations of all sizes, in both the private and public sector, to develop better managers and leaders'.[145] The Council acknowledged a 'direct link between leadership capability and sustained high performance'.[146] Its research findings included the following:

☀ There are still shortages in the quality and quantity of people with leadership skills. Yet the need for those with leadership skills is increasing all the time. There need to be some 400,000 new entrants to management and leadership positions each year.
☀ Larger organizations prefer customized leadership development programmes.
☀ Few professional associations require any management learning prior to membership and Continuing Professional Development (CPD) requirements, despite a recognition by professionals of the importance of leadership development.
☀ There is a lack of data on leadership development for benchmarking purposes.

The CEML research was the basis for proposals and an agenda for action on leadership development. However, according to research carried out in 2010 by the Kenexa Research Institute, an American talent management consultancy, surveying some 29,000 employees in 21 countries, the UK was ranked 17th on a leadership effectiveness index.[147] The UK lagged behind the United States and Germany and also behind China and India, who ranked joint first, but was ahead of bottom-ranked Japan. Kenexa identified two key priorities for leadership development in the UK:

1. *Building trust by employees in their leaders.* Jack Wiley, executive director of the Institute, says:

   The abilities to inspire trust [in leaders] and to remain trustworthy are essential qualities for any leader ... We found that certain actions and behaviours are important for developing leadership trust. These include working ethically and with integrity, supporting whistle-blowers, 'walking the talk' and giving credit where it is due.

2. *Engaging in open, honest, two-way communication.* Wiley says:

   There's also a need to communicate openly, to listen and to remain approachable. Direct reports need to feel safe enough to tell their leader the truth.

We discuss the values underlying leadership in Chapter 6 and leadership development in Chapter 11.

The importance of leadership is commonly judged in terms of its impact on the *effectiveness* of an entity that is led. 'The ultimate measure of effectiveness for leaders', according to Bill George, 'is the ability to sustain superior results over an extended period of time'.[148] However, leadership is a more widely pervasive phenomenon than this. Its primary significance, according to some scholars, is not economic, rather it is its importance in stemming the loss of meaning associated with 'modernity', for example the moral collapse of firms.[149] Richard Hackman also believes that the leadership role is best seen not in terms of its economic impact but in terms of its shaping of the organizational context, such as goals, membership, incentives and culture.[150]

In addition Nitin Nohria and Rakesh Khurana argue that its scope and importance need to be addressed not only in terms of their impact on performance effectiveness but also, and more importantly, in terms of their influence on organizational life – such as meaning, morality and culture.[151] They also argue convincingly that these require urgent attention with respect to leadership education and development in institutions of higher education – and, I would add, in business school MBA programmes especially.

Leadership throughout the Hierarchy: Individual, Shared and Distributed Leadership

Until recently many of the texts on leadership had assumed that leadership was 'a solo act – a one-person undertaking – regardless of whether the organization being led … [was] a nation, a global corporation or a scout troop'.[152] The conventional view of leadership is that individual leaders make a significant and even crucial impact on the performance of their organizations, though research findings are inconsistent.

For example, Alan Berkeley Thomas in a study of large retail firms in the UK found that individual CEOs *do* make a difference.[153] More recently Noam Wasserman and colleagues also found in their study that, while industry structure and company history may explain a greater variance in company performance over time, the influence of CEO leadership is also substantial, although it may vary across industries.[154] However, Bruce Pasternack and colleagues claim there is little correlation between CEO leadership behaviour and organizational performance.[155] And Richard Wellins and Patterson Weaver Jr quote a study of 83 leadership successions in 1997 and 1998 by Margaret Wiersma that showed little relationship between the loss of a CEO and company performance.[156]

The 'heroic' model of solo leadership that attributes greatness, charisma and near-infallibility to a single leader is flawed: 'both dangerous and dangerously naïve' according to Keith Grint.[157] Totalitarian regimes 'led' by a single leader – whether in countries or companies – are testimony to this view. What CEOs who are effective leaders themselves do is to create a 'leadership culture' that is characterized by collective or distributed leadership and therefore a multitude of leaders throughout the organization. In the words of Henry Kissinger, former US Secretary of State, 'A leader becomes great if he institutionalizes a system, if it doesn't become totally dependent on one person.'[158] British supermarket chain Tesco's long-serving chief executive Sir Terry Leahy's announcement in June 2010 that he was to retire in nine months' time led to a significant fall in the share price, suggesting just such a dependency.

This dependency has been reinforced by executive education and leadership development programmes that emphasize the individual leader:

> The parsing of leadership styles has become de rigeur in American business schools. Professors teach students to adopt the right leadership style for themselves, using '360-degree feedback' to make them aware of how they are perceived by others – and how to manage those perceptions. A growth industry called executive coaching caters to the leadership-impaired.[159]

Dennis Tourish and colleagues studied transformational leadership education in 21 leading business schools and found a confusing conflict between the widely posited purposes of leadership and an undue emphasis on the individual 'heroic' leader.[160] This conflict concerns the 'unresolved tension between two ... ideas': the purpose of a collective interest and common purpose that characterizes transformational leadership and the purpose of self-interest (derived from agency theory) in which transformational leaders exert a top-down influence over the activities of others in pursuit of their visions, missions and objectives. Each purpose or aim undercuts the other. And Tourish and colleagues say: 'Business school educators tend ... to uncritically exaggerate the contribution [individual] leaders make to business success' and 'use stories which chronicle how powerful and charismatic leaders routinely rescue organizations from the precipice of failure'.

New 'post-heroic' ideas, however, have emphasized the value of more collaborative and less hierarchical practices that are enacted through fluid, multi-directional interactions, networks and partnerships.[161] While these ideas about 'shared', 'distributed', 'collaborative' and 'networked' leadership are not necessarily interchangeable, they all imply a more collaborative and shared notion of power and authority.

Individual Leadership

Solo leadership is not necessary, not desirable, and probably impossible in today's organizations, according to James O'Toole and Bruce Pasternack and colleagues.[162] The new view of leadership is that the traditional role of a single leader who 'leads' by command-and-control can no longer work because the challenges and problems facing organizations today are too complex and difficult for one person or even a small group of executives to handle on their own.[163] 'Contextualists' argue that many situational factors constrain solo leaders.[164] What is needed, Wilfred H. Drath says, is a 'relational dialogue ... people making sense and meaning of their work together... [creating] a world in which it makes sense to have shared goals or shared knowledge'.[165]

The 'heroic' model of leadership attributes greatness and infallibility to individual leaders, according to Keith Grint, which, to repeat, is 'both dangerous and dangerously naïve'.[166] Business leadership that depends on one all-powerful leader, Pasternack and colleagues say, is 'unstable in the long run'.[167] The examples they give are the disintegration of the ITT Corporation after CEO Harold Geneen's retirement and the way in which General Motors after Alfred Sloan, Polaroid after Edwin Land, and Coca-Cola after Roberto Goizueta seemed to lose their way.

There are many examples of once-lauded heroes falling out of favour: *The Economist* quotes Bernie Ebbers of WorldCom, Diana Brooks of Sotheby's, Jean-Marie Messier of Vivendi Universal, Percy Barnevik of ABB, Kenneth Lay and Jeffrey Skilling of Enron, and even the iconic Jack Welch of General Electric.[168] Stefan Stern cites Tony Hayward, former CEO of BP, whose star waned over the disastrous Gulf oil spill in 2010 owing to his inflexibility and lack of dynamism, his appearance as 'a rabbit in the headlights of a car' and, above all, his ill-considered and clumsy public statements.[169] Stern says that Hayward's 'pleasing self-effacing' style when he took over from Lord Browne in 2007 'didn't cut it at the height of the crisis of 2010 ... A reminder that the best leaders do not simply adopt one fixed (heroic) [style], but are able to adapt to suit the circumstances' (as we will see in Chapter 2 when we discuss situational leadership).[170] Tony Blair, as a former UK prime minister, is another example of a heroic leader eventually falling out of favour.

One problem is the celebrity status that is accorded to solo leaders which feeds their egos and reinforces their ambitions. The result is that:

> Nearly all CEOs think of themselves as the sort of all-knowing, tough, take-charge leader whose photo appears on the cover of *Forbes*, and they find irresistible the temptation to centralize authority in their offices, making all important ... decisions themselves.[171]

This phenomenon is not limited to 'heroes' in the business world of capitalism. It is apparent in communist cultures too. For example, personality cults developed around communist leaders like Jiang Zemin and Zhu Ronji in the People's Republic of China. Says Susan V. Lawrence of the Beijing Bureau of the *Far Eastern Economic Review*, 'China's state media [are] increasingly given over to paeans to Jiang', and he has engaged in adorning public buildings with his calligraphic inscriptions 'with enthusiasm'.[172]

Individual leadership, nevertheless, still has a place. It is necessary in small and start-up companies and in organizations where inspiration is needed to bring about transformational change, say Pasternack and colleagues.[173] But they also add:

> CEOs of large companies should ... see that it is more productive and satisfying to become a leader of leaders than to go it alone.[174]

Shared and Distributed Leadership

Various references in the literature have been made to leadership that is shared, distributed, distributive, dispersed, collective, or (not a pre-possessing term) institutional. *For clarity's sake, distributed leadership may be regarded as the (hierarchically) vertical dispersal of authority and responsibility and shared leadership as the 'horizontal' aspects of these phenomena.* House and Aditja say:

> The process of leadership cannot be described simply in terms of the behavior of an individual: rather, leadership involves collaborative relationships that lead to collective action grounded in the shared values of people who work together to effect positive change.[175]

Burdening the lexicon, they distinguish among 'delegated leadership', 'co-leadership' and 'peer leadership'. And co-leadership itself is interpreted in different ways, for example in terms of one co-leader 'playing second fiddle' to another[176] or as two leaders working side by side with equal managerial responsibility.[177] Others use the term to mean the same as leadership that is shared among many individuals. Shared leadership is nothing new, having been recorded in ancient times:

> Republican Rome had a successful system of co-leadership that lasted for over four centuries. This structure of co-leadership was so effective that it extended from the lower levels of the Roman magistracy to the very top position, that of consul.[178]

A survey by the Manufacturing Foundation found that leadership in successful middle-market manufacturing firms in the UK tended not to reside in one person at the top but existed as a shared role among the top management team.[179] Shared leadership reflects a shared ownership of problems; an emphasis on learning and development (empowerment) to enable sharing, understanding and contribution; and a culture of openness, mutual respect and trust. Michael Kocolowski suggests that healthcare and education (in the United States), where most studies have been conducted, are two sectors that are especially open to shared leadership.[180] The successful recovery of British supermarket Asda as part of Walmart in the 1990s was overseen by co-leaders Archie Norman and Allan Leighton.

Michael Useem found that 'The best projects [by MBA students] come from the teams that learn to act together and exercise shared leadership.'[181] Shared leadership is characterized by:

※ The quality of interactions among people rather than their position in a hierarchy.
※ The effectiveness with which people work together in solving a problem rather than a solo performance by one leader.
※ Conversations rather than instructions.
※ Shared values and beliefs.
※ Honesty and a desire for the common good rather than self-interest, secrecy and spin.

In 2001 Bruce Pasternack and colleagues, in collaboration with the World Economic Forum and the University of Southern California, surveyed over 4,000 people in leadership roles in 12 large organizations on three continents and interviewed 20 to 40 in each one. They found that many successful companies – such as the Intel Corporation, Motorola, and the Hyundai Electronics Industries Company in South Korea – were developing an institutional leadership capacity rather than depending on a charismatic CEO: 'Rather than an aria, leadership can be a chorus of diverse voices singing in unison.'[182] The measure they developed is known as the Leadership Quotient (LQ). Leadership, James O'Toole says, is an 'organizational trait'.[183]

However, O'Toole and colleagues reported on the indifferent reception these findings had at the 2000 World Economic Forum in Davos, Switzerland, despite evidence being provided of a sufficient number of cases of shared leadership that could attest to its success:

... this resistance to the notion of shared leadership stems from thousands of years of cultural conditioning [starting perhaps with Plato's views]. We are dealing with a near-universal myth: in the popular mind, leadership is always singular.[184]

Marianne Döös and Lena Wilhelmson reported on a study showing that two-thirds of Swedish managers had a positive attitude towards shared leadership (or co-leadership).[185] They studied four pairs of leaders in four Swedish organizations that were concerned with product development, management consulting, communications and soccer. Their common characteristics included shared values, mutual confidence, shared approaches to planning and visualizing, capitalizing on differences and a receptivity to new ideas, and a joint recognition of setbacks and successes. The Amana Corporation's CEO Paul Staman commented:

> [Shared leadership] allows more time for leaders to spend in the field; it creates an internal dynamic in which the leaders constantly challenge each other to higher levels of performance; it encourages a shared leadership mindset at all levels of the company; it prevents the trauma of transition that occurs in organizations when a strong CEO suddenly leaves. [What makes this work is] a shared set of guiding principles, and a team in which each member is able to set aside ego and 'what's in it for me' thinking.[186]

Jay Carson and colleagues, studying 59 consulting teams, found that shared leadership predicted team performance as rated by clients.[187] They also found that external coaching and the internal team environment, consisting of a shared purpose, social support and a voice, were associated with the emergence of shared leadership.

Leadership involving two people can, however, prove very dysfunctional despite its lasting many years. For example, during the period 1997–2007 in the UK the relationship between the then prime minister Tony Blair and his Chancellor of the Exchequer (finance minister) Gordon Brown was, *The Times* said, seriously flawed, with a consequential 'terrible, wasteful cost in allowing governance to play second fiddle to psychodrama'.[188]

The idea of distributed leadership (also known as institutional or dispersed leadership) takes shared leadership further. It was first described by Philip Selznick in 1957.[189] Jeff Gold and Alma Harris highlighted a study of distributed leadership in two schools and how it occurred through 'mediation in the form of [dialogue] and representational symbols' with the aim of identifying actions for improvement and monitoring any subsequent progress.[190]

Peter Gronn, in his meta-analysis of empirical studies in 20 organizations with distributed leadership, observes that this often begins spontaneously but eventually becomes institutionalized.[191] He identifies two features of distributed leadership: interdependence and coordination. Interdependence is characterized by an overlapping of leaders' responsibilities and the complementarity of responsibilities. Coordination and alignment among co-leaders are key to success, but not only at the top.

O'Toole found that 'many of the key tasks and responsibilities of leadership [are] institutionalized in the systems, practices, and cultures of the organization'.[192] Institutionalized leadership is characterized by an empowerment to act like owners and entrepreneurs rather than 'hired hands'; to take the initiative and accept accountability; and to create and adhere to agreed systems and procedures. O'Toole and colleagues suggest that the reason for the continued success of companies under the successive tenure of several CEOs – and for the failure of previously successful CEOs in new companies – is to do with organizational variables like systems, structures and policies, 'factors that are not included in research based on a solo leadership model'.[193]

Flexible distributive leadership is required to cope with the increasing volatility, complexity and variety of organizations' external environments, according to Michael Brown and Denny Goia.[194] And distributive leadership, in Peter Gronn's view, has emerged as a result of the development of new organizational forms – such as flatter structures that are more organic and virtual organization – that require greater interdependence and coordination.[195] The current interest in institutional leadership reflects a post-industrial division of labour that is characterized by distributed workplaces, which include such phenomena as 'hot-desking' and working from home. This kind of working has been made possible by developments in IT. But Keith Grint warns that, 'In attempting to escape from the clutches of heroic leadership we now seem enthralled by its apparent opposite – distributed leadership: in this post-heroic era we will all be leaders so that none are.'[196]

Yet a study of 12 universities in the UK by George Petrov of the University of Exeter's Centre for Leadership Studies found that distributed leadership was being used as 'a cloak to hide an increasing lack of consultation with staff … used by those in positions of real power to disguise power differentials, offering the illusion of consultation and participation while obscuring the mechanisms by which decisions are reached and resources distributed'.[197] Petrov sees distributed leadership not as a successor to individual leadership but as a parallel process.

Bruce Pasternack and colleagues suggest that whether (and how) a CEO builds institutional leadership, as did Jack Welch at General Electric and Yotaro 'Tony' Kobayashi at Fuji Xerox, can make a difference to organizational performance.[198] Pasternack says:

> **Too much is being written about the CEO as the great leader and not enough about organizations that demonstrate leadership capacity throughout the organization … Really good leaders take their skill and abilities and build into their organizations the capacity for leadership all the way down the line.[199]**

And Mary Curnock Cook, chief executive of UCAS, the UK's university and college student admissions service, sees distributed leadership as the organization's DNA:

> **Leadership can and should take place at all levels in an organisation. It's not something that comes only from the top. I like to think of leadership being the DNA of a company.[200]**

Hierarchical Level and Leadership

If distributed leadership is important, then it would be interesting as well as useful to explore the similarities and differences in leadership behaviour and effectiveness across the various levels of an organization's hierarchy. Most early empirical research studies of leadership focused on first-line or middle-level managers owing to the availability of access and large enough sample sizes.[201] However, in line with the growing acceptance of qualitative research, in more recent times we have seen many more studies of CEOs that have been based on interviews with them – indeed there has been a plethora of such studies.

Organizational hierarchy is associated with 'command-and-control' leadership. On the one hand, Robert Fuller says, authority and hierarchy are associated with inflexibility, slow decision making and a lack of responsiveness towards customers, and, on the other hand, if 'rank matches with experience, expertise and judgement … [these] ensure that the person who is best qualified to make the decision is the one with the authority to make it'.[202] Fuller makes the point that 'the problem is not hierarchy *per se*, but the abuse thereof', such as self-aggrandizement and self-preservation.[203] Frances Hesselbein says 'when people move into a circular system, enormous energy is released'.[204] But many organizations will probably always have hierarchies, and leadership in relation to organizational level is therefore a worthwhile consideration.

Leadership has been traditionally conceived as a top-down, hierarchical and formal role.[205] Clearly there are many people with formal leadership titles throughout hierarchical organizations – not just CEOs – who are effective leaders, however we would choose to define what 'effective' means here. Nevertheless, Scott DeRue and Susan Ashford correctly question why some people in formal leadership positions are not seen as leaders and why some people are seen as leaders even though they do not hold formal leadership positions.[206] Leadership theory has come to encompass more than formal, traditional leadership, namely a broader relationship of mutual influence 'composed of reciprocal and mutually reinforcing identities as leaders and followers [that] is [dynamic and] endorsed and reinforced within a broader organizational context'.[207] In other words, according to several scholars, leadership is a socially constructed and reciprocal relationship between leaders and followers.[208]

However, traditional, hierarchical and formal organizations with leadership of one kind or another in evidence do still exist today, and they do so in abundance. For example, leadership for Scott Goodwin, CEO of Voxclever, an IT and telecoms company founded in 2008, is 'to provide a clear framework for the business and make it abundantly clear to my managers what their roles and responsibilities are'.[209] And in such organizations we can indeed find effective leaders – and effective and happy 'subordinates' who may or may not be 'followers' in the currently fashionable sense. Are work situations commonplace where 'individuals "claim" an identity and others affirm or "grant" that identity as the underlying process by which leader and follower identities become socially constructed and form the basis of leader-follower relationships'?[210] I have yet to witness any CEOs or indeed any managers throughout an organizational hierarchy 'claiming' their leadership role and their staff 'granting' it. In formally *leaderless* groups, where leaders may emerge because of their value, contribution and esteem in a group, as described by Bernard Bass in his classic 1954 article,[211] what DeRue and Ashford describe certainly makes sense.

But such democracy in commonplace conventional organizations is still a long way off for many if not most corporate cultures and national cultures. Indeed in some cultures 'democracy' is a deception, an illusion, wishful thinking, or is even regarded as subversive. And yet the uprisings in many Arab countries in early 2011 would seem to signal an accelerated change in this unhappy state of affairs towards a more truly democratic, inclusive and participative form of leadership that resonates with the self-actualization of humanity.

Any comprehensive theory of leadership therefore would need to encompass leadership – its nature, occurrence and development – both in formal organizations and in informal groups. Moreover, such a theory must not lose sight of what the word 'leadership' means – 'showing the way and drawing people with you' – and eschew fanciful and impertinent constructions of what one or another academic *wants* it to mean. This is the approach that this book takes.

Likely hierarchical differences in leadership behaviour were pointed out long ago by Philip Selznick.[212] According to Robert Lord and Karen Maher, 'the perceptual processes that operate with respect to leaders are very likely to involve quite different considerations at upper versus lower hierarchical levels'.[213] Top-level leaders are responsible for the vision and mission of the organization – where it is heading, the development of appropriate strategies and strategic goals, and creating and promoting shared values throughout the organization. Lower-level leaders are responsible for formulating plans to implement strategies, accomplishing routine tasks and encouraging individual involvement and team working. Amatai Etzioni sees top management as being concerned with ends rather than means, middle management with means rather than ends, and first-level management with daily operations.[214] At all levels, however, there are two needs: to empower people – to *enable* people to do what needs to be done – and to engage them – to get them to *want* to do what needs to be done.

Richard Wellins and Patterson Weaver Jr argue that first-level and middle managers are:

> ... the leaders who really make or break a company, and who offer the greatest return on a development investment ... Working daily on the front lines, these people *see* problems, opportunities, and challenges. They are the most visible level of leadership to employees and customers. They bear the brunt of the responsibility for engaging the workers, building morale, and retaining key players ... [They] are the lynchpin between the strategy set at the top and the execution of that strategy through the ranks.[215]

At lower organizational levels, Daniel Katz and Robert Kahn, however, suggest little leadership as such is required, as the focus is on administrating to maintain effective operations.[216] This is contentious: leadership is needed wherever there are subordinates or followers. And administrative tasks are a means by which objectives and performance standards are achieved: plans have to be formulated to carry out tasks and achieve objectives. Katz and Kahn say that, at middle levels, administrative procedures are developed and implemented, and human relations skills are important. At the top level of an organization these administrative procedures are initiated to reflect new policy. Executives with overall responsibility for an organization will practise *strategic leadership*,[217] which we discuss in the chapter on leadership and strategy.

However, any division, department or section in a company can have a vision of where or what it needs to be. It can, and ought to, have the strategies to pursue this. And, while it may – and hopefully does – share the core corporate values, it can also define additional values, for example the performance standards that are particularly important to that part of the company and guide its members' behaviour. Examples are external or internal customer service, production quality and data accuracy. Conversely, CEOs must also be concerned with individual involvement and team working among their board members and senior management. Stephen Zaccaro and Richard Klimoski argue that a leader's position in the organizational hierarchy determines the choices available to him or her, the impact of those choices, and the requirements of the leader.[218]

In addition to a critical review of the major theories and models of leadership, we explore in Chapter 3 how transformational and transactional leadership – an important and useful current model of leadership – is distributed throughout organizational hierarchies.

The collective leadership capacity of an organization is the sum total of distributed leadership at all hierarchical levels. And, as Peter Drucker says, this is the basis for its survival and success: it provides an organization's ability to act as its *own* change agent.[219] When the collective leadership capacity of an organization is strong, we may say that that organization has a strong *leadership brand*. Dave Ulrich and colleagues state:

> **Leadership brand occurs when leaders at every level are clear about which results are most important, develop a consistent approach to delivering these results, and build attributes that support [their] achievement ...[220]**

Creating and sustaining a leadership brand[221] is a way to build employee engagement and commitment to the company,[222] just as a product or service brand is a way to build client or customer loyalty. Brand loyalty, in the case of leadership, requires employee engagement and commitment.

 Further Reading

John Adair (1989), *Great Leaders*. Guildford: The Talbot Adair Press.

John Antonakis, Anna T. Cianciolo and Robert J. Sternberg, Editors (2004), *The Nature of Leadership*. Thousand Oaks, CA: SAGE Publications.

Bernard M. Bass (2008), *The Bass Handbook of Leadership: Theory, Research, and Managerial Applications*, Fourth Edition. New York, NY: Free Press.

Warren Bennis, G.M. Spreitzer and T.G. Cummings, Editors (2001), *The Future of Leadership*. San Francisco, CA: Jossey-Bass.

Alan Bryman, David Collinson, Keith Grint, Mary Uhl-Bien and Brad Jackson (2011), *The SAGE Handbook of Leadership*. London: SAGE Publications.

James MacGregor Burns (1978), *Leadership*. New York, NY: Harper and Row.

Roger Gill, Editor (2005), *Leadership under the Microscope*. Ross-on-Wye: The Leadership Trust Foundation.

Keith Grint (2005), *Leadership: Limits and Possibilities*. Basingstoke: Palgrave Macmillan.

Keith Grint (2010), *Leadership: A Very Short Introduction*. Oxford: Oxford University Press.

Brad Jackson and Ken Parry (2008), *A Very Short, Fairly Interesting and Reasonably Cheap Book about Studying Leadership*. London: SAGE Publications.

Barbara Kellernan (2008), *Followership: How Followers Are Creating Change and Changing Leaders*. Boston, MA: Harvard Business Press.

Donald G. Krause (1997), *The Way of the Leader*. London: Nicholas Brealey.

Antonio Marturano and Jonathan Gosling (2008), *Leadership: The Key Concepts*. Abingdon: Routledge.

Joseph Masciulli, Mikhail A. Molchanov and W. Andy Knight, Editors (2009), *The Ashgate Research Companion to Political Leadership*. Farnham, Surrey: Ashgate.

Nitin Nohria and Rakesh Kumar, Editors (2010), *Handbook of Leadership Theory and Practice*. Boston, MA: Harvard Business Press.

Peter G. Northouse (2010), *Leadership: Theory and Practice*, Fifth Edition. Thousand Oaks, CA: SAGE Publications.

John L. Pierce and John W. Newstrom (2008), *Leaders and the Leadership Process*. New York: McGraw-Hill.

Ronald E. Riggio, Ira Chaleff and Jean Lipman-Blumen, Editors (2008), *The Art of Followership*. San Francisco, CA: Jossey-Bass.

Birgit Schyns and Tiffany Hansbrough, Editors (2010), *When Leadership Goes Wrong: Destructive Leadership, Mistakes, and Ethical Failures*. Charlotte, NC: Information Age Publishing.

Simon Western (2008), *Leadership: A Critical Text*. London: SAGE Publications.

Gary Yukl (2009), *Leadership in Organizations*, seventh Edition. Upper Saddle River, NJ: Prentice Hall.

Stephen J. Zaccaro and Richard J. Klimoski, Editors (2001), *The Nature of Organizational Leadership: Understanding the Performance Imperatives Confronting Today's Leaders*. San Francisco, CA: Jossey-Bass.

Discussion Questions

1. Why is there no agreed paradigm for leadership?
2. 'Leadership is showing the way and helping or inducing others to pursue it'. Discuss.
3. What is 'good' leadership?
4. 'Leaders are people who do the right thing; managers are people who do things right' (Warren Bennis). Discuss.
5. 'And when we think we lead, we are most led' (Lord Byron). Discuss.
6. Why is the study of followership useful to understanding leadership?
7. Change management or change leadership? Which is more important?
8. Do leaders behave differently across hierarchical levels in organizations?
9. Is the day of the individual, 'heroic' leader giving way to the age of collective leadership?
10. How might collective organizational leadership enable an organization to be its own 'change agent'?

2 Sectoral Similarities and Differences in Leadership

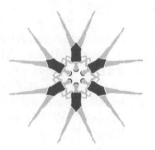

Q. What do business, politics, public service, higher education, charities and the armed forces have in common? A. The need for leadership.

OVERVIEW

- This chapter reviews similarities and differences in leadership, its impact and challenges across selected sectors: namely business, politics, public service, higher education, not-for-profit and the armed forces.
- Studies of the impact of leadership across sectors primarily comprised of large-scale surveys, interviews and objective measures of leadership effectiveness justify its importance and its contribution to human achievement and happiness.
- One of the big issues for business leadership in the first decade of the twenty-first century has been greed and the increasing gulf in mutual understanding between the top leadership of businesses and both their staff and the general public. Yet there are also well-documented cases of good leadership and good companies to work for.
- Political leadership has also suffered from an increasing credibility deficit. We consider, with examples, its development and the characteristics and challenges that make it unique.
- The public sector is the instrument used by elected politicians to pursue their visions and missions. Leadership in the public sector is also idiosyncratic: as one senior civil servant says, 'top civil servants are leaders, but they are on a lead'. Differences in attitudes and approaches and in the challenges and constraints that leaders face largely explain the differences in leadership characteristics between the public and private sectors.
- Higher education institutions in the UK are experiencing management and leadership issues that are specific to the sector and pose interesting leadership development challenges. The overriding challenge for higher education, apart from funding cuts and uncertainties, is to achieve a sustainable balance between academic freedom and scholarship and business managerialism.
- Organizations in the voluntary, charity and not-for-profit sectors focus on visions, missions and values that generally are different from those in the private and public sectors. This implies the need for some different leader characteristics and competencies.

(Continued)

(Continued)

- The armed forces are often regarded as paragons of virtue in respect of leadership. Their leadership style has evolved through command-and-control and directive leadership to mission command and more democratic forms of leadership. We also consider the demands that highly dangerous situations place on leadership and the increasingly varied roles that the armed forces are called upon to perform.

Leadership in Business

In 2001 Lyn Offermann commented that public confidence in business leaders had deteriorated in the preceding years, with a disillusionment that focused largely on issues of ethics and values.[1] This has continued to be the case, with notable headline failures, public outcries and various disasters in the intervening decade up to 2011. Ineffective or bad leadership has been estimated to have cost anything between $500,000 and $2,700,000 in an organization, with adverse impacts in the forms of lost intellectual or social capital, disengaged employees and missed business opportunities, according to Adrian Furnham.[2] And on the basis of several studies, he calculates the overall failure rate for managers in leadership positions at around 50 per cent.

Also in 2001, the highly respected management and strategy scholar Henry Mintzberg said, 'There's a greed in the air which is just mind-blowing … corporations have been captured by one insatiable group – the greediest of all – the shareholders.'[3] Shareholders, however, have been overtaken in this respect in the 10 years since then by top corporate executives themselves. The huge salaries and bonuses for CEOs that focus their attention on the short-term share price rather than building the company are both dysfunctional and irresponsible. Yet, as journalist Alison Eadie said in 2001, despite a 'publishing blizzard' on leadership and the great array of available leadership development programmes, we [were] 'turning out duds'.[4] It appears that we are still doing so.

Despite their CEOs' explanations of factors beyond their control – which are occasionally correct – companies usually fail because of leadership errors. Ram Charan and Jerry Useem comment, 'What undoes them is the familiar stuff of human folly: denial, hubris, ego, wishful thinking, poor communication, lax oversight, greed [and] deceit.'[5] Richard Tedlow chronicles a litany of leaders in denial, starting with Henry Ford, whose denial of customers' wishes in 1922 – 'Any customer can have a car painted any color that he wants as long as it is black' – led to customer flight and near-bankruptcy in the 1940s.[6] In his investigation of why CEOs fail, Sydney Finkelstein discovered 'surprisingly few causes':

* They ignore the need for change.
* They have the wrong vision: the logical and practical limitations of the 'one big idea' are not considered.
* CEOs 'get too close' to their companies: they treat these as extensions of themselves.
* They have arrogant attitudes.
* They revert to using old formulas that once worked but no longer do so.[7]

Strategy is a key area of weakness. For example, Kmart, Tyco and AT&T followed the 'strategy *du jour*'; Tyco, WorldCom and AT&T were beset by 'acquisition lust'; and Cisco Systems failed in strategic thinking – they omitted to test their basic assumption of growth and ignored the indicative data.[8] The UK's General Electric Company (GEC), after its long-serving chairman Lord Weinstock's retirement in 1996, followed divestment and investment strategies that virtually destroyed the company.[9]

Culture and corporate values are another key area of weakness. Ram Charan and Jerry Useem quote 'dangerous' cultures that encourage profit taking without disclosure and conflicts of interest without safeguards: 'rotten cultures produce rotten deeds'.[10] Brian Baxter, senior partner at Kiddy and Partners, sees a shift from a 'nurturing', people-oriented leadership to a 'tough, driving' style, which is 'not liked or admired but [is] widely respected'.[11] A notable example of this style together with the wrong strategy and putative 'fat-cat' greed is Sir Fred ('the Shred') Goodwin, former CEO of the Royal Bank of Scotland. The consequences of this shift, which can be explained by at least one major theory of leadership (situational leadership), are unfortunately the opposite of what is actually needed. These consequences are resentment, alienation and a psychological withdrawal from work – and corporate damage that is sometimes terminal.

Warren Bennis and James O'Toole suggest that boards often do not understand what defines real leadership today.[12] Finding it hard to 'measure' vision, inspiration and conviction, they focus on 'hard' facts like shareholder value, market share, merger experience and technical skills as evidence of effective 'leadership'. Yet when they do focus on CEOs' visions, Bennis and O'Toole say:

> **Boards are often seduced by articulate, glamorous – dare we say it – charismatic dreamers who send multiple frissons down their collective spines. William Agee seduced many boards with his 'chasing rainbows' number, creating rhapsodic scenarios for a vision-starved board and proceeding to 'fail upwards' because his glossy pitch always fell short of the directors' expectations.[13]**

Leaders also have a 'shelf life' that expires through burnout, thereby diminishing energy. Changes in working methods associated with globalization and the digital economy – a decentralization of operations and increased team working – are also influencing the nature of the leadership that is required: global virtual teams are becoming more widespread.[14] These consist of individuals who are culturally diverse and geographically or organizationally distributed worldwide and who interact in carrying out inter-dependent tasks guided by a common purpose and use computer-mediated communication technologies.

While there is considerable evidence for the positive effect of leadership on organizational effectiveness and employee satisfaction, the performance measures used in studies have usually been subjective evaluations.[15] This has led to less-than-compelling evidence for the importance of leadership.

A Conference Board study of some 400 *Fortune 1000* companies in the United States in the late 1990s found that 47 per cent of executives and managers rated their companies' overall leadership capacity as poor or fair, while only 8 per cent rated it as excellent.[16]

And a survey by Development Dimensions International in 1999 found that only 36 per cent of employees, including senior management, said they had confidence in their leaders.[17] Employees identified weaknesses in 13 out of 14 leadership skills, including strategic decision making, coaching and facilitating change. Only 49 per cent of employees perceived empowering leadership in senior management; only 30 per cent believed that their leaders had a vision; and 25 per cent criticized strategic decision making. Robert McHenry, chairman of OPP, suggests that:

* Managers do not think strategically or long term.
* People are expected to lead and manage without training.
* Too many leaders are choosing entrepreneurship over strategic focus.
* Managers often lack communication skills.[18]

A Chartered Management Institute (CMI) survey of leadership in the UK from the perspective of followers revealed that many leaders were failing to inspire the next generation and were also struggling to meet today's business challenges, though organizations with leadership development programmes in place were doing significantly better.[19] More than one-third of all executives and nearly one-half of junior managers perceived the quality of leadership in their organizations as very poor. The chair of the project's advisory panel, Sir John Egan, commented:

> Today's senior people have a new accountability to the people they lead. Good leadership is not elusive to describe nor to develop, but many companies have yet to rise to the challenge of creating programmes of leadership for all their managers.[20]

While 55 per cent of managers identified inspiration as one of the three most important leadership characteristics, only 11 per cent said their leaders provided it. They were more likely to see their leaders as knowledgeable (39 per cent) and ambitious (38 per cent) – characteristics that were perceived as important to their leaders' promotion but not as important to leadership *per se*. The other most significant leadership attributes were the ability to provide a vision, to look to the future, and to handle change – all of which were perceived as often lacking. The majority of executives favoured a role for leaders where they could create a sense of purpose and a central vision or set of goals and then develop others around them to achieve those goals. Commenting on the survey results, Mary Chapman, director-general of the CMI (2002), said there was a 'mismatch between what people want from their leaders and what they are experiencing': what they wanted was vision and inspiration, but what they got was ambition and technical knowledge.[21] The survey also revealed that leadership development was still a low priority. Almost half of respondents' organizations had no specific leadership development budget. However, where their organizations addressed leadership development, 57 per cent of respondents rated quality of leadership highly in comparison with 21 per cent of those in other organizations.

An interview survey of 1,000 employees in British companies with more than 500 staff at the beginning of 2004 revealed many employees as bored at work, lacking in commitment, alienated, and ready to quit.[22] The managing director of the firm conducting the survey, Steve Newhall, said:

> Our research shows that organisations that fail to create a sense of meaning through their activities simply don't earn people's loyalty ... We all have hard jobs; we want to be sure they are worth the effort and help us grow.

The 'inspiration gap' the CMI survey identified in the UK in no way applied to the top companies in a 2004 survey by *The Sunday Times* of the 100 best companies to work for and their 20,000 employees. Adèle Collins commented, 'The energy and inspirational qualities of a company's leader emerge this year as the major factors in making a company one of the best to work for.'[23]

Another Conference Board leadership survey in 2002 had revealed a decline in the perceived strength of leadership in American companies. In 1997 about one-half of respondents had rated their company's leadership strength as good or excellent; in 2001 only about one-third did so.[24] And a survey by OPP in 2002 also revealed a significant dissatisfaction with leadership:[25]

❄ Only 40 per cent of respondents were satisfied with the leadership of their organizations.
❄ The main cause of dissatisfaction was a lack of trust.
❄ 69 per cent felt that the most important leadership quality was trustworthiness, but only 22 per cent believed it was their boss's best attribute.
❄ Almost 40 per cent believed that the quality of leadership had declined in the previous 10 years.
❄ The greatest dissatisfaction was associated with taking risks or being entrepreneurial: 'People want leaders they can trust and with whom they feel confident about their future rather than those offering disruption.'[26]

In another 2003 survey by the Manufacturing Foundation of successful middle-market manufacturing firms in the UK, in more than half of the firms leadership style was ranked second, after strategic planning, in respect of its impact on company performance.[27]

Annual surveys by *Fortune* magazine in the United States and *The Sunday Times* in the UK track 'the world's most admired companies' and the '1000 best companies to work for' respectively. They consistently identify leadership as a key factor contributing to high (and low) rankings. For example, Scott Spreier and Dawn Sherman of management consultants Hay Group, who conducted the 2002 *Fortune* survey, point out that the most admired companies are more focused on strategic issues, more successful at maintaining employee morale and commitment, and better led, with a greater emphasis on teams rather than individuals.[28] *Fortune* magazine reported that:

> The truth is that no one factor makes a company admirable, but if you were forced to pick the one that makes the most difference, you'd pick leadership ... people are voting for the artist, not the painting.[29]

In *The Sunday Times* 2002 survey of the *100 Best Companies to Work For*, W.L. Gore & Associates, the Gore-Tex manufacturer, was ranked 16th overall, top for 'the most approachable management', and sixth for both 'the best work/life balance' and the 'most trusting managers'.[30] Mike Cox, technical director of the industrial products division, said:

> Teamwork is everything. Gore is structured entirely differently from a classical organisation, to encourage everyone to contribute and to be inventive and creative. There is no positional power: you are only a leader if teams decide to respect and follow you, and we assess each other, which is rare but generates feedback and a sense of meritocracy.[31]

By 2004, W.L. Gore was ranked as the best company to work for in the UK, and also had the top score for putting into practice strong values and principles.[32] Between 80 and 90 per cent of Gore's staff believed they could make a difference to the company, felt they made a valuable contribution to business success, and also felt the company was 'principled'.[33] And the majority of staff thought that Gore's corporate values did not reflect only one person's leadership. The 2004 survey supported the relationship between leadership and corporate values. Commenting on this, Adèle Collins said:

> ... where staff perceive the values and principles within their company to be strong they are more likely to have a strong leadership and are more likely to view their company as a better place to work overall.[34]

In the 2005 survey, W.L. Gore was the first company to rank first in two successive years, also leading the leadership category.[35] In 2007, for the fourth successive year, Gore ranked top overall in the mid-size firm category (between 250 and 4,999 employees).[36] Between 2008 and 2011 the company dropped in the rankings but remained in the top 13 each year (see the chapter on leadership and values for a further discussion of Gore's values and culture).

The top ranking company for leadership in 2004 was Beaverbrooks, the jewellers. Beaverbrooks also ranked as the second best company to work for overall. Alastair McCall reported one employee as saying, "The more senior people are a real inspiration. They have taught me so much about myself and continually support me. I feel a true sense of belonging here.'[37] McCall also said:

> Giving workers a sense of ownership is one of the key ingredients in creating the best companies to work for. Most often, the lead for achieving this comes from the top, making quality of leadership – and the ability of the boss to inspire the workforce – the single biggest influence on a company's ranking.[38]

Jim Collins and Jerry Porras claimed that the research evidence shows that companies' sustained success is clearly associated with leadership.[39] However, David Day and Robert Lord argued that the effects of strategic (top-level) leadership could not be assessed in less than two years.[40] Thomas Lenz explained:

> Literature on corporate decline and failure indicates that such measures are 'lagging indicators' ... [whereas] use of behavioral referents affords a means to evaluate leadership with 'leading indicators ... [which] may open the way for more rapid corrective action, if deficiencies are present.[41]

The best companies to work for in 2002 on average outperformed the rest of the FTSE-listed companies, with investment returns over the previous five years of 25.4 per cent compared with –2 per cent, 6.3 per cent and 21.2 per cent over the previous three years.[42] Apart from the benefits to employees, being 'a good company to work for' makes a company an attractive investment. Numerous other studies show a relationship between leadership and financial performance, market share, organizational and work group climate, and employee job satisfaction, commitment and productivity.

A survey by the Accenture Institute of Strategic Change in the United States found that the stock prices of companies perceived to be 'well led' – creating cultures of adaptation – grew 900 per cent over a ten-year period versus 74 per cent for companies perceived to lack good leadership in this respect.[43] In research with Harvard Business School, executive search consultants Odgers, Ray & Berndtson found that the quality of leadership accounted for some 15–20 per cent of the total variance in companies' performance, using a methodology that measured ROL ('return on leadership').[44]

The importance of leadership has been recognized by the UK's Council for Excellence in Management and Leadership (CEML) in a radical recommendation for the voluntary reporting of leadership by public and private sector organizations in their annual reports, using evidence-based statements.[45] Sue Law made the point that the reporting of leadership was an 'inevitable next step' in the increasing emphasis on business accountability, including business ethics, the environment and social responsibility as a whole.[46] The CEML has established several areas of leadership capability that might be included: morale (including employee job satisfaction); motivation (including surveys of employees' understanding of their companies' vision and strategy); and long-term development, including reviews of potential for leadership capability.

Leadership in Politics

In our discussion of leadership in politics we define 'politics' as concerning the individual and collective activities and behaviour of people in governing a country or region. In relation to leadership, we are interested in the role and effects of status, values and the use of power in social relationships and decision-making processes in various cultural contexts. A useful way of understanding political leadership as individual agency – the product of individual action – is the framework proposed by Fred Greenstein[47] and Joseph Nye:[48]

✳ Contextual intelligence and practical wisdom – interpreting situations and contexts (we discuss this as part of cognitive intelligence in our chapter on the multiple intelligences of leadership).
✳ Emotional intelligence and courage (also discussed in the same chapter).
✳ Ethical vision (discussed in our chapters on leadership and vision and leadership and values).
✳ The contemporary art of political communication.
✳ The skills of diplomacy and political negotiation.
✳ Organizational skills (such as choice of advisers).

The last two attributes are classified by Joseph Masciulli and his colleagues as related to 'hard' power and resources and the first four to 'soft' power and resources (but these are not necessarily mutually exclusive).[49] And Masciulli and colleagues[50] point out the dilemmas that political leaders face today and tomorrow, using three forms of political activity that critical theorists such as Mark Stier[51] have proposed:

* The interpretive conception – the analysis and development of meanings on the basis that human beings are 'intentional and meaningful in their actions'.
* The technical conception – using knowledge as a means of changing the social and natural worlds.
* The educative conception – 'enlightening people about which means are effective for the ends that they desire to pursue'.

Reconciling all three forms of political activity in relation to liberal-democratic, human rights and ethical commitments, Masciulli and colleagues say, is elusive and requires 'exceptional' leadership.[52]

In his discussion of political leadership Dennis Kavanagh contrasts *reconcilers* with *mobilizers*.[53] He cites, as British examples of the latter, Lloyd George, Joseph Chamberlain and Tony Benn, who were primarily concerned with achieving policy goals rather than reconciling different interests, usually through radical change. Mobilizers therefore may be transformational leaders (whom we introduced in Chapter 1) who emerge in conditions of dissatisfaction or crisis, like Lloyd George in 1916 and Winston Churchill in 1940. But in British politics, leaders who start out as mobilizers – as Harold Wilson and Edward Heath did – do not last long as such and eventually become reconcilers as a result of the pressures of the consensus culture of political parties and government.

On the other hand, while the 'Iron Lady', British prime minister Margaret Thatcher, transformed British society in the 1980s as a mobilizer, she was eventually rejected because of her unwavering authoritarian leadership style. Her successor, John Major, according to historian Anthony Seldon, lacked the 'essential attributes of a leader': the ability to define an agenda, mobilize support for that agenda, and then inspire followers with a vision of the destination.[54] Similarly, Kevin Theakston says:

> No one would or could look to Major for visionary or innovative leadership. His skills were primarily those of a political manager – his approach was reactive, tactical and problem solving ... a details man ... But he was not good on policy or on medium- and long-term strategy and objectives. He did not project a clear ideological position or a strong sense of policy direction.[55]

Following a good start as Leader of the Opposition along with his party's election in 1997, Tony Blair began to appear in a shaky position as prime minister from 2003 onwards, with declining ratings on 'trust' as a result of joining the controversial war in Iraq and increasing scepticism over his policies at home. He was perceived as committed to goals and values, and, Peter Riddell says, he preferred the 'big picture' strategy, values and images over policy detail.[56] His 'Third Way', however, was unclear and his 'modernization' mantra lacked direction and application. Meanwhile the opposition Conservative Party elected four leaders in quick succession. David Cameron, elected in December 2005, was destined to become prime minister in a coalition government with the Liberal Democrats in May 2010.

Political parties may from time to time lose their way, as evidenced by the disastrous performances of the British Labour Party in the 1982 general election and the Conservative Party in the 1997 and 2001 general elections. Such events have to do with leadership: failure is usually to do with vision, values and strategies that lack an intellectual or emotional appeal. Robert Elgie, in a discussion of political leadership, suggests that any differences in leaders' traits and styles are exercised through – and limited by – the institutional culture in which they operate.[57] This is a point we shall return to in our discussion of leadership, strategy and culture.

Former US president Richard Nixon is said to have used bargaining rather than display 'leadership', and he suffered a fatal credibility crisis over the Watergate affair.[58] The charismatic president Bill Clinton was castigated for lying about his sexual misconduct. His successor George W. Bush, whose venture into Iraq to topple its president, Saddam Hussein, ostensibly on the grounds of his possession of weapons of mass destruction, divided the American nation, still won a second term in the 2004 presidential election with a 2 per cent margin in the popular vote.

Doris Kearns Goodwin, the Pulitzer Prize-winning historian and biographer, contrasts the leadership styles of three American presidents whose legacies loomed large over several decades after they left office.[59] Lyndon B. Johnson's greatest strengths, she says, were his understanding of the legislative process, his brilliance on both a one-to-one basis and in small groups, his ability to create team spirit, and his sense of timing. John F. Kennedy was his opposite in all of these respects. But he understood the power of language and the importance of symbolism, humour and image in mobilizing people towards a common goal. Among American presidents, however, it is Franklin D. Roosevelt who perhaps offers the best case study in leadership, Goodwin says. His greatest gift as a leader was his absolute confidence in himself and, even more importantly, in the American people. All three knew how to channel people's best impulses towards positive outcomes. Their strengths lay in their extraordinary ability to reach out and move others, despite their human weaknesses. Their stories offer useful lessons for today's leader in any kind of organization. In alluding to the office of President of the United States, Tony Blair, as a former British prime minister, said:

> **Leadership is personal. People often think of leaders as the repositories of unique knowledge, who by reason of their office can survey things that others cannot ... there is still a sense in which the leader, and most particularly the President of the United States, remains on the Olympian heights. Mere mortals are still inspired by a certain awe – at least for the office of the presidency, if not always for the human being that occupies it. ... the real test of leadership – amongst all the tests of policy, judgment, politics and ability – is whether, in the final analysis, you put the country first; that ultimately you are prepared to put what you perceive to be the common good of the nation before your own political self. It is the supreme test. Very few leaders pass it.[60]**

However, according to research by clinical psychologists Steven J. Rubenzer and Tom Faschingbauer, American presidents who are rated most highly by historians tend not only to be intelligent but also to have ambitious goals and to be willing to bend the truth.[61] Tony Blair suffered accusations of lying in relation to the case for going to war in Iraq in 2003. Rubenzer says that 'being a better liar than the others ... seems to increase their chances of putting their policies in place'.[62] But perhaps it is also one reason why electorates are so cynical about their political leaders.

The decline and eventual collapse of the Soviet Union and the introduction of *perestroika* and *glasnost* brought the heroic leadership of Michail Gorbachev to prominence. The French president, Jacques Chirac, was accused of financial corruption, though in 2003 he displayed strong leadership in standing firm against the US campaign in Iraq. The German Chancellor, Helmut Kohl, was accused of improper fund-raising for his party. And the Spanish government was unexpectedly defeated in elections in 2004, partly owing to Spain's participation in a coalition with the United States and the UK in post-war Iraq, but also as aresult of a perceived dishonest misrepresentation, for political purposes, of the identity of the perpetrators of a terrorist bombing in Madrid. In Northern Ireland the Ulster Unionists led by David Trimble were overtaken by the more hard-line Democratic Unionist Party led by the Reverend Ian Paisley, thereby putting the peace process in jeopardy. Indeed Trimble lost his parliamentary seat in the 2005 elections.

Asia too has witnessed a series of political leadership crises. The Philippines president, Joseph Estrada, was accused of corruption and resigned. The Japanese prime minister Mori was criticized for his inability or unwillingness to define his vision for Japan as a leader in IT and support it with tangible strategies, and he also eventually resigned. Thailand's prime minister Thaksin Shinawatra promulgated 'new action, new thought' but took an antagonistic stance towards new civic reformist institutions and came to be regarded by some as an autocrat. Amid accusations of fraud and corruption, he fled the country. Indonesia has had a succession of presidents since the fall of its dictator Suharto in 1998, as it gradually attempts to engage with democracy. And in the aftermath of bloody wars new political systems in Afghanistan and Iraq have also been introducing democratic leadership.

January and February 2011 saw the start of uprisings among the people of several Arab countries – Tunisia, Egypt, Yemen, Bahrain, Syria and Libya – with various skirmishes occurring elsewhere too. 'Freedom' was the call, and democracy the people's vision. New leadership was being sought.

Democracies, however, in which leaders are elected are beginning to meet with signs of disillusionment, says Anthony Giddens.[63] Fewer people are voting and more people are eschewing politics, believing the worst of politicians and political leaders. Broadcaster and writer Jeremy Paxman believes that this attitude towards politics and political leaders is due to governments' remoteness from the people and from communities, and their increasing inability to make changes and get things done.[64]

Ironically this may be due to government ministers behaving more like managers than leaders. Mark Goyder of the Centre for Tomorrow's Company points out that government ministers are drenched in statistics on progress, are questioned about specific cases in their functional domain, and are always expected to be in the 'know':

New plans, new initiatives new targets are thrown out to feed critics ... Ministers are drawn into managing when their job should be leadership. We want a minister for health, not a minister running the health service. Perhaps our political leaders could get back to being leaders, and let the people appointed to manage ... [manage].[65]

Goyder imagines what one might hear in the House of Commons at Question Time:

Member for Early Bleating: 'What is the minister doing about lengthening [National Health Service] waiting lists in my constituency?' Minister: 'There is a three-year plan to deal with waiting lists as part of a wider preventive programme, on which parliament was consulted. It is the responsibility of the chief executive of the NHS, together with the local line management, in whom I have every confidence. These things take time. Ask me again in two years.'

Leadership in the Public Sector[66]

A veteran ex-permanent secretary in the British Civil Service is reported as having said that he had 'never been sure that leadership is not regarded partially as a crime within Whitehall'; another stated that top civil servants 'are leaders, but they are on a lead'.[67]

The public sector is the instrument of elected politicians for pursuing their visions and missions. 'In public services', Paul Joyce says, 'it is important to recognize the primacy of politicians in creating strategic visions'.[68] Public sector managers are expected to articulate and sell the vision to employees at all levels. Sir Norman Bettison, Chief Constable of West Yorkshire, says: 'The best leaders are those who can secure long-term public value and a vision for their staff.'[69]

However, '[... the] UK's poorly managed and union-dominated public sector is ill-equipped for a decade of fiscal austerity' read the caption for an online blog in late 2009 by John Philpott, the Chartered Institute of Personnel and Development's chief economic adviser and visiting professor of economics at the University of Hertfordshire.[70] Philpott contends that poor public service performance[71] is due in part to 'under-management' in terms of management quality, which is in turn the result of inadequate or insufficient training in managing people productively. If he is right, a lack of leadership is one ghost that apparently still haunts the public sector despite government attempts to exorcise it.[72]

The public sector is often adversely compared with the private sector.[73] Leadership is at the heart of organizational effectiveness and employee engagement. So what does recent research say about the similarities and differences in leadership between the sectors?

The public and private sectors have traditionally been regarded as very different.[74] In recent years, however, they have been moving culturally closer to one other. In the United States, for example, the 'Reinventing Government' movement of the 1990s sought to change the mission and culture of the public sector by instilling such concepts as innovation and entrepreneurship and customer and employee empowerment.[75]

However, the US federal government appears to be still lagging well behind the private sector in fostering employee engagement and accountability according to a McKinsey survey, although government managers understand and embrace their organizations' vision and direction and are more motivated to make a difference than their private sector counterparts.[76]

A very similar need in the UK around the turn of the twenty-first century was reflected in the government's public sector modernization agenda.[77] We are now witnessing a greater commercialization of services in the public sector, previously mainly the concern of the private sector, and greater responsiveness to a wider range of stakeholders in the private sector, previously mainly the focus of the public sector.[78]

However, there are significant differences as well as similarities in leadership and leadership development in the UK public and private sectors. Separate surveys of leadership and management issues in the UK public and private sectors by Ashridge in collaboration with the National School of Government in 2008 found similarities between the two sectors in:

* Emphasis on social and environmental responsibility (expressed by 94 per cent of respondents in both sectors).
* Perceived effectiveness of respondents' immediate managers (77 per cent of respondents in the public sector and 80 per cent in the private sector).
* Adequate availability of immediate managers (71 per cent and 69 per cent respectively).
* Satisfactory communication of top-level leadership with staff (46 per cent and 49 per cent respectively).[79]

Significant differences in leadership and leadership development between the public and private sectors concern perceptions that:

* Top-level leadership is effective (55 per cent of respondents in the public sector and 74 per cent in the private sector).
* Their organization is doing enough to develop the next generation of leaders (36 per cent and 48 per cent respectively).
* Their organization's approach to motivation is right (39 per cent and 55 per cent respectively).
* People feel more involved in decision-making processes than three years previously (51 per cent and 69 per cent respectively).

Leadership in the public sector needs to be valued more, particularly in the NHS, according to Clare Chapman, director-general of the workforce for the Department of Health:

> If quality is going to become the organizing principle ... Leaders have got to free staff up to be able to wrap the service around patients and communities rather than looking up at government targets. And the NHS must value leaders and leadership in a far more significant way.[80]

Turning doctors into leaders is a major challenge for the NHS – and perhaps also more widely within the healthcare sector. Thomas Lee argues that in the United States, in the healthcare system, leaders first 'need to absorb three painful messages': performance matters (how patients fare); 'value' is not a bad word (achieving good outcomes as efficiently as possible); and improvements in performance require teamwork ('Individual clinicians have only limited control over the fate of their patients [despite their passion for patients' interests and personal need for autonomy] ... superior coordination, information sharing, and teamwork across disciplines are required if value and outcomes are to improve').[81]

The first annual survey of the best places to work in the public sector by *The Sunday Times* in 2010 shows that public sector employees are 'more content with and engaged by certain key aspects of their working environment' – pay and benefits and the contribution their organizations make to their local community and society more generally – than their private sector counterparts.[82] The introduction of performance-related pay in the public sector was criticized by Sir Norman Bettison because it did not reflect why people chose to work in public service:

> **People join, and remain in, the public sector because of a sense of vocation – to make a difference to society or to the quality of people's lives ... Now, one by one, they find themselves castigated over their pay.[83]**

However, with respect to leadership and well-being, the picture is the opposite. The survey report also says:

> **The public sector is falling behind at a time when it is faced with a barrage of negative messages from both the main political parties concerning the sector's prospects after the [then] imminent general election.[84]**

Compared with the private sector, confidence in the leadership skills of senior management and inspiration from the top leader in an organization are significantly lower among public sector employees. Jonathan Austin, CEO and founder of Best Companies Ltd, which conducts the surveys for *The Sunday Times*, says, 'Leaders need to communicate and listen to feedback from employees more than ever.'[85]

Outstanding leaders are often perceived as charismatic: they attract and inspire followers, which we discuss in later chapters. Charismatic leadership in the public sector in Canada is perceived in terms of vision, risk taking, challenge and encouragement, and energy and determination, according to Mansour Javidan and David Waldman.[86] However, they found that charismatic leadership overall was not strongly related to motivation or operating performance. Yet motivation was found to be predicted by risk taking, challenge and encouragement by the leader, which engendered higher self-esteem in subordinates. Risk taking, however, may be discouraged or avoided in the public sector. In the words of Senator Dwight Nelson, a Jamaican government minister:

> **In the private sector we have what we call risk management; we have leadership that is prepared to take risks and we do not have that in the public sector. We play it by the rules, whether those rules are productive or not.[87]**

The relationship between charismatic leadership and operating performance is much stronger in the private sector than in the public sector,[88] probably because of political or bureaucratic constraints on leaders' behaviour or accomplishments.[89] This relationship is much stronger still in the private sector when there is a high degree of uncertainty, for example in times of crisis or turbulence.[90] Such uncertainty is stressful for subordinates, which results in a lack of self-confidence, greater receptiveness to a charismatic vision, and a greater freedom among leaders to exercise discretion. According to research at Cranfield School of Management, individual leadership is favoured in difficult business circumstances, whereas in the public sector collective leadership and consensus are favoured during difficult times, even at the expense of individual leadership.[91] However, while bureaucracies in the public sector have often been characterized by a lack of turbulence or uncertainty, crises may reduce the difference between them and the private sector in respect of the effects of charismatic leadership.[92] In any case, the relentlessly increasing pace of change in the public sector is a constant challenge to public sector leaders.[93]

A unique leadership challenge in the public sector appears to be the shift away from traditional technical or operational roles on the one hand and from advisory roles on the other to more collaborative, networked leadership roles.[94] These leadership roles carry with them high levels of accountability yet less authority, implying a need for greater political awareness, more collaborative and engaging leadership behaviour, and exceptional influencing skills. 'Engaging leadership', John Alban-Metcalfe and Beverly Alimo-Metcalfe say, is about *how* leaders strive to lead competently: they show concern for others, enable them to do what needs to be done, encourage them to question, build a shared vision, inspire others, focus team effort, support a developmental culture, network, and facilitate change in a sensitive manner.[95]

Engaging leadership is much more about using personal power (influence) than using position power (authority). Authority is the power or right to give orders and enforce obedience[96] that is associated with rank, status or position in an organization, industry or nation. Personal power on the other hand is the power to influence people, regardless of rank, position or status, due to one's personal attractiveness, expertise, knowledge, characteristics or social skills (which we discuss further in the chapter on leadership and engagement). That others are willing to be influenced is the prerequisite of personal power. Today there is a trend towards the use of personal power and away from the use of authority that is common to both the public and private sectors. The 2008 Ashridge survey showed that there is the same perception of this trend (by 74 per cent of respondents) in both sectors.[97]

'The popular image of an empowered, proactive leader fails to reflect the reality of senior managers' roles in public sector organizations in the UK', according to Frank Blackler.[98] Based on a 2006 study of NHS chief executives, he says:

... the study of leadership in the public sector cannot be divorced from broader study of the institutions of the state and, in this case, from the centralized performance audit regime that government developed to drive forward its modernization policy.

By 2010 leadership in the public sector was still an intractable issue. But it also faced an additional, unavoidable challenge – a prolonged period of scarce resources – according to the executive director of the Institute for Government and former permanent secretary in two ministries, Lord Bichard:

> **The test will be to deliver better services at a lower cost, rather than merely identify a series of cuts to existing services – and that provides public sector leaders with their biggest challenge in a generation.[99]**

While the familiar needs still existed, Bichard also highlighted that today's needs required:

※ Less risk-averse and more innovative organizations.
※ More engagement between leaders and the front line.
※ A better management of risk.
※ The valuing, recognizing and promoting of successful innovators.
※ The removal of process-based targets that stifled people's creativity.
※ An attack on energy-sapping and needless paper, reports and meetings.
※ The development of genuine collaborations with partner organizations and measuring their success in terms of outcomes.
※ An emphasis on the skills of influencing, negotiating, building trust and sustaining coalitions.
※ Caution to be exercised over any further restructuring that would consume energy and give marginal benefits.

Bichard underscores the need for a clear sense of purpose (mission), direction (vision), values and engagement – four of our six core themes and practices of effective leadership with the fifth one, empowerment, implicit in his recommendations, though there is nothing directly about strategy. He comments: 'When resources are scarce, there is a premium on well-targeted, client-centred services – and outstanding leadership.'[100]

So is leadership different in the public and private sectors? It is similar in relation to social and environmental responsibility and employees' attitudes to their immediate managers – two favourable characteristics. It is different in relation to perceptions of top-level leaders, risk taking, the adequacy of leadership development, and organizational approaches to motivation and decision-making involvement. Differences in attitudes and approaches and in the challenges and constraints that leaders face probably largely explain the differences in leadership characteristics between the public and private sectors.

Leadership in the UK's Higher Education Institutions[101]

Higher education institutions in the UK are experiencing management and leadership issues that are unique to the sector and pose interesting leadership development challenges. A leadership development programme conducted by the Leadership Trust in the UK as part of an organization development initiative in a new university – Sheffield Hallam University – revealed some of the tensions that were typical in the sector.[102] Wider research findings published in November 2006 also underscored some of the very same issues.[103]

The myth of the 'gifted amateur' – that anybody who is highly educated and highly intelligent can naturally manage or lead – is still perpetuated in the cloisters of academia.[104] This myth, of course, is patently false. The challenge is to transform 'knowledge workers' – academics and professionals – first into managers and then into leaders. Time and time again we see remarkable academics transformed into unremarkable managers or leaders – and we lose gifted academics in the process. Perhaps this danger is implicitly understood, though it is seldom articulated: many academics will eschew formal management and leadership roles (such as head of department, director, dean or pro-vice-chancellor). And when such positions are sought, they are sometimes sought for the wrong reasons.

Why is there this resistance in higher education institutions (HEIs) to taking on management and leadership roles? The reasons suggested are a lack of rewards; loyalty to one's discipline rather than the institution; career structures in these research assessment-obsessed times that reward research over teaching, programme development and administration;[105] and the potentially negative impact on research performance, prestige and peer relationships.

While HEIs must operate in a business-like way, they are not simply businesses, says Sir Ivor Crewe, master of University College, Oxford, and former vice chancellor of the University of Essex and president of Universities UK.[106] In the UK almost all HEIs are part of the public sector. These rely on public funding for less than half of their income and they have a more democratic, critical and dissenting culture than that which is typical of the public sector.[107] The purpose of higher education – to address society's needs, the priorities of the government of the day, or the creation of knowledge for knowledge's sake – continues to be hotly debated. The core mission or purpose of a university, Crewe says, is the creation and communication of knowledge and ideas.[108] Higher education 'is a good in itself, and an end in itself', says Boris Johnson, former UK shadow higher education minister and, currently, mayor of London.[109]

Yet market forces have clashed with such traditional academic missions and values. The academic landscape has changed in several ways as a result of the following:

※ The rise of mass education.
※ Increasing competition for students (especially international non-EU students, who pay full economic fees).
※ Increasing competition for funding from both government and non-government sources.
※ The lure of increasingly competitive overseas markets.
※ The competing demands of diverse stakeholders, such as the expectations of self-funding students and the demands of corporate sponsors.

Such conditions call for responsiveness and speedy decision making in the context of 'managerialism'. But higher education is 'selling its soul' as managerialism, regulation and the drive to get 'bums on seats' supersede the wider good of academia, according to survey findings in 2006.[110] A majority of academic staff believe that higher education has lost its role as the 'conscience and critic of society' and that higher education's 'humanity and excitement' and its association with the 'joy of learning' have been sacrificed to targets and performance measures.

Criticisms of the 'corporatization' of universities – with its attendant emphasis on return-on-investment and 'customer' happiness – pose a challenge to university leaders. According to Steven Schwartz, vice chancellor of Macquarie University in Australia, modern universities are too much obsessed with money and are failing to teach their students 'wisdom':

> We once were about character building but now we are about money. We live in the age of money, and money is what the modern university is all about. Apparently we need more circus performers and salon managers. For some reason, no one seems to worry about a shortage of philosophers, historians and ethicists ... [but] successful careers depend on the practical application of wisdom.[111]

Managing academics has been likened to 'herding cats' – notoriously independent, uncontrollable and selfish creatures. It has even been suggested that laissez-faire leadership[112] – or no leadership at all – is the preference. A lack of leadership implies a lack of followership. In a letter to *The Times,* a correspondent asked:

> ... how often are our leaders in higher education hamstrung by academic subordinates quite unable to control their propensity to cavil, carp and criticise whenever new initiatives are tabled? The problem, surely, is that 'followership' capabilities are so underdeveloped in the academic workforce.[113]

Academic values and 'leadership' are uneasy bedfellows.[114] The presence of two distinct sub-cultures in HEIs – academic and administrative – is reminiscent of C.P. Snow's 'two cultures' of science and the arts in society.[115] This implies the need for leadership in creating a sense of unity of vision and purpose through *shared* values: vision and purpose are the starting point – and the driving force – of successful organizations.[116] Collegiality and managerialism need not be mutually exclusive.[117]

Tensions exist, however, between administrative leadership and faculty leadership; between corporate leadership and departmental leadership; between autonomous collegiality and controlling managerialism; and between academics' allegiance to discipline and their allegiance to the institution. One reason for academics' lack of 'loyalty' may be that HEIs fail to use the expertise within their own walls – the academics themselves – for example in strategy development, scenario thinking, change facilitation, and not least leadership development.

The value placed by academics on individual autonomy and academic freedom must be recognized and responded to, as must their discipline allegiance, which is usually greater than their institutional allegiance.[118] This poses a challenge for leadership in respect of a shared vision and mission, strategies and a corporate identity for an institution. For some top and senior academics and managers in HEIs this 'displaced' loyalty shows itself in a lack of personal engagement with leadership development. Moreover, those who most need it appear to be those least likely to desire it: they are indifferent, resistant or 'unavailable' (owing to other priorities or being 'too busy').

Good governance must be high on any government's HEI agenda. The challenges for non-executive leadership and HEIs as 'holding companies' are comparable with those in the private sector. However, the governing bodies of older universities like Oxford, Cambridge and Durham in the UK may be more representative of the range of their stakeholders and therefore more sympathetic to academic-led senates. They have a more 'collegial' form of governance that fits with a 'first among equals' leadership style: the authority of professional expertise over position power, academic autonomy and self-regulation.[119] On the other hand those of the newer universities tend to be faster decision makers and more involved and informed commentators on university strategies, less familiar or comfortable with the academic culture but arguably more in touch with the 'real world'. Furthermore, they may have less clear and more ambiguous goals that risk conflict and competition rather than achieve consensus and unity of action.[120] This may be true for their visions and missions too.

The overriding challenge for higher education is to achieve a sustainable balance between academic scholarship and business management. This means, on the one hand, communities of scholars engaged in teaching, research and learning and the creation and communication of knowledge for the common good and, on the other hand, the institutions that scholars inhabit being managed with efficiency, entrepreneurial flair, marketing savvy and fund-raising wizardry – and well led ... That is the leadership development challenge for the UK's HEIs.

Leadership in the Not-for-Profit Sector[121]

Organizations in the voluntary, charity and not-for-profit sectors focus on visions, missions and values that generally are different from those in the private and public sectors. This implies a need for some different leader characteristics and competencies.

'The absolute most important issue confronting the nonprofit sector today and into the near future relates to leadership', said Thomas J. Tierney, former chief executive of the global management consulting firm Bain & Company, and co-founder and chairman of The Bridgespan Group, Inc., a not-for-profit strategy consulting firm.[122]

Commercial organizations will use financial measures of success such as profitability and shareholder value, though it is argued elsewhere in this book that these measures of success may be ill-advised as their *raison d'être*. Charities and not-for-profit organizations (NFPs), however, place more emphasis on other measures of success – those associated with their pursuit of their mission or purpose, the quality of the services they provide and their efficiency in doing so. Yet income and cash flow are crucial to their survival and growth. Some 52 per cent of charities in the UK have been affected by the economic recession and over half of those affected have seen their income drop.[123]

While there are many identical requirements for executive effectiveness in the commercial and NFP worlds, just as there are in the commercial and public sectors,[124] there are some leadership-related requirements that are particularly important for NFPs, among them:

* ※ A deep commitment to the organization's mission.
* ※ Understanding and communicating the unique tradition and role of the NFP sector.
* ※ A commitment to the common good and practising what is preached.
* ※ Building an organization that cares about the people and the clients it serves.
* ※ Providing psychological, rather than financial, recognition and rewards.[125]

NFPs generally cannot afford high salaries and bonuses and, according to Tierney, many are too small to provide meaningful career development opportunities for next-generation leaders[126]. Psychological recognition and rewards therefore become even more important than in the commercial world.[127] These requirements define the kind of leadership that NFPs need – transformational leadership. And studies of a diverse range of organizations in the NFP sector consistently show the comparative advantage of transformational leadership over transactional leadership alone – leadership that is characterized by transactions between leaders and the led, such as management-by-exception and rewards that are contingent on performance (which we discuss in Chapter 3).[128] This is not to say, however, that transformational leadership is necessarily more important in NFPs than in the commercial sector, though there is some evidence that this may be so because of the strong emphasis on mission and the nature of the requirements for success in the NFP sector.[129]

NFPs figure in the rankings in *The Sunday Times'* annual survey of the best companies to work for. Christians Against Poverty (CAP), the Bradford-based debt counselling charity, was the top small company to work for in the 2009 survey, which was the third year running that the 100 best small companies to work for had been headed by a charity.[130] CAP gained an almost perfect score from employees for making a positive difference to the world, and the leadership was perceived as inspiring, non-hierarchical, receptive, moral and respected.

In the 2009 general rankings of the 100 best companies to work for,[131] London & Quadrant Housing Trust (L&Q), the London-based social housing charity, was the top NFP, ranked 22nd: 71 per cent of L&Q's employees said that managers help them fulfil their potential, 75 per cent found their work stimulating, and 76 per cent felt they would really make a difference at work. L&Q clearly took leadership seriously, having established its own leadership academy in partnership with Cranfield University. Other NFPs ranked in the top 100 were the Royal Society for the Protection of Birds (36th); Thames Reach, the homeless charity (44th); Look Ahead Housing & Care (46th) and Great Places Housing Group (61st), both housing associations; and Prospects for People with Learning Disabilities (67th).

Innovation is key to survival, growth and effectiveness in NFPs as much as in commercial organizations and the public sector. And it is well accepted that leadership plays an important part in stimulating and sustaining creativity and innovation.[132] However, in NFPs this may not necessarily be the case; nor may it be a simple relationship. A study of NFP human service organizations in the United States found no direct relationship: their leadership practices created a strong cultural consensus around values that could inhibit innovation.[133] Examining the link between leadership and organizational culture, therefore, is important to understanding how leadership and innovation in NFPs are related.

Many initiatives are in place to publicize and improve leadership and leadership development specifically among NFPs, such as the annual Charity Awards – sponsored by the Leadership Trust – and the Third Sector Excellence Awards, the Third Sector Leadership Centre and the Clore Social Leadership Programme. Yet 95 per cent of the 150 leaders surveyed by the Third Sector Leadership Centre and Henley Business School said they were unable to access the leadership development support they needed to enhance their leadership effectiveness, needing more creative and flexible forms of support such as coaching, mentoring, networking and internet-based learning rather than a traditional classroom-based education.[134] While the then Third Sector Minister, Angela Smith, paid tribute to the voluntary sector in the UK in 2009 as 'the best in the world',[135] the leadership development effort in the sector still needs to be continuously applied and sustained, informed and underpinned by relevant and valid research.

Leadership in the Armed Forces

Military leaders like Hannibal, Rommel, Patton, Nelson and Wellington are legends. And the armed forces are often regarded as paragons of virtue in respect of leadership. For example, journalist Godfrey Smith claims that, in the Battle of Britain in the Second World War:

> We won not because our pilots were better but because they were much better led. [Keith] Park [AOC, 11 Group, Fighter Command] has been compared to Wellington, but whereas Wellington had to concentrate for five hours at Waterloo, Park had to do it for five months.[136]

'Military command has been and remains a standard dictionary meaning of leadership', Joseph Masciulli and colleagues suggest.[137] They say:

> In the military, people in positions of command show followers the way, but are not open to debates in which the force of the better argument decides the course of action.[138] Their hard power of command with coercive enforcement is always in reserve to 'guide' the followers in the direction chosen by the leaders.[139]

Examples of outstanding leadership are frequently drawn from the armed forces in civilian leadership development programmes. Yet leadership in the British Army came under criticism in the 1970s in a seminal analysis by Norman Dixon. He pinpointed, among generals, their fundamental conservatism and outmoded traditions – their tendencies to reject or dismiss information that challenged their pre-conceptions, to under-estimate the enemy, to persist in pursuing an obviously doomed task, to prefer frontal assaults and brute force to proper reconnaissance and surprise, and to suppress or distort news from the front in the interest of morale – as well as their 'unnatural attachment' to mystical forces such as fate and luck.[140]

It is with reference to the armed forces that the term 'command and control' first appears in 1838 in the writings of Baron Antoine Henri de Jomini (1779–1869).[141] A section of his book is entitled 'The Command of Armies and the Supreme Control of Operations'. The term comes into common usage in the mid-twentieth century when General MacArthur is instructed by President Truman to 'take command and control of the forces'.[142] The Royal Navy defines command and control as follows:

> **Command is the *authority* [my italics] granted to an individual to direct, coordinate and control military forces. Control of the actual process through which the commander organises, directs and coordinates the activities of forces allocated to him. Command and control, supported by a system of people, information and technology, enable the maritime force commander to apply military force effectively.[143]**

While the term is commonly used and indeed in the battlefield 'the "true" centre of effective command and control (C2) remains the commander himself',[144] David Alberts and Mark Nissen suggest its meaning is 'totally antithetical to the way in which these functions need to be accomplished in many of the 21st century missions'.[145] Military units increasingly find themselves in non-traditional roles such as peace-keeping operations and humanitarian aid support that involve multinational task groups and increasingly decentralized command and control systems,[146] networked leadership and delegated authority.[147] These ideas are the basis for *mission command*, a key aspect of British military doctrine. This entails empowering subordinates to exercise leadership through delegated and decentralized decision making and giving freedom of action and initiative.

The US Army's vision statement states: 'We are about leadership; it is our stock in trade, and it is what makes us different.'[148] When abuse of war prisoners occurs, as happened in Iraq after the 2003 war and during the subsequent occupation by coalition forces, it is worthwhile remembering the US Army mantra: 'The commander is responsible for everything the unit does or fails to do.'[149] In parallel with the rise in corporate scandals in the world of business, the military faces ethical criticism for its tactics and behaviour. Leonard Wong and colleagues say:

> **For military leaders at the systems [strategic] level, new issues in ethics are ... being confronted ... American military leaders are accustomed to waging war guided by moral obligations based on Western values, allegiance to the Constitution, and adherence to the laws of war. With the attacks of September 11th and the global war on terrorism, the U.S. military now finds itself in a situation of ethical asymmetry – fighting an enemy that does not follow the same moral guidelines [e.g. targeting civilians, using suicide bombers, etc.].[150]**

The demands that highly dangerous situations place on leadership have been little explored, according to Donald Campbell and colleagues at the United States Military Academy at West Point.[151] A dangerous environment is one 'in which leaders or their followers are *personally* faced with highly dynamic and unpredictable situations and where the outcomes of leadership may result in severe physical or psychological injury (or death) to unit members'.[152]

What precisely *is* leadership in dangerous situations? What does danger *do* to leadership – to shaping and drawing out specific characteristics and behaviours? And what distinguishes effective leaders from less effective leaders in dangerous environments?

Francis Yammarino and colleagues propose a multilevel model of leadership and team dynamics for dangerous military situations comprising key propositions relaying to pragmatic leadership at the individual level, individualized leadership at the level of pairs (dyads), and shared leadership at the team level.[153] Dangerous situations are characterized by ambiguous, uncertain, shifting and unexpected events that are typically the cause of lethal errors because of the increased frequency of multiple and conflicting interpretations.[154]

Benjamin Baran and Cliff Scott suggest that leadership in dangerous situations becomes a collective sense-making activity, among all team members regardless of rank, that both reduces ambiguity and promotes resilience in the face of danger.[155] Sense making, they suggest, takes the form of 'framing', 'heedful interrelating' and 'adjusting'. *Framing* is 'converging on an understanding of what is significant and what is not significant in the setting' to reduce ambiguity and provide a shared focus. *Heedful interrelating* is developing a shared understanding of the level of risk and danger and that any new action by any member of the team may 'radically (and sometimes unintentionally) alter the *status quo*'. *Adjusting* is about maintaining awareness of the surroundings 'but simultaneously [remaining] poised to shift action should … collectively held assumptions prove to be mistaken'.

In dangerous situations *trust* – 'one's willingness to be vulnerable to another group member's actions' – plays a crucial role.[156] Patrick Sweeney in a study of 72 combat soldiers found that a majority reassessed their trust when faced with the danger of imminent battle, focusing on their perceptions of their leaders' character and situational competence – leaders' ability to manage stress, display technical and tactical proficiency, take care of group needs, solve problems and be candid.[157] Kelly Fisher and colleagues found that trust also results from 'mateship' – the development of mutually close, supportive relationships that reflect loyalty, stoicism and egalitarianism.[158]

Operating in dangerous environments such as urban warfare may 'severely strain the moral character and ethical discipline of individual leaders', according to research by Olav Olsen and colleagues.[159] The leader's actions, they suggest, can both enhance trust among followers and influence followers' sensitivity to ethical issues and shape their ethical decisions. Ultimately it is the leader's own moral integrity that 'determines the choices made in a hostile, threatening environment': ethical behaviour is a vital aspect of leadership in dangerous environments.

Two further issues, Fisher and colleagues suggest, challenge leaders in dangerous environments.[160] A culture of violence, such as the use of torture and the unprovoked killing of civilians, may emerge. So may a culture of corruption – the abuse of power and position. But they also describe how some leaders' competencies – physical courage, adventurousness, comfort with risk, ability to learn and use new knowledge, and willingness to lead by example – can enhance leader effectiveness in dangerous environments.

The military is not a monolithic organization, Leonard Wong and colleagues say, but a 'diverse collection of organizations – army, navy and air force – roles, cultures and people'.[161] Individual leaders, in a traditional hierarchy in which authority is distributed accordingly, will command large numbers of subordinates and therefore will have a significant impact on people.

The military's role has become much more varied since the end of the Cold War, with a lesser emphasis on conventional warfare and a greater involvement in anti-terrorist combat and peace-keeping operations in a wide variety of situations, many with considerable ambiguity and uncertainty, and often with extraordinarily far-reaching consequences. Leadership is required at strategic, operational and tactical levels, reflecting respectively national (or, in the case of UN forces, global) interests, policy and resource usage; major campaigns; and battles, engagement and close combat. An under-rated ability for strategic leadership is 'cognitive capacity' (which is discussed in the chapter on multiple intelligences and leadership). Wong and colleagues report on research that stresses the importance of an independent perspective of the strategic environment and the use of abstract conceptual models in senior military leaders.[162]

Retired Vice Admiral John Lockard of the US Navy and Chief Operating Officer of Boeing Integrated Defense Systems points out that aligning individual people with the goals of the larger organization is much simpler in the military than it is in industry.[163] And an alignment with team goals is easier in the armed forces, he says, because people in industry tend to be rewarded for their individual achievement rather than teamwork. Moreover, he believes, the armed forces provide opportunities for leadership earlier and more continuously than industry does: '… the military has a continuous focus on leadership, which has a direct correlation to mission accomplishment'.

One of the major contributions to leadership development in the UK's armed forces from the 1960s onwards has been that of John Adair. Adair's Functional Leadership model, later known as Action-Centred Leadership,[164] and employing the Three Circles model (discussed in the next chapter, on leadership theory), was adopted at the officer training centres for the Army, Royal Air Force and Royal Navy at Sandhurst, Cranwell and Dartmouth respectively. This model views leadership as concerned with meeting task needs, team needs and individual needs. Greg McMahon describes how this method has been applied, for example, in the Australian Army.[165] Air Chief Marshall Sir Brian Burridge says the Adair approach to leadership development 'represents a timeless model which should continue to be the bedrock of RAF leadership teaching and development'.[166]

It is not surprising that the armed forces today are held in high esteem in respect of leadership and leadership development, and that lessons are frequently drawn from them for their application in the commercial and other sectors. But leadership in the armed forces nevertheless has its unique features and challenges.

Further Reading

Joseph Masciulli, Mikhail A. Molchanov and W. Andy Knight, Editors (2009), *The Ashgate Research Companion to Political Leadership*. Farnham, Surrey: Ashgate.
Kevin Theakston (1999), *Leadership in Whitehall*. Basingstoke: Macmillan.
Kevin Theakston, Editor (2000), *Bureaucrats and Leadership*. Basingstoke: Macmillan.
Gary Yukl (2009), *Leadership in Organizations*, Seventh Edition. Upper Saddle River, NJ: Prentice Hall.

 Discussion Questions

1. In what ways is leadership different across the sectors discussed in this chapter?
2. What are the common and different ways of judging leadership effectiveness or success across sectors?
3. What are the key challenges facing leadership in the various sectors?

3 Leadership Theory: A Critical Review, Synthesis and Redefinition

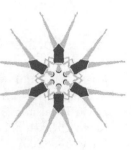

The Questioner, who sits so sly, Shall never know how to Reply. He who replies to words of Doubt Doth put the Light of Knowledge out.

William Blake (1757–1827), 'Auguries of Innocence'.

OVERVIEW

- The major theories and models we find in textbooks have each helped us to understand leadership. Each one is a piece in the jigsaw puzzle of leadership. This chapter reviews not only the major theories of leadership and how they help us to understand it, but also how none of them on its own provides a complete picture.
- Trait theories of leadership, also known as 'Great Man' theories, postulate on the common qualities or characteristics of effective leaders. These theories raise the question of whether such qualities are inherited or acquired.
- Theories of emergent leadership, including 'servant leadership', postulate that leaders may emerge who have the characteristics and skills to meet the needs of their group, organization or society at a given time.
- Leadership style theories describe what leaders do and classify it into two categories: people focused and task focused. Action-Centred Leadership is a development of leadership style theory, focusing on task, team and individual.
- The Bradford model of leadership focuses on the interpersonal 'micro skills' of effective leadership behaviour – ways in which effective leaders structure their interactions with followers and others, gather information, give information, influence behaviour and handle emotion.
- Psychodynamic theory, or leader-member exchange theory, explains the effectiveness of leaders as a function of the psychodynamic exchange that occurs between leaders and group members. Leaders provide direction and guidance through the influence permitted to them by members.
- The path-goal theory of leadership employs the 'expectancy model' of work motivation. According to path-goal theory, the leader increases the personal payoffs to subordinates for achieving work goals and paves the way to these payoffs by clarifying the path, removing or reducing roadblocks and pitfalls, and enhancing personal satisfaction along the way.
- Contingency and situational leadership theories suggest that there is no one best style of leadership. Successful and enduring leaders will use different styles according to the nature of the situation and the followers.

(Continued)

(Continued)

- The 'New Leadership' comprises visionary, charismatic and transactional trans-formational leadership theories. Transformational leadership occurs when leaders raise people's motivation and sense of higher purpose. It is distinguished from transactional leadership, which involves an exchange between leader and followers that typically provides a material or psychological reward in return for their compliance with the leader's wishes, policies and procedures. Engaging Transformational Leadership is a newer UK variation. Other theories discussed include strategic leadership, pragmatic leadership and evolutionary leadership.
- No theory or model of leadership so far has provided a full and satisfactory explanation of leadership. There is a widespread view that a new, more integrated conceptual framework for leadership is both possible and necessary. This chapter attempts to provide such a framework with a model of six themes and practices that have emerged in the scholarly and practitioner leadership literature.

It will come as no surprise to learn that leadership theory, like the very definition of leadership that we discussed in Chapter 1, is beset by a 'definitional quagmire'.[1] Just as it is said that there are as many theories of economics as there are economists, it seems that this is also true for leadership too: there appear to be as many theories of leadership as there are leaders! And some leaders go into print on their personal ones. For example, Vice Admiral Sir Adrian Johns of the Royal Navy considers leadership to have six pillars: delegation, subordinate development, loneliness, adaptability, humour and heritage (not letting down the people who preceded you)[2] – a collection of heterogeneous elements that, it may be argued, constitute a category mistake.[3]

Mary Ann Glynn and Rich DeJordy's review of the leadership literature found that research approaches focus variously on the personality or traits of the leader, the process of leadership, the impact of leadership, and leadership performance (assessed by the performance or effectiveness of individuals, groups or organizations).[4] They also see four successive groups of leadership theories: trait-based, behaviour-based, contingency-based and transformational.[5]

I use this classification in this chapter and, recognizing that each successive group of theories is a further piece added to the jigsaw, develop it with a 'post-transformational' (integrative) category. I start with trait theories.

Trait Theories of Leadership: The Heroic Leader

Review

Trait theories of human behaviour emerged in ancient Greece, India and China around 2,500 years ago. Euripides (c. 480–406 BC), for example, in *The Suppliant Women* says: 'Rashness in a leader causes failure; the sailor of a ship is calm, wise at the proper time. Yes, and forethought: this too is bravery.'[6] And Sun Tzu (c. 500 BC) said, 'Command [leadership] is a matter of wisdom, integrity, humanity, courage and discipline.'[7]

For hundreds, perhaps thousands of years, effective leaders were believed to show common characteristics that would cause them to behave in certain ways. This was the era of so-called 'Great Man' theories.[8] In 1926 Luther Lee Bernard attempted to explain leadership in terms of the 'internal' qualities that a person was born with.[9] And Ralph Stogdill, based on his research from the 1940s, listed many traits (and some behavioural skills) that he said were crucial to leadership: dependability, cooperativeness, assertiveness, dominance, high energy, self-confidence, stress tolerance, responsibility, achievement orientation, adaptability, cleverness, persuasiveness, organizational and speaking abilities, and social skills.[10]

Leadership trait studies are mostly psychological in approach. Sociologists frame leadership in terms of relationships among people rather than in terms of individual traits or characteristics, often focusing on power and dominance.[11] The sociological approach is to analyse the characteristics of leaders that result from their position in society: social class, education, gender and religious, ethnic and kinship networks.[12] An example of how traits are associated with occupation and advantage is what Catherine Hakim calls 'erotic capital': the economic and social advantages that good looks will have for people in certain occupations.[13]

The problem with the resulting social elite theory is that it deals with position in social strata and its associated dominance and control rather than with the analysis of the personalities and behaviour of leaders. As James MacGregor Burns said, leadership involves not simply the power of control, but the power to motivate: 'one must look for motives as well as the weapon'.[14] And in the words of the poet, W.B. Yeats:

> The Light of Lights Looks always on the motive, not the deed, The Shadow of Shadows on the deed alone.[15]

The idea that leadership is associated with superior intelligence originated in the teachings of Aristotle, Plato and Socrates and it gained currency during the Age of Enlightenment. Intelligence is a particularly interesting trait:

> ... people who provide effective leadership in big jobs appear to be always above average in some basic form of intelligence, although they rarely seem geniuses.[16]

Timothy Judge and colleagues, in their meta-analysis of studies of intelligence and leadership, found that intelligence and leadership were significantly associated.[17] And Dean Simonton found that differences in intelligence accounted for about 10 per cent of the variation in the 'greatness' of US presidents.[18]

Superior intelligence in a leader, however, can have disadvantages as well as advantages.[19] For example, I have shown that too high a level of intelligence may interfere with effective decision making, probably because of excessive 'intellectualizing' about the decision: 'paralysis through analysis'.[20] And there is evidence that leadership effectiveness is impaired when a leader's intelligence substantially exceeds that of the follower group,[21] perhaps as a result of a mutual lack of intellectual empathy. Dean Simonton suggests that 'The [US presidents] who are the most intellectually brilliant are often barely elected ... They have trouble speaking in sound bites and communicating with the public.'[22] The only US president rated as intelligent and with a PhD degree, Woodrow Wilson, was elected, Simonton notes, with only 20 per cent of the popular vote.

Early studies of leadership and personality, in the 1930s and 1940s, assumed that effective leaders had special traits in common and aimed to identify these. Following a period during which research results were generally inconclusive, more promising results have emerged more recently. Peter Northouse's analysis suggests that the main qualities appearing to be important for leadership are integrity, self-confidence, sociability and determination, as well as cognitive ability.[23] In another study, employing the 'Big Five' factor model of personality, Timothy Judge and colleagues also found significant relationships between several personality traits and leadership that were even higher than those for intelligence and leadership, namely extraversion, agreeableness and conscientiousness, in addition to openness to experience (intelligence).[24] Another analysis, of successful CEOs, suggested the following characteristics:

✳ Integrity, maturity and energy.
✳ Business acumen (a deep understanding of the business and a strong profit orientation).
✳ 'People' acumen (judging people, leading teams, coaching and growing people, and cutting losses [mismatches between people and jobs] where necessary).
✳ Organizational acumen (engendering trust, sharing information, listening expertly as well as diagnosing under-performance, delivering on commitments, change orientation, and being both decisive and incisive).
✳ Curiosity, intellectual capacity and a global mindset (being externally oriented, eager for knowledge of the world, and adept at connecting developments and spotting patterns).
✳ Superior judgement.
✳ An insatiable appetite for accomplishment and results.
✳ A powerful motivation to grow and convert learning into practice.[25]

Most of these characteristics are cognitive, emotional or interpersonal, and some are deeply embedded in individual values. Whether these are exhaustive, or consistently displayed, is highly questionable. And some also tend to emphasize the individual in isolation rather than the relationship he or she has with others.

In a study of 17 CEOs, their top management teams (TMTs) and organizational performance, Randall Peterson and colleagues found significant associations between CEO personality and TMT dynamics and between TMT dynamics and organizational performance.[26] CEO conscientiousness was associated with a TMT concern for legality and a sense of control over the environment; CEO emotional stability with team cohesion, intellectual flexibility and leader dominance; CEO agreeableness with team cohesion and power decentralization; CEO extraversion with leader strength (dominance); and CEO openness with team risk taking and intellectual flexibility

Joyce Bono and Timothy Judge, in a meta-analysis of 26 studies of personality and the six dimensions of transactional and transformational leadership identified by Bruce Avolio, Bernard Bass and Don Jung (which we discuss later in this chapter),[27]

found weak relationships between personality and leadership.[28] With regard to transformational leadership in particular, the 'Big Five' personality traits[29] – neuroticism, extraversion, openness, agreeableness and conscientiousness – explained 12 per cent of the variation in charisma (idealized influence and inspirational motivation combined) and only 5 per cent of the variation in intellectual stimulation and 6 per cent in individualized consideration. Extraversion was the strongest and most consistent correlate of transformational leadership. Correlations between personality traits and transactional and laissez-faire leadership were generally weak and of little practical significance.

Based on their research for their model of *breakout strategy*, Sydney Finkelstein and colleagues propose five key leadership capabilities:[30]

※ *'Positive' Capabilities* – the ability to enable transformation: visioning, articulating, inspiring, persuading, deciding, resolving, selling.
※ *'Negative' Capabilities* – the ability to deal with negative situations, people and contexts: waiting, listening, thinking, testing, feeling, absorbing, debating.
※ *Conceptual Capabilities* – the ability to master systems, processes and procedures and take calculated risks: analyzing, auditing, appraising, planning, researching, theorizing.
※ *Creative Capabilities* – the ability to think 'outside the box': experimenting, interacting, harmonizing, patterning, imagining, questioning.
※ *Relational Capabilities* – the ability to relate to people and to build trust and confidence: communicating, empathizing, building solidarity, reaching out, giving, demonstrating competence.

Adam Grant and colleagues, in a study of store leaders and employees in a US national pizza delivery company, found that when employees were proactive – taking the initiative and speaking out – introverted managers would lead them to earn higher profits; when employees were not proactive, extraverted managers – who were outgoing, bold, talkative and dominant – would lead them to higher profits.[31] They commented:

... because extraverted leaders like to be the center of attention, they tend to be threatened by employee proactivity ... Introverted leaders, on the other hand, are more likely to listen carefully to suggestions and support employees' efforts to be proactive.

According to research by Andrew Johnson and colleagues using monzygotic and dizygotic twin studies, which we discuss in relation to the heritability of personality and leadership in our chapter on the assessment and development of leadership, there are personality differences between transformational and transactional leaders (which we discuss later in this chapter).[32] In terms of the 'Big Five' personality characteristics, they say: '[Transformational leaders] are ... outgoing, broad minded, and most likely to respect their followers (high conscientiousness). In contrast, [transactional leaders] have an opposite personality ...': they tend to be unconscientious, introverted and disagreeable. They also tend to be low in endurance and in their need for both achievement and affiliation, impulsive, disorganized, aggressive and dominant.

Critique

The picture of personal qualities for leadership is still not complete – despite a long list of putative traits – and it is not agreed. For example, Jim Collins' research of databases of corporate results for companies that had been transformed into great companies, going back to 1965, came up with only one finding: they all had leaders who displayed 'a paradoxical mixture of personal humility and professional will' – an unusual mix of being 'timid and ferocious, shy and fearless' at the same time – that is also known as 'Level 5' leadership.[33]

Adrian Furnham points out that the list of traits comprises a 'rag bag' of individual differences: physical characteristics such as height, body-mass index and energy; social backgrounds such as education and social status; abilities such as intelligence and fluency; personality such as self-confidence and stress tolerance; and social skills such as assertiveness and emotional intelligence.[34] In their research for the UK's Council for Excellence in Management and Leadership, Lew Perren and John Burgoyne identified some 83 management and leadership attributes that had been distilled from over 1,000![35] What is needed, Nitin Nohria and Rakesh Khurana say, is a synthetic meta-analysis.[36]

It cannot be disputed that leaders who do not possess all of the traits, whatever they are, are often effective (in whatever sense). And leaders who possess many of them are often not effective. It is inconceivable that an effective leader possesses *all* the traits that are associated with effective leadership and conversely that an ineffective leader – or a 'non-leader' – possesses none. A set that is appropriate to the situation is called for. Mike Pedler and colleagues say:

There is no one correct definition of leadership, or any one set of personal qualities or competencies that characterise leaders.[37]

Even if trait theory stood up to scrutiny, it can still be argued convincingly that some strengths in excess can become weaknesses. For example, in the armed services, poor decision making can result from 'cognitive dissonance'[38], where decision makers will reject new information after they have made a decision that suggests it was wrong.[39] Imbalance among traits can be dysfunctional: complementarity is needed.

Furnham points out several shortcomings of the early work on traits:

* It was not explained how traits were rank-ordered or related to one another.
* The trait approach was retrospective: were traits a cause or a consequence of leadership style?
* It was not clear if traits were both necessary *and* sufficient.
* It ignored the role of both subordinates and situational and organizational factors (context).[40]

Richard Bolden and Jonathan Gosling make a really good point about the importance of context:

Whilst personal qualities of the leader are undoubtedly important they are unlikely to be sufficient in themselves for the emergence and exercise of leadership. Furthermore, the manner in which these qualities translate into behaviour and group interaction is likely to be culturally specific and thus depend on a whole host of factors, such as the nature of the leader, followers, task, organisational structure, and culture (national, corporate and group).[41]

According to Adrian Furnham, people who are chosen to lead are those who are self-confident, bold, strategic, ambitious, astute, persistent, vigilant or articulate.[42] It is an interesting link between trait theory and the emergence of leaders which we now turn to.

Theories of Emergent and Servant Leadership

'Asking who should be the leader', Henry Ford said, 'is like asking who should sing tenor in the quartet'.[43] The man with the tenor voice, of course! Leaders may emerge who will have the characteristics and skills to serve the needs of others – a group, organization or society – at a given time.

Emergent Leadership

Emergent leaders are likely to be viewed as being most prototypical of the group.[44] The classic study of this was of a street corner gang in the United States.[45] Such leaders may emerge regardless of, or in the absence of, any formal leader appointed by others. Theories of emergent leadership emphasize the importance of followers:[46] leadership depends on an interaction between the goals of the followers and the leader. Vertical dyad linkage theory, or leader–member exchange (LMX) theory, has grown out of work in this area.[47]

The emergence of 'natural' leaders is usual in political leadership where leaders need to conform to followers' expectations. The nineteenth-century French politician Alexandre Ledru-Rollin was aware of this: *'Eh bien! Je suis leur chef; il fallait bien les suivre'* – 'Ah well! I am their leader; I really ought to follow them!'[48]

Perhaps the most infamous example of an emergent leader was Adolf Hitler. However misguided, flawed and evil, Hitler's vision, values and oratory inspired a nation during a time of a collective depressed psyche. It was not only Mao Zedung who led people on a 'long march' in the wrong direction; in Hitler's case it was to total defeat and desolation.

Servant Leadership

The ability or desire to serve the needs of other people is usually (but not always) the reason why leaders emerge. Great leaders serve others, according to the theory of 'servant leadership' associated with Robert Greenleaf.[49] Socrates and his pupil Xenophon saw leadership as serving others – as meeting their needs.[50] And in the Bible St Paul said, '...I have made myself every man's servant, to win over as many as possible'.[51] Great leaders, then, will display humility. And as Major-General (Rtd) Tim Cross says, '[Jesus] served those who served the cause ... but He certainly wasn't a

doormat, rather a man of tremendous physical and moral courage'.[52] It is no coinci-
dence that the motto of the UK's Royal Military Academy at Sandhurst is *Serve to
Lead* and that the Service prayer says, ' ... help us to be masters of ourselves that we
may be servants of others, and teach us to serve to lead'.

Servant leadership in public service, then, is all well and good, but what place does
it have in the world of business? The CEO of the Toro Company, Ken Melrose, believes
that 'the great leader is a great servant': he says, 'I came to understand that you best
lead by serving the needs of your people. You don't do their jobs for them; you enable
them to learn and progress on the job.'[53] And the founder of SouthWest Airlines, Herb
Kelleher, says:

**Leadership is being a faithful, devoted, hard-working servant of the people you lead and
participating with them in the agonies as well as the ecstasies of life.[54]**

Retailer Asda appears to be the only organization in the UK that uses the term 'servant leader', though many others encourage the idea and put it into practice.[55] Service
to other people is also part and parcel of leadership in the trade union movement. As
(Lord) Vic Feather once said to one company's management when General Secretary
of the UK's Trades Union Congress, 'They work for you, and I work for them.'[56]

Many leaders have problems with the notion of servant leadership, especially if it
is inconsistent with their self-image. Tom Marshall asks:

**After all, leaders lead, servants serve. If leaders are going to be the servants what are the
servants going to do, and who is going to do the leading?[57]**

Robert Greenleaf identifies two kinds of leaders: strong natural leaders, who take
charge, make the decisions and give the orders, and strong natural servants, who
assume the leadership role because they see it as a way in which they can serve.[58]
Strong natural leaders, he says, are assertive and driven by the need for acquisition or
dominance, whereas strong natural servants are driven by the need to serve a cause.
Greenleaf goes on to say that only natural servants ought to lead. The leadership issue
here is natural servants who have the ability to lead but do not do so. Servant leadership is not a matter of leadership style, but of character and motivation – and thus of
traits?

Servant leadership entails strong values: servant leaders will take on leadership
roles because they want to serve others. And people will follow servant leaders because
they trust them. In Greenleaf's words:

**The servant-leader is servant first ... It begins with the natural Feeling that one wants to
serve, to serve first. Then conscious choice brings one to aspire to lead. He or she is
sharply different from the person who is leader first, perhaps because of the need to
assuage an unusual power drive or to acquire material possessions.[59]**

Greenleaf suggests the test of servant leadership is whether those served 'become
healthier, wiser, freer, more autonomous, more likely themselves to become [servant

leaders]'.[60] Servant leaders will help followers develop their own values that will then support the organization in its mission or purpose.

The servant leader, Danah Zohar and Ian Marshall say, 'serves the ultimate source of meaning and value'.[61] They cite as examples Mahatma Gandhi, Mother Theresa, Nelson Mandela and the Dalai Lama. Less well known is Katsuhiko Yazaki, the Japanese owner of a global mail-order company, Felissimo. Zohar and Marshall describe how, after becoming wealthy through an inherited business, Yazaki emerged from a monastery with a new self-awareness and a vision of the 'proper' role of business as enhancing human happiness.[62] He pursued this vision by helping his customers to imagine and achieve more fulfilling lifestyles and investing his money in educational projects and saving the environment.

Critique of Emergent and Servant Leadership Theories

A key issue for emergent leadership and servant leadership theories is that they ignore the many demands that the wider organization or society presents in addition to those of a particular group of followers. Nelson Mandela in South Africa and Václav Havel in the Czech Republic are each examples of emergent leaders who did address such demands. But another issue is that these theories do not provide a sufficiently complete or sufficient *explanation* of effective leadership.

Mitch McCrimmon, a psychologist and executive development consultant, argues compellingly that servant leadership is 'paternalistic and gets in the way of employee engagement'[63] (see our chapter on leadership and employee engagement). He argues:

> Just when we need to empower front line knowledge workers to think for themselves and take more ownership, the last thing they need is to be served by their managers. John F. Kennedy got the direction of service the right way round when he said: 'Ask not what your country can do for you but what you can do for your country'.

McCrimmon also contends that servant leadership is interesting but false. It may be appropriate, he says, in those situations where leaders are elected – such as politics or clubs where such leaders are expected to serve their colleagues' wishes, needs or interests or be voted out of office – but not in business, where managers are usually expected to serve their companies' owners first and foremost (or be fired):

> The harsh reality in business is that employees are a means to an end. Effective managers will, of course, do all they can to engage, motivate, consider and include employees but that does not amount to being their servant. The truth is that while managers fire employees who aren't performing, no servant can fire his master. Therefore, this sense of servant leadership is interesting but clearly false.

McCrimmon overlooks the possibility that servant leadership may entail serving the nation ('Queen and country', in the case of the UK), shareholders, or even a inanimate but compelling cause (a mission or purpose): the idea of servant leadership is still valid.

However, McCrimmon also says that servant leadership is true but trivial. It is not distinctive or preferable, he says, compared with a multitude of post-heroic leadership models that emphasize the need to abandon traditional models of autocratic and hierarchical leadership in favour of models based on teamwork, community, an involvement in decision making, caring, selflessness, and so on. He says that servant leadership (in transactional analysis terms,[64] the nurturing parent) also risks the same adverse consequences – demotivation and disengagement – as autocratic leadership (the critical parent). McCrimmon argues as well that servant leadership is less empowering for employees – and therefore less engaging – than employees serving their managers. And a religious rationale for servant leadership, such as Jesus Christ as a role model, he says, is based on personal values rather than business value.

Leadership Style Theories

Overview

The lack of a consistent set of leadership traits – who effective leaders are – stimulated a new focus of attention – what effective leaders *do*. The 'scientific management' of Frederick W. Taylor at the start of the twentieth century promoted the importance of organizational goals and efficient methods and procedures and the associated task-focused leadership in a mechanistic bureaucracy. This found its highest expression in Henry Ford's factories. The 'human relations movement', emerging from Elton Mayo's work in the 1920s and 1930s at the Hawthorne Works of Western Electric, refocused leadership on the importance of employees' feelings, attitudes and needs. This disjunction between task and human relationships, and later their conjunction, has characterized much of subsequent leadership theory.

The Michigan and Ohio State Studies and their Legacy

The first development was a set of influential theories that were popular from the 1950s to the 1960s. These theories of leadership style were articulated in various ways:

※ 'Concern for task' – production orientation – and 'concern for people' – employee *orientation, in the Michigan studies.*[65]
※ 'Initiating structure' and 'consideration' in the Ohio State leadership studies,[66] and the similar 'structuring' and 'consideration'.[67]

The development of these ideas by Rensis Likert led to a categorization of exploitative autocratic, benevolent autocratic, consultative and democratic leadership styles, based on the Michigan studies.[68] Robert Tannenbaum and Warren Schmidt likewise produced a similar continuum of leadership styles: autocratic, persuasive, consultative and democratic.[69] Another expression of the leadership styles model was that the leader must fill two roles:[70]

✳ Task direction – defining the goal, planning the solution, supplying the necessary knowledge.
✳ Social specialist – maintaining the morale and motivation of the group.

The leadership styles model gave rise to Robert Blake and Jane Mouton's Managerial Grid,[71] later renamed the Leadership Grid.[72] The original Managerial Grid describes leaders as '9,9' when they emphasize both the task and the people: '9,1' when they emphasize the task but not the people; '1,9' when they emphasize the people but not the task; and '1,1' when they emphasize neither (see Figure 3.1). Blake and Mouton later added a third dimension, 'flexibility'. This model gained, and indeed still has, considerable popularity, particularly with leadership development specialists.

The purely descriptive model was replaced by a more prescriptive one that suggested that people-centred behaviour was more effective in getting results. Preference, however, appeared to vary: while leaders' subordinates preferred their leaders to be people-centred, leaders' bosses preferred them to be task-centred.[73] This posed a dilemma for leaders 'in the middle'.

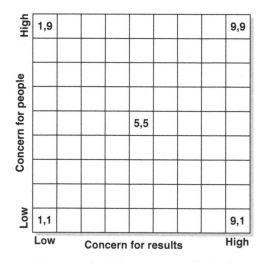

Figure 3.1 Blake and Mouton's Leadership Grid

Bernard M. Bass and colleagues developed this simple model into one describing five styles, defined in Table 3.1 below.[74]

Table 3.1 Bass and Colleagues' Five Styles of Leadership

Leadership Style	Definition
Directive	You tell subordinates what to do and how to do it. You initiate action. You tell subordinates what is expected of them, specifying standards of performance and setting deadlines for completion of work. You exercise firm rule and you ensure that they follow prescribed ways of doing things. You also ensure they are working to capacity, reassigning tasks to balance the workload.
Consultative	You tell subordinates what to do, but only after discussing matters with them first and hearing their opinions, feelings, ideas and suggestions.
Participative	You discuss and analyze problems with your subordinates to reach a consensus on what to do and how to do it. Decisions are made by the group as a whole and your subordinates have as much responsibility for decisions as you do. They participate as equals in decision making.
Negotiative	You employ political means and bargaining to gain desired ends, making political alliances, promising subordinates rewards for meeting expectations, releasing information to suit your interests, maintaining social distance, 'bending' the rules, encouraging subordinates to compete, and 'selling' decisions to them.
Delegative	You describe the problem or need and the conditions that have to be met, and you make suggestions, but you leave it to subordinates to decide what to do and how to do it.

Employeeship

The very idea of leadership that connotes the abrogation of responsibility of people to think for themselves and to act of their own volition – with or without the warm cookies[75] – has, satire apart, attracted the critical analysis of Noam Chomsky and others[76] and the development of an approach known as 'employeeship'.[77] 'Employeeship' replaces the traditional view of leadership as associated with hierarchy and subordination with a model of partnership and co-ownership between managers and non-managerial employees.

This model conceives of managers (leaders) in a facilitation role in which employees are authorized to decide and act for themselves. This participative leadership approach contrasts with the traditional view of employee compliance, hierarchical authority and limited employee discretion. Employeeship is an element in – as a necessary precondition for – empowerment, which we discuss later in our chapter on leadership and empowerment.

Action-centred Leadership

A British model of leadership that develops the earlier American ideas of task and people orientation as defining leadership style is 'Action-Centred Leadership' (ACL). This was a term coined in 1968 by the Industrial Society (later known as The Work Foundation), according to John Adair,[78] for a model that had its origins with Henry Harris in the

British War Office Selection Boards of the late 1940s.[79] The model took shape as 'Functional Leadership' (FL) in the 1960s at the Royal Military Academy, Sandhurst, and was further developed by Adair himself.[80] His 'Three Circles' model of ACL was the result of 'the careful analysis of leaders' actions' rather than any conventional scientific method and conceptually very simple. Adair's theory describes the domain within which leadership occurs and prescribes in general what leaders do (or ought to do).

A key difference in Adair's model compared with the American models was that 'people orientation' focuses separately on the individual and the team rather than 'people' as a whole. Effective leaders, for Adair, must address needs at three levels: the task, the team and the individual (see Figure 3.2):

> **The Biblical image of the shepherd well illustrates [the] three-fold responsibility [for meeting task, team and individuals' needs]. The shepherd [provides] direction, [maintains] the unity of the flock and [meets] the individual needs of the sheep.**[81]

The ACL model dismisses the idea that effective leaders possess a common set of traits but does propose that they must possess the competence to handle a wide range of different situations. The more there is overlap, and the more balanced the needs of the task, team and individual, the more effective the leadership will be. David McClelland cautions that a strongly achievement-motivated leader will focus on the task, sometimes to the detriment of the individual and the team, and may demand too much of others who may not be similarly motivated.[82]

If 'task' here is taken literally to mean 'a piece of work to be carried out', then the scope of the model will be limited to the everyday operational context. For example, Wing Commander Arthur Adamson reports on a case study of FL in officer cadet leadership training in the RAF in which 'task' encompassed defining the task, making a plan, allocating work and resources, controlling the quality and tempo of work, checking performance against the plan, and adjusting that plan.[83] This was merely an operational interpretation and application of the concept of 'task'.

Figure 3.2   Adair's Three Circles Model (John Adair (2009), *Effective Leadership: How To Be an Effective Leader*, New Revised Edition. London: Pan Books, 38. Reproduced with kind permission)

The model gains more generality and value by explicitly extending 'task' to encompass direction (mentioned by Adair in his Biblical metaphor) – vision and mission – and the road map – strategy; and, because values inform vision, mission and strategy, this element of leadership is also associated with task.[84] This is a more strategic interpretation and application of the notion of 'task' and reflects key elements in the new model of leadership described later in this chapter. Indeed 'tangible vision, values and strategy' rank in the top three globally valued leadership capabilities.[85] Marian Iszatt White, drawing on ethnographic research in the further education sector in the UK, provides practical examples of using the ACL model in four different situations showing various relationships between task, team and individual.[86]

The ACL model has been extensively used in leadership development in the UK armed forces (see Chapter 2) and the public sector. Scholars on both sides of the Atlantic, however, have shown little academic interest in the model. Yet testimony as to its usefulness and popularity is such that 'John Adair has led the British "rush" to leadership for longer than anyone can care to remember', says Keith Grint,[87] as the world's first (full) professor of leadership studies (at Surrey University in 1979);[88] over one million people have attended ACL courses; and he was appointed to the UNESCO Chair in Leadership Studies in 2006.

Critique of Leadership Style Theories

Leadership-style approaches have remained largely unfulfilled owing to their undue emphasis on the leader, followers and the task at the expense of the leadership situation.[89] Leadership style theories also fail to consider the contingencies in the leadership situation.[90]

In addition these approaches do not account for the behaviour of middle-level leaders who are expected to translate for subordinates the vision and strategies usually set by top-level leaders.[91] And leadership style theories focus on behaviour, but do not address values, except by implication: which values are relevant and effective in getting the job done and relating to subordinates and others, and what do these values mean to them? Moreover, Rob Goffee and Gareth Jones, reverting to trait theory, argue that it is not leadership style that makes a great leader but the underlying personal qualities that make the style effective.[92] This probably explains why autocratic leadership is a strong predictor of observed bullying.[93]

Research findings on the effectiveness of different leadership styles appear to be inconsistent.[94] No one style consistently produces better results, though a people or relationship orientation is more often associated with improvements. However, methodological shortcomings mean that it is difficult to identify the impact of leadership style because of extraneous factors in the situation. Most of the research findings have assumed rather than suggested that the leadership style leads to performance and satisfaction, whereas in fact the reverse is sometimes the case.[95] Studies have also mostly focused on the leader in relation to a group of followers, involving averaging their assessments of the leader, and thus failing to account for differences that reflect different behaviour by leaders towards different individuals.[96] This criticism, however, cannot be levelled at ACL, which introduces the idea of responding to and meeting individual needs.

Leadership style research studies have also failed to take account of informal leadership, whereby leaders emerge regardless, or in the absence, of any formal structure, which was discussed earlier. Problems in leadership style research are that the research instruments may not have been administered to the most appropriate persons, that formal and informal leaders will vary in their behaviour patterns, and that these studies suffer from common problems of measurement that are associated with questionnaire instruments.[97]

Nevertheless, one recent study has rehabilitated the two components of leadership identified in the Ohio State studies: consideration and initiating structure. Timothy Judge and colleagues carried out a meta-analysis of their relationship with leadership. They found moderately strong correlations between these and leadership (0.48 for consideration and 0.29 for initiating structure), with consideration more strongly related to follower satisfaction, motivation and leader effectiveness, and initiating structure slightly more strongly related to leader job performance and group-organizational performance.[98]

The Bradford Model: The Micro Skills of Leadership

The Bradford model of leadership, developed by Gerry Randell and colleagues, focuses on the interpersonal 'micro skills' of effective leadership behaviour.[99] These are ways in which effective leaders will structure their interactions with followers and others, gather information, give information, influence behaviour and handle emotion. The core skills of leadership, according to this model, comprise the perception of others' thoughts and feelings through their behaviour, appropriate questioning, making judgements from the answers, and responding appropriately both verbally (using active listening by paraphrasing meaning) and non-verbally through body language (reflecting implied feelings). The model was initially used in training managers in performance appraisal but was later extended to leadership development more generally.

This is a highly practical and useful model as a basis for leadership development that gained popularity with many organizations in the UK from the 1970s onwards (in which I was involved) and was supported by empirical validation studies.[100] The model is highly focused on behaviour at the 'micro' level, but it could be argued that it is narrow in its coverage of the behavioural domain of leadership.

Psychodynamic Theory: Leader–Member Exchange (LMX)

Review

This LMX approach defines the effectiveness of leaders as a function of the psychodynamic exchange and relationship that occurs between leaders and group members (followers or subordinates). Leaders provide direction and guidance through the influence permitted to them by members. Exchange theory – known also as LMET or

Vertical Dyad Linkage Theory – focuses on the characteristics of the leader, their individual followers and their relationship.

In contrast to leadership style theories, LMX theories argue that leader–member relations are sufficiently variable to warrant focusing on each pair of leaders and members (each 'dyad') separately: members will differ markedly in their descriptions of the same leader.[101] The essence of psychodynamic theory is an understanding of the self and others and, as a result, the transactional nature of the leader–follower relationship.[102]

This theory was apparently in use in ancient China. The 'Great Plan', dating from around 2200 to 1121 BC (a date mentioned in the text) and drawing on astrology, morality, physics, politics and religion, prescribed how leaders should behave with their followers or subordinates – considering their attitudes towards social order and towards work:

> **The three virtues are rules, firmness, and gentleness. Spell out rules for peaceful people; deal firmly with violent and offensive people; deal gently with amenable and friendly people. Employ firm supervision with those who shirk or lack initiative, gentle supervision with those who are distinguished by their talents and good dispositions.**[103]

This prescription – some 1,700 years before Confucius – resembles Robert Liden and Feorge Graen's Vertical Dyad Linkage model in which leaders will reward subordinates who show commitment and work hard by showing consideration and, towards others, will act impersonally and rigidly.[104]

According to Douglas Brown and Robert Lord, leadership researchers have defined leadership mainly in terms of easily observable behaviours and their direct impact on outcomes or results rather than in terms of explanations of the underlying processes that lead to such outcomes.[105] For example, they describe communicating a vision rather than why and how that vision will influence followers. This, they say, limits our ability as leaders to exercise influence over individuals, groups and organizations.

Attributional and social-cognitive theories of leadership focus on the perception of leaders' traits and behaviour by followers, such as charisma. We need, therefore, to emphasize the importance of feedback from followers and the use of appropriate leadership behaviour, which the introduction of 360° feedback has helped us to understand.

Critique

While LMX theory is useful in emphasizing the relationships between leaders and followers or subordinates, it appears to support the notion of privileged groups in organizations, which is contrary to our human value of fairness, Peter Northouse argues.[106] The theory also does not explain how high-quality exchanges are developed or how LMX exchanges are analysed or validly measured: the measures used and reported thus far are not comparable and lack content validity.[107] LMX theory is not very helpful in explaining the specific leadership behaviours that create high-quality relationships, merely implying generalities about the need to promote trust, respect, openness, autonomy and discretion. However, the theory does support the notion of 'individualized consideration', which is a key element of transformational leadership (discussed later in this chapter): treating individuals according to their needs and recognizing their uniqueness.

Path–Goal Theory

Review

The path–goal theory of leadership employs the 'expectancy model' of work motivation.[108] This proposes that a person's motivation (effort) depends on his or her assessment of whether their effort would lead to good performance, the probability of a reward, either material or psychological, as a result of the good performance, and the 'valence' (value of the reward to the person). The expectancy model of motivation is discussed in the chapter on leadership and engagement.

According to path–goal theory, the leader increases personal payoffs to subordinates for achieving work goals and paves the way to these payoffs by clarifying the path, removing or reducing roadblocks and pitfalls, and enhancing personal satisfaction along the way. Effective leaders will adopt different styles – supportive, instrumental, participative or achievement-oriented – in different situations. The situational factors that moderate subordinate performance and satisfaction are the personal characteristics of the subordinates and environmental and structural factors. Path–goal theory is primarily about transactional leadership: the leader will offer rewards to others for their successful achievement of the leader's goals.

Critique

Path–goal theory suffers from many of the same deficiencies as leadership style theory, for example inconsistent findings, a group averaging of ratings, a lack of consideration of informal leadership, dubious causality, and measurement problems. These have been well documented elsewhere by Alan Bryman.[109] But even if such research findings were more consistent in predicting subordinate performance:

> ... the plethora of leadership styles and situational factors that the theory and research have put forward do not provide leaders with clear guidance as to how they should behave.[110]

Path–goal theory develops Fiedler's contingency theory and takes into account employee motivation in the choice of leadership style. However, the theory is questionable in situations in which goals are constantly changing and in which leaders cannot offer task direction owing to the highly specialized nature of work.

Situational and Contingency Theories of Leadership

Overview

'Chaos is the midwife of dictatorship', said Will Durant, the American writer and philosopher.[111] Disarray and crisis – bad social, political or economic situations – tend to spawn authoritarian leaders. We have seen many companies and countries where this has happened. A given situation calls for a particular leadership style.

Contingency theories suggest that there is no one best style of leadership. Successful and enduring leaders will use various styles according to the nature of the situation and the followers. Differences among these may relate to the maturity of followers or subordinates, the favourableness of the relationship between them and their leader, the clarity and structure of the task or work, the position power and personal power of the leader, the corporate and national culture, and the degree of urgency of a task or activity and the time available.

Effective leaders know how to adopt a different style for a different situation, regardless of how effective any one particular style has been in the past. The effectiveness of a particular style of leadership depends on the relationship between the characteristics of the leader, the followers and the situation. Bernard Bass and colleagues found that specific leadership styles were associated in different ways with organizational, task, personal and interpersonal characteristics.[112] And Philip Hodgson and Randall White argue, 'Effective leadership is finding a good fit between behaviour, context, and need.'[113]

Once again, contingency theory is nothing new. The ancient Chinese 'Great Plan' can be interpreted as advising leaders to behave differently according to two kind of contingency – the social context and the nature of the followers or subordinates.[114]

Fiedler's Contingency Theory

Fred Fiedler was the pioneer of contingency theories in the late 1960s. His contingency theory suggests that the effectiveness of a leadership style – whether task oriented or people oriented – will depend on the favourableness of a situation in terms of:

* How defined and structured work is.
* How much position power (authority) the leader has.
* The relationship between the leader and the followers.[115]

A situation is highly favourable when work is clearly structured and the leader has great position power (authority) and good relationships with the group. An unfavourable situation is one that is characterized by unstructured work, little position power and poor relationships with the group. Fiedler's prescriptive model, however, is complicated;[116] he suggests that it is more difficult for a leader to change his or her style to suit the situation than it is to change the leader according to the situation.[117] The research underpinning Fiedler's model has been criticized for inconsistent results and confusion over the measurement instruments.[118]

Hersey and Blanchard's Situational Leadership Theory

Situational Leadership as a model of leadership behaviour developed by Paul Hersey and Kenneth Blanchard has gained even greater popularity than the Managerial Grid, with a range of assessment instruments. It relates four leadership styles – 'telling' (directive), 'selling' (consultative), 'participating' and 'delegating' – to followers' or subordinates' readiness for them (their maturity).[119]

Readiness is defined as the ability and confidence to carry out a task. Followers or subordinates who lack a sense of responsibility or knowledge of a task will need clear instructions from their leader, who will accordingly adopt a directive or 'telling' style. As they grow in ability and confidence, so the leader should move to a more relationship-oriented and ultimately delegative (empowering) style. This model assumes a flexibility of style in the leader – their behavioural skills – as well as the ability to diagnose the situation and the style that is needed – their cognitive ability.

Reddin's 3-D Theory of Managerial Effectiveness

Bill Reddin's 3-D model of leadership goes one step further: it describes four styles that can be effective or ineffective, depending on their appropriateness to the situation (Figure 3.3).[120] The four effective styles are the bureaucrat (similar to Blake and Mouton's 1,1 or Hersey and Blanchard's delegative style); the developer (1,9 or a participative style); the executive (9,9 or a consultative/selling style); and the benevolent autocrat (9,1 or a directive style). Ineffective styles, which are the same four foregoing styles respectively but used inappropriately, are the deserter, the missionary, the compromiser and the autocrat.

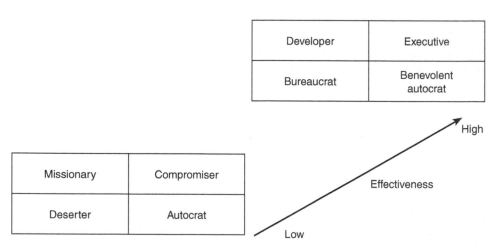

Figure 3.3   Reddin's 3-D Model of Leadership

Reddin uses the term 'situational sensitivity' to refer to the ability to 'read' a situation for what it contains and know what behaviour would most likely be effective. He uses the term 'style flexibility' to refer to the ability to change behaviour according to situational needs. And he proposes the idea of 'situational management' to describe changing the situation to increase managerial effectiveness, for example overcoming resistance to change.

Critique

The various contingency theories have contributed the idea that situational factors need to be considered when examining leadership behaviour. There is no doubt that one leadership style that works well in one situation will not necessarily work well in another.

These theories, however, do not explain *how* leadership styles vary according to organizational level or (top) executive level.[121] And they do not explain how leaders can change either their style or the situation.[122] They also do not explain the leadership processes of acquiring and interpreting the meaning of information, social networking and strategic decision making.[123] As Rob Goffee and Gareth Jones say, '... given that there are endless contingencies in life, there are endless varieties of leadership ... the beleaguered executive looking for a model to help him is hopelessly lost'.[124] Situational and contingency theories do not refer explicitly to values, a key aspect of leadership, except perhaps by implication. Joanne Ciulla says:

> In some situations a person with particularly strong moral values must emerge as a leader ... [for] example, Nelson Mandela and Václav Havel seemed to have been the right men at the right time ... [they] both offered the powerful kind of moral leadership required for peaceful revolutions in South Africa and the Czech republic.[125]

There is little conclusive research evidence to support situational and contingency models of leadership. Problems to do with methodology, analysis and ambiguity in its implications led to much disillusionment with the contingency approach – though never an outright rejection. It was, however, something else that stimulated the development of alternative approaches that collectively have been called the 'New Leadership'.[126]

The 'New Leadership': Vision, Charisma and Transformational Leadership

Vision, charisma and transformation are the keywords for the New Leadership. The concept of transformational leadership arose from the study of rebel leadership and revolution in the early 1970s.[127] However, it was a political historian and biographer, James MacGregor Burns, who, in a seminal book published in 1978, first described 'transforming leadership' and contrasted it with 'transactional leadership'.[128]

Transforming or transformational leadership occurs when both leader and followers raise each other's motivation and sense of higher purpose. Transactional leadership on the other hand involves a transaction, or exchange, between leader and followers, such as providing a material or psychological reward in return for followers' compliance with the leader's wishes, with no sense of any higher purpose. Transforming leadership, according to Burns, addresses people's higher-order needs for achievement, self-esteem and self-actualization. It encourages them to look beyond self-interest for the common good. Transforming leadership raises both leaders and followers to 'higher levels of motivation and morality',[129] whereas transactional leadership merely reflects what or how people are, appealing to their existing needs, desires and preferences.

Transformational leaders have strong values. Burns' theory distinguishes between the morality of ends and the morality of means. Transactional leadership, Joanne Ciulla suggests, concerns values that are implicit in the means of an act – 'modal' values like responsibility, fairness, honesty and keeping promises.[130] Transformational leadership, on the other hand, is concerned with end-values like liberty, justice and equality. Rabindra Kanungo and Manuel Medonca say that the moral aspects of transformational leadership are a prosocial orientation, a concomitant vision and values that reflect a concern for others.[131]

Micha Popper and Ofra Mayseless argue, 'The impact of transformational leadership is reflected in motivation, empowerment, and morality [values].'[132] In terms of Maslow's hierarchy of needs[133] (see the chapter on leadership and engagement), they quote Burns as suggesting that transformational leaders motivate followers to pursue the highest level of need satisfaction, namely self-actualization. Transformational leaders, they say, empower followers to think independently, critically and creatively and raise their levels of self-efficacy, self-worth, self-confidence, competence, autonomy and risk taking. And, again quoting Burns, they say, as do Kanungo and Medonca, that transformational leaders emphasize prosocial values such as justice and equality rather than modal, instrumental values such as loyalty.

Transactional and transformational leadership are probably the most influential leadership theories in current thinking.[134] And the Full Range Leadership model is perhaps the most well known among these.

The Full Range Leadership Model

Overview

Probably the most important recent model of leadership that includes and extends these ideas is Bernard Bass and Bruce Avolio's Full Range Leadership model: laissez-faire, transactional leadership and transformational leadership.[135] This model resulted from extensive empirical research by Bass in the early 1980s, stimulated by Burns' ideas.

Laissez-faire Leadership

Laissez-faire leaders avoid taking a stand, ignore problems, do not follow up and refrain from intervening. In terms of leadership style theory (directive, consultative, participative and delegative styles), they use no particular style to a significant extent.[136]

Laissez-faire is non-transactional leadership, if indeed it is leadership at all. This behaviour may result in conflict and a lack of achievement. An example is former US president Calvin Coolidge, who is reputed to have slept 16 hours each day. Researchers at the University of Bergen in Norway found that laissez-faire leadership behaviour was the most prevalent destructive leadership behaviour in a representative sample of the Norwegian workforce.[137]

Transactional Leadership

Transactional leaders practise management-by-exception and contingent reward.

Management-by-exception. Management-by-exception is practised in two forms: passive and active.[138] Passive management-by-exception is displayed when a leader sets work objectives and performance standards but then waits for problems to arise, reacts to mistakes and intervenes reluctantly. The active form entails monitoring for deviations and errors and then correcting them, and enforcing rules and procedures.

Contingent reward. Contingent reward entails setting work objectives and performance standards, providing feedback, and also providing financial or psychological rewards in exchange for performance that meets expectations. This may result in motivating people to achieve goals and to develop themselves, but not to the extent of transformational leadership.

Transactional leaders appear to be strongly directive and they tend not to use the consultative, participative or delegative styles.[139] They set objectives and performance standards, but do so in a directive rather than participative manner. Transactional leaders, according to the Bradford micro skills theory of leadership, are also more likely than transformational leaders to use closed and leading questions in their interactions with others.[140] These behaviours run the risk of gaining only compliance rather than commitment. Transactional leaders also tend to use rewards for performance on the basis of directives about objectives. And, while this can result in short-term achievement, it runs the risk of stifling human development, with the consequential loss of competitive advantage.

Transformational Leadership

Transformational leaders do more than 'transact' with subordinates or followers, and this is what makes a significant difference to people's motivation and development. They achieve, Bass says, 'performance beyond expectations' in their subordinates or followers.[141] They stimulate followers to transcend their own immediate self-interest for the greater good of the group, organization or society. Transformational leadership makes a positive impact on empowerment, motivation and morality. According to the Bass and Avolio model, transformational leaders tend to use one or more of the four 'I's: individualized consideration, intellectual stimulation, inspirational motivation and idealized influence.

Individualized Consideration. Transformational leaders display individualized consideration: they listen actively; they identify individuals' personal concerns, needs and abilities; they provide matching challenges and opportunities to learn in a supportive environment; they delegate to them as a way of developing them; they give developmental feedback; and they coach them. Transformational leaders practise MBWA – 'management by wandering around'. This 'I' is similar to the dimension of consideration or socio-emotional orientation in leadership style theories.

Intellectual Stimulation. Transformational leaders use intellectual stimulation. They question the *status quo*. They present new ideas to followers and challenge them to think. They encourage imagination and creativity in rethinking assumptions and old ways of doing things. And they do not publicly criticize errors, mistakes, failure or ideas or approaches that differ from their own. Socrates, in his famous question-and-answer dialogues, was probably the greatest example of an intellectually stimulating leader.[142] Such leaders will use and encourage intuition as well as logic. This is a recipe for personal growth. In the words of the American Supreme Court justice, Oliver Wendell Holmes, Jr: 'A mind once stretched by a new idea never regains its original dimension.'[143] With the increased emphasis today on knowledge work, intellectual stimulation is particularly important.[144] Knowledge-based organizations require leaders who can create and maintain an environment where innovation thrives. Intellectual stimulation, together with individualized consideration, is the basis for an effective coaching and mentoring role.

Inspirational Motivation. Transformational leaders display inspirational motivation. They communicate a clear vision of the possible future; they align organizational goals and personal goals so that people can achieve their personal goals by achieving organizational goals; and they treat threats and problems as opportunities to learn. They provide meaning and challenge to the work of their followers. And they speak (and write) in an appealing and exciting way. In Bass's words:

> Quantum leaps in performance may be seen ... when a group is roused out of its despair by a ... leader who articulates revolutionary new ideas about what may be possible.[145]

As a result, followers want to meet expectations and they display their commitment to, and not merely their compliance with, the vision, goals and tasks. They are motivated and inspired.

Idealized Influence. Transformational leaders also display idealized influence, something closely related to charisma. They express confidence in the vision; they take personal responsibility for actions; they display a sense of purpose, determination, persistence and trust in other people; and they emphasize accomplishments rather than failures. US football coach Paul 'Bear' Bryant captures this dimension of transformational leadership thus:

> There's just three things I ever say. If anything goes bad, then I did it. If anything goes semi-good, then we did it. If anything goes really good, then you did it. That's all it takes.[146]

Such leaders also gain the admiration, respect, trust and confidence of others by personally demonstrating extraordinary abilities of one kind or another. They put the needs of other people before their own, and they display high standards of ethical and moral behaviour. Trust is perhaps the single most important factor in transformational

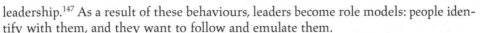

leadership.[147] As a result of these behaviours, leaders become role models: people identify with them, and they want to follow and emulate them.

Transformational leaders tend to use the consultative, participative and delegative styles as well as the directive style.[148] The four 'I's are related to these four leadership styles in different ways. Transformational leaders are also more likely than transactional leaders to use open and probing questions and reflective responses. These findings are consistent with what Tom Peters and Bob Waterman called 'loose–tight' leadership behaviour[149] and with those of Abraham Sagie and colleagues in respect of the participative and directive styles.[150] The latter researchers found that integrating these styles can be effective. The implication is that transformational leaders are more active and more flexible in their leadership behaviour.

Hierarchical Level and Transactional and Transformational Leadership

Bruce Avolio and Bernard Bass suggest that transformational leadership should be observed at all levels in an organization.[151] Deanne Den Hartog and colleagues found that charismatic/transformational leadership behaviour was valued almost equally at top and lower levels of management.[152] A study of commonalities and differences in leadership behaviour and effectiveness at different hierarchical levels in manufacturing organizations by Gareth Edwards and me using a 360° leadership assessment instrument, Bass and Avolio's Multifactor Leadership Questionnaire,[153] revealed the following:

- Transformational leadership is displayed more at higher levels than at lower levels but its effectiveness is the same at all levels.
- The use of both transactional leadership and laissez-faire leadership was found not to vary across the hierarchy.
- The effectiveness of transactional leadership was found to decrease above middle-management level.[154]

In summary, there are differences across hierarchical levels in organizations in the *use* of transformational leadership and the *effectiveness* of transactional leadership (see Figure 3.4). These findings are consistent with those of previous research that have shown transformational leadership to be more prevalent at upper levels than lower levels in organizations[155] and consistently conducive to extra effort, effective and satisfying at all hierarchical levels.[156]

Another study of leadership and organizational hierarchy, by Titus Oshagbemi and myself, also showed that, overall, transformational leadership was displayed more at higher levels than at lower levels while transactional leadership did not vary (except specifically for contingent reward, which differed between middle and first-level managers).[157] The particular dimensions of transformational leadership that varied were intellectual stimulation and inspirational motivation. This study also showed that senior managers were less directive and more participative in their leadership style than first-level managers. There were also significant differences between senior, middle and first-level managers in their use of the delegative style, which was positively associated with hierarchical level: senior managers used this style most.

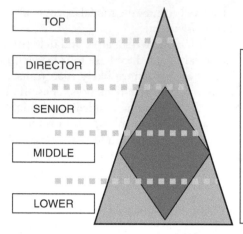

Notes: The reason for the diamond shape for transformational and transactional is that while transactional leadership was conducive to extra effort, effective and satisfying at middle management levels, it was conducive to extra effort mainly at senior levels and effective and satisfying mainly at lower levels. *Laissez-faire* was inhibitory to extra effort, ineffective and unsatisfying at all levels.

☐ Transformational leadership

■ Transformational and transactional leadership

Figure 3.4 A Working Model of Transformational and Transactional Leadership across Hierarchical Levels

Hierarchical position therefore appears to be a moderator of the use of transformational leadership (a positive relationship) but not its effectiveness, which is constant throughout organizations. It is also a moderator of the effectiveness of transactional leadership (a negative relationship) but not its use, which in general is also constant across the hierarchy. Stephen Zaccaro and Richard Klimoski suggest that organizational context, of which hierarchical position is one feature, is often understated as a moderator: it is a boundary condition for theory building and model specification.[158] More empirical research on the commonalities and differences in leadership across organizational hierarchies is needed.

Pseudo-transformational Leadership

Transformational leadership may also take a dark form, what Bass and Avolio call 'pseudo-transformational leadership'.[159] Such leaders encourage an 'us-and-them' competitiveness and pursue their own self-interests rather than the common good. They use symbols of authority and hierarchical differentiation.[160] Pseudo-transformational leaders may possess a dysfunctional charisma: their values are highly questionable, and they are likely to lead their followers towards disaster and perdition.

Critique of the Full Range Leadership Model

Bass and Avolio's Full Range Leadership theory is supported by a meta-analysis of 87 relevant studies by Timothy Judge and Ronald Piccolo, though contingent reward was found to be strongly associated with transformational leadership as a whole.[161] Bass claims universal applicability of his Full Range Leadership model across national cultures, though he does say that the specific behaviours that characterize the dimensions may vary.[162] However, while the Full Range Leadership model has enjoyed popularity, it is not beyond criticism.

Issues concern the validity of its factor structure[163] and the transformational leadership scales.[164] The results of various studies, including a confirmatory factor analysis by Bass and Avolio themselves, have led to the conclusion that a six-factor model is the best representation of this model, though there is low discriminant validity among the transformational and contingent reward (transactional) scales.[165]

Bass's model of transformational leadership incorporates communicating a vision as a source of 'inspirational motivation' and expressing confidence in it as 'idealized influence', but little more is said of vision, and nothing at all is said of mission or strategy. Vision is one of the key differences between a manager and a leader, according to Stanley Deetz and colleagues.[166]

Generalizability of the Full Range Leadership model across hierarchical levels in organizations has been questioned,[167] though Bass found transformational leadership at all levels.[168] Other studies, however, have found it to be displayed significantly more at higher levels.[169] Zaccaro and Klimocki point out that hierarchical level as a moderator in the use and effectiveness of leadership behaviour has been a long-held theoretical assumption.[170] And John Antonakis suggests that hierarchical level moderates Bass's 'full-range leadership' model.[171] Kevin Lowe and colleagues, however, had previously found that the effectiveness of transformational leadership did not differ across organizational levels.[172] Indeed top and middle-level managers appeared to display transformational leadership more than lower-level managers did but it was still effective at all levels.[173]

Another criticism of the transactional/transformational leadership model is twofold: transactional leadership appears to relate more to 'management' than to leadership; and the concept of transformation over-emphasizes the role of the leader in the change process.[174] In fact, Alan Bryman says, transactional leadership can be equated with 'management' and the theories of 'leadership' style discussed earlier actually concern 'management' style rather than leadership.[175] Transactional leadership reflects a control orientation, whereas transformational leadership is empowering and inspirational, resulting in changes in people's abilities, attitudes, values, beliefs and motivation. But Kets de Vries and Florent-Treacy rightly argue that concentrating on transformational or charismatic leadership role without considering the transactional one is too narrow: both roles are needed.[176]

Engaging Transformational Leadership

Beverly Alimo-Metcalfe and Robert Alban-Metcalfe emphasize the importance of distinguishing between 'distant' leadership and 'close' or 'nearby' leadership.[177] They contrast interview studies with top-level managers and studies at all levels of the *perceptions* of top-level managers ('distant' leadership) and immediate bosses ('nearby' leadership). Support for this contrast comes from the literature on leadership and social distance. For example, Boas Shamir's study of Israeli students showed the following differences (see Table 3.2):[178]

Table 3.2 Differences between Distant and Close Leaders

Distant Leaders	Nearby Leaders
Ideological orientation	Sociable and open
Strong sense of mission	Considerate of others
Courageous, rhetorical expression	Have a sense of humour
Little concern for personal criticism	High level of specific expertise
or sanction	Dynamic and active
	Impressive physical appearance
	Intelligent or wise
	Setting high performance standards
	Unconventional behaviour

Alimo-Metcalfe and Alban-Metcalfe used a grounded theory approach to determining the nature of 'nearby' leadership to ensure adequate content validity. This involved using a sample that was inclusive with reference to age, ethnicity, gender and level in the organization.[179] Research, using the same methodology and undertaken in the UK by the Home Office among police officers and staff and among FTSE 100 companies, confirmed the initial findings.[180] Initial analyses in local government suggested the existence of nine scales. Subsequent analyses, additionally involving a total of 3,477 managers and professionals in local government and the National Health Service (NHS), indicated the existence of 14 scales, with high levels of reliability and construct, criterion and discriminant validity. These scales were assessed using the Engaging Transformational Leadership Questionnaire (TLQ).

The TLQ assesses 'engaging transformational leadership' behaviours in the contexts of leading individuals, leading the organization, and moving forward together, along with personal qualities and values (see Figure 3.5). The model consists of 14 scales, with a total of 98 items:

❋ Leading Individuals

  ❋ Showing genuine concern.
  ❋ Being accessible.
  ❋ Enabling.
  ❋ Encouraging change.

❋ Leading the Organization

  ❋ Supporting a development culture.
  ❋ Inspiring others.
  ❋ Focusing the team effort.
  ❋ Being decisive.

❋ Moving Forward Together

  ❋ Building a shared vision.
  ❋ Networking.

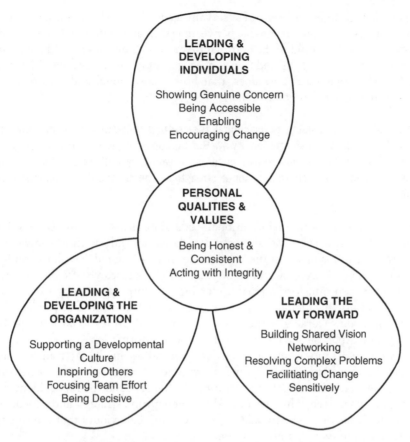

Figure 3.5 The Engaging Transformational Leadership Model (© Real World Group, 2011. Reproduced with kind permission)

> * Resolving complex problems.
> * Facilitating change sensitively.

* Personal Qualities and Values

> * Being honest and consistent.
> * Acting with integrity.

This model has undergone research using a longitudinal design to establish cause–effect relationships between leadership behaviours and performance in organizations, something that is unusual in leadership research. After controlling for contextual factors, a national longitudinal study, using a leadership culture tool based on the TLQ with multi-professional teams in the NHS, found evidence of a direct cause–effect relationship between an engaging style of leadership and productivity, measured objectively.[181] In contrast to models of 'distant', often 'heroic' leadership, the whole tenor of the TLQ is one of leadership as a shared process, with an emphasis on openness, connectedness, empowerment, humility and humanity.

This is close to Robert Greenleaf's 'servant leadership'.[182] It emphasizes the social influence process in 'connectedness' between leader and individual. This model of leadership breaks the mould of the dominant American 'Full Range Leadership' model in emphasizing the 'engaging' and 'serving' aspects of leadership. Alimo-Metcalfe and Alban-Metcalfe suggest, as Bass does, that both transactional and transformational leadership are needed in organizations:

> ... the real skill is in being transactional (i.e. setting objectives, planning, providing feedback, etc.) in a transformational way. But perhaps the greatest challenge is, how willing will those in the most senior positions – who may well have been appointed precisely because of their transactional strengths – be to adopt a transformational style?[183]

Andrew Kelly found that transformational leadership, as assessed by Alimo-Metcalfe and Alban-Metcalfe's TLQ, was strongly correlated not only with Maslow's higher-level motivators in his model of the hierarchy of needs,[184] but also with the mid-range motivators of loyalty, security and belonging.[185] Kelly's research also demonstrated a correlation between transformational leadership and employee resource commitment (in the form of organizational commitment behaviour), and this was particularly the case for knowledge workers – those who contributed professional and specialized knowledge and expertise and controlled the flow of information.

In reviewing Alimo-Metcalfe and Alban-Metcalfe's model of transformational leadership, Malcolm Higgs and Victor Dulewicz note how it accounts for the organizational context and situational considerations.[186] In particular the model identifies the following factors in leadership: vision, values and culture, strategy and a 'people' factor. This people factor implicitly addresses leadership behaviours that are to do with empowerment, motivation and inspiration.

Other Theories and Models of Leadership

Noel Tichy and Mary Devanna's concept of transformational leadership proposes that transformational leaders are visionaries; see themselves as change agents; display courage in the face of resistance and risk; emphasize the need for motivation, empowerment and trust; are driven by strong values; see mistakes, errors and failures as learning opportunities; and cope with complexity, uncertainty and ambiguity.[187] This model, however, is based on observations of only 14 business leaders.

Alannah Rafferty and Mark Griffin propose another variation that they determined empirically, with the following five dimensions of transformational leadership:

❋ Vision – expressing an idealized picture of the future based around organizational values.
❋ Inspirational communication – expressing positive and encouraging messages about the organization, and making statements that build motivation and confidence.

☀ Intellectual stimulation – enhancing employees' interest in and awareness of problems, and increasing their ability to think about problems in new ways.

☀ Supportive leadership – expressing concern for followers and taking account of their individual needs.

☀ Personal recognition – providing rewards such as praise and acknowledging effort in the achievement of specified goals.[188]

Visionary Leadership

Marshall Sashkin's visionary leadership concerns transforming an organizational culture in line with the leader's vision of the organization's future.[189] Sashkin and Rosenbach also suggest that there are three personal characteristics that guide the leader's behavioural strategies: self-efficacy (self-confidence), power orientation (use of power in different ways) and cognitive capability.[190] Cognitive capability concerns understanding complex cause-and-effect chains that enable action at the right time to achieve the desired outcomes.[191] Sashkin's theory is but a single piece in the leadership jigsaw puzzle.

Charismatic Leadership

Outstanding leaders are often perceived as charismatic: they attract and inspire followers. Charismatic leadership is found at all levels in the organization, though most frequently at the top, Bernard Bass says, and it is associated with greater trust in their leaders and achievement among followers.[192] The charismatic leader 'weaves a spell' outside the organization, too, attracting shareholders and investment in troubled times, according to research by Francis Flynn and Barry Staw.[193] David Waldman and colleagues, however, in a study of senior managers in Fortune 500 companies in the United States, found that charismatic leadership was associated with net profit margin, but only under conditions of environmental uncertainty.[194] Charismatic leadership appears to be dysfunctional in predictable conditions, perhaps because it may generate unnecessary change.

Max Weber, the German sociologist, wrote the classic work on charisma.[195] He saw this as primarily a social relationship between leader and follower resulting from extraordinary personal qualities but which also required continual validation: followers' perception of the leader's 'devotion to … exceptional sanctity, heroism or exemplary character [and] the normative patterns of order revealed or ordained by him'. Weber saw charisma as a process of influence and commitment that would arise in opposition to traditional bureaucracy.

A more contemporary view is that charisma is not something that is possessed by a leader but a consequence of the relationship between leader and followers.[196] Followers appear to be attracted to different types of leaders, and followers' work values – favouring participation, security and extrinsic rewards – will contribute to their leadership preferences.[197] Joanne Ciulla comments on charismatic leadership and values: 'The values of charismatic leaders shape the organization, but in some cases these values do not live on when the charismatic leader is gone'.[198]

Organic Leadership

Gayle Avery suggests that organizations of the future will require an 'organic' form of transformational leadership.[199] She characterizes this as:

✳ Mutual sense making within the group.
✳ The emergence rather than the appointment of leaders.
✳ A buy-in to the group's shared values and processes.
✳ Self-determination.
✳ The emergence of vision from the group (rather than from a leader).
✳ Vision as a strong cultural element.

The organic paradigm of leadership, she says:

> ... involves letting go of conventional notions of control, order and hierarchy, replacing them with trust and an acceptance of continual change, chaos and respect for diverse members of the organization ... the members are expected to be self-managing and self-leading.[200]

Centered Leadership

Theory creation is not the exclusive preserve of academics in the field of leadership. Management consultants McKinsey and Company have proposed a theory of leadership capability based on interviews with leaders, academic literature reviews, client workshops and global surveys. They identify five 'capabilities' that they call 'centered leadership'.[201] McKinsey claim that this model is valid across different regions, cultures and seniority levels as well as for men and women equally. The five capabilities are as follows:

✳ *Meaning.* Infusing life and work with meaning, associated with 'signature strengths', purpose and happiness.
✳ *Positive Framing.* Framing the world optimistically,[202] such as seeing opportunity (rather than danger, which is pessimism) in change and uncertainty, associated with self-awareness, 'learned' optimism[203] and 'moving on'.
✳ *Connecting.* Managing complex webs of communication chains and connections, associated with network design, sponsorship, reciprocity and inclusiveness.
✳ *Engaging.* Engaging with risk, fear and opportunity and helping people to summon the courage to act, associated with voice, ownership, risk taking and adaptability.
✳ *Managing Energy (Energizing).* Sustaining and restoring personal energy and commitment – physical, mental and emotional – and helping others to do likewise.

Preconditions for centered leadership, McKinsey say, are intelligence, a tolerance for change, a desire to lead and communication skills, and their impact is manifest as 'presence', resilience and a sense of belonging. As part of an ongoing validation process, it was found that all five capabilities were important to how men and women rated their own performance as leaders and their satisfaction with life in general.[204]

This research should be treated with caution: misleading results may arise from common method variance that results from correlated data being gathered from the same respondents.

Critique of the 'New Leadership' Theories

The various theories commonly categorized as the 'New Leadership' – charismatic leadership, visionary leadership and transformational leadership, with the exception of the organic paradigm – have been challenged as focusing on the individual rather than the organization as a whole. Critics say they fail to explain distributed leadership.[205] Gary Yukl and Peter Gronn criticize contemporary leadership theories such as transformational and charismatic leadership for their assumption that one individual ('the leader') will lead all of the other people in a group or organization towards its goals.[206]

Transformational leadership has rejuvenated leadership research since the mid 1980s.[207] It adds to the previously well-established dimensions of leadership, consideration and the initiation of structure, the visionary aspect of leadership, and the emotional involvement and development of followers or employees.[208] What it does not do is explain the nature of effective visioning and the organizational mission or the place of values, culture and strategy in leadership.

Pragmatic Leadership

Is effective leadership always concerned with organizational transformation? Clearly such a transformation may be necessary when an organization or nation is performing poorly, there is a new opportunity, or the business or economic environment changes adversely. But organizational transformation may not be necessary, and it may even be dysfunctional, when the organization or nation is performing well in conditions of relative stability. While radical organizational transformation may not be appropriate, transformational leadership is still desirable, entailing 'custody of the company's direction and its culture and values'.[209] Perhaps effective leadership, then, is about being 'right at the time'. As Sir Peter Parker, chairman of Mitsubishi Electric Europe BV, points out:

> The world of business is like a pendulum. So leadership is about being right at the time. At present, the pendulum favours Branson rather than Hanson: modern, open, accessible, informal and egalitarian.[210]

'Being right at the time' raises the question of pragmatic leadership. It has been argued that outstanding leaders, like Benjamin Franklin for example, may be neither transactional nor transformational or charismatic but pragmatic.[211] In considering 10 cases of noteworthy leadership by Benjamin Franklin, Michael Mumford and Judy Van Dorn suggest that outstanding leaders may simply take a functional, problem-solving approach based on their knowledge about, and sensitivity to, both social relationships and the problems people face.[212]

Warrior Leadership

A version of this is David Nice's warrior leadership.[213] Nice's model describes how political and military leaders will behave in conflict and pre-settlement periods. They will enter freely into conflict and strive to overcome the opposition; control information; emphasize results over methods; get to know those they seek to lead and defeat; and use intermediaries as buffers. Political leaders in Northern Ireland displayed such behaviours during the peace process.

This brings us to the place of strategy in relation to leadership. One idea is that strategy is a core theme and practice in effective leadership, as can be seen in our model that we discuss later in this chapter. Another idea is that leadership may emphasize strategy as 'strategic leadership'.

Strategic Leadership

Strategic leadership rejoices in a plethora of definitions. Gerry Johnson and Kevan Scholes define strategic leadership as encapsulating entrepreneurial processes and strategic vision.[214] They also see strategic leadership as concerned with strategy development and change.[215] In research by Philip Stiles, one interviewee said, 'The mission is why we are in business. The vision is where we want to be. These are fundamentally the responsibility of the board.'[216] Some writers argue that the sole role of the strategic leader is providing a vision, mission and guiding principles (values and rules).[217] Beverley Mobbs, a quality management consultant, calls vision, mission and values 'critical success factors' in the pursuit of excellence.[218] Katherine Beatty and Laura Quinn give examples of strategic leadership: creating a shared vision of the future; linking the efforts of everyone in the organization to the organization's goals; not just accomplishing objectives but also steadily improving the organization.[219]

Strategic leadership, according to upper echelons theory, refers essentially to the top management team.[220] A key role of top-level leaders is to decide and implement strategy.[221] Using a model of strategic leadership developed by Michael Hitt and colleagues,[222] Abdalla Hagen and colleagues found that American CEOs ranked its six components in the following order of importance:

1. Determining a strategic direction.
2. Developing human capital.
3. Exploiting and maintaining the core competencies.
4. Sustaining an effective corporate culture.
5. Emphasizing ethical practices.
6. Establishing strategic control.[223]

Katherine Beatty and Laura Quinn describe the model of strategic leadership used by the Center for Creative Leadership in the United States:

> ...individuals and teams ... exert strategic leadership when they think, act, and influence ... in ways that enhance the organization's sustainable competitive advantage ...[224]

Apart from competitive advantage, shareholder value also emerges in definitions of strategic leadership. John Sosik and Don Jung define strategic leadership as 'The capacity to orchestrate complex business processes and to leverage these opportunities into financial rewards for shareholders.'[225] This definition of strategic leadership sounds more like management than leadership and is very narrow if not misguided in its focus on shareholders only. We discuss this in a later chapter.

Management consultant Bruce Nixon,[226] in his work on helping companies to deal with global forces, effectively uses a strategic leadership model that focuses on:

*   Global forces – environmental trends, issues and opportunities.
*   Current state – how well the company is responding.
*   Purpose and values – both individual and corporate; the company's unique positioning.
*   Vision of a desirable future – for the world and for the company; the culture needed.
*   Strategy – key strategic actions, influence, networking, obstacles, implementation and support.

Strategic leadership concerns developing the organization's vision, mission, strategies and culture, and monitoring progress and changes in the business environment to ensure strategies are focused, relevant and valid. A key competency in strategic leadership is decision making – about whether or not to act and if so when. Strategic leadership is concerned with monitoring how well an organizational culture, including values, is supporting the organization's vision and mission. And it also concerns the monitoring of human capital – employees' competencies, budgets and organizational structure and systems. However, little or no attention is paid in strategic leadership theories to the need for empowerment, motivation and inspiration. The place of strategy in effective leadership is discussed in Chapter 7.

Evolutionary Leadership Theory

An attempt to make sense of the great diversity of leadership theories is evolutionary leadership theory (ELT), postulated by Mark Van Vugt and Anjana Ahuja.[227] The central idea is that the behaviours associated with leadership and followership emerge through natural selection during human evolution. Such behaviours – adaptive behaviours – enhance human beings' chances of surviving and reproducing by enabling them to adapt to their environment. And such behaviours eventually become 'hard-wired' in the human brain: they become automatic and usually beneficial. So leadership and followership become virtually instinctive and natural. Some people naturally lead and some people naturally follow (and perhaps some people just naturally get out of the way!).

Evolutionary leadership theory draws on an eclectic range of disciplines – psychology, biology, neuroscience, economics, anthropology and primatology – to explain how differing leadership styles and behaviour have emerged. Van Vugt and Ahuja suggest a primitive yet enduring characteristic of human beings:

> ... we do seem happiest when our working environments echo facets of ancestral tribal life – a close-knit structure governed loosely by trusted elders, in which every member [is] valued for his or her unique contribution to group living and survival.[228]

As a scientific theory ELT generates hypotheses and predictions that they claim can be tested. A major one, the Mismatch Hypothesis, is that:

> ... our relatively primitive brains, which prime us for membership of fairly small, egalitarian tribes, find it tough to cope with the mammoth corporations and civic structures of the 21st century ... [we still] seek out leaders who display physical and behavioural traits that our ancestors would have prized on the savannah (which is why we like tall, strong-jawed leaders).[229]

Before we evaluate this hypothesis, let us consider how leadership has evolved in the human race. According to Van Vugt:

> ... leadership cannot be studied without examining the needs and desires of followers. From an evolutionary perspective, it is not surprising why individuals choose to lead given the obvious benefits. It is more puzzling why people would voluntarily defer to a leader given what is known about the process of evolution through natural selection.[230]

Anthropologists have studied leadership because of the consistency with which leaders appear in human societies, say Jelmer Eerkens and colleagues.[231] They comment:

> Most anthropologists agree ... that small-scale human societies of the late Pleistocene [126,000 to 12,000 years ago] generally lacked formalized and permanent leaders with authority to make decisions about a broad range of activities (such as economics, religion, and politics). Only during the early Holocene [from 12,000 years ago to the present] do we see the expression (or re-expression) of such leaders among human societies.[232]

Van Vugt says that evolutionary biology and social psychology as scientific disciplines have both studied leadership but have scarcely influenced each other, though this is now changing under the umbrella of evolutionary psychology. Van Vugt poses several questions. What selection pressures might have led to the emergence of leadership and followership in hominid evolutionary history? Is leadership designed to solve a set of adaptive problems? What has evolutionary thinking to say about the origins of leadership? And what are the implications of an evolutionary-based analysis of leadership?

Van Vugt offers two perspectives on how leaders and followers emerge. The evolutionary biology perspective suggests that adaptations for dominance and submission have led only incidentally to leadership and followership. He says, 'Dominant individuals undertake leader-like activities because the costs are negligible to them.' A prediction that leadership is correlated with dominance based on this has not received much support in the psychological literature: '... leadership and dominance', he says, 'are different evolutionary pathways to obtaining status'. The evolutionary game-theory perspective, he says, 'views leadership and followership as complementary social strategies in coordination situations' according to their benefits to those adopting them,[233] particularly in situations of group movement, peacekeeping within groups and intergroup competition.[234] Van Vugt and colleagues use ethologist Nikolaas

Table 3.3 Van Vugt and Colleagues' Four-Functions Analysis of Psychological Adaptations in the Evolution of Leadership

Proximate Mechanisms	
Causation	Ontogeny*
• What kind of people make good leaders?	• When do leader–follower patterns emerge in the life span?
	• Does developmental history predict leadership propensity?
Phylogeny**	Adaptation***
• When did leadership emerge in our species?	• Did leadership promote the survival of our forebears so that it became part of
• Are there parallels in other species?	our evolved psychology?
Ultimate Mechanisms	

Notes:
* equated with development
** equated with evolution
*** equated with function

Tinbergen's four-functions model[235] to analyse psychological adaptations associated with the evolution of leadership, as shown in Table 3.3.

Leadership has had a long evolutionary history from the earliest hominids some 2.5 million years ago. Evolutionary psychology and evolutionary leadership theory in particular provide a framework for understanding how leadership and followership have resulted from adaptations that have taken place in human development to facilitate group action. Such theory can also take into account personality and ability differences in leadership. However, more knowledge is needed about the interplay between genetic and environmental influences on leadership.

In their discussion of evolutionary leadership Van Vugt and colleagues argue credibly that leadership cannot be studied without considering the psychology of followers. They also say that the relationship between leaders and followers is ambivalent because their respective goals are not always shared, which also makes sense. And the way we respond to leadership today, they suggest, has been shaped by 2.5 million years of living in small egalitarian communities, again a reasonable opinion. A problem emerges in why Van Vugt and colleagues say that evolutionary leadership theory is useful:

> We are often required to defer to people in leadership roles whose behavior is markedly inconsistent with qualities important in ancestral leadership. This may lead to frustration, alienation, and efforts to change leaders, jobs, or careers. If we want to know why leadership sometimes fails in modern society, we should consult the lessons from our past.[236]

Not all psychologists are convinced. For example, Glynis Breakwell, an eminent social psychologist and vice chancellor of Bath University in the UK, while 'engaged' with evolutionary leadership theory, questions the evidence that is claimed to support it.[237] In particular, she criticizes the key claim by Van Hugt and Ahuja that 'people feel uncomfortable in organisations that do not resemble the social groupings that they would have experienced in ancestral tribal communities', that we hunger for leaders whose attributes are like our ancestors (such as those who are tall and strong-jawed). This mismatch hypothesis, she counters, 'cannot be tested in any meaningful way': we cannot establish what people in prehistoric times valued in their leaders.

Leadership Theory: Current Status

No theory or model of leadership so far has provided a full and satisfactory explanation of leadership; indeed there is no consensus on the meaning of leadership in the first place. Many theories are partisan or partial, reflecting particular philosophical or ideological points of view. Many are based on limited, even biased, research: the answers one gets depend on the questions one asks. As a result the theories that emerge are often self-fulfilling prophecies and at best explain only some aspects of leadership. Gary Yukl's wide-ranging review of the leadership literature in 1989 – and still a valid criticism more than 20 years later – concluded:

> Most of the theories are beset with conceptual weaknesses and lack strong empirical support. Several thousand empirical studies have been conducted but most of the results are contradictory and inconclusive.[238]

A related shortcoming of current leadership thinking is the separate tracks – cognitive, emotional, moral, spiritual and behavioural – along which leadership research and theory have moved. For example, none of the theories and models reviewed, other than servant leadership, addresses the spiritual element of people's lives – the need for meaning.[239] Some theories do attempt to combine the different tracks, but only superficially.

For example, research in 1996 by the Industrial Society (later known as the Work Foundation) identified 'observable leadership skills and behaviours, beliefs and trust' as the three key elements of 'liberating leadership'.[240] In terms of our model, these elements relate to the emotional and behavioural dimensions of leadership. But the 'Leader Ship' model proposed by the Industrial Society, in which the superstructure, hull and keel of a ship metaphorically represent these three elements respectively, omits any reference to vision and strategy. Current theories of leadership have failed to integrate the disparate tracks and put the pieces of the jigsaw puzzle together to produce a clear, coherent picture.

Strategy and leadership, for example, are topics that have been greatly researched and written about, but 'we still seem to be a long way from fully understanding these two concepts and how they are interrelated'.[241] None of the theories that have been reviewed deals much with strategy.

Understanding leadership as a process centred on a relationship rather than on the individual has been receiving much attention recently. Leadership is exercised in all relationships, including upwards. Joseph Rost says that management takes place between managers and *subordinates*, whereas leadership takes place between leaders and *collaborators*: the essence of leadership is not the leader but the relationship.[242] Leadership involves both leaders and collaborators in aiming to make real changes in an organization, where these changes reflect the common purpose of the leaders and collaborators, whereas management involves coordinating activities that reflect the organization's purpose.

Richard Whipp and Andrew Pettigrew point out that there has been insufficient attention to leadership as a process and to the interaction between leadership and context, in particular the difference that leadership can make to competitiveness by comparing firms.[243] Alimo-Metcalfe and Alban-Metcalfe's model of close/nearby leadership contrasts with American models of distant leadership, also suggesting differences in leadership according to context.[244]

This chapter so far has reviewed the contribution and limitations of key leadership theories. The range of leadership theories has been likened to the periodic table in chemistry: we are still discovering (or creating) new elements.[245] The variety of different theoretical frameworks constitutes a relatively fragmented and disparate body of knowledge, and this reduces their value.[246] Such a variety of theories frequently serves to confuse those who wish to understand, practise or develop leadership in all its aspects and complexity. On the other hand, such fragmentation, Michael Katzko suggests, is a sign of the richness of a field of academic study.[247]

Current leadership theory appears to be a product of the economic and social context of the time. Peter Gronn suggests that '… theories of leadership wax and wane in keeping with wider cultural and economic shifts and developments'.[248] They reflect the changing nature of work and authority in society as whole. The mechanistic, bureaucratic organizations of the twentieth century spawned a traditional exchange or transactional leadership.

Gayle Avery shows how the various approaches to leadership – theories from trait theory to visionary, charismatic and transformational theories – can be classified into four leadership paradigms: classical, transactional, visionary and organic.[249] Organizations of the future, reflecting technological advances and societal change, and with organic forms and a greater proportion of knowledge workers, will require a form of transformational leadership beyond current models, such as Avery's organic leadership paradigm. Very few theories and models of leadership, Avery says, span all four paradigms.

Bruce Avolio and colleagues, in reviewing current leadership theories and research and pointing out trends and future directions, suggest that there is a growing emphasis on the role of the followers in leadership and that leadership is increasingly being distributed and shared in organizations,[250] which we have already considered in Chapter 1. They also indicate a growing interest in how leadership develops, which we consider in our chapter on the assessment and development of leadership, and in how a 'more holistic' view of leadership is evolving. We now turn, therefore, to a theory of leadership that attempts to draw together the range of current theories and ideas about leadership and provides a new, more holistic view of the core leadership themes and practices that are appropriate for the challenges ahead.

Redefining Leadership

The Need for a More Integrated Conceptual Framework for Leadership

James MacGregor Burns suggests that an integrative theory, a general theory of leadership, that draws on different disciplines is needed.[251] In November 2001 he convened an interdisciplinary group of leadership academics and outlined his vision for a 'general theory of leadership' – a set of principles that were universal and that could be adapted to different situations,[252] supported by Roseanne Foti and John B. Miner: it would be 'entirely possible that a single over-arching theory of leadership is beginning to emerge from [the] conglomeration' of overlapping current theories of leadership.[253]

I believe that leadership can be redefined to integrate the different tracks of research and thinking. After all, Edwin Locke has made an attempt to create an integrated model of work motivation, a field blessed (or cursed) with as much fragmentation and richness as leadership.[254] Frank Schmidt has also recommended using 'mega-analysis' to build integrated theories or models.[255] Mega-analysis combines all known meta-analyses of empirical studies that are relevant to each path or connection in a theory or model. Schmidt and colleagues have already done this on a small scale in the field of human resource management.[256] Creating an integrated theory or model of leadership that is based on just such mega-analysis is the next step and an exciting and worthwhile challenge. Now we turn to the set of core themes and associated practices of effective leadership that I have identified in taking a 'helicopter view' of the extant theories, models and concepts as a contribution to this development.

Six Core Themes and Practices of Effective Leadership

Six propositions in an integrative model of leadership (see Figure 3.6) are each explained in the following six chapters. They reflect the core themes and associated practices of leadership distilled from the extant literature and explain what leaders do and how they do it in showing the way and helping or inducing others to pursue it.

> *Vision*. Effective leaders define and communicate a valid and appealing vision of the future.
>
> *Purpose*. Effective leaders define and communicate a valid and appealing mission or purpose.
>
> *Values*. Effective leaders identify, display, promote and reinforce shared values that inform and support the vision, purpose, and strategies.
>
> *Strategy*. Effective leaders develop, communicate and implement rational strategies that are informed by shared values and enable people to pursue the vision and purpose.
>
> *Empowerment*. Effective leaders empower people to be *able to do* what needs to be done.
>
> *Engagement*. Effective leaders engage people to *want to do* what needs to be done by using their personal power to influence, motivate and inspire them.

The new model of leadership is an attempt to bring together research findings, the findings of leadership surveys, and what organizations have found to constitute best practice. An earlier version of the model comprised five core themes and practices of leadership.[257] The first theme/practice – vision and mission/purpose – has been split into separate themes as a result of further analysis. A second change in the model relates to the theme/practice labelled 'influence, motivation and inspiration'. Since the original model was published, the term 'engagement' has come into popular usage in discussions about leadership. This term, very aptly in one word, denotes the consequences of the effective and ethical use of power in influencing, motivating and inspiring people in a way that is

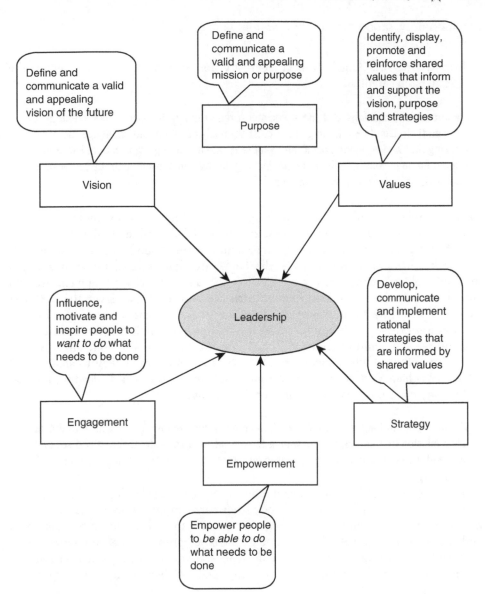

Figure 3.6 Model of Six Core Themes and Practices of Effective Leadership

consistent with its popular usage. Therefore this theme/practice has now been re-labelled 'engagement'. The relationship between engagement and empowerment is worthy of conjecture and, of course, further research. For example, is empowerment a precondition of engagement, or is engagement a precondition of empowerment?

This chapter and Chapters 1 and 2 have already provided some evidence for the validity and utility of the model. Additional evidence in support of it follows below, together with further discussion and evidence of the individual themes and practices in the following chapters.

Additional Evidence for the Six Themes and Practices
of Effective Leadership

Robert Kreitner and Angelo Kinicki identify vision, values and empowerment as the
new leadership paradigm:

> Traditional organizations and the associated organizational behaviors they created have
> outlived their usefulness. Management must seriously question and challenge the ways of
> thinking that worked in the past if they want to create a learning organization. For example,
> the old management paradigm of planning, organizing and control might be replaced with
> one of vision, values, and empowerment.[258]

In their studies, Arthur Yeung and Douglas Ready found that expressing 'tangible
vision, values and strategy' ranks in the top three globally valued leadership capabilities.[259] And according to a survey by the Manufacturing Foundation, successful middle-market manufacturing firms in the UK[260] are characterized by visionary and
inspirational leadership, a clear strategic direction, a supportive corporate culture, and
employees who are empowered to make decisions and act.[261] Moreover, the '100 Best
Companies to Work for in America'[262] have three common characteristics: an explicit
mission or purpose, a strategy for achieving that purpose, and cultural elements that
support the mission and strategy.[263] And one highly successful company's former
chairman and CEO who supports vision, values and strategy as key to shareholder
value is William W. George of Medtronic, Inc., one of the world's leading medical
technology companies, based in Minneapolis. He says:

> The best path to long-term growth in shareholder value comes from having a well-articu-
> lated mission that employees are willing to commit to, a consistently practiced set of val-
> ues, and a clear business strategy that is adaptable to changing business conditions.[264]

Economists historically have not paid much attention to leadership in organizations,
viewing an organization as a 'black box' that turns inputs (human resources, raw
materials, etc.) into outputs – goods and services – for consumption by customers
and clients. However, Patrick Bolton and colleagues propose an economic model of
leadership that comprises defining a mission statement; setting out a vision and
communicating it to followers; developing and implementing a strategy; and
empowering others.[265]

Other models closest to our six-theme/practice model are Kotter's and Kouzes and
Posner's. John Kotter says that leadership concerns the following:

- ❋ Setting a direction.
- ❋ Developing a vision of the future and expressing it in terms of the values of the
  followers.
- ❋ Developing strategies for achieving the vision in a participative way.
- ❋ Aligning people (obtaining their commitment to the pursuit of the vision).
- ❋ Motivating and inspiring people.[266]

Kotter's original elements that are in common with our model are direction and vision, which we conceived as one and the same thing ('what or where we want to be'), strategies, and motivating and inspiring people, which, together with influencing and aligning people (to get their commitment), we conceive of as engaging people. Kotter and Hesketh say that there may be unusually capable people at the top but that their effectiveness is based on communicating 'their visions and strategies broadly ... [obtaining] understanding and commitment ... [motivating] large numbers of their middle managers ... [and building] coalitions'.[267] And in this later writing, Kotter and Hesketh also say that leadership is also about empowering people, which our model also proposes. However, Kotter's model does not directly address mission or purpose.

Also close to our model is James Kouzes and Barry Posner's model of leadership as five key practices:[268]

* Modelling the way.
* Inspiring a shared vision.
* Challenging the process.
* Enabling others to act.
* Encouraging the 'heart'.

Modelling the way is in essence what we call clarifying one's own values as a leader and building and reinforcing shared values that inform and support the vision, mission and strategies for their pursuit. Inspiring a shared vision reflects two of our leadership themes and practices of vision and of engagement. Challenging the process (seizing the initiative, creating and innovating, taking risks and learning from mistakes) and enabling others to act contribute to our themes and practices of strategy and empowerment. And encouraging the heart – recognizing contributions and celebrating values and victories – reflects aspects of our leadership theme and practice of engagement. But as with Kotter's model, Kouzes and Posner's model does not explicitly address mission or purpose.

In Chapter 1, I described how Bruce Winston and Kathleen Patterson drew on their extensive literature review to create an integrative definition of leadership. In describing how leaders exercise leadership, they refer to vision, mission (purpose), values, empowerment and behaviours that in my model of leadership constitute engagement.[269]

The Burke-Litwin model proposes that individual and organizational performance are a function, in part, of mission, strategy, culture, individual knowledge and skills (an element of empowerment), and motivation – the key idea in Warner Burke and George Litwin's concept of leadership.[270] They define individual and organizational performance in terms of productivity, customer satisfaction, self-satisfaction, profit and quality. Fred Cannon's model, resulting from an empirical study of 462 managers at all levels in one financial services organization, proposes that leadership is a function of personal and professional qualities, the creation of a vision, building and sustaining commitment, and ensuring execution, with strategy and culture as two situational or contextual factors.[271]

Stephen Zaccaro and Deanna Banks suggest that most models of leader effectiveness specify setting the direction – defining the organizational purpose and a vision of the future as 'a direction for collective action' – as a central role of organizational leaders.[272] It also entails 'facilitating or enabling' people to achieve it, according to Stephen Zaccaro and Richard Klimoski, and this is done 'through mission, vision, strategy, goals, plans, and tasks'.[273] They also suggest that, in addition to the 'social or interpersonal influence processes … cognitive processes [are] equally critical to leader effectiveness', for example interpreting environmental demands and strategic thinking. The role of top-level organizational leaders is to align the organization and its environment.[274] This entails making sure that strategic choices and their implementation are effective.

Cynthia Montgomery at the Harvard Business School says that we need to think about strategy in a way that recognizes the need for leadership: frameworks, tools, techniques have abounded but, alone, they are wanting:

> **The teaching of strategy has both led and followed suit. At many top business schools, general management departments have been replaced by strategy groups made up of experts who delve into the economics of competitive advantage but rarely acknowledge the unique role leaders play in the process of formulating and implementing strategy.[275]**

Not only is strategy a key practice of effective leadership; strategy itself also requires effective leadership that draws on other key practices to be itself effective. In Michael Porter's words,' … strategy and leadership are inextricably linked'.[276] Developing or revising a strategy depends on leadership, he says, with leaders using a clear intellectual framework, providing discipline and focus in decision making, and being prepared to make difficult choices. Robert Staub also sees strategy as part of the leadership role: a leader, he says, provides guidance to followers in strategic planning, thereby focusing their attention on the organization's mission and objectives.[277] And Arthur Yeung and Douglas Ready include strategic change in their conception of leadership.[278] Strategic thinking is now widely regarded as an essential aspect of leadership.[279] But in many models of leadership, especially those from psychologists and sociologists, strategy does not appear.

I would argue that strategy is a core practice in effective leadership and that oratory, heroism and charisma each may play a part too. Motivation and empowerment, however, each require a stimulus in order to occur. These stimuli might include a vision of a desired future, a compelling sense of purpose, shared values, or effective strategies for the pursuit of vision and mission.

Bill George, former CEO of Medtronic and subsequently a professor at Harvard Business School, conceives of achieving and sustaining a superior performance as serving customers, aligning people around mission and shared values, and empowering leaders and collaboration throughout the organization.[280] He cites Johnson & Johnson as a company that has achieved such alignment.

Practical Application of the Model of Six Core Leadership Themes and Practices

The model, or parts of it, has been used in leadership development programmes with groups of top-level, senior and middle-level managers in the UK in a variety of industries and sectors. The most effective leaders will display all six core practices, though the relative importance of the six practices may vary according to the particular situation. For example, how might this model apply to the leadership of individuals or groups who will vary in respect of their ability to do what needs to be done and their willingness or desire to do what needs to be done and to do it in accordance with corporate values? Table 3.4 suggests which practices might be most applicable in showing the way and helping or inducing others to pursue it.

Table 3.4　Application of the Model: Ability and Willingness

Unable and Willing	Able and Willing
Vision	Vision
Purpose	Purpose
Strategy	
Empowerment	

Unable and Unwilling	Able and Unwilling
Vision	Vision
Purpose	Purpose
Values	Values
Strategy	Engagement
Empowerment	
Engagement	

Issues with the Model of Six Leadership Themes and Practices

There are several questions and issues with the proposed model.

Are shared values – in contrast to an individual leader's values – a prerequisite, something desirable, a goal or an outcome of effective leadership? Any one or more of these features may apply, depending on the nature of the leadership situation and its specific or unique needs.

The model of six themes and practices does not recognize situational differences as is the case with contingency and situational leadership theories. Such differences may not be significant: all six themes and practices apply in all situations but may do so in varying ways and to varying extents.

This model may not appear to address followership explicitly. On the other hand, it does so implicitly, explaining the issues and ways of gaining voluntary, willing and engaged followership. The model may also be seen as leader-centric. It can be countered that followership entails leadership and vice versa. And it is argued that it is leaders who 'show the way' for others voluntarily and willingly to engage with and follow.

The model also does not explicitly account for cultural differences in whether and how it may be applied. However, much of the evidence for each theme and practice transcends different cultures, as it does sectoral and organizational–hierarchical differences, and an argument – a hypothesis – similar to that for them may be made here, namely that cultural differences, for example differences in values, may entail differences in the way and extent to which the six themes and practices apply.

Is the model valid? No empirical evidence is presented for its validity as a holistic model, and this could be and should be addressed. However, there is a plethora of evidence to support the importance of each theme and practice both in its own right in respect of human behaviour in groups and organizations and in leadership as a whole.

Another issue is whether the model applies as much to lower levels of management as it does, perhaps more obviously, to top management levels. It can be reasonably argued that it does. Research into leadership across the organizational hierarchy suggests that we will find leadership throughout, not just at the top or middle of an organization, as was explained earlier in this chapter.

This issue appears to concern terminology more than concepts. For example, asking a first-level manager such as a foreman or office supervisor for a vision may at first sight seem inappropriate. There are two reasons why it is not. First, it would be unarguably good leadership for first-level managers – indeed all managers – to be promoting the (shared) vision, purpose and values for the organization as whole and to be empowering and engaging their people in pursuing them in relation to what they specifically do in their part of the organization. And that leads us to the second reason.

First-level managers need to be developing and implementing a vision, purpose and strategies for their part of the organization that are informed by and support the corporate vision, purpose and strategies. Values apply generally, though there may be additional, unique, idiosyncratic values pertaining to particular parts of the organization, for example, legal affairs, HR, customer service, etc., that first-level managers need to address and promote. And there is no reason why the staff of a warehouse, computer centre, marketing department or finance office cannot or should not have a vision of what or where they want it to be or it needs to be and a sense of mission or purpose in what they do: indeed quite the contrary. Moreover, they can and should have strategies for this. These strategies may be more like specific plans than the corporate strategies that we find in the boardroom, but that is acceptable: the leadership model works with that interpretation. And lastly, but not least, empowerment and engagement are equally important at this level as they are anywhere else.

A further issue is corporate and national culture. It can be argued that all of the themes and practices are universal. What is more culturally sensitive is how leaders behave in their practices in relation to vision, mission or purpose, shared values, strategy, empowerment and engagement. The landmark GLOBE studies make a distinction between practices and values, which represent preferences. We explore this relationship between leadership and culture further in a later chapter.

Let us now consider in more detail the flowers that make up Montaigne's flower arrangement.[281] The next chapter discusses the first (and fundamental) core theme and practice of leadership: defining and communicating a valid and appealing vision of the future.

Further Reading

Bernard M. Bass (1985), *Leadership and Performance Beyond Expectations*. New York: Free Press.

Bernard M. Bass with Ruth Bass (2008), *The Bass Handbook of Leadership: Theory, Research and Managerial Applications*, Fourth Edition. New York: Free Press.

Bernard M. Bass and Ronald E. Riggio (2006), *Transformational Leadership*, Second Edition. Mahwah, NJ: Lawrence Erlbaum Associates.

George R. Goethals and Georgia L.J. Sorenson (2006), *The Quest for a General Theory of Leadership*. Cheltenham: Edward Elgar.

Robert Greenleaf (1977), *Servant Leadership*. New York: Paulist Press.

Keith Grint, Editor (1997), *Leadership: Classical, Contemporary and Critical Approaches*. Oxford: Oxford University Press.

Donna Marie Ladkin (2010), *Rethinking Leadership: A New Look at Old Leadership Questions*. Cheltenham: Edward Elgar.

Peter G. Northouse, Editor (2010), *Leadership: Theory and Practice*, Fifth Edition. Thousand Oaks, CA: SAGE Publications.

Mark van Vugt and Anjana Ahuja (2010), *Selected: Why Some People Lead, Why Others Follow, and Why It Matters*. London: Profile Books.

 Discussion Questions

1. What traits or personal characteristics do you think effective leaders have in common?
2. Do effective leaders always 'emerge'? Or can an effective leader have been 'appointed'?
3. Do effective leaders always vary their style or behaviour according to the nature of the group of people they lead and the situation they are in?
4. Is having charisma essential to being an effective leader?
5. What contribution has the Full Range Leadership model made, and what are its limitations in helping us to understand leadership fully?
6. What can we learn from the theory of evolutionary leadership?
7. Do you think it is possible to create a single inclusive and over-arching theory or model of leadership? If not, why? If so, what are the issues that need to be resolved?

4 Leadership and Vision

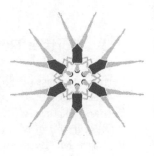

Without vision, a people perish.

The Bible, *Proverbs*, 29: 18

OVERVIEW

- The proposition of this chapter is that effective leaders define and communicate a valid and appealing vision of the future. This is the first core theme and practice in our model of leadership, and one of two that underpin leadership overall.
- Vision is an image in the mind of what the future will or could be like. A vision defines what or where the organization wants or needs to be. It represents 'true north', and a vision statement is your compass. Vision is fundamental to effective leadership and is the driving force for organizational change.
- Having a vision that is brief, clear, valid and desirable, contains relevant imagery, and is communicated and implemented in everyday actions and behaviour makes a vital difference to organizational performance.
- While entrepreneurs usually have a vision already, creating a vision should be a participative process, concluding with one that all stakeholders share.
- Effective leaders ensure that people understand and are committed to vision throughout the organization: that the vision is shared.
- Vision without effective leadership is impotent. Effective leadership ensures that vision is translated into reality.

Without a common vision, an organization flounders. As Marshall Sashkin says, it is 'rudderless in a sea of conflicting demands, contradictory data, and environmental uncertainty'.[1] There is plenty of evidence for this statement. For example, the Swiss watch industry initially was overtaken (pre-Swatch) in non-luxury markets by cheap Asian digital watches because of a lack of vision. Success in what one does may hinder imagining what may be possible or even what is happening elsewhere.

A vision provides a 'compass' for everybody in the organization, Stephen Covey says.[2] And James Kouzes and Barry Posner depict vision as the 'magnetic north'.[3] We need to have a compass and keep it with us at all times in order to gain a clear sense of direction.

Having a dynamic and inclusive vision is associated with company success. For example, Sydney Finkelstein and colleagues describe how Harley-Davidson transformed itself from industry follower on the verge of collapse to thriving industry leader through revitalizing its vision, purpose and consequential strategies.[4]

A vision of change can determine survival. An example of this was FDR's 'New Deal' – a series of economic programmes introduced in the United States between 1933 and 1936 during the first term of Franklin Delano Roosevelt as president of the United States in response to the Great Depression, focusing on the 'Three Rs': relief for the unemployed and poor, recovery of the economy, and reform of the financial system to prevent a repeat depression. ICI in the UK was revitalized under Sir John Harvey-Jones in the 1980s, and in the United States Jack Welch rescued General Electric in the 1980s – both with a clear vision of a desirable future. Having a vision for change can prevent failure or demise.

A Chartered Management Institute survey of 1,900 managers in the UK public sector found that vision was the most sought-after feature of leadership, together with engaging employees with the vision as one of the top three skills expected of leaders.[5] The report includes a telling quotation from one borough council (local government) manager:

> **We are suffering the syndrome of jumping on every latest bandwagon, often with no clear sense of direction as to where the next journey will take us.**

'The very essence of leadership', as stated by Theodore Hesburgh, former president of Notre Dame University in the United States, 'is that you have to have a vision'.[6]

What is Vision?

The Meaning of Vision

Vision, according to the *Concise Oxford English Dictionary*, is 'a mental image of what the future will or could be like'; it involves 'the ability to think about or plan the future with imagination or wisdom'.[7] Vision defines what or where the organization wants or needs to be. It is a statement of the likely, necessary or desired future of a group, organization or nation.

Stephen Zaccaro and Deanna Banks give several definitions of what visions are.[8] They identify what is common among the many definitions:

* 'Visions provide an idealized representation of what the organization should become.' For example, McDonald's wants to be 'the world's best quick service restaurant experience' – 'consistently satisfying customers better than anyone else through outstanding quality, service, cleanliness, and value'.[9]
* Visions relate to a longer time span than strategies. Visions may have a time span of three to twenty years, while strategies will typically last for one to five years.[10]
* Visions reflect values – preferences – and in that respect do not change.[11] In this sense visions may be ideological and expressed in moral terms.[12] However, environmental factors will dictate how they are translated into strategies.
* Visions are symbols of change for harnessing the collective effort of organizational members. They are means of giving meaning to work and inspiring people.[13]

Jill Strange and Michael Mumford, in reviewing vision studies, concluded that vision serves five purposes:

※ Specifying the direction, purpose and uniqueness of a venture (though purpose is a separate concept which is often confused with vision – see Chapter 5).
※ Providing a motivational force by organizing action around an evocative future goal.
※ Providing a meaning for the work that needs to be done and a sense of identity.
※ Enabling the coordination of activities by providing a framework for action.
※ Providing a basis for developing organizational norms and structures.[14]

Stanley Deetz and colleagues concur:

> Visioning is essential to creating the norms, mission, and rules of an organization, components that make up the organization's formally espoused goals ... Vision [is] an organizational *ideal*.[15]

Vision is not the preserve of top management only, but a feature of effective leadership at any level, in any function, in an organization. The nature and content of visions will vary at different levels and in different functions in any organization but they must be compatible with, and support, the overall corporate vision for there to be a shared sense of unity. The top-level leader or board of directors will define a broad, long-term (often ambiguous) vision and translate it into specific organizational strategies. The middle-level leader will then translate the organizational vision into a departmental vision or goals and more short-term strategies. And the lower-level leader in turn will translate these goals and strategies into more short-term goals and operational plans and tasks.[16] Progressing down the organization, vision and goals will change from the abstract to the concrete, from the long term – from years, even decades – to the short-term – monthly, weekly and daily.[17] In this respect top-level leaders will set the stage; lower-level leaders will be the actors.

CASE EXAMPLES OF VISIONS

- First Quench Retailing, a drinks retailer that in 2002 was one of the UK's '100 Visionary Companies', with a vision of being 'an enjoyment and celebration company'.[18]
- General Electric's then CEO, Jack Welch, promoted the following famous vision in 1990:

  > Our dream for the 1990s is a boundaryless company ... where we knock down the walls that separate us from each other on the inside and from our key constituents on the outside.[19]

(Continued)

(Continued)

- The University of Strathclyde's vision is still, more than 200 years since its founding by John Anderson, driven by his vision of the university as 'a place of useful learning', recently strengthened as '*The* place of useful learning'.
- Durham University, England's third oldest university, sees itself as 'shaped by the past, creating the future', with the ambition (vision) of being:

  ... recognised as an international exemplar of the best in research and research-led education ... [and aiming] to be widely recognised as one of the top 5 universities in the UK and the top 50 in the world.[20]

- Henry Ford's vision of 'a car for the great multitude [the Model T Ford introduced in 1908] ... so low in price that no man will be unable to afford one' led to a mass market for cars and the invention of the dealer franchise system for selling and servicing them.[21]
- Former prime minister Lee Kuan Yew's vision in 1984 foresaw Singapore as 'the Switzerland of the East by 1999', based on the similarity between Switzerland's reality and Singapore's aspirations in respect of their possession of only one natural asset – human resources – their status as a major financial centre, their high-tech/high-wage economy, and the discomfort of being surrounded by potential enemies.
- Former prime minister Mohamed Mahathir's 'Vision 2020' for Malaysia was that Malaysia would be a fully developed nation by 2020 according to OECD criteria in respect of literacy, education and health.
- The Nigerian government's 'Vision 2020' for the nation: by 2020 Nigeria will be one of the 20 largest economies in the world, able to consolidate its leadership role in Africa and establish itself as a significant player in the global economic and political arena.[22]

Characteristics of Visions

Both findings from academic research and the practical experience of business leaders suggest that a clear vision is essential to the survival and success of an organization.[23] The lack of a clear vision from any of the major party leaders in the run-up to the May 2010 general election in the UK has been widely criticized.

Stuart Cross, a management consultant, says: 'I have little idea of what kind of country and society they are likely to build, what level of ambition they have for improving things, and how we will know whether or not we are on track'.[24] The Conservative Party's 'Big Idea' – 'The Big Society' – he says, was set out in its manifesto but disappeared in communications and debates. And, he adds, the Labour and Liberal Democrat party leaders focused on the concept of fairness, with no clear picture of the kind of society they envisioned. Fairness, Cross states, could mean 'simply ... [sharing] the misery equally' – not a vision that an effective leader would promote. Laura Frith, psychologist and managing director of Reed Consulting, says: 'Having a clear vision and direction comes up as the top critical success factor for good leaders across all industry sectors.'[25]

A vision has to be aligned to the needs and expectations of the organization's stakeholders. Where strongly held personal visions are not aligned, individuals will resort to political means to pursue their own. This will leave the organization without a sense of direction and less capable of responding to the need for change.[26] Positioning the organization for change is essential to the leadership role.[27] Warren Bennis refers to vision as an outcome, goal or direction when he speaks of the 'management of attention' as a key leadership competency.[28] Aligning people with the vision, he says, is a matter not just of communicating the vision – by explaining or clarifying it – but also of creating the meaningfulness of intentions.

The research literature stresses the importance of certain attributes of vision, the imagery of the vision content, and the way the vision is communicated. Gerry Robinson, former chief executive of Granada, says:

> There is a tendency to think of vision as something rather sophisticated and complex but actually most visions are terribly simple ... You do have a vision as to what it is you are trying to do, at both a personal level and at a corporate level. It is very important to be very clear, very repetitive, very simple about that. It is essential that people know what success is.[29]

Tom Peters says a good vision is challenging, effective and inspiring.[30] He quotes Steve Jobs, who wanted to revolutionize the way people process information, think and deal with the world. In probably the only such study, Robert Baum and colleagues investigated entrepreneurial firms and their growth (sales, employment and profit) over two years in relation to the attributes and content of their visions and the way these were communicated.[31] The criteria they used were brevity, clarity, abstractness, challenge, future orientation, stability, and the desirability or ability to inspire. The visions they found were various mixtures of mission, strategy, values and goals: the particular mixture adopted seems to be the way that a particular leader creates a guide to future action. They discovered several relationships between vision and growth:

⁎ Those firms with a vision grew significantly more than those without one.
⁎ The brevity, clarity and desirability of the vision are particularly important.
⁎ Imagery of growth in the vision statement is related to actual growth. For example, in one firm, wanting to be 'known nationally as the manufacturer of leading-edge, highly technical and deeply designed artistic architectural woodwork' was related to actual growth in the firm.
⁎ Communicating the vision effectively entails oral, written and non-verbal means – dramatic gestures, role modelling, and the way the firm selects, trains and rewards employees. Simply having and communicating a vision is not enough: leaders must show that they are pursuing the vision in their actions and behaviour.

Organization growth is clearly associated with the characteristics of the vision, its content, and the extent to which it is communicated to employees. Visionary leadership behaviour is also associated with enhanced individual performance, trust and satisfaction among subordinates and with business unit performance.[32] Visions likely to enhance organizational performance, according to Paul Nutt and Robert Backoff,[33] have several features:

1. They offer new possibilities: they are 'innovative ... unique, vibrant ... inspirational, and ... offer a new order'.
2. They are desirable, '[drawing] upon the organization's values and culture, and [connecting] the possibilities to these values'.
3. They are actionable, '[pointing] to activities that people can undertake to move towards a desirable future'.
4. They can be articulated using powerful imagery representing what people want.

Visions must have an explicit ethical or moral component to them;[34] they must at least be in line with values, says Lindsay Levin, chairman of the Whites Group.[35] Visions may even be expressed in terms of values. Kees Van der Heijden quotes the example of Levi Strauss's vision: 'To be a company that our people are proud of'.[36] Stephen Zaccaro and Deanna Banks suggest that the ethical and moral aspects are perhaps the most important features of a vision.[37] Boas Shamir shows how a vision is most effective when it is congruent with followers' personal values.[38] Subordinates or followers will judge vision in terms of what is 'good' and 'right'. And values, because they create a passion and conviction about the vision, are central to it.[39] Effective visions reflect values that are associated with an aspiration for growth and change.

A six-year study by Jim Collins and Jerry Porras compared 18 successful and long-lived companies that had all out-performed the stock market between 1925 and 1975 by 12 times. These companies included Hewlett-Packard, 3M, Johnson & Johnson, Procter & Gamble, Merck, Sony, Motorola and Nordstrom, and they were compared with 18 of their major competitors. Collins and Porras found that successful companies have a core ideology – core values and a core purpose – and a vivid vision of the future 10 to 30 years ahead – a 'BHAG' (a 'Big, Hairy, Audacious Goal').[40] Figure 4.1 shows Collins and Porras's components of vision. These go beyond a strict definition of vision, reflecting ideology, which is determined by values and purpose.

Collins and Porras define core ideology as:

... what we stand for and why we exist ... the enduring character of an organization ... a consistent identity that transcends product or market life cycles, technological breakthroughs, management fads, and individual leaders.[41]

Their 'envisioned future' is what we aspire to become, to achieve, to create. Core values are a system of 'timeless' guiding principles and tenets. And core purpose is 'the organization's most fundamental reason for existence, which we discuss later in the next chapter.

Ira Levin says vision should be future oriented, compelling, bold, aspiring and inspiring, yet believable and achievable.[42] According to John Kotter, a good vision has six characteristics:[43]

* ※ Imaginable – conveying a picture of what the future will look like.
* ※ Desirable – appealing to the long-term interests of all stakeholders.
* ※ Feasible – realistic and attainable.

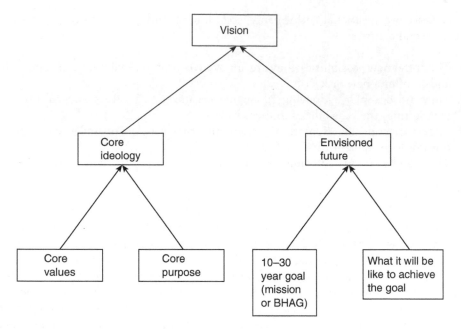

Figure 4.1 Collins and Porras's Components of Vision

※ Focused – clear enough to provide guidance in making decisions.
※ Flexible – allowing individual initiative and differing responses in the light of changing conditions.
※ Communicable – easy to communicate (and able to be explained within five minutes).

Kotter says as well that vision must also meet the needs of the organization's stakeholders – particularly shareholders, employees and customers – and it must be easily translated into strategies that can improve its competitiveness in its industry.[44] One reason for the failure of so many dotcom companies, internet guru Patricia Seybold says, is their lack of vision in how they can competitively deliver market needs.[45] Stanley Deetz and colleagues point out that 'A strong long-term vision gives cohesion to the work of an organization.'[46] Without it, initiatives like TQM, BPR, quality circles, benchmarking, and so on, become ineffectual fads.

So how specific should visions be? According to Gregory Dess and Joseph Picken:

> **The most powerful visions are clear about the direction and objectives and proactive in approach, but deliberately vague about the means – leaving room for flexibility in developing viable strategic options and solving complex problems.**[47]

David Butcher and Mike Meldrum point out that visions can sometimes be 'short-lived, misguided and even embarrassing once the world has moved on', as with British Airways' self-image as 'the world's favourite airline' – 'a label at odds with its poor results and sustained adverse publicity'.[48]

Visions must also be backed up by action that is consistent if they are not to invoke distrust. Sally Lansdell describes how in February 2000 CEO Matthew Barrett of UK-based Barclays Bank described his vision of 'superiority in the range of products, services, and value propositions available to customers'.[49] This was badly received by the customers of small village branches, 171 of which were to be closed within two months, thereby causing hardship for them. And the City does not like false promises contained within vision or mission statements, as a sliding share price reflecting Rentokil's unfulfilled goal of a 20 per cent annual increase in profits neatly illustrated.[50]

The Importance of a *Shared* Vision

A study of top teams in telecommunications, airlines, computer software and manufacturing in the United States by the Hay Group found that they frequently did not have a *shared* vision of what they were trying to achieve.[51] The risk of a lack of shared vision is a potentially dysfunctional situation in which each top-team member promotes his or her own agenda. People in successful organizations will have a shared view of the future.

Getting commitment to a vision is 'part and parcel' of the process of engaging people in the work and future of the organization or nation. John Kotter and Lorne Whitehead say:

Anyone who is trying to help an organization, public or private, to go through large-scale change ... needs to communicate the new vision in a way that helps people not simply to understand it but to buy into it.[52]

This means *emotional commitment* as well as intellectual understanding, together gained by 'winning hearts and minds'. Reasoning using data and logic is no substitute for appealing to people's feelings: both are necessary. Gaining people's commitment to a vision so that it becomes a *shared* vision is the goal here.

A shared view of the future that stretches the organization beyond its current capabilities is an important determinant of achievement and effectiveness.[53] A shared vision creates alignment. Peter Senge puts it this way:

In a corporation, a shared vision changes people's relationship with the company. It is no longer 'their company'; it becomes 'our company'. A shared vision is the first step in allowing people who mistrusted each other to begin to work together. It creates a common identity.[54]

John Kotter makes the valid point that, for organizational change, only an approach based on vision will work in the long term.[55] He says a shared vision:

* Clarifies the direction of change and ensures that everything that is done – new product development, acquisitions, recruitment campaigns – is in line with it.
* Motivates people to take action in the right direction.
* Helps to align individuals and coordinate their actions efficiently.

A vision is the driving force for strategy formation, Kees Van der Heijden says: for the individual entrepreneur this is personal, but in a management team the driving force is a shared vision.[56] In large, mature organizations the management team shares the decision making and creates a shared vision through 'strategic conversation'.[57] Van der Heijden states, '[The] shared vision [is] arrived at through communicating and modifying personal views in the team through a conversational process.' 'Visions', he points out, 'tend to be tacit, taken for granted ... seldom made explicit ... [operating] in the background'. Peter Senge and colleagues add:

> Visions which tap into an organization's deeper sense of purpose, and articulate specific goals that represent making that purpose real, have [a] unique power to engender aspiration and commitment ... The content of a true shared vision cannot be dictated: it can only emerge from a coherent process of reflection and conversation.[58]

James Kouzes and Barry Posner also emphasize the need for a shared vision:

> Leadership isn't about imposing the leader's solo dream; it's about developing a *shared* sense of destiny ... A vision is *inclusive* of the constituents' aspirations ...[59]

Creating the Vision

Visions Start with Dreams

'The future belongs to those who believe in the beauty of their dreams', Eleanor Roosevelt is reputed to have said. And a Nepalese Buddhist mantra says 'Never laugh at anybody's dreams. People who don't have dreams don't have much.' A vision starts with a dream, as Robert Greenleaf says:

> Not much happens without a dream. And for something great to happen, there must be a big dream. Behind every great achievement is a dreamer of great dreams. Much more than a dreamer is required to bring it to reality; but the dream must be there first.[60]

Journalist Sal Marino takes up this theme:

> Dreaming things that never were is not a science. It's an art practiced by visionaries who manage by faith instead of by formula. They are driven by an unquestioning belief that the lessons of the past will inevitably invent the successes of the future. They see visions where others see vacuums. They say 'We can' when others say 'We can't'.[61]

This is a theme that was taken up by Barack Obama in his 2008 US presidential campaign: 'Yes, we can. We can change. Yes, we can.'

John Middleton and Bob Gorzynski say:

> Vision is deeply paradoxical. It is partly mystical, partly common sense. It is sometimes a picture of the future, sometimes a feeling. It is sometimes fully-formed, often not. But it is almost always the ability to see things differently or to integrate disparate and seemingly

unrelated information in new ways. Sometimes it is merely asking questions that others cannot or will not ask. As John F. Kennedy put it: 'Some people see things and ask "Why?" I see things and ask "Why not?"'[62]

The poet David Whyte says, 'If you can see more than one step ahead of you, it is not your path.'[63] The path 'well trod' is not one's unique way. 'Effective leaders go against the grain', says Jo Owen.[64] What makes the difference, he says, is being 'unreasonable' – having a vision and goals that are not based on reason and logic alone, that are based on translating dreams into reality, that involve taking risks, that stretch the organization, and that make a huge difference, and whose promulgators are remembered for it. The examples he gives are Sir Richard Branson's taking on of British Airways; US President Kennedy's vision of putting a man on the moon by the end of the decade; CNN's creation of 24-hour news; and Dell's displacement of Apple and Compaq. He reminds us of Henry Kissinger's definition of leadership: 'the art of taking people where they would not have gone by themselves'.

Vision and Entrepreneurship

The two main roles of the founder of a company, according to Edgar Schein, are creating a vision – the critical step – that leads to strategies and creating an organizational culture that reflects the founder's philosophy.[65] The individual entrepreneur personally decides on the vision and takes the risk of failure, though in large, mature organizations the management team will share in the decision making and create a shared vision through a 'strategic conversation'.[66] Andrew Kakabadse says that:

> Effective visioning requires a willingness to consider all the options and to share information that is needed to develop them. It also demands that staff commit to a plan of action that is in the best interests of the organisation ... [it] is not a managerial fad ... but a fundamental element of best practice for senior executive teams. It provides an effective organisational force, a binding cohesion, initially at senior management levels, but then throughout the organisation, guiding and motivating people's actions.[67]

A useful vision contains an entrepreneurial idea, and a strategic vision is a view of an organization's future 'in terms of a business idea, size, scope or success formula ... that will indicate direction for action'.[68]

Some outstanding leaders do sense an opportunity, create a new vision, communicate it in an inspiring way, build trust in it, and achieve the vision through empowering people. As a result they are often perceived as charismatic.[69] The vision challenges the *status quo*, addresses followers' personal aspirations, and often involves the leader in taking a risk. It can be argued, therefore, that entrepreneurs, in order to be successful, *must* also be effective leaders.

Requirements of a Vision

Vision must have intellectual acceptance among those led: it must make sense in being challenging but achievable.[70] Those who are led may be composed not only of subordinates or employees, but of all stakeholders – investors, suppliers and customers too: in a sense they are also part of the organization.

Most people in a company will expect the CEO to have a personal vision of where it should be going, but Sir John Harvey-Jones believed this vision needed much discussion and consideration of the processes required to get there.[71] This was essential to getting commitment to the vision. He said:

> I do not believe in the myth of the great leader who can suddenly engender in his people a vision and lead them to an entirely new world. I believe that the reality is more traumatic and more demanding ...[72]

Kees Van der Heijden says: 'The vision needs to have the power to convince people that the proposed future is not a "pipe-dream" but that a feasible process can be envisaged which will cause its realisation.'[73] Arriving at such a vision entails discussing the following:

※ The business environment, particularly developments in society and new ideas.
※ Definition of the business and areas for exploitation.
※ The distinctive competencies and resources that now exist in the organization or can be developed.
※ The constraints to imitation by other organizations and making the organization's distinctive competencies and resources sustainable.
※ The feasible path from the present to the future situation by which new distinctiveness can be developed from existing distinctiveness – the 'formula for success'.[74]

Keith Denton describes how senior and middle-level managers in a medical centre in the United States had many and varied visions of its future.[75] They had common threads, but there was no common vision. There will usually be several competing entrepreneurial visions in an organization. The foregoing considerations will provide a process – and objective and rational criteria for the organization's potential for survival, development and success – for converging towards a common understanding and thereby towards organizational learning and progress. Sydney Finkelstein and colleagues describe how in successful companies the vision remains constant in essence across global borders, though its implementation may vary according to local circumstances. They cite Dell Computer, Starbucks, McDonald's and HSBC as examples.[76]

Formulating a Vision

Visions emerge from two sources, according to Stephen Zaccaro and Deanne Banks: from 'sense-making and consensus-seeking and [consensus]-making processes' and from the values of the top-level executive.[77] Visions may result from interpreting the misalignment between the organization and its environment and the need for organizational change and negotiation among the top-level team.[78] Zaccaro and Banks suggest that the influence of visionary leaders:

> ... resides not in their environmental analysis or negotiation skill but rather in the values they seek to propagate through organizational change.[79]

Andrew Dubrin suggests several sources as a basis for creating a vision: annual reports, management books and magazines, group discussions (with both work colleagues and friends), the work of futurists, and not least one's own intuition.[80] Creating a vision can be viewed as an entrepreneurial activity involving imagination, perception, analysis, interpretation and synthesis. Vision may be formulated rationally[81] *and* intuitively.[82] It requires both reflection and intuition, both insight and foresight. It is an intellectual activity, and its outcome requires validity in the minds of followers.

In formulating a vision, Richard Allen suggests several key questions should be considered:

1. What is our purpose?
2. What is our driving force?
3. What are our core values?
4. What do we do best?
5. What do we want to accomplish?
6. What do we want to change?[83]

Thomas Bateman and colleagues provide a useful taxonomy of goal content and goal hierarchy for top-level leaders in business organizations that could be used in the visioning process.[84] And Monica McCaffrey and Larry Reynolds describe a useful workshop approach to creating a vision using a facilitator, described in the following case example.[85]

CASE EXAMPLE: MCCAFFREY AND REYNOLDS' APPROACH TO CREATING A VISION

This successful approach comprises several phases: setting the scene, taking stock, scenario planning, agreeing the vision and taking action.

1. Setting the scene.
   - Clarify the purpose of the process.
   - Ask participants what they find both enjoyable and frustrating about their jobs, which may imply the kind of vision that would be exciting.

2. Taking stock produces a picture of where the organization is at present.
   - Participants in small groups identify and report positive and negative features of the organization under several headings, e.g. customers, competitors (or, in the absence of competitors, regulatory or political matters), people (employees) and processes (organization and systems).
   - Based on the feedback, participants then are asked to say where they would like to see the organization going.

3. Scenario planning, whereby a range of possible futures is identified, with the implications for action now (explained in Chapter 7).
   - Small groups use a PESTLE framework (see Chapter 6), including customers, competitors and demographics, to identify the political, economic, social, technological, legal and ecological forces that could lead to change for the organization.

(Continued)

(Continued)

> Different groups focus on optimistic, pessimistic, *status quo* and 'wild card' scenarios (whereby a group imagines an unpredictable event that would have huge consequences for the organization).
> - Based on the groups' reports, implications for action are discussed for each scenario.

4. Agreeing the vision.

- Each small group creates a vision in words or pictures and then presents it to all participants.
- The whole group discusses each vision's merits and demerits and identifies the common themes of all the visions.
- A single vision statement is created through rewriting until it meets with a consensus.

5. Taking action.

This involves discussing:
- How and when the vision will be communicated.
- What needs to be done to create strategies to pursue the vision and turn it into reality.

Writers on leadership will usually attribute *creating* a vision to leadership.[86] Effective leaders will invariably communicate their vision in an inspiring way, whether they have created it or not. But many business and political leaders will not have created the vision they communicate. For example, it was the vision of Karl Marx ('entrepreneur') that underpinned the leadership of Lenin and Stalin ('managers') in the former Soviet Union, according to Gareth Edwards.[87]

Nevertheless, the most effective leaders will spend some 20 per cent of their time in creating a vision for the future, according to Andrew Kakabadse and Nana Kakabadse.[88] Chris Rodriguez, then CEO of the Bradford & Bingley Building Society, said:

... the process of creating a vision is a combination of listening a lot, getting creative input from a wide variety of people and then thinking hard.[89]

Typically a board of directors will work together to produce a vision, and the chief executive will then communicate it to the rest of the organization. But visionary thinking is not the exclusive province of the CEO or even the board. Gregory Dess and Joseph Picken point out: 'Broad participation in the formulation of a strategic vision offers multiple perspectives and encourages commitment.'[90]

They quote the case of Sears' dramatic transformation after 1994 when 120 of the firm's senior executives formed taskforces and heroically came up with a vision for the company: to be 'a compelling place to shop, work, and invest' – a remarkable achievement considering the potential variety of ideas and the potential for their incompatibility and dissensus.

Visioning is not important, however, only for top-level leaders. Robert House says leaders at any organizational level may formulate visions.[91] Indeed every department or business unit should have its own vision. But such visions need to be framed within the context of the organizational vision.

Involving people in the visioning process gathers people around a shared, common vision and achieves their maximum commitment to it. Individual leaders who already have a vision will have a more difficult task. Richard Olivier states that, if a group rejects a leader's vision, it is difficult to revisit it.[92] The leader has to explain the reasoning behind the vision and the values that inform it. Values are the subject of Chapter 6, and we will see how important it is for vision and leadership to reflect shared values in a group or organization. Olivier uses the following exercise in helping individuals to create a vision:

1. Think about your experience and your core values. What do you really care about in your life? What kind of things, habits, people, behaviours, activities and situations do you tend to gravitate towards? And avoid or move away from? Answering these questions may yield some common themes not previously apparent.
2. Now think about times when you felt closest to inspiration and vision, and the times you felt farthest away from them. What was happening at those times, who was involved, what were you doing, and how did you feel? This process likewise should produce some signposts.[93] Hopefully these signposts point the same way!

Sally Lansdell describes other useful ways of developing visions:[94]

Pictorial Vision Statements. An abstract verbal statement is translated into a colourful image that communicates both the cognitive and emotional aspects of the vision. Small groups of three to six members, each representing a business function, will meet for one hour with the CEO's liaison and an artist-facilitator. The artist-facilitator draws how group members see the business today and tomorrow and their role in it. The artist-facilitator later produces illustrations representing the patterns and issues arising in each group. These are used by the CEO and group of senior managers to develop a single picture for the vision of the organization as a whole.

Storytelling. Beverly Kaye and Betsy Jacobson say that storytelling essentially comprises telling the story, understanding the implicit metaphor by the listeners, and creating a shared meaning.[95] 'Storytelling is how we make sense', say Michael Lissack and Johan Roos: 'The power of a story is that it allows the listener to recreate an experience in their mind … The power of storytelling helps us consolidate our experiences to make them available in the future, whether to ourselves or to others.'[96] Stories tap into both the intellect and the emotions and, when stories are vivid and memorable, they also help people to understand in relevant and meaningful ways. Steve Hoffmann of Agilent Technologies uses stories to help frame and simplify messages, such as the organization's vision and its importance, because they are more memorable than slide presentations or speeches.[97] And they help in achieving a shared vision because storytelling is a collective act.

Tara Jones at Lane4 Management gives two examples of the visioning process, one positive and the other negative.[98]

CASE EXAMPLE 1: VISIONING WITH NEGATIVE IMPACT

In [this] company, rather than galvanize its people in a motivating way, the visioning process demotivated them. The company, a large retail organization, had recently made an acquisition. The acquiring company was conservative, autocratic, and slow in decision making. The organization being acquired was progressive, collaborative, fast-moving, and innovative. The leaders knew they had to develop a compelling vision that would bring everyone together and harness their energy. They made two big mistakes. First, the Board created the vision in isolation rather than consult with people in both companies. And the Board was primarily comprised of members of the acquiring company. The resulting vision was biased towards the acquiring company. Hence, the new vision demotivated those from the acquired company who felt that their success, philosophy, and approach had been ignored. They became less committed. The resulting reduction in morale and engagement, which in turn led to more turnover of high performers from the acquired company, hurt performance. By failing to integrate the successes of both companies, the new Board lost many of the great people and things that had made the acquired company so appealing.

The second mistake they made was to communicate the vision solely through one-way *town hall* speeches, at which a Board member presented the vision passionately, but in a prepared and polished way. In the Q & A session, many employees felt uncomfortable asking questions, and so left feeling unclear about the message, how the vision was to be lived, and how things would be different. The Board had not allowed people to discuss and make sense of the vision and what it *really* meant to their day-to-day work life.

CASE EXAMPLE 2: VISIONING WITH POSITIVE IMPACT

A global financial institution ... had just undergone a restructure, resulting in much uncertainty and ambiguity. The senior leadership team (SLT) recognized the need to update their vision to provide a future view which would re-engage their people and restore belief in the company. The SLT ran focus groups comprised of people from various levels to understand employees' opinions about the direction the organization needed to go, the future they hoped for, and the type of place they wanted the company to be. Armed with this information, the SLT generated a compelling vision that captured the hopes of employees.

They then shared the new vision in a way that engaged the employees and minimized their uncertainty and ambiguity. The SLT delivered the usual *roadshows*, but also ensured that employees attended mini-workshops in which the SLT shared their understanding of the vision, and explained what it meant to them and how people could see how the leaders' new behaviours aligned to the vision. These sessions enabled employees to make sense of the new vision in an environment clearly supported by the leaders; their commitment to the vision was clear. People understood where the vision came

(Continued)

(Continued)

from, how others interpreted it, and what it meant to them individually. The SLT also described how the goals and performance measures related to the vision. Employees asked how these new performance expectations aligned to and supported the new vision. They had the chance to make sense of the vision and gain clarity about the direction, relate it to their job, clearly see what was expected of them and their performance, and have the tools to achieve those performances.

Going forward, the vision was kept alive through continual reference in communications and in team meetings. The high engagement ultimately increased productivity and profitability.

Communicating and Sustaining the Vision

Effective leaders ensure that people throughout the organization understand and are committed to vision. The need to communicate and explain the organization's vision is a continuous and sustainable one so that all members of the organization are always clear about where it is heading.[99] Stephen Zaccaro and Deanne Banks explain how communicating and implementing a vision for growth can make a crucial difference:[100]

※ Visions provide a frame of reference for both leaders and followers for the strategic direction of the organization.
※ They provide 'a source of impassioned empowerment that motivates followers'. This comes from the values and ideology implicit in the vision. For example, according to James MacGregor Burns, effective leaders 'emphasize fundamental values such as beauty, order, honesty, dignity, and human rights'.[101]
※ The way that leaders articulate and communicate the vision may galvanize commitment to it.

Communicating a vision in a confident and attractive way and taking overt action to implement and pursue the vision are two core components that are common across current leadership theories. In fact vision is far more powerful than charisma or personality in its effects on the performance and attitudes of followers.[102] Key to this is the link between the values expressed in the vision and the self-concepts of the followers.[103] The way a vision is communicated determines whether and how much followers identify with it, their loyalty to it, and their motivation and efficacy to pursue it through strategic and tactical goals.[104]

Failing to communicate a vision effectively is one of the main reasons for the failure of strategies to implement it.[105] Top-level leaders are responsible for communicating the organizational vision and making sure all members of the organization understand it, are committed to it, and implement it. Sally Lansdell says it is not necessary to have a *written* vision.[106] More important is the leader's ability to explain the organization's vision 'in a compelling way in five minutes or less'. Otherwise it will be ineffective. James Kouzes and Barry Posner state that communicating a vision:

> ... isn't a one-way process; on the contrary, it's a process of engaging constituents in conversations about their lives, about their hopes and dreams ... Leadership isn't about imposing the leader's solo dream; it's about developing a *shared* sense of destiny ... A vision is *inclusive* of the constituents' aspirations; it's an ideal and unique image of the future for the common good.[107]

Having a vision, and even translating it into goals and strategies, is not enough. Effective leadership entails communicating it in a way that attracts followers. Tom Marshall suggests, perhaps controversially, that people do not follow visions: they follow leaders.[108] Such leaders, he says, not only have the 'right' visions and goals that reflect the aspirations of people. They also effectively use persuasion and build relationships with their followers.

The vision must point the way forward. It must be sustainable. It must be exciting and fire the imagination. It must challenge people to participate in pursuing it. Timing in communicating a vision is of the essence in leadership. A premature vision may be rejected because it leaves too many questions unanswered. The leader's task is never accomplished until people own the vision for themselves. And communicating the vision does not stop there. Organizations will go through good times and bad, and initiatives, promoted – and received – with enthusiasm, can fade away. Therefore the leader's role, as Tom Marshall says, 'is to continually reiterate, reinforce, clarify and redefine goals along the way'.[109] As Stanley Deetz and colleagues argue, 'people respond to the vision they hear, not the one that was meant':

> To be effective ... a vision statement must be collaboratively constructed and 'owned' by members across organizational levels. Unless the vision is clearly communicated and integrated into organizational practices, it is likely to have little effect ... some of the world's premier organizations have turned a commitment to a strong vision into unparalleled success.[110]

Ways in which commitment to vision may be achieved, they say, include:

✳ Involving all stakeholders in creating it.
✳ Linking the vision explicitly to shared values or guiding principles, the work objectives of all groups and individuals to create alignment and the criteria for performance appraisal and improvement, and reinforcing individuals' behaviour that relates to it.
✳ Using inspirational language to communicate it and constant repetition in team briefings and workshops, supported by brochures or booklets, internet dissemination, 'roadshows', videos with the CEO talking about the vision, and a vision jingle or song.
✳ Surveys on employees' understanding of the vision and their attitudes to it, with remedial action where necessary.

The importance of communicating the vision passionately is clear:

> You have got to know where you are going, to be able to state it clearly and concisely – and you have to care about it passionately. That all adds up to vision, the concise statement/picture of where the company and its people are heading, and why they should be proud of it … The issue here … is not … the substance of the vision, but the importance of having one, *per se*, and the importance of communicating it consistently and with fervor.[111]

It is one thing to formulate a vision but quite another to communicate it in a way that gains people's commitment to it and their everyday action on it.[112] This requires *framing* the vision. Framing entails aligning people's understanding with what is meant through the use of language, for example metaphors. We return to this theme – communicating in an inspiring way – in the chapter on leadership and engagement.

Communicating the vision in an inspiring way has both content and stylistic aspects. On content, this is characterized by emphasizing the importance of the vision; expressing confidence in people's self-efficacy and ability to achieve it; making reference to values and moral justification; emphasizing the common goal and collective identity; and referring to hope and faith.[113] On communication style, an inspiring communication of the vision is characterized by a captivating tone of voice, pacing and sitting, leaning forward, direct eye contact and animated facial expressions.[114] Michael Frese and colleagues concluded from their experimental study that the inspirational communication of a vision can be trained.[115]

Yet because communicating a vision is difficult, some companies have resorted to specialist agencies to help them do it, says Roger Eglin.[116] He reports the managing director of one such agency as saying:

> Many companies are still using old-fashioned methods. You get a typical situation where a large company has been through a merger and the chairman wants to communicate a new vision. He appears on stage backed by expensive audiovisuals and tries to sell the vision in an Orwellian sort of way. It is generally appalling and doesn't work.

Creative ways of communicating the vision in global companies can go beyond company newsletters and e-mail. Federal Express used an internal private business television network called FXTV, operated via satellite, with a daily five-minute broadcast to employees around the world that focused on how their individual efforts contributed to the company's vision.[117] Immediately after the annual meeting of its top 500 executives, General Electric circulated a video of the CEO's speech on the company's direction with instructions to attendees on how to use it with their teams.[118] Within a week 750 videos in eight languages had been distributed worldwide.

Sally Lansdell provides several more case examples of how companies communicated and implemented their visions and the impact on their businesses as a result.[119] One example, shown below, is Boehringer Ingelheim GmbH, a multinational German pharmaceutical company, whose vision statement was *'Werte schaffen durch Innovation'* – 'Value through Innovation'.

CASE EXAMPLE: BOEHRINGER INGELHEIM'S APPROACH TO COMMUNICATING AND IMPLEMENTING A VISION

The process followed these steps:

1. Analysis of the company environment and competitors' corporate philosophies.
2. Research into how the company would grow and rank among the best.
3. Testing of the resulting vision in terms of likely consequences.
4. Communicating the vision in novel ways at the group's annual top management conference.
5. Workshops on the vision for all employees.
6. Reinforcement of the vision in action by using rewards for new ideas.
7. Introduction of a new company magazine called *Vision*.
8. Development of a set of associated leadership principles accompanied by workshops.
9. An annual 'Value through Innovation' event to maintain the momentum.

After the process was introduced, collaboration internally and externally improved, recruitment became easier, morale increased, processes speeded up, purchasing waste dropped, and sales tripled over seven years.

Vision as a Driving Force

Vision is the driving force for motivation and achievement. To be a driving force, a vision must be positive, not negative:[120] energy is better directed towards making something happen rather than preventing it from happening.

For example, following the merger of UMIST and the Victoria University of Manchester in the UK in October 2004, the vision for the new University of Manchester was 'a 21st century university that will become an international research powerhouse and a favoured destination for the best students, teachers, researchers and scholars in the world'. In 2011 its vision – the 'Manchester 2015 Agenda' – is for The University of Manchester to be 'one of the top 25 universities in the world', an ambitious one, its president and vice chancellor Professor Dame Nancy Rothwell admits, '[whose] realisation will demand energy, commitment and superb execution'.[121] This vision is seen as the driving force for the university.

Positive visions connote a sense of power rather than the powerlessness associated with negative visions. And positive visions persist, whereas negative visions last only as long as the threat exists. Vision reflects ambition. And as James Champy and Nitin Nohria say, 'ambition is the root of all achievement'.[122]

Richard Olivier, drawing from Shakespeare, supports this view but also cautions against excessive or misdirected ambition.[123] He cites examples from *Macbeth*, *Richard III* and *Coriolanus*, where over-ambitious leaders turn into tyrants. He points out that the word 'ambition' comes from 'ambit', the Greek root of which also means 'wingspan'. 'Ambition' therefore is associated with how far we can stretch our wings. Too little, and we will never fly; too much, and we may crash to the ground.

Translating Vision into Reality

The effectiveness of leadership is most likely in practice to be judged by the extent to which a vision becomes a reality. There are mixed opinions on this, and the issue really depends on the nature of the vision. Nevertheless, 'action without a vision is stumbling in the dark, and vision without action is poverty-stricken poetry', says Warren Bennis.[124] In a speech in 1997, the then Federal President of Germany, Roman Herzog, said: '… we do not only need the courage to see visions; we also need the strength and the will to turn them into reality'.[125] But, Stanley Deetz and colleagues suggest: 'A vision is always just out of reach.'[126] It is a state of affairs to strive for, Bert Nanus says, something that exists only in the imagination and that 'may never become a reality … [requiring] an act of faith'.[127] This idea of a vision is commonplace among leaders. For example, Domino Pizza's chairman said that the company's vision was a 'finishing line' – 'if there ever is one' – in a 'marathon rather than a sprint'.[128]

Translating a vision into reality is a leadership responsibility throughout the organization. Beverley Mobbs says there is often a 'lack of linkage between vision, strategy and day-to-day activities' but that linkage may be achieved by using the 'Balanced Scorecard' (see the chapter on leadership and strategy).[129] Figure 4.2 shows my simple model for translating a vision into reality.

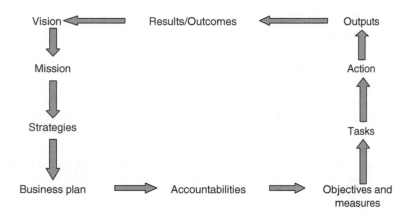

Figure 4.2   Translating Vision into Reality

'Vision without resources is a hallucination', says Louis Andre of the United States Defence Intelligence Agency.[130] Having a vision of change without the prerequisite resources and commitment to change will lead to demise or failure. Examples in political history include Spartacus and Hannibal, the French Revolution and the Third Reich; in business – Polaroid, Bethlehem Steel, PanAm, ABN Amro and (almost) BP.[131] And however good a vision is, change – at a group, organizational, national or global level – can come only through an effective implementation of the vision. This entails not just adequate resources but also effective management overall: a clear sense of purpose (which we discuss in the next chapter); values and ethical principles, goal set-ting and strategies (which we discuss in later chapters); action planning, action, monitoring and the evaluation of progress, corrective action, and the evaluation of accomplishment against the vision and the associated purpose, values and goals.

The Impact of Vision

By 2001 vision and mission statements were being used by some 70 per cent of orga-nizations across the world.[132] Their main benefit was reported as to 'strengthen inte-gration effort across an organization'. A survey in the UK by the Leadership Trust in 2002 revealed that 27 per cent of its companies either did not have a vision or had one that was unknown to most employees.[133] In those companies that were known have a vision, over 90 per cent of managers said it was coherent, consistent and well under-stood. But only 42 per cent saw their companies as fully on track in pursuing their vision.

The right vision can have several benefits for an organization, according to Bert Nanus:

❋ It stimulates commitment to the organization and energizes people.
❋ It provides meaning to people's lives.
❋ It provides a standard of excellence to aim for and encourages improvement.
❋ It focuses the organization on a desired future state.[134]

A viable vision when articulated well will have an impact on organizational perfor-mance,[135] people's implicit conceptions of leadership,[136] and effective group interac-tion.[137] Dave O'Connell and colleagues provide a useful review of vision and the visioning process as well as an integrated model.[138] They summarize the impact of vision as:

❋ Keeping organizations in touch with their environments and helping stakeholders understand the reasons for action by management.
❋ Central to strategic planning.
❋ Leading to challenging goals.
❋ Leading to growth in entrepreneurial firms.
❋ Enhancing group effectiveness, organizational commitment and overall organiza-tional performance.
❋ Shaping people's views of leadership.
❋ Creating the spark that moves the organization beyond the mundane and key to successful leadership.

Danny Miller and John O'Whitney argue that a vision gives a company 'character and direction, harmonizes strategy and processes, and motivates people to work towards a common objective'.[139] Mark Lipton identified five benefits of managing with a vision, based on an analysis of over 30 international studies:

❄ Performance improvement on measures such as profit, return on shareholder equity, employee turnover, and rate of new product development.
❄ Promotion of change by serving as a guide during organizational transformation.
❄ Provision of the foundation for a strategic plan.
❄ Motivation of employees and attraction of talented people.
❄ Keeping decision making on track, providing focus and direction.[140]

One obvious problem with visions and vision statements is that they may not actually provide direction, set a common goal, or inspire anybody. They may be an ego exercise by the CEO: '... some corporate leaders [can't] distinguish between vanity and vision ... implementation and basic blocking and tackling are increasingly regarded as more important than vision'.[141] Questions start to be asked about 'this vision thing'.

But clear visions, according to James Kouzes and Barry Posner, are associated with high levels of job satisfaction, motivation, commitment, loyalty, *esprit de corps*, clarity about the organization's values, pride in the organization and organizational productivity.[142] Joseph Boyett and Jimmie Boyett point out, 'It is next to impossible to have an energetic, creative, innovative, flexible, competency-driven company without a vision.'[143]

It is important for the leader to model the attitudes, values and beliefs implicit in the vision. This fosters trust, sets high performance expectations, and shows confidence in people's ability to meet these expectations. Leaders exert charismatic influence when their visions encompass current organizational problems or crises, when their visions are perceived to represent a solution to them, and when their visions are perceived as rational, cogent and persuasive in doing so.[144]

Stephen Zaccaro and Deanne Banks present a model that shows how visions influence organizational effectiveness (see Figure 4.3).[145] In the model, 'inclusive language' refers to language that unifies rather than divides – using words like 'we' and 'our' rather than 'them' and 'they'.[146] This is an aspect of *framing* our speech, which we discuss in the chapter on leadership and engagement.

Visionary Leadership in Action

Visionary leadership is a theory of leadership in its own right (see Chapter 3). A 1989 global survey of 1,500 CEOs representing companies producing 10 per cent of the Gross World Product identified the overwhelming importance of visionary leadership in anticipating the company's future and its place in global business, setting ambitious corporate goals and inspiring managers to achieve them.[147] The need for a vision is universal.

Visionary leadership is the cornerstone of corporate survival.[148] Yet in fewer than half (42 per cent) of the UK's PLCs in 2001 was the board of directors exclusively responsible for creating the vision and mission, according to research by Philip Stiles, and in over 17 per cent it was exclusively or mostly management's responsibility.[149]

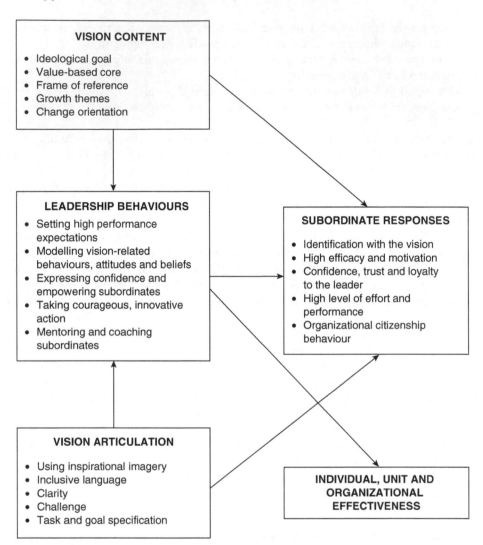

Figure 4.3 Model of Leadership Vision and Organizational Effectiveness

(Adapted from Stephen J. Zaccaro and Deanna J. Banks (2001) Leadership, vision, and organizational effectiveness. In Stephen J. Zaccaro and Richard J. Klimoski (Editors), *The Nature of Organizational Leadership: Understanding the Performance Imperatives Confronting Today's Leaders.* San Francisco, CA: Jossey-Bass, 197)

'The best way to predict the future is to create it', says Peter Drucker.[150] According to Joseph Jaworski, true leaders 'create the future' through their commitment to others, through 'synchronicity'.[151] Larry Reynolds calls this 'transcendental' leadership'.[152] It is leaders that make companies appear visionary, according to a study of 18 companies by Jim Collins and Jerry Porras.[153] Their leaders consistently promoted an organizational identity and a set of organizational values not just through 'framing' them but also through programmes for their implementation, socialization and recognition. According to Glenn Rowe:

> [Visionary leadership] is future-oriented, concerned with risk-taking, and visionary leaders are not dependent on their organizations for their sense of who they are. Under visionary leaders, organizational control is maintained through socialization and the sharing of, and compliance with, a commonly held set of norms, values, and shared beliefs.[154]

The ability to craft a compelling vision, a story of where the organization is going, is a characteristic shared by charismatic leaders, Jay Conger says.[155] But having a vision statement is not the same as being visionary. Based on in-depth interviews and biographical research, Conger found that there were different ways of being a visionary leader:

☀ Those who have an idea about the way the world is heading and focus the organization in that direction, e.g. Fred Smith, FedEx head.

☀ Those who are opportunists who see a gap in the marketplace and take advantage of it with a vision of a new product or service, e.g. Yvon Chouinard, founder of recreational clothing company Patagonia.

☀ Those who are not visionaries in the usual sense, such as those who have visions in more than one form, e.g. Ray Kroc, who took two McDonald brothers' idea and set up a new form of franchise and real estate leasing.

Visionary leaders, James Champy and Nitin Nohria say, 'see the world [or their company] differently and dare to make [the] dream come true', quoting the Wright brothers and their vision of powered flight.[156] Visionary leadership concerns creating and communicating the mission of the organization – what it stands for – and a vision of its future. The everyday concept of vision has to do with a broad world-view, a deep understanding or insight, and future orientation.[157] Alan Bryman says:

> ... it is often not easy to see what is visionary about ... visions ... there is little to distinguish leaders' visions from ... strategy. In the case of [Steve] Jobs, the term seems warranted because he was concerned at Apple to transform people's lives through computers ... It is not surprising that it tends to be those leaders whose 'visions' are either innovative or deal with ultimate values ... [who] are typically regarded as charismatic. Leaders who adopt visions that are barely distinguishable from strategic intent or from broad aims and which lack innovativeness (for example, stereotyped proclamations about competitiveness, emphasis on quality or the customer) are creating visions in name only.[158]

Robert House and Jane Howell distinguish between a vision focused on the enhancement of a social institution (that of a 'socialized' leader) and a vision focused on enhancing a leader's personal power (that of a 'personalized' leader).[159] Jill Strange and Michael Mumford analysed the biographies of 60 notable historical leaders of both kinds and found that, in constructing their visions, ideological leaders emphasized personal values and standards and charismatic leaders emphasized social needs and change.[160] They suggested that leaders formed mental models based on their experience that they then used to do this.[161] Examples of well-known leaders they give using this classification are shown in Table 4.1.

Table 4.1   Ideological and Charismatic Leaders

	Ideological	*Charismatic*
Socialized	Charles de Gaulle	Franklin D. Roosevelt
	Margaret Thatcher	Henry Ford
	Eleanor Roosevelt	John F. Kennedy
	Mohandas Gandhi	Jomo Kenyatta
	Ronald Reagan	Winston Churchill
	Woodrow Wilson	J.P. Morgan
Personalized	Che Guevera	Benito Mussolini
	Deng Xiaoping	Idi Amin
	J.D. Rockefeller	J. Edgar Hoover
	Vladimir Lenin	François Duvalier (Doc)
	Mao Zedong	Neville Chamberlain
	Joseph Stalin	Nicolae Ceausescu
	Joseph McCarthy	Huey Long

Unsurprisingly, socialized charismatic leaders are more likely than personalized charismatic leaders to articulate visions that result in positive outcomes for society.[162]

Visionary leaders may transcend the bounds of reality: Colin Wilson says that the visionary 'starts from a point that everybody can understand, and very soon soars beyond the general understanding'.[163] Visionary leaders, Glenn Rowe points out, tend to take risks, create disorder and excitement, and change 'the way people think about what is possible, desirable and necessary ... They work in, but do not belong to, organizations.'[164] They are also often driven by strong personal values.[165]

The visionary leader is an outsider. The outsider is a person who perceives the unstable foundations on which human life is built and feels that chaos and anarchy lie deeper than the order that most others believe in – a person not at home in the world and who cannot accept its values. H.G. Wells' hero in *The History of Mr Polly* typifies the visionary as an outsider: 'If you don't like your life you can change it.' The visionary wants to 'go out and *do* something'.[166]

The self-confidence of the visionary may result from a long period of self-doubt, leading to a discovery of what he or she may be capable of.[167] We all possess a 'visionary faculty'.[168] But living from moment to moment clouds vision: for example, the need for short-term profit and the trouble-shooting and fire-fighting that preoccupy the lives of many managers at work. Our visionary faculty is impaired by excessive stress in our everyday lives. Too often we see only what is the case, not what may be possible. Visionaries are lateral thinkers. Colin Wilson says, 'imagination is the instrument of self-knowledge'.[169] And imagination and creativity come into play when we are relaxed and we daydream.

One difference between visionaries who are leaders and those who are not is the time-frame in which they operate. Tom Marshall states:

> The visionary or the dreamer lives almost entirely in the future, he dreams his dreams or
> she paints her visions of what could be, but neither of them have to do anything to

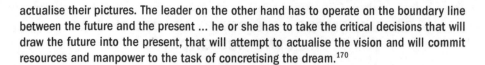

actualise their pictures. The leader on the other hand has to operate on the boundary line between the future and the present ... he or she has to take the critical decisions that will draw the future into the present, that will attempt to actualise the vision and will commit resources and manpower to the task of concretising the dream.[170]

A visionary does not necessarily make things happen. Robert Craven, considering The Beatles' Paul McCartney as the creative leader who masterminded the group's success, quotes Yoko Ono, widow of the John Lennon, as saying:

John did not make the phone calls, he was not on that level as a leader – he was on the level of a spiritual leader. He was the visionary and that is why the Beatles happened.[171]

For Glenn Rowe, visionary leaders will probably create more wealth than 'managerial leaders', but with a high degree of risk, particularly in the short term, though an organization needs managerial leaders too. What is also required, however, is strategic leadership, which is discussed in the chapter on leadership and strategy.

Visionary companies share several features, according to Jim Collins and Jerry Porras:[172]

* A fundamental belief in, and passion for, the business they are in.
* Remaining true to an enduring set of values while adapting strategies and other aspects of culture according to environmental demands.
* An enduring core ideology, reflected in their values, that transcends customer demands and market conditions, guides and inspires people, and creates alignment and *esprit de corps*.
* BHAGs ('big, hairy, audacious goals') that motivate people to achieve greatness in the long term – for example, NASA's goal in the early 1960s to put a man on the moon by the end of the decade.

Organizations can become visionary through 'strategic innovation' and through individual entrepreneurs who are not blamed for failures (rates will always be high) but who learn from them and try again ... and again. Also important here is developing a culture that values innovation along with its associated core values. Visionary companies all have a deep dedication to the customer. Becoming more visionary comes from understanding the customer, trends in the industry, connections with things beyond the business that are changing, and front-line staff who know how the world is changing every day. It also comes from brainstorming not why or how things will not work but how to create something that will work.

A visionary leader puts into words a compelling vision for a nation, organization or group of people, persuades or influences people to commit to it, and then empowers and inspires people to achieve it. But Collins comments:

[The] difference between being an organization with a vision statement and becoming a truly visionary organization ... lies in creating alignment – alignment to preserve an organization's core values, to reinforce its purpose, and to stimulate continued progress towards its aspirations.[173]

CASE EXAMPLE – VISIONARY LEADERSHIP AT THE GENERICS GROUP

Part 1 (1986–2001)[174]

Visionary leaders will bring change by designing a new future for their organizations rather than settling for incremental improvement. The Generics Group was a technology incubator organization whose vision was to turn intangibles into tangibles. The Generics Group had a design approach and a vision that had been created and implemented by someone who demonstrated clarity, judgement and a total commitment to success – a person who stood apart from the rest.

Professor Gordon Edge founded the Generics Group with the clearly expressed vision of creating wealth through technology. By 2001 his Cambridge-based ideas factory had gained a global reputation not only for technological consulting but also for turning brainwaves into businesses.

Since 1986, the Generics Group had established or invested in more than 40 companies in areas such as telecommunications, biotechnology and materials engineering. With 250 employees, research laboratories in Cambridge, Stockholm and Baltimore, and offices in Boston, Stockholm, Zurich and Tokyo, Generics was valued at more than £220 million when floated in December 2000.

Edge's visionary approach to turning technology ideas into revenues was honed during a training that began in the 1970s at Cambridge Consultants. Later he started PA Technology as an offshoot of the PA Consulting Group, before leaving to establish Generics in 1986. Edge's vision for Generics was to create a radically new environment in which to foster technology entrepreneurship. 'You can't organise people into being more creative, but you can create an environment in which creativity is part of the culture', he said.

At Generics' headquarters, employees from various fields such as biotechnology and engineering worked together. 'It's an interdisciplinary culture,' Edge stressed. Employees were encouraged to invest personally in spin-off companies and the entrepreneurial among them were encouraged to develop their own ideas.

A novel feature of Generics' innovation process was its Innovation Exploitation Board (IEB). The IEB was a large committee of employees drawn from across the company that discussed all the technology and business opportunities that Generics received. 'It's a peer-group review process that is effective in providing a rigorous challenge to an emerging opportunity', argued Edge. The IEB could also draw on a £1 million fund to test ideas further if required.

Creativity was so important to Generics that it was measured using a mixture of objective and subjective metrics. 'Objectively, we can point to numbers such as how many patents a person has produced', said Edge. 'But we also use the mechanism of peer-group review, as no-one is better than your colleagues at assessing your performance as a creative worker'.

Edge's vision for his company was so strong that the strategy, culture and organization remained unchanged after fourteen years – only the size was different. The secret of his leadership success, he believed, was always to recruit people whom you genuinely believed to be better than yourself.

Part 2 (2001–2011)

Less inspiring is Generics' history since 2001, illustrative of the process of perishing due to a loss of vision and a failure to gain a new one. Shortly after flotation, increasing pressures from

(Continued)

(Continued)

the stock market stifled the company's creativity and innovation. Gordon Edge left, together with many long-standing colleagues who had shared his vision that had enabled and nourished the egalitarian entrepreneurial environment that underpinned Generics' value.

Management of Generics by visionless accountants after flotation dismantled its innovative investment activities in favour of more controllable but regrettably loss-making consulting. By 2007, Generics, rebranded as Sagentia in 2006, was valued at around £14.55m – some 7 per cent of that at flotation.[175] However, following the appointment of a new CEO – Brent Hudson – in 2009 and subsequent major gains, Sagentia's market capitalization had risen by March 2011 to just under £30m.[176]

Jim Collins and Jerry Porras provide a suitable concluding note for this chapter: 'Visionary leaders die. Visionary products become obsolete. Visionary companies go on forever'.[177]

However, a vision without purpose is doomed to fail. To be effective, vision has to be translated first into a mission or purpose (or vice versa) for the organization and then into specific goals or objectives and action plans. We consider leadership and purpose in the next chapter.

Further Reading

Talula Cartwright and David Baldwin (2007), *Communicating Your Vision*. San Francisco, CA: Jossey-Bass.

James C. Collins and Jerry I. Porras (1996), *Built to Last: Successful Habits of Visionary Companies*. London: HarperBusiness.

Corey Criswell and Talula Cartwright (2011), *Creating a Vision*. San Francisco, CA: Jossey-Bass.

Stanley A. Deetz, Sarah J. Tracy and Jennifer L. Simpson (2000), *Leading Organizations through Transition*. Thousand Oaks, CA: SAGE Publications.

James L. Kouzes and Barry Z. Posner (2010), *The Leadership Challenge Vision Book*, Fourth Edition. San Francisco, CA: Jossey-Bass.

Sally Lansdell (2002), *The Vision Thing*. Oxford: Capstone Publishing.

Dave O'Connell, Karl Hickerson and Arun Pillutla (2011), Organizational visioning: an integrative review. *Group & Organization Management*, 36, 103–125.

Discussion Questions

1. Is vision just a dream?
2. How can you create a vision that all stakeholders will share?
3. How can you ensure that people throughout the organization understand and are committed to the vision?
4. Should a vision be attainable or not quite attainable?
5. How could Generics Group's vision have been sustained?

5   Leadership and Purpose

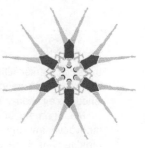

Great leaders are those who can articulate a company's vision and inspire their employees to work toward its realization, bound together with a shared purpose.

Roger Fisher, Samuel Williston Professor of Law,
Emeritus, at Harvard Law School[1]

OVERVIEW

- The proposition of this chapter is that effective leaders define and communicate a valid and appealing mission or purpose. This is the second core theme and practice in our model of leadership, and one of two that underpin leadership overall.
- A sense of mission or purpose is the hallmark of great organizations. And we human beings need a purpose in what we seek and do.
- The terms 'mission' and 'purpose' are usually used interchangeably, though some organizations will interpret them differently.
- A mission statement or statement of purpose describes an organization's purpose, distinctiveness, intended products or services and markets, and often its core values. It captures and provides its identity.
- Such statements need to be short enough to be easy to remember and generic enough to encompass likely developments in the organization's business environment.
- Shareholder value is a frequently espoused purpose in commercial organizations. However, this is also misguided and potentially dysfunctional. A 'good' purpose enhances the lives of those the organization serves and those who serve it and provides meaning, guidance and inspiration.
- An organization's vision and purpose will inform each other. Either may flow from the other. Therefore either may be the basis for creating or refreshing the organization. But a clear vision and purpose are both necessary for the organization to be most effective.
- A purpose based on a vision of its future and its core values is the fundamental driving force of an organization: it is the 'glue' that holds the whole organization together. And the creation and sustenance of a shared purpose are the 'heart and soul' of leadership.
- A case study of the UK's Royal National Lifeboat Institution provides an illustration of shared purpose in an organization.

Thucydides was the first to write about the importance of purpose in leadership.[2] A sense of purpose is the hallmark of great organizations. 'Purpose is preparation for doing what is right and what is worthwhile', says Nikos Mourkogiannis in a seminal book on purpose.[3] It is, he says, the organization's *animus* – its driving force. Effective leaders are people, he says, who 'evoke a clear, consistent purpose that attracts followers'.[4]

Mourkogiannis cites examples of noted leaders who display strong purposefulness through different kinds of purpose.[5] He tells four 'great stories of purpose': Tom Watson's passion for discovery, Warren Buffett's excellence in financial artistry, Sam Walton's altruistic commitment to the customer, and Henry Ford's and Segmund Warburg's heroic purposes. Warren Buffett at Berkshire Hathaway, he says, 'has always pursued excellence … [considering] himself an artist, and investment his "canvas"'. In addition, Bill Gates at Microsoft displays heroism, pursuing achievement 'on a scale beyond that of any other company'. Richard Branson at Virgin Group 'embodies discovery in each of his enterprises' and in creating distinctive innovations. And Herb Kelleher's altruism at Southwest Airlines focused on customer value-for-money and comfort.

Joel Kurtzman cites Google as a 'famously common-purpose organization' that has 'an outsized mission and an inspiring leadership team that brings together head and heart in the service of higher goals'[6] and FM Global likewise as an exemplar of 'how common purpose leadership works … and how the vision, mission, values, and practices of common purpose leaders can be highly profitable without eroding over time [since its formation in 1835]'.[7]

Defining and embedding a sense of purpose in an organization is a way of aligning – binding together – the interests not only of its employees but also of all its stakeholders. While Marxists believe that the interests of capital and wage-labour are diametrically opposed, 'great leaders,' says Joel Kurtzman, 'motivate people by building a sense of inclusiveness' through a common purpose.[8] Purpose is a fundamental and vitally important part of leadership – our second core theme and practice of effective leadership. Roger Fisher says:

> From the war on terror to human rights to domestic politics, we inhabit a world that, perhaps more than ever, is defined by competing values and ideas. Yet somehow this basic insight is too often lost on corporate leaders, who constitute one of the world's most influential communities. Business is often mistakenly thought of as a dispassionate, value-free pursuit, reducible to quarterly earnings reports and valuations of brand equity. But just as there are no atheists in a foxhole, there are no automatons bound by the laws of finance found in a company's executive offices. There is a fundamental human need for guiding ideals that give meaning to our actions.[9]

This is the need for purpose in what we seek and what we do. Employees and followers need to understand the organization's purpose for strategies to succeed, and they need to know not only *what* but also *why*.[10] Spiritually intelligent leaders will understand these needs and respond to them.[11]

Marshall Goldsmith comments on why effective leaders will focus on a common purpose:

... leaders and their followers ... make the right decisions on their own because they have internalized the organization's mission, values, strategy, and brand. Companies that understand this ... [they] hire leaders who focus on common purpose – building a sense of inclusiveness within the organization where people know what to do and why, and understand what the organization stands for – and stand with it![12]

Hillary Rodham Clinton, United States Secretary of State, commented that 'American leadership has been at its best when it rallies the world around common challenges and shared aspirations'.[13] And in Joel Kurtzman's words, '... the heart and soul of leadership is the creation of *common purpose*'.[14]

What is Organizational Purpose?

Mission in the organizational context, according to the *Concise Oxford Dictionary*, is 'a strongly felt aim or calling'.[15] So mission is not about where or what the organization wants to be, which is vision, but about how it sees its purpose or task. The same source also defines 'purpose' as 'the reason for which something is done or for which something exists ... resolve or determination'.[16] The term 'mission' goes beyond purpose with its connotation of a 'calling', which may not be appropriate in many non-religious contexts. But the terms 'mission' and 'purpose' are close in meaning and they are usually used interchangeably, though the term 'purpose' may be more concrete for most of us.

Nikos Mourkogiannis, however, distinguishes between purpose and mission, primarily because, he says, mission statements are often 'utterly trivial' and insincere.[17] This may well be the case, but it is not a sound basis for abandoning mission statements or making a distinction between them and purpose: changing the words does not make the concepts different. The fact that many mission statements are inadequate means that their owners need to reconsider their mission – or purpose.

Elizabeth Gordon, however, explains how mission and purpose may differ in the way they are interpreted.[18] Some organizations, she says, use mission statements to define why they exist – 'what are we here to do?' – and also define their purpose as what they hope to achieve in the future and how they contribute to the 'greater good' of society. Their 'purpose' answers the question of 'why do our mission and vision matter?' In this chapter I use the terms 'mission' and 'purpose' to mean the same thing, though 'purpose' is my preferred term.

The UK's Chartered Institute of Personnel and Development (CIPD) defines 'purpose' as 'an organization's ... identity, the reason why it exists and the golden thread to which its strategy should be aligned'.[19] A sense of shared purpose should extend not only to all employees but also to all stakeholders both within and outside the organization.

An organization's purpose, then, defines why the organization exists and what it does. It also defines *how* the vision will be attained. A purpose is a practical way of putting that vision into action. A statement of purpose therefore will include some or all of the following:

- ※ Who are we? A definition of the business we are in.
- ※ What do we do? The markets we serve.
- ※ Why do we exist? Our corporate values, beliefs and guiding principles.

A purpose may depend on the vision. A vision of what the future will be like, or what a desirable future could be like, could form the basis for a reason for existing and doing something with resolve or determination – a reason for a purpose. On the other hand, a vision may depend on the purpose. Wanting to do something with resolve or determination, for example because of the beliefs or values one has or because of a felt need or duty, could form the basis for a vision of a desirable future state of affairs.

Stephen Covey says, 'Go and ask people what the purpose of the company is and you'll get 10 different answers ... They don't know the purpose of the company.'[20] Richard Scase agrees, adding that:

> ... mission statements are rarely taken seriously and are usually seen as irrelevant. Too often, they are simply the manufactured product of some PR consultancy. Companies have them because they are supposed to.[21]

'The secret of success is constancy of purpose', noted the nineteenth-century British prime minister Benjamin Disraeli.[22] 'Constancy' for Disraeli referred to a leader's constancy in the sense of an unwavering purpose, but we might also interpret it to mean constancy among everybody in a group or organization – a common purpose. Common purpose is a rare phenomenon, according to Joel Kurtzman, but it can be achieved and recognized:

> [Common purpose is displayed] when a leader coalesces a group, team, or community into a creative, dynamic, brave, and nearly invincible we. It happens the moment the organization's values, tools, objectives, and hopes are internalized in a way that enables people to work tirelessly toward a goal.[23]

Are purpose and goals the same? Marshall Goldsmith puts it well:

> Goals are specific objectives we strive to achieve, usually within defined parameters of space, time and resources. Purpose is the 'why' behind any thought or deed. Purpose is not about achieving a goal – it's more a way of life. Purpose is enduring, whereas goals can be created, adjusted and discarded ... Purpose should be what the goals serve ... a greater overarching aim, one that benefits all stakeholders.[24]

However, research in the UK by the CIPD revealed that a sense of shared purpose was strengthened when shared values, objectives and actions were integrated into employees' goals as part of a performance management process.[25] And this was even more important in periods of uncertainty and change. In contrast to this, a sense of shared purpose may be weakened by changes in the organization's environment such as globalization or when there are competing goals or conflict between departments in the organization. This, the CIPD said, would require 'leaders … to reassert the wider organisational purpose and … vision [of the future]'.[26]

The CIPD also commented that 'Shared purpose is closely aligned to both leadership and engagement.'[27] It is argued in this chapter that shared purpose is not merely 'aligned' to leadership but is a core theme and practice in effective leadership. And thus it is too with engagement, which we discuss in the chapter on leadership and engagement, with a clear connection between a sense of shared purpose and engagement. The CIPD again:

> **Leaders need to engender a strong sense of shared purpose and when achieved this keeps employees motivated and engaged by working towards the same ultimate goal. A strong sense of shared purpose can also ensure that various parts of the organisation stay in alignment with a common aim.[28]**

In two pieces of action research on leadership in strategic business units, Leopold Vansina found that successful general managers engaged in large-scale organizational change would 'direct their efforts towards the "embodiment of purpose" within the *whole* company', shaping or strengthening corporate identity.[29] The purpose was regarded as realistic and achievable but also challenging, appealing to the competitive spirit and energizing. Richard Scase sees purpose this way when statements of purpose are taken seriously by top management, quoting (in 2004), for example, the appeal to young people of 3M's emphasis on innovation and BP's commitment in its statement of purpose to environmental sustainability[30] (which has since been called into question, however, as a result of the disastrous oil spill in the Gulf of Mexico caused by the explosion on the Deepwater Horizon rig in April 2010).

What are the different forces that hold together organizations with a common purpose and those without one? In the case of common-purpose organizations it is, Kurtzman says, caring, compassion and values such as authenticity.[31] In the case of organizations without a common purpose, he says, 'they are held together … [by] interesting work, various types of incentives, and money. [They] need powerful retention packages where payments for an employee's accomplishments are stretched out into the future.' This latter suggestion – for rewards over the long term – is very timely and sensible in light of the global banking crisis that created economic chaos in many countries in 2008 and had causes that were related to an emphasis on generating short-term profits.

Vision and Purpose as Distinct

Vision is about the future of the organization – its future positioning, what or where the organization wants or needs to be. Michael Raynor sees vision as determined by the organization's purpose and by the recognition of the market forces that will impact on its future.[32] However, one may argue conversely that an organization's purpose may be a consequence, not a precursor, of vision. While some scholars would debate this, practitioners generally regard vision as the first step – the foundation – for developing the organization's purpose.[33]

Alex Miller and Gregory Dess contrast vision and purpose: vision is a group's or an organization's aspirations for the future that will appeal to the emotions and beliefs of its members; purpose is a matter of group or organizational identity and comprises its purpose, distinctiveness, intended products or services and markets, as well as its core values.[34] Stanley Deetz and colleagues point out:

> **Most organizations have a mission statement that articulates the overall purpose that the organization was founded to accomplish ... A mission tells you where the organization wants to go ... A vision, however, helps you see the importance of getting where you want to go and understand why some paths there are better suited ...[35]**

Keith Denton quotes Disney as a good example: its purpose is 'to make people happy', and its vision is 'to become the leading entertainment company in the world'.[36]

Vision and purpose, however, are often confused or ill-defined. An example of this confusion is the British Civil Service Management Board's Vision for the Civil Service: 'To make a difference to the success of the country; to serve with integrity, drive and creativity.'[37] This is a statement of purpose.

FirstGroup plc similarly confuses its vision with its purpose. It states its vision as 'to transform travel, providing public transport services that are safe, reliable, high quality, personal and accessible'.[38] This is also a statement of purpose. However, its vision is expressed as a stated 'aim': 'to be the number one public transport provider'. The Chairman's Report does not make reference to the company's vision or purpose, focusing only on financial performance and strategy.

An early statement of purpose by Cadbury-Schweppes Beverages, that was later changed, proclaimed the company's purpose as 'To be the biggest non-cola company in the world.'[39] This is actually a vision statement: it states what the organization wants to be, not what it does. And it also lacks appeal: as Rhymer Rigby says, it is better 'to define yourselves in terms of what you are, not what you aren't'.[40]

Another example of the confusion between vision and purpose is the 'vision' of Perot Systems in the United States: 'to deliver innovative services and solutions that serve the particular needs of our clients and their customers' – really a purpose – though later in its annual report for 2001, director Ross Perot, Jr, said:

> **Our vision for Perot Systems is to become the most admired information services company in the world. Admired for the service we provide, the commitment and expertise of our employees, and the results and value we bring to our customers.[41]**

Even the American association of management scholars, the Academy of Management, confuses purpose and vision. The President's Message on 7 July 2010 reported that 'the AOM's entire leadership group' endorsed its vision as the following: 'We inspire and enable a better world through our scholarship and teaching about management and organizations.'[42] This was actually a statement of purpose. Yet AOM stated its purpose as follows: 'To build a vibrant and supportive community of scholars by markedly expanding opportunities to connect and explore ideas.'

Different writers posit different, and sometimes conflicting, characteristics of useful statements of purpose.[43] And such statements often appear to be 'either banal [or] situation specific',[44] or 'a muddled stew of values, goals, purposes, philosophies, beliefs and descriptions'.[45] Several writers also confuse the issue:

> The mission statement, or purpose, of your organization is the broad description of its reason for existence. It is the single statement that differentiates your organization from other organizations in the community. It is the source from which all of your organizational plans and dreams, strategies, objectives, policies and outcomes flow.[46] An effective mission statement describes the firm's fundamental, unique purpose ... [it] indicates what the organization intends to accomplish, identifies the markets in which the firm intends to operate, and reflects the philosophical premises that are to guide actions.[47] ... mission [is] the intent, spirit, or rallying cry which constitutes the organization's and its members' primary duty or way of behaving, the foundation and force which throws, sends or casts itself into the future towards its goals and targets.[48]

This selection of examples is a *pot-pourri* of references to a 'reason for existence', a 'rallying cry', identifying markets, and indicating 'what the firm intends to accomplish', says Michael Raynor.[49] And yet the statement of purpose, according to Stephen Covey, should be 12 words or less, easily memorized and inspirational.[50] These multiple demands only give weight to the argument for well-developed cognitive skills in defining purpose. But, Raynor says, 'Like the panoply of Greek gods, it is just possible that these concepts [vision and purpose and many other, related ones] are so tied together that to speak of one is to invoke them all.'[51] One response to this confusion has been to create several statements:

⁕ A vision statement – describing what or where the organization wants to be.
⁕ The statement of purpose – describing the nature and purpose of the organization's business and its competitive positioning.
⁕ An ethics statement – providing guiding principles for handling conflicts of interest.
⁕ A statement of operating philosophy or core values – providing guiding principles for employee behaviour.

Richard Olivier describes how activities (with their own laudable purpose) may get out of line with the organization's overall 'core purpose', quoting the case of a group of British police officers:

> [The] constabulary had done their best to take on board the recommendations of the Stephen Lawrence Report and combat 'institutional racism'. One of their new missions was to build a community centre where they could meet local youths, play football, table tennis, etc, and generally come into contact in a non-confrontational way. Sounds great. The trouble was that the crime rate was going up and the local community now felt less safe than they had before the project started. The mission had so involved and stimulated everyone around it that the core purpose of 'Making Britain safer' was no longer

being served. The mission, however noble, had got out of line ... and the core purpose was suffering. Those concerned had to rein in the runaway mission and re-focus in order to serve the core purpose.[52]

The terminology Olivier uses – 'mission' and 'core purpose' – unfortunately adds to the confusion over these terms. Here 'mission' is treated as a specific project in line with the core purpose, whereas the 'core purpose' is our concept of the purpose or mission. It is perhaps best to use the term 'purpose', define it and then stick to it.

SIX KEY POINTS ABOUT PURPOSE

1. Purpose is based on well-established moral ideas: ideas that have lasted help a business to last.
2. Purpose advances both competitiveness and morality: purpose creates synergy by integrating them.
3. Purpose relates people to plans and leaders to their colleagues.
4. Purpose cannot be decided quickly or in an *ad hoc* way: it has to be discovered by trial and error over time.
5. Purpose is a matter of life-or-death: its presence may transform an organization; its loss may destroy it. As a result it is more valuable than anything else.
6. Purpose is a paradox: it may boost profits, but only if pursued for its own sake; it may boost morale, build a brand, but it should never be just a tool in doing so.

Adapted from Nikos Mourkogiannis (2006), *Purpose: The Starting Point of Great Companies.* New York: Palgrave Macmillan, 17–18.

Creating a Statement of Purpose

Characteristics of Good Statements of Purpose

Statements of purpose need to be short enough to be memorized and generic enough to encompass likely developments in the organization's business environment, which may be extremely rapid in some sectors. Examples are Tesco's 'core purpose': 'Creating value for customers, to earn their lifetime loyalty';[53] and Marks & Spencer's purpose: 'Making aspirational quality accessible to all.'[54] The purpose of The Co-operative Group in the UK is: 'To serve our members by carrying on business as a co-operative in accordance with co-operative values and principles.'[55] The Group's values relate specifically to those of a cooperative[56] and to more general ethical values. Principles are the way that values are put into practice, which we discuss in the next chapter.

The organizational purpose, Stephen Covey suggests, will determine the organization's goals, context and coherence.[57] The lowest common denominator for a statement of purpose, he says, might read like this: to improve the economic well-being and quality of life of all stakeholders. Covey argues cogently for these elements in a statement of purpose. Organizations largely serve economic purposes by providing goods and services, and employment provides livelihoods. Quality of life, and quality of work life in particular, is of increasing moral, psychological and social importance.

Gary Yukl says that the organization's statement of purpose is the core of a vision.[58] He states that this statement is an overall picture, reflecting the important themes and values of the organization, rather than a detailed blueprint. 'A good mission statement should be distinctive, relevant and memorable', says Hilary Scarlett.[59] Michael Raynor points out that there is a lack of agreement on how to create both a vision and a purpose: what is needed is clarity about the meaning of these concepts.[60] He suggests that the organization's purpose should emerge from an understanding of its core competencies and be informed by its core values.

Statements of purpose are too often 'a collection of business buzzwords', says Sally Lansdell.[61] Our friend Scott Adams in *The Dilbert Principle* goes somewhat further in his usual satirical way: he describes a mission statement as 'a long awkward sentence that demonstrates management's inability to think clearly'.[62] Sally Lansdell relates a story from the *Dallas Morning News* on how Adams duped Logitech's senior executives (with the connivance of the company's co-founder and vice chairman):

> [Scott Adams] was asked ... to pose as ... a management consultant who was going to help executives draft a new mission statement for the company's New Ventures group. Adams disguised himself with a wig and a false moustache, before deriding the existing statement – 'to provide Logitech with profitable growth and related new business areas' – and leading an exercise in which managers brainstormed words and ideas for a new one. The result? 'The New Ventures Group is to scout profitable growth opportunities in relationships, both internally and externally, in emerging, mission inclusive markets, and explore new paradigms and then filter and communicate and evangelize the findings'. Drawing a last diagram, a picture of Dilbert, Adams took off his wig and the Logitech managers realized they'd been duped, although they apparently enjoyed the joke.

Nikos Mourkogiannis provides a useful framework for thinking about purpose.[63] This comprises eight multiple-choice questions, the answers to which when taken together will imply any one of the four likeliest types of purpose – discovery, excellence, altruism or heroism – for the organization as a basis for developing and implementing an appropriate concept of purpose. He then also provides a framework of 10 generic steps for developing and disseminating a clear understanding of the organization's purpose and putting it into action.

Gail Fairhurst and Robert Sarr describe how one company framed the purpose using metaphor.[64] The public affairs team came up with a good threefold statement of purpose for their department: to disseminate corporate information; to communicate responsibly with the public; and to engage in more dialogue with the public through membership of stakeholder organizations. Each of these elements was regarded as equal in importance and interdependent in carrying out the overall purpose of winning public trust. Thus was born the metaphor of a 'three-legged stool' for their purpose.

What is a 'Good' Purpose?

An example of the kind of purpose that makes people proud to be associated with a company comes from Percy Barnevik, CEO of the Swedish–Swiss company that owns Asea-Brown Boveri. He says:

I would like to create and develop an image of us as helping to improve the world environment. For example, transferring sustainable technology to China or India, where they have a tremendous need to clean up their coal-fired power plants. Our employees can ... see that we contribute something beyond shareholder value.[65]

Another good example here comes from the National Trust in the UK. Its original purpose in 1895 was 'to act as a guardian for the nation in the acquisition and protection of threatened coastline, countryside and buildings'.[66] In the words of one of its co-founders, Octavia Hill, the National Trust looks after beautiful places 'for the everlasting delight of the people' – for everyone, rich and poor, city and country dweller, young and old. Today, its aim (purpose) 'is unchanging: to conserve and defend our precious but vulnerable heritage of buildings and landscapes for the benefit of the nation'. It is 'for ever, for everyone' and can never end.

Nikos Mourkogiannis identifies four types of purpose[67] that 'drive action in all walks of life':

⚛ Discovery – the *new*. '[Seeking] action that is freely chosen for the sake of advancing into new places.'

Discovery, Mourkogiannis says, 'involves a love of the new and the innovative, and it animates many technological businesses. At Sony, the "joy of technological innovation" was explicitly stated by its founder as one of the reasons for the company's existence.'[68]

⚛ Excellence – the *intrinsically beautiful*. '[Seeking] action that constitutes innate fulfilment for its own sake ...'

Mourkogiannis says that the pursuit of excellence is defined by the craft itself rather than the customer and is a never-ending struggle.[69] Achieving excellence in our various roles in life – work, home, sport, etc. – is associated with happiness – the supreme good (see Chapter 9 on leadership and engagement for a discussion of this). And the ultimate aim of human activity, according to Aristotle, is happiness (*eudaimonia*) or, perhaps more precisely, fulfilment, 'flourishing' or success.

⚛ Altruism – the *helpful*. '[Seeking] action that increases happiness.'

Altruism is a characteristic of organizations that focus primarily or exclusively on serving their customers, clients or members. Two examples are Nordstrom's personal service to its customers beyond its obligations and Marks & Spencer's established tradition of treating its staff as 'part of the family'.[70] One's happiness is achieved by causing or increasing happiness in others.

⚛ Heroism – the *effective*. '[Seeking] action that demonstrates achievement.'

Heroism, Mourkogiannis says, is not the winning itself but the ambition or daring that is evident in the pursuit of goals.[71] The examples he cites are Bill Gates' desire to put Microsoft's operating system into everybody's desktop computer and Henry Ford's ambition to 'improve the world' through 'democratizing' the automobile.

Mourkogiannis also identifies types of purpose based on moral ideas, although these characterize fewer organizations these days than in the past:

✳ *Patriotism* – concerned with defence of a community and typified by nationalism, seen in Korea and still in the United States.
✳ *Universalism* – the spirit driving a universal basis for duties seen, for example, in the UK's National Health Service, railway services and the World Wide Web.
✳ *Religion* – represented in the idea of a calling or vocation as in the Protestant 'work ethic', Quaker charities like Rowntree and businesses such as Islamic banks.
✳ *The law* – exemplified in one particular form of religion, namely the Roman Catholic Church and the 'divine law' it enforced.[72]

The relationship in some organizations between their purpose and vision poses problems, as the following example shows. 'To give excellent advice on leadership development to major corporations and the public sector' is a reasonable and adequate statement of purpose, and it has what Mourkogiannis would call a 'moral twist' (excellence).[73] 'To be the world's foremost leadership development adviser to major corporations and the public sector' likewise is a reasonable and adequate vision statement, but it is also, Mourkogiannis would say, 'amoral': it is about the future success of the company. If we then say to our employees, 'If you carry out our mission (a good thing to do anyway), we will achieve our vision':

> Curiously, the amoral vision becomes a justification for the quasi-moral mission, rather than the other way around. This breeds cynicism, with the result that the mission is seen as just another management tool, a way of getting from here to there.

Shareholder Value, Customer Value and Stakeholder Value as Organizational Purpose

A frequently stated purpose is to maximize shareholder value, for example Lloyds TSB Group's 'governing' objective.[74] 'Leaders are not measured by vision, mission statements or codes of ethics', Iain Mangham comments, 'but like the wrapping on Christmas presents these serve as appropriate decoration. They are measured by the growth in shareholder value ... Not surprisingly, leaders give their full attention to that.'[75] James Collins and Jerry Porras say: 'A primary role of core purpose is to guide and inspire. Maximizing shareholder wealth does not inspire people at all levels of an organization, and it provides precious little guidance.'[76] Sharon Turnbull argues that:

> Where organisations define themselves as simply being 'for profit' there is a lack of meaning for employees that is rarely sustainable. Greed by shareholders and leaders breeds unrest amongst employees and quickly extends to the contempt of customers. All too rare in the west are those companies with a clearly defined purpose that transcends money, and for whom profit is the by-product - not the raison d'etre.[77]

Another frequently stated purpose is to meet market demands and needs and satisfy customers or clients. Peter Drucker has always argued that companies should exist not to make profits but to create and satisfy customers. He says:

> **Aristotle said there can only be one end, but there can be many means. Profit is a means, very much like oxygen to the human body. It is absolutely necessary, but you don't exist for its sake.**[78]

Peter Doyle states that a purpose which is focused on short-term profits and return on capital makes it very difficult to maintain market share in competitive markets.[79] Companies like BMW, Siemens and Hewlett-Packard, he says, with returns on capital of much less than the average, are the first choice for customers. Focusing on providing customer value, and not shareholder value, paradoxically produces greater shareholder value.

This is very persuasively argued using several examples by Bill George, former chairman and CEO of Medtronic, Inc. – one of the world's leading medical technology companies based in Minneapolis – and the Academy of Management's 2001 'Executive of the Year'.[80] Focusing primarily on maximizing shareholder value, he says, may lead to short-term improvements but not to sustainable long-term growth.[81] This is what happened to GEC in the UK, leading to its virtual demise, according to its embittered former chairman Lord Weinstock after his retirement in 1996.[82]

Bill George also argues that people today seek meaning and purpose in their work – a spiritual aspect that we discuss in a later chapter. When they find it, '[they] will buy into the company's mission and make the commitment to fulfilling it'.[83] Gregory Dess and Joseph Picken quote Xerox PARC guru John Seely Brown as saying: 'The job of leadership today is not just to make money: it's to make meaning.'[84]

Richard Ellsworth emphasizes the importance of corporate purpose, and he denigrates the preoccupation with shareholder value on both economic and humanistic grounds.[85] Instead, he says, only 'a customer-focused corporate purpose provides the key to outstanding performance and to enhancing the lives of those the company serves and of those who serve it'. In his commentary on Ellsworth's thesis, Scott Snook says:

> **Everything flows from a customer-focused purpose. A singular focus on serving customers defines the ultimate end for corporate visions, missions, and strategies. Ultimately, all strategic direction flows from this clearly understood answer as to why the corporation exists.**[86]

A slightly different view is that organizations exist to serve the interests of *all* their stakeholders. In 1995, the Royal Society for the Encouragement of Arts, Manufactures, and Commerce (RSA) published a report on its inquiry into 'Tomorrow's Company: the role of business in a changing world'. The report argued:

> **The companies which will sustain competitive success in the future are those which focus less exclusively on shareholders and on financial measures of success – and instead include all their stakeholder relationships, and a broader range of measurements, in the way they think and talk about their purpose and performance. In short it is this inclusive approach which differentiates Tomorrow's Company from yesterday's companies.**[87]

Every organization has a range of stakeholders – customers, owners and investors (shareholders), suppliers, distributors, the government, the community in which it operates, society at large, and not least its employees. Each stakeholder will ask how the organization serves its interests. Stakeholder interests therefore have to be taken into account in the round in deciding the organizational purpose – why the organization exists and what it does. An example of a purpose that does so is Barclays', focusing on customers, employees and communities as key stakeholders: 'to be an innovative, customer focused Group that delivers superb products and services, ensures excellent careers for our people and contributes positively to the communities in which we live and work'.[88]

A 2009 survey by the CIPD revealed that organizations had four different types of purpose that were not necessarily mutually exclusive:

✳ Making the most profits for investors and owners (49% of cases).
✳ Balancing the needs of all stakeholders (25%).
✳ Creating the most value for customers (20%).
✳ Giving the most benefit to society (6%).[89]

It is sadly ironic that the most common purpose was also the least engaging for employees and the least likely to be shared.

The CIPD report states:

> **People want to have a purpose beyond making money. A purpose of maximising shareholder value leads to employee disenchantment and a lack of loyalty and commitment.**

Maximizing shareholder value as a widely promulgated *raison d'être* of commercial business is a harmful statement of its purpose – a self-deluding mantra. Most companies start out to provide products or services to a present or future market (and, in doing so, provide employment). Eventually many will go public to attract investors and raise funds in order to further that end, not to provide a return to shareholders as an end in itself. If maximizing shareholder value were the sole purpose or even the main purpose of a company, then it would hop from one industry, product or service to another to achieve the highest margins and hence maximize shareholder value.

This just does not happen in successful companies. And where it does happen, the inevitable outcome will be sub-optimal or self-destructive. One reason for this is that employees will be less than engaged with the business; influenced – or even inspired – not by the company's vision or purpose but by what they, like their equally amoral management or investors, can materially get out of the business. They will be, or they will become, Oscar Wilde's cynics: '[people] who know the price of everything and the value of nothing'.[90] Selling products or services that meet market needs and wants – and not aiming to maximize shareholder value – is the route to sustainable success.

John Kay, noted economist and former director of the Saïd Business School at the University of Oxford, argues that the direct pursuit of wealth – manifest as greed and materialism – can damage individuals and their organizations.[91] In support of his argument he quotes several mega-rich business magnates, the richest of all during their working lives:

'The man who dies rich thus dies in disgrace.' (Andrew Carnegie) 'I believe it is my duty to make money and still more money, and to use the money I make for the good of my fellow man, according to the dictation of my own conscience.' (John D. Rockefeller)

Says Chris Hohn, '… organizations with a moral purpose are the long-term winners because they are motivated by something more powerful than money'.[92]

Yet the mantra of shareholder value is still perpetuated, even among noted leadership theorists. For example, John Sosik and Don Jung emphasize the responsibility of top corporate leaders to create wealth for their shareholders and 'to motivate organizational members to create the strategies, structures, markets, and talent pools required to achieve their financial goals'.[93] And they define *strategic leadership* accordingly as 'The capacity to orchestrate complex business processes and to leverage these opportunities into financial rewards for shareholders.'[94] Ian Buckingham suggests that 'the drive for delivering shareholder value in quarterly increments', for example in investment banking, has led to a dysfunctional culture – euphemistically called a 'performance culture'.[95]

Nevertheless there are positive developments. For example, the United Nations in 2007 ratified the use of a 'triple bottom line' in public sector accounting. This approach adds to the traditional idea of organizational effectiveness – economic success – to include 'people' and 'planet' as well as 'profit'.[96] The benefit of this approach is to broaden the concept of organizational effectiveness not only in the public sector but also in the private sector, where the notion of corporate social responsibility is more commonly used to encompass 'people' and 'planet'. The Triple Bottom Line is a sound basis for enlightened organizational visions and purpose, for example 'green' visions and the purposes of BP, General Electric and Unilever.[97]

In recent years, especially as a result of the financial crisis, the wisdom of focusing on shareholder value as the 'be-all' and 'end-all' of business has been questioned. Even Jack Welch has changed his view: 'On the face of it, shareholder value is the dumbest idea in the world.'[98]

Commercial businesses, of course, do have to make a profit to survive and grow. It is a fiduciary duty of directors to the shareholders in many countries, including the United States and the UK. However, it is not the only duty and should not be so. Some commentators also argue that maximizing profits is a way of maximizing happiness in the world, which most certainly is not as frequent a phenomenon as they may think. In the words of Nikos Mourkogiannis, 'In any case, if happiness is the real goal, then maximizing profits is only a rule of thumb, not a moral duty.'[99]

The origin of the obsession with shareholder value was an article in 1976 by two economists, Michael Jensen and William Meckling, that argued that company shareholders were not being well served by company managers because their interests were different.[100] Shareholder value became the mantra. Stakeholder interests – those of customers, suppliers, employees, and society in general – were regarded as being of lesser importance. And not long before that, in 1970, Milton Friedman had asserted, with evangelical zeal, that the one and only responsibility of business was to make money for its owners.[101]

Working for the customer, not the shareholder, has become a common contemporary idea. Richard Lambert, head of the Confederation of British Industry, says:

> **If you concentrate on maximising value to shareholders over the short term, you put at risk the relationships that will determine your longer-term success.[102]**

Roger Martin argues for the replacement of shareholder value by customer value – 'customer-driven capitalism' – in which customer satisfaction is the purpose.[103] 'I don't work for the shareholder. I work for consumers and my customers', says Unilever's CEO, Paul Polman.[104] Bill George, former CEO of Medtronic and now a Harvard Business School professor, says that a new generation of leaders is now replacing hierarchy-oriented, top-down leaders serving their companies' short-term oriented shareholders, and focusing instead on their companies' customers and clients as their *raison d'être*. By way of an example, George quotes Medtronic's purpose as 'restoring people to full life and health', a motivational force for the company's 38,000 employees. He believes, as many scholars and commentators do, that people are increasingly searching for 'satisfaction and meaning from their work, not just money'. Organizations' purposes, and the reasons why those organizations exist, now increasingly focus on those who benefit from their products and services, and not on those who merely want to make money from them in providing those products and services. He holds that:

> **The leader's first obligation is not to shareholders, but rather to customers. CEOs who spend too much time listening to Wall Street risk ignoring their most important stakeholder – their customers. Any organization that doesn't provide its customers with superior value relative to competitors will find itself going out of business. Employees are much more motivated by serving customers than they are by getting stock prices up, and that's what leads to innovation and superior customer service.**

Many critics of shareholder value as the central purpose of business now take a different view, proposing *stakeholder value* instead. Michael Porter and his colleague Mark Kramer have joined in this debate with their idea of creating 'shared value': pursuing a corporate self-interest while also acting for the common good.[105] They admit to this diminished trust in capitalism as a result of the excessive emphasis on profits and capitalism's crisis of legitimacy from 2008. But they also criticize the effects of the corporate social responsibility (CSR) movement (see our next chapter), which they say has attempted to address social weaknesses at the expense of business. They quote examples of attempts by General Electric, Google, IBM, Intel, Johnson & Johnson, Nestlé, Unilever and Walmart to replace both old-fashioned capitalism and CSR with shared value. Their idea is nothing new: for example, in 2000 William Clay Ford Jr as chairman of the Ford Motor Company stated that:

We see no conflict between business goals and social and environmental needs. I believe the distinction between a good company and a great one is this: a good company delivers excellent products and services; a great one delivers excellent products and services and strives to make the world a better place.[106]

However, Porter and Kramer do add weight to the argument that the sole pursuit of profit will prove counterproductive.

Steps in Creating a Statement of Purpose

Kim Kanaga and Sonya Prestridge provide a useful procedure for creating a statement of purpose.[107] The key questions to be considered are as follows:

❋ What purpose does the organization serve?
❋ Who are the organization's customers?
❋ What do the organization's customers have to gain from it?
❋ What are the organization's distinctive competencies?
❋ What does the organization want to change (represented in its vision)?
❋ What energizes the organization?
❋ What are the organization's core values, and how do they inform its vision and purpose?
❋ What legacy should the organization aim to leave (hypothetically)?

These questions are then subjected to a brainstorming process:

1. One sheet on a flip chart is devoted to each question. Members of the group call out ideas, either randomly or in turn, that relate to each question, considered one at a time. All suggestions are recorded, regardless of quality or repetition, and this process is continued until ideas dry up.
2. The sheets are posted around the room. All members study them and then identify and report patterns and themes, looking for common words and repetition.
3. The themes and patterns are then discussed to identify the key ideas for a statement of purpose.
4. All members individually write a statement of purpose.
5. Members form groups of three or four and share their statements and create a common one.
6. The whole group reconvenes, shares the small groups' statements of purpose, and creates a single, agreed statement. A sub-group may be assigned to add the finishing touches for approval by the whole group if desired.

Fran Ackermann and Colin Eden take a different approach to developing a clear purpose, which they call a 'statement of strategic intent', thereby eschewing the common 'mission statement'. This results from strategic goals, which in turn result from an analysis of strategic issues and distinctive competencies.[108] They say that this should encompass the business idea. They also suggest that a purpose, and even a vision, may result from the process of making strategy. Whether this is logical or effective is arguable: I have proposed that strategies are the ways and means of pursuing a purpose or a vision, or both, and therefore they must presuppose a clear, shared purpose or vision.

To consolidate a shared sense of purpose in an organization, Mourkogiannis recommends establishing a 'community of purpose' in the organization.[109] The top management team must set an example with their actions and behaviour being in accordance with the purpose they espouse, ensuring that the purpose is translated into strategies, goals, plans and action throughout the organization and that momentum is maintained, and monitoring its validity and utility in the light of changing circumstances. Characteristic drivers of a shared purpose in organizations, according to the 2009 CIPD research, would be that:

✳ The purpose is invigorating – it is uplifting and deliverable.
✳ The purpose is brought to life through using crafted language and storytelling.
✳ The purpose is at the heart of the organization's vision and strategy.
✳ Employees are consulted on key issues and decisions.
✳ Employees understand what is expected of them, receive clear performance feedback, receive coaching and discuss their training and development needs.
✳ Other common practices – such as quality management – exist in the organization that also break down functional and physical boundaries.[110]

The Importance and Benefits of a Shared Purpose

A statement of purpose serves three functions, according to Chris Bart and J.C. Tabone:

✳ To provide a focused basis for allocating resources.
✳ To motivate and inspire people throughout the organization (or group or nation) to achieve a common goal or purpose.
✳ To create a balance among the competing interests of the various stakeholders in the organization.[111]

Paul Joyce and Adrian Woods add some further reasons for having a statement of purpose:

✳ To refocus the organization during a crisis.
✳ To create standards of behaviour.
✳ To provide a common purpose or direction.
✳ To define the scope of the business.
✳ To allow the CEO to assert control over the organization.
✳ To develop shared values or culture in the organization.
✳ It is expected.[112]

Both the vision statement and the statement of purpose provide a context for people in an organization to make sense of the tasks they are performing. Both vision and purpose can be inspiring and motivating in themselves. As Sanjay Menon says, 'The energising power of a purpose or valued cause has often been noted in the context of religious or missionary work and sovereignty movements.'[113] In the not-for-profit sector, faced with 'compassion fatigue' among the general public, Owen Hughes says, 'charities need to make people understand not only what they do but also what they are like as an organisation.'[114] He also says images help to do this when they reflect the core idea of what the organization stands for, illustrate benefits rather than problems, and connect and inspire rather than shock.

When all employees share a belief in the purpose, they are enthusiastic, according to Milton Moskowitz and Robert Levering, who carry out an annual survey of the best US workplaces for *Fortune* magazine.[115] In 2000 C. William Pollard, then CEO of ServiceMaster, one of the world's most respected companies, and ranked the top service company among the *Fortune 500*, stated that:

> **People want to contribute to a cause ... When we create alignment between the mission of the firm and the cause of its people, we unleash a creative power that results in quality service to the customer and the growth and development of the people who do the serving. People find meaning in their work.**[116]

Nikos Mourkogiannis suggests three reasons why purpose is crucial to an organization's success:

1. Wealth creation and success result from a sense of purpose.
2. Purpose reflects motivation and behaviour: it is 'the core energy ... that fuels everything else'.
3. Purpose is central and paramount in successful leaders' minds in what they value.[117]

How can a leader tell that something is wrong with the organization's purpose? Mourkogiannis suggests some symptoms and opportunities:

* A lack of energy among people in the organization, associated with a perception that the top management team do not really believe in what they say.
* Calls for a new strategy, which may really mean the need for a new direction for rediscovery or a reassurance of the purpose – an opportunity for which may be the appointment of a new chairman or CEO.
* Action does not happen after strategies have been decided.
* Problems occur with the organization's reputation, such as criticisms or scandals.
* A major structural change such as a merger or acquisition that requires a review of the direction and identity.[118]

While some 47 per cent of UK employees in the 2009 CIPD survey reported a strong sense of a shared purpose at work, some 28 per cent did not feel this.[119] This survey linked employees' feeling of a shared purpose with their engagement, which in turn was linked with organizational performance and effectiveness. The CIPD research identified three benefits to a strong sense of shared purpose:[120]

✳️ High levels of employee engagement – absorbing and meaningful work, motivation and a commitment to the organization.

✳️ A strong sense of community – a shared purpose engenders collaborative working, especially in smaller, single sites.

✳️ Effective teams – fostering both a 'local' team spirit and a 'global' commitment and enabling distributed leadership, which we discussed in Chapter 1.

The CIPD research report illustrated this with the case study in this chapter and added:

An organisation's shared sense of purpose is its identity and 'the golden thread' to which its strategy should be aligned.[121]

High-performing organizations display a strong sense of shared purpose, not just among managers and employees but also among external stakeholders.[122] There is growing evidence for the positive and sustainable impact of a strong sense of a shared purpose on organizational performance and effectiveness. For example, Richard Ellsworth found that delivering value to customers as companies' espoused purpose is significantly more profitable than either maximizing shareholder value or trying to balance the needs of all stakeholders.[123] This is one irony that continues to escape some business school academics in the field of strategic management, finance and accounting in their teaching about shareholder value.

A 2010 survey of 2,042 employees for the CIPD in the UK revealed that some 35 per cent felt that the core purpose of their organization was detached from what they actually did.[124] Yet organizations with a sense of shared purpose had more engaged employees and outperformed those without it, according to the survey findings. There also appeared to be a gap between knowing the organization's core purpose (76 per cent of employees) and sharing it (28 per cent). These statistics implied a serious leadership shortcoming in respect of this key driver of organizational success and alignment to it.

The CIPD survey revealed that some six out of every ten employees in the private sector considered 'to make the most profits for investors and owners' to be their organization's purpose. This is hardly likely to be inspiring to employees – a seeming blind spot in many leaders. 'I feel demotivated that all my hard work and effort is going into the pockets of investors and owners' is a typical comment by respondents. Many employees, however, are prepared to accept this and 'live' the values of the organization. Alignment to the organization's purpose is the key issue – even more important than the nature of the purpose itself. Alignment between the employee's goals and values and the organization's goals and values is also important for engagement[125] (which we discuss in the chapter on leadership and engagement). Nikos Mourkogiannis, however, believes that people do *not* need to be aligned in an organization where there is a clear purpose because they have already been attracted to it – by its purpose.[126] In my opinion this begs the question: is this indeed the case?

In the CIPD survey slightly fewer than six out of ten employees in the public sector and slightly more than five out of ten employees in the voluntary sector considered their organization's purpose to be 'to give the most benefit to society' – around half of all respondents considering this explicitly mentioned that this was stimulating and encouraging. Among those who considered their organization's main purpose was to create the most value for customers, a typical comment by respondents in all sectors was: 'By focusing on customers, in the long run we are benefiting ourselves – the more satisfied customers are the more loyal they will be and the more successful the organization will be.'

How deep does the sense of shared purpose go? Slightly more than one-quarter of employees believed that this permeated the whole organization, but not for the majority. The evidence on whether or not this mattered was not clear. Says the CIPD:

> **Organisations can't impose a sense of shared purpose and manipulated top-down selling of a common purpose creates cynicism and resistance. Shared purpose is not just for charities or the public sector. By encouraging employees to find their own meaning at work, they connect and create a true sense of what they are at work to do, that's beyond profits or short-term efficiency measures and regardless of the sector they operate in.**[127]

A sense of shared purpose is strongest, the CIPD states, when employees develop an emotional relationship with the organization's purpose.[128] The CIPD quotes several examples in the private sector:

* *Standard Chartered Bank:* 'employees have an emotional connection with the bank's reputation and the many corporate social responsibility (CSR) and volunteering opportunities that are open to them'.
* *Pfizer (Grange Castle):* 'employees have an emotional connection with improving patients' lives'.
* *Xerox Global Document Outsourcing Service Delivery team:* 'employees have a strong bond around providing excellent customer service'.
* *Birmingham City Council (BCC):* 'Employees have interpreted the core purpose of the council [to provide services to citizens of Birmingham] in terms of what it means for their job role, suggesting that they have internalised it' as providing the 'highest quality information or service which gives value for money' when the citizens of Birmingham 'contact BCC by whatever means they choose'.

Dr Reto Francioni, CEO and Chairman of the Executive Board of Deutsche Borse, links purpose to strategy: '... true transformation of an organization depends on ... anchoring strategy to purpose ... Strategy that has no purpose is merely tactics ....'[130] Likewise, I argue in support of the integrated model of leadership in this book that vision and purpose need to be enacted through strategies.

The fundamental driving force of the organization is a purpose based on a vision of its future and its core values. It is, Richard Scase says, 'the glue holding the whole business together'.[131]

CASE STUDY: SHARED PURPOSE IN PRACTICE AT THE ROYAL NATIONAL LIFEBOAT INSTITUTION (RNLI)[132]

Organizational Purpose and Vision

Founded in 1824, the RNLI is recognized as one of the most successful charities. Although the organisation has significantly expanded its services and its geographical presence since 1824, its core purpose remains the same. It is *'the charity that saves lives at sea'*. This unifying purpose underpins the organization's vision, values and strategic and operational priorities.

The organization's vision is *'to be recognised universally as the most effective, innovative and dependable lifeboat and lifeguard service'*. A clear operational focus underpins this vision, including: having a strategically located fleet of lifeboats (coastal and inland) that can be launched in all weathers; providing lifeguard services on a seasonal basis; and ensuring resources are allocated to supporting safety education and accident prevention at and by the sea. A clear set of performance targets underpins these operational targets and these are published in the organization's strategic plan for all stakeholders to refer to.

Factors that have Contributed to the Organization's Success

A number of factors have contributed to the organization's success. First, it operates a long-term planning timeframe. This includes a twenty-year strategic plan supported by a five-year business plan and an annual operating budget.

Second, given the nature of its business, the RNLI has to maintain adequate financial reserves. Innovative fundraising has played a key role in building these reserves. A large percentage of the organization's funding (60 per cent) comes from legacies. The general public give to the RNLI because they respect the work the lifeboat crews do. They perceive lifeboat crews as being courageous, selfless (that is, they put their lives at risk to save others) and independent (the public are aware that the RNLI does not receive any central funding). It is this independence that generates tremendous respect amongst the general public, without which the organization's future may not be sustainable. However, changing external factors mean that the organization cannot afford to be complacent: an ageing population, the increasing cost of elder care, as well as reduced investment funds could all affect its future financial base. Long-term financial planning is already difficult for the organization. Despite knowing that a donor has set up a legacy, it is difficult to plan for when that legacy will arrive.

Third, and something that is aligned to the organization's core values, is maintaining a strong volunteer ethos. This ethos enables the organization to prioritize spending on areas that will allow it to achieve its core purpose, as opposed to covering staffing costs.

(Continued)

(Continued)

Maintaining the organization's reputation amongst the general public and other key stakeholders is thus key to sustaining its business model.

The organization has identified a number of external factors that could impact on its current and future success:

- The impact that the current economic situation could have on the RNLI's own operations as well as those of its key suppliers, including the supply of funding and the supply of volunteers.
- Technological advancements and changing legislation linked to risk taking that could affect the future demand for RNLI lifeboat services.
- Climate change and the potential increase in demand for lifeguard services on UK beaches.
- Changing demographics and the effect that this could have on the number of people who choose to spend their time volunteering.

Organizational Structure and Resourcing

Currently, just under 1,300 staff work at the RNLI. In addition, there are large numbers of volunteers: 5,000 of these work in roles that directly involve saving lives, for example as lifeboat crew and shore helpers (these are people who help run the lifeboat stations). The majority of those who head up the lifeboat stations are volunteers, rather than paid employees. There are also numerous volunteers working in various fundraising roles as well as trustees.

Having access to such a quantity of volunteers enables the organization to prioritize its expenditure around achieving its core purpose – saving lives at sea.

Building and maintaining a volunteer pipeline are crucial to the organization's sustainable future and form a key element of the strategic people plan. It is recognized that a number of external factors could affect the volunteer pipeline in the future: changing demographics and the attractiveness of the RNLI to different age groups; the general state of employment opportunities; as well as the perception of volunteering amongst different groups within society. The multiple priorities and opportunities that the 'Baby Boomer' generation, for example, have access to have been identified as a key risk that the organization needs to actively manage.

Developing a Shared Purpose

Perhaps the strongest sense of connection with the organization's purpose can be found in the lifeboat stations. The operational benefit of this connection with the organization's purpose is that staff and volunteers in lifeboat stations invest their energy in making sure that the lifeboats and other essential lifesaving equipment are kept in peak condition and are thus ready to be put into action at all times and in all conditions. While this does lead to a strong sense of responsibility and accountability amongst lifeboat crew members, the organization has to work hard to ensure that lifeboat crew engage with the work of the whole organization and not just their particular lifeboat station. Maintaining this strong sense of a shared purpose is thus something that needs to be

(Continued)

(Continued)

continually reviewed alongside changing operational priorities. An example of this is the development of dual-purpose lifeboat stations, that is, as a base for developing both lifeguard and lifeboat services.

Having such a clear purpose has helped the organization maintain a continuing supply of staff, both volunteers and employees. It helps with high levels of organizational engagement too. Staff turnover is particularly low, currently averaging around 9 per cent.

While most staff find it relatively easy to identify with the organization's core purpose, not all of them find it quite so easy to appreciate the impact of their individual contribution on the wider purpose of saving lives at sea.

To address this, a number if changes have been introduced by the HR and training team. These include: creating development opportunities for staff working in support roles to spend time experiencing what life in a lifeboat station is like; encouraging staff and volunteers working in lifeboat stations to share stories of their work with staff and volunteers in other parts of the organization; and using more visual communication approaches to bring the business of saving lives at sea more alive for everyone, such as the TV/video footage used to promote the 'Train One Save Many' fundraising campaign.

Despite these changes, the HR team recognizes that more could be done to help people develop a greater sense of connection with the organization's purpose. One way of doing this is to develop the awareness and capabilities of line managers so they are more equipped to help staff and volunteers develop a better sense of this connection. Another way to do this would be to encourage lifeboat crews to take personal responsibility for helping colleagues in other parts of the organization connect with this core purpose through personal feedback.

HR's Role in Supporting the Organization's Shared Purpose

The HR team is currently reviewing the organization's people plan to ensure that HR practices can support the priorities laid out in the 2010 to 2030 strategic plan.

Some of the key strategic priorities include:

- Ensuring a continuing supply of highly skilled volunteers who are capable of filling operational and fundraising roles in the future: linked to this priority is ensuring more transparent career development frameworks so that current and future staff are more aware of what a career at the RNLI could look like.
- Introducing a competency framework, reflecting organizational values, that will underpin recruitment, performance management and development activities for staff in all roles.
- Providing an enhanced performance management system that will reflect the need for personal excellence by focusing on continuous improvement to ensure enhanced organizational efficiency and effectiveness.
- Building line management capability so that managers will be more skilful in creating an environment where all volunteers and staff will perform at their best and continue to connect with the organization's purpose: this initiative will include helping line

(Continued)

(Continued)

managers understand their role in creating opportunities for staff to experience the 'sharp end', as well as providing managers with the necessary tools to do so; in addition, it will be important to ensure that managers take more accountability for making difficult decisions relating to individual and organizational performance.

Case Discussion Questions[133]

1. What do you think of the RNLI's vision in comparison with the criteria for a good vision?
2. How sustainable is the RNLI's purpose?
3. Comment on the extent to which you believe the RNLI's purpose is shared.
4. Much publicity has surrounded the issue of salaries, bonuses and pensions during the adverse economic conditions following the banking crisis in 2008. Charities should not be exempt from this concern, said two newspaper correspondents.[134] They cited high salaries in the RNLI (e.g. 40 senior executives earning between £60,000 and £139,999) and final-salary pension 'black holes', all increasingly funded by donations from members of the public, and the fact that the RNLI also has many volunteers and low-paid lifeboat crews who are actually the people who are saving lives at sea.

   Two other correspondents have defended and praised the RNLI. One, an RNLI volunteer himself, professed no grievance over senior executives' salaries and admired the proper and professional administration of donations; both correspondents pointed out the efficient management of operations and the considerable pleasure and pride that volunteers and local communities had in contributing to the service.[135]

   Discuss these opinions in the context of 'good' leadership in the RNLI.
5. What do you think are the leadership challenges for the RNLI's management as they face the future?

 Further Reading

CIPD (2009), *Shared Purpose and Sustainable Organization Performance,* Research Insight. London: Chartered Institute of Personnel and Development.

CIPD (2010), *Shared Purpose: The Golden Thread?* Survey Report. London: Chartered Institute of Personnel and Development.

Richard R. Ellsworth (2002), *Leading with Purpose: The New Corporate Realities.* Stanford, CA: Stanford Business Books.

John Kay (2010), *Obliquity.* London: Profile Books.

Joel Kurtzman (2010), *Common Purpose: How Great Leaders get Organizations to Achieve the Extraordinary.* San Francisco, CA: Jossey-Bass.

Nikos Mourkogiannis (2006), *Purpose: The Starting Point of Great Companies.* New York: Palgrave Macmillan.

Discussion Questions

1. Which comes first: vision or purpose? Why?
2. Should the purpose of a company publicly quoted on the Stock Exchange simply be to maximize shareholder value?
3. How can you create a purpose that all stakeholders share?
4. How can you ensure that people throughout the organization understand and are committed to the purpose?
5. How permanent should a purpose be?

We now turn to examine the place of values in leadership, a significant determinant and feature of culture and a basis for, or at least an influence on, the organization's vision and purpose.

6 Leadership and Values

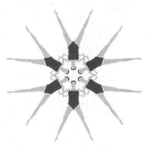

Open your arms to change, but don't let go of your values.

Nepalese Buddhist mantra

OVERVIEW

- The proposition of this chapter is that effective leaders identify, display, promote and reinforce shared values that inform and support the vision, the purpose and strategies. This is the third core theme and practice in our model of leadership.
- Values are principles or standards that are considered to be important or beneficial. 'Moral' values are values that are regarded as good as opposed to bad, right as opposed to wrong. They serve as guiding principles for behaviour for everybody in a group or organization. Moral values in a business context that are translated into rules of conduct are known as business ethics.
- A useful distinction here is that personal values are individual, subjective and 'internal', whereas corporate values (the core values of the organization) are impersonal, objective and external – the guiding principles for people's behaviour in the organization.
- Key core values in the best companies to work for include honesty and truthfulness, integrity, and trust and trustworthiness.
- An effective leader lives the values of the organization and sets an example as an inspiring role model. A mismatch between actions and espoused values denotes hypocrisy, which destroys credibility and trust.
- The more personal values and corporate values are aligned, and the more values are shared, the stronger the corporate culture will be and the happier and more effective people in the organization will be. And a strong culture with the right values – those that inform and support the organization's vision, purpose and strategies – characterizes an effective organization.
- To create a culture of shared values in the organization, it is necessary to involve people in discovering the range and commonality of existing values; determining which values are desired in light of the organization's vision, purpose and strategies; communicating these via internal channels and organizational systems; and ensuring that organizational systems can facilitate, promote and reinforce these in people's actions and behaviour.

(Continued)

(Continued)

- Moral values translated into rules of conduct in business are known as business ethics. Business ethics are supposed to govern actions and behaviour. A decline in ethical standards in business over the last decades of the twentieth century has continued into the first decade of the twenty-first century. This is the responsibility of leaders and poses a significant challenge.
- The argument continues to run that there is one and only one social responsibility for business: to maximize profits and shareholder value. However, corporate social responsibility (CSR) can be justified because of its social and economic benefits: it reflects stakeholders' values and maximizes the long-term competitive advantage, profitability and value.
- Effective leaders identify, display, promote and reinforce the shared values that inform and support the vision, the purpose and strategies. They must behave and act with responsibility and conviction in doing so. We discuss why and how they do so in this chapter.
- Shared values in part will determine corporate and national cultures. Leadership has a crucial role in shaping the culture of an organization and a nation. We consider the characteristics of corporate cultures, both advantageous and dysfunctional. A case study of Goldman Sachs provides an opportunity to consider the nature of the values that are associated with a strong, positive corporate culture.
- Leadership *sans frontières* poses another leadership challenge. Cross-cultural and multicultural situations call for leadership behaviour that is a mix of universal principles and cultural empathy. We explore what is universal across cultures and what is culture-bound. The challenge to organizational leadership is to develop a corporate culture that incorporates those human values that are universal, recognizes the diversity of other values across national cultures, and reconciles those values within a corporate culture that supports the organization's vision and strategies.

What are Values?

Effective leaders will identify, display, promote and reinforce shared values that will inform and support the vision, purpose and strategies. Values are principles or standards that are considered to be important or beneficial.[1] We evaluate aspects of our existence – objects, behaviour, events, activities, motives, intentions, goals and outcomes – on the basis of our values.[2] 'Moral' values are values that are regarded as 'good' as opposed to 'bad', 'right' as opposed to 'wrong'. These are the basis for a system of ethics and professionalism. They serve as a 'normative regulatory guide' for individuals.[3] 'Values', Jo Silvester says, 'determine where individuals invest effort'.[4]

In the context of leadership, values provide us with a sense of the desirability of, and therefore a preference for, particular states of existence – for example, a clear vision of the future, purposeful behaviour, a particular goal, or a particular outcome of our behaviour. Values therefore also inform and support our strategies for pursuing a vision and a purpose as well as the particular vision and purpose themselves. And values, together with their associated systems of ethics, are an important determinant of both corporate and national culture.

There is a widespread belief that a poisoned culture in companies was a major contributor to the financial and banking crisis of 2008 and 2009. Then chief executive of the UK's Financial Services Authority, Hector Sants has argued that regulators should play a greater role in assessing how culture influences companies' behaviour.[5] Sants has also criticized the emphasis on shareholder value as the defining characteristic of 'success', which I have already discussed in this book, in stating that: 'There must be a stronger and more explicit obligation to wider society. There must be a clear recognition of the need for institutions to contribute to the common good.' Whether leaders in banks and financial institutions have learned this and put it into practice still remains to be seen.

However, Niall Ferguson also argues that 'regulation alone is not the key to financial stability' because it can encourage a 'culture of box-ticking "compliance" rather than individual moral judgment'.[6] It is better education, he says, that will repair the damage to our financial system. That better education, he points out, in agreement with Sants, will include the understanding that shareholder value is not the overriding measure but something along the lines of a Hippocratic oath. The problem is that it would probably amount to a 'Hypocritic' oath.

The need for more emphasis on ethical behaviour is greater than ever before, says the Archbishop of Wales, Dr Barry Morgan.[7] He cites recent events in the banking sector that question for whose benefit banks are run and a widespread view that to talk about ethics in business is not 'businesslike' but 'irrelevant, pious or even weak'. Clearly this is a serious leadership issue. Morgan quotes Simon Longstaff of the St James's Ethics Centre in Australia who proposed six questions that needed to be asked:

1. Would I be happy for this decision to be on the public record?
2. What would happen if everybody did this?
3. How would I like it if someone did this to me?
4. Will the proposed course of action bring about a good result?
5. What will the proposed course of action do to my character or the character of my organization?
6. Is the proposed course of action consistent with my espoused values and principles?

In educating our current and future leaders business schools are contributing to ethical improvements in business and society. In the Harvard Business School, Morgan reports, MBA students take an oath pledging that their purpose is 'to serve the greater good of society' and commit themselves to behaving ethically and responsibly. Sandra Sucher at the Harvard Business School provides the literature-based course that has been run there since the 1980s based on her book *The Moral Leader*.[8]

Ethical behaviour can and must become second-nature, Morgan says: '... in the end, conventional regulations cannot cure moral blindness or human greed'. Leadership is about showing the way and inducing or helping others to pursue it. Ethical behaviour is an increasingly important area for what leadership is about – for the greater good of both individuals and society at large. And moral intelligence[9] – the ability to distinguish between right and wrong – is an underlying leadership competency (which we discuss in the later chapter on the multiple intelligences of leadership).

Leadership and Personal Values

In a study of the leadership behaviour and value orientations of Australian executives, James Sarros and Joseph Santora found a close association between transformational leadership behaviours and the use of contingent reward (transactional leadership) and the values of achievement, benevolence, self-direction (intellectual autonomy) and stimulation (intellectual challenge).[10] Unsurprisingly they also found a scant association of these values with management-by-exception (transactional leadership) and laissez-faire leadership behaviour.

A study of middle-level managers in the UK and Canada suggested that a higher level of moral reasoning tended to be associated with transformational leadership.[11] James O'Toole suggests that effective leaders who are moral listen to their followers because they honestly believe that the welfare of those followers is the 'end' of leadership, not that followers are merely the means to achieving the leader's goals.[12]

Transformational leaders display a strong morality both in their prosocial orientation – a desire to benefit others in the organization or in society at large – and in behaviour that reflects values of empathy, care, concern and respect for others: they take an altruistic rather than egotistical stance.[13] Transformational leaders model pro-social and altruistic behaviours: Micha Popper and Ofra Mayseless see transformational leaders as 'good parents'.[14]

UK business schools, for example Cass, Manchester and Nottingham, are recognizing that leaders' education may have had a bearing on the banking and financial crisis in 2008 by promoting an undue emphasis on shareholder value, according to Ian Buckingham.[15] He reports that these business schools have made business philosophy and ethics modules mandatory in their MBA programmes. The aim is to refocus students away from shareholder value, balance sheet management and 'short-termism' and towards a greater recognition of the link between 'boom and bust' and the management of culture.

Leadership and Corporate Values

Personal values and corporate values are different though they may overlap. Personal values, Stephen Covey says, are individual, subjective and internal, whereas corporate values, which he calls 'guiding principles', are impersonal, objective and external.[16] He points out that:

> **Principles apply at all times in all places. They surface in the form of values, ideas, norms, and teachings that uplift, ennoble, fulfil, empower, and inspire people.[17]**

The 'corporate values' defined by many companies are guiding principles for people's behaviour in the organization. Metaphorically speaking, personal values come from the 'heart' while guiding principles come from the 'head'. Nevertheless, the corporate values officially espoused and promoted by an organization do reflect personal values. They are beliefs about what is good for its business and accordingly how people in the organization are expected to behave. In a study of a culture change programme in a large engineering company in the UK, Sharon Turnbull discovered that the content of the company's new corporate values was less important than the fact that corporate values now existed: employees apparently wanted to identify with *something*.[18]

A survey carried out for the Chartered Institute of Personnel and Development in the UK in 2010 (discussed in the previous chapter in relation to common purpose) revealed a brighter picture for organizational values than it did for organizational purpose (which we discussed in the previous chapter), with some 82 per cent of all respondents expressing an awareness of organizational values to a great or lesser extent.[19] Figures for the voluntary sector, public sector and private sector were 97 per cent, 93 per cent and 77 per cent respectively. Only 5 per cent said they did not know their organizations' values and 4 per cent that their organization did not have any stated values. When asked to identify an organization that had a strong set of values and was embraced by its employees, employee-owned retail store John Lewis topped the list by a large margin (35 per cent of all respondents).

Ralph Larsen, CEO of Johnson & Johnson, emphasizes the importance of core values regardless of their commercial pros and cons:

> The core values embodied in our credo might be a competitive advantage, but that is not why we have them. We have them because they define for us what we stand for, and we would hold them even if they became a competitive disadvantage in certain situations.[20]

Peter Drucker, the father of modern management, gives a practical example of differences in values that many companies will identify with:

> In any conflict between short-term results and long-term growth, one company decides in favour of long-term growth; another company decides ... in favor of short-term results ... this is not primarily a disagreement on economics. It is fundamentally a value conflict regarding the function of a business and the responsibility of management.[21]

Companies' statements of values are often criticized for being no more than a belief in 'motherhood and apple pie'. The 2004 Roffey Park survey in the UK found that 52 per cent of the 735 managers surveyed were sceptical about their companies' values statements.[22] Many companies' values statements are meaningless and even harmful, says Patrick Lencioni.[23] He cites some common ones – communication, respect, integrity, excellence. However, according to the company's 2000 annual report, these were also Enron's – hardly a paragon of virtue. Lencioni says:

> Most values statements are bland, toothless, or just plain dishonest ... Empty values statements create cynical and dispirited employees, alienate customers, and undermine managerial credibility.

Ever since Jim Collins and Jerry Porras in 1994 published *Built to Last*, which argued that the best companies would adhere to an explicit set of core values, many companies have created their own statements of core values, Lencioni says, because they felt they had to do so:

> Today, 80% of the *Fortune 100* [companies] tout their values publicly – values that too
> often stand for nothing but a desire to be au courant or, worse still, politically correct.

Such actions, Lencioni states, debase values statements, create cynicism – the very
opposite of what is intended – and waste the opportunity to define what distinguishes
a company from its competition by 'clarifying its identity and serving as a rallying
point for employees'. True core values, he says, 'inflict pain':

✳ They make some employees feel like outcasts.
✳ They limit the organization's freedom, strategically and operationally, and con-
  strain, as well as guide, their people's behaviour.
✳ They require leaders in the organization to be role models and paragons of virtue.

Lencioni also suggests that there is much confusion about values. This in turn hinders
any clear debate. He defines several types of values:

✳ *Core values.* Inherent, sacrosanct values that distinguish a company and serve as
  guiding principles for everybody's behaviour. They are often the values of the
  founders, as with Hewlett-Packard's 'The HP Way'.
✳ *Aspirational values.* Values that an organization needs to be successful in the
  future but currently lacks. Lencioni quotes an example of a *Fortune 500* company
  which cited 'a sense of urgency' as a core value because employees were complacent: this is not a core value but an aspirational value.
✳ *Permission-to-play values.* Like core values but merely reflect the minimum
  behavioural standard required of all employees. It is these – such as integrity,
  teamwork, quality, customer satisfaction, innovation – that we can see as common
  to many companies, but they do not create a distinctive identity.
✳ *Accidental values.* Arising spontaneously, these reflect the common interests or
  values of employees, such as dress code, thus creating a sense of inclusivity, but
  they may also limit a company's opportunities and development by being too
  exclusive. They are false core values.

Values, and the behaviour that reflects them, are the basis for effective relationships
in business organizations, and they shape the business persona on which a brand and its
reputation depend, says Mark Goyder.[24] Thomas J. Watson Jr, son of the founder of IBM,
has argued that beliefs (values) – IBM's were respect for the individual and liberating
the talents and energies of its people – must inform the vision, purpose and culture:

> Any organization, in order to survive and achieve success, must have a sound set of beliefs
> [values] on which it premises all its policies and actions. Beliefs [values] must always
> come before policies, practices and goals. The latter must always be altered if they are
> seen to violate fundamental beliefs [values].[25]

'Don't be evil' is Google's mantra and its Code of Conduct shows how this should
pervade all its actions and behaviours.[26]

Values in business organizations appear to be a field which academics will shy
away from. Sally Stewart and Gabriel Donleavy suggest several reasons for this.[27]

First, they risk charges of ethnocentricity and of promoting a particular set of values. Second, they tend to be unwilling to counter the argument that business needs only to obey the law. Third, the theoretical problems of dealing with such an abstract subject are formidable. Business school academics tend to leave this to their philosophy colleagues who will treat the subject 'academically'. The result, according to Simon Webley, is the neglect of business ethics and values as a subject.[28]

Professional bodies, such as the Chartered Management Institute and the Institute of Directors in the UK, promote professional codes of practice.[29] But there are cross-cultural organizations that promote values-based leadership. For example, Webley quotes the International Chamber of Commerce based in Paris and the Caux Principles, which were published in 1996, reflecting a stakeholder model and promoting the shared values of the common good (*kyosei*) and human dignity.[30] The Interfaith Declaration on International Business Ethics was published in 1994 under the auspices of the Duke of Edinburgh, Crown Prince Hassan of Jordan and Sir Evelyn de Rothschild.[31] This declaration, based on a common religious heritage, promoted four key values: justice, mutual respect, stewardship and honesty.

Societal culture influences organizational values and culture both directly and indirectly through its influence on individuals' values and on the nature of tasks in the organization such as aggressiveness in competition, the nature of the organization's industry and dominant professions, and access to the internet[32] (e.g. the United Arab Emirates restricted the use of BlackBerry telephones in 2010 for security reasons).

UK corporations appear to be reticent about using value-based terms and they confuse values with performance criteria.[33] The reason is unclear, but perhaps it is that values are subjective and largely culture-related and therefore difficult territory when compared with objective data. William Loges and Rushworth Kidder make an attempt to define generally accepted societal values.[34] A review of codes of business ethics of 15

Table 6.1 Frequency of Mention of Values in 15 Corporate Codes (Adapted from Simon Webley, 1992, *Business Ethics and Company Codes*. London: Institute of Business)

Value	No. of Mentions
Integrity	11
Highest ethical standard	9
Responsibility	8
Reputation	7
Honesty	6
Openness	4
Fairness	3
Competitiveness	3
Trustworthiness	2
Profitability	2
Truthfulness	2

large UK corporations by Simon Webley revealed the espoused values shown in Table 6.1. Two examples of corporate (core) values that are linked to the organizations' vision, purpose and strategies are shown below.

CASE EXAMPLE: CORE VALUES OF DURHAM UNIVERSITY[35]

Durham University in the UK is committed to the following core values that support its vision and purpose and underpin its strategies:

- Defence of freedom of thought and the cherishing of intellectual debate and new ideas.
- The valuing of knowledge and learning for their own sake, and for their ethical, cultural, social and economic benefits.
- The creation of communities in which critical thinking and creativity are combined with opportunities for personal growth and development, so that all can realize their full potential.
- The fostering of cross-disciplinary and cross-cultural thinking and working.
- The communication of knowledge and learning for the benefit of all.
- The promotion of diversity, respect for others and equality of opportunity.
- Striving for excellence in everything that is done, as a single and purposeful organization.
- The measurement of all that is done against the standards of an ethical and sustainable world.

CASE EXAMPLE: CORE VALUES OF THE NATIONAL TRUST

The UK's National Trust states: 'Instead of material wealth or status, we take comfort in family and community, places we love, the appreciation of beauty, fresh air, and a sense of kinship, with each other, with the past and with the natural world.'[36] Leadership is about reinforcing shared values and sometimes about changing values and, as a result, the organizational culture. The National Trust says, for example, 'Our people [must be] free to be creative. Our culture required too much approval and consensus, slowing up decision-making. We are now handing power to our staff and volunteers at properties and slashing the rulebook, rewarding individual initiative, tempered by responsibility and the need to sustain our charity for the long term.'

Corporate Values and Corporate Identity

Corporate identity is a concept that came into popular use some 50 years ago. But one of the earliest recorded examples is Pericles's funeral oration in 431 BC in his effort to inspire unity among the Athenians in their war with Sparta. In effect he made it clear in an inspiring way what was different about them.[37] Organizational leaders commonly articulate and claim what is unique, central and enduring about their organization.[38] Corporate identity, though, is what members perceive it to be.[39]

Corporate identity reflects an organization's purpose, strategies, values and vision: what it does, why it does it, how it does it, what it stands for and, above all, what or where it wants to be. However, with superficial catchy names, logos and advertising taglines, corporate identity – 'that rich and varied set of characteristics that fuels differentiation and fires contribution' – has not been fully appreciated as 'a powerful force ... in shaping the fortunes of organizations', according to Laurence Ackerman.[40]

Corporate Values versus Personal Values

The more personal values and corporate values (guiding principles) are aligned – the more the 'maps of the territory reflect the reality of the territory' – the more effective they will be in building a strong, favourable culture, says Stephen Covey.[41] Effective leadership therefore includes creating shared values in the organization.

Congruence between employee values and organizational culture is positively related to employee commitment.[42] And value congruence among group members is associated with lower conflict in their relationships and their enhanced performance and satisfaction.[43] Shared values also have a clear economic benefit, says Mark Tannenbaum:

> An analysis of these successful companies and their competitors demonstrated that focusing first on alignment of values and strong cultural norms were distinguishing factors with measurable bottom-line revenue and profitability results.[44]

A study of 11 US insurance companies showed that those whose managers did not share the same perception of corporate values performed less well than those with shared values.[45] Ann Nicotera and Donald Cushman point out an ethical issue:

> If the value systems of individuals do not complement the value system of their organization, those individuals will eventually be faced with insoluble ethical dilemmas.[46]

And Peter Drucker highlights the poor performance and frustration that can result from incompatibility between the individual's values and the organization's values:

> To work in an organization the value system of which is unacceptable to a person, or incompatible with it, condemns the person both to frustration and to non-performance ... Organizations, like people, have values. To be effective in an organization, a person's values must be compatible with the organization's values. They do not need to be the same. But they must be close enough to coexist.[47]

Value congruence mediates the relationship between leadership style and performance outcomes.[48] When the values of the leader and the followers coincide, the leader gains legitimate power through credibility. Legitimate power is the ability to motivate people because of their belief in the leader and in what that person is trying to accomplish.[49] Former UK prime minister Margaret Thatcher's departure in 1990 – after a successful start in this respect – was at least partly due to her failure to maintain or reflect the shared values among her followers in her leadership behaviour.[50] The very essence of transformational leadership, says Terry Price, is the achievement of 'value congruence within the group, organization, or society [that] gives rise to behaviour that is itself congruent with these values'.[51] Transformational leaders create and promote a culture of shared values and beliefs that support and facilitate the pursuit of the vision, purpose and strategies of the group, organization or society.

If personal values are distinct from corporate values, can an organization create an organization-wide value system? Can it have a culture of shared values? An example of an effective guiding principle was the promise to customers of insurance company Commercial Union (now part of Aviva) that 'We won't make a drama out of a crisis.' Following this principle became a source of pride for employees and they succeeded in retaining customers even when premiums rose. Miranda Kennett says: '"values" are valueless if they are not relevant to those who buy or use your products or services'.[52]

Key Values and the Behaviour of Leaders

Honesty and Truthfulness

Honesty and truthfulness are core values proclaimed by many organizations. But leaders will understandably often face a dilemma here. They will have to tread a fine line between the truth, the whole truth and nothing but the truth. While truthfulness is desirable, it may also sometimes be unhelpful when pursuing honourable motives.[53] As the philosopher Bernard Williams says, there is a moral difference between inaccuracy and truthfulness when it relates to intent or motive.[54]

Practical issues for leaders include questions like 'How accurate do we need to be to be regarded as truthful?'; 'How honest should we be about our mistakes and failings?'; 'How do truthfulness and authenticity relate to each other?'; 'How much should we disclose?'

Richard Olivier recounts the experience of a human resources director who learned that one scenario which the company was planning for entailed redundancies and relocation for many employees.[55] When frequently asked what was happening, he was not free to reveal what he knew. He therefore faced a dilemma: tell the truth and breach the confidence entrusted to him, pre-empt the management's decisions and action and worsen morale, or lie. Instead, he decided to be truthful about the extent to which he could be honest. He said: 'I do know what is being planned and at the moment there are good reasons why I can't tell you all about it. Here's what I can tell you … and this is when I will be able to tell you more ….' In this way he was able to retain the trust and respect of the employees despite not being able to tell them what they wanted to know. Telling the whole truth in this case may have proved to be a disastrous self-fulfilling prophecy.

Richard Reeves says that 'Leadership requires both a respect for the truth and a recognition that honesty is not always the best policy.'[56] I would say that honesty – about what you cannot disclose – is *always* the best policy.

One of the ways to develop a sustainable culture of trust in an organization is to ensure total honesty at all times, even at a cost – in the short term – to morale. As consultant Bernard Buckley suggests: 'If anything you are doing doesn't fit with what you've said, don't do it, or explain why not.'[57]

Integrity

Stephen Covey says that honesty is telling the truth – it is 'conforming our words to reality'.[58] Integrity 'includes but goes beyond honesty': it is 'conforming reality to our words – in other words, keeping promises'. And Warren Bennis and Joan Goldsmith comment that 'Leaders walk their talk; in true leaders, there is no gap between the theories they espouse and their practice.'[59] Integrity demands consistency in what one says and does.

The importance in leadership of setting an example as a model for the behaviour of followers is nothing new: it was recognized in the ancient writings of Sun Tzu (*The Art of War*) and Confucius (*The Analects*).[60] Tony Simons calls the perceived fit between espoused and enacted values 'behavioural integrity'.[61] He points to a pattern of increasing divergence between managers' words and deeds, driven, he says, by managerial fads and organizational change efforts. He goes on to say:

> ... the divergence between words and deeds has profound costs as it renders managers untrustworthy and undermines their credibility ... [and sacrifices] the trust and commitment of their subordinates.

And Stephen Covey adds:

> Many executives say they value capitalism, but they reward feudalism. They say they value democracy, but they reward autocracy. They say they value openness and glasnost, but they behave in ways that value closeness, hidden agendas, and politicking.[62]

Integrity is essential to good leadership, both morally and in terms of effectiveness. Adrian Furnham says: 'A lack of integrity is usually accompanied by a lack of conscience – one sign of a psychopath.'[63] He comments on so-called 'integrity tests', pointing out that, because people without integrity lie, this is an obvious limitation. He recommends asking people who know them, such as their work colleagues, not about their misdeeds but about their 'sins of omission rather than commission ... [about their] absence of integrity'. For example:

* My manager is always trusted by people in the work group.
* My manager always maintains high personal standards.
* My manager always tells the truth.
* My manager always puts the organization's interests above his own.
* There is always consistency between what my manager says and what he does.[64]

A telling example of the mismatch between values and behaviour comes from the Revlon Corporation:

> At the Revlon Corporation the story is told about Charles Revlon, the head of the group, who insisted that employees arrived for work on time, but seldom arrived himself much before noon. One day Charles wandered in and began to look at the sign-in sheet, only to be interrupted by the receptionist who had strict orders that the list should not be removed.

Both insisted that they were in the right until finally Charles said 'Do you know who I am?' And she said 'No sir, I don't'. 'Well, when you pick up your final pay check this afternoon, ask 'em to tell ya'.[65]

True leaders practise what they preach. Unfortunately this is not very widespread.[66] When espoused values do not match behaviour, this is hypocrisy. But perhaps even behaviour is less important than motive (reflecting values). One view of values-based guiding principles is that these govern behaviour rather than motives.[67] Motives in fact reflect personal values. In the words of the poet W.B. Yeats:

The Light of Lights Looks always on the motive, not the deed, The Shadow of Shadows on the deed alone.[68]

Bill George, former chairman and CEO of Medtronic in the United States, points out that companies vary little in their stated values – customer orientation, quality, integrity in business dealings, respect for employees, and good citizenship – and that it is difficult to create a unique set of values.[69] He says that what makes the difference is the reinforcement and *practice* of these values, particularly by top management. Without this integrity, trust evaporates. And so does belief in the organization's purpose. George argues that: 'Integrity is everything. It takes many years to establish the reputation for integrity, yet it can be lost in a single act. Witness ... Union Carbide Bhopal ....'

Leaders do sometimes lack the ability, moral courage, time or energy to act in accordance with their values. Moral courage is standing up for a set of beliefs and values when the sands are shifting beneath one's feet. Yet, Adrian Furnham says, few companies have courage as a core value.[70]

Trust and Trustworthiness[71]

Trust in banking and the capital markets has seriously declined over the past few years. But the best companies to work for are still forging ahead (which we discuss later in this chapter) and research on trust and trustworthiness has revealed why this is so.

'Leaders at Luminus engage employees by making the time to talk, help and support them, resulting in an atmosphere of trust and loyalty.' So says Nick Rodrigues about the second-best company to work for in the UK, a community housing provider, and the best company for leadership, according to *The Sunday Times* 2010 annual survey.[72] This climate of trust and loyalty is associated with employee perceptions of the company being run on 'sound moral principles' and 'senior managers truly [living] its values'. They listen to employees and whose skills have their confidence, with those employees having faith in an inspiring chief executive, Chan Abraham.

But elsewhere trust and trustworthiness are in serious short supply. As US president Barack Obama said in his State of the Union Address on 27 January 2010, 'We have to recognize that we face more than a deficit of dollars ... We face a deficit of trust.' This is no less true here in the UK.[73] So what is trust, how does it relate to leadership, and how do we build – or rebuild – trust and trustworthiness?

Trust is an elusive concept in the academic literature. It is viewed differently through the various lenses of psychology, sociology and economics. Yet trust is well understood in practice.[74] The *Oxford English Dictionary* defines trust as confidence in an attribute of a person or thing or the truth of a statement without evidence or investigation.[75] 'Trustworthy' means being able to be relied on as honest or truthful. In a recent survey by the Work Foundation of what leaders themselves believe leadership to be and how they practise it, trust is among the most important aspects.[76] 'Good' leaders, it found, will have trust as a personal value but 'outstanding' leaders will understand how to use trust to create the conditions for exceptional employee engagement and performance.[77]

Yet deceit and deception are unfortunately commonplace today in public services, politics, business – and sport: the highly publicised extra-marital affair of the England football captain John Terry, for example, was associated with breach of trust and the adverse impact these had on many people. The consequence of a breach of trust is disenfranchised and disengaged employees and managers: trust is the foundation on which employee engagement is built.[78]

Several surveys paint the same picture. The Edelman Trust Barometer revealed a decline in public trust in business in the United States 'to do the right thing', from 58 per cent in 2008 to 38 per cent in 2009.[79] The CIPD reported a significant lack of trust by employees in both their immediate managers and their senior managers.[80] Overall only one-third of employees said they had confidence or trust in their senior managers, resulting in part from a perceived lack of consultation on important decisions. The situation appeared even worse in the public sector than in the private sector: 22 per cent versus 39 per cent respectively.[81] According to the CIPD:

> **The underlying problem seems to be a lack of trust and confidence in the ability, motivation or willingness of public sector employees, including front-line managers and professionals, to perform appropriately if given autonomy and discretion over service delivery. And part of this undoubtedly stems from a long-standing pattern of often mutually suspicious relations between government and trade unions or professional bodies representing vested public sector employee interests.[82]**

According to Brian Amble, trust in banks in the UK has fallen from 41 per cent in 2007 to 21 per cent in 2010 and trust generally in business fell to a historic low in 2009, with small increases since and significant scepticism about their sustainability after the recession.[83] 'A sceptical public', he says, 'now views trust and transparency as more important than the quality of a company's products and services'.

The prognosis for the banking and finance sector is not good. The thirteenth PricewaterhouseCoopers' Annual Global CEO Survey published in January 2010 found that as many as 65 per cent of CEOs in banking and capital markets did not accept that trust in their industry had declined significantly.[84] Many business leaders in these industries appeared to be unable or unwilling to grasp the message.

On the brighter side, however, a Roffey Park Institute survey in the UK in 2009 found that more managers than in the previous year reported that their organization's stated values were being displayed in behaviour, which was promising for the retention and sustainability of trust.[85]

A reputation for trustworthiness is necessary for cooperation. When people are perceived as trustworthy, they are also seen as having integrity and dependability.[86] This in turn enhances the likelihood of cooperation.[87] There are three elements in trustworthiness: perceived integrity, ability and benevolence.[88] The characteristics of benevolence include exploring failure and accepting errors and mistakes, knowing that people will achieve great things only if they have the support and opportunity to experiment and learn from mistakes. Honesty and empathy are related elements that have been identified in the research, but these rank lower than reliability and capability in their relative importance.[89] David Butcher identifies two types of trust, based on competence and motives.[90] Trust in people's competence is easier to win, he says, than trust in their motives.

Trust plays a central role in organizational effectiveness. Leaders have a responsibility, therefore, to build trust through establishing their trustworthiness. Pamela Shockley-Zalabak and her colleagues suggest there are five key drivers of trust:

※ Competence.
※ Openness and honesty.
※ Concern for employees as stakeholders in the organization.
※ Reliability (keeping commitments).
※ Identification (where employees believe their values are reflected in the values the organization as a whole exhibits in day-to-day behaviour).[91]

Areas that need to be monitored, they recommend, are the organizational culture, policies and practices for messages about trust and relationships, performance appraisals, accounting and reporting practices, decision making and leadership behaviour.

In a democracy, whether specious or real, trust in political leaders can fail. Bagehot in *The Economist* describes how, in the UK, 'bitter revelations' about them have led to 'corrosive cynicism' among the voting public.[92] Bagehot gives examples of the causes: the belief that the Iraq War was mis-sold, parliamentary expenses scandals, 'a slew of memoirs by Tony Blair and his allies, casually admitting their long-held belief that Gordon Brown – the man they had publicly backed for re-election as prime minister weeks before – was more or less a dangerous lunatic', and 'secretly recorded Liberal Democrat ministers saying mildly disobliging things about their Tory coalition partners'. The result: voter trust in their political leaders is now in a 'catastrophic shape'.

How well trusted are CEOs and line managers? We have a national index of trust in the UK, introduced in 2009 by the Institute of Leadership and Management and *Management Today* magazine, that measures perceptions of integrity (honesty), ability (to do the job), fairness (concern for employee welfare), consistency (reliability and consistency of behaviour), openness (accessibility and receptivity) and understanding (of employees' roles and responsibilities). The 2010 Index of Leadership Trust (ILT) showed no change in respect of line managers (60/100) but a small increase, from 59 to 63 for CEOs, over the previous year, presumably reflecting how well many CEOs have navigated the economic storm.[93] The ILT showed that trust in CEOs was strongly associated with job losses; that the public sector lagged slightly behind the private sector in trust; and that female CEOs were more trusted than their male counterparts.

People who trust others are generally optimistic, happier than mistrustful people, feel in control of their destinies, are tolerant of people who are different from themselves, indeed welcome dealings with strangers, and see opportunities rather than threats.[94] In the words of Marek Kohn: 'Trust is to be sought for its own sake, and because it keeps good company.'[95] And, as political historian and school headmaster Anthony Seldon says, 'A presumption of trust rather than a presumption of mistrust helps individuals and organisations flourish … The duty to be trusting and the responsibility for being trustworthy are incumbent on all: no one can opt out.'[96] Trust and trustworthiness are liberating. And the best companies to work for demonstrate this in their policies and practices.

The Relationship between Leaders' Values and Organizational Performance[97]

The best companies to work for have exemplary leadership: managers at all levels are respected and valued by employees for their leadership (we discuss this further later in the chapter). Senior managers in these companies truly live the values of the organization and act as inspiring role models for others.[98] Over 60 years ago, a Chief of Staff in the US Army said: 'The leader must be everything that he desires his subordinates to be.'[99] And leaders today are in front of the camera every time they speak or act: everything they say or do is visible, and therefore not leading by example is not an option.[100]

An effective leader sets an example as a role model. But CEOs who are also founders of their firms have an even more demanding role. Their values affect the performance of their firms, but not in a straightforward way.

Research by the Chartered Institute of Personnel and Development underscored exemplary leadership in creating a learning culture in organizations.[101] And '… the day when director pay is directly linked to how they [directors] behave is not far off', according to John Drysdale.[102]

Founders of companies can exercise a particularly strong influence on corporate values that will often endure for a long time. Bill Hewlett and Dave Packard's *The HP Way* is one example. Founders' and CEOs' values can influence the strategies and organizational structures they choose.[103] But whether and how founders' personal values can influence the *performance* of new ventures is less well researched.[104] Organizational life-cycle theory suggests that organizations pass through different stages, with each stage presenting different challenges that will require a variety of business philosophies and strategies[105] and, by implication, various values. The influence of CEOs' values therefore may be moderated by their firms' age and size, which will reflect these life-cycle stages.[106]

Recent research involving 92 CEOs and 313 members of top management teams of small and medium-sized enterprises in New England, in the United States, investigated the impact on their companies' performance of two personal values held by CEOs: collectivism and novelty.[107] Collectivism is the subordination of personal interests to the goals of the larger work group, an emphasis on sharing, cooperation, group harmony, a concern for group welfare and hostility towards out-group members.[108] Novelty is the tendency to value change, the new and the different.[109] These two values were drawn from an established model of personal values[110] and are relevant to new venture management and the creativity and cooperation that are required.[111]

The impact of founder-CEOs' value of collectivism on firm performance was found to be moderated both by the age of the firm and its size, with a positive effect in larger firms but none in small firms. The effects of collectivism are beneficial in older firms but disadvantageous in younger firms. Founder-CEOs' value of novelty and firm performance showed a positive relationship in young firms but no relationship in older firms, with no difference between larger and smaller firms. Mature firms headed by collectivist founder-CEOs displayed an average sales growth of 37 per cent versus 8 per cent in those headed by founder-CEOs low in collectivism. And young firms headed by founder-CEOs that were high in novelty displayed an average sales growth of 39 per cent compared with 14 per cent for those with founder-CEOs that were low in novelty. Founder-CEOs' values of collectivism and novelty can therefore influence firms' performance at different points in the organizational life cycle.

Companies' leaders' values clearly do matter to their organizations. Apart from collectivism and novelty, other values may also be important, for example (drawing on the values model used in the research) duty, rationality, materialism and power. A superior performance can be expected in firms when founder-CEOs' values are aligned to the requirements associated with the age and size of their firms. This suggests that founders of firms may have a shelf-life and should expect to step down one day for the good of their firm. Trying to change a CEO's values is more likely to fail the firm than changing the CEO.

The Importance and Identification of Shared Values

There is a widespread belief among corporate executives in the need to create strong, shared values to unite people in a fragmented world, according to James O'Toole.[112] If there is one organizational characteristic that provides the 'glue' for uniting people, it is trust. And trust, O'Toole suggests, 'emanates from leadership based on shared purpose, shared vision, and especially, shared values'.[113]

Importance of Shared Values

Shared vision, purpose and values in an organization or nation constitute a strong positive culture. In Levi Strauss, for example, shared values contribute to competitive success: 'values drive the business' and provide a common language that unites employees and leaders.[114] Shared values also have a significant impact on both the job satisfaction and morale of people in an organization as well as their job performance and contribution.

A culture that is strong – where values are widely shared and deeply held – tends to endure, and the founder's vision and strategies are likely to become a legacy – or a hangover – depending on their flexibility and environmental conditions.[115] As John Gardner says:

> One of the tasks of leadership – at all levels – is to revitalize ... shared beliefs and values, and to draw on them as sources of motivation for the exertions required of the group.[116]

A survey of senior and top-level managers by Ashridge Management College in the UK revealed significant tensions between their personal values and corporate ethics.[117] One respondent reported: 'My organisation has one mission – maximise shareholder value – everything else they do is secondary … environmental destruction is the result.' Some 44 per cent of respondents said they had supported social or environmental campaigns in their private lives and one-quarter of these believed their actions to be inconsistent with what they were expected to do at work. These findings called into question the extent to which corporate values were genuinely shared.

The leadership challenge is to create 'transcendent' values that will accommodate different aspirations. This appeal to common, higher-order values that transcend narrow self-interest reminds us of transformational leadership – that raises us to go beyond our self-interest and pursue the common good. One example that James O'Toole quotes is Václav Havel, former president of the Czech Republic.[118] Havel made decisions on the basis of his principle of 'civility' – the collective practice of respect for people. He did just this in reluctantly allowing the dissolution of Czechoslovakia into the Czech Republic and Slovakia.

Ian Davis suggests that people will increasingly be seeking employment with companies that will uphold their personal values:

> The best companies will create jobs and roles where employees feel they have some control over what they do, where professional relationships are valued, where more than lip-service is paid to work-life balance and where there is real belief in the social and ethical responsibility of the employer.[119]

Shared values are at the heart of the well-known McKinsey '7S' framework (see Figure 6.1), which is useful for understanding the culture of an organization together with its strengths and weaknesses, and for considering the factors affecting strategy implementation.[120]

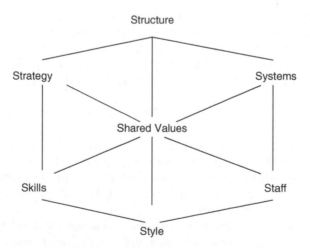

Figure 6.1 The McKinsey Seven S Model

Shared work values are important for the performance of team members and their satisfaction with the cooperation among them. This was demonstrated in a study of

411 members and their team leaders in 72 Taiwanese corporate teams by Li-Fang Chou and colleagues.[121] Trustworthiness was found to mediate the relationship between shared values and team-member performance, and trustfulness to mediate the relationship between shared values and satisfaction with cooperation.

Identifying Shared Values and Shaping a Culture

If an organization wants to have genuinely shared values, it is necessary first to discover the existing values and then determine what values are desired.[122] This discovery process should be led, but not dictated, by the organization's leadership. In the Barnsley Alcohol and Drug Advisory Service in the UK, Peter Wickens successfully applied this process by following 10 steps:

1. Introduce the concept of values.
2. Identify possible relevant values, both positive and negative.
3. Ask everybody individually to select six that best describe their perception of the current values of the organization as demonstrated by the behaviour of themselves, the top management and others.
4. Have small groups of people (of about the same organizational level) reach consensus on six to eight of the perceived current values.
5. Report the conclusions to a plenary session (in the Barnsley Alcohol and Drug Advisory Service only 'humour' emerged as common, and many values were negative) and get plenary session consensus.
6. Returning to the original list, ask everybody individually to select values that are desired, have small groups, this time multi-functional and multi-level, reach consensus on about six.
7. Following reports again back to the plenary session, distil desired values into a final list.
8. After the workshop, ask participants to discuss the results with their colleagues, aiming to involve as many people as possible as 'insiders'.
9. Reconvene to report and discuss the consultation process and refine the values.
10. Translate the values into behaviour, goals and measures, including working to eliminate the negative current values that were identified earlier.

Ownership of the values is a key issue. Patrick Lencioni does not believe that this should be achieved by seeking consensus.[123] He says this risks including suggestions from employees 'who don't belong in the company in the first place' and '[creating] the false impression that all input is equally valuable'. The best values initiatives, he says, are 'driven by small teams that include the CEO, any founders who are still with the company, and a handful of key employees'. This is viable provided that the teams are representative of all employees.

Effective leaders provide ways to recognize, encourage and develop shared values among followers. Stanley Deetz and colleagues say: 'If leaders want to ensure that their values are inculcated into organizational members, then they must also provide organizational systems that correlate with their espoused goals.'[124] Creating a sense of shared core values that will support the organization's vision, purpose and strategies requires their integration into every policy, procedure and process that concerns employees: recruitment, assessment and selection, performance management and appraisal, training and development, promotion and rewards.

Successful companies reflect their shared values in their recruitment processes to attract the 'right' people and in their culture by introducing them into their corporate literature, communication policies and practices, competency models, training and development programmes, promotion practices and performance appraisal processes. In its recruitment and selection strategy, the RAF uses a procedure that first assesses an individual's values and then his or her skills for a role. This reduces the risk of incompatibility with the organization's culture: it is easier to train a person in skills than in values.

Another strategy that organizations use to create a strong corporate culture is utilizing performance appraisals and their linked rewards and promotion. Here those whose actions and behaviour reflect or promote organizational values or guiding principles enjoy rewards and promotion. This is contingent reward (transactional leadership) in action (see our earlier chapter on leadership theories). Employees may feel that the organizational values are being 'forced' upon them and that their own values are less important. This may then result in disaffection and alienation. However, transformational leadership has an advantage over transactional leadership in creating trust, respect and confidence in management.

In the context of culture change, some organizations go further, using indoctrination, or what Edgar Schein calls 'coercive persuasion'.[125] He says this is more typical of companies in some east Asian countries, and is known as *xinao*, or a 'cleansing of the mind.' As an example in the United States, Schein quotes GE's Jack Welch's non-negotiable requirement: 'if you wanted to stay at the company, you had to learn what he wanted you to learn. Heavy socialization is back in style in American corporations.' Schein also says that a culture change is more difficult than is perhaps appreciated and takes a long time – for example, 25 years in the case of Procter & Gamble. He argues that coercive persuasion is the only viable alternative to starting with a completely new set of employees who already possess the desired values. This view is debatable: this approach would not succeed in some cultures, such as that in the UK and other parts of Europe, and in any case it is not the only option.

The revitalization of values in a collaborative way as the basis for employee engagement is illustrated by the Strathclyde Fire & Rescue Service (SFR).[126] Focus group discussions were held with 800 of the 3,500 employees followed by a service-wide staff survey during 2009 and 2010. The resulting list of shared core values was composed of professionalism, respect, integrity, dedication and excellence, known as 'PRIDE'. The Head of Organisation Development for SFR, Diane Lauder, said that employee consultation and involvement in producing the core values was essential to their validity.

Business Ethics, Social Responsibility and Leadership

Moral values translated into rules of conduct in business are known as 'business ethics'. Business ethics are supposed to govern actions and behaviour. Ethics, philosopher Anthony Grayling says, 'is about one's "ethos", one's whole way of life … what sort of person one is'.[127] Business ethics are about the organization's way of doing business, the sort of organization it is – its culture.

A decline in ethical standards in business over the last decades of the twentieth century has continued into the first decade of the twenty-first century. An increasing emphasis on short-term financial performance in the commercial sectors, especially banking and finance, has accompanied this decline. Leadership is a key factor here. Leaders either encourage or discourage followers to behave in an ethical or unethical way;[128] and they influence ethical conformity.[129] Corporate culture, including business ethics, is established by the founders of organizations[130] and their successors.

In response to the spate of corporate scandals over greed and corporate wrongdoing, many university business schools have introduced business ethics and social responsibility courses into their MBA programmes. However, scepticism exists, and indeed has increased, towards the practice of business ethics and corporate social responsibility – evident in 2004 in the words of Philippe de Woot, chairman of the University of Louvain:

The protagonists of the recent financial scandals in the United States were successful students of business ethics in prestigious international business schools. Some even taught business ethics.[131]

Little has changed since.

Even apparently transformational leaders may act in their own self-interest rather than 'morally' correctly. Terry Price argues that leaders may act in accordance with other values that they think override general moral requirements.[132] Transformational leadership, he says, is about more than being authentic – being true to oneself – it is also about sacrificing some values when generally applicable moral requirements legitimately compete with them. Adolf Hitler, for example, while in some respects an 'effective' leader, infamously failed this crucial test. So have several nations' leaders and CEOs in business organizations in more recent times.

The ethical leadership challenge is to identify, display, promote and reinforce, in every way possible, corporate values and ethical standards of behaviour that both reflect the shared personal values of individuals in the organization and its other stakeholders *and* serve its vision, purpose and strategies. This is the basis for corporate social responsibility (CSR).

In 1962 the Nobel Prize-winning economist, Milton Friedman, famously argued that:

... there is one and only one social responsibility of business – to use its resources and engage in activities designed to increase its profits so long as it stays within the rules of the game ... Few trends could so thoroughly undermine the very foundations of our free society as the acceptance by corporate officials of a social responsibility other than to make as much money for their stock-holders as possible. This is a fundamentally subversive doctrine.[133]

We have come a long way since then in our thinking and practice in respect of CSR. CSR – concern for the environment, concern for the working conditions of suppliers' employees, and supporting human rights around the world – is justified, Geoffrey Colvin argues, on grounds of corporate self-interest – if only to maximize long-term profitability.[134] He argues that it is also justified on grounds of consumer demand: increasing capitalism and prosperity around the world has 'made room for those issues on the mainstream agenda'.

In the first edition of this book in 2006 I presented an array of studies showing the social *and* economic benefits of CSR and examples of its practice.[135] Yet CSR has not yet been sufficiently internalized in the culture of business organizations: indeed there are companies that practise CSR to the benefit of all stakeholders (including shareholders), but there are also companies that say they do so but do not. Good leadership entails showing the way with CSR. And this characterizes the best companies to work for.

The Best Companies to Work for[136]

Aristotle recognized the characteristic spirit and beliefs of a community – its *ethos*. A strong culture is characterized by values that inform and support the vision, purpose and strategies of the organization and are shared by everybody throughout it. And the most effective organizations are communities that share ethical values.[137] Where this is the case, leaders are most likely to get commitment to its vision, purpose and strategies. But what values? And how can leaders ensure the 'right' values are shared and inform everybody's behaviour?

Since the landmark book *In Search of Excellence*[138] was published in 1982, *Fortune* magazine has listed the most admired US companies. Manfred Kets de Vries suggests these are distinguished by a common set of values: trust, teamwork, customer focus, change orientation and a learning environment.[139] Leadership is one of the several reasons why companies are seen as good to work for. The best companies in the UK have the happiest and most productive employees. Becoming the best is not easy, but remaining one of the best is an even greater challenge. One company, however, managed to do this – as Number One for four successive years.

Every year *The Sunday Times* publishes its survey on the '100 Best Companies to Work for' in the UK. The 2007 survey covered some 150,000 employees in 650 companies. And in that year, for the fourth successive year, W.L. Gore & Associates of Livingston in Scotland – manufacturer of the famous 'Gore-Tex' fabrics and materials – ranked top overall in the mid-size firm category (between 250 and 4,999 employees).[140] Gore's success reflected a strong culture of shared values – a large overlap between the personal ethos of the staff and the corporate ethos of the company they work for. This was one outcome of truly effective leadership.[141] And the biggest improvement in general had been in the perceived extent to which senior managers 'truly live the values of [the] organisation'.[142] Managers had become better role models and more inspiring as leaders.[143]

While Gore's ranking has slipped in the intervening years to 2011 when it was ranked 13th overall, perhaps because other companies had improved more, the company has nevertheless maintained its reputation among its employees for innovation, creativity and teamwork, with no 'managers' or a traditional chain of command.[144] The 2011 report shows 85 per cent of employees 'love their job so much they wouldn't leave tomorrow even if they were offered another job', and 87 per cent say they are proud to work for the company.

In the best companies to work for, managers at all levels are respected and valued by employees for their leadership, employee well-being is taken seriously, the company is seen as contributing to the local community and society at large, and work is seen as fulfilling. Citing workplace engagement and its unique culture as a competitive advantage, Gore's manufacturing plant leader, John Housego, said: 'We are successful because of the ability of our associates [employees] to grow, explore and learn in an environment of freedom and trust.'[145]

Goldman Sachs, the banking, investment management and securities company, has fared very well as a 'best company to work for' in terms of leadership and values in the UK,[146] but its recent record in business ethics and social responsibility in the United States has almost branded it as a pariah. Our case study at the end of this chapter describes this contrast.

While employees who are highly engaged with their work and their company will always go the 'extra mile', those in leadership positions must never take advantage of this to the detriment of employees' well-being.[147] Goldman Sachs in the United States, if not in the UK, might be criticized in this respect. But the biggest enemy of any workplace, says Alastair McCall, the Best Companies survey report's editor, is worker disengagement, running at over 25 per cent in companies that failed to make the top 100 compared with about 9 per cent in the best companies to work for.[148]

Why do employees become disengaged? 'If the idea of people in your company working together towards a common goal looks about as likely as world peace, you are not alone', says Nick Rodrigues.[149] The survey results, he says, show many firms actively encouraging unhealthy competition with internal teams pulling in different directions, thereby creating a blame culture and a disillusioned workforce.

The surveys by *The Sunday Times* show that the best companies to work for do have exemplary leadership. To remain among these, as standards rise, however, means innovating in a highly competitive environment, says Richard Caseby, *The Sunday Times'* managing editor.[150] Jonathan Austin, chief executive of Best Companies Ltd, points out:

> [The real heroes of these surveys are] the companies which have taken the findings each year and used them to improve the working environment for their employees ... The companies that deserve the greatest recognition are those that view their appearance there as a journey rather than a destination.[151]

Effective leaders identify, display, promote and reinforce shared values that inform and support the vision, purpose and strategies. They behave and act with responsibility and conviction in doing so. We conclude this chapter with why this is the case and how they achieve this.

Leading with Responsibility and Conviction[152]

The right to lead, like all rights, carries with it *responsibility* – a legitimate requirement, duty or obligation to do something,[153] for example to use personal power in an ethical way. And it is hard to imagine effective leadership without showing that one is firmly convinced of something – namely *conviction*.[154]

Following the UK general election in May 2010, party leaders David Cameron and Nick Clegg (Conservatives and Liberal Democrats respectively) have, according to many commentators, shown both responsibility and conviction in joining their political parties together to form a coalition government. Both showed responsibility – to act in the national interest above and beyond party interest – as well as conviction – their strong shared belief that together they could form a viable and strong government that would reflect both party seats won and the popular vote. They both did so despite opposition from some followers in their respective parties, which was particularly strong in the case of the Liberal Democrats.

Psychologist Jo Silvester worked with political parties in the UK in identifying the competencies required to be a Member of Parliament – a role that entails both representation and leadership. The Conservatives identified conviction as 'seeking opportunities to present views and persuade others to adopt their ideas'; the Liberal Democrats emphasized 'values in action' – 'promoting beliefs and key messages through [one's] own actions'[155] – a notion that is virtually identical to conviction.

The practice of campaigning on the basis of a politician's own fundamental ideology, values or ideas rather than an existing consensus or popular position is known as conviction politics. Examples of conviction politicians are the UK's Margaret Thatcher and Gordon Brown, and in the United States George W. Bush and Senator Paul Wellstone. Conviction politicians appear more honest: they say what they believe rather than what the audience wants to hear. But leaders are accountable not just for what they preach but also for practising it, as we discussed earlier with respect to integrity. They are accountable in the sense that they have an obligation or duty to *answer for and explain* the fulfilment or non-fulfilment of a responsibility.[156]

American leadership consultant Eileen Rogers explains the importance of leaders having conviction:

> **To sustain the vision despite adversity, challenges, obstacles and delays, leaders must have personal conviction in the mission, believe that it can be achieved, and create a new strategy to ensure that the vision endures.**[157]

She makes the point that conviction entails optimism, which Warren Bennis says is 'all about possibilities, change, hope ... without [this], how can any leader succeed?'[158] One of the most prominent examples of a charismatic leader with conviction and optimism is Aung San Suu Kyi, the leader of the Burmese democracy movement and Nobel Peace Prize winner. She has stood up for her unrelenting belief in democracy and freedom in the face of great adversity under many years' house arrest by the military junta in Burma.

Conviction in a leader is a prerequisite for influencing, motivating and inspiring people – for engaging them in wanting to do what needs to be done. For example, believing in the vision or purpose of your organization is essential to engaging people in pursuing it. But in positions of leadership there are risks associated with strong convictions, for example arrogance, hubris and the fostering of 'dissensus'.[159]

Max Weber, the father of modern social science, pointed out the relationship between the two sets of ethical virtues – conviction (*Gesinnungsethik*) and responsibility (*Verantwortungsethik*).[160] He said that the virtue of responsibility was in understanding the possible causal effect of an action and then choosing how to achieve a desired end. And the virtue of conviction, he said, was in choosing the right end. Responsibility and conviction were therefore complementary to each other.

Taking on a leadership role entails responsibilities. It entails accepting the obligation to engage and enable people to pursue a vision, purpose and supporting strategies and to behave ethically and in accordance with the values of the organization. It also entails accepting personal accountability for success and failure. 'Too many leaders', Robert L. Joss, Dean of Stanford Graduate School of Business, said in his valedictory speech, 'get caught up in thinking about power rather than their responsibility to those they lead'.[161]

C.K. Prahalad, the distinguished management thinker who died in April 2010, always ended his MBA and executive education courses by sharing his perspective on how his course members could – and should – become responsible managers, and exhorting them to 'strive to achieve success with responsibility'.[162] This message never changed in 33 years.

Responsibility without conviction however, is unengaging; and conviction without responsibility is impotent. Leadership requires both conviction and responsibility in showing the way by identifying, displaying, promoting and reinforcing shared values that will inform and support the vision, purpose and strategies. Effective leaders behave and act with responsibility and conviction in doing so.

Shared values and beliefs are 'the templates through which groups and group members interpret their shared experience ... [and] ... are an essential component of group culture'.[163] So now let us consider leadership in the broader context of culture.

What is Culture?

'Culture is to people what software is to computers – the programming of people's thinking and behaving', say Martha Maznevski and Joe DiStefano.[164] This simile raises a question about the compatibility of the software with – to introduce a metaphor – the hardware or the operating system: a question of cross-cultural fit and conflict.

Culture has been described in many ways, and it is difficult to find a consensus here. In any case, culture describes what an organization *is*.[165] Andrew Leigh and Michael Maynard see culture as 'a heady mixture of vision, values, tradition, ethos and self-image'.[166] Harry Triandis states that culture is reflected in 'shared cognitions, standard operating procedures, and unexamined assumptions'.[167] And Work Systems Associates describes culture as:

> ... the lifestyle of [the] organization: the core values; hidden assumptions or beliefs; [the] systems, policies, and procedures; the way [it does] business every day.[168]

Understanding the corporate culture – and, by implication, the national culture in the case of expatriate managers – is essential for effective leadership.

[The] ability to perceive the limitations of one's own culture and to develop the culture adaptively is the essence and ultimate challenge of leadership. The most important message for leaders at this point is 'Try to understand culture, give it its due, and ask yourself how well you can begin to understand the culture in which you are embedded.'[169]

The case for the importance of corporate culture in business organizations has been strongly argued. For example, Gideon Kunda and Stephen Barley say:

Culture enhances social integration; social integration eliminates the need for bureaucracy, and increases levels of investment which, in turn, enhance performance and productivity. Thus, by manipulating culture, substantial increments in profitability should accrue.[170]

However, Jennifer Chatman and Sandra Eunyoung Cha take a more measured view:

We [do] not claim that by simply managing culture, leaders will be assured of organizational success, or by neglecting culture they will be doomed to failure. Leveraging culture is but one of a number of key leadership tools. We [do] claim, however, that by actively managing culture, an organization will be more likely to deliver on its strategic objectives in the long run.[171]

Our understanding of culture was advanced in the early 1980s by three complementary, hugely popular books that focused our attention on vision, values and leadership: William Ouchi's *Theory Z*, Terrence Deal and Allan Kennedy's *Corporate Cultures: The Rites and Rituals of Corporate Life*, and Tom Peters and Robert Waterman's *In Search of Excellence*.[172] Ouchi's *Theory Z* argued for the need to integrate the typically Western values of individual achievement and advancement with the Japanese sense of community.[173] This sense of community, however, has its downside. Michiyo Nakamoto argues that Japan's culture of group solidarity may have to give way to the entrepreneurial spirit of the individual.[174] He quotes Martin Reeves at Boston Consulting Group as saying that such group solidarity has often counted for more than results, and Ichiro Hatanaka of Accenture as suggesting:

... the skill that has been most valued at Japanese companies has been the ability to coordinate the various elements of the group so as to maintain the harmony of the whole. And that is why Japan's business leaders break down in tears as they announce a drastic restructuring or a corporate failure: they have failed the group.

Organizational Culture and Leadership

The literature in this area is rather sparse, though the indications are that leadership has a crucial role in shaping the culture of the organization.[175] Bernard Bass argued that transactional leaders worked within the organizational (corporate) culture while transformational leaders changed it.[176] And Edgar Schein suggested that leaders shaped the culture of the organization in the early stages of the organizational life cycle but their

actions and behaviour were increasingly influenced by it as the organization matured.[177]
Founding an organization as an entrepreneur, for example, will require a clear focus on
a vision and purpose for it together with core values that will support the vision and
purpose and inform the organization's strategies in pursuing them.

Terrence Deal and Allan Kennedy identified five components of a strong organizational culture: the organization's external environment, corporate values, the existence of heroic figures in the organization, rites and rituals, and the cultural network.[178]
And Tom Peters and Robert Waterman discovered eight cultural features that characterized 'excellent' companies: a bias for action, closeness to the customer, autonomy
and entrepreneurship, productivity through people, being hands-on and value-driven,
sticking to the knitting, having a simple form and lean staffing, and having simultaneously loose–tight properties.[179]

Meanwhile Emmanuel Ogbonna and Lloyd Harris caution that 'the complexities
and intricacies of the concept of organizational culture have done more to confound
executives and researchers than to enlighten them'.[180] They explain that organizational culture is not the same as organizational climate or power and politics, and it is
not a unitary concept.

Warner Burke and George Litwin define culture similarly as 'the way we do things
around here' and the collection of overt and covert rules, values and principles that
guide organizational behaviour, and climate as:

> **The collective current impressions, expectations, and feelings that members of local work
> units have that, in turn, affect their relations with their boss, with one another, and with
> other units.[181]**

Organizational culture comprises multiple sub-cultures, typically of a departmental,
occupational and professional, and geographical kind. Ogbonna and Harris carried out
an in-depth case study of three UK retailing companies and found that the cultural
perspectives of their employees were directly linked to their hierarchical position in
their organizations.[182] Head office managers tended to perceive organizational culture
in an integrative way, emphasizing consistencies (and possibly neglecting sub-culture
differences). Store managers perceived it in a differentiated way, recognizing the existence of sub-cultures (e.g. head office) and balancing their demands. Shop floor staff
perceived organizational culture as fragmented and in a constant state of flux, and also
indicated confusion about the company's values.

Ogbonna and Harris concluded that 'any change initiative which is based solely on
head office values and perceptions is likely to be ineffective'. They suggested that:

> **There is an inherent difficulty in achieving an organization-wide consensus in values ...
> [and that] it may be advisable to ... recognize the existence of subcultural differences ...
> and look for ways of reconciling only the key differences which directly impact upon the
> performance of the organization.**

A study of a large Danish insurance company by Geert Hofstede also revealed not one
corporate culture but three distinct sub-cultures – a professional sub-culture, an

administrative sub-culture and a customer-interface sub-culture.[183] Failure to understand this led to values-based rifts and adverse consequences in the form of losses and a change in ownership and top management.

The major manifestations of culture, according to Edgar Schein, are:

* The behavioural regularities observed when people interact – such as language, traditions and rituals.
* Group norms, standards and values.
* Espoused or articulated values.
* A formal philosophy.
* Rules of the 'game'.
* A corporate climate – the feeling portrayed through the organization's physical layout and the way people relate to one another.
* Embedded skills or the special abilities of the organization.
* Habits of thinking, mental models and other linguistic paradigms.
* Shared meanings.
* 'Root metaphors', or integrating symbols.
* Formal rituals and celebrations.[184]

Corporate values are perceived in the artefacts of corporate culture: organizational structure, office layout, dress codes, stories and legends, the distribution and sharing of power, reward systems, communication style and methods, behavioural norms and expectations, unwritten rules, and the taken-for-granted beliefs and assumptions at the heart of corporate culture.

Values affect behaviour, and behaviour affects values. Karen Legge says:

> ... [culture] is both produced and reproduced through the negotiation and sharing of symbols and meanings – it is both the shaper of human action and the outcome of the process of social creation and reproduction.[185]

However, in building a corporate culture, Stanley Deetz and colleagues say:

> ... leaders have more direct control in shaping communication patterns and overt behaviors than they do in changing deep-rooted value systems. Therefore ... leaders [need to] create and change a culture through the way they communicate ... [affecting] the espoused values, norms, and rules of their organization through visioning ... [shaping] employees' identification with the organization ... [and framing] organizational stories, myths, and everyday communication ... in line with the values that are best for the organization.[186]

The need for leaders to create and manage organizational culture is consistent with the increasingly accepted importance of organization-wide leadership – shared or distributed leadership.[187]

Culture operates at the emotional level and therefore is a powerful force. Janice Beyer and David Nino suggest five ways in which culture shapes emotions:[188]

✳ *Managing the anxieties arising from uncertainties.* Organizational culture, Edgar Schein argues, provides meaning, stability and comfort for members.[189]

✳ *Providing ways to express emotions,* for example rites and rituals. Rites and rituals are held on to long after they have ceased to be useful because they have emotional meaning. Steve Fineman says it is our self-control, and not managerial control, that manages the tension between private feelings and public display and enables social control.[190]

✳ *Encouraging and discouraging emotional experience.* Culture, say Dennis Tourish and Ashly Pinnington, may shape emotions in a subtle way, sometimes insidiously, whereby people, assured they are empowered and free, may 'roam [but] at the end of a leash, constrained ... by the governing cultural assumptions of the organization'.[191]

✳ *Engendering identification and a commitment to the organization.* Cultures provide a social identity and thereby an emotional bond or attachment among organizational members and with the organization itself.

✳ *Producing ethnocentrism.* A 'strong' culture is characterized by 'like-minded, like-feeling, like-behaving employees' who may yield a competitive advantage, say Dennis Tourish and Ashly Pinnington,[192] but might also create an unhealthy organization, for example in the case of a lack of diversity and a lack of openness to diversity.[193] The dangers of 'groupthink'[194] and unquestioning compliance or obedience in respect of orders from superiors[195] are well known.

Martha Maznevski and Joe DiStefano have developed a Cultural Orientations Framework that identifies six areas that need to be addressed in considering culture:

✳ Relationship of people to the environment: harmony, mastery or subjugation.
✳ Relations among people: collective, individualistic or hierarchical.
✳ Mode of activity: being, doing or thinking.
✳ Human nature: 'blank slate', predisposition to 'goodness' or predisposition to 'badness'.
✳ Time: monochronic (linear time, requiring its measurement and management), polychronic (time viewed as flexible), and past, present or future orientation.
✳ Space: sense of shared or personal ownership (public or private).[196]

A distinctive and strong corporate culture can give one business a competitive advantage over another in the same industry.[197] Companies that outperform their competitors and enjoy better returns on their investment, higher net income growth and bigger increases in share value tend to have stronger corporate cultures, where values and behavioural norms are widely shared and strongly held.[198] For example, in their analysis of the Silicon Valley cluster of interconnected companies, John Micklethwait and Adrian Wooldridge identify what they call 'the ten habits of highly successful clusters':

✳ A strong belief in meritocracy.
✳ A very high tolerance of failure.
✳ A tolerance of 'treachery' – talent-intensive businesses inevitably lose both secrets and employees.

* Collaboration – short-term alliances between companies and individuals.
* Risk orientation – one winning idea pays for scores of failures.
* Re-investment – the money that is made is ploughed back into the company.
* Change orientation – getting stuck in a rut risks demise.
* An obsession with a winning product.
* The opportunity and achievement orientation – success is admired and aspired to rather than begrudged.
* The sharing of wealth – founders share proceeds with employees when firms are sold.[199]

Emmanuel Ogbonna and Lloyd Harris carried out a multi-industry study in the UK involving 1,000 business units, investigating the relationship between leadership style, organizational performance and organizational culture.[200] They identified four distinct types of culture – innovative, competitive, bureaucratic and communitarian – and three leadership styles – participative, supportive and instrumental (akin to directive or transactional leadership). Performance was measured by a composite of customer satisfaction, sales growth, sales volume, market share and competitive advantage.

They found that competitive and innovative cultures were associated with organizational performance. They also found that strongly held shared values were associated with organizational performance, but only if the organizational culture was oriented towards the external environment. With regard to leadership style, they found 'significant, indirect pervasive effects on organizational performance' and strong causal associations with competitive and innovative cultures (and hence on organizational performance). Supportive and participative leadership styles were positively related to organizational performance, and instrumental leadership was negatively related. Ogbonna and Harris's overall conclusion was that the organizational culture mediated the relationship between leadership style and organizational performance.

Jesper B. Sorensen found that firms with stronger cultures also performed more consistently, except when industry volatility increased.[201] The reason, Stephen Ackroyd and Philip Crowdy said, could be that a strong culture was able to impede adaptability:

> The findings of a good deal of case study work in industry, and particularly that with an ethnographic or an anthropological focus, have suggested that work cultures are highly distinctive, resilient and resistant to change.[202]

Employees are often more satisfied when they work in a 'strong culture' in which values are widely shared.[203] But too strong a commitment to the values and 'desired' behaviours might decrease flexibility and inhibit creative problem solving.[204] Stanley Deetz and colleagues suggest:

> ... a strong culture can become a limitation when important shared beliefs and values interfere with the goals of the organization or members and the direction it needs to go to

stay competitive ... [it] can actually hurt an organization or even lead to unethical behavior. Therefore, a strong culture may best be thought of as a balance between extremes.[205]

Empirical studies of the relationship between corporate culture and performance, however, do not always show clear-cut results. One study, by John Kotter and James Heskett, for example, showed a positive but weak correlation between the strength of the corporate culture and economic success.[206] However, what they did find was that high-performing companies – those producing a shareholder value four times greater over 10 years compared with low-performers and a return on capital of 11.3 per cent compared with 7.7 per cent – were characterized by the greater value they placed on leadership, customers, employees and shareholders. And 'visionary companies', in which vision was not merely the preserve of the CEO but was embedded in the organization, were differentiated from 'also rans' by displaying an historical continuity in values, actions consistent with values, investment in people, objectives beyond profit, and investment for the long term.[207] Their average return on an investment over 50 years was 15 times the stock market average.

David Buchanan and Andrzej Huczynski comment, '... the popular view that a strong corporate culture [leads] to economic success [is] just plain wrong'.[208] Perhaps the truth of the matter, however, is that the corporate culture should not just be *strong* but should also be *positive* in terms of the values supporting and informing the organization's vision, purpose and strategies. So a question for a leader is to decide whether the organization's 'strong' culture is the appropriate culture in relation to its vision, purpose and strategies. The existing culture may be at odds with these – a huge challenge for leadership. This question must be addressed using input from all stakeholders, particularly employees. For this to happen, employees need to be empowered to provide such input, a question considered in Chapter 8 on leadership and empowerment.

Ross Perot, chairman of Perot Systems Corporation, emphasized the importance of corporate culture in the company's 2001 annual report by stating the intention to 'Create an environment where the hopes and dreams of every person can materialize if the company is successful.'[209] The company believed that its 'unique culture' – reflecting the values of initiative, flexibility, accountability and integrity – produced 'energy and results'. Its annual report was itself unique in providing examples of how its values were translated into real-life behaviour.

Founders of companies can create organizational cultures that will often endure long after their passing.[210] They will often create a company in order to put their deeply held values into practice. These values will appear in their companies' statements of purpose and in their visions of a desired future as well as in 'the way we do things around here'. So why do such organizational cultures endure?

One explanation comes from the study of memes, a term coined by Richard Dawkins.[211] Memes are items of information through which culture is inherited. These lead to 'copycat' behaviour and enduring cultural characteristics such as dress, diet, ceremonies, customs and technologies.[212] Richard Hooker gives examples of memes that characterize the way proponents of 'manoeuvre warfare' talk about the Wehrmacht's *Sturm und Drang, Schwerpunkt* and *Auftragstaktik* rather than 'main effort' and 'mission tactics'.[213] He argues that in talking this way the speakers are promoting an authoritative and warlike image characteristic of the German Second World War military machine. Modern examples of memes are the use of the terms 'boat people' and 'asylum seekers' and George W. Bush's 'axis of evil'. 'Mimetic engineering' is the term for embedding desirable values into the collective minds of people in an organization through the use of memes.

Successful leaders create strong, positive cultures: the culture supports the vision and purpose of the organization or group and facilitates their pursuit. Deetz and colleagues say:

> If company values are consistent with national and community values and with different levels in the organization and across the industry, the strength of the culture is increased. If the various systems are contradictory, the strength is reduced ... Cultural strength is increased when company values are carefully integrated with deeply held values of employees ... [and when] pay systems, employee relations, and espoused values are consistent.[214]

Research in the early 1990s reported by Amin Rajan showed that a large majority of companies still had 'strong elements of paternalism and bureaucracy in their culture'.[215] This research also noted that 'their change programmes sought to replace them by elements of democratic culture of high performance and employee empowerment' and that some 'also tried to embrace elements of the anarchic culture of excellence and continuous improvement', on which the 'jury' was still out seven years later. One problem, according to a chief executive whom Rajan quotes, was the 'leadership gap':

> It is one thing to talk about creating a new organisation for the new age. But not creating the requisite leadership qualities at the outset is like putting the cart before the horse.

Shared values and homogeneous corporate cultures are strong in Japanese companies. Values underpin the vision and purpose of a Japanese company and inform its strategies, even to the extent that *wa* – harmony – among employees may be prioritized over profitability. Corporate visions are strong in Japan as well and more enduring than in the West, reflecting corporate values developed over a long period and service to Japanese society as a whole and not just the company's stakeholders. Strategy tends to be more intuitive, a creative art, and people-centred rather than task-centred. And empowerment tends to take place more with groups or teams (collectives) than with individuals. Engaging with followers or employees, however, is not achieved through rhetoric and charisma as much as through leading by example, listening humbly to employees, coolness and modesty.[216] This comment on corporate culture in the context of national culture leads us now to explore national culture and its relationship to leadership.

National Culture and Leadership

Can there be 'leadership *sans frontières*'?[217] Those who work in multinational or global organizations may have a particular interest in the similarities and differences in the behaviour of effective leaders in different cultures. In the UK, Tom Cannon says, the nature of effective leadership is changing because we have moved from a mono-culture to a multi-culture.[218]

Examples of areas in business in which understanding cross-cultural aspects of leadership styles and behaviour can help are dealing with global competition, international mergers and acquisitions, assessing new market opportunities, the international transfer of executives, a localization of management, and international management development programmes. As a result of working in multinational organizations managers can better predict the problems arising in adopting parent-company organizational policies and leadership practices. Cross-cultural studies suggest the need to avoid global generalizations and to focus on local cultures.[219]

Values define both corporate and national cultural differences. So if effective leaders create a strong culture of shared values, is leadership universal or culture specific? Cultural differences pose a special challenge for leaders in global and multinational organizations. For example:

> **Exporting participative leadership to countries with authoritarian cultures is like preaching Jeffersonian democracy to [those] who believe in the divine right of kings.**[220]

Research evidence tends to support travellers' tales about differences in the behaviour of leaders in different cultures, says Bernard Bass.[221] But popular views or stereotypes of cultural characteristics do not always stand up. For example:

> **The idea of consensus has a powerful appeal for Japanese, who seem convinced, despite abundant evidence to the contrary, that their society and culture are built on a foundation of *wa*, harmony.**[222]

The way of Lao Tzu, however, is still reflected today in Japanese culture. John Adair writes:

> **... the Japanese practise a more self-effacing style of leadership than is customary in the West. In Japan the group is still valued more highly than the individual.**[223]

Yet 'leadership' is a universal phenomenon: there are leaders everywhere, and they exercise leadership. In democracies effective leaders gain the voluntary commitment of people – not merely their compliance – to strive towards goals: they get people to *want* to do the things that will help the organization succeed. And they empower them to do so. According to a survey by the PA Consulting Group, universal aspects of leadership across cultures are vision, inspiring people, and creating a learning organization.[224] British Telecom focuses on five key skills and characteristics in its cross-cultural leaders and their leadership development: emotional resilience, flexibility and openness, perceptual acuity and sensitivity, personal autonomy, and humility.[225]

In a comparative study of Southeast Asian and UK managers, the Southeast Asians emerged as seeing themselves as significantly more directive and less delegative than UK managers would see themselves.[226] Both groups were about the same in their use of the consultative and participative styles. Southeast Asian managers, however, varied more in their use of the latter two styles.

The greater directiveness and lesser delegativeness of Southeast Asian managers are not surprising. The cultures they work in are generally more authoritarian than UK culture. In some traditional Asian cultures, people expect to be told what to do and how to do it. They regard initiative and decision making on direction and methods as the manager's responsibility. Moreover, they do not necessarily even want to be consulted. Being consulted about what to do or how to do it may be seen as a weakness in the manager (suggesting that he or she does not know) rather than a strength – helping the individual to develop and grow or gaining his or her commitment through the ownership of ideas. This means that participative (Western) management practices such as management-by-objectives may not work as well as they do in the West. Southeast Asian managers might well find their subordinates more dependent on them. They may also find themselves more overloaded as the result of a lack of delegation. The greater variation in Southeast Asian managers' use of consultation and participation might reflect a more heterogeneous management culture than in the UK, with its mix of Western-educated managers and traditional Asian managers.

Consultative and participative styles of leadership in the Near East and Middle East, according to Hayat Kabasakal and Ali Dastmalchian, cannot be equated to those in the West.[227] The consultative style, they say, is used to 'pander to egos' rather than to improve the quality of decision making, and the participative style is used to induce feelings of belonging to the group rather than to achieve consensus on decisions. Mansour Javidan and Ali Dastmalchian suggest, in respect of Iranian managers, much like Southeast Asian managers, that they 'have become accustomed to autocratic leaders who make decisions without much participation from their employees … They expect the leader to develop a vision and communicate it to them.'[228]

Southeast Asian managers also emerged as seeing themselves as more *laissez-faire* than UK managers do.[229] Perhaps Southeast Asian culture conditions them to avoid conflict, and therefore to avoid confronting people, and to be more 'psychologically distant' from their subordinates. The greater use of management-by-exception that also emerged might reflect their greater workload as a result of a disinclination to delegate. And, with respect to their greater use of contingent reward, other findings suggest that extrinsic rewards like money are more effective for Southeast Asian managers in motivating employees than for UK managers. Performance-related pay has become increasingly controversial in the UK in recent years. Uma Jogulu, using Bass and Avolio's Multifactor Leadership Questionnaire and objective ratings of their performance, found the same cultural differences in leadership behaviour between Malaysian and Australian managers.[230] Higher performers in Malaysia were transactional leaders and in Australia were transformational leaders.

A greater psychological distance between Southeast Asian managers and their subordinates may also explain another finding: their lesser individualized consideration. In general, the differences in leadership styles and in transactional and transformation leadership between Southeast Asian countries and the UK are consistent with Geert Hofstede's model.[231] According to this model, national cultures will vary in terms of power distance, uncertainty avoidance, independence and 'masculinity/femininity'.

While transformational leadership has universal applicability and similar outcomes, more specific leadership behaviours, such as a directive style, vary in respect of outcomes.[232] This is true also for a participative style, which is more effective in egalitarian cultures.[233]

A study of national cultural differences in a large international chemical company across several European countries and including the United States revealed differences in people-oriented leadership but not in task-oriented leadership.[234] For example, managers in the Czech Republic tended to rely more on their own experience when making decisions than UK managers did.[235] This has implications for empowerment, participation and consequently the commitment of those who have to implement management decisions. The Latin European countries value people-oriented leadership more.

Cultural values appear to affect organizational commitment. Arzu Wasti, in a study in Turkey, found that, for employees who endorse individualist values, satisfaction with work is a key determinant of emotional attachment to the organization and a feeling of obligation to remain with it.[236] On the other hand, for those with collectivist values, satisfaction with the supervisor is more important.

That many values differ between the West and Asia is scarcely contested. Lee Kuan Yew, former prime minister of Singapore, has frequently argued this. But Malaysia's former prime minister, Dr Mahathir Mohamad, said: 'Asian values are actually universal values and Western people used to practise the same values'.[237] He has a point.

Fons Trompenaars proposes that the solution to the problem of cultural differences is not ethnocentric domination or even compromise, but the reconciling of opposing values.[238] The challenge to organizational leadership is to develop a corporate culture that incorporates those human values that are universal, recognizes the diversity of other values across national cultures, and reconciles those values within the corporate culture that supports the organization's vision and strategies. Sally Lansdell quotes, for example, global management consultants McKinsey & Co. as achieving just such a balance.[239] By 1999, she says, only 40 per cent of its 4,800 consultants were from the United States with the rest representing some 80 nationalities. All consultants were expected to adhere to a set of corporate values and aspirations, for example an obligation to see things from others' points of view (empathy). But within this framework there is freedom to act in line with what is best for the company.

The GLOBE Project and Follow-up Studies

A major contribution to understanding the relationship between national (societal) culture and leadership was made by the long-term GLOBE project which began in 1993.[240] This project sought to identify the 'etic' (the universal characteristics) and the 'emic' (the culture-specific characteristics) of effective leadership. It aimed to develop a culturally endorsed implicit leadership theory of shared cognitions and beliefs about leadership in culturally defined groups. It also sought to answer, among others, the following questions:

1. Are there leadership behaviours and attributes that are universally effective across cultures?
2. Are there some that are effective only in some cultures?
3. How do societal and organizational cultures affect leadership behaviour that is effective?
4. What is the effect of violating cultural norms relevant to leadership behaviour?

The project gathered data from 17,370 managers in some 951 organizations in 62 societies. It studied nine cultural dimensions drawing on previous work on culture, including Hofstede's. These were uncertainty avoidance, power distance, societal collectivism, group collectivism, gender egalitarianism, assertiveness, future orientation, performance orientation, and humane orientation.[241]

The GLOBE studies empirically derived 21 primary leadership behaviours, which, as a result of second-order factor analysis, reduced to six global leadership dimensions, the core of the 'culturally endorsed leadership theory' (CLT):

- ☀ Charismatic/Value-based.
- ☀ Team-oriented.
- ☀ Participative.
- ☀ Autonomous.
- ☀ Humane.
- ☀ Self-protective.[242]

Seven of the 21 primary leadership behaviours from across five of the leadership dimensions (all except team-oriented) emerged as culturally contingent. These were:

- ☀ Status Conscious.
- ☀ Bureaucratic (formerly labelled Procedural).
- ☀ Autonomous.
- ☀ Face Saving.
- ☀ Humane.
- ☀ Self-sacrificial/Risk Taking.
- ☀ Internally Competitive (formerly Conflict Inducing).[243]

A sub-study of over 6,000 managers in European countries revealed that leadership concepts varied by culture within Europe.[244] Countries that shared cultural values also shared leadership concepts. However, Deanne Den Hartog and colleagues found that certain aspects of charismatic/transformational leadership are strongly and universally endorsed across cultures.[245]

A qualitative analysis of data from 25 countries in the GLOBE project used data from focus groups, ethnographic interviews, the media, participant observations and unobtrusive measurements to draw conclusions about conceptions of leadership that were (a) universal – for example, that the leader is inspirational – and (b) culture-specific – for example, that the leader invests in the future.[246]

An analysis of the GLOBE data for future orientation – planning and forecasting, investing in the future, and delaying gratification – revealed that Iran, Kuwait, Turkey and Qatar were similar to one another but below the world average.[247] The concept of 'fate' or destiny in Islam[248] – that all past and future deeds are pre-ordained – influences future orientation negatively. However, this appears to be true only at the overall societal level and not in organizations, where leaders are expected to be future-oriented and 'visionary'.[249]

As part of the GLOBE project, Felix Brodbeck and colleagues found that middle-level managers in the telecommunications, food processing and finance industries in

Germany shared a strong performance orientation and a lack of compassion and interpersonal consideration.[250] The authors believed that sensitivity to the feelings of people was an important development need among business leaders in Germany to cope successfully in the future with the challenges of globalization and multicultural teams.

Members of the original GLOBE team themselves pointed out two weaknesses in study reports:[251]

1. The reduction of leadership factors to six entails losing rich data that were camouflaged. Mansour Javidan and colleagues gave an example. Charismatic/ value-based leadership was one of the six CLT dimensions and universally endorsed. However, one of the primary leadership factors that contributed to this CLT dimension was self-sacrificial leadership, which was highly culturally contingent (namely, endorsed in some cultures but not in others).
2. The 21 primary dimensions comprised a mix of leadership attributes that were variously endorsed universally, rejected universally, or culturally contingent.

Javidan and colleagues therefore, in a further analysis of the GLOBE data, focused on the more specific primary factors and on the clearly culturally contingent factors within them. They found strong support for the connection between both organizational culture and national culture and leadership in the following ways:[252]

- ※ Power distance predicts status-conscious, bureaucratic and internally competitive leadership behaviour.
- ※ Institutional collectivist values predict bureaucratic, non-autonomous (dependent) and self-sacrificial leadership behaviour.
- ※ Uncertainty avoidance predicts status-conscious and bureaucratic leadership behaviour.
- ※ Humane orientation predicts humane leadership behaviour [hardly surprising!].
- ※ Performance orientation predicts self-sacrificial and non-face-saving (not avoiding embarrassing or shaming oneself or others) leadership behaviour.
- ※ In-group collectivism predicts non-autonomous (dependent) and self-sacrificial leadership behaviour.
- ※ Gender egalitarianism predicts internally non-competitive leadership behaviour.

Mansour Javidan and colleagues said that further research into the actual manifestations of leadership behaviours and their outcomes in different cultures had been carried out and was in the process of being reported on. Meanwhile, they suggested that the practical implications of the findings so far on cultural commonalities, similarities and differences for leadership were as follows:

- ※ The relationships between organizational culture and leadership and national culture and leadership need to be examined and considered together, not in isolation.[253]
- ※ The role of global leaders in engaging individuals, groups and organizations in different parts of the world will be enhanced by an understanding of their diversity and an understanding of how cultural upbringing and organizational values shape the implicit leadership theories of managers in different cultures.[254]

☀ Global leaders who reflect managers' implicit leadership theories in different cultures are likely to be better equipped and better able to engage them, thereby building stronger relationships with their stakeholders around the world.[255]

CASE STUDY: CORPORATE VALUES AT GOLDMAN SACHS

Goldman Sachs in the UK took the Number One slot overall in *The Sunday Times* 100 Best Companies To Work For survey in 2007 in the big companies category (5,000-plus employees).[256] A global leader in banking, investment management and the securities industry, the company headed the 'Leadership' ranking by a large margin. Its striking leadership characteristics were perceived as the company's vision of the future, strong ethical principles, its senior managers living the values, the leadership skills of the senior management team, and the huge level of employee engagement with the company. Employee engagement was so strong that it was producing an adverse impact on the ratings for personal well-being (e.g. excessively long working hours), though 'not enough to dim [employees'] esprit de corps'.[257]

Several events in the three years after 2007, however, revealed that, while Goldman Sachs in the UK may have been a great place to work, in the United States it had misled investors and 'overlooked' its obligations to its customers, calling into question its ethical behaviour.[258] *The Times* pointed out 'a severe cultural problem for the bank in appearing to safeguard its own interests to the detriment of those of its customers'.[259]

In July 2010 Goldman Sachs agreed to pay a fine of US$550 million to settle accusations that it had misled investors over a mortgage-backed security. Moreover, the company had allegedly been a major player in the American banking crash of 2008 and had helped Greece to mask the true amount of its indebtedness. In the words of *Rolling Stone* magazine, the company had behaved like 'a great vampire squid wrapped around the face of humanity, relentlessly jamming its blood funnel into anything that smells like money'.[260] On 20 July 2010 the company reported a slide in earnings of 82 per cent in the second quarter.

Goldman Sachs is a prime example of how leadership at the top is critical to the sustained well-being of a company and its reputation. Sathnam Sanghera suggests the problem was the company's internal culture: what made the company peerless in the world of finance had also made it 'the most dysfunctional institution this side of the Simpson family'.[261] He says serious issues were an excessive insistence on conformity, chronic 'workaholism', sanctimoniousness and extreme arrogance, with the 'central belief that working at Goldman is the best thing that can happen to you ... The basic problem with Goldman Sachs is that it has succumbed to evil.' *The Times* commented:

> There will be questions whether Lloyd Blankfein, the bank's chief executive and a gifted trader, is the right leader for such an institution. The bank sorely needs statesmanship. Goldman once quietly prided itself on being a relationship bank that, first and foremost, cared for its clients. In the years since its flotation and under Mr Blankfein's leadership, the biggest charge against it is that it has made a fortune and lost its culture.[262]

(Continued)

(Continued)

In the UK, however, the company has continued to do well. In *The Sunday Times* 25 Best Big Companies to Work For survey in the UK in 2011, Goldman Sachs International ranked second for the second successive year. The survey reported high levels of satisfaction among staff with respect to leadership, personal growth, how they felt about the company, giving something back, and getting a fair deal. Pay and benefits were seen to be second to none, as might be expected. And, as in 2007, staff still saw their bosses as 'truly [living] the values of the firm', as good listeners, and as having two co-chief executives who 'run the organisation on sound moral principles ... and are a source of inspiration'. Goldman Sachs in the UK won the 2011 'Best Leader' special award.

Case Discussion Questions

1. What differences with respect to leadership, values and culture do you see in Goldman Sachs in the UK and the United States? What do you attribute them to?
2. Is Lloyd Blankfein 'the right leader' for Goldman Sachs? Why or why not?
3. Can a high level of employee engagement ever be bad?

 Further Reading

N.M. Ashkanasy, C. Wilderom and M.F. Peterson, Editors (2000), *Handbook of Organizational Culture and Climate.* Thousand Oaks, CA: SAGE Publications.

Joel Bakan (2004), *The Corporation: The Pathological Pursuit of Profit and Power.* New York: Free Press.

Andrew D. Brown (1995), *Organisational Culture.* London: Pitman.

Jagdeep S. Chokar, Felix C. Brodbeck and Robert J. House (2007), *Culture and Leadership Across the World: The GLOBE Book of In-Depth Studies of 25 Societies.* Hove, East Sussex: Psychology Press.

Joanne B. Ciulla (1998), *Ethics: The Heart of Leadership.* Westport, CT: Praeger.

James C. Collins and Jerry I. Porras (1997), *Built To Last: Successful Habits of Visionary Companies,* Second Edition. London: Century/Random House Business Books.

Mary L. Connerley and Paul B. Pedersen (2005), *Leadership in a Diverse and Multicultural Environment: Developing Awareness, Knowledge, and Skills.* Thousand Oaks, CA: SAGE Publications.

Andrew Crane and Dirk Matten (2007), *Business Ethics,* Second Edition. Oxford: Oxford University Press.

Stanley A. Deetz, Sarah J. Tracy and Jennifer L. Simpson (2000), *Leading Organizations through Transition.* Thousand Oaks, CA: SAGE Publications.

Francis Fukuyama (1995), *Trust: The Social Values and the Creation of Prosperity.* London: Hamish Hamilton.

David Grayson and Adrian Hodges (2004), *Corporate Social Opportunity! 7 Steps to Make Corporate Social Responsibility Work for Your Business.* Sheffield: Greenleaf Publishing.

Geert Hofstede, Gert Jan Hofstede and Michael Minkov (2010), *Cultures and Organizations: Software for the Mind,* Third Edition: *Intercultural Cooperation and Its Importance for Survival.* Maidenhead: McGraw-Hill Professional.

Robert J. House, Paul J. Hanges, Mansour Javidan, Peter W. Dorfman and Vipin Gupta, Editors (2004), *Culture, Leadership, and Organizations: The GLOBE Study of 62 Societies.* Thousand Oaks, CA: SAGE Publications.

Marek Kohn (2008), *Trust: Self-Interest and the Common Good.* Oxford: Oxford University Press.

J. Kotter and J.L. Heskett (1992), *Corporate Culture and Performance.* New York: Free Press.

Manuel Mendonca and Rabindra N. Kanungo (2007), *Ethical Leadership.* Maidenhead: McGraw-Hill Education/Open University Press.

Edwin Schein (2010), *Organizational Culture and Leadership,* Fourth Edition. San Francisco, CA: Jossey-Bass.

Anthony Seldon (2009), *Trust: How We Lost It and How To Get It Back.* London: Biteback.

Pamela Shockley-Zalabak, Sherwyn Morreale and Michael Z. Hackman (2010), *Building the High-Trust Organization: Strategies for Supporting Five Key Dimensions of Trust.* San Francisco, CA: Jossey-Bass.

Sandra J. Sucher (2007), *The Moral Leader: Challenges, Tools and Insights.* New York: Routledge.

? Discussion Questions

1. What values would you wish to promote in an organization, and why?
2. Who decides what the corporate values should be? And how can we create a culture of 'shared values'?
3. Why are some managers hypocrites?
4. Why have business ethics declined?
5. Why do corporations practise corporate social responsibility and why do some say they do but do not?
6. How effective are business schools in teaching business ethics and corporate social responsibility?
7. How can we know that an organization's culture is the 'right' culture for it?
8. How transferable across organizations and industries is leadership?
9. What are the most challenging leadership issues in working in a cross-cultural or multicultural environment?
10. Can there be a leadership philosophy and practice called 'global leadership'?

Shared values inform not only vision and purpose in effective leadership but also the strategies for pursuing them. So we now turn to strategy, the fourth core theme and practice in our model of leadership.

7 Leadership and Strategy

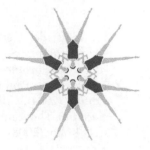

Without strategies, vision is a dream.

OVERVIEW

- The proposition of this chapter is that effective leaders develop, communicate and implement rational strategies that are informed by shared values. This is the fourth core theme and practice in our model of leadership.
- Expressed in the simplest possible way, strategy is about how to get from where we are now to where we want to be. It is a journey plan and a route map for travelling to the destination (represented in a vision). Strategy also serves an organization's or nation's purpose and is informed by its core values.
- Strategies, as a core theme and practice in leadership, are ways of pursuing the vision and purpose, identifying and exploiting opportunities, anticipating and responding to threats, and not only responding positively to the need for change but also creating change.
- Strategic thinking can be classified into various approaches or schools of thought: the classical, evolutionary, systemic and processual. And strategies are developed at several levels: corporate, business and functional.
- Studies show that a lack of strategic thinking and poor strategies are common management weaknesses, except in the most admired companies and those that are most successful. We discuss the characteristics and consequences of strategy in these respects. Several examples of corporate strategies are provided.
- This chapter discusses the concept of core competencies and distinctive capability in strategic thinking and the Balanced Scorecard as a useful basis for developing strategy.
- Developing strategy entails a 'strategic conversation' within the organization – a participative approach – and alignment of people's tasks and actions. We discuss how this can be done through 'sense making' and the cognitive skills and social and emotional processes involved. We also discuss the effects of emotion and mood in the strategy process.
- We discuss methods of strategic analysis, in particular environmental scanning, PESTLE analysis, industry and competitor analysis, SWOT analysis, benchmarking and scenario planning.

(Continued)

(Continued)

- Deciding on a strategy may entail reconciling a variety of individual interpretations and choices to achieve consensus in strategy development. Decisions reflect decision makers' mental maps and political processes (including their use of power), which in turn reflect the organizational culture. Strategies on the other hand may emerge: they may *form* rather than be *formulated*. Influences on this process are history and context.
- Leadership is also about ensuring that strategy is implemented effectively and sustained during its life. This entails enabling and ensuring commitment to it through ownership of it as well as the control mechanisms that are part and parcel of 'management'. Strategic leadership is showing the way through strategies, informed by shared values, in the pursuit of a vision or purpose.
- A case study is provided for analysis and discussion: a well-known company that suffered a decline due to poor strategies and its subsequent recovery, reversal and then success.

One of the greatest disasters in British manufacturing industry was the result of catastrophic leadership with respect to strategy (and purpose). After building the General Electric Company (GEC) over 30 years into the UK's largest and most important manufacturing company, the late Arnold (Lord) Weinstock retired in September 1996 only to see the company decline, as the renamed Marconi, into virtually a 'penny stock'.[1] According to Stephen Aris, Weinstock believed the reason for this dreadful decline was a preoccupation with maximizing shareholder value as the company's purpose, its strategies of divesting the Marconi defence electronics business and investing in little-known American IT companies, and the lack of cost and management controls that had been a feature of Weinstock's management of the company. Weinstock is alleged to have said of his successor Lord Simpson and his colleague John Mayo:

> They knew nothing about the business they were in, and nothing about the businesses they were buying ... From the moment he [Simpson] arrived, all the controls I had put in place, the five bench-marks and so forth, were dropped. After that there was only one budget meeting.[2]

Disastrous strategies, serving a misguided purpose, together with poor strategic controls led to the virtual collapse of this one-time flagship British company and its absorption into Ericsson in 2006.

Leadership starts with a dream – a vision of what or where we want to be. We pursue that vision through strategies, which are the first step in transforming the dream – the vision – into a reality. Effective leaders develop, communicate and implement rational strategies that are informed by shared values. And rational strategies concern intelligent choices that determine whether an organization survives, prospers, or dies. GEC is a classic case example.

What is Strategy?

The word 'strategy' comes from the Greek, *strategos*, which originally referred to a general in command of an army. Its meaning evolved over several centuries BC to mean successively the art of the general, managerial skills as well as oratory and power, and ultimately 'the ability to employ forces to defeat opposing forces and to develop a unified system of global governance'.[3] But what is the general's role? Donald Hambrick and James Fredrickson state:

> The general is responsible for multiple units on multiple fronts and multiple battles over time. The general's challenge ... is in orchestration and comprehensiveness. Great generals think as a whole. They have a strategy; it has pieces, or elements, but they form a coherent whole ... a central, integrated, externally oriented concept of how an organization will achieve its objectives ... [therefore] choices about internal organizational arrangements are not part of strategy.[4]

John Middleton and Bob Gorzynski argue the association of business strategy with military usage is unfortunate:

> ... we tend to think of [strategy] in terms of plans of attack or defense, competitive battlefields, and winners and losers ... strategy is as much to do with understanding the *process of change* as with the tactics employed to deal with it. Moreover, strategy is more than a zero-sum game. It is not simply about competing for a bigger share of a finite market, it is about creating new markets to meet human needs in new and exciting ways. It is about *creating the future*.[5]

The military association of strategy is also unfortunate in connoting a top-down approach to developing and implementing strategy – leadership by command and control. The 'generals' or directors may often rationalize this by arguing that the required expertise resides only with themselves. Or perhaps it may reflect their arrogance and conceit. As we shall see later, strategy development requires a participative or consultative style of leadership, tapping the wisdom of all members of an organization, to be most effective.

Modern thinking about strategy and its application to business starts with Alfred Chandler in the 1950s and 1960s. He defined strategy as:

> ... the determination of the long-term goals and objectives of an enterprise, and the adoption of courses of action and the allocation of resources necessary for carrying out these goals.[6]

Nowadays, 'asking a management theorist to define strategy', *The Economist* says, 'is rather like asking a philosopher to define truth'.[7] Undaunted, Moshe Farjoun defines strategy as:

> ... the planned or actual coordination of the firm's major goals and actions, in time and space, that continuously co-align the firm with its environment.[8]

Goals 'state what is to be achieved and when results are to be accomplished, but do not state how the results are to be achieved'.[9] Actions are '… resource deployments, initiatives, responses, moves, deals, investments, and developments'.[10] Coordination refers to goals and the means for achieving them, resources and the administrative infrastructure. Strategy reflects vision and purpose and core values. Co-alignment refers to adapting to, and at times adapting, the environment.[11] Strategy is therefore a matter of content (goals and action), coordination and context, and it is interactive, adaptive and integrative.[12]

Expressed in the simplest possible way, strategy is about how to get from where we are now to where we want to be. It is a 'journey plan'.[13] Strategy is generally viewed as 'a posture and a plan', where posture is 'a fit or alignment … between [for example] activities and organizational structure, and environmental elements, such as a customer group'.[14] Christopher Bartlett and Sumantra Ghoshal pointed out in the late 1980s the need for multinational and global organizations to meet demands for both global efficiency and local responsiveness at the same time.[15] This, they argued, would entail replacing centralized, hierarchical structures with networks made up of far-flung teams and resources.

Strategies are route maps. They are ways of pursuing the vision and purpose of the organization, identifying and exploiting opportunities, and anticipating and responding to threats. According to Michael Porter, strategy is about optimum competitive positioning in the market. However, the turbulence of today's business environment requires a redefinition: strategy is not about position but about process – about developing processes to enable the exploitation of advantages.[16] In the chairman of Bain & Company Orit Gadiesh's words, this entails having a 'strategic principle', grounded in economic reality, about company direction.[17] Orit Gadiesh and James Gilbert advocate the *strategic principle* to drive an organization's strategy.[18] This principle guides the allocation of scarce resources and decisions about what to do and what *not* to do. It is similar to a statement of purpose but different in several ways, as shown in Table 7.1.

Table 7.1 Statements of Purpose and Strategic Principles Compared (based on Orit Gadiesh and James Gilbert (2001), Transforming corner-office strategy into frontline action. *Harvard Business Review*, 79 (5), May, 72–79)

Statements of Purpose	Strategic Principles
Inform a company's culture	Drive a company's strategy
Aspirational: something to strive for	Action oriented: enable action now
Intended to inspire frontline workers	Enable frontline workers to act quickly and make strategically consistent choices

Gadiesh and Gilbert cite Admiral Lord Nelson's simple strategic principle as an example: 'Whatever you do, get alongside an enemy ship.' This is a rule of engagement that every sailor could easily learn by heart – and one that was effective and enduring. C.K. Prahalad sees the differences between the traditional and emerging views of strategy as follows (see Table 7.2).

How the strategy process is incremental and informed by shared values is depicted in the model shown in Figure 7.1. This view has been taken further by David Grayson and Adrian Hodges. They point out that corporate social responsibility (CSR), which we discussed in

Table 7.2 The New View of Strategy (based on C.K. Prahalad (1999), Changes in the competitive battlefield. Mastering Strategy: Part Two. *Financial Times*, October 4, 2–4)

Traditional View	*Emerging View*
Strategy as *fit* with resources	Strategy as *stretch and leverage*
Strategy as *positioning* in existing industry space	Strategy as *creating* new industry space
Strategy as *top management* activity	Strategy as *total organizational process*
Strategy as an *analytical* exercise	Strategy as an *analytical and organizational* exercise
Strategy as *extrapolating* the past	Strategy as *creating the future*

Chapter 6, is widely perceived to add costs and extra regulatory burden, yet it has simultaneously created untapped opportunities for product innovation, market development and non-traditional business models.[19] They argue that 'corporate social opportunity' – exploiting the opportunities arising from stringent social, ethical and environmental standards – 'lies in building CSR *into* business strategy, not adding it *on* to business operations'.

Figure 7.1 The Process of Strategy

Schools of Strategy Theory

Alfred Chandler's approach was based on the assumption that organizations act in a rational and sequential way. His famous dictum that 'structure follows strategy' was challenged only in the 1980s, by writers like Tom Peters and Richard Pascale. Igor Ansoff developed Chandler's ideas by providing a prescriptive approach to strategy, using analytical tools.[20] Ansoff and Chandler, together with Michael Porter of Harvard Business School, are advocates of the 'classical school' of thinking about strategy. This view assumes that there is one best answer to the strategy question and that rational thinking will lead to it. Profitability is the supreme goal; rational planning is the means to achieve it.

Another school of thought is the evolutionary school, which argues that markets, not managers, determine success. Success is achieved through 'survival of the fittest', which entails adaptability rather than a deliberate strategic choice. So the best strategy is flexibility. The systemic school of thought argues that the social context is all-important. The social and economic contexts in which firms are embedded vary. Competitors' strategies need to be analysed in terms of their social and economic contexts. Therefore there can be no universal model of strategy. The 'processual' school of thought rejects the notion of 'rational economic man'. This view asserts there are cognitive limits to rational action, varying personal objectives and agenda, and cognitive biases. Emotion also plays a part. Strategy is about 'satisficing': achieving solutions that are not perfect or ideal but are good enough and workable.[21] Satisficing (sufficing and being satisfactory) is an emotional acceptance that there are too many uncertainties and conflicts in values for there to be any hope of obtaining the ideal solution.

Firms in the same industry vary in their performance and competitive advantage. Why? One explanation in strategy theory, the resource-based view, is that market position derives from a firm's 'unique bundle of resources and capability'.[22] To be a source of competitive advantage and to maintain a unique and sustainable position in the market, such resources and capability according to this view must be valuable, rare (available in short supply relative to demand), and not easily transferred, imitated or replicated.

The resource-based theory of strategy originated in the work of Bo Wernerfelt, developing ideas that had first been set out 20 years earlier by Edith Penrose.[23] From the standpoint of leadership, the resource-based view implies the need to develop a strong culture and set of shared values that will support the firm's vision, purpose and strategies as well as distinctive competencies among its employees. An even broader implication of the resource-based view is the need to develop the firm's collective leadership capacity – 'institutional leadership' – and its leadership 'brand' (which was introduced in Chapter 1).

Central to the resource-based theory of strategy is the idea of core competencies. 'Core competencies [attributed to C.K. Prahalad and Gary Hamel] is one of the most used and abused phrases in business strategy', says the economist John Kay.[24] The term is used variously, he says, to describe the resources an organization has (such as economic and business knowledge), what it does (such as solving problems and project management), and the characteristics it needs but may not have (such as innovation and customer focus). The main strategic question for any organization, he argues, is how well what the organization is matches what it does. He makes the distinction between distinctive capability and skills. Distinctive capability is idiosyncratic to an organization; skills can be readily bought in the marketplace – or trained.

An example of distinctive capability that Kay gives is from his own company, London Economics: its exceptional economic expertise and an established position in the market that other organizations – competitors – would find it difficult to replicate. Another example is from the Saïd School of Business at the University of Oxford: the Oxford brand, which, he says, 'immediately implies an intellectual, relatively academic, positioning'.

In defining a strategy, a company must begin by identifying the markets where its distinctive capability is relevant and must then acquire and deploy the skills required to capture and serve these markets. As Andrew Pettigrew and Richard Whipp point out, to compete successfully depends on two abilities: '... to comprehend the competitive forces in play and how they change over time ... [and] the linked ability ... to mobilise and manage the resources necessary for the chosen competitive response through time'.[25] Competitive advantage, Kay says, is associated with distinctive capability, not with pursuing new lines of business just because they provide easy pickings in markets that are growing or profitable. A leadership responsibility, he argues, is 'to put together the resources which complement the organization's distinctive capability in achieving [its] market position'. It follows, he says, that 'any effective strategy is specific to the business that deploys it'. One size does not fit all.

Strategies that have turned out to be highly effective have also often challenged pre-conceived views of the world, the apparently rational and what is possible.[26] Such strategies reflect a state of mind rather than the expert use of strategy tools and techniques. Such strategies therefore are the consequence of leadership that breaks the mould, of leadership with an unconventional, pioneering or innovative vision. John Middleton and Bob Gorzynski suggest that the challenge of strategy lies in its inherent paradox: for example, 'a vision of the future' and 'a firm footing in reality', 'stretching the organization beyond what is currently possible' and 'core competencies', and 'seeing the big picture' and 'attention to detail'.[27] Effective leadership goes beyond merely choosing between such opposites or even reconciling them: it must, as Gary Hamel and C.K. Prahalad say, "find the higher ground'.[28]

The Characteristics and Consequences of Strategy

The difference between 'what we are' and 'what we want to be' creates what Leopold Vansina calls 'psychic tension', which requires both our will and coordinated action for its resolution in the form of strategy.[29] John Kotter states, 'Strategy without vision can only go so far and vision without strategy translates into hope without a practical reality.'[30] In the words of the Chinese proverb: 'It is not the call of the duck, but its flight, that makes the flock to follow.' It is perhaps not the leader *per se* who creates followers, but the leader's vision and strategies. As with vision, strategies require intellectual validity, spiritual meaning and emotional appeal in the minds and hearts of followers. Winston Churchill as a leader in wartime achieved all these with his proactive strategies:

> **To [Parliament] he gave the realisation of his unrivalled grasp of the grand design that must unfold through the years ahead.[31]**

Good strategies result from the organization's vision and statement of purpose, and good strategic planning reflects the values of the organization and its environmental realities.[32] Psychologist Leonard Goodstein argues that strategic planning should include clarifying the organization's core values.[33] Strategic decisions reflect such values, which need to be articulated and shared throughout the organization. We have argued that this process is a key leadership theme and practice in its own right (see Chapter 6).

In a celebrated lecture at the Harvard Business School in 1931, Alfred North Whitehead, the eminent philosopher, identified strategic foresight as 'the crucial feature of the competent business mind'.[34] By this he meant the ability to anticipate future developments – to reflect on change and novelty, see through confusion, foresee trends, discern emerging patterns, and understand the social currents that were likely to shape future events. Some 500 years ago, the Japanese military leader Miyamoto Musashi said: 'In strategy it is important to see distant things as if they were close and to take a distanced view of close things.'[35]

Today's leaders, when contemplating mergers and globalization, James Champy and Nitin Nohria say, will frequently have great visions, but 'getting from A to B is often as dangerous and mysterious as sailing off into unknown waters was in the age of exploration'.[36] Markets and competition are increasingly complex and dynamic. Global integration and the coordination of operations, the demand for local country and market responsiveness, and the need for innovation and new business development pose ongoing challenges.

Strategic leadership models emphasize the thought processes of leaders. They propose that strategic decisions reflect a careful analysis of the environment and organizational strengths and weaknesses, opportunities and threats, using defined criteria.[37] Senior executives may consistently misinterpret environmental threats and opportunities.[38] How this can happen is well understood in the concepts of cognitive dissonance[39] and the perseverance effect.[40] This can lead to strategic drift[41] and serious consequences. Gerry Johnson and Kevan Scholes identify several cognitive characteristics of strategic leaders: visionary capacity, mental ability and the ability to cope with complexity, and expressing ideas simply.[42]

Strategic thinking is a crucial cognitive competency for leaders. And yet, according to John Adair, the UK's business culture is sadly short term and pragmatic: 'We don't even believe in strategy, let alone strategic leadership.'[43] Only 44 per cent of companies' annual reports mentioned corporate strategies, with only 36 per cent stating clear objectives for the company and few stating its direction, according to a 2002 study in the UK, Europe and United States.[44] In that same year the best reports were from GlaxoSmithKline, BT, Vodafone, AstraZeneca and Aviva; the worst were from UBS, Tesco, Berkshire Hathaway, Deutsche Telekom and Kingfisher. However, the world's most admired companies (headed by GE, Walmart and Microsoft), according to a survey conducted for *Fortune* magazine, did possess clear and focused strategies.[45]

A 1998 survey of small and medium-sized enterprises in one UK region revealed that 64 per cent had a formal strategic planning process.[46] And according to a 2001 survey of 451 senior executives across the full range of organizations by management consultants Bain & Company, strategic planning was used by 76 per cent of respondents' organizations.[47] The main benefits of strategic planning were reported as strengthening integration efforts across the organization and improving competitive positioning, performance capabilities and financial results. For example, a 2003 study by management consultants PricewaterhouseCoopers found that companies with documented human resource strategies typically showed a 35 per cent higher revenue per employee than the 42 per cent of companies without one.[48] And, Michael Mankins and Richard Steele report, strategies delivered on average only 63 per cent of their potential financial performance, with one-third of executives indicating less than 50 per cent.[49]

Bureaucratic organizations are notoriously poor in strategic behaviour. Universities, for example, are weak in competing with one another and slow in responding to a fast-changing environment, according to Michael Diamond.[50]

Kasturi Rangan reports that many not-for-profit organizations do not have any strategy and most make programme decisions based on their purpose rather than a strategy.[51] However laudable their actions, acting this way, Rangan points out, 'can stretch an agency's core capabilities and push it in unintended directions', citing as an example a children's aid agency, SOS Kinderhof, based in Austria. This is not to denigrate loyalty to the purpose, for this is the source of inspiration for the organization and its funding sources. On the other hand, the organizational purpose must keep pace with the times.

Competitive advantage plays a central role in defining strategy.[52] Michael Porter is well known for his theory of strategy development and implementation based on an understanding of competitiveness and the environment and for his 'Five Forces' model:

* The threat of new entrants and the appearance of new competitors.
* The degree of rivalry among existing competitors in the market.
* The bargaining power of buyers.
* The bargaining power of suppliers.
* The threat of substitute products or services that could shrink the market.[53]

Porter's model provides generic strategies for managing the future that capture the maximum value embodied in the firm's products and services.[54] However, John Middleton and Bob Gorzynski suggest that Porter's approach is flawed:

> It is based on a static view of the world, in which the size of the economic pie is given and finite ... all that is left to be decided is how the pie is to be divided up, and corporate profits must ... come at a cost to society.[55]

And Chan Kim and Renée Mauborgne's research suggests that this approach may well be dysfunctional: it discourages creativity, with old, young and new industries alike, and it focuses on the competition – a 'vicious cycle of competitive benchmarking, imitation and pursuit ... [that achieves] mere incremental advantage over market rivals' – instead of value and innovation for the customer.[56] The customer, not the competition, should be the focus of strategy. Kim and Mauborgne quote Pret A Manger, Starbucks, Bloomberg and Ikea as examples of success in this respect. Gary Hamel and C.K. Prahalad concur. They argue that businesses need to focus on aligning their own strengths – their core competencies – with customer needs rather than focusing on the competition.[57] And they also need to focus on innovation that is aimed at exceeding customer demands – thereby staying ahead of the competition.[58]

In a very different context Sir Ernest Shackleton, who was particularly interested in the 'mental' side of leadership, thought out brilliant strategies for survival in terrible conditions. He made highly detailed contingency plans while still remaining flexible. Today we would call this scenario planning. In every way, from planning his adventures – including fund raising – to responding to threats and opportunities during his voyages, Shackleton set the standard for 'best practice' in strategy formation and implementation. He taught us lessons that are particularly relevant to today's high-risk, turbulent and entrepreneurial business environment

Strategy as Part of Leadership

Thinking about strategy during the 1990s moved away from 'long-term planning' to a concern with aligning the organization to the demands of a rapidly changing world and providing a leadership dimension to the strategy process. Perhaps the most prominent thinkers here are Christopher Bartlett and Sumantra Ghoshal, who argued that:

※ Leaders need to change their focus from devising formal systems to developing organizational purpose.
※ They should replace top-down vision and direction with bottom-up initiatives from those people who are closest to the customer.
※ Top-level leaders should replace directing and controlling middle and front-line managers with creating an environment whereby they can manage themselves.[59]

Creating strategies first requires a clear, shared vision, purpose and values for the organization and empowering people to manage themselves (à la United Technologies Corporation)[60] and pursue these. Donald Hambrick and James Fredrickson depict the place of strategy as shown in Figure 7.2. This shows strategy as driven by strategic analysis and strategic objectives that reflect the organization's purpose and values.

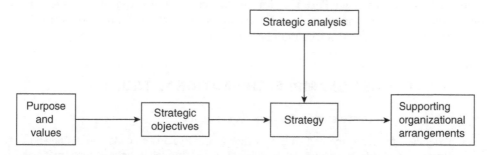

Figure 7.2 The Place of Strategy in Leadership (Adapted from Donald C. Hambrick and James W. Fredrickson (2001), Are you sure you have a strategy? *Academy of Management Executive*, 15 (4), 48–59)

Organizational arrangements relating to structure, processes, policies, people and rewards will support strategy.

Robert Kaplan and David Norton explain the characteristics strategy and how it is used:

* Strategy is a continual process, through linking it to budgets, strategic learning and information systems.
* Strategy is everyone's job, using strategic assessments and personal 'scorecards'.
* The organization is aligned to its strategy through business and support unit synergies.
* Strategy is translated into operational plans by using strategy maps and the 'Balanced Scorecard' (see below).
* Change is mobilized through executive leadership.[61]

The psychologist Leonard Goodstein regards strategic planning as 'the most important function of any leader'.[62] This contention might be arguable in a narrow sense – that strategic planning only or essentially concerns *how to pursue* the vision and purpose of the organization and not necessarily the development or definition of the organization's vision, purpose or values. Indeed he says it 'involves more than drafting some airy statement of purpose and posting it on the wall of every cubicle'.[63] Nevertheless Goodstein places strategy as a central theme and practice in leadership. This is to be applauded.

As we have seen, different commentators will variously regard vision, purpose and even values rather than strategy as the most important or the fundamental leadership concern. My view is that strategy is part of leadership: leadership is not part of strategy – unless of course it is a strategy itself (which presumes there has been inadequate leadership previously). Goodstein, however, defines strategic planning in terms of establishing goals (presumably in the context of organizational vision and purpose) and the pathways to reaching them, clarifying the organization's values, and identifying and planning how to avoid or minimize potential obstacles.[64] He says: 'A strategic plan should be a clear statement of the organization's desired future and the path to reach this future'.[65]

Strategies are ways of pursuing the vision and purpose, anticipating and responding to threats and identifying and exploiting opportunities. Effective leadership entails not only responding positively to the need for change but also creating innovative, beneficial change. Michael Porter endorses this view, saying that advantage comes only from innovation and upgrading in the context of a vision.[66] Indeed opportunities that are not identified and seized may become threats.[67]

CASE EXAMPLE: THE NATIONAL TRUST

The UK's National Trust's strategy has several elements:

* Working to preserve and protect the buildings, countryside and coastline of England, Wales and Northern Ireland, in a range of ways, through practical conservation,

(Continued)

(Continued)

learning and discovery, and encouraging everyone to visit and enjoy their national heritage.

- Educating people about the importance of the environment and of preserving our heritage for future generations.
- Contributing to important debates over the future of the economy, the development of people's skills and sense of community and the quality of the local environment in both town and country.
- Helping to shape external policy and issues of public debate for the benefit of our national and cultural heritage.[68]

CASE EXAMPLE: DURHAM UNIVERSITY

An example of strategies in the higher education sector in the UK are those of Durham University, whose strategies for 2010–2020 cover the two key strategic areas of research and education, in which three 'ideals' are embedded: world university, community and place, and sustainability (long-term social, environmental and financial responsibilities).[69] 'Key targets' are associated with the research and education strategies as well as with the ideals underpinning them.

Research Strategies

1. Demonstrate international research excellence across the entire academic base and take a leading part in developing the academic agenda in each discipline.
2. Increase significantly the number and proportion of both postgraduate Masters and PhD students, and postdoctoral researchers, providing each with the best possible quality of experience.
3. Shape and respond to international, national and local research agendas.
4. Raise the university's research profile nationally and internationally by effectively disseminating research successes and outcomes.
5. Establish a culture of prioritizing support for research by all communities across the university, enhancing external research funding and embedding policies which protect research time.

Education Strategies

1. Provide an academic education that is research-led and transformative, a curriculum underpinned by excellence in teaching facilities and a culture of reflective practice.
2. Provide students with outstanding and distinctive opportunities for personal development, ensuring future success and employability.
3. Ensure a diverse and international student experience.

CASE EXAMPLE: THAILAND'S NATIONAL ECONOMIC AND SOCIAL DEVELOPMENT BOARD

An excellent example of strategies in the public sector – a 'national development plan' – comes from Thailand's National Economic and Social Development Board. Thailand's Eleventh National Development Plan 2011-2015 is designed to pursue a vision for national transformation and a tripartite purpose derived from it.

The plan was announced by the Thai government in October 2010.[71] It is a framework for medium-term national development designed with the participation of all development partners at community, regional and national levels. The plan reflects a 'Philosophy of Sufficiency Economy' as a guiding principle together with an integrated people-centred development approach. It serves a vision of Thailand as ' ... a happy society with equity fairness, and resilience'. This vision is characterized by people living peacefully and well-prepared for changes within a society based on consolidated social foundations, quality economic growth, sustainable natural resources and environmental management and good governance.

Since its inception in 1961 with the First Plan (1961–1966), national development planning has evolved in accordance with the changing context of the external environment and internal conditions. In line with the Thai Constitution (1997), the State incorporates ideas and suggestions from public participation in policy making and national and economic social planning processes. The risk of unsustainable development – the adverse impact of previous development efforts on society, natural resources and the environment – is intended to be reduced through aiming for a 'Sufficiency Economy' endorsed by the King.

Vision

A happy society with equity, fairness and resilience.

Tripartite Mission

- To promote better income distribution, and a fair, harmonious and democratic society in order for people to achieve a better quality of life.
- To create socio-economic security through strengthening of production of goods and services based on knowledge, creativity and environmental friendliness, improving social protection for better coverage and ensuring food and energy security.
- To strengthen resilience to changes and crises and develop human resources.

Strategies

1. Promoting the just society.
2. Developing human resources to promote a life-long learning society.
3. Balancing food and energy security.
4. Creating a knowledge-based economy and an enabling environment.
5. Strengthening economic and security cooperation in the Region.
6. Managing natural resources and the environment towards sustainability.

Implementation

The vision for the nation will be translated into a reality through implementing the six strategies using specific objectives, targets, plans and key performance indicators and a participative approach. This entails the empowerment of development partners and a clear division of responsibilities among them and concerted effort among all stakeholders.

CASE EXAMPLE: MEDTRONIC

Based in Minneapolis in the United States, Medtronic is one of the world's leading medical technology companies and an example of constancy of values and purpose – 'restoring people to full life and health' – with a focus on intelligent strategies and customer value rather than shareholder value.

Bill George, former chairman and CEO of Medtronic in the USA and now a Harvard Business School professor, argues that employees can adapt to major strategic shifts provided that the company's purpose and values remain constant, which is an important factor in maintaining their trust in top management.[72] He describes how Medtronic was 'completely reinvented' every five years in respect of its business strategies. For example, between 1989 and 1994, the company was transformed from a pacemaker company into a broader cardiovascular business, with subsequent revolutionary new therapies and further innovation, reflecting its 'Vision 2010' and the constancy of its purpose and values. Table 7.3 shows how the company's revenues, profits and shareholder value grew as a result of Medtronic's commitment to its purpose, values and flexible strategies. Price-to-earnings ratio has consistently been 40 to 50 times.

Table 7.3 Medtronic's Growth in Revenues, Profits and Shareholder Value ($), 1985–2001

	1985	2001	Annual Increase
Revenue	363m	5.5b	18%
Earnings per share	0.04	1.05	23%
Shareholder value*	400m	60b	37%

* $25,000 when the company was set up in 1949

Developing the Strategy

A McKinsey global survey of some 2,000 multi-business company executives in December 2010 reported that more than a quarter of their companies lacked a consistent process for developing strategy.[73] And only 20 per cent of these addressed choices about their portfolios and the allocation of resources – the best corporate strategies in McKinsey's view.

'Strategy development', Colin Eden says, 'is about discovering how to manage and control the future … It is concerned with capturing the experience and wisdom of organizational members about how they believe an attractive vision of the future can be attained.'[74] This is exactly what the British Geological Survey (BGS) did. With a clear, new vision of what he wanted BGS to be, when he was appointed as its head, David Falvey immediately invited all non-managerial employees to apply to join a strategy team.[75] Seven 'pillars' of new or better ways of working were agreed in the team within 21 months and a project-based organizational structure was introduced within 27 months. A 2003 survey by the Manufacturing Foundation of successful middle-market manufacturing firms in the UK reported that the commitment and ownership of members of the organization in respect of strategic vision and plans would be critical to its success.[76] BGS is a good example here.

'Mere consultation and the broadcasting of messages', James Champy says, are not sufficient in achieving commitment to and ownership of strategy.[77] Peter Linkow makes the point that organizations that do not involve employees in the strategy process in what Kees Van der Heijden calls 'strategic conversation'[78] – simply conversation among people in the organization intended to contribute to its strategy – will not survive.[79] The usefulness of strategic conversation is well supported by research findings.[80]

Organization-wide strategic thinking, Linkow says, is a source of competitive advantage. This is an essential element of what Bruce Pasternack and colleagues call the organization's strategic leadership capacity[81] – an outcome of distributed leadership, which we discussed in Chapter 1. Linkow says that unrelenting environmental pressures require a strategic agility in 'constantly monitoring the competition, scanning for changes in the external environment, and identifying emerging market opportunities'. As a result of delayering and downsizing, he comments, more middle-level managers need to be part of the strategic conversation process and hence be the first to understand it. This has leadership implications for empowerment, which is discussed in Chapter 8.

Strategy results from design, experience or ideas.[82] It most often results from design: analysis, evaluation and planning by top management. However, this process is influenced by the individual and collective experience of people in the organization and by the organizational culture, for example the procedural routines and subconscious assumptions that are taken for granted. This may lead to future strategies, Gerry Johnson and colleagues say, that are merely adaptations of past strategies.[83] Innovative strategies, they would argue, result from more than experience – namely, from diversity and variety of ideas. Organizations will therefore respond to the often rapidly changing and uncertain business environment through a process of 'logical incrementalism' – learning by doing – which relies more on emergent strategy than on top-down direction and control. Encouraging strategic conversation in the context of distributed leadership in the organization has the potential to enhance innovation in strategy.

Steps in Strategy Development

According to Colin Eden, strategy development involves:

- ※ Articulating a strategic vision.
- ※ Identifying the major strategic issues facing the organization that require both insight and foresight.
- ※ Generating options and building scenarios.
- ※ Identifying stakeholders and their possible response in relation to their own goals.
- ※ Developing goals.
- ※ Setting strategies within the goal context.

❋ Establishing strategic programmes.
❋ Creating a statement of purpose.
❋ Developing strategic controls.[84]

In the business context, Donald Hambrick and James Fredrickson maintain that a strategy provides the answers to five questions:[85]

1. Where will we be active?
   This question concerns product categories, market segments, geographical areas, core technologies and value-creation stages.
2. How will we get there?
   The options are internal development, joint ventures, licensing or franchising, and mergers and acquisitions.
3. How will we win in the marketplace?
   The differentiators are image, customization, price, styling, and product or service reliability.
4. What will be our speed and sequence of moves?
   This question concerns speed of expansion and the sequence of initiatives.
5. How will we obtain our returns?

Leonard Goodstein and colleagues advocate 'applied strategic planning'.[86] The steps are:

1. Preparing for the strategic planning process – assessing readiness, those to be involved, time frame, and the communication of progress.
2. Clarifying the core values.
3. Formulating the organization's purpose.
4. Strategic business modelling – developing specific, detailed plans.
5. Performance audits – assessing the implications of current performance for implementing the strategic business model.
6. Gap analysis and closure.
7. Integrating action plans.
8. Contingency planning.
9. Implementing the strategic plan.

Action plans that are not integrated or, even if integrated, are not managed are unfortunately a commonplace phenomenon. We can often see this in larger corporations and in government where the 'right hand' appears not to know what the 'left hand' is doing or is doing something incompatible with it. We can also witness a lack of cooperation, collaboration or coordination among leaders in major functions, departments and ministries in governments – 'barons in their fiefdom' – and incompatibilities among the various strategies or in the way these are being implemented. Accountability for both integration and implementation rests fairly and squarely with the 'superordinate' leader – for example, in the UK this would be the permanent secretary, the cabinet secretary/head of the Civil Service, the CEO or, ultimately, the prime minister.

Goodstein's approach is similar to Colin Eden's. Integrating these two, together with some minor modifications, creates a useful synergy, shown in the text box below.

STEPS IN THE STRATEGY PROCESS

1. Preparing for the strategic planning process – assessing readiness, those to be involved, time frame, and communication of progress.
2. Clarifying the core values.
3. Formulating and/or articulating the organization's mission/purpose and vision of the future.
4. Identifying the major strategic issues facing the organization.
5. Generating strategy objectives and options and building scenarios.
6. Evaluating strategy options and deciding strategies.
7. Identifying stakeholders and assessing their possible responses to these strategies in relation to their own goals.
8. Developing specific goals and detailed plans.
9. Assessing the implications of current performance for implementing the chosen strategies – gap analysis.
10. Revising strategies.
11. Integrating strategy implementation plans.
12. Developing strategic controls.
13. Contingency planning.
14. Implementing the strategic plan.
15. Managing strategy: monitoring, feedback, and correction of action or change of strategy.

Cognitive, Social and Emotional Aspects of Strategy Development

Understanding the strategy process has been aided by research in the field of managerial and organizational cognition.[87] The cognitive element of strategy development entails individual attention, encoding, storage and information retrieval as a basis for action and, within the strategy team, the cognitive processes of sharing meanings, constructing interpretative frameworks and socialization processes for choosing and coordinating action.[88] CEOs have the additional task of collating and making sense of their top teams' views.[89]

The strategic leader is a 'sensemaker',[90] and CEOs and top-level executives must be 'sense-makers' rather than 'grand strategists'.[91] Christopher Bartlett suggests that they 'rarely have the detailed business and technical knowledge to set anything but the general direction of a complex organization'.[92] He describes how Intel was forced to move from making memory chips to making microprocessors not as the outcome of a strategic decision reflecting a clear corporate vision but as a result of the wisdom of front-line managers who, as Intel's CEO Andy Grove said, 'really knew what was going on'. Bartlett believes that top-level executives need to focus not on strategic fit and organizational alignment but on creating 'dynamic disequilibrium, challenging the organization's working assumptions, and creating the discomfort that prompts creative action'. This is 'intellectual stimulation' – an aspect of transformational leadership that we discussed in Chapter 3.

Managers in leadership roles have to make sense of their strategic environments – for example, by using mental models – as a basis for making informed strategic choices. An organization's managers may not share the same perceptions of the strategic environment, according to Kevin Daniels and colleagues.[93] They say that effective behaviour in this case is to start from a cognitive commonality and to work on reconciling any diversity later. This latter task requires encouraging dissent and expert opinion, empathy – appreciating others' perspectives – and coming to a consensus that reflects multiple perspectives and multiple-stakeholder acceptability – an example of participative leadership that we also discussed in Chapter 3.

How individuals make sense of information and use knowledge (through mental models) in strategic thinking has been explored using 'cognitive mapping' methods.[94] Mental models, Phyllis Johnson and colleagues point out, 'can hasten decision making, but can also lead to misdiagnosis of strategic issues'.[95] The importance of leader briefing and team interaction skills in developing mental models and communication processes for handling unfamiliar situations has been established by research.[96] This has important implications for strategy formation in novel and adverse business environments.

Edward de Bono, the renowned formulator of 'lateral thinking' (see Chapter 10 on multiple intelligences of leadership), rightly criticizes those who decry thinking 'inside the box' in favour of 'thinking outside the box' because, he believes, there is a place for both.[97] He says:

We do not all need to be 'off-track thinkers' [those who think innovatively]. Individuals who learn patterns about an organisation and its values, and stay true to them, become very effective ... 'in-the-box-thinking' ... is unfair and implies that people 'in the box' do not get anywhere.

Both logical thinkers (inside the box) and creative, lateral thinkers (outside the box) are needed when formulating and deciding strategy: leaders need both abilities to different extents according to the circumstances.

The strategy development process is not only a cognitive process but also a social and emotional process. There is some empirical evidence of the effect of emotion and mood ('affect') on strategic leadership and management, for example the desire to conform to group expectations and 'social loafing' (not sharing the consensus but also not being willing to make the effort to change it).[98] Moreover, and complicating this analysis, individuals may vary in their behaviour both from situation to situation[99] and from one to another because of personality traits such as introversion or extraversion.[100] Information processing may be adversely affected by 'emotional contagion', where one person's affective state induces that state in others through unconscious signals.[101]

Emotion and mood might also influence the environmental information that is attended to or the recall processes in information processing.[102] Anxious individuals will attend more to the threatening or negative aspects of a situation.[103] Kevin

Daniels found significant relationships between negative affectivity – the tendency to experience the negative emotions of anxiety and sadness – and poor organizational performance, industry decline and industry competitiveness.[104] This suggests that individuals with negative affectivity might tend to favour strategies that reflect pessimistic interpretations of the strategic environment.[105] Daniels suggests that anger could influence individuals to allocate more resources to existing strategies or to re-position them against the sources of such anger, for example competitors.[106] He also suggests that positive affectivity may influence individuals to initiate a radical strategic change and that fatigue makes individuals less likely to consider fully all the strategic options.

A recent study by Roderick Gilkey and business school and medical science colleagues reinforced this connection between cognitive and emotional processes.[107] Strategic thinking appears to be associated with at least as much emotional intelligence as cognitive intelligence.[108] 'Managers appear to integrate their brain processes', they say, 'as they become better strategists', which implies the need to view strategy and its execution holistically rather than as separate activities.

The Balanced Scorecard: A Framework for Creating Strategy

Robert Kaplan and David Norton introduced the 'Balanced Scorecard' as a framework for creating strategy in the early 1990s.[109] The Balanced Scorecard underpins 'a strategic management system that institutionalizes the new cultural values and processes into a new system for managing'.[110] It is based on a strategy map that defines the 'architecture' of strategy:

❀ Financial – the strategy for growth, profitability and risk, viewed from the shareholder's perspective.
❀ Customer – the strategy for creating value and differentiation from the customer's perspective.
❀ Internal Business Processes – the strategic priorities for various business processes that create customer and shareholder satisfaction.
❀ Learning and Growth – the priorities to create a climate that supports organizational change, innovation and growth.

Kaplan and Norton say that 'organizations build their strategy maps from the top down, starting with the destination and then charting the routes that lead there'. This first requires senior executives to review their statement of purpose (why the company exists) and core values (what the company believes in). On this basis, a strategic vision is developed – what the company wants to become. Strategies then identify the paths for reaching that destination.

John Sosik and Don Jung explain how the Balanced Scorecard can be used in strategic leadership.[111] This starts with identifying and communicating a vision that is translated into organizational goals, which are measured and monitored in relation to the four perspectives of the Balanced Scorecard. Sosik and Jung cite Mutual of Omaha as a company that has effectively used this approach to revitalize itself and pursue its vision.

The Place of Strategic Analysis in Leadership

Leadership is showing the way and helping or inducing others to pursue it; therefore credible leadership must result from a credible process of deciding the way. Several processes and techniques can enable us to develop credible strategies, for example environmental scanning, PESTLE analysis, industry and competitor analysis, SWOT analysis, benchmarking and scenario planning.

Environmental scanning and strategic analysis. The initial task in the strategy process is environmental scanning and strategic analysis[112] – on the face of it a cognitive process. Its purpose is to determine the favourable and unfavourable trends – and hence the opportunities and threats – that could impact on organizational performance.[113] This process is fraught with difficulties and risk, such as the misinterpretation of threats and opportunities. For example, Phyllis Johnson and colleagues suggest:

> [Individuals may] selectively attend to information that is consistent with their mental models when scanning and analyzing their strategic environment ... [and they may be] ... pressured by [a lack of] time ... [or] other cognitive demands or feel they are already familiar with the issues.[114]

Environmental scanning is particularly important during uncertain times. Bruce Pasternack says, 'The leadership challenge is to read economic signals to understand if they presage either recovery or harder times ahead.'[115] Uncertainty, however, is more than just economic: it is also political, social, technological, legal and ecological.

PESTLE analysis. Political, economic, social, technological, legal and ecological factors or forces will affect organizations and nations.[116] Their analysis is commonly known as PESTLE analysis. This has its origins in 'ETPS', Francis Aguilar's acronym for economic, technical, political and social factors,[117] later more popularly known as STEP or PEST, and eventually as PESTLE. PESTLE analysis is a powerful tool for understanding the environment or context in which change is taking place or being contemplated, especially in conjunction with SWOT analysis (see below). It is therefore indispensable in the leadership and management of change.

Industry and competitor analysis. This focuses on competitors, business ideas and distinctive competencies in the industry. Michael Porter's 'Five Forces' model, which was discussed earlier in this chapter, is a popular framework for competitor analysis.[118] Competitive advantage essentially grows out of the value a firm is able to create for its customers or clients that exceeds the firm's cost in creating it.

Chan Kim and Renée Mauborgne suggest the use of a 'strategy canvas' in which the horizontal axis identifies the factors in which the industry competes and the vertical axis shows the extent to which firms in the industry offer these competitive factors.[119] The strategy canvas provides a strategic profile of firms in the industry. One example they give is the hotel industry in France, which emerges from their analysis generally as comprising hotels that copy one another, fail to stand out in the eyes of customers, do not have a devoted following among them, and fail to generate significant economic returns. An exception that they describe is the successful Formule 1 hotel group, which has a clear, divergent and focused strategy, along with a memorable 'tagline' – 'Two-star comfort, one-star price'.

The process for developing a strategy canvas involves four steps:

1. Creating a common perception of reality among the company's senior managers.
2. Visits by the managers themselves to customers or clients (not commissioned reports) to assess the latter's opinions on the company's products or services, identify what is valued by them, and draw up strategic profiles depicting how the company could stand out in the market.
3. Presentations by teams of managers of their strategy canvases, voting on them, and drawing up a strategic profile for the future.
4. Communicating the new strategy on a single page – so that it is readily understood by all employees, can remain constantly visible, and clearly states where the company currently stands and where it has to focus its efforts for the future.

SWOT analysis. This refers to the organization's strengths, weaknesses, opportunities and threats. SWOT analysis is a basis for identifying key issues in matching the organization's internal resources and distinctive competencies with environmental threats and opportunities.[120] A strategy is chosen that will capitalize on the organization's strengths; control, reduce or avoid its weaknesses; neutralize threats; and exploit its opportunities.[121]

Benchmarking. This is a commonly used technique for identifying 'best practice' and improving business performance. According to Morgen Witzel, the process entails asking three questions:

1. What tasks are we not doing well?
2. Are others performing these tasks better than we are?
3. Can we adapt their methods to our own business to improve our performance?[122]

Proponents of benchmarking, Witzel says, argue that benchmarking, through learning from others' successes and failures, diffuses best practice and innovation. Companies may not, of course, wish to disclose such information. And, more seriously, benchmarking may lead to a convergence whereby companies will try to imitate one another rather than focus on innovation, as was discussed earlier in this chapter. A competitive advantage results not from following current best practice but from the creativity and innovation that go beyond it.

Scenario planning. What does the future hold for the organization? And how does the future affect strategies for pursuing the organization's vision and purpose? According to Gary Hamel and C.K. Prahalad, most managers on average will devote less than 3 per cent of their time to thinking about the future.[123] The urgent drives out the important. The future is left unexplored. And the capacity to act, rather than think and imagine, becomes the measure of leadership. Yet on the other hand, Bruce Pasternack says:

> When I meet with CEOs these days, I usually hear the same questions: When will our business recover? What risks does our company face? How can we gain more control over our destiny?[124]

Uncertainty is an unavoidable feature of the business environment. Pasternack and his colleague, James O'Toole, call the kind of leadership required in these conditions 'yellow-light' leadership.[125] We cannot forecast merely by extrapolating the past into the future. Scenario planning focuses on assumptions, values and mental models in thinking 'outside the box' and on identifying possible future scenarios and planning for them. Thinking outside the box is about escaping from the patterns of experience that are stored in the brain and do most of our thinking. Merely using these patterns will create all manner of heuristics and biases which will then prevent us from *imagining* what might be. The antidote to such cognitive constriction in strategy formation is scenario planning. This kind of planning makes a difference in strategy development: thinking 'outside the box' results in more creative strategies and these can provide a route map should any of the futures that are anticipated change.

Invented by Herman Kahn of the Rand Corporation in the 1940s, scenario planning is a process that has gained currency after Shell pioneered the approach in the early 1970s in the business context. All possible futures for the company are identified, evaluated and planned for.[126] This process enabled Shell to become one of the strongest oil companies in the world, foreseeing the energy crises of 1973 and 1979, the rise in the importance of energy conservation, the development of the global environment movement, and the break-up of the Soviet Union.[127] Through scenario planning Shell was able to react quickly to the 1973 oil embargo by Opec and emerge as the world's most profitable oil company. It has since updated its scenarios to look ahead to 2050. Kees Van der Heijden says:

> Scenario thinking now underpins the established way of making decisions at Shell. It has become part of the culture, such that people throughout the company, dealing with significant decisions, normally will think in terms of multiple but equally plausible futures to provide a context for decision making ... The distinguishing feature of the scenario culture is that it has invested in assumptions, values and mental models.[128]

Scenarios are stories about the future. Scenario planning takes the views of managers and external experts to identify how social, technological, economic, environmental (ecological) and political forces might affect the organization in the long term and how it might respond through contingent strategies. Peter Schwartz, president of the Global Business Network, and the architect of Shell's scenario planning, has stressed the need for companies to add security issues to scenario planning, as a result of the 9/11 terrorist attacks on the United States.[129] In particular, he has identified the extent to which Islamic fundamentalism might hinder the spread of Western capitalism and democracy.

Following Henry Mintzberg's distinction between strategy formulation and strategy formation,[130] several scholars have argued that we need to take account of history and context in strategy development by exploring how leadership, context and history can interact in forming an organization's strategy and how this can change over time.[131] Understanding this interaction is important in gaining a complete picture of leadership, for the same leader may succeed in one organizational context and fail in another.[132]

Strategic Decision Making and Emergent Strategy

Deciding on a strategy entails reconciling a variety of individual interpretations and choices in order to achieve consensus.[133] Strategic decision making is usually described either as a sequence of steps or phases or in terms of a set of characteristics or dimensions, such as comprehensiveness and rationality, politicization, centralization and formalization.[134] Strategic decisions are essentially unusual in that they will have no precedents, will entail the commitment of substantial resources, and will influence or dictate decision making throughout the organization.

Although there is little evidence that top management teams influence the process of making strategic decisions,[135] some research suggests that the personality and demographic characteristics of CEOs and the top management team as a whole do play an important part.[136] High achievers tend to favour formal processes both for decision making and for communication, and risk-averse CEOs reduce uncertainty by exercising greater control and direct supervision.[137]

Gerry Johnson suggests that strategic decisions reflect political processes as much as analysis: managers' perception is influenced by mental maps as well as analysis, and these maps are the product of the organization's culture.[138] This relationship is depicted in Figure 7.3.

Indeed the corporate culture interacts with all aspects of business strategy. As Stanley Deetz and colleagues highlight:

A positive business strategy and positive corporate culture go hand in hand. An effective strategy must grow out of the culture and the culture must be strategically shaped.[139]

The political processes involved in strategic decision making include the use of power. The misuse of power may lead to the repression of the least powerful members in the group.[140] For example, in their leadership role, non-executive directors will need to draw on both their political will and their political skill to exercise influence.[141] We discuss power more fully in our chapter on leadership and engagement.

Henry Mintzberg uses the analogy of the potter's wheel to describe the strategy process as a craft.[142] He says strategies do not need to be deliberate but can emerge

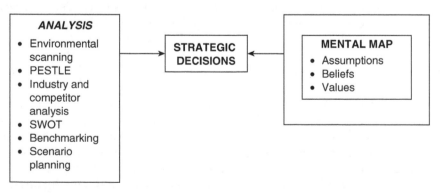

Figure 7.3 Relationship between Analysis, Mental Maps and Strategic Decisions

through circumstances. Strategies can *form*; they need not necessarily be *formulated*. What often happens is that strategy emerges – not necessarily in line with strategic intent – as a result of the unexpected patterns or consistencies that are perceived.[143] The strategies that are implemented may be the result of an emergent stream of actions that are recognized as a pattern *post hoc*. Strategic learning is key here: effective strategies may be formed and discovered by experimentation rather than by formal analysis and decision making.[144] Emergent strategy is more viable during times of turbulent environments.

Implementing Strategy

Thomas Stewart, former editor of the *Harvard Business Review*, says that the 'most pernicious' of the 'false distinctions that dog business thinking' is 'the separation of strategy (where the company should go) from execution (getting there)'.[145] However, strategy is *not* about *where* the company should go (this is vision) but about *how* it will get there, and execution is actually carrying out the strategy – making the journey. Given this clarification, his claim that 'strategy without execution is daydreaming' – that a plan for how to get there without actually doing it is daydreaming – makes complete sense.

In the aftermath of the dotcom bubble burst in the early 2000s, it became fashionable, according to Roger Martin, to say 'A mediocre strategy well executed is better than a great strategy poorly executed.'[146] Martin says that '[any] strategy that fails to produce a great outcome is simply a failure'. A good strategy is one which has accounted for what may impede its successful implementation, for example resources (including capability).[147]

Management consultants the Hay Group surveyed 100 senior managers just below board level in FTSE 350 companies and found, in the respondents' view, an astonishing failure by CEOs to execute strategy properly.[148] Nearly 80 per cent did not believe their businesses would achieve the CEOs' targets; one-third did not understand the CEOs' strategies well enough to carry them out; more than 25 per cent disagreed with messages from their CEO; and some 25 per cent were 'just plain bored'. Caution is required when interpreting these findings because of the small sample and possible response bias (more contented senior managers may not have responded). However, Stefan Stern, who reported these findings, suggested that the problem was poor communication: the need for clearer, simpler and honest messages – both down and up.

Implementing strategy is above all a process of communication. The aim of communication is gaining an understanding of and a commitment to strategy. These are necessary for joined-up thinking and action and effective teamwork in the implementation process. This means reaching not just managers throughout the organization but also all employees and to do so within the different ethnic and national cultures in which they live and work.[149]

The need to communicate and explain the organization's strategy as well as its vision and purpose is a continuous one so that every member of the organization is always clear about where it is heading and how it is striving to get there.[150] Robert Mittelstaedt relates how people will time and time again complain that they do not understand their companies' strategies, yet CEOs will also typically say, 'They've been briefed a hundred times – they should understand it by now.'[151] He believes that multiple strategies will often reflect a lack of focus. And 'corporate wordsmiths massage [their] communication … until [they become] all things to all people … and mean nothing to the person trying to do his or her job every day'. Mittelstaedt recommends using performance indicators and rewards that are aligned to strategy (though this is an example of transactional leadership), easily remembered mnemonics (but not slogans) and corporate storytelling to bring strategy alive for every employee. A case example of an approach to communicating strategy is Durham University's as shown below.

CASE EXAMPLE OF IMPLEMENTING AND SUSTAINING A STRATEGY: DURHAM UNIVERSITY

Durham University strives to ensure that people are engaged with its strategy in a number of ways.[152] Senior managers are supported via workshops and the provision of appropriate tools in order that they can communicate the strategy and interpret its meaning for individual departments, divisions and sections. A representative communications focus group coordinates strategy communications. And five-year operational plans are developed by all departments, divisions and sections in line with the university's corporate strategy to enable the achievement of those parts of the strategy that are relevant to them.

Staff are kept informed of progress through periodic performance reports that have been integrated into existing internal communications – the *Vice Chancellor's Bulletin*, *Dialogue Newsletter* and *Dialogue Updates* – as well as annual performance presentations and 'roadshows' for staff. The strategy is also communicated in an outline form to current students and externally to key stakeholders including alumni, schools and the media to ensure a consistent understanding of the university's vision and its pursuit and to encourage advocacy. Staff members in individual departments are involved in developing departmental plans to deliver the strategy through their own objectives and priorities which have been aligned with it.

Few strategic plans will turn into action, according to Chan Kim and Renée Mauborgne, because of 'paralysis by analysis'.[153] This paralysis, they say, is caused by the muddle of a:

> … lengthy assembly of a mishmash of data and analysis into a hefty tome teeming with industry assessments, jargon-laden presentations on cost savings or market share expansion, topped off with a torrent of budgetary spreadsheets … One company we worked with had so many strategic priorities it called a general meeting to prioritise the priorities.

Jocelyn Davis and colleagues say that more than half of all strategies are abandoned because they have failed to take hold of or to achieve the desired results in the time expected.[154] They found in their research that executives, when pressed to speed up implementation, may focus on 'efficiency' by manipulating processes, systems and technologies and ignoring the human element because of the need to 'wade through a morass of human emotions, questions, quirks, and complaints' that will slow them down. Yet *people* are, they say, the 'key differentiator between slower and faster organisations'. Davis and colleagues identified three traps that would slow down the implementation of strategy:

1. Over-attention to pace – trying to do everything faster, throwing resources at tasks and problems, and cutting corners.
2. Over-attention to process – ignoring human motivation (needs, wants, motives, aspirations, etc.) in favour of efforts to improve processes and technologies.
3. Measuring speed 'as if it were nothing more than a race', thereby overlooking *value*: the need both to speed up the time it takes for people or initiatives to start contributing net value and to achieve sustained value over time.

'The key issue with strategy for the chief executive', says Colin Eden, 'is not its development, content or correctness but making it have an impact throughout the organization, gaining commitment to it, ownership of it and strategic control'.[155] Ultimately it will be the CEO who is accountable for all this.

Strategic Leadership

While our model of leadership posits strategy as a core theme and practice in leadership, leaders who focus on strategy in pursuing a vision or purpose are generally called strategic leaders. A key function of a leader, and particularly the CEO, Roland Calori and colleagues agree, is strategic leadership in forming and implementing strategy.[156] The CEO and top management team certainly play a significant role in strategic leadership.[157] But Brian Leavy and David Wilson suggest that top management's role in strategy formation may be any of the following:

✳ Directly formulating the content of strategy.
✳ Shaping the strategy indirectly through managing the organizational context and the strategy process.
✳ Overcoming the institutionalized forces for continuity in an organization – inertia – in pursuing new strategic departures.[158]

Strategic leadership, like emotional intelligence and empowerment as we will see in later chapters and indeed leadership itself, tends to suffer from a diversity of further interpretations and definitions. Richard Byrd regards it as anticipating, envisioning, maintaining flexibility and empowering others to create strategic change.[159] John Adair sees it as direction (vision, purpose and communication), teambuilding and creativity.[160] Alan Hooper and John Potter view it as vision, purpose, communication and values.[161] Duane Ireland and Michael Hitt consider it as determining the firm's purpose or vision, exploiting and maintaining core competencies, developing human capital, sustaining an effective organizational culture, emphasizing ethical practices, and establishing balanced organizational controls.[162] Strategic leadership entails strategic thinking: environmental scanning, strategic analysis, strategy formation and strategy implementation, according to Francis Milliken and David Volrath.[163] Donald Hambrick is more specific but also narrower: strategic leadership involves aligning the organization with anticipated external forces such as technological developments, market trends, regulatory constraints and competitors' actions.[164] And Paul Shrivastava and Sidney Nachman suggest that strategic leadership is the creation of an overall sense of purpose and direction (vision) that guides the formulation and implementation of integrated strategies in organizations.[165]

Strategic leadership, according to Sydney Finkelstein and colleagues, underpins the strategy process in the manner shown in their model (Figure 7.4). Strategic leadership is seen as producing the vision for the organization, a value proposition, a customized business model, and a set of projects and programmes for implementation. Strategic leadership, they say, entails four processes:

✳️ *Strategic Thinking* – critical thinking and analysis that create the 'big picture' and produce the vision.
✳️ *Strategic Definition* – identifying and refining an attractive value proposition – the distinctive offering made by the business to its customers or clients.
✳️ *Strategic Alignment* – configuring and developing the business model to deliver the value proposition.
✳️ *Strategic Enactment* – taking all the actions necessary – projects and programmes – to implement the business model, deliver the value proposition and realize the vision.[166]

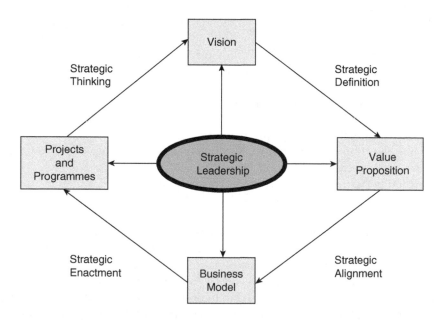

Figure 7.4 Strategic Leadership and the Breakout Strategy Cycle (Adapted from S. Finkelstein, C. Harvey and T. Lawton (2007), *Breakout Strategy: Meeting the Challenge of Double-Digit Growth*. New York: McGraw-Hill, 14)

The common thread in these conceptions is that all of these activities are informed by the vision and purpose of the organization. As a possible synthesis of these ideas, we might say that *strategic leadership is showing the way through strategies, informed by shared values, in the pursuit of a vision and purpose.*

Gerry Johnson and Kevan Scholes underscore the importance in strategic leadership of a vision, purpose and 'the (perhaps few) guiding rules [values and guiding principles] associated with these'.[167] They also suggest that 'strategic leaders are often applauded because such a vision can provide sufficient clarity within which the discretion of others in the organization can be exercised' and that the use of intuition together with more formal approaches to decision making can make an important contribution to strategy development. And Jim Collins and Jerry Porras say:

Companies that enjoy enduring success have core values and a core purpose that remain fixed while their business strategies and practices endlessly adapt to a changing world.[168]

CASE STUDY: LEADERSHIP AND STRATEGY AT MARKS & SPENCER

Reaping profits of over £1bn in 1997 and a British icon, Marks & Spencer (M&S) was acclaimed in the *Guardian* as 'The Manchester United of British business'.[169] Yet within 18 months, Christmas sales had slumped and M&S was in trouble.

The company's serious decline in the late 1990s from its pre-eminent position in the retail industry was an example of poor strategic leadership and management. When Luc Vandevelde took over as chairman and CEO in 2000, he identified the major problem as a lack of understanding of the company's fundamental strengths – what customers valued most about the business – and then using that information to develop its brand.[170] He said:

Once you lose your confidence, the tendency is to spread your risks and then you start becoming average in everything you do – and your customers know that.

His strategy for recovery was two-pronged. The first phase, 2001–2002, he described as 'simple, radical and all-encompassing':

- To focus on the heart of the business – the retail and financial services operations in the UK and to get back to the fundamental strengths that had made Marks & Spencer (M&S) great in the past.
- To stop all activities which were non-core or making a loss.
- To achieve the right capital structure to make the balance sheet more efficient to generate greater value for shareholders.[171]

This strategy was carried out successfully: within two year M&S around. The cover of the annual review for 2002 declared 'thing

(Continued)

Two, from 2002 on, addressed future growth, looking at 'how we deliver value, both for our shareholders and for the communities in which we operate'. The company had to:

- Regain our leadership in clothing and speciality food by translating our scale and authority into superior quality, value and appeal.
- Build on our unique customer relationships through new products and services, particularly in Home and Financial Services.
- Shape our store locations, formats and product offer to meet the changing needs of our customers.
- Reassert our position as a leading socially responsible business.

By early 2004, however, improvements had reversed in certain areas and M&S had announced that Vandevelde was to step down as chairman because of 'personal commitments' once a successor was appointed. Having become a part-time executive chairman in September 2003, Vandevelde was now being criticized for not spending enough time on the company, which he accepted (his other commitments included Vodafone, a private equity fund and Carrefour). It was said that 'the miracle he is credited with performing is nothing more than a mirage'.[172] Sales of food, clothing, general merchandise and homewares had fallen, the company's teenage fashions were failing, and M&S shares had plummeted. Critics also pointed to a failure to respond to a trend towards low-carbohydrate food.

At this point in 2004 Stuart Rose was drafted in to fend off a takeover attempt from Philip Green, owner of BHS and Topshop. Rose had an M&S pedigree: he had started his career there in 1972, had spent 17 years there, and had then left because of bureaucracy and internal politics. He was CEO of the Burton group for 10 years and then became the CEO of Argos with a brief to defend the company from a takeover (where he did in fact eventually sell the business but after having made a good deal several months later). He then joined Arcadia, the owner of Topshop and Burton, which was then in trouble with debts of over £250m. Having turned the company around, he then sold it to Philip Green for £855m, with a substantial reward for himself too.

Rose's initial approach on rejoining M&S was to lead a turnaround strategy based on 'retail housekeeping'.[173] This entailed cutting prices, smartening up stores, and enhancing fashions. Rose then introduced Plan A ('There is no Plan B') in January 2007. Plan A was composed of 100 commitments that had to be achieved over five years, that were subsequently extended in 2010 to 180 commitments by 2015, with the ultimate goal of becoming 'the world's most sustainable major retailer'.[174] At the heart of Plan A are five pillars: combating climate change, reducing waste, using sustainable raw materials, ethical trading, and helping customers to lead healthier lifestyles. Rose stated:

> We aim to engage all of our 21 million customers with Plan A. Our new commitments will mean Plan A is built into every one of the 2.7 billion individual Marks & Spencer products our customers buy from us each year. We also aim to help 3 million of them develop their own personal Plan A by 2020. Despite the recession, our customers are still concerned about social and environmental issues, but believe that business and government need to do the 'heavy lifting' by taking the lead, driving change and making it easy for them to get involved when they can make a difference.[175]

(Continued)

(Continued)

Underpinning how the company does business, the company says, are its core values of quality, value, service, innovation and trust, for which, it maintains, it has 'an unrivalled reputation'.[176]

Rose became executive chairman in 2008, combining the roles of CEO and chairman. This caused controversy among shareholders and commentators as it was out of line with best corporate governance practice and especially because it was also in light of a profit warning that had caused a plunge in the company's share value of over 30 per cent. M&S's progress stalled during the recession and profits tumbled from £1bn to around £600m. However, with a better-than-expected fourth-quarter performance in early 2010 and trading having improved generally, Rose quit his CEO role to make way for a new CEO, Marc Bolland, from Morrisons, the supermarket chain, though he was to stay on for a year as non-executive chairman. Meanwhile, Rose agreed to a 25 per cent pay cut during his remaining months with M&S.

In April 2010, Rose handed out an £80m 'farewell bonus' to M&S's 78,000 staff, reflecting the company's 'outperformance against expectations at the start of the year'.[177] Yet its market value at £5.8bn was still below the £9.1bn offered by Green in 2004. Says Rose: 'When I came here in 2004, you couldn't get a team on the pitch that didn't have either a broken leg or a Rooney ankle. Now we've got lots of strong people on the bench'.[178] In the words of retail analyst Philip Dorgan:

> [Rose] was neither the messiah many thought when M&S's profits stormed through £1bn ... [nor] the pariah many have painted him as. He oversaw the company through the worst recession in living memory ... There are things that Rose did right and things that he did wrong, but he leaves M&S in a much healthier position than he found it.[179]

Rose was named the '2006 Business Leader of the Year' by the World Leadership Forum for his efforts in restoring the fortunes of M&S, knighted in the 2008 New Year Honours, and appointed Chairman of Business in the Community in January 2008.

Case Discussion Questions

1. What leadership action with respect to strategy could Luc Vandevelde have taken to avoid or deal with the reversal in M&S's fortunes in 2004?
2. What was different and more effective about the strategies that Stuart Rose adopted after he took over as CEO?
3. How would you characterize the way Stuart Rose exercised leadership after he took over as CEO?
4. Should the roles of CEO and chairman ever be combined? What are the implications for effective leadership of doing so?

Suitable words with which to conclude our four chapters on vision, purpose, values and strategy, in line with our model of leadership, come from Bill George:

> Pursue a worthy mission with a passion that inspires your employees, stay true to your purpose, practice your values with an unyielding consistency, and employ an adaptable business strategy to match changing market conditions. The long-term increases in shareholder value will far surpass the highest expectations of those who would seek only to maximize shareholder value.[180]

Vision, purpose and strategies, informed by core values, need to be turned into a reality. This requires the ability and desire to pursue them. We therefore now turn our attention to our two remaining themes and practices of effective leadership: the empowerment and engagement of people.

 ## Further Reading

Christopher A. Bartlett and Sumantra Ghoshal (1998), *The Individualized Corporation*. London: Heinemann.

Bob De Wit and Ron Meyer (2005), *Strategy Synthesis: Resolving Strategy Paradoxes to Create Competitive Advantage*, Second Edition. London: Thomson Learning.

Gary Hamel (2001), *Leading the Revolution*. New York: McGraw-Hill.

John Hendry, Gerry Johnson and Julia Newton, Editors (1993), *Strategic Thinking: Leadership and the Management of Change*. Chichester: John Wiley & Sons.

Gerry Johnson, Kevan Scholes and Richard Whittington (2009), *Exploring Corporate Strategy: Text and Cases*, Ninth Edition. Harlow, Essex: Pearson Education.

Brian Leavy and David Wilson (1994), *Strategy and Leadership*. London: Routledge.

John Middleton and Bob Gorzynski (2002), *Strategy Express*. Oxford: Capstone Publishing.

 ## Discussion Questions

1. Why is strategic thinking a common management weakness?
2. Should strategy be geared solely or largely to maximizing shareholder value? If so, why? If not, what should strategy chiefly be geared to?
3. Should strategy be formulated or allowed to 'form'?
4. How can a commitment to strategies be achieved throughout the whole organization?
5. What is 'strategic leadership'? Is it really any different from 'effective leadership'?

8 Leadership and Empowerment

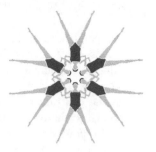

As for the best leaders, the people do not notice their existence. The next best the people honour and praise. The next, the people fear. And the next, the people hate. But when the best leaders' work is done, the people say, 'We did it ourselves'.[1]

Lao Tzu (c.500 BC)

OVERVIEW

- The proposition of this chapter is that effective leaders empower people to be *able to do* what needs to be done. This is the fifth core theme and practice in our model of leadership.
- The various definitions and concepts of empowerment are reviewed in this chapter. As a synthesis of these I propose that empowerment is giving people the knowledge, skills, self-confidence, opportunity, freedom, authority and resources to manage themselves and be accountable for their performance.
- Studies show that empowering people generally enhances both job satisfaction and organization performance measured in various ways.
- Empowerment is a topic that is much misunderstood and is interpreted in different ways. Unsurprisingly, therefore, it often arouses passion and heated debate whenever it is mentioned. One of the issues concerns the belief that, in empowering other people, managers have to 'give away' some of their power.
- Barriers to empowerment include bureaucracy, risk aversion, the need for control over others, fear of a loss of control, a lack of trust, the skill and time required to do it, and resistance to being empowered among those receiving it due to their distrust of the motives and consequences. Empowering others requires both an ethical justification and emotional intelligence.
- We review cultural variations and considerations in empowerment and examples of empowerment practices, including delegation, and the risks involved and reasons for resistance to it.
- If knowledge is power, then empowering people also means sharing knowledge with them. We review how empowerment is necessary to create a learning organization in which people can be creative.

The 'best' leaders will have followers or employees whom they empower and whose satisfaction comes from a sense of self-efficacy – the feeling of capability or competence to perform a task – and the feelings associated with achievement. Such leaders may be invisible, or at least in the background, but they are among the most effective leaders, says Thomas Lenz.[2] 'At the other extreme', he says, 'is the leader who takes on the mantle of "hero" or "messiah" ... who positions himself or herself as the central protagonist of organizational drama and origin of ideas and actions crucial to the future of an enterprise'.[3]

Empowering people is a principle that Nelson Mandela followed. For his wish, as president of a newly liberated South Africa, was not merely to lead his people but to empower them to lead themselves.[4] 'Good leaders', Mark Goyder says, will keep out of the way; having found the best managers they will create the conditions in which the managers can best manage.[5]

What is Empowerment?

The essence of empowerment, according to the *Oxford English Dictionary*, is giving people authority or power[6] – giving people the ability, or making them able, to do something or act in a particular way.[7] 'Power' has connotations of vigour, energy, authority, influence. Effective leadership entails enabling people to do what needs to be done to pursue a vision, purpose, objective or strategy and to fulfil their potential. Robert Heller sees empowering people as 'setting them free to think for themselves'.[8] Richard Olivier says: 'Alignment happens when the right "thing" (outside) is linked to the right "feeling" (inside).'[9] And in this respect, as Goethe in the eighteenth century remarked: 'Whatever you can do, or dream you can, begin it. Boldness has genius and power and magic in it'.[10]

Empowerment was also understood by St Thomas Aquinas, the thirteenth-century philosopher and Dominican friar. He believed it was immoral to abuse people and under-use them.[11] Developing this point, Francis Yammarino stated:

> ... it is 'immoral' not to develop others or to not allow them to develop to their fullest potential because of the resulting tremendous waste of human talent.[12]

The roots for its modern empirical study lie in the Hawthorne studies at Western Electric in the United States in the 1920s.[13] These purported to demonstrate that the workers being studied improved their work performance simply in response to the fact that they were being studied, that management was taking an interest in them, rather than the fact that their working conditions were being improved.

One of the first books about empowerment, written in the genre of a modern fable and also a best-seller, was that by William C. Byham.[14] Byham defined empowerment as '[having] responsibility, a sense of ownership, satisfaction in accomplishments, power over what and how things are done, recognition for ... ideas, and the knowledge that [one is] important to the organization'.

The term 'empowerment' has now become part of everyday management language,[15] though it is sometimes ridiculed by journalists as mere jargon. Patrick Waterson and colleagues note that empowerment is now 'a theme in contemporary strategic thinking as well as a prescription for good management practice'.[16] But while the term is relatively new, the practice is not – for example, giving decision-making authority to employees, enriching their jobs and delegating to them. The underlying concepts of empowerment are also not new, for example McGregor's Theory Y,[17] Likert's 'new patterns of management',[18] Herzberg's job enrichment,[19] Hackman and Oldham's Job Characteristics Model,[20] and the Quality of Working Life movement of the 1970s.[21] Empowerment also captures the two dimensions of individualized consideration and intellectual stimulation in Bass's model of transformational leadership.[22] It is only recently, however, that the idea of empowerment has extended to encompass sharing power, energizing employees, enhancing self-efficacy – belief in one's own capabilities to do what needs to be done – by reducing powerlessness and increasing the opportunities for intrinsic motivation at work.[23]

Empowerment is not a clear-cut concept according to Toby Wall and colleagues.[24] Sometimes it refers to employees' feelings of competence, meaningful work, autonomy and contribution and sometimes to the managerial or leadership practices that determine such feelings. Chris Argyris argues that there is a great deal of confusion about empowerment.[25] One problem, he says, is the conflict between 'internal commitment' and 'external commitment'. This is the inconsistency of asking employees to 'own' situations and problems and to behave like owners (internal commitment), yet expecting them to meet job requirements as specified by bosses (external commitment). The problem occurs when managers ask for internal commitment and the organizational system rewards external commitment. Asking people to act like owners when they have not set the objectives is a psychological paradox. Argyris points out:

> When someone else defines objectives, goals, and the steps to reach them, whatever commitment exists will be external. Employees may feel responsible for producing what is required of them, but they will not feel responsible for the way the situation is defined.

This chapter attempts to synthesize the various concepts, ideas and opinions about empowerment as an essential and meaningful theme in leadership theory and an important management and leadership practice. Definitions of empowerment have been many and varied, leading to some confusion in management circles. Peter Mills and Gerardo Ungson say that scholars will use the term when they mean other things, such as an empowered *feeling*, and that the term is also used to mean the same as delegation and employee participation.[26] And Jerald Greenberg and Robert Baron define empowerment as:

> ... the passing of responsibility and authority from managers to employees [involving] power being shifted down the ladder to workers who are allowed to make decisions themselves.[27]

This is a very limited view of empowerment, focusing only on giving authority power and expecting responsibility in return. This is not true empowerment: it is merely delegation. Holly Rudolph and Joy Peluchette make the point that delegation (and participation) 'only create[s] the conditions necessary for empowerment to take place'.[28]

Peter Mills and Gerardo Ungson use the term *structural empowerment* to denote the 'formal horizontal decentralization of authority such that decisional power flows to employees from the formal structure'.[29] Structural empowerment, they say, arises in conditions of uncertainty and 'information asymmetry' and where employees need to exchange information and other resources. In addition to individual variables, group and organizational characteristics – group effectiveness, worth of the group and status in the hierarchy – also influence feelings of empowerment, according to a 1999 study in the healthcare sector.[30]

Roy Herrenkohl and colleagues identify several different uses of the term 'empowerment':

* Sharing power with, or transferring power to, those who do the work.
* Redistributing authority and control.
* Sharing equal responsibility (between employees and managers) for results.
* Maximizing employees' contribution to an organization's success.
* The full participation of workers and leaders in decision making.
* The pursuit of a shared vision and purpose through team effort.
* Self-motivation through a full understanding of responsibility and authority.
* The capability to make a difference in the attainment of goals.
* A synergistic interaction among individuals that emphasizes cooperation and leads to an expansion of power for the group.[31]

Herrenkohl and colleagues define empowerment as a shared vision, a supportive organizational structure and governance, a responsibility for knowledge and learning, and institutional recognition.[32] All of these together encourage employees into using their initiative to improve processes and take action. A shared vision provides meaning and value in work. Self-efficacy and personal control – a belief that one can make a difference by influencing the environment and outcomes – are also important features of empowerment. Bradley Kirkman and Benson Rosen similarly define empowerment in terms of potency, meaningfulness, autonomy and impact.[33]

Kirkman and Rosen make a distinction between self-managing teams and empowered teams. Both are autonomous, they argue, but empowered teams 'also share a sense of doing meaningful work that advances organizational objectives ... team empowerment is a much broader concept'. They found that team effectiveness was determined by team empowerment in addition to individual autonomy, and that highly empowered teams were more effective than less empowered teams.

Scott Seibert and colleagues investigated empowerment at the level of the work unit, the 'empowerment climate' – a shared perception of the extent to which an organization will use structures, policies and practices that support employee empowerment.[34] They found that the empowerment climate is empirically distinct from psychological empowerment and positively related to work-unit performance. Psychological empowerment, empowerment at the individual level, they define as an individual's experience of intrinsic motivation based on personal cognitions in relation to work role – meaning, competence, self-determination and impact. The relationship between the empowerment climate and individual performance and job satisfaction, Seibert and colleagues found, was mediated by the extent of psychological empowerment.

A popular view of empowerment – sharing information, encouraging participation, teambuilding, providing training and development, and rewarding people for taking initiatives and risks – involves a leader in *doing something to employees*. An alternative view is that true empowerment comes from self-determination and intrinsic motivation.[35] This is captured in Phil Lowe's definition of empowerment:

The process as a result of which individual employees have the autonomy, motivation and skills necessary to perform their jobs in a way which provides them with a genuine sense of ownership and fulfilment while achieving shared organizational goals.[36]

Empowering people literally *is* giving people power – making them *able to* ... Sir John Harvey-Jones says that 'the leader is an enabler as much as a driver'.[37] Sanjay Menon suggests that power has to do not only with control but also with competence and being energized to achieve valued goals.[38] He says:

The psychologically empowered state is a cognitive state characterised by a sense of perceived control, competence, and goal internalisation.

Goal internalization reflects a belief in, and a commitment to, the vision, purpose, causes and goals of the organization. This, Menon says, is the 'energizing aspect of empowerment', which we noted in Chapters 4 and 5. Menon found in his study that goal internalization and perceived control were strongly related. He maintained that:

Goal internalisation is ... the ownership of the organisational goal, while perceived control is ... ownership (or control) of the means (e.g. decision-making authority) to achieve that goal.

An empirical study of empowerment by Menon explains empowerment as self-perceptions of competence (self-efficacy), a perception of control over the work environment, and the internalization of organizational goals.[39] Self-efficacy is an important ingredient in feeling empowered and can be explained by the expectancy–valency theory of motivation[40] (which we discuss in the next chapter on leadership and engagement). Perception of control results from delegation and autonomy. Menon's work adds to our understanding of empowerment, however, by emphasizing the importance of goal internalization. Goals can be motivating if they are valued as a cause or worthy purpose. If personal needs and objectives are congruent with the organization's objectives, people will feel they control their own lives and that their actions make a difference.

Underlying empowerment, however, is self-awareness and 'perceived competence' or self-efficacy.[41] In fact, in Conger and Kanungo's model, empowerment is a process of psychological enabling, primarily through enhancing the belief in self-efficacy.[42] In a more recent extension of this model, Sanjay Menon adds perception of control over the work environment and the internalization of organizational goals.[43] He notes:

If employees in modern organisations are to be ... enjoined in the organisational cause, then they need to internalise the goals of the organisation.

Francis Yammarino sees empowerment displayed where people are allowed to write their own job descriptions, work in self-managing teams, take part in decision making, and are delegated meaningful and challenging tasks and responsibilities.[44]

My definition synthesizes a range of key ideas and research findings in the practitioner and scholarly literature:[45]

Empowerment is giving people the knowledge, skills, self-confidence, opportunity, freedom, authority and resources to manage themselves and be accountable for their performance.

One key aspect of empowerment that is often overlooked, much to the cost of performance and achievement, is resources. Many an 'initiative' (particularly those from governments) has failed or suffered because of a lack of appropriate or sufficient resources – people (human capital), money (funds/budgets), materials, equipment, facilities, technology, information, time, natural resources and reputation.

Along with empowerment comes an accountability for behaviour and performance. Just as rights entail responsibilities, power entails accountability. So my definition of empowerment includes an accountability for one's behaviour and performance. Rob Lebow says:

... unless you link accountability and responsibility ... you'll never get accountable employees. It's the 'strings' that are placed on employees – policies, incentives and performance standards – that destroy accountability. [46]

My definition also includes 'opportunity'. Nannerl Keohane, a distinguished leader in business and academia in the United States, criticizes the lack of opportunity associated with a lack of empowerment. 'Micromanaging subordinates', she says, 'gives them little opportunity to develop leadership skills of their own and reduces the energy available for the work of the organization'.[47]

Empowerment and Leadership Styles

Research at the Leadership Trust in the UK suggests that transactional leaders – who emphasize management by exception and reward contingent on performance – are primarily directive in their leadership style, and strongly so, while the more effective transformational leaders (who display Bass's four 'I's) use all the leadership styles – directive, consultative, participative and delegative.[48] They are likely to use such styles according to the situation, as situation leadership and contingency theories suggest. Using a participative leadership style is a feature of empowering people. And a positive relationship has been established between participation, satisfaction, motivation, quality, productivity and performance.[49] The implication here is that transformational leaders are more empowering than transactional leaders.

This is consistent with the research finding that psychological empowerment is an important moderator in the relationship between transformational leadership and innovative behaviour: transformational leadership is positively related to innovative behaviour when psychological empowerment is high and transactional leadership is negatively related to innovative behaviour but only when psychological empowerment is high.[50]

Micha Popper and Ofra Mayseless sum up the relationship between transformational leadership and empowerment as:

* Increasing followers' autonomy and encouraging them to think independently and critically.
* Raising their level of self-efficacy, self-confidence, competence, self-worth and self-management.
* Augmenting their creativity and risk taking.[51]

The Practice of Empowerment

Ken Blanchard and colleagues suggest that empowerment requires two things:

* First, recognizing the importance of knowledge, experience and intrinsic motivation in improving performance.
* Second, releasing power by sharing accurate information, creating autonomy within boundaries and replacing hierarchy with self-managing teams.[52]

Robert Quinn and Gretchen Spreitzer say that 'this promising concept [of empowerment] often proves elusive'.[53] A basic problem, they state, is the lack of consensus on what empowerment is and how to implement it. For example, half of the 12 most senior executives in a *Fortune 50* manufacturing company believed that empowerment was about delegation and accountability. Their implicit strategy for empowerment, they said, was to:

* Start at the top.
* Clarify the organization's vision, mission and values.
* Clearly specify the roles, tasks and rewards for employees.
* Delegate responsibility.
* Hold people accountable for results.

The other six senior executives, Quinn and Spreitzer report, viewed empowerment very differently, as about risk taking, growth and change. This meant:

> ... trusting people and tolerating their imperfections ... [asking] for forgiveness rather than permission ... [acting] as entrepreneurs ... with a sense of ownership in the business ... engaging in creative conflict, constantly challenging each other.

Their implicit strategy for empowerment was to:

* Start at the bottom by understanding the needs of employees.
* Model empowered behaviour for employees.
* Build teams to encourage cooperative behaviour.
* Encourage intelligent risk taking.
* Trust people to perform.

A fear expressed by one senior executive (in the first group) was: 'We can't afford loose cannons around here', to which another, from the second group, retorted, 'When was the last time you saw a cannon of any kind around here?' Quinn and Spreitzer point out an important and incorrect assumption in mechanistic, top-down strategies for empowerment: that 'empowerment is something managers do to their people'. They argue that truly empowered people have a sense of:

⁕ Self-determination: they are free to choose how to do their work – they are not 'micro-managed' (or, if we follow United Technology Corporation's advice literally, they are not 'managed' at all but led).
⁕ Meaning: they feel their work is important to them, and they care about it.
⁕ Competence: they are confident about their ability to do their work well.
⁕ Impact: they believe they can influence their work unit, that others will listen to their ideas.

The three major barriers to empowerment, according to research by Quinn and Spreitzer, are a bureaucratic culture that emphasizes maintenance of the *status quo* and impedes change; conflict among organizational functions such as production and customer service; and personal time constraints due to workload. They describe how an empowerment programme such as The Ford Motor Company's can create the shared values and beliefs necessary for true empowerment. The organizational requirements are a clear vision, mission and challenge, openness and teamwork, individual goals aligned clearly to the vision, with clear boundaries for decision making and clear task responsibilities, and mutual support and a sense of security. The last requirement here is about reinforcing efforts to take the initiative and risk rather than punishing failure when people do this.

A survey by Development Dimensions International found that British companies, such as Shell UK Exploration & Production and the telecommunications company Orange, empowered their staff more than those in other countries through information sharing and 'high-involvement' strategies with employees.[54] Shell estimated it had saved £19 million in production costs as a result of its high-involvement programme. One useful approach to empowering people at work focuses on achieving several conditions:[55]

⁕ Win–win agreements whereby followers satisfy their own needs, goals and aspirations by achieving what is expected of them at work. This is done by ensuring a clear mutual understanding and commitment regarding expectations in five areas:
  ⁕ Specifying desired results.
  ⁕ Setting guidelines.
  ⁕ Identifying and providing available resources.
  ⁕ Defining and agreeing accountability and how results will be evaluated.
  ⁕ Clarifying and delivering the consequences – in terms of rewards or benefits.

⁕ Self-management, whereby people manage themselves according to that agreement. The leader provides help and support, together with the necessary organizational structures and systems. People appraise themselves according to the agreed results and criteria.

※ The character traits associated with a genuine desire for other people's accomplishment and success:

　　※ Integrity, whereby the leader's habits are congruent with corporate values, words are congruent with actions and expressions with feelings.
　　※ Maturity, whereby courage is balanced with consideration, for example clear and assertive expression moderated by listening and empathy.
　　※ 'Abundance mentality', whereby the leader is willing to share the rewards and benefits of success.

※ Skills of communication, planning and organization, and synergistic problem solving to enable the foregoing conditions. Synergistic decision making entails getting several people at different levels in the organization to work together on a problem and make a recommendation.

Empowering people includes delegating challenging tasks and assigning responsibility and authority to others.[56] Delegation is often *not* carried out deliberately to develop people, which would be true empowerment. Managers will delegate to others for a variety of reasons – often to improve their own time management, get more things done, or simply to avoid doing uninteresting things themselves. These aims may reflect a preoccupation with self-interest on the part of the leader: a concern with his or her own personal needs, goals, interests or agenda without a genuine concern for the well-being of subordinates.[57] This is not true empowerment. Effective leaders will empower people through delegation by taking account of both the long-term goals and the interests of the individual as well as those of the organization (and, of course, the immediate needs of both).[58]

Delegation carries with it two main benefits. It empowers and develops people: it enhances their knowledge and skills, it provides opportunities for growth and advancement, it increases people's motivation and job satisfaction, and it enhances their value to the organization. Second, it frees up time for other, more critical tasks that need to be carried out personally. Barriers to effective delegation centre on a reluctance to delegate and managers' lack of delegation skills. How often do we hear, 'If you want something done right, do it yourself'? Such reluctance arises from the fear that the task will be done badly, a desire for personal control and achievement, the perceived staff workload, and the lack of time to do it – a 'chicken-and-egg' situation. A lack of delegation skills tends to concern the inability to analyse the staff workload, critical tasks, and staff abilities, interests and potential, as well as poor communication skills in explaining and gaining commitment to objectives, tasks and responsibilities.

Phil Lowe describes the process of effective empowerment as follows:

※ Coaching – whereby leaders help people to apply or improve knowledge and skills on the job.
※ Sponsorship – sponsoring projects by employees.
※ Facilitating – suggestion schemes, quality circles, self-directed work teams, training events and project teams.
※ Mentoring – providing counselling and guidance to less experienced or mature employees.
※ Providing learning and development opportunities – e.g. job rotation schemes.

※ Accrediting – recognizing the acquisition of specific competencies.
※ Taking ownership of employee development.[59]

An example of empowerment comes from the British Army. 'Mission Command' recognizes that success on the battlefield is related to the speed with which commanders make decisions. It involves telling subordinate commanders what to achieve and why, but not what to do and how. They are allowed to take the initiative within defined limits. Ronit Kark and colleagues found in their study that transformational leadership was simultaneously associated with both empowerment and dependence on the leader.[60] Whether this is a paradox will depend on what kind of dependency is present. In the British Army example, this is clear and consistent with true empowerment. Mission Command has five key elements:

※ Commanders ensure that subordinates understand their intentions, their own missions, and the strategic, operational and tactical context.
※ They tell subordinates what effect they are to achieve (the objective) and the reason why it is necessary.
※ They allocate sufficient resources to subordinates to carry out their missions.
※ They use a minimum of control to avoid unnecessarily limiting subordinates' freedom of action.
※ Subordinates decide for themselves how best to fulfil their missions or achieve their objectives.[61]

Eileen Shapiro suggests, however, that the best examples of employee empowerment are found not in organizations that educate and coach their managers to empower people but in 'fast-paced entrepreneurial companies typified by high-growth Internet start-ups'.[62] These circumstances – with extremely rapid speed and growth – require high-impact decisions by junior people without consultation with bosses, motivated by the prospect of huge rewards appearing fairly quickly afterwards. This is, Shapiro says, empowerment 'by default' rather than 'by design'. Shapiro expressed this view in 2000, before the internet 'bubble' burst: 'Entrepreneurs often have an abnormally high need for control; that's partly why they dump … employers and start their own enterprises.' But it is those entrepreneurs who are genuinely empowering of their employees, she says, who succeed most.

An interesting form of empowerment is that which is practised and promoted by John Timpson, chairman of Timpson Ltd, a UK chain of key-cutting and shoe-repair businesses in the UK. Timpson practises 'upside-down management' – a model of management and leadership that inverts the traditional triangle and puts customers at the top and the board of directors at the bottom, representing metaphorically the support (and freedom) that the top management will provide managers, front-line employees and customers (see Figure 8.1).[63]

The essence of this approach, developed by Timpson from 'The Nordstrom Way'[64] and widely acclaimed in the UK, is a focus on customer needs and the trust shown by top management in their staff in around 850 shops throughout the country. Trust shows itself in the autonomy that employees have in running their businesses, for example in respect of pricing, ordering and display arrangements.

Figure 8.1   'Upside-down Management'

Vineet Nayar, CEO of HCL Technologies, which employs some 70,000 people in 26 countries, takes a different approach: 'employees first, customers second'.[65] He states its purpose as:

To concentrate the company's attention and resources on the employees who operate in the 'value zone', the place where employees and customers interface and where real value is created.

Nayar says he cannot understand why this should not be so, and he makes a compelling case why employees and not customers should come first. This philosophy is implemented by building trust through transparency – for example, by opening up processes and sharing information – and having management ('enabling') functions, including finance and HR, accountable to employees in the value zone in the same way that those employees are accountable to their managers. This inversion of the management pyramid is similar to Timpson's. Nayar says: 'The chief executive … [becomes] the one asking the questions, rather than the one giving all the answers'. The past four years have seen a tripling of revenues and operating income, a fall in employee attrition of 50 per cent, and 70 per cent of all major deals closed by HCL won against the big four global IT players.

Perhaps the epitome of empowerment is the practice of a Brazilian company called Semco SA.[66] This is a company that does not use conventional management practices or even leadership practices such as a mission statement. It is a 'test case' of putting the 'annual report-speak of "trust" and "delegation" into practice', enabled by 'huge peer pressure and self-discipline', says Simon Caulkin.[67] Employees choose their managers; decide their pay, which is made public, as is all financial information; decide when they work: meetings are voluntary; and nobody apparently is in control. Yet the company, under Ricardo Semler, a Harvard MBA, has 'surfed Brazil's rough economic and political currents with panache', Caulkin says, 'often growing at between 30 and 40 percent a year'. The model only works, Semler maintains, if dissent, argument and diversity remain real. Semco is a company 'out of control', with empowered employees.

Sir Ernest Shackleton, the Antarctic explorer, was an empowering leader. He spelt out exactly what was required of each man and provided the best possible equipment. He understood and accepted each man's quirks and weaknesses, identified his unique talents, matched what needed to be done with these abilities, and helped each one to reach his potential through challenging and meaningful work. Perhaps above all, he was a nurturing, caring leader, even serving tea in bed to the ship's 'cry-baby'.

What specific actions or behaviour – in leaders or followers – constitute empowerment? My review of the literature suggests the following:

❋ Self-awareness of one's strengths and limitations, interests, preferences and motivational drivers, and values, beliefs and attitudes.
❋ The delegation of challenging tasks and the authority to make decisions and take action.
❋ Stimulating people's intellects, imagination and intuition, questioning the *status quo*, and getting them to do likewise.
❋ Providing the opportunity, resources and support for people to perform.
❋ Sharing knowledge and rewarding *learning* as well as performance.
❋ Coaching and training for skills acquisition or improvement.
❋ Allowing or encouraging self-determination and autonomy – the freedom of people to manage themselves.
❋ An acceptance of responsibility (sense of duty or obligation) and accountability (the willingness to admit to being the source of actions or decisions that caused given outcomes).

In their study of managers in the United States, Alan Randolph and Edward Kemery found a positive relationship between empowerment practices and psychological empowerment that is mediated by employees' perceptions of their managers' use of power bases.[68] Psychological empowerment comprises a sense of meaning, competence, self-determination and impact.[69] And the model of power bases they used in their research was the well-established one of John French and Bertram Raven (Table 8.1).[70]

More specifically, Randolph and Kemery found that the uses of reward and referent power were positively associated with employee psychological empowerment and the use of expert power was negatively associated with employee psychological empowerment. The use of expert power appeared to disempower employees by undermining the use of their own expert power. The implication of these findings is that managers need to be careful to use reward and referent power and to avoid using expert power (and the three position power bases) in developing an appropriate context for their empowerment actions to be effective.

Table 8.1　Power Bases

Position Power	*Personal Power*
Reward power	Expert power
Coercive power	Referent power
Legitimate power	

Empowerment and Culture

It should be clear from our discussion in Chapter 6 on leadership and values that empowerment would interact with both organizational and national culture. Implementing empowerment in a multicultural organization or environment is likely to be more difficult than in a single culture. Empowerment varies according to culture and leadership style, which in turn are determined by situations and other contingencies. For example, Amin Rajan quotes a senior director involved in an empowerment initiative:

> We made a mess of our empowerment initiative at the outset. We did not think about the changes in corporate values that would be needed to make it work. We simply thought our people would be glad to have a job in this once-proud organisation and thus go along with our blueprint for change ... we forgot to ask the basic question: 'Why would staff want to be empowered in a climate of exponential change?' But more than that, we forgot to ask, 'What's in it for the staff?'[71]

Empowerment varies across cultures according to cultural values, requiring an understanding of local values and flexible leadership behaviour. Ignoring cultural differences in empowering people may make the effort a failure. Despite its shortcomings, Hofstede's model of the dimensions of culture, which we discussed in Chapter 6, can provide a useful framework for understanding the implications of culture for empowerment.[72] Alan Randolph and Marshall Sashkin suggest the following guidelines.[73]

When the power-distance is high, people may not feel comfortable in making decisions and taking actions that have previously been the prerogative of their managers. There may be a mutual reluctance to share information and replace the established hierarchy with self-managing teams. When the power-distance is low, managers and employees are more likely to welcome empowerment.

When uncertainty avoidance is high, employees prefer goals, policies, procedures and assignments to be precisely spelled out for the sake of clarity and certainty. Information sharing, provided the information is understandable, and clarifying boundaries to establish the limits to autonomy are welcomed. When uncertainty avoidance is low, people tolerate an unclear structure in relation to roles and procedures, though empowerment may lead to chaos. But a greater tolerance of ambiguity does not excuse accountability, so boundaries that set limits are still needed. Empowered, self-managing teams tend to be comfortable with setting their own goals, roles and procedures.

When individualism is strong, there may be difficulty in moving towards team empowerment. However, individualistic people prefer control over their own destinies, and they therefore seek information that gives them such control. Moreover, those with such information feel a stronger compulsion to act responsibly.[74] Individualistic people respond positively to autonomy, but they may have difficulty in self-managing teams. When collectivism is strong, information sharing and team accountability are preferred.

The effects of 'masculinity/femininity' as a cultural dimension on empowerment are likely to be moderated by other cultural elements. In masculine cultures (where assertiveness and a focus on results are strong), information relating to results is likely to be shared, and clear and meaningful goals and responsibilities will be sought. In feminine cultures (where the emphasis is more on nurturing and caring), information is more likely to be sought on processes and relationships, which are emphasized over tasks and goals, and there is also likely to be a focus on the team development process.

The Benefits of Empowerment

Empowerment is seen as liberating – as simply good leadership. Chris Argyris reports one CEO as saying, 'No vision, no strategy, can be achieved without able and empowered employees.'[75] And Gregory Dess and Joseph Picken say:

> Inspiring the organization and its stakeholders with a clear vision and compelling sense of purpose is a *necessary* but not a *sufficient* condition for the development of an organization that can learn, adapt, and respond effectively to a rapidly changing environment. Empowerment, providing motivated employees with the responsibility and authority to implement the vision, is equally important.[76]

Empowerment can also help the move towards a stronger culture of initiative, creativity, innovation and accountability. The relationship between empowerment and education and its implications for leadership certainly were recognized in the nineteenth century by the Scottish lawyer and Lord Chancellor, Lord Brougham: 'Education makes a people easy to lead, but difficult to drive; easy to govern, but impossible to enslave.'[77]

David Myers points out that 'study after study finds that when workers have more control – when they can help define their own goals and hours and when they participate in decision making – their job satisfaction rises'.[78] He quotes the case of Herman Miller, the American office furniture manufacturer and in 1989 one of *Fortune* magazine's top 10 most-admired companies, whose investment in employee empowerment was repaid with a 25-times increase in stock value between 1970, when it went public, and 1991.[79] The $1.6b company Herman Miller has become well known as a laboratory for testing new ideas and effective innovation with a long line of successes, including a suite of 'programmable' office environments named 'Convia'.[80] Participative management – inherited from the De Pree family who founded the company in 1923 – is a key principle as well as a core value and practice in the company. The founder's son Max De Pree says:

> Each of us, no matter what our rank in the hierarchy may be, has the same rights: to be needed, to be involved, to have a covenantal relationship, to understand the corporation, to affect our destiny, to be accountable, to appeal, to make a commitment.[81]

Peter Turney found that empowered employees have a sense of ownership and responsibility, satisfaction in their accomplishments, a sense of control over what and how things are done, and the knowledge that they are important to the organization.[82] Gervase Bushe and colleagues, in a 1996 study of empowerment, reported increased productivity and efficiencies, measured by increased customer satisfaction and innovation.[83] Continuous improvement, responsiveness to customers, quality and efficiency were achieved by empowered workers rather than bureaucrats.[84]

John Seddon reported on a 1991 UK study of customer satisfaction and staff attitudes in a service organization.[85] The study found that customers were more satisfied when staff said they understood the company's mission, they felt empowered, they felt they had good inter-unit relations, and their manager was open to suggestions for change. Similar findings resulted from a 1998 study in a US retail store, the Sears Corporation,[86] and a study in the same year of restaurants in the UK.[87]

When challenges engage our skills, we often become so absorbed in the flow of an activity that we lose our awareness of self and time.[88] Writers and painters, for example, know this sensation of 'flow' only too well. Challenge is essential to satisfying work. Moreover, leaders often do not change because they are not challenged.[89] A lack of empowerment can lead to no change, even when that change is needed. Being empowered, Philip Hodgson and Randall White say, means being willing and able to challenge the *status quo*:

> **Visions don't work unless the people who have to find their way to the vision are given sufficient empowerment to take the actions necessary to reach the vision without continually needing to refer back to their leader.[90]**

Empowerment can enhance organizational performance. Edward Lawler and colleagues report a greater return on sales when people are given more control and responsibility.[91] In fact supervisors who are more empowered are perceived by their subordinates as more innovative, influential upwards and inspirational.[92]

David Myers says: 'As people accumulate a history of productivity in high-challenge, high-skill situations they develop positive self-esteem.'[93] Gretchen Spreitzer and Robert Quinn found that managers with low levels of self-esteem, negative feelings about their jobs, and poor support from their colleagues and bosses were less likely to effect organizational change through transformational leadership.[94] Self-esteem, for the nineteenth-century psychologist and philosopher William James, was 'the ratio of a person's successes to his or her pretensions', where pretensions were viewed as goals, purposes or aims.[95] Self-esteem is a powerful motivator. And self-esteem is perfectly acceptable morally, and indeed desirable, as what Sir Kenneth Wheare called 'proper pride', and as distinct from the 'sin of inordinate pride', which shows itself as 'self-love, self-satisfaction, self-admiration ... and self-glorification', as we can see in Malvolio or Mr Toad.[96]

An empirical study of operators of complex technology by Des Leach and colleagues showed that empowerment could result in employees' increased job knowledge and self-confidence, but not necessarily their motivation or job satisfaction.[97] However, Daniel Dennison suggests that empowerment can also lead to improvements in employee absenteeism and turnover, which may reflect poor morale.[98]

Leadership Issues and Problems with Empowerment

The term 'empowerment' often arouses controversy whenever it is mentioned. It is a term like 'total quality management' and 'business process re-engineering', and even 'servant leadership', that often provokes strong negative reactions among many senior executives – and indeed among employees at large.

There are several reasons for this. The meaning of empowerment is anything but consistent across different organizations or even people in one organization.[99] And its implementation has not been easy for many organizations, meeting with resistance at all levels. As Chris Argyris says, empowerment of employees is notably difficult to achieve.[100] A strong organizational culture can either help or hinder a move towards greater empowerment.

There are those who reject the idea as dangerously subversive to managerial authority and control. Is the (moderate) need for power that characterizes effective leaders incompatible with empowering followers? Empowerment must be distinguished from the need for control. Sharing power does not diminish power; in fact sharing power multiplies power. Some regard 'empowerment' as merely another word for delegation, as nothing new. And there are those who would immediately reject the idea as yet another management fad – although it has been around for at least 2,500 years.

Empowerment implies the need for a concomitant capability. Henry Coleman describes how Airtouch wanted, through cross-training, to empower its call centre staff in dealing with customers.[101] Unfortunately these lowly paid staff did not have the intellectual capacity to take on the additional responsibility. Chris Argyris points out that there is also a limit to employees' emotional commitment to their work and employer and hence their desire for empowerment.[102] Stress may increase as a result of greater responsibility,[103] although this may be due to fear of failure and its consequences.

People cannot perform unless they have the opportunity to do so. Providing opportunities to people and the freedom and resources to do what they can do – and to do what they have not done before – is part of good leadership. Giving people the knowledge and skills they need to perform, for example through training and coaching, is hardly a case that needs to be argued. In the words of the ancient Chinese saying: 'Give a man a fish and you feed him for a day. Teach him how to fish and you feed him for a lifetime.' Empowerment, however, does not always enhance work performance.[104] It is likely to be more effective when there is a high degree of operational uncertainty than when work processes are more predictable and understood.

Is the empowering leader at risk of becoming laissez-faire and losing control? Bernard Bass suggests that, if a person's goals are not aligned with the organization's, then, through being empowered, he or she may pursue self-interest at the expense of the organization.[105] He also suggests that 'groupthink' and 'social loafing' may occur in self-managing teams: members may avoid being critical of one another and nobody will take responsibility. To avoid this, perhaps more rather than less structure is needed in empowered teams.[106] In this respect *The Economist* is somewhat cynical about empowerment:

The empowered, flattened organisational structure is fatally flawed. Empowerment has an unintended and paradoxical effect upon organisations whereby employees attempt to maximise the degree of individual freedom and responsibility during expansionist times, then abdicate leadership responsibility and actively undermine innovative strategic solutions when threatened by potential loss of power and income.[107]

Empowerment in Bureaucratic Organizations

Empowerment as a management practice, Adrian Wilkinson says, is the very antithesis of the principles of scientific management according to Frederick W. Taylor, namely clear limits to authority, the separation of planning from operations, the need for incentives for workers, task specialization and management by exception.[108] One of Henry Ford's patriarchal aphorisms intoned: '… leadership is perfect when it so simplifies operations that orders are not necessary'.[109] Leadership may be 'perfect' when orders are not necessary, but not because operations are so simple. Bureaucracy is at odds with empowerment: it is associated with powerlessness, a lack of initiative, non-fulfilment and emotional 'homelessness'.[110]

The bureaucratic organization is the antithesis of the learning organization. As far back as 1964, Michel Crozier depicted the bureaucratic organization as unable to learn from past mistakes, therefore engaging in a retreat from reality.[111] This results, in terms of transactional leadership, either from passive management by exception that reinforces the *status quo* or from active management-by-exception that punishes initiative and the risk taking that is necessary for learning.[112] Long ago Tom Burns and George Stalker suggested that bureaucratic organization and leadership styles would disadvantage companies operating in fast-moving and unpredictable environments, including those occupying a particular technological niche.[113]

The restructuring of traditional bureaucratic organizations to encourage 'intrapreneurship' and create a learning organization, Bala Chakravarty and Martin Gargiulo argue, requires employee empowerment during the process.[114] They describe how, typically, such a transformation is characterized first by an authoritarian restructuring and then by a more participative revitalization. This, they say, often fails. It is due to top management's inability to empower employees because of a loss of trust that is necessary during restructuring.

Senior staff in the UK higher education sector complain of institutional bureaucracy that discourages teaching initiatives and innovative teaching and learning methods, according to Ian McNay.[115] Bureaucracy is an enemy of empowerment, for which it substitutes system controls. McNay suggests that one reason for this problem may be senior staff's lack of confidence and a lack of leadership training:

This lack of confidence leads to control strategies where even minor decisions have to go further up the decision-making hierarchy than is efficient … Subsidiarity is a good principle … [whereby] … leadership and management are distributed, and small, agile, adaptive units are created.

Empowerment and Trust

A lack of trust is the enemy of empowerment. So is fear of the consequences of taking risks. Such distrust and fear can lead to a desire for control. The 'control freak' is a common phenomenon. However, control does not necessarily mean controlling other people: 'it means the organization is "in control" – the parts work together responsibly to create the desired results'.[116] Empowerment means letting go. Fear of losing control and a lack of trust are emotional responses.

Distrust is the enemy of empowerment. Trust in fact is a *sine qua non* for empowerment, as Warren Bennis affirmed in conversation with Richard Hodgetts:

> **Hodgetts:** '... even if you have the best vision in the world, if you can't generate trust, it doesn't matter. And it's not just trust in an abstract sense. It's the ability to connect with people in their gut and in their heart and not just in their head.'

> **Bennis:** 'Absolutely, and that's particularly true in this era of re-engineering and downsizing, where trust continues to be a major concern for the employees. If leaders can't establish that trust, then participation and empowerment will be cynical relics of a distopian nightmare. The problem is squarely in the hands of management, and it's a challenge that will confront us well into the next century.'[117]

It is only when we learn to manage our emotions and have the courage to make changes that we can be truly empowering.

When intentions and decisions are challenged, a single-minded leader may ignore this and lead an organization or nation into difficulty or disaster: witness Hitler's refusal to heed his generals' advice that led to Germany's defeat and Tony Blair's diminishing popularity after joining the Iraq War in early 2003 (contrasted with Winston Churchill's acceptance of dissent over his strategies).

In a BBC2 television series on the *Secrets of Leadership*, Andrew Roberts described how Hitler at first deliberately empowered his commanders but then, as his trust in them waned, reversed his leadership strategy.[118] Initially he introduced 'Mission Control', whereby he empowered his army leaders in the field. High Command set the objectives and commanders in the field were enabled to act on their own initiative and respond to situations without waiting for orders. Lower ranks were trained in leadership on the rationale that every follower had the potential to be a leader. Hitler displayed trust in his commanders to use their initiative and expertise to fulfil the mission, and he adopted this approach in his leadership of the German government, devolving decision-making responsibility to ministers while he happily stayed in his Bavarian retreat. However, his growing distrust of his army generals in the struggle to take over Russia led him to abandon his empowerment strategy and Mission Control and to 'micro-manage' activity at the fighting front. The outcome was disastrous: hundreds of thousands of German soldiers were killed, the fight against Russia was lost, and the Allies broke through in western Europe. Abandoning empowerment was the disastrous result of distrusting his subordinates. In fact it is not uncommon for managers to recall empowerment and take control when the chips are down.

Empowering people means taking the risk that mistakes will be made and, when they are made, treating them as opportunities to learn. During the Second World War, Winston Churchill won the confidence of his service chiefs through empowerment:

... he brought [to them] the sure knowledge that they might take calculated risks of even the most hair-raising kind without having to look over their shoulders.[119]

The extent of empowerment by the leader depends on the leader's need for control of others, self-awareness, self-control, self-confidence, trust in others, interpersonal skills, and a desire for empowerment or acceptance of it by subordinates or followers. Another enemy of empowerment is involvement in 'the minutiae of management' – expense claims, sick leave, etc.[120] To empower people means letting go. It means taking the risk that mistakes will be made and, when this happens, treating them as opportunities to learn. This requires courage – the courage to fail, as Adrian Furnham puts it.[121] In failure, it is important to acknowledge the failure and even more important to learn from it.[122] Risk aversion, a lack of trust, and selfishness or self-centredness on the part of the manager impede this. Organizational initiatives to empower people have often failed because of managers' inability to delegate effectively, their need for power, their own job insecurity, and role ambiguity.[123]

Empowerment, Risk and Resistance

A Nepalese Buddhist mantra says: 'Take into account that great love and great achievements involve great risk.' Empowerment carries risks. One is the risk of perceived abdication by a leader; others are fear of a loss of control and fear of failure. For example, in one telecommunications company I worked with, some managers expressed discomfort with the risk of anarchy as the result of empowerment. They preferred limits to subordinates' authority. Empowerment requires a distinction to be made between *leading* an organization and *controlling* it.

When the Bank of Scotland failed to gain control of NatWest in 2000, CEO Peter Burt said, 'People have to learn to fail ... If you don't try you may never lose, but you'll never win.'[124] The Bank of Scotland's arch-rival, the Royal Bank of Scotland, pipped it to the post – after two failed attempts at taking over Barclays Bank and Birmingham Midshires. People learn more from failure than from success. In fact failure is necessary for success. This requires us to understand *why* we have failed in a particular situation and to use this understanding in future risk taking. A Nepalese Buddhist mantra says: 'When you lose, don't lose the lesson.' Empowering people, therefore, may carry a risk of failure, but this risk is necessary and worthwhile if we are to help them to succeed.

In their economic model of leadership, Patrick Bolton and colleagues argue the importance of empowerment and discuss its difficulties. They recognize that there is a limit to how much any individual leader can do and emphasize the importance of communication and developing followers' knowledge base and skills as part of the empowerment process.[125] But they also recognize leaders' reluctance to delegate for several reasons: a lack of trust, an unwillingness to empower others because of the desire to retain power and a fear of competition from their up-and-coming, and perhaps smarter, staff.

The effect that empowerment has on people has been well researched. But leaders often fail to empower followers and subordinates. What motivates leaders to empower them? In two studies by Natalia Hakimi and colleagues, they show how leaders' trust in their followers' performance and integrity influences empowerment and that this influence is moderated by the leader's conscientiousness.[126]

Loss of control is an issue for empowerment. Peter Mills and Gerardo Ungson say:

> The success or failure of employee empowerment depends on the ability of the organization to reconcile loss of control inherent in empowerment practices with the fundamental organizational need for goal congruence.[127]

They propose two ways of exercising control for the risks of empowerment: the organizational constitution and the building of organization-wide (routine) trust. The organization constitution is, Mayer Zald says, 'a set of agreements and understandings that define the limits and goals of the group ... as well as the responsibilities and rights of participants'.[128] Mills and Ungson distinguish between 'routine trust' and 'basic trust'. The former is a limited form of trust built up over time and seen in everyday relationships, entailing the belief that a person has the ability to perform specific tasks under specific conditions.[129] Basic trust arises in situations where people have little information about the object of their trust,[130] and it carries greater risk than routine trust.[131] Basic trust, according to Blair Sheppard and Dana Sherman:

> [has] the potential for the individual to behave in ways contrary to the interests of the organization, primarily because the empowered employee's behavior is often outside the purview of the organization and therefore difficult to control.[132]

According to Graham Clark, the need for control determines the extent to which empowerment is possible.[133] Organizations with a strong need for control and a low tolerance of risk – 'compliant organizations' – include mass-production firms, fast-food restaurants, retail financial services and airlines.

Empowerment has disadvantages, both perceived and real. Some employees may abuse the increased power they gain. Some may not have the desire or aptitude for the increased responsibility. Many employees might be happy with the *status quo*. Managers of empowered employees need to have new or better skills in facilitation and information sharing. Some may fear a loss of control.[134] The vertical chain of command, and its associated emphasis on control, is still common in organizations. The problem is that control seeks conformity to the plan, policies and procedures. The emotional reaction it engenders is captured in the saying, 'Trust flees authority.' This problem has greatest adverse impact in the realms of middle-level management. Yet middle managers are expected, and ought, to be leaders themselves.[135] In fact most resistance to empowerment comes from middle-level managers.[136] John Scully says that some employees may regard empowerment as an abdication by managers that will lead to organizational anarchy.[137]

Some managers 'are like parents who want their children to make decisions for themselves but want them to make only the decisions that [they] ... would have made', say Stanley Deetz and colleagues.[138] This approach creates mutual distrust and cynicism and leads to the defensive assertion by managers that empowerment does not work. The Harbridge House survey revealed that some 62 per cent of middle-level managers and one-third of senior and junior managers felt threatened by empowerment: the three most common barriers to empowerment were an unwillingness to let go, a fear of the new, and risk aversion.[139] Even CEOs may have a problem; for example, Robert Haas, CEO of Levi Strauss, said: 'It has been difficult for me to accept the fact that I don't have to be the smartest guy on the block.'[140]

Chris Argyris describes such resistance to empowerment by managers as examples of what he calls 'Model 1' – unilateral control.[141] This is characterized by:

* Needing to maximize winning and minimize losing.
* Perceiving challenges to authority, policies and strategies as signs of weakness.
* Going to great lengths to avoid such conflicts and covering up efforts to do so.
* Achieving the desired outcomes while minimizing the stimulation or expression of negative feelings.

On the other hand Argyris's Model 2 managers will:

* Confront issues.
* Debate assumptions.
* Share information.
* Express feelings.
* Involve and empower people.
* Focus on winning collectively as an enterprise rather than winning as an individual.

Eileen Shapiro, in a review of Argyris's models, questions the assertion that empowerment is the result of confronting issues, debating assumptions, sharing information and expressing feelings. Instead she posits the structural circumstances of the economy as an alternative explanation for empowerment described earlier in this chapter, quoting fast-paced entrepreneurial situations with empowerment 'by default' as an example.[142]

More junior managers and non-managerial employees may resist empowerment because of several forms of anxiety. Their new freedom to take risks may also lead to a fear of lack of support from their bosses when they fail. They may fear failure itself in what they perceive to be a 'blame' culture. And they may fear losing their job either because of failure or because of handing it away and becoming redundant. They may also fear that accepting greater responsibility and accountability may mean it is harder to blame others when things go wrong. Empowering people includes giving them the power to say 'no' to being empowered – if they do not want it. Judith Bardwick suggests that leaders can empower in small increments others who are anxious about the responsibility and its accompanying risk of failure.[143]

Managers may also fear a loss of power and control when they delegate authority to subordinates, with little benefit in return for themselves. In fact, empowering subordinates implies a redefinition of the manager's role – as a leader, rather than a manager, of people. As we said in Chapter 1, 'We manage *things* and *processes*, but we *lead* people.'

Empowerment, the Learning Organization and Creativity

If knowledge is power, then empowering people means sharing knowledge with them. Yet, according to research on strategies for the knowledge economy by Windle Priem and David Finegold, nine out of every ten people in global firms say they do not have access to lessons learned by their firms.[144] In their report Priem and Finegold say:

> Leaders should participate in development programmes, mentor high-potential managers, have executives share publicly their mistakes and what they learned, recognise those who took carefully calculated risks but didn't succeed, and promote people who actively share knowledge to help the whole organisation.

Priem and Finegold's report also makes the point that employees must feel that sharing knowledge is part of their job and that it is recognized and rewarded. Many leaders sadly miss the mark by failing to ensure this: they reward performance but not learning. Most people feel they do not share in the success of the organization, and half feel they do not have a stake in improving corporate performance.

Knowledge management is nothing new. And it is an example of leadership through empowerment. Knowledge management is about people, not IT: it is about learning, communication, using knowledge from various sources and developing a culture of knowledge sharing.[145] Effective leaders share information and ideas across the organization and encourage and cultivate informal sources of information.[146]

Creating a learning organization is about learning how to learn, facilitating the learning of all its members and continuous organizational change.[147] A survey of 532 CEOs and senior managers in the top 100 companies in 15 countries by the PA Consulting Group in 1996 revealed a significant global consensus on the need to create learning organizations characterized by agility, continuous adaptation, creativity and innovation, facilitated by empowering leadership.[148]

A model organization in this respect, management consultant Chris Collison says, is BP.[149] In 1996 Sir John (later Lord) Browne, the company's Group CEO, initiated a successful knowledge management programme using an intranet that saved millions of dollars. This programme involved a task force to identify best practice, teams about to carry out a new project getting together with peers from other parts of the organization to identify the best way to do it, reviews of action taken compared with those intended and the lessons learned, and proof of learning about what the firm knew about running a similar project before getting approval and funding for a new project.

Nurturing the creativity of gifted people entails empowering them. There are three kinds of creative people in organizations. Some create new things and ideas from scratch. Some rearrange existing things or ideas and put them into a new order or perspective. And creative people require leaders who themselves are creative. What do we mean by 'creativity'? Creativity is the ability to generate new and original ideas, associations, methods, approaches and solutions – a process known as 'ideation' – and to relate them to a given problem. Creativity – popularly associated with the right hemisphere of the brain – is characterized by artistic, intuitive, conceptual, emotional,

holistic, 'divergent' and 'lateral' thinking and the associated behaviour. Analytical thinking – 'left-brain' – by contrast is logical, rational, mathematical, technical, controlled, administrative, 'convergent' and 'vertical'.

Creativity must be contrasted with *innovation*. Innovation is not invention; that is, creativity. Innovation is a process of implementation, Joe Prochaska says, 'identifying an existing resource and, through knowledge, elevating it to a new level of utility and value to the customer'.[150] He believes:

> **The biggest roadblocks to innovation are a lack of understanding of when to take intelligent risks ... and insufficient knowledge of the skills and principles needed to develop innovation into a managerial practice ... innovation is largely knowledge driven.**

The intelligence shown by creative people is evident through their conceptual fluency and flexibility, originality and preference for complexity.[151] Conceptual fluency is the ability to generate many ideas rapidly. Conceptual flexibility –'dimensionality' – is the ability to 'shift gears', to discard an approach or a frame of reference in favour of another. Originality is the ability to give unusual interpretations or responses to situations. And creative people display a preference for complexity as an enjoyable challenge. This preference has important implications for leading creative people.

Creativity is impaired by a belief that there is always one right answer, by the discipline and requirements of bureaucracy, such as standard operating procedures, and by authoritarianism in managers. This, together with a fear of evaluation – often premature – and a fear of criticism, leads to conformity or convergent thinking. Another barrier is the lack of recognition and use of creativity in people. Prochaska believes that creativity is often misunderstood by top management in an organization:

> **The biggest roadblock to creativity is that it is not precisely defined or well understood as a managerial practice that can have an attractive return on investment when put to work in an organization. It is especially misunderstood among top management, from whom a high level of support is needed to sponsor any change in an organization.[152]**

What does this mean for empowering leadership? John Hafile says that creative people need appropriate roles and goals, appropriate infrastructure and support, the permission and freedom to experiment and make mistakes, and a recognition and reward of their achievements and for these to be put into use.[153] Using the results of creative work will sometimes result in failure: 'The operation was a success though the patient died.'

There are some further implications for leadership. Creative people's bosses must welcome disagreement and contrary views, using empathy and suspending judgement. Creative people must be made accountable for the changes they suggest. Creative ideas must reach the decision makers. In addition, in their analysis of 'breakthrough thinking', Gerald Nadler and Shozo Hibino suggest that those who are expected to implement others' creative solutions must be involved in creating the thinking process at the group level, with flexibility in applying this.[154] All of this is necessary in order to create or reinforce a culture of creativity.

My concept of empowerment explicitly includes self-confidence or self-efficacy – the feeling or belief that one is *able to do* what needs to be done. This is a form of intrinsic motivation. And intrinsic motivation is a feature of *engagement* – the desire and commitment to do what needs to be done. This is the topic of the next chapter.

 ## Further Reading

Chris Argyris (2000), *Flawed Advice and the Management Trap*. Oxford: Oxford University Press.

K. Blanchard, J.P. Carlos and A. Randolph (1995), *Empowerment Takes More Than a Minute*. San Francisco, CA: Berrett-Koehler.

William C. Byham (1988), *Zapp! The Lightning of Empowerment*. Pittsburgh, PA: Development Dimensions International Press.

Neil Thompson (2006), *Power and Empowerment*. Lyme Regis, Dorset: Russell House Publishing.

 ## Discussion Questions

1. Why is empowerment much misunderstood? Why do some managers resist empowering their people?
2. How can the barriers to empowerment be overcome or reduced?
3. Is empowerment universally applicable and effective? What are the cross-cultural considerations?
4. Can leadership be effective without empowering other people?

9 Leadership and Engagement

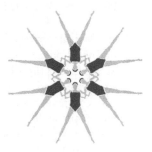

Inspire others and you will feel inspired yourself.

Theodore Zeldin[1]

OVERVIEW

- The proposition of this chapter is that effective leaders engage other people by influencing, motivating and inspiring them to want to do what needs to be done. This is the sixth core theme and practice in our model of leadership.
- Influencing, motivating and inspiring people are what is most commonly associated with leadership. The outcome of transformational leadership is employee engagement: employees who are motivated to levels beyond what is normally the case.
- Employee engagement is the extent to which people in an organization willingly, even eagerly, give of their discretionary effort over and above doing what they have to do. They are willing and eager to give of their best, display creativity and use their initiative.
- Yet engaging leadership is a major weakness among many of those in leadership positions, both in what they stand for and how they communicate it and in the example they set. It is the area of leadership that calls for the greatest attention and improvement.
- Understanding what motivates people at work, how it does so, what leaders do when they motivate employees, and how they create the conditions in which motivation can emerge is essential to engaging employees with their work and the organization. Employees are engaged and inspired in their work when there is meaning, worthiness and challenge in it.
- Leaders engage employees through the way they use various forms of personal power, not position power (authority).
- The rhythms and sounds of speech and language are closely associated with feelings and emotion. The way we talk to others – our authenticity, use of 'framing', rhetoric and 'body language' – can be a source of inspiration to them.
- This chapter reviews the major concepts and theories of motivation and how understanding and applying them can contribute to leadership effectiveness, the different forms of power and its use in the influencing process, the relationship between inspirational leadership and charisma, authenticity, and the use of inspirational language and speech in leadership, in particular the framing of language and the use of rhetoric.

The vast majority of senior executives – some eight out of every ten across Europe and the Middle East – believe that employee disengagement is one of the three biggest threats facing their business.[2] Yet, according to 43 per cent of them, issues concerning morale and motivation are rarely discussed at board level and some 90 per cent of their companies simply choose to ignore the problems caused by disengaged staff. Could this be due to ignorance, admitted or otherwise, of how to deal with it?

Brian Amble reports these stark research findings from the Economist Intelligence Unit (EIU). Also thought-provoking – and paradoxical – is the EIU's finding that CEOs apparently highly overrate their personal impact on employee engagement and underrate the impact of middle managers.

Nevertheless, there has been an increasing interest in employee engagement, especially employee involvement and motivation, in recent times, which has probably been fuelled by the even greater need to engage employees during times of economic hardship. In the UK the Talent Foundation noted in September 2010 that the topic was the most frequently read one on their website, superseding even leadership.[3] Research by Transparent Consulting suggests that large companies in the UK are making more of an effort to engage with their employees, though there are still concerns about whether meaningful change will result.[4] In 2009 the UK government published the findings of a study of a wide range of public and private sector organizations, concluding that the key enablers of engagement were line management, employee voice, integrity and leadership.[5]

Businesses headed by effective leaders have employees who are significantly more engaged, creative and innovative, and these businesses make more money than those run by less effective leaders, according to research carried out by Kenexa, surveying some 29,000 employees in 21 countries.[6] Using an employee engagement index, the research found that engagement ranged from 91 per cent where leaders were rated as effective to 17 per cent where they were rated as neutral or ineffective: employee engagement was five times higher in businesses with effective leadership. In addition, the research had lessons for leadership development, which we discuss in Chapter 11.

Zoe Thomas makes the point that, during tough economic times, firms have more to gain than ever from strongly engaged employees.[7] She quotes the Sytner Group, the prestige car retailer, ranked third in the 25 Best Big Companies to Work For 2010, posting record profits in a year in which, according to the company's chief operating officer, it had consciously 'put its staff first'. An Ipsos Mori poll of 100 board directors from the 500 largest UK companies showed that they appreciated the importance of increasing employee engagement during the difficult economic conditions prevailing in 2010.[8] Supermarket J. Sainsbury's strategy is to ensure open, two-way communication, and not just to listen but also to act on suggestions, says CEO Justin King.[9] John Lewis's employee (partner) ownership model is 'a huge reinforcer for engagement', says Patrick Lewis, partners' counsellor: 'Leaders are effectively working for their owners. And the commitment we get from partners can be very impressive.'[10]

In a McKinsey survey, virtually all of the executives surveyed who characterized their companies' change initiatives as 'extremely successful' said that employees contributed ideas to shape the efforts.[11] Nearly 25 per cent of the extremely successful transformations were planned by groups of 50 people or more, compared with 6 per cent of unsuccessful transformations. The involvement and engagement of people is a key leadership process in organizational transformation.

So What Exactly is Engagement?

In this chapter we first discuss the nature of employee engagement. We then consider in turn the relationships between engagement and motivation, power and influence, and inspiration, followed by how employee engagement can be enhanced as a core practice of effective leadership.

What is Engagement?

Unfortunately, like 'leadership', employee engagement has no universal definition, though its simplest expression is 'passion for work'.[12] It is most commonly defined as intellectual and emotional commitment to the organization or as the discretionary effort shown by employees in their work.[13]

Employee engagement is the extent to which people in an organization will willingly, even eagerly, give of their discretionary effort, over and above doing what they have to do. They are willing and eager to do more than they have to – giving of their best, displaying creativity, and using their initiative. The UK's Chartered Institute of Personnel and Development defines employee engagement as 'a combination of commitment to the organisation and its values plus a willingness to help out colleagues (organisational citizenship) ... [going] beyond job satisfaction and ... not simply motivation'.[14] The outcome produced as a result of engaging leadership has been defined as 'a measure of the extent to which employees put discretionary effort into their work'.[15] Key ideas that constitute the concept of employee engagement are:

* Positive attitudes towards, and a commitment to, work, colleagues, the organization and its leaders.
* Attentiveness to, enthusiasm for, and absorption in work.
* The motivation to work – to do what needs to be done (and more) – that results from influence and inspiration not only from the nature of the work or the organization itself but also from leadership behaviour displayed in the organization.

Ivan Robertson and Cary Cooper suggest that current concepts and models of engagement emphasize employee commitment and the benefits to the organization.[16] They also suggest further research needs to be carried out in order to explore a fuller notion of engagement that includes personal well-being as a better basis for sustainable benefits to both the organization and the individual. For example, a lack of employee engagement may be associated with boredom, which is a killer, according to research in the UK public sector.[17] Annie Britton and Martin Shipley at University College London found a correlation between boredom and death: civil servants who admitted to being extremely bored at work were 2.5 times more likely to die of cardiovascular disease. Chronic boredom is dangerous: it can lead to depression, which in turn is associated with a high risk of heart disease.

Engagement among employees is also linked to their personality traits: adjustment (the absence of neurosis), conscientiousness (prudence), altruism and agreeableness, which, Adrian Furnham says, means that 'some people are thus easy to engage by head and heart, and others not'.[18] Effective leaders engage other people through their charisma or ability to inspire. Engagement results partly from effective leadership, whereby people see how their work fits into the 'big picture' and they feel they are listened to and dealt with fairly. As Furnham says, 'those who are intrinsically motivated don't need very much extrinsic motivation'.

Optimists are perceived by other people to be more charismatic and more likely to succeed than pessimists, according to researchers at the National Bureau of Economic Research in the United States.[19] They define 'dispositional optimism' as 'a personality trait associated with individuals who believe, either rightly or wrongly, that in general good things tend to happen to them more than bad things'. Leaders who are optimists rather than pessimists, I contend, are more likely to attract followers and to be engaging: they are more likely to be influential, motivating and indeed inspiring.

Employee engagement may suffer as a result of a process-driven and hierarchical culture that does not sufficiently recognize the value of leadership. This has been the case in Germany, according to some commentators.[20] Some companies, however, are taking the lead in introducing initiatives to increase employee engagement, for example Allianz, Europe's largest insurance company, is using customer feedback and dialogue with staff to do so. Conference Board research in Germany has shown that providing economic security during difficult times is a primary factor in maintaining and enhancing employee engagement.[21]

A 'perfect example' of how employee disengagement can damage a business comes from British Gas (BG).[22] The majority of the 3,000 unionized employees who responded to a trade union survey in BG voiced several serious complaints. These related to the company's management style, being overworked, being made to 'oversell' to customers – 'Now it's all profit and no customer service' – and being micromanaged and subjected to draconian discipline over the slightest infringements, including missing performance targets for the first time. Such disengagement was the basis for an impending strike ballot. Yet a BG statement in response to these complaints referred only to an accusation of job cuts, apparently ignoring the issue of disengagement. Sadly, in the past the company had been seen as a great place to work.

Employee engagement is often misunderstood, even by business journalists. For example, in reporting on the topic and quoting Rob Briner, a professor of organizational psychology in the UK, Carly Chynoweth says:

> ... Briner [does not] have much time for the concept of employee engagement – the idea that organisations should make staff feel happy and involved with corporate goals.[23]

This is not an adequate definition of employee engagement. On this false premise – which Chynoweth, and perhaps even Briner, is not alone in assuming – an invalid criticism of employee engagement emerges. However, according to Chynoweth, Briner does make a good point:

Broadly speaking, just because people are happy at work does not mean they will perform better. The strongest link really is that if you perform well at work you feel more satisfied, so employee-engagement enthusiasts might have it the wrong way round.[24]

Trying to make people happy so that they will perform better is unlikely to work, though helping people to perform better may well help to 'improve their mood'.[25] It is well established that happy workers are not necessarily productive workers.[26] The relationship between happiness and job performance is equivocal in the research literature, mainly because of differing ways of defining and measuring 'happiness'. These are job satisfaction, the presence of positive affect (feelings), the absence of negative affect, the lack of emotional exhaustion, or psychological well-being. Peter Warr adds to these kinds of happiness the following: joy, contentment, and a sense of personal meaning – all of which are different from one another.[27]

However, there is support in the literature to suggest that a relationship exists between affective well-being, intrinsic job satisfaction and managers' performance, according to Peter Hosie and colleagues.[28] They say that indicators of managers' affective well-being and their intrinsic job satisfaction were shown to predict aspects of their contextual and task performance. But are well-being and satisfaction to be treated as means to an end or as an end in themselves?

Cynthia Fisher, reviewing the extant literature on happiness at work, concludes that past research has underestimated its importance.[29] She suggests that the concept of happiness at work should include not only job satisfaction but also work engagement and affective organizational commitment. She also points out that there is evidence that happiness at work has consequences for both individuals and organizations as a whole.

Research into happiness can be a controversial political issue. For example, in 2010 the UK government announced a plan to use a questionnaire-based measure of general well-being rather than measures of income or wealth as a basis for policy and planning. A group of psychologists in the UK fiercely criticized this initiative as 'pernicious and cynical'.[30] They argued that introspection on one's own subjective experiences was not a reliable way of generating knowledge, simple self-report measures were inadequate for assessing affective states, no such 'concocted' measures could represent a unitary quality of 'happiness', and that more objective and reliable indexes – of unhappiness – were strongly associated with social inequality, which was concentrated among the 'marginalised, excluded and dispossessed'. The political issue that these psychologists raised concerns the motives of the government: whether happiness, rather than economic equality (whatever this is and regardless of whether it can ever be achieved), can be the more valid indicator of societal well-being.

However, other psychologists have taken issue with this stance. For example, Steve Reicher and Alex Haslam say:

Leaving aside the inconvenient fact that this [that self-reported ratings of happiness are not only poor predictors of important things such as people's mental and physical health but also meaningless] simply isn't true, one might retort that 'objective' measures of economic performance are themselves highly problematic by this criterion. [Moreover],

happiness, most of us would agree, is important not as a means to something else but as an end in itself. Hence the key question is not 'What does happiness predict?' but 'What predicts happiness?' – and one can only answer this question if one has taken the trouble to try to measure happiness in the first place.[31]

Reicher and Haslam point out the constantly repeated finding in research that 'the quality of one's social relations is a far better and more robust predictor of happiness than … one's wealth', but with one proviso. This is true for people in affluent societies: personal wealth and the provision of public services play a part in making possible such social relations. Government therefore may also perform a role in making sure that people do have the services they need to be part of society – and engaged with it. Indeed in March 2011 the UK's coalition government launched a new Employee Engagement Taskforce aimed at driving growth and boosting productivity.

ENGAGEMENT – A MUSICAL EXAMPLE

… there's something missing in our orchestral culture… a vital spark of intensity and engagement … Simon Rattle [resident conductor of the Berlin Philharmonic Orchestra] … told me [Tom Service] … that one of the principal players in Berlin … was amazed at the brilliance of … British musicians in the first rehearsal … the technical standard was much better than … at the Berlin Phil at a first rehearsal. The problem was, the final concert wasn't any more exciting than that first run-through. That's the exact opposite of what happens in Berlin …, Vienna …, or Amsterdam … The payoff is … that the concerts [by those cities' great orchestras] often have an expressive intensity that British orchestras rarely manage. It's a different way of thinking about what performance is. The goal in Berlin or Munich is to get to a place where the music is in the bones of the players; in Britain, the problem is getting further into the music than playing all of the notes in the right order … into the x-factor of the thrill of performance.

Extracts from Tom Service (2011), Do British orchestras play too perfectly? Critic's notebook, g2, *Guardian*, 17 February, 21.

What does it take to engage people and gain their commitment to the work of the organization, to pursue its vision and purpose? The ability to motivate, influence and inspire followers or subordinates is one of the biggest challenges facing leaders today across the range of human endeavour. We first address the relationship between motivation and engagement.

Engagement and Motivation

Engaged employees are motivated to exert effort, perform the work that needs to be done and thereby pursue the vision, purpose and strategies of the organization.

Understanding how this happens entails understanding what motivates people at work, how it does so, what leaders do when they motivate employees, and how they create the conditions in which motivation can emerge to the extent that employees are engaged with their work and the organization.

What is Motivation?

The study of motivation, George Miller says, 'is the study of all those pushes and prods – biological, social and psychological – that defeat our laziness and move us, either eagerly or reluctantly, to action'.[32] A good working definition of motivation is: 'those psychological processes that cause the arousal, direction, and persistence of voluntary actions that are goal-directed'.[33] Unless we are motivated, we will do nothing. Motivation reflects our needs and wants.[34]

'Motivation' comes from the Latin *movere*, 'to move'. A motive thus is something that moves us into action – a push or a pull. Effective leaders, then, tap people's psychological processes that arouse, direct and maintain voluntary behaviour towards goals. Motivating people means stimulating, instilling or arousing thoughts or feelings that will animate or energize them to act in a particular way.

The motivation that leaders, through their actions, create in people is extrinsic: people are motivated to do something or not to do it as a result of a leader's behaviour.[35] Motivation is not only a consequence of good leadership. People may be motivated to achieve the required results through bullying or fear in order to avoid unpleasant consequences. This is associated with negative reinforcement. People may be motivated by the prospect of extrinsic rewards, such as money, recognition (such as public praise) and other externally provided rewards and benefits. Extrinsic motivation entails a feeling of compulsion to do things for an external source to achieve an outcome that usually satisfies lower-order needs like having enough money to survive. Extrinsic motivation entails seeking and securing a reward from work.

On the other hand people may be motivated by intrinsic needs – for example, a need for the pleasure or satisfaction that accompanies performing meaningful, interesting, enjoyable or challenging work, a need to belong to a social group, a sense of responsibility, achievement, self-esteem, creativity, or making a difference in some way. This is intrinsic motivation. People may be motivated in the absence of leaders, managers or anybody else: they may perform an activity for the inherent satisfaction of the activity itself.

Mihaly Csikszentmihalyi studied why people such as artists, musicians, chess players, mountaineers and actors love to do what they do, despite the absence of material reward. He found that they all said, 'experiencing the activity was in itself the reward … This is the feeling I labelled "flow"', says Mihaly Csikszentmihalyi.[36] The leadership challenge is to structure work according to individuals' needs and interests so that it is the reward in itself. Richard Ryan and Edward Deci argue that intrinsic motivation relates to three innate psychological needs: competence, autonomy and relatedness (an interaction with other people and security in relationships).[37] With intrinsic motivation, 'my work is my reward'.[38]

The motivation of creative people poses a special leadership challenge. Extrinsic motivation, such as deadlines and performance-related pay, appears to be detrimental to creativity. Intrinsic motivation, on the other hand, seems to be conducive to it. The single best stimulus to creativity is freedom – the power to decide what to do and how to do it and a sense of control over one's destiny.[39]

There can be no better way of being intrinsically motivated at work – to be doing what needs to be done – than when organizational goals are aligned with our individual goals. This, Stephen Covey says, enables people to create a 'win-win agreement' – a psychological contract between them and their leaders – that 'represents a clear mutual understanding and commitment regarding expectations in five areas: ... desired results, ... guidelines, ... resources, ... accountabilities, and ... consequences [rewards or benefits]'.[40]

Leadership, then, is in part concerned with eliciting motivation in people by creating motivational environments. Motivation is an individualized phenomenon. Leaders therefore have to know their followers and provide the opportunities for individuals' idiosyncratic needs to be satisfied, as Bass's theory of transformational leadership suggests in its component of individualized consideration.

Major Theories of Motivation

Motivation theories, like theories of leadership, are many and varied. What follows are a brief review and a synthesis of the major ones that are particularly useful in the context of employee engagement.

Maslow's 'Hierarchy of Needs'. Needs exist at several successive levels, according to Abraham Maslow: survival, safety and security, affiliation, challenge, achievement, recognition and self-esteem, and self-actualization (self-fulfilment).[41]

McGregor's Theory X and Theory Y. Douglas McGregor contrasts two sets of assumptions and attitudes in managers in respect of human nature: Theory X and Theory Y.[42] Theory X postulates that the average human being inherently dislikes and tries to avoid work, has little ambition, wants security above all, and therefore must be coerced, controlled, directed and threatened to do what needs to be done. Theory Y on the other hand postulates that human beings will exercise self-direction and self-control in pursuing objectives to which they are committed; commitment results from rewards associated with achievement; the average human being will not only accept responsibility but also even seek it; the capacity to exercise imagination, ingenuity and creativity is widely, not narrowly, distributed; and the potential of the average human being generally is only partially utilized.

Herzberg's Motivation–Hygiene Theory. This theory proposes that there are some elements in the work situation that, when present, tend to lead to satisfaction and other elements that, when present, tend to lead to dissatisfaction.[43] The former are motivators, the latter hygiene factors. Motivators include the nature of the work itself, achievement, recognition and opportunities for advancement. Hygiene factors – dissatisfiers – include poor technical supervision, pay and working conditions. The implications for leadership are clear. Effective leaders minimize dissatisfiers and maximize motivators.

Expectancy-Valence Theory. This theory explains how individuals are motivated to take action that they perceive as maximizing the likelihood of desirable outcomes for themselves, such as, for example, to avoid pain, enhance pleasure or meet collective interests.[44] Self-efficacy, moderated by task complexity and locus of control, is a significant determinant of motivation and performance at work.[45] One might reasonably infer here that empowerment is a necessary condition for motivation: a self-perception of a lack of empowerment or of disempowerment is likely to lead to a lack of motivation.

Equity Theory. In evaluating the outcome of reward, one consideration is the fairness or equity of that reward, not only in relation to effort expended but also in relation to other people.[46] The tension that results from a sense of inequity creates the motivation to resolve it through several kinds of corrective or, more usually, dysfunctional behaviour.

Goal Theory. Appropriate and compatible goals, resources and rewards are motivational in energizing individuals and sustaining their action and serve the interests of both individuals and their organizations.[47] Related to this theory is the 'Pygmalion effect'.[48] This refers to the phenomenon whereby the greater the expectation placed upon people, the better they perform. The term derives from a Cypriot sculptor in a narrative by Ovid in Greek mythology, Pygmalion, who fell in love with a female statue he had carved out of ivory. The Pygmalion effect is a form of self-fulfilling prophecy: people with poor expectations internalize their negative label and those with positive labels and associated self-esteem succeed accordingly.

McClelland's Motivational Needs Theory. The style and behaviour of human beings is characterized by a mix of the needs for affiliation ('n-affil'), authority or power ('n-pow') and achievement ('n-ach').[49] David McClelland suggests that a strong affiliation need undermines a manager's objectivity because of the need to be liked; a strong power need may be associated with strong work ethic and commitment to the organization but not necessarily with flexibility and interpersonal skills; and a strong achievement motivation is associated with effective leadership.

Towards a Synthesis in Motivation Theory

A recent development in motivation theory known as 'Positive Organizational Behavior [or Scholarship]' has emerged: studies of 'positive deviance' in organizations have suggested that it is associated with a high level of employee motivation.[50] This brings together some key ideas from earlier theories of motivation and personality theory. Positive deviance, Kim Cameron says, is characterized by appreciation, collaboration, virtuousness, vitality, optimism and meaningfulness reflecting a culture of trust and trustworthiness, resilience, humility, authenticity, respect and mutual forgiveness among employees.[51] *Welcoming* feedback from others, a rare phenomenon in my opinion, is one example. Kim Cameron reports that focusing on the positive attributes of employees, rather than on their weaknesses and problem solving, leads to a significantly better performance by their organizations.[52] And treating threats, problems and failures as opportunities to learn and improve can be a source of great inspiration among one's subordinates or followers. It prevents, removes or reduces the emotional contagion of loss of self-esteem. Indeed quite the contrary: together with a focus on positive attributes, it can maintain or enhance self-esteem – generally a powerful motivator.

So what does motivate people at work? We can tentatively draw together a list of the human needs that theories of motivation describe. These are shown in the text box below. These needs, of course, will vary from individual to individual. Various combinations of them would produce interesting variations both in one's personal 'profile' of needs and goals in work and life and in how one behaves specifically in a leadership role with other people. For example, understanding and responding appropriately to other people's needs, both individually and collectively, is associated with effective leadership. This is known as emotional intelligence, which we discuss in the next chapter.

HUMAN NEEDS

- The need to survive.
- The need for money (as a means to survival and other ends such as recognition, self-esteem, physical comfort and power).
- The need to belong – affiliation.
- The need for fairness or equity.
- The need to influence others – power and control.
- The need for autonomy.
- The need for self-efficacy.
- The need for interesting, meaningful and challenging work.
- The need for recognition, status and self-esteem.
- The need to achieve and contribute.
- The need for exploration, novelty and discovery.
- The need to fulfil aspirations and potential.

CASE EXAMPLE: EMPLOYEE ENGAGEMENT – A MATTER OF MOTIVATION[53]

What does employee engagement from a motivational perspective look like in practice? John Smythe, from the Engage for Change consultancy, offers two scenarios to illustrate it. Imagine two different employees, called Ruby and Geraldine, who work for different businesses.

Scenario 1

In the first scenario, Ruby is invited to attend a morning meeting titled 'Help our recovery'. 'The invitation confirms recent open communication about the poor performance

(Continued)

(Continued)

of all parts of the company, and that its parent is unable to subsidise it, let alone provide more cash for investment, and that fast action must be taken to stabilise the situation', Smythe explains. 'But it also says there are no secret pre-hatched plans for radical action. It says: "We want you and your colleagues to take ownership with management to solve the crisis, recognising that unpalatable options will have to be on the table."'

Ruby is both concerned and flattered. She arrives at the meeting feeling like a player rather than a spectator. A two-month timetable is laid out in which she and her colleagues are invited to use their knowledge to find achievable cost savings without harming key business areas.

In this process, Smythe says, there are three good questions employees can be asked. What would they do if they had a free hand in their day job? What would they do if they were a director of the company? What would they do if they had survived a takeover but were given two months by the acquirer to propose small but radical changes? In this way, employees can own the decisions that are necessary, and not become disengaged or demotivated even as tough measures are put in place.

Scenario 2

The alternative scenario, which concerns Geraldine, is less appealing. She is also invited to a meeting described as a 'cascade briefing'. Rumours have been spreading, directors have gone to ground, and communication from the company has been sparse.

'At the "cascade", her fears are confirmed when, in a PowerPoint presentation, the full extent of the dire state of the business is revealed for the first time', Smythe says. 'Detailed top-down plans for restructuring and efficiencies are revealed. The focus is all on reduction with no hint of new business opportunities. Geraldine feels less like a spectator and more like a victim. To varying degrees, her colleagues leave the meeting in shock and immobilised.'

These examples are based on real situations, Smythe says. 'The first adult-to-adult example resulted in very fast action from a large group of workers, who all, or nearly all, felt they were driving change where they worked, and fast results were achieved. The second disenfranchised those who could contribute, resulting in a huge task of execution by an overworked "change team"', he states.

'When have you have felt most engaged, most valued and most implicated in a successful project or period at work?' he asks. 'Absolutely none of us is going to report that it was more like Geraldine's experience.'

Engagement means sharing power, which can scare some managers. It also means developing a culture of 'distributed leadership': selecting and developing leaders at every level who will engage people in the decision-making and change process.

'A culture of distributed leadership means challenging assumptions about the primacy and effectiveness of a command-and-control approach to leadership', Smythe says. 'It primarily means individual leaders assessing how they have learnt to make decisions, how they engage others in decision making and how they transition from being a "god" with all the answers to being a "guide" helping to liberate the creativity of others.'

Engagement, Power and Influence

If leadership is showing the way and helping or inducing people to pursue it, where does the leader's ability to do this come from? Leaders get things done through using their power. They influence, motivate and inspire people to do – or much better, to *want to do* – what needs to be done by using various forms of power. Power in this context is the ability to influence the thoughts and actions of another person or group of people.

Using power is exhilarating. Indeed it may be, as former American secretary of state Henry Kissinger famously said, 'the greatest aphrodisiac'.[54] Yet true leaders are willing to share power with those they lead – to empower them to be freer, more autonomous and hence more capable of doing what they need to do.[55]

Forms of Power

While managers are appointed to their position, leaders are not. Leaders *emerge* or are *elected* as leaders, as we have discussed in Chapter 3. Managers, especially those with employees reporting to them, usually are expected to behave like leaders, though, as we have discussed in previous chapters, many fail to do so adequately. Those who do can be very effective leaders as well as managers. And, of course, some people are effective leaders without being managers.

Managers have authority or 'position power', which is associated with their rank, status or position in an organization. This is the power that entitles them to give direction and material or financial rewards to subordinates or others. However, managers who rely on authority to get things done will usually foster only reluctance or compliance at best. Managers or would-be leaders who rely on 'personal power' instead of position power are much more likely to achieve people's commitment – a belief in, and desire to do, what needs to be done – and their engagement than those who rely solely on position power.

It is very important for would-be leaders to understand the difference between these two forms of power and to be able to use them appropriately. Using position power or authority does influence or motivate people to do what needs to be done. But personal power is the basis for 'winning hearts and minds' – influencing, motivating *and* inspiring people to *want to do* what needs to be done and to be committed and engaged in doing it.

There are several forms of power described in a classic model by John French and Bertram Raven: legitimate power, coercive power, reward power, referent power, expert power, and information power.[56] These forms of power depend for their effectiveness on followers' perceptions of them in leaders. Reward power straddles position and person: it requires the authority to dispense material or financial rewards, but it is within a leader's personal power to dispense psychological rewards (in the form of recognition and praise). Table 9.1 shows my classification of these forms of power.

Position Power (Authority)
Legitimate Power. Legitimate power is associated with authority and is a form of position power. It is based on people's perception of the manager's or leader's right or

Table 9.1 Forms of Position Power and Personal Power

Authority (Position Power)	Personal Power
• Legitimate Power • Coercive Power • Material/Financial Reward Power	• Psychological Reward Power • Referent Power • Expert Power • Information Power

authority to make them do something because of his or her role or position in the organization or cultural custom and practice (and it has nothing to do with personality or personal relationships). Robert Isaac and colleagues make this distinction: 'Managers use legitimate power to push employees towards desired ends, whereas leaders use their influence to pull followers towards goals.'[57]

Coercive Power. Coercive power, associated with position or authority, is based on the perceived ability of a leader or manager to bring about undesirable or unpleasant outcomes for those who do not comply with expectations, instructions or directives. Examples of such outcomes are the withholding of pay rises or bonuses, promotion or privileges; the allocation of undesirable or unpleasant tasks or responsibilities; reprimands or disciplinary action including dismissal; and even the threat or infliction of physical punishment including pain and death.

Coercive power does not bring about voluntary action, only necessary action; nor does it foster followership. The least effective leaders will use coercive power, which creates fear among people of the adverse consequences of not complying with the wishes of a leader. It is temporary in its impact and it creates negative feelings and attitudes. It is associated with an extreme form of the directive style of leadership – tyranny. One example was Saddam Hussein, who used authority, manipulation and coercive power with the Iraqi people and pain and death as threats and punishments. John Laughland says he 'inspire[d] terror in Iraq but loyalty too': he combined 'extraordinary brutality with occasional acts of exceptional kindness – the classic hallmarks of a psychopath'.[58] George Orwell recognized how dictators use power; for them:

Power is not a means, it is an end. One does not establish a dictatorship in order to safeguard a revolution; one makes the revolution in order to establish the dictatorship.[59]

Material/Financial Reward Power. Material or financial reward power offers a material or financial benefit in return for acquiescence, cooperation or even followership, for example a pay increase, bonus, privileges or promotion. This is a common feature of transactional leadership (in the form of contingent reward), and such reward power is associated with the position and authority to dispense a material or financial reward. One problem with reward power when used in a one-to-one situation is that it tends to encourage individualism at the expense of teamwork.[60] But conversely team-based reward can alienate individuals who are the high achievers that will stand out in a team. And of course such power may be abused or regarded as manipulation or bribery.

Personal Power

Personal power comes from many sources and is not necessarily based on charisma. A study of American presidents suggested that those who were regarded as charismatic – Jefferson, Jackson, Lincoln, Theodore Roosevelt, Franklin Roosevelt and Kennedy – possessed stronger needs for power than those regarded as low in charisma – Tyler, Pierce, Buchanan, Arthur, Harding and Coolidge.[61]

Personal power is 'the ability to affect others' attitudes, beliefs and behaviours without using force or formal authority', say Fiona Dent and Mike Brent.[62] Former US president George W. Bush, for example, is said 'not [to] have Ronald Reagan's or Bill Clinton's skills at crowd-pleasing politics, but he is a master at the one-on-one politics of personal persuasion', according to Irwin Stelzer.[63] In contrast, historian A.J.P. Taylor said of Lord Northcliffe: 'He aspired to power [authority] instead of influence, and as a result forfeited both.'[64]

Psychological Reward Power. This form of power is using recognition and praise as a reward for achievement. Like providing material or financial reward, however, it is a form of contingent reward (and hence transactional leadership). But it should be remembered, as was discussed in Chapter 3, that contingent reward is more closely associated with effective leadership overall than Bass's original Full Range Leadership model postulated.

Referent Power. This is the influence that leaders can exert as a result of their perceived attractiveness, personal characteristics or social skills (e.g. charm), reputation or charisma in the eyes of the followers and the respect or esteem that followers have for them. It is power that leaders have as a result of followers' belief in them and what they are trying to do. It is associated with being trusted and respected, shared values, and with followers' desire to follow. Idealized influence, in Bass's model of transformational leadership, is related to referent power.

People will identify with leaders when leaders display insight into their needs, values and aspirations and respond positively to them (with emotional intelligence) in a timely fashion. They will display empathy in passionate ways with them.[65] Showing courage and taking personal risks and responsibility will instil trust. The leader gains referent power. Leaders like Churchill and Eisenhower took the blame for their failures; Hitler did not. Effective leaders will also display a sense of purpose, persistence and trust in others. An example of purposefulness and persistence and its inspirational effects based on her resulting referent power, her vision, values and purpose notwithstanding, is Margaret Thatcher, former British prime minister. In her former Cabinet secretary (Lord) Robin Butler's words:

> **What cannot be doubted is her belief in her basic principles and her unflinching courage in holding her corner when she has decided that a battle must be fought – qualities that brought so many people to her banner.[66]**

Thatcher saw having conviction and principle as incompatible with consensus politics[67] and, presumably, with the participative style of leadership.

Displaying the values leaders espouse in their behaviour has been shown to motivate others to behave similarly. For example, morally 'beautiful' behaviour can lead to an emotion in others ('elevation') that creates this desire, felt physically in the chest.[68] Confidence in oneself and in others counts: this means not only having self-confidence but also extending this faith to others and sincerely believing in their talents.[69] This leads to respect, trust and confidence in the leader, a willingness to exert extra effort, to 'go the extra mile', and the desire to achieve to show support for the leader. An important source of referent power for leaders is credibility. People look for credibility – honesty, inspiration and competence – in their leaders.[70] Jean Vanhoegaerden says: 'Credibility means doing what you say you will do.'[71] He quotes one manager:

> I worked for someone who proclaimed that he was really committed to empowerment. He bought the entire department a book on the topic so we could better understand his management philosophy. As the book suggested, the limits of autonomy were agreed. But, the first time I took a decision within that limit which he did not like, he resorted to bullying. His actions were completely alien to what he had preached.[72]

Sir Ernest Shackleton, the explorer, was an example of inspirational leadership through referent power that was gained by treating people with respect and encouragement when things went wrong.[73] Interestingly, Shackleton also had the intellectual skills to back up his inspirational leadership: he paid painstaking attention to detail and used what we would now call scenario planning.

Expert Power. This is another form of personal power, based on others' perception of a leader's competence, skills or expertise. People are willingly influenced by those who are perceived as knowledgeable or skilful in a way that is relevant to the task or work. Socrates placed great emphasis on the right of those who have knowledge to lead. However, there are dangers in expert power. Research at the London School of Economics suggests that, while leaders who display a powerful 'leader' demeanour may boost their appearance of competence, they may also stifle contributions by followers or subordinates in participative decision-making interactions.[74] And St Paul said that knowledge 'puffs up',[75] to which Tom Marshall adds:

> [Knowledge] feeds our feelings of self-importance to know things that other people don't know and to be able to make decisions on the basis of inside knowledge.[76]

Information Power. This form of personal power is related to expert power but concerns information rather than a person's competence, expertise or skills. People are influenced by those who have information that they need or want for their work but do not have or who control access to it. A favourite example of this is the boss's secretary.

Mike Clayton suggests two further forms of power that are useful to consider. *Connection Power* arises from networking – being able to use links to influential people to support or supplement more direct personal power.[77] Neither information power nor connection power, Clayton argues, satisfactorily accounts for the power that certain 'gatekeepers' have in organizations to control access to wider resources such as funds, equipment, supplies, etc. These resource gatekeepers are often middle-ranking, junior or administrative colleagues with little legitimate power, and as such, he says, they wield *Resource Power* as a proxy to meet their need for control in their workplace.[78]

Use of Power by Leaders

From a political science perspective, Joseph Nye views power and leadership as inextricably intertwined.[79] He sees effective leaders as using both a hard form of power (coercion) and a soft form (attraction), according to the nature of the leader, followers and situation, in exercising 'smart power': 'Bombing an enemy into submission is quite different from persuading others to follow.'[80] Nye's model is a simplification of French and Raven's taxonomy: coercive and reward power relate to his hard-power category and legitimate, referent and expert power to soft power. Hard power is about using 'carrots' (inducements) and 'sticks' (threats).

Power pervades human relationships. So how does it relate to engagement – to gaining people's attention, interest, cooperation, commitment, enthusiasm and dedication? And how do effective (and ethical) leaders use power in influencing, motivating and inspiring people?

Clearly, using coercive power, for example threats, may well achieve the outcome one wishes: a person's efforts to do so will be motivated primarily by fear. Using reward power is similar except that a person's efforts are motivated by the promise (probability) of a sufficient material or psychological reward: in terms of Bass's Full Range Leadership theory it is a 'transaction'. Hard power is associated largely with transactional leadership, though reward power in the form of contingent reward is also somewhat associated with transformational leadership.

Coercive power employs a negative reinforcement – 'the strengthening of a response as a consequence of its being followed by the cessation or avoidance of an aversive stimulus'[81] – whereby (transactional) leaders may threaten such an 'aversive stimulus', punishment, for a failure to comply, thereby motivating followers or employees through fear to do their bidding. Reward power employs a positive reinforcement – the provision of a reward immediately following a response to increase the future frequency or probability of the behaviour – which works well with rats, dogs and donkeys and is the basis of human performance-related pay systems. Neither form of hard power is likely to be seen as 'engaging' in the sense in which we normally use the term.

An exception perhaps exists where reward power and the associated rewards that are delivered are perceived as sufficient to procure huge employee engagement. An example here is the global investment banking and securities firm Goldman Sachs, the top-ranked 'best company to work for' in the large-company category in 'The Sunday Times 100 Best Companies to Work for 2007' survey.[82] In such situations employee well-being may suffer, both health-wise and in domestic relationships, which ultimately may be self-defeating for 'excessive' engagement.

Nye suggests that leaders in authoritarian cultures may use coercive power and issue commands, but those in democracies must use soft power – a combination of inducement and attraction.[83] Former US Army Chief of Staff Eric Shinseki explained why soft power is applicable even in the armed forces:

> You can certainly command without that sense of commitment, but you cannot lead without it. And without leadership, command is a hollow experience, a vacuum often filled with mistrust and arrogance.[84]

Power may be misused. Probably most senior executives are highly competent at planning, organizing, directing and controlling, but some are 'control freaks' and some are bullies. They get things done, but by using coercive power, to various degrees, by using fear or the threat of sanctions to obtain compliance by others. Such power-mongers may succeed but they will do so *despite* and not because of dysfunctional behaviour. Such leaders possess unsocialized power motives. As a result, they will fail to empower their subordinates (I use this term deliberately), they will even disempower them, and they will certainly not inspire or engage them.

Criticism of the Power Base Model

Criticism of the French and Raven power bases is two-fold. First, they are arbitrary and under-researched though they do explain and even predict behaviour. The second criticism, however, is more philosophical. The strength – and therefore the validity – of the positional power bases has become greatly diminished in modern times. There have been periods and places in history where positional power reigned supreme, only to be challenged by individuals with uncommon personal power who were ready to use it in opposition to the established regime or hierarchy. This is what started to happen in early 2011, initially among the North African Arab states and then spreading to the Gulf region and the Middle East. The value of information power is also eroded today by the ready access to information afforded by the internet.

Engagement and Inspiration

'Transformational leaders,' Bernard Bass and Bruce Avolio say, 'inspire those around them by providing meaning and challenge to their followers' work'.[85] Inspiration is a high level of motivation. The word 'inspiration' comes from the Latin *inspirare*, which means 'to breathe in', so inspiration is like 'a breath of fresh air, it gives energy'.[86] In a religious context, 'inspiration' in the Koran (*wahy*) can be read as 'revelation' and 'the inspired' (*yuha*) as 'the revealed'.[87] This implies that being inspired is associated with a revelation of a vision, purpose or meaning. When people understand and identify with the vision and purpose of an organization, they are very likely inspired.

Inspiring leaders are often regarded as charismatic – they are perceived to have a special talent or power to attract followers and inspire them with devotion and enthusiasm. One view is that charismatic leaders are emotionally expressive, self-confident, self-determined and free from internal conflict.[88] They also show empathy with followers; they use compelling, emotive language; they display personal competence; they display confidence in their followers; and they provide followers with opportunities to achieve.[89] However, whether, and to what extent, charisma is essential to effective leadership – or the result of it – is arguable:[90] George Binney and Colin Williams say:

> Many of the organisations we know do not have charismatic leaders ... [Their leaders] are usually modest, sometimes even self-effacing, losing no opportunity to stress that real achievement has come from teamwork, not the inspiration of just one individual.[91]

This raises the question of ego. Michael Maccoby stimulated a debate about whether effective leaders are egotistical and narcissistic, arguing that, because of their vision, charisma and energy, they help organizations, which they see as extensions of their egos, become great.[92] But Jim Collins found in a research programme that the most effective leaders – who have successfully transformed their business organizations – will suppress their egos: they are self-effacing, humble and shy, but resolute.[93] An example of this was Edward Stobart.

The real issue is authenticity: inspirational leaders inspire others because they communicate themselves – their virtues and their flaws.[94] An example was Mahatma Gandhi, who said, 'My life is its own message.'[95] While charisma is generally viewed as a social process between leader and follower, where the leader might well have some very special gifts, such as oratory, charisma is very much a 'manufactured' phenomenon today,[96] especially among politicians.

Manipulation is an issue too. Richard Olivier says there is a 'thin line' between inspiring and manipulating others.[97] He says:

> Sometimes managers need to inspire those around them to do what they want them to do. This is justifiable when all parties know the purpose and agree that there is a potential benefit to individuals and the organisation. In this respect, inspiration is a part of the persuasion process.

And inspirational leadership is questionable, as Bernard Bass points out:

> Inspirational leadership has been most applauded by the masses and most derided by skeptical intellectuals who [equate] it with demagoguery, manipulation, exploitation, and mob psychology. Its emphasis on persuasive appeals to faith rather than reason, to the emotions rather than to the intellect, and to various mechanisms of social reinforcement rather than to logical discourse has made it seem fit only for the immature and the undereducated.[98]

Inspiration is associated more with transformational leadership than with transactional leadership, which itself may be motivational. James MacGregor Burns relates transformational leadership to Maslow's theory of the hierarchy of needs: followers of transformational leaders are motivated to achieve the highest possible level of need satisfaction – self-actualization.[99] Bernard Bass's research for the Full Range Leadership Model suggests that transformational leaders:

> [provide] meaning and challenge to their followers' work. Team spirit is aroused. Enthusiasm and optimism are displayed. Leaders get followers involved in envisioning attractive future states; they create clearly communicated expectations that followers want to meet and also demonstrate commitment to goals and the shared vision.[100]

Intellectual stimulation is often also inspiring.[101] It contributes to subordinates' or followers' independence and autonomy by encouraging them to think for themselves, to look at problems in new ways, to think through an action before taking it. However, Bass says that leader competency alone does not guarantee intellectual stimulation and the inspiration of subordinates or followers. He cites former US presidents Jimmy Carter and Herbert Hoover as technically competent but failures at inspiring people, and John F. Kennedy and Franklin Roosevelt as less intellectually astute but superior in intellectual stimulation and inspirational leadership. He says:

A sine qua non of intellectual stimulation is arousing consciousness and awareness in followers of what is right, good and important, which new directions must be taken, and why.

Sir Ernest Shackleton, the explorer, was an inspirational leader. He drew inspiration from his faith, other people and the literature of great thinkers. He set an example, made personal sacrifices, focused on the future and not the past, and inspired his men with his unflinching confidence of success, insisting on being treated no differently from others and never asking anybody to do anything that he would not do himself. Shackleton made a lifelong impact on his men: some were still gathering to honour him 50 years after the *Endurance* mission of 1914–1916, some 42 years after his early death at 47 in 1922. He was the archetypal transformational leader: he transformed the expectations and motivation of his men beyond what they had ever thought possible

Is effective leadership necessarily visionary and inspiring? Not everybody believes it is. John Roulet, a management consultant and a former director of organizational development in a large technology company in the United States, recommends 'obliterating' the 'myth' that 'leadership is visionary and inspiring'. He writes:

We tend to associate leadership with individuals who are effective communicators, visionary and inspirational. Our view of leadership, however, becomes hopelessly distorted when it is based on such personal characteristics. Leadership is about work, not personality and social behaviours. As in any work endeavour, an individual's personal traits are an entirely different issue from his or her performance. The common characteristics associated with leadership are appealing, but they are not synonymous with leadership. This mistake, which is made over and over again, results in the confusing, mediocre and poor leadership we have become accustomed to in business, government and the military.

So what is leadership? Leadership is simply the quality of the leader's performance. There are three components to leadership and these enable us to determine the achievement of something of value:

1. *Accomplishment.* The leader's performance must result in the achievement of something of value.
2. *Cost-effective use of resources.* The leader must use resources wisely.
3. *Adherence to values.* What the leader does and achieves must not violate what the group holds as important (i.e. values).

The correctness of the criteria presented above becomes clear when we compare them to the current leadership paradigm. That paradigm defines leadership as being visionary, inspirational, etc. History has provided us with countless leaders who were visionary and inspirational and possessed many of the traits commonly associated with great leadership. Many, however, were colossal failures as leaders.

But those leaders who accomplished great things, used the resources they commanded wisely, and adhered to their groups' values *were* great leaders. It is indisputable and that is what makes these leadership criteria correct. Leadership criteria based on personality traits and social skills simply do not measure the work of a leader. Organizations wanting to take a realistic and optimally effective approach to leadership must first embrace a new leadership paradigm. That paradigm established the criteria for organizational leadership as accomplishment, cost-effective use of resources and adherence to group values.[102]

This polemic requires analysis and comment. One – but not the only – criterion of effectiveness of leadership undoubtedly is accomplishment, defined and measured in ways that are appropriate to the specific work context of the leader and followers or group members. Examples of such ways are customer satisfaction, financial goals, service delivery, employee morale, etc. Adherence to group values is another appropriate criterion: one of our propositions is that effective leaders identify, display, promote and reinforce the shared values that will inform and support the vision, purpose and strategies. However, proposing a cost-effective use of resources as a criterion of effective leadership confuses leadership with management, which we discussed in Chapter 1. Moreover, Roulet's two legitimate criteria of effective leadership that are part of his 'new leadership paradigm' are only two of several, indeed perhaps many, possible criteria for leadership. Roulet's concept of effective leadership is false in one part and inadequate in the other part and it diverts our attention from the essence of leadership: showing the way.

A further criticism of Roulet's 'new paradigm' is his confusion that leadership is 'simply quality of the leader's performance' defined in terms of 'accomplishment, cost-effective use of resources and adherence to values'. He wrongly decries personal characteristics and social behaviours as relevant to effective leadership, citing as 'colossal failures' many leaders who were 'visionary and inspirational and possessed many of the traits commonly associated with great leadership'. It is true that vision and inspiration are associated with effective leadership, though it cannot be claimed that they are sufficient or even necessary in themselves for effective leadership or that they are undesirable or contra-indicated because some leaders who displayed them were 'colossal failures'.

So let us now consider another way in which leaders inspire people. Inspiration also come from communicating a clear vision eloquently, confidently and with confidence in it, using appealing language and symbols, which we now turn to.

Inspirational Language and Speech

'Nothing is so akin to our natural feelings as the rhythms and sounds of voices', wrote Cicero.[103] The Chinese translation of the word 'speech' is two words that separately mean 'act' and 'talk'. So to make a speech is 'to perform a talking show'.[104] Inspirational speeches contain simple language and imagery and play on words in a colourful way.

They are delivered with sincerity and passion, with confidence and conviction, and often with expansive body language – in particular facial expressions, gestures of the hand, head movements and eye contact. Eye contact gives the audience the impression of spontaneity and being addressed directly.[105] Inspiring leaders express emotions through their body language. For one CEO, John Robins of Guardian Insurance, '... leadership is about communicating emotions and excitement'.[106]

Does 'style' win over 'substance' in engaging people? This became a topical issue in the UK's 2010 general election campaign. In the run-up to the election, the performances of the three main parties' leaders in a series of televised debates were analysed. According to the media consensus, the Liberal Democrat leader Nick Clegg unexpectedly made an extraordinary impact on the mass TV audience and 'won' the first televised debate by the three main party leaders – Gordon Brown (Labour and then current prime minister), David Cameron (Conservative) and Clegg – and he did so owing to his style rather than the substance of what he said. Clegg went 'from near obscurity to hero in the space of 90 minutes', says psychologist Peter Honey.[107]

Honey points out Clegg's 'style' in engaging the audience:

⁎ Looking straight into the camera, which is the equivalent of making eye contact.
⁎ Keeping his eyebrows level and calm, thereby inviting the audience to 'trust me'.
⁎ Engaging with questioners by using their names and being sufficiently relaxed to risk having his left hand in his trouser pocket for some of the time, which communicates an air of authority.

Honey suggests that Clegg's performance is an example of the paramount importance of behaviour when trying to influence people: to other people 'you are your behaviour'. He says:

It is only ... when people have become accustomed to how someone looks and behaves that substance takes centre stage ... To be persuasive and effective we need style and substance, not one without the other. Substance without style devalues substance; style without substance is not sustainable.[108]

Peggy Noonan captures the essence of inspirational public speaking:

A speech is a soliloquy, one man on a bare stage with a big spotlight. He will tell us who he is and what he wants and how he will get it and what it means that he wants it and what it will mean when he does or does not get it, and ... He looks up at us ... and clears his throat. 'Ladies and gentlemen ... ' We lean forward, hungry to hear. Now it will be said, now we will hear the thing we long for. A speech is part theatre and part political declaration; it is personal communication between a leader and his people; it is an art, and all art is a paradox, being at once a thing of great power and great delicacy. A speech is poetry: cadence, rhythm, imagery, sweep! A speech reminds us that words ... have the power to make dance the dullest beanbag of a heart.[109]

Language is one's most powerful tool: without communication skills a leader will fail to have an impact.[110] Yet most senior executives 'don't make the strong audience connection – visceral, personal, emotional – needed to inspire trust and action,' according to Nick Morgan, a communications consultant.[111]

Brian MacArthur, like Simon Schama, laments the lack of oratory in leaders today: 'Where are the visions and where are the words that inspire men and women to greater things and make them vote with enthusiasm, even passion?'[112] Modern egalitarianism may have tended to discourage flights of high rhetoric. Disraeli said of his legendary adversary William Gladstone: 'A sophisticated rhetorician, inebriated with the exuberance of his own verbosity.'[113] Using an esoteric, even if right, quote or allusion may seem pretentious, but politicians today sometimes forget that the common people are actually educated. According to Peggy Noonan, they 'go in for the lowest common denominator – like a newscaster'[114] – or perhaps a tabloid newspaper. But Morgan suggests that people in business increasingly expect speakers to connect with them 'viscerally, personally and emotionally'.[115]

Jeremy Paxman, the broadcaster, writer and political commentator, describes how 'the Leader' at party conferences has 'largely discarded the rousing vision, the cloudy imagery and the rhetorical resonance of even twenty years ago'.[116] The reason is, he says, that such oratory does not suit television, which is 'a medium of impressions and more intimate tone'. Political conference speeches therefore have become 'an awkward hybrid, part talk, part declamation'. And, he says, it is all 'a sham', for such speeches, and the punctuating and final euphoric hand-clapping and subsequent theatrical departure, are engineered, timed and planned, and the speeches are not even written by the speaker but by teams of speechwriters.

Outstanding leaders do influence and persuade people through inspirational language. This is perhaps the most obvious behavioural characteristic of an outstanding leader. But this poses a problem, even a paradox. If humility is a characteristic of effective leadership, as we find in the teachings of Jesus and Lao Tzu and in the opinion of many successful business leaders, how does this square with the power of oratory, exalted by the Greeks and Romans? 'Silence is of the gods', says a Chinese proverb; yet 'Silence is the virtue of fools', said Francis Bacon (Watts, tr. 1640).[117] John Adair suggests the solution to this is listening: humility lies in listening rather than speaking or waiting to speak.[118]

Great leaders, however, have often been elevated to iconic status through their use of language. How do they do it? They inspire people, Brian MacArthur says, through what they say and how they say it:

The speeches of Moses, Jesus of Nazareth and Muhammad to their followers are still inspiring men and women to lead lives based on a moral code and still, today, changing the course of history ... the greatest speeches ... move hearts or inspire great deeds [and] uplift spirits ...[119]

The prophet Muhammad, Safi-ur-Rahman al-Mubarakpuri says, 'was noted for superb eloquence and fluency ... [as] an accurate, unpretending straightforward speaker ... [with] the strength and eloquence of bedouin language and the decorated splendid speech of town'.[120] MacArthur points out that inspirational speeches by leaders 'articulate dreams, offer hope, stir hearts and minds, and offer their audiences visions of a better world'.[121]

Ken Rea of the Guildhall School of Music and Drama explains how leaders can learn a lot from actors, not by 'acting' but by using their techniques 'to make their story clear and hold the attention of the audience'.[122] This way, he says, leaders gain 'the confidence to be more authentically themselves and gain credibility'. They learn to master their voice, body and emotions, which in turn conveys 'presence, charisma and personality'. Rea criticizes Ed Miliband, the newly elected leader of the British Labour Party, at the October 2010 party conference, in which he displayed sincerity but no passion, thereby making him look 'light-weight, lacklustre and devoid of charisma'. Rea says:

> You can have all the bright ideas and be on top of the figures, but you can also let yourself down on the behavioural things – what you look and sound like.

The ability to communicate a clear, simple vision is a key characteristic: 'The power of language ... [gives] life to vision', James Kouzes and Barry Posner say.[123] And David E. Berlew argues: 'Leaders must communicate a vision in a way that attracts and excites members of the organization.'[124] In the words of William Hazlitt in 1807:

> The business of the orator is not to convince, but persuade; not to inform, but to rouse the mind; to build upon the habitual prejudices of mankind (for reason of itself will do nothing) and to add feeling to prejudice, and action to feeling.[125]

The text box shows the famous key phrases of well-known inspirational speeches by Martin Luther King Jr, Abraham Lincoln, Winston Churchill and John F. Kennedy.

Martin Luther King Jr delivered his before a crowd of 250,000 in Washington, DC. That speech, Kouzes and Posner say, was rooted in fundamental values, cultural traditions and personal conviction, and stirred hearts and passions.[126] It remains a masterpiece of connecting with an audience and crafting rhetoric. Abraham Lincoln, who 'demonstrated ... passionate conviction allied to simple but eloquent words, quietly spoken'[127] in 270 words spoken in three minutes gave possibly 'the greatest and noblest speech of modern times' – his famous Gettysburg address. Former speechwriter for Tony Blair, Philip Collins, describes how President John F. Kennedy asked his speechwriter Ted Sorensen, preparing his inaugural presidential address, to discover Lincoln's secret. It was two-fold: using poetic images and '[not using] a two or three-syllable word where a one-syllable word would do'.[128] His address on 20 January 1961 rallied the youth of his country and had a far-reaching influence – on George W. Bush after the 9/11 terrorist attack on the United States.[129] Winston S. Churchill's Battle of Britain speech[130] and his Dunkirk speech[131] inspired the nation. And Tony Blair's speech to his first Labour party conference as newly elected prime minister[132] was both triumphal and indicative of radical change in the ideology of Labour.

INSPIRATIONAL LANGUAGE

Martin Luther King, Jr

'I have a dream ….'

Abraham Lincoln

'… government of the people, by the people, for the people, shall not perish from the earth'.

Winston Churchill

'Never in the field of human conflict was so much owed by so many to so few.'

'We shall fight on the beaches … we shall fight in the fields and in the streets, we shall fight in the hills, we shall never surrender.'

John F. Kennedy

'Ask not what your country can do for you; ask what you can do for your country.'

'Let every nation know, whether it wishes us well or ill, that we shall pay any price, bear any burden, meet any hardship, support any friend, oppose any foe, in order to ensure the survival and the success of liberty.'

Tony Blair

'Now make the good that is in the heart of each of us serve the good of all of us. Give to our country the gift of our energy, our ideas, our hopes, our talents. Use them to build a country each of whose people will say that "I care about Britain because I know that Britain cares about me." Britain, head and heart, will be unbeatable. That is the Britain I offer you. That is the Britain that together can be ours.'

Barrack Obama

'Yes, we can. Yes, we can change. Yes, we can.'

… [emphasizing] duty over rights, the importance of family life, zero tolerance on crime and a more positive approach to European unity as he appealed for Britain to become a beacon to the world. Even right-wing commentators hailed the speech as a historic statement of intent.[133]

Political leaders may express core values and beliefs in inspirational speech, with potentially dangerous consequences. Examples of where these are more likely to lead to negative outcomes show a sense of superiority, a perceived injustice to oneself or one's group, a sense of vulnerability, distrust and a sense of helplessness.[134] Effective leaders through their rhetoric may inspire their followers to change the *status quo*, even violently,[135] especially when they also communicate innocence and victimization.[136]

We cannot leave this discussion of inspirational speech without a comment on Adolf Hitler. 'Hitler, undoubtedly the greatest speaker of the century … changed a nation by his oratory', says Brian MacArthur.[137] He was able to arouse a mass audience and work it up to a frenzy, with a mixture of appeals to idealism, power, hatred and action, the use of symbols, the assertion of a grandiose identity – 'Deutschland über Alles'. His moving speeches captured the minds and hearts of a vast number of the German people:

he virtually hypnotized his audiences. The inspirational effect of a brilliant speech can be illustrated by Hitler's address in 1932 to the Düsseldorf Industry Club. On his arrival:

> ... his reception ... was cool and reserved. Yet he spoke for two and a half hours without pause and made one of the best speeches of his life, setting out all his stock ideas brilliantly dressed up for his audience of businessmen. At the end they rose and cheered him wildly. Contributions from German industry started flowing into the Nazi treasury.[138]

Norman Lebrecht concurs: 'Hitler was nothing if not a spellbinder ... Mixed with revulsion at the deeds he inspired, one cannot avoid a sneaking admiration for a lone individual who overturned an entire civilisation.'[139]

Central to inspirational language are two skills: framing and rhetorical crafting.[140] Inspirational language is not the exclusive domain of the speaker's podium or rostrum. The skills of framing and rhetorical crafting apply just as much in any one-to-one conversation between leader and follower, manager and subordinate, or indeed between any two people – where the purpose is to motivate or inspire.

Framing Language and Speech

Framing is connecting your message with the needs and interests of those whose commitment you need.[141] This means you must first know your audience. Framing is the management of meaning, which requires careful thought and forethought.[142] Meaning is found in the image of the organization, its place in the environment, and its collective purpose, according to Bernard Bass.[143] And Jay Conger says that:

> ... the most effective leaders study the issues that matter to their colleagues ... in ... conversations ... they collect essential information ... They are good at listening. They test their ideas with trusted confidants, and they ask questions of the people they will later be persuading. These explorations help them think through the arguments, the evidence, and the perspectives they will present.[144]

Framing is about developing a shared sense of destiny through dialogue,[145] something both Martin Luther King Jr and Nelson Mandela did very well. Leadership is about building connections with people: *effective leaders*, Doris Kearns Goodwin says, *make people feel they have a stake in common problems*.[146] Giving people an identity as stakeholders creates shared ownership and thereby a wholehearted commitment to solving problems and building futures together. Framing involves several specific behaviours.

Catching attention. First, catching people's attention at the start with something surprising or attention grabbing. Nick Morgan recommends avoiding a joke or rhetorical question and instead telling a carefully crafted 'personal parable' or anecdote that the audience can identify and which captures your overall theme.[147]

Timing. Timing is (almost) everything: knowing when to introduce an initiative and when to hold off is a crucial skill.[148] John Hunt calls this exercising 'theatre'.[149]

Appealing to common interests. Your message must be linked to the benefits for everybody involved. This extends to incorporating the values and beliefs of those you are communicating to, appealing to common bonds – noting, Vincent Leung says, that 'what is white in one culture may be black in another'.[150]

Avoiding statistics. Using statistics usually should be avoided. Statistical summaries are regarded by most people as mostly uninformative and unmemorable: 'information is absorbed by listeners in proportion to its vividness'.[151] However, as Nick Georgiades and Richard Macdonnell say, telling a group that a project has an 80 per cent chance of success rather than a 20 per cent chance of failure is more likely to win over the group.[152]

Use of vocabulary. Framing also entails using a vocabulary that matches the listeners' and generally not using a two- or three-syllable word where a one-syllable one will do. Charles Goldie and Richard Pinch also advocate 'economic representation' in communication: using one word rather than several words to express oneself.[153]

Showing feelings. A key element in framing is showing that you are feeling what you are saying, speaking with passion and emotion, and reinforcing the verbal message by using appropriate body language. As Shakespeare's Hamlet said to the travelling players – 'Suit the action to the word, the word to the action.' This refers to tone of voice, posture and gestures – what Nick Morgan calls the 'kinesthetic connection' with the audience.[154] This kinaesthetic connection, of course, requires authenticity to be effective.

Authenticity. Actions speak louder than words. They demonstrate one's authenticity – one's feelings about what one is saying. Mary-Louise Angoujard, a communication consultant, says: 'Body language accounts for a great deal in influencing people's perceptions, but it should be interpreted in context – your movements, expression and voice will betray you if you don't believe what you are saying.'[155] Unspoken signals that are processed subconsciously include hand movements, stance, a tilting of the head and facial expressions.

Framing language may be difficult for a speaker who has strong emotion about a subject, whose authenticity is all too obvious.[156] Inspiring others requires first finding out what inspires you and speaking 'from the heart', according to Richard Olivier: 'If the speaker is inspired and moved, it generally follows that the audience will empathise.'[157] Brian MacArthur points out that:

> However brilliant the words, it is also the manner of delivery, the sincerity of the speaker, that makes a speech great ... Speeches succeed, according to Lloyd George, by a combination of word, voice and gesture in moving their audiences to the action the orator desires.[158]

Authenticity has become a big issue for leaders, particularly those in politics and government. The professional speechwriter has been used for a long time. Public orators in ancient Greece employed rhetores to produce speeches. Simon Schama notes that former US president Andrew Jackson's best speeches were written by Chief Justice Roger Taney and that Samuel Rosenmann wrote for Franklin D. Roosevelt.[159]

But the rise of the adviser – the 'spin doctor' – has created scepticism among audiences about whether leaders are speaking their own words sincerely or those invented by experts in image management. In fact leaders themselves have been 'invented'. Howard Gardner says 'even the claim for authenticity can be manufactured ... good actors know how to feign sincerity'.[160] Image management, or impression management, when taken to extremes, however, can backfire and have a 'boomerang' effect.[161]

Leaders in the public gaze will often present a desirable or impressive image of themselves. Adrian Furnham captures typical (male) examples: being seen jogging, playing soccer with some children, fishing while stripped down to jeans, kissing babies.[162] He also illustrates how such leaders desperately try – and sometimes fail – to avoid presenting an unfortunate image: stumbling on the beach (former Labour Party leader Neil Kinnock), smoking (deputy prime minister and Liberal Democratic Party leader Nick Clegg), nodding off to sleep at a conference or in Parliament (Lord Chancellor and Secretary of State for Justice Ken Clarke), or drinking wine rather than tea (champagne is a no-no). 'The PR gurus are in direct conflict with the paparazzi and gossip journalists who seek out shots of politicians getting it wrong', Furnham says. 'They believe it is their job to puncture the pomposity of leaders and celebrities by showing them as they are.'

Authenticity, however, like so many other usually positive leadership characteristics, may have adverse consequences. Saying what you mean may demonize sections of a community, as, for example, it has done in Northern Ireland.[163] And authenticity, when it occurs accidentally, may positively destroy or at least severely damage a leader's credibility and reputation.

For example, take the case of Gordon Brown, then leader of the British Labour Party and prime minister, campaigning in the run-up to the general election on 6 May 2010. Just eight days before voting, he engages with a long-standing Labour voter, listening attentively, smiling and even joking. Then he gets into his car and declares to an aide, 'That was a disaster ... Whose idea was that? ... Just ridiculous' – and also that the woman was a bigot (in connection with the immigration issue). As one journalist said, and most agreed, 'It was *not* a disaster. Whoever had the idea deserved some praise. It was not ridiculous',[164] but Brown's reaction to the meeting was an unmitigated disaster. How do we know? He had left his microphone switched on after getting into his car and his words were broadcast for all to hear. The woman was not amused; Labour lost her vote, and more.

Apart from the issue of whether the meeting was a success or a disaster (he seriously misread the situation in the first place), the authenticity issue was the public image of the leader that he intended to display versus his private opinions and feelings – the *real* Gordon Brown – that he intended to hide, unsuccessfully. His credibility – and therefore his ability to engage effectively with others, to influence and inspire them – was forever damaged.

Authenticity sometimes creates a dilemma. Top executives, such as presidents, prime ministers and the CEOs of high-profile companies, will sometimes unwittingly gain unwelcome publicity by speaking out forthrightly. Should they do so? If they do they may engage with a particular community, disengage with another, or simply cause trouble for themselves and others around them. Stefan Stern reports three views: from a PR and communications guru, a lawyer and an academic. Alastair Campbell, adviser to former British prime minister Tony Blair, believes discretion in appearing indiscreet is the better part of valour.[165] Lawyer David Morley says: '... speak up but assume that what you say will come to the attention of those inclined to be offended by it.[166] Be ready to defend your views to their face.' And Rob Goffee says:

We have had our fill of carefully scripted, well-spun leaders. We don't trust them any more. Great leadership always involves personal risk and a capacity to speak up on important issues, to care enough to say things others have thought but not publicly articulated. We

want leaders who are authentic rather than contestants in a popularity contest. Effective leaders are authentic chameleons – adjusting and adapting language, style and behaviour – but without losing a sense of self.[167]

The need for authenticity is nothing new. As Polonius, adviser to the king in Shakespeare's *Hamlet*, advised his son Laertes:

This above all: to thine own self be true. And it must follow, as the night the day, Thou canst not then be false to any man.

Inclusivity. In framing your speech, you must move from 'I' to 'we' – using words like 'we' and 'our' rather than 'them' and 'they'. This characterizes inclusive language that unifies rather than divides followers.[168] This extends to comparing your group and situation with other groups and situations, for example with competitors ('We can do better than …'), with ideals ('We can achieve our best performance yet'), with goals ('We can achieve whatever we set our mind to'), with the past ('We can do better than we've ever done before'), with traits ('This is what we could look like if …'), and with stakeholders ('We can make our employees our strongest advocates').[169]

Presenting a solution and a challenge. Finally, framing includes presenting a solution, challenging the audience to implement it,[170] and then 'reading' the audience's reaction – their non-verbal signals – of receptivity, engagement with you, an agreement and commitment to your message and adjusting to it accordingly and – better still – involving the audience in some form of physical activity related to your message.[171] This technique can also go further. David Greatbatch and Timothy Clark suggest the speaker can also offer the solution,[172] for example:

Tony Blair: 'And here's one for us to put back down the Tory throats …'. [problem]
'… fewer days lost in strikes than in any of the eighteen years of Tory government'. [solution]
Audience: Applause.

Television has made a difference in public speaking, whether for education, entertainment or to win hearts and minds for a cause. Nick Morgan says that the 'grand gesture … sweeping phrases, the grand conceits' and voice projection were *de rigueur* for centuries[173] and, of course, still are so in theatre. But television (and video) has enabled the illusion of people talking to you from a few feet away, more personally, more intimately and therefore more trustworthily. Trust in the speaker – and winning hearts and minds – depends on the connection between the verbal message and the kinaesthetic message, in other words, authenticity in communication.

Rhetorical Crafting of Language and Speech

Rhetoric is the art of verbal expression. Inspiring leaders not only frame their language, but also craft their rhetoric. Speaking in West Berlin in 1987, then US president Ronald Reagan said:

> General Secretary Gorbachev, if you seek peace, if you seek prosperity for the Soviet Union and eastern Europe, if you seek liberalization: come here to this gate. Mr Gorbachev, open this gate. Mr Gorbachev, tear down this wall.[174]

Reagan is widely regarded as having been a great communicator, skilled in both framing his message and in crafting his rhetoric.

Jesse Jackson, 1988 US presidential candidate, 'touches hearts' in the way he speaks. P.J. O'Rourke, the American journalist, says of him:

> He is the only living American politician with a mastery of classical rhetoric. Assonance, alliteration, litotes, pleonasm, parallelism, exclamation, climax and epigram – to listen to Jesse Jackson is to hear everything mankind has learned about public speaking since Demosthenes.[175]

Assonance is 'the resemblance of sound between syllables in nearby words arising from the rhyming of stressed vowels (e.g. *sonnet, porridge*), and also from the use of identical consonants with different vowels (e.g. *killed, cold, culled*)', according to the *Concise Oxford English Dictionary* (OED).[176]

Alliteration is 'the occurrence of the same letter of sound at the beginning of adjacent or closely connected words'.[177]

Litotes is 'ironical understatement in which an affirmative is expressed by the negative of its opposite (e.g. *I shan't be sorry* for *I shall be glad*)'.[178]

Pleonasm is 'the use of more words than are necessary to convey meaning (e.g. *see with one's eyes*)'.[179]

Parallelism is giving two or more parts of a sentence a similar form so as to give the whole a definite pattern (e.g. *The inherent vice of capitalism is the* unequal sharing *of blessing; the inherent virtue of socialism is the* equal sharing *of miseries* [Winston Churchill]).

Exclamation (ecphonesis) is 'a sudden … remark expressing surprise, strong emotion, or pain'[180] (e.g. *O tempore! O mores!*).

Climax is 'a sequence of propositions or ideas in order of increasing importance, force, or effectiveness of expression',[181] (e.g. And from the crew of Apollo 8, we close with *good night, good luck, a merry Christmas, and God bless all of you, all of you on the good earth* [Frank Borman, astronaut]).

Epigram is 'a concise and witty saying or remark',[182] sometimes a pun or a paradox (e.g. *I am not young enough to know everything* [Oscar Wilde]).

According to Adrian Beard, rhetoric was taught in British schools long before English language and literature as we know it came into being.[183] Bernard Bass describes how inspirational leaders will substitute simple words, metaphors and slogans for complex ideas, such as *glasnost* and *perestroika* representing complex social, economic and political change in the former Soviet Union, and 'Never again!' to convey a response to the Holocaust.[184] Inspiring leaders will also give examples, tell anecdotes, produce quotations and recite slogans. They tell stories.

Storytelling. Screenwriting coach, and award-winning writer and director, Robert McKee believes that 'most executives struggle to communicate, let alone inspire'.[185]

He argues for engaging people's emotions not through 'dry' memos, missives, PowerPoint slides or conventional rhetoric but through storytelling. He says that the former methods are an intellectual exercise whereby one tries to convince or influence people on the basis of facts and logic but that 'people are not inspired to act by reason alone'. A much more powerful way is to unite an idea with feeling – by telling a story. Talula Cartwright says:

> People naturally gravitate to stories. Nearly everyone can remember stories from childhood that captured the imagination, touched the heart, and helped determine ideals, heroes, religious beliefs ...[186]

McKee suggests that people identify more with a story about struggle against adversity than with rosy pictures because they see it as being more truthful. Once again, as has been discussed earlier, self-knowledge is a *sine qua non*. McKee says:

> A storyteller ... [asks] the question, 'If I were this character in these circumstances, what would I do?' The more you understand your own humanity, the more you can appreciate the humanity of others ...

Use of rhythm, metaphor and symbols. Inspiring leaders will vary their speaking rhythm. They will use familiar images, metaphors and analogies to make the message vivid – as did Nelson Mandela with the image of the new South Africa as the 'Rainbow Nation'. They will choose symbols which capture the imagination – for example, the eagle symbolizes strength, the olive branch peace, the lion courage.[187] The cross symbolizes suffering, sacrifice and redemption; 'the hammer and sickle signifies the worker and peasant whose proletarian dictatorship would bring forth a communist utopia', Bernard Bass says.[188] Hitler used to great effect symbols such as the swastika, the goose step, the 'Heil Hitler' salute, and the 'Horst Wessel' song.[189]

Tihamér von Ghyczy says, 'Metaphors ... [involve] the transfer of images or ideas from one domain of reality to another.'[190] The rhetorical metaphor is well known and heavily used in the business world. It is part of inspirational language, for example 'winning the match', 'star performers', and so on. But linguistics scholars say such metaphors have a 'shelf life', eventually becoming 'dead metaphors'. The 'cognitive metaphor', von Ghyczy points out, serves a different function. He quotes Aristotle's view that good metaphors will surprise and puzzle us: while they will have familiar elements, their relevance and meaning will not be immediately clear. It is in this 'delicately unsettled [state] of mind that we are most open to creative ways of looking at things': '... something relatively unfamiliar (for example, evolutionary biology) [is used] to spark creative thinking about something familiar (business strategy)'.

Expression of hope. Inspiring leaders will express hope and possibilities. They will wax lyrical, as did Martin Luther King Jr, with phrases like '... the jangling discords of our nation ...' and 'a beautiful symphony of brotherhood'. But, as John Adair says, such leadership is about having the courage to take people forward in a positive way, not about demoralizing them through language that is filled with threats and fears.[191]

Lists. Lists can strengthen and enhance a message. Three-part lists are particularly effective, even those including identical items.[192]

Repetition. Inspiring leaders will also use repetition. This promotes easier recall.[193] As Churchill said:

> If you have an important point to make, don't try to be subtle or clever. Use a pile-driver. Hit the point once. Then come back and hit it a second time – a tremendous whack![194]

The way we speak may either engage or disengage other people. And Jim Gray says:

> The ability to speak convincingly to others – to compel them – has to rank as one of the most important skills in business and in life. It's the mark of a true leader. For many who occupy positions of leadership, it's the one missing element that prevents them from fully realizing all that they can be. Audiences in today's communication-saturated age ... are more demanding and critical than ever. They want leaders who can address them with clarity and authenticity.[195]

Philip Collins suggests that in the UK rhetoric has become 'a casualty of progress'.[196] He quotes Matt Ridley's central thesis in his book *The Rational Optimist*[197] that it is 'wonderful to be alive in the 21st century' – because of life expectancy, prosperity and peace – in support of the idea that rhetoric now '[seems] out of proportion to the facts ... The essential ingredient of a great speech [is] a sense of injustice or outrage.' Collins explains:

> Language [has become] less courtly and more colloquial ... Lloyd George once referred to 'the great pinnacle of sacrifice, pointing like a rugged finger to Heaven' and was admonished in the newspapers for being too low brow. If George Osborne[198] said that about the deficit he'd be carted off to the funny farm or made poet laureate.[199]

The very best leaders, Jim Collins says, will have ambitions 'first and foremost for the organization, the cause [the organization's vision, purpose and values], the work – not [themselves]'.[200] This is why, he says, such leaders can get people to do what they might otherwise not do – and like doing it. Ultimately, the American journalist Walter Lippmann said, the final test of all leaders is that they will leave behind them in other people 'the conviction and the will to carry on',[201] which is perhaps the hallmark of authentic, sustainable engagement.

The company responsible for *The Sunday Times* 'Best Companies to Work For' survey – Best Companies Ltd – has created a model for showing how managers can affect employee engagement: great managers motivate, converse with, consider and care for the people they lead.[202] Carly Chynoweth reports examples of greater employee satisfaction and company performance as a result of engagement programmes.[203] She cites, for example, Spire Healthcare, which introduced a new way of managing that gave staff in its 37 private hospitals more control with, after initial scepticism, an 83 per cent increase in a sense of ownership among employees and a 9 per cent increase in its financial performance.

We have discussed above the six themes and practices of effective leadership. These practices require a variety of skills – multiple forms of intelligence – for their effectiveness. We now turn to considering what these multiple intelligences are and how they are used in effective leadership.

Further Reading

Kim S. Cameron, Jane E. Dutton and Robert E. Quinn, Editors (2003), *Positive Organizational Scholarship: Foundations of a New Discipline*. San Francisco, CA: Berrett-Koehler.

Mike Clayton (2011), *Brilliant Influence*. Harlow: Pearson Education.

Stephen Denning (2007), *The Secret Language of Leadership: How Leaders Inspire Action through Narrative*. San Francisco, CA: Jossey-Bass.

Gail Fairhurst and Robert Sarr (1996), *The Art of Framing*. San Francisco, CA: Jossey-Bass.

Nick Georgiades and Richard Macdonnell (1998), *Leadership for Competitive Advantage*. Chichester: John Wiley & Sons.

Jim Gray (2010), *How Leaders Speak*. Toronto: Dundurn Press.

David Greatbatch and Timothy Clark (2005), *Management Speak: Why We Listen to What Management Gurus Tell Us*. Abingdon, Oxford: Routledge.

Brian MacArthur (1999), *The Penguin Book of Twentieth-Century Speeches*, Second Edition. London: Penguin Books.

Marks & Spencer (2005), *Speeches that Changed the World*. London: Smith-Davies Publishing.

L.W. Porter, G.A. Bigley and R.M. Steers, Editors (2003), *Motivation and Work Behavior*, Seventh Edition. Burr Ridge, IL: Irwin/McGraw-Hill.

Mark C. Scott (2000), *Reinspiring the Corporation: The Seven Seminal Paths to Corporate Greatness*. Chichester: John Wiley & Sons.

 Discussion Questions

1. List and prioritize what motivates, engages or inspires you (in the context of work, study or home).
2. Consider the forms of power and influence that you exercise with work colleagues, friends and relatives and apply the descriptions outlined in this chapter under the headings of 'authority (position power)' and 'personal power'.
3. Is the use of power in interactions with other people always manipulation?
4. Do effective leaders motivate people or do they create the conditions in which people are motivated?
5. What do you think are the major problems in the way managers speak to their staff?
6. Can people be trained to speak inspirationally?
7. How can leaders convince you that they are authentic?
8. Is an 'engagement programme' a viable initiative for an organization?
9. What is the relationship between empowerment and engagement? Which, if either, is a necessary precondition for the other?

10 Multiple Intelligences of Leadership

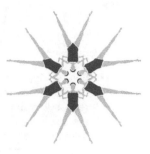

I have striven not to laugh at human actions, not to weep at them, nor to hate them, but to understand them.

Baruch Spinoza (1632–1677), *Tractatus Politicus*, 1, iv

OVERVIEW

- 'Intelligent leadership' is leadership that depends not only on cognitive intelligence but also on several other types of intelligence – emotional, social, cultural, moral, spiritual and behavioural. However, variations in the definition of 'leadership' among scholars and practitioners may cause differences in their assessment of the extent to which these types of intelligence contribute to leadership behaviour and effectiveness. Some scholars, however, argue that cognitive intelligence is the sole form of intelligence.
- Cognitive intelligence comprises the abilities, among others, to perceive, recall, simplify and understand ideas and information, reason with them, take a 'helicopter' view, imagine possibilities, use intuition, make judgements, learn, solve problems and make decisions. It is particularly useful in creating and developing vision, purpose, shared values and strategy.
- Emotional intelligence comprises understanding the needs and feelings of both oneself and others, practising self-control, and responding to the needs and feelings of other people in appropriate ways. It is generally considered to be the most important form of intelligence in effective leadership, though some scholars believe the concept to be a false one.
- Social intelligence extends the notion of emotional intelligence to social situations, encompassing social awareness and social competency.
- Cultural intelligence is the ability to connect with other people in different cultures and to cope effectively with cultural diversity, which is important for leadership in cross-cultural and multicultural settings.
- Moral intelligence is 'the ability to differentiate right from wrong according to universal moral principles'. Universal moral principles include empathy, responsibility, reciprocity, respect for others and caring for others. One major theory of moral intelligence considers moral intelligence to have four constituents: integrity, responsibility, compassion and forgiveness. Moral intelligence has taken on increasing importance as a result of a perceived decline in business ethics, thereby posing a new leadership challenge.

(Continued)

(Continued)

- Spiritual intelligence is the understanding that human beings have an animating need for meaning, value and a sense of worth in what they seek and do and responding appropriately to that need. More and more people, especially managers, are seeking higher meaning, value and worth in what they do and are willing to forsake materialism for it.
- Leaders may be able to discern and understand the need for particular leadership behaviour, but they may not necessarily be able to *act* in that way. Behavioural intelligence – the behavioural dimension of leadership – comprises the skills of both using and responding to emotion, for example through body language, communicating in other ways (through writing, speaking and active listening), using personal power, and physical activity.
- We need to understand the interaction that takes place among the cognitive processes, emotions and volitional action (behavioural skills) in leadership, for example in effective time management and in the effects of stress, anxiety, anger and mood on cognitive functioning.
- Leadership is both an art and a science. It is an art in terms of the imitative or imaginative skills needed to achieve form, function and meaning. It is a science in terms of the systematic cognitive processes and formulated knowledge that effective leaders use in the forming and testing of ideas and practices.

Blue-chip employers and governments have typically scrambled for graduates with the top grades, grade point average or degree classes from the 'top' universities in the belief that these graduates are their future top leaders. They have equated a high-class degree with 'intelligence' – cognitive intelligence. They have often made a big mistake. Many scholars and practitioners now believe that cognitive intelligence is only one of the several 'intelligences' that are required to be an effective manager or leader and that it is not necessarily the most important one for effective leadership.

Forms of Intelligence

In his analysis of attitudes, Tom Marshall identifies three basic components: a cognitive element, which he defines as intellectual beliefs or convictions; an emotional element, which comprises the feelings we have about these beliefs; and a volitional element, which he defines as the behavioural responses we make because of our beliefs.[1] Manfred Kets de Vries and Elizabeth Florent-Treacy describe effective leadership in terms of cognitive and emotional 'competencies' and the behavioural characteristics that contribute to them.[2] Marshall Sashkin and Molly Sashkin describe the elements of transformational leadership as 'ABC': affect (emotion and feelings), behavioural intent (confidence to act) and cognition (the basis for vision).[3]

Research in AT&T identified cognitive skills, the need for power and interpersonal skills as associated with the career advancement of managers.[4] The ability to motivate and inspire followers draws upon sources of power as well as a set of interpersonal skills. Gilbert Fairholm describes a 'spiritual' dimension to leadership associated with integrity, independence and justice,[5] one that is concerned with meeting people's needs for meaning and value in what they do. And Constance Campbell suggests that 'holistic' leadership reflects four components of the inner person: cognition; spirituality, emotion and 'being'.[6]

Studies of how and why leaders succeed, Dave Ulrich and colleagues suggest, focus separately on three clusters of leadership factors:

✳ *What to know.* The knowledge cluster, which includes knowing *how*, concerns setting the direction (understanding the business environment and developing a vision), mobilizing individual commitment, and creating organizational capability.
✳ *How to be.* The second cluster, about *being*, concerns personal values and motives such as integrity, ambition, a concern for others, loyalty and self-awareness.
✳ *What to do.* The *doing* cluster refers to the behaviour and actions of leaders, such as where, how and with whom leaders spend their time.[7]

Howard Gardner introduced his concept of multiple intelligences in 1983.[8] He defined intelligence as 'the capacity to solve problems or to fashion products that are valued in one or more cultural settings'.[9] Intelligence, he argued, was composed of the following eight forms:

✳ *Linguistic intelligence.* The ability to think in words and use language to express and understand complex meaning. Gardner gives T.S. Eliot's facility with speech and language as an example.
✳ *Logical–mathematical intelligence.* The ability to detect and understand cause-and-effect connections and the relationships among actions, objects, events or ideas, for example Albert Einstein.
✳ *Musical intelligence.* The ability to recognize and appreciate musical patterns, pitches, tones and rhythms, and to compose and perform music. Musical intelligence operates in parallel to linguistic intelligence. An example is the pianist Arthur Rubinstein.
✳ *Visual–spatial intelligence.* The ability to think in pictures, use imagination and perceive the visual world accurately in three dimensions. Architects require this form of intelligence.
✳ *Intrapersonal intelligence.* The ability to understand and manage oneself, one's thoughts and feelings, strengths and weaknesses (part of what is now known as emotional intelligence), and to plan effectively to achieve personal goals.
✳ *Interpersonal intelligence.* The ability to understand other people, display empathy, recognize individual differences, and interact effectively (also related to social intelligence, cultural intelligence and emotional intelligence), for example Mahatma Gandhi.
✳ *Bodily kinaesthetic intelligence.* The ability to use the body in skilful and complicated ways, involving a sense of timing, coordination of movement and the use of the hands, for example Martha Graham, the creator of modern dance, who exemplified the ability to use one's body.
✳ *Naturalist intelligence.* The ability to recognize, categorize and draw upon features of the natural world, for example Charles Darwin.

Most of the intelligences in Gardner's theory – if not all according to him – are to do with thinking or cognition. Russell Moxley has called for a more holistic view of leadership that integrates four arenas of the human condition: the mind (rational thought), the heart (emotions or feelings), the spirit and the body.[10] Gardner considers the notion of spiritual intelligence but finds it difficult to separate it from its religious connotations, preferring to consider what he calls 'existential intelligence', of which spiritual intelligence is 'one variety'.[11] Even then he believes its distinctiveness from other intelligences and the supportive empirical evidence to be insufficient to propose it as a valid ninth form of intelligence. Neither does Gardner accept moral intelligence as a valid intelligence, arguing, in 1999, that there was no consensus on what it was and that, again, there was little evidence to support it.[12] We revisit these issues in our model of multiple intelligences later in this chapter.

Gardner's theory of multiple intelligences has met with greater support among practitioners such as educators than among academics: his criteria for what may be called a form of intelligence have been questioned and criticized as too subjective.[13] And his theory has been challenged for being grounded too much in reasoning and intuition without the compelling empirical evidence to support it. In 2001 Ronald Riggio and colleagues reported on research into how multiple forms of intelligence – cognitive intelligence (IQ), emotional intelligence and social intelligence – were associated with effective leadership.[14] This suggested that:

⁕ The possession of multiple forms of intelligence was important for effective leadership.
⁕ We were just beginning to understand the breadth, depth and potential applications of non-IQ domains of intelligence.
⁕ Incorporating multiple intelligence constructs into existing leadership theories would improve our understanding of effective leadership.
⁕ Research on multiple intelligence had important implications for both the selection and training of future leaders.

Robert Sternberg defines human intelligence as 'mental activity directed toward purposive adaptation to, selection and shaping of, real-world environments relevant to one's life'.[15] He proposes a 'triarchic' model of intelligence, comprising three elements:

⁕ *Analytical intelligence.* The ability to solve abstract problems quickly.
⁕ *Practical intelligence.* The ability to apply concepts to real-world contexts entails the use of tacit knowledge.
⁕ *Creative intelligence.* The ability to deal with novel situations, imagine possibilities and generate new ideas.[16]

When these three forms of intelligence are present and balanced, Sternberg would label this 'successful intelligence'.[17] However, Linda Gottfredson has challenged Sternberg's triarchic theory, arguing its non-empirical basis and that practical intelligence is simply a specific set of task-related skills and knowledge that people learn so that they can cope with specific environmental challenges.[18]

In our model of multiple intelligences, we posit seven forms of intelligence underlying leadership effectiveness: cognitive, emotional, social, cultural, moral, spiritual and behavioural. Let us consider each of these in turn and how they interact in producing leadership behaviour.

Cognitive Intelligence

'Few characteristics are more valued, or valuable, in modern Western society than intelligence', say Timothy Judge and colleagues.[19] Indeed they found a significant but moderate association between intelligence and leadership. Moreover, intelligence was found in a study by Robert Lord and colleagues to be the *only* attribute that was critical to a leader.[20] Sir Christopher Hogg, former chairman of the UK's Financial Reporting Council, Courtaulds, Reuters Group, SmithKline Beecham, GlaxoSmithKline and Allied Domecq, says:

> Whatever else it is, business is an intellectual exercise ... it [is] fantastically demanding on intellectual resources. You are dealing with an enormous range of variables. You are always trying to make decisions on inadequate information and against time. It means a constant process of selection of priorities.[21]

One the other hand Fred Fiedler argues that 'Intellectual abilities ... do not predict leadership performance to any appreciable degree'.[22] And others (as we will see later in this chapter) demote intellectual abilities in favour of other abilities, particularly those to do with feelings and emotion. Gerry Robinson, former CEO of Granada, says:

> The danger of a high intellect is that it can veer into over-intellectualising a business problem that is essentially very simple. People with lots of nous but average intelligence can be enormously successful in running large companies.[23]

I suspect that the reason for such disagreement rests with the variation in definitions of leadership in the first place. However, most scholars and commentators would agree that effective leadership does require the abilities to perceive, interrelate, organize and understand information, reason with it, imagine possibilities, use intuition, make judgements, solve problems and make decisions. These abilities play a large part in producing vision, purpose, shared values and strategies for pursuing the vision and purpose that will 'win' people's minds if not their hearts.

The Cognitive Skills of Leadership

Tom Peters and Robert Waterman argue that:

> An effective leader must be the master of two ends of the spectrum: ideas at the highest level of abstraction and actions at the most mundane level of detail.[24]

This resembles what is commonly known as a 'helicopter view': the ability both to see a problem or issue in context (from a high vantage point) and to focus on the detail and move easily between each activity – to be able to 'see both the forest and the trees'. The helicopter view is an example of 'complementarity': the ability to do one thing without prejudice to the opposite. For example, Gerry Johnson and Kevan Scholes describe strategy creation and implementation as involving both detailed analysis and visioning about the future.[25]

The cognitive skills that make up what Robert Sternberg calls 'successful intelligence' are memory, analytical abilities and creativity, and he believes that these are important for effective leadership.[26] But while they are necessary they are not sufficient, for Sternberg argues that wisdom is also important. He defines wisdom as:

> ... the extent to which [a leader] uses successful intelligence as moderated by values to ... seek to reach a common good ... by balancing intrapersonal (one's own), interpersonal (others'), and extrapersonal (organizational/institutional/spiritual) interests ... over the short and long term, to ... adapt to, shape, and select environments.

Nigel Holden and colleagues define wisdom somewhat differently: 'prudence shaped by the capacity to anticipate tendencies towards positive/successful/effective or negative/unsuccessful/ineffective outcomes'.[27] More light-heartedly, writer and broadcaster Nigel Rees quotes an Israeli writer: 'It is said that a clever person knows how to get out of a trap into which a wise person would not have fallen in the first place.'[28]

Underlying the intellectual or cognitive dimension of leadership are several more specific forms of intelligence, according to Howard Gardner: the ability to think in words and use language to express and understand complex meaning (linguistic intelligence); to understand cause-and-effect connections and relationships among actions, objects, events or ideas (logical–mathematical intelligence); and to think in pictures, use imagination and perceive the visual world accurately in three dimensions (visual-spatial intelligence).[29]

Leopold Vansina studied successful general managers in a multinational company.[30] He found they would think holistically, backed up by subsequent analysis, in attempting to understand a situation, which in turn would lead to a vision of what the company should be like in the future. Future orientation is a necessary requirement for effective leadership. Leaders, Tom Marshall says, must be able to deal with the future and they also need foresight.[31] Foresight in turn, he says, requires vision – seeing possible futures, identifying opportunities and possibilities, and knowing how to respond – and intuition – a sense for the unknown (which we discuss later).

Both visioning and strategy development require a well-developed cognitive ability. High-level leaders in particular have to produce a fit between the organization and its anticipated environment at some distant future time.[32] They have to process ambiguous and complex information and produce a logical framework, understand how their organizations may evolve in the context of the vision, and develop the appropriate strategies and tactics.[33] This requires both logic and creativity. John Kotter says:

> Great vision emerges when a powerful mind, working long and hard on massive amounts of information, is able to see (or recognize in suggestions from others) interesting patterns and new possibilities.[34]

Turning vision into goals or objectives also requires cognitive skills. This process takes disjointed, inconsistent and 'sometimes apparently contradictory ideas, phenomena and opinions and builds them into a mental image in which each element has a logical and integral relationship with the whole'.[35] Based on a study of the research literature, Stephen Zaccaro and Deanna Banks suggest that high-level leaders need 'meta-cognitive' skills – inductive reasoning, deductive reasoning, divergent thinking, information processing skills, and verbal reasoning.[36] Such skills – for example, the selective encoding, combination and comparison of information – are particularly important for unstructured problems requiring insight and creativity.[37]

Another cognitive ability in effective leadership is being to take the adversary's perspective on one's own frame of reference – one's mental model – for strategy development.[38] Research reported by Owen Jacobs and Michael McGee suggests that cognitive ability is associated with reflecting on experience, being open to new ideas, and having the capacity to form and integrate multiple perspectives on one's environment and experience.[39] Strategists will implicitly use mental models in scanning, analysing and making sense of the competitive environment. A mental map is known as a paradigm: 'the set of assumptions and beliefs that resides deep within [the organization's] culture and influences the thinking, decisions and actions of its members'.[40] Drawing on this idea, cognitive mapping has been used to describe individuals' mental models and to understand how leaders will formulate visions, interpret the competitive environment and develop strategies.[41]

Peter Linkow proposes the following cognitive competencies required for strategy formation:[42]

❊ *Reframing*. Challenging and restating the underlying beliefs, values and assumptions – mental models – that form the basis of organizational relationships and action, for example through brainstorming.
❊ *Scanning*. The constant search for information that relates to beliefs, values and assumptions. Demographic and cultural information (part of the social context) and industry and market information (part of economic analysis) might be included here. Conclusions as a basis for decision making are made iteratively – through a successive approximation.
❊ *Abstracting*. Grasping the essential message in disparate information. An example would be capturing and describing the essence of Charles Rennie Macintosh's architectural design based on studying the houses he designed. Many tools are available for this, such as the nominal group technique and cluster and factor analysis.
❊ *Multivariate thinking*. Balancing many dynamic variables simultaneously to discern the relationship among them. In metaphorical terms, it is about seeing the forest *before* seeing the trees, but nevertheless also seeing the trees and the spaces around them ('helicopter view'). Multivariate thinking enables seeing how actions or decisions affect one another. Mathematical modelling and simulation are useful tools.
❊ *Envisioning*. Seeing future states as vivid mental images. Vision is the result of analysis, imagination and intuition. Useful tools are the Delphi method[43] and scenario planning (discussed in Chapter 7 on leadership and strategy).

* *Inducting.* Arriving at beliefs and generalizations from specific or limited information. The converse process is deduction, which starts with a theory from which hypotheses are generated and tested and leads to confirmation or disconfirmation. An example of induction is the small-scale piloting of a programme in a low-risk situation before introducing it organization-wide.
* *Valuating.* Seeking to know and understand the underlying beliefs, values and assumptions of stakeholders. The rationale is that their interests are important and that successful strategic action requires incorporating a balance of interests. This process involves stakeholder analysis (see Chapter 7).

When managers fail to use (or do not have) effective cognitive processes and models of their organizations, they will tend to resort to simplistic management 'fads'.[44] Naomi Brookes and Michel Leseure, investigating the relationship between managers' cognitive processes and organizational performance, found three themes to be emerging: managers would use extremely simple models, cognitive processes were characterized by a small series of steps in chronological order, and their cognitive models were highly pictorial in nature.[45]

Philip Hodgson and Randall White usefully suggest four perspectives of leadership that characterize the intellectual dimension:[46]

* *The economic and strategic perspective.* This focuses on what the organization should be trying to do – its 'strategic intent'.[47] It seeks a good fit between what the organization needs to become and the constraints and opportunities in its business environment.
* *Internal culture*: developing the organization's culture to enable it to do what needs to be done. This means first establishing a clear vision and set of corporate values. Leaders then take one or more of three stances: command-and-control, empowerment, or 'difficult learning'. Command-and-control might work in an organization where expertise is highly valued and senior executives are expected to make the right decisions. Empowerment assumes – and ensures – that people can produce the necessary solutions to problems. In difficult learning the leader responds to uncertainty through 'an evolving, continuous process of discovery and reinvention', which leads to a competitive advantage.
* *The overall aims of the leader*, e.g. maintenance of the *status quo* or revolution.
* *The leader's own knowledge and skills,* such as (a) strategic knowledge concerning the needs and goals of stakeholders and competitors and planning techniques; (b) tactical knowledge of how to identify emerging threats and opportunities and respond to them quickly and appropriately, within the strategic framework, through innovation and improvisation;[48] and (c) in particular, handling uncertainty during change. Another track to the research that has contributed to our understanding of the cognitive processes in leadership is the organizational systems approach. This approach, exemplified by the work of Daniel Katz and Robert Kahn,[49] emphasizes the role of leaders in spanning organizational boundaries and coordinating activity across them. Such boundaries are composed of interfaces with the external environment or between organizational levels.

The American writing guru, Albert Joseph, says: 'Thinking is the process of simplify-ing the relationships between ideas. Therefore simplicity is not only desirable – it is the mark of the thinking person.'[50] The danger of over-intellectualizing on problems carries some credence. In a study that explored management potential as a concept of 'trainability', I found that the most intelligent individuals (as measured by Heim's AH5 high-level cognitive intelligence test[51]) did not improve their ability to prioritize items in their in-basket or to make effective decisions as a result of coaching as much as those of above-average (but not high) intelligence.[52] Intelligence was related to prioritizing and decision making in a curvilinear manner (a ∩-shaped relationship). The conclusion was that the most intelligent individuals tended to analyse problems more, at the expense of effective decision making, though intelligence plays a part up to a point and then becomes dysfunctional.

Intuition[53]

In addition to analytical and reasoning skills, intuition and imagination are generally regarded as important characteristics of effective leadership. Intuition is often called the 'sixth sense' or 'gut feeling'. This gut feeling, Baroness Susan Greenfield says, is due to the release of peptides in the abdomen that serve as chemical messengers to the brain.[54] 'First the feeling, then the thought': the feeling occurs faster than the thought, often accompanied by physical reactions. Intuitive feelings guide decision making so that the mind can make good choices. Leaders' ability to recognize and use intuition will depend on both their cognitive and emotional intelligence.[55]

'Intuition' and 'instinct' are often casually used interchangeably, but a distinction is necessary here. Intuition is immediate understanding, knowledge or awareness, without any conscious cognitive process.[56] Erik Dane and Michael Pratt say that 'intuition draws on our inborn ability to synthesize information quickly and effec-tively.'[57] The *process* of intuition is known as 'intuiting' and the *outcome* of intuition 'intuitive judgments.'[58] Intuitions are emotionally laden judgements that arise from rapid, non-conscious, holistic associations. These associations in turn arise from the linking of disparate pieces of information and recognizing features or patterns in doing so. We are unaware of these processes as they happen. Rational analysis may even prevent us from 'seeing the obvious'.[59] The processes to do with experience are emotionally driven.[60] Intuition and emotion appear to operate through a common neural mechanism: the basal ganglia. The confidence that people feel about their intuitive judgements is therefore probably due to a combination of their associative and emotional characteristics. Instinct, on the other hand, is an innate, 'hard-wired' tendency to respond in a particular way to a stimulus.[61] Examples we are all familiar with are the instincts of sex, hunger and self-preservation. Instinctive behaviour is unlearned and largely genetically programmed.

Intuition is also confused sometimes with insight. Insight is the sudden under-standing or appreciation of the meaning or significance of a pattern or a solution to a problem.[62] An example is Archimedes' sudden discovery while in his bath of his famous principle concerning the displacement of fluid by a body immersed in it. Insight is the sudden conclusion to a lengthy process of reasoning and incubation.

Transformational leaders who use intellectual stimulation will encourage followers to recognize their intuitions as well as using logical reasoning.[63] Intuition can be critical in differentiating successful top executives from dysfunctional ones.[64] Ralph Larsen, former chairman and CEO of Johnson & Johnson, said that when successful middle managers reach senior management, where problems become more complex and ambiguous, their judgement – intuition – 'is not what it should be ... it's a *big* problem'.[65] In uncertain and ambiguous situations, intuitive decisions appear to be more effective than rational ones,[66] and this is also the case for moral and aesthetic judgements.[67]

Leaders in cultures low in what Geert Hofstede calls 'uncertainty avoidance'[68] may be more inclined than those in other cultures to favour intuitive judgements.[69] This may also be true for leaders in 'feminine' cultures in comparison with those in 'masculine' ones.[70] Intuitive leaders may be less dominating with their subordinates than analytical leaders, and they tend to be more liked and respected by analytical subordinates than analytical leaders are by intuitive subordinates.[71]

Ignoring intuition, whether for rational or emotional reasons, risks error and failure, as no doubt many of us – and many leaders – have discovered. In the words of the Arab proverb, 'Dawn does not come twice to awaken a man.'[72] However, intuition should not be taken at face value: as Daniel Kahneman, psychologist and Nobel Laureate, says, 'Overconfidence is a powerful source of illusions, primarily determined by the quality and coherence of the story that you can construct, not by its validity.'[73]

Intuitive capacity is nevertheless important to strategic vision. Gerry Johnson and Kevan Scholes point out that there are leaders who see what other executives do not see and who champion new ways of working.[74] Albert Einstein regarded intuition as a gift possessed by great people.[75] Yet sadly many senior executives hesitate to share their intuitions for fear of being laughed out of the boardroom. Randall White and colleagues argue:

> Most executives can't and won't talk about [their intuitions]. Shareholders and institutional investors are particularly unimpressed by intuitive decisions and judgements. As a result, annual reports and the like have become works of incredible fiction. If a chief executive hits on a brilliant idea while in the bath, it is not something that he will proclaim at the AGM.[76]

There are many anecdotes of defining moments of intuition. Sir Richard Branson's decision in 1984 to go into the airline industry was based on intuition, against all the advice of colleagues and friends that was based on rationality.[77] He has since created a successful airline with a unique brand.

Another such moment defined the survival of Chrysler in the 1990s. One weekend in 1988, the then-president of Chrysler, Don Lutz, was driving his Cobra. Relaxed and ruminating on criticisms about the company, he formed a vision of a car that would be a 'muscular, outrageous sports car that would turn heads and stop traffic'. He put his intuitive decision into action that Monday. The Dodge Viper was to become a 'smashing success', the right car at the right time. His intuition, Lutz says, was 'this subconscious, visceral feeling ... [that] just felt right'.[78] But it all started with an image in his imagination.

Imagination

Imagination, says Ralph Rolls, is a human being's 'most powerful weapon for attack, defence, survival – but above all for invention and creativity'.[79] In the words of the poet William Wordsworth, imagination is 'that inward eye which is the bliss of solitude',[80] and with which, in the words of Ralph Rolls, 'man can see beyond himself, beyond his immediate environment and circumstances'.[81] Imagination is 'the vanguard or advance scouting party of thinking', says John Adair.[82] It leads to the exploration of uncharted waters, experimentation, creativity, invention and innovation. While imagination may be fanciful, silly or cranky, it characterizes the pathfinder. Richard Olivier quotes Einstein as saying:

> **Imagination is more important than knowledge – for while knowledge points to all that is, imagination points to all there will be ...[83]**

Susan Greenfield describes how even learning skills may occur through imagination: it helps to establish more neural connections in the brain.[84] She quotes the example of learning to play the piano, which can be aided by imagining one is playing it as well as by actually doing so.

Emotional Intelligence

Emotion at Work

We know that emotion has far-reaching impact on judgement, performance, relationships with other people, and well-being at work.[85] 'First the feeling, then the thought': the emotional mind (in the more primitive part of the brain called the amygdala) is far quicker than the rational mind (in the prefrontal cortex), springing into action without pausing even for a moment to consider what it is doing.

We all experience emotion in our lives, not least at work. While psychologists have studied emotion for many decades, it has not figured much in the study of work in general and leadership in particular until recently. Moreover, 'The emotional impact of a leader is almost never discussed in the workplace, let alone in the literature on leadership and performance', say Daniel Goleman and colleagues.[86] Why? Steve Fineman suggests a reason:

> **Deeply rooted in Western (especially male) cultural beliefs about the expression of emotion is the belief that organizational order and manager/worker efficiency are matters of the rational, that is non-emotional, activity. Cool strategic thinking is not to be sullied by messy feelings. Efficient thought and behaviour tame emotion. Accordingly good organizations are places where feelings are managed, designed out, or removed.[87]**

Guy Lubitsh and John Higgins describe how ignoring emotions can result in tragic consequences – for example, in the *Challenger* disaster.[88] Engineers did not feel they could let management know of a crucial fault in the Space Shuttle because of their unwillingness to listen to opposing or unpopular views and bullying – a failure of leadership. Peter Frost describes how the emotionally insensitive attitudes and behaviour of managers in organizations may create 'emotional pain' that becomes toxic and debilitates the organization.[89] Listening to employees, he says, is a way of 'cleansing' emotional toxins. We need feeling as well as thinking people, says Kjell Nordstrom:

> In an excess economy success comes from attracting the emotional consumer or colleague, not the rational one ... We need not only agile thinkers, but acting, feeling and communicating human beings as well.[90]

The expression of positive emotions may have very positive outcomes. For example, excitement is contagious: it can stimulate others into action.[91] Daniel Goleman and colleagues argue:

> When the leader is in a happy mood, the people around him view everything in a more positive light. That, in turn, makes them optimistic about achieving their goals, enhances their creativity and the efficiency of their decision making, and predisposes them to be helpful.[92]

Emotions may have adverse effects on one's own judgement, task performance and well-being, as well as on one's relationships with others.[93] Kevin Daniels suggests that negative emotions, for example, may affect the way managers make major strategic decisions about their organizations.[94] Time and time again we see calmness under pressure – self-control – as a characteristic of effective leaders. It is emotions that explain why irrational decisions are often made. The 'heart' may rule the 'head' with adverse consequences even at the top level in an organization

In practice it is difficult, and perhaps even unrealistic, to separate feeling from thinking. For the 'emotional brain', housed in the structure in the limbic system called the amygdala, works very closely and speedily with the 'thinking brain' in the prefrontal cortex. This relationship provides us with what we call 'emotional intelligence'.[95] It is well known that effective learning, for example, depends on the interaction between cognitive and emotional processes.

We now understand a great deal about emotion and its relationship to our behaviour. And we have come to accept the need to 'manage' both our own and other people's emotions. Sharon Turnbull makes the point that 'charismatic and transformational leadership has at its heart the assumption that the control of emotion is the most effective way to lead'.[96] But this is not about encouraging the exploitation of other people's feelings. It is instead about enabling both ourselves and people we interact with to function effectively, achieve results, and enjoy job satisfaction. It is about emotional intelligence.

Emotional Intelligence: An Overview

Emotional intelligence (known as 'EQ', as distinct from 'IQ') is the extent of our self-awareness, our ability to manage our own feelings, our awareness of the needs and feelings of other people, and our ability to respond appropriately. In the words of Warren Bennis:

> **Emotional intelligence is much more powerful than IQ in determining who emerges as a leader. IQ is a threshold competence. You need it, but it doesn't make you a star. Emotional intelligence can.**[97]

And Daniel Goleman says:

> **High IQ makes you a good English professor; adding high EQ makes you chairman of the English Department ... High IQ makes you a brilliant fiscal analyst; adding high EQ makes you CEO.**[98]

That more emotionally intelligent people perform better at work, and that this applies both to workers in general[99] as well those specifically in leadership positions,[100] is a popular but nevertheless challenged view today. The concept of EQ developed rapidly during the 1990s. Its roots go back to the 1920s with Thorndike's concept of 'social intelligence',[101] defined by Kimberley Boal and Robert Hooijberg as the understanding of one's social environment[102] (which we discuss later in this chapter). One of the earliest definitions of EQ comes from Howard Gardner in 1985: the ability 'to notice and make distinctions among other individuals ... in particular, among their moods, temperaments, motivations, and intentions'.[103] Peter Salovey and John Mayer later re-conceptualized it as 'the ability to monitor one's own and others' feelings and emotions, to discriminate among them and to use this information to guide one's thinking and actions',[104] and subsequently developed the definition as follows:

> **Emotional intelligence refers to an ability to recognize the meanings of emotions and their relationships, and to reason and problem-solve on the basis of them. Emotional intelligence is involved in the capacity to perceive emotions, assimilate emotion-related feelings, understand the information of those emotions, and manage them.**[105]

Two forms of intelligence identified by Howard Gardner underlie the emotional dimension of leadership: the ability to understand and manage oneself, one's thoughts and feelings, strengths and weaknesses, and to plan effectively to achieve personal goals (intrapersonal intelligence); and to understand other people, display empathy, recognize individual differences, and interact effectively (interpersonal intelligence).[106] Together, these constitute EQ.

Notable models of EQ have been developed by Robert Cooper and Ayman Sawaf,[107] Daniel Goleman and Richard Boyatzis, and Victor Dulewicz and Malcolm Higgs.[108] A comparison of the characteristics of emotional intelligence that these authorities agree on is provided in Table 10.1. Comparable terms are grouped together.

Robert Cooper and Ayman Sawaf suggest that there are three broad aspects of EQ – emotional literacy, emotional competencies, and values and beliefs – with 14 factors within them.[109] Unique to their model are emotional expression, intentionality, creativity, constructive discontent, outlook, intuition, and trust radius.

Table 10.1 Characteristics of Emotional Intelligence

	Cooper and Sawaf	Goleman and Boyatzis	Dulewicz and Higgs
Self-awareness	✓	✓	✓
Awareness of others Organizational awareness Interpersonal sensitivity	✓	✓	✓
Resilience	✓		✓
Interpersonal connections Building bonds	✓	✓	
Compassion Empathy	✓	✓	
Personal power Influence Persuasion	✓	✓	✓
Integrity Trustworthiness	✓	✓	✓
Conscientiousness		✓	✓
Achievement orientation Motivation		✓	✓

According to Goleman, 'emotional intelligence refers to a different way of being smart. It's not your IQ. It's how well you handle yourself and handle your relationships, how well you work on a team, your ability to lead.'[110] And it is 'the capacity for recognizing our own feelings and those of others, for motivating ourselves, and for managing emotions well in ourselves and in our relationships'.[111] Research by Goleman and Boyatzis produced four dimensions of EQ – self-awareness self-management, social awareness, and social skills – and 20 factors within them.[112] Unique to Goleman's model are accurate self-assessment, self-confidence, self-control, adaptability, initiative, service orientation, developing others, leadership (in its own right), communication, change catalysis, conflict management, and teamwork and collaboration. Research by Victor Dulewicz and Malcolm Higgs suggests there are seven dimensions of EQ.[113] Unique to their model is decisiveness.

Ernest O'Boyle and colleagues carried out a meta-analysis, classifying EQ studies into three streams: ability-based models that use objective test items, self-report or peer-report measures, and 'mixed models' of emotional competencies. All three streams correlated positively with job performance, cognitive ability and the 'Big Five' personality characteristics of neuroticism, extraversion, openness, agreeableness and conscientiousness, the results supporting the overall validity of the concept of EQ.[114]

Is EQ merely a recycling of what we used to call the 'soft' skills of management and leadership? Is it not just another case of 'old wine in new bottles'? I do not believe this is so. So-called soft skills generally concern *interpersonal intelligence* – relating to others – whereas EQ also includes *intrapersonal* intelligence – knowing oneself, which is necessary before one can understand others.[115] The former leader of an executive team at Ford Motor Company, Nick Zenuik, says: 'Emotional intelligence is the hidden competitive advantage. If you take care of the soft stuff, the hard stuff takes care of itself.'[116]

Emotional Intelligence and Self-awareness

'We lie loudest when we lie to ourselves', says Eric Hoffer, the American sociologist.[117] How can we recognize and respond to other people's feelings if we fail to recognize and respond to our own? Self-awareness includes seeing ourselves as others see us. In the immortal words of Scottish poet Robert Burns:

> **O wad some Pow'r the giftie gie us To see oursels as others see us! It wad frae mony a blunder free us, And foolish notion.[118]**

Awareness of the importance of self-awareness is nothing new: sociologist Charles Cooley coined the term 'the looking glass self' over a century ago.[119] Yet there are some commentators, such as journalist Lucy Kellaway, who dismiss self-awareness as 'tosh'.[120] Referring to the UK's Home Office selection criteria for recruiting bankers, she asks: 'Have you ever met anyone who was "fully aware of their own strengths, weaknesses and motivations"?' She suggests that what people say about themselves, for example about how they learned from failure, may have nothing to do with their actual ability to lead effectively. Owing to her exaggeration and misunderstanding of the concept, she is not convincing.

Nevertheless, as leaders we need to know and control ourselves first before we can lead and enable others. This is not a new principle: Philip Massinger in 1624 said: 'He that would govern others, first should be the master of himself.'[121] Understanding ourselves helps us to better understand other people. In an important study Allan Church has shown that high-performing managers are significantly more self-aware than average performers.[122]

A lack of self-awareness may result in reading other people's responses wrongly, incorrect assumptions about people and situations, and inappropriate behaviour.[123] Self-awareness gives individuals greater perceived control over interpersonal events.[124] And transformational leaders who are self-aware display high levels of self-confidence.[125] Rob Goffee sums up the importance of self-awareness: 'At the heart of good leadership is self-knowledge: knowing your strengths and weaknesses and using them to your advantage.'[126] Self-awareness, then, is the starting point for self-development, and this is a prerequisite to become a good leader. What characterizes self-awareness?

❋ *Personal insight* is awareness of how we are feeling and why we are feeling that way.
❋ *Accurate self-assessment* adds to personal insight and entails understanding our strengths and limitations as well as our emotional needs.
❋ *Humility* is taking responsibility for one's actions, admitting to mistakes and being prepared to apologize. The poet John Ruskin recognized this: 'The first test of a truly great man is his humility.'[127]
❋ *Self-confidence.* Self-confidence is undoubtedly a characteristic of effective leaders.[128] According to journalist and broadcaster Jeremy Paxman it is a *sine qua non* for political leaders.[129]
❋ *Personal vision* – understanding what we want from life, what our values are, what we stand for.

Emotional Intelligence and Self-control

The emotionally intelligent leader exercises self-control. David Gilbert-Smith, founding CEO of the Leadership Trust, says:

> **... all leadership starts with oneself, with learning to know and control oneself first, so that then and only then can one control and lead others.**[130]

Goleman refers to the ability to manage our emotions. Cooper refers to 'effectively applying' them. Our ability to effect personal change, and indeed to influence others, depends on how we manage our emotions. In exercising self-control, it is important to deal with a person's emotional reaction, Alistair Ostell and colleagues say, before attempting to resolve the problem.[131] What may get in the way of this, Ostell adds, is 'unconstructive mood matching'.[132] This is what happens when we display an emotional state that is similar to that of another person, with adverse consequences, for example displaying anger with somebody because he or she is angry with you. Self-control means avoiding the use of emotive verbal expressions and negative body language that would exacerbate another person's negative emotion. Self-control involves self-awareness, displaying integrity, self-empowerment and being agile in our behaviour.

Emotional Intelligence and Awareness of Others' Needs and Feelings

Self-awareness and self-control are critical pre requisites if we are to excel in the third major competency of EQ – awareness of others. Interpersonal insight is characterized by understanding others' motivation, aspirations, needs, interests, preferences, likes and dislikes, and feelings.

Key to an awareness of others is empathy. Says Peter Drucker, 'The number one practical competency for leaders is empathy. Today, perceptiveness is more important than analysis.'[133] The essence of empathy is sensing what others feel without their saying so. We sense other people's feelings not through the words they use but through their body language – their eye contact, tone of voice, facial expression, gestures and posture. Simon Baron-Cohen extends the notion of empathy to include appreciating that a response to another person's feelings or situation is required and then responding appropriately.[134]

How do we achieve empathy? For Nelson Mandela, 'To see the world through another man's eyes, you have to walk a mile in his shoes.'[135] Emotionally intelligent leaders who do display will use well-developed questioning skills – open and probing rather than closed and leading questions. They will also use active listening skills – paraphrasing the meaning or content of what the other person has just said and reflecting the feeling displayed through that person's body language. Active listening confirms to another person your understanding of his or her meaning and feelings. Such understanding builds trust. And trust breeds powerful relationships. But Baron-Cohen would add that powerful relationships depend not only on awareness and understanding but also on taking appropriate action.

Emotional Intelligence and Leadership

According to Daniel Goleman, EQ is twice as important as cognitive or technical skills for high job performance.[136] And at the top level, he says, EQ is almost all-important, according to findings from profiles of top executives in 15 global companies including IBM, PepsiCo and Volvo. Robert Sternberg says that IQ accounts for as little as 4 per cent of exceptional leadership, job performance and achievement; EQ may account for over 90 per cent.[137] A study of 100 management and business leaders in the UK over seven years by Malcolm Higgs and Vic Dulewicz revealed that 'emotional intelligence was more highly related to success than IQ alone', consistent with Goleman and Sternberg.[138] Dulewicz and Higgs found that EQ and IQ together are even better predictors of managerial success.[139]

The concept of EQ has helped us to understand empowerment as a core leadership practice. EQ is about being aware of one's own abilities, needs and feelings, recognizing those of others, managing one's feelings, and responding to others in appropriate ways through well-developed interpersonal skills. Awareness of – and overcoming – one's own need for control, for example, is necessary if one is to empower people sincerely and effectively.

Openness and curiosity in leaders stimulate exploration and learning and the creative problem solving that is necessary in visioning and strategy development.[140] Risk propensity is also important: visionary leaders are intellectually and emotionally courageous.[141] They know when to confront painful situations and they can resist conforming as the easy, less effective option. Effective leaders also display skills in complex interactions with others, behavioural flexibility, conflict management, social awareness and reasoning, persuasion and empathy.[142] Understanding the moods and emotions of stakeholders is important to leaders, for example in deciding how to communicate strategies.[143] Chief executives need to understand and manage the dynamics of the top team, which calls for EQ, in ensuring clear goals and cooperation. Studies by the Hay Group clearly reinforce the need for EQ:

> ... the most successful teams are distinguished by empathy and integrity, rather than brainpower ... [they] excel at working with others and are adaptable, capable of self-control and able to manage 'productive conflict' ... over ideas rather than personalities.[144]

A study of 12 skippers in a BT Global Challenge Round-the-World yacht race, using Dulewicz and Higgs' model, found that the more successful ones displayed greater EQ, in particular interpersonal sensitivity, and that their intuitiveness increased during the race.[145] Interviews reported by Jane Cranwell-Ward indicated the importance for success of self-confidence, self-belief, a strong set of values and an ability to cope with emotions.[146] And Malcolm Higgs and Vic Dulewicz report several studies that indicate a link between EQ and leadership.[147] They speculate that leadership effectiveness is a sum of EQ, intellectual or cognitive intelligence (IQ) and managerial competence, an idea that is worth exploring.

In a 2001 study of innovation and enterprise course participants at the Swinburne University of Technology in Australia, Benjamin Palmer et al. found that EQ correlated with elements of transformational leadership – individualized consideration and inspirational motivation – and (as Julian Barling and colleagues also found) with the contingent reward element of transactional leadership.[148] In a further study, Lisa Gardner and Con Stough, studying 110 senior managers, found that EQ correlated highly with all aspects of transformational leadership (individualized consideration, intellectual stimulation, inspirational motivation, and idealized attributes and behaviour (derived from idealized influence)).[149] Understanding others' emotions and emotional management were the best predictors of transformational leadership, and unsurprisingly there was a negative relationship with laissez-faire behaviour.

Strategic thinking commonly is associated with the prefrontal cortex in the brain, which performs an executive function involved in problem solving. However, a study by Roderick Gilkey and colleagues suggests that strategic thinking is associated with less neural activity in that region of the brain than in the areas associated with 'gut' responses, empathy and EQ, namely the insula, the anterior cingulated cortex and the superior temporal sulcus.[150] Unconscious emotional processing appeared to be operating more freely than the conscious executive function in the prefrontal cortex. Strategic thinking therefore appears to require as much EQ as IQ.

Effective leadership, then, requires well-developed EQ – the ability to understand oneself and others, to manage one's emotions, and to use interpersonal skills to respond to other people in appropriate ways. Effective leaders 'win people's hearts'. They use personal power (interpersonal skills) – an element of EQ – rather than position power (authority). EQ, in addition to cognitive intelligence, is essential to identifying, displaying, promoting and reinforcing the shared values that support the pursuit of a vision, purpose and strategies and to empowering and engaging people in doing what needs to be done. 'Emotional leadership,' Daniel Goleman and colleagues say, 'is the spark that ignites a company's performance, creating a bonfire of success or a landscape of ashes'.[151]

Criticisms of the Concept of Emotional Intelligence

The concept of EQ has not received universal acclaim. Some scholars regard the concept as unintelligible and invalid. For example, Edwin Locke asks:

> What is the common or integrating element in a concept that includes introspection about emotions, emotional expression, non-verbal communication with others, empathy, self-regulation, planning, creative thinking and the direction of attention? There is none.[152]

Locke asks rhetorically: 'What does EI [emotional intelligence][153] not include?' In defence of EQ one might argue that cognitive intelligence is also a multi-faceted concept and 'general intelligence' even more so. One might also point out that some of the components of EQ that Locke posits are really not part of EQ or central to it: planning, creative thinking and the direction of attention, for instance. However, he does argue the interesting point that EQ is not another form of intelligence but cognitive intelligence – the ability to grasp abstractions – applied to a particular aspect of life: emotion.[154] Whatever it is called, therefore, he says, it is a skill, not an 'intelligence'. While John Antonakis agrees with Locke, Neal Ashkanasy and Marie Dasborough dismiss this idea: 'If you like to believe that how people solve spatial and verbal puzzles is good enough to explain leader behaviour ... we have to disagree.'[155]

Distinguished psychologist the late Hans Eysenck agreed with Locke; however, he also lambasted the claims of EQ proponents as unproven:

> **Goleman exemplifies more clearly than most the fundamental absurdity of the tendency to class almost any type of behaviour as an 'intelligence' ... If these five 'abilities' define 'emotional intelligence', we would expect some evidence that they are highly correlated; Goleman admits that they might be quite uncorrelated, and in any case if we cannot measure them, how do we know they are related? So the whole theory is built on quicksand: there is no sound scientific basis.**[156]

Frank Landy points out correctly a difficulty with the coherence of EQ theory. He says that this is adversely affected by a lack of stability in the concept of EQ and the ways EQ is measured, making meta-analysis difficult to carry out.[157] He claims that the few validity studies carried out show that EQ has little substantial predictive value. He also points out the strong commercial EQ movement that is at odds with the many academics who criticize its expansive claims as exaggerated or false. Moreover, the databases of EQ proponents, he says, are 'proprietary', that is they are not freely available to independent researchers for confirmatory analysis, replication or verification, a critical requirement for proper science.

A major issue in the development of EQ models, Konstantinos Petrides and colleagues say, has been the lack of differentiation between 'trait' EQ and 'ability' EQ – based on self-reports and performance measures respectively.[158] They point out, for example, that asking someone whether they believe they are good at abstract reasoning is very different from actually doing it. Self-reports are the common basis for developing trait models, while performance measures are needed to develop ability models. Trait EQ and ability EQ, Petrides and colleagues say, 'are two distinct constructs differing in many important ways ... As expected, the conceptual differences between the two constructs are directly reflected in emerging empirical findings',[159] which show very low correlations between measures of trait EQ and ability EQ.[160] Ability EQ measures are more likely to have predictive validity for EQ (if EQ actually exists), according to John Antonakis and colleagues.[161]

Stéphane Côté and Christopher Miners suggest a compensatory model for the relationship between EQ and IQ: the relationship between EQ and job performance becomes more positive as cognitive intelligence (IQ) decreases and, for low-IQ individuals, job performance increases as EQ increases.[162] Petrides and colleagues also found that, among school pupils with low IQ, the higher their trait EQ, the greater their task performance and organizational citizenship behaviour,[163] thereby supporting Cote and Miners' model.[164] EQ appears to compensate for low IQ on task performance.

John Antonakis also rejects the validity of the concept of EQ because of the insufficiently rigorous research that underlies it. While granting that leaders do need to manage emotion, he also asserts this to be a function of IQ and not EQ. In a debate with Ashkanasy and Dasborough he says that we must 'leave open the possibility that EI [EQ] might one day go the way of *Raphus cucullatus*, the dodo bird, destined for extinction'.[165]

Ashkanasy and Dasborough, however, believe that Antonakis's criteria for the academic respectability of EQ are much too strict, to the extent of representing a perfect study that can virtually never be achieved in practice. They make the point that there is much research literature on EQ that is published after peer review in rigorous scholarly journals that supports the concept of EQ and its role in leadership. Indeed a review of the literature on EQ up to 2007 published in the *2008 Annual Review of Psychology* concluded that ability measures of EQ exhibited test validity as a group: EQ was a significant predictor of outcomes across diverse samples in a number of real-world domains.[166] Emotions do play a part in leadership. And leaders need to be aware of emotions and to manage them both in themselves and in other people.

Criticism of claims for the positive relationship between EQ and transformational leadership has focused mainly on methodological issues, especially the possibility of common method variance (CMV)[167] in the correlated data because the data come from the same respondents in a given piece of research. The presence of CMV undermines the validity of research findings and hence any conclusions one might draw. This has been explored by Dirk Lindebaum and Susan Cartwright using the Wong and Law Emotional Intelligence Scale (WLEIS) and the Transformational Leadership Questionnaire (TLQ). They used multi-rater assessment to avoid the risk of CMV and compared same-source data and non-same-source data to identify its potential presence. They found no significant relationship between trait EQ and transformational leadership.[168]

However, even this conclusion should be accepted only tentatively because context – in this case the construction industry in which project managers were the respondents – may have affected transformational leadership behaviour adversely owing to role expectations in the construction industry. Lindebaum and Cartwright conclude that the relationship between EQ and transformational leadership needs to be reconceptualized and studies of it also need to be more rigorous than they have been in the past in avoiding or controlling for CMV.[169] And Frank Walter and colleagues, in their critical review of the empirical evidence for EQ, provide a fitting conclusion to our discussion of EQ and leadership:

> ... in spite of conflicting perspectives on the definition and measurement of EI [EQ], and in the midst of a continued debate on EI's construct validity, empirical research on EI and leadership has produced notable findings. Even though the scholarly literature does not support hyperbolic claims regarding EI's relevance for leadership processes, evidence does suggest that EI has the potential to help scholars better understand leadership emergence, specific leadership behaviours, and leader effectiveness. That said, we also believe a lot remains to be accomplished.[170]

Social Intelligence

The idea of 'social interest' – the natural inclination to work together with others to achieve personal and societal goals – started to be explored in the 1920s. Psychologist Edward Thorndike was the first to define 'social intelligence' – as 'the ability to understand and manage other people and to engage in adaptive social interactions'.[171] Further definitions followed: 'the ability to get along with others' (1927);[172] and 'the ability to get along with people in general, social technique or ease in society, susceptibility to stimuli from other members of a group, as well as insight into the temporary moods or underlying personality traits of strangers' (1933).[173] Karl Albrecht defines social intelligence as 'the ability to get along well with others while winning their cooperation'.[174] And Daniel Goleman suggests that social intelligence is an extension of emotional intelligence and comprises social awareness and social facility:[175]

※ *Social awareness* is the ability to instantaneously sense and understand others' inner states, feelings and thoughts as well as the states of social situations. The four sub-dimensions of social awareness are primal empathy, attunement, empathic accuracy and social cognition.
※ *Social facility* is competencies of performing social tasks effectively, comprising four sub-dimensions of synchrony, self-presentation, influence and concern.

David Wechsler, however, like Hans Eysenck would have done, regarded social intelligence as 'just general intelligence applied to social situations'.[176] And several early research attempts failed to support social intelligence as a sufficiently distinctive construct, though Robert Schneider and colleagues eventually produced a model of social intelligence as having seven dimensions: extraversion, warmth, social influence, social insight, social openness, social appropriateness and social maladjustment.[177] John Kihlstrom and Nancy Cantor point out, however, that their model is compromised by a reliance on self-report measures, needing objective performance measures for the seven dimensions.[178] They say, 'as psychologists are fond of saying', that further research is needed because, while social intelligence has been conceptualized, its assessment is beset with methodological psychometric problems. And, they add, what is needed are 'assessments of social intelligence which are grounded in an understanding of the general social-cognitive processes out of which individual differences in social behaviour emerge'.

Social intelligence appears to be culture-related. E. Willman and colleagues, in a study of Chinese and Germans, found that the Chinese were strongly influenced by the traditions and thinking of Confucianism, for example a preference for actions that would conform to and fulfil the interests of the community as a whole rather than those of the individuals in it.[179] For them, socially desirable and socially engaging behaviour were highly prototypical of social intelligence. Germans, however, showed significantly less of such behaviour.

Social intelligence as a set of social skills that constitute an 'intelligence' in their own right may well contribute to effective leadership over and above emotional intelligence, but this needs further research. The same may be said of cultural intelligence.

Cultural Intelligence

Christopher Earley first used the term 'cultural intelligence' to refer to an individual's ability to connect with others outside their own culture – to cope with cultural diversity.[180] David Thomas and Kerr Inkson refer to cultural intelligence as 'a multi-faceted competency consisting of cultural *knowledge*, the practice of *mindfulness*, and a repertoire of *cross-cultural skills*'.[181] Soon Ang and colleagues define cultural intelligence as 'an individual's capability to function and manage effectively in culturally diverse settings … a specific form of intelligence focused on capabilities to grasp, reason, and behave effectively in situations characterized by cultural diversity'.[182] They posit four components of cultural intelligence: cognitive, metacognitive, motivational and behavioural:

1. *Cognitive* cultural intelligence concerns knowledge of the norms, practices and conventions in different cultures acquired from education and personal experience: 'those with high cognitive cultural intelligence understand similarities and differences across cultures.'
2. *Metacognitive* cultural intelligence comprises the mental processes that individuals use to acquire and understand cultural knowledge: 'those with high metacognitive cultural intelligence are consciously aware of others' cultural preferences before and during interactions [and they] adjust their mental models during and after interactions.'
3. *Motivational* cultural intelligence concerns the desire to 'direct attention and energy toward learning about and functioning in situations characterized by cultural differences'.
4. *Behavioural* intelligence concerns the '[ability] to exhibit appropriate verbal and nonverbal actions when interacting with people from different cultures'. This ability involves the flexibility of behaviour that enables a person to behave or act appropriately in a wide range of situations occurring in a global context. It can be regarded as an element in our concept of 'behavioural intelligence', which we discuss later in this chapter.

Ang and colleagues have developed a cultural intelligence scale, the CQS.[183] This is a twenty-item scale with four meta-cognitive items, six cognitive items, five motivational items and five behavioural items. Reliability coefficients for the four scales all exceed 0.70 (cognitive = 0.86, metacognitive = 0.72, motivational = 0.76 and behavioural = 0.83), and Ang et al. established good evidence of validity of the CQS. High levels of cultural intelligence are associated with:

* Flexibility and appropriateness of behaviour and actions when interacting with people from different cultures.
* A desire to learn how to behave in different cultural situations.
* An awareness of cultural norms.
* An ability to adjust mental models accordingly (similar to Thomas and Inkson's 'mindfulness').

Low levels of cultural intelligence are associated with:

❋ Difficulty in interacting with people from different cultural backgrounds.
❋ A low tolerance for others' cultural norms.
❋ A lack of desire to learn about them and behave accordingly.[184]

Cultural intelligence is claimed to be distinct from EQ because it entails being able to switch between national contexts and learn new patterns of social interaction as well as produce appropriate responses to these patterns. Whether cultural intelligence is also distinct from social intelligence is also debatable: as we said earlier, social intelligence is culture-related. Ilan Alon and James Higgins suggest that cognitive intelligence, EQ and leadership behaviours are moderated by cultural intelligence in determining global leadership success.[185] Kok-Yee Ng and colleagues suggest that cultural intelligence itself is a key determinant of the extent to which global leaders learn from their international assignments and thereby enhance their effectiveness.[186] The more people from different cultural backgrounds – especially leaders – interact with one another, the more opportunities and likelihood there are for misunderstanding and conflict and learning from them.

Global leaders and leaders operating globally need to have cultural intelligence. How cultural intelligence predicts conflict resolution strategies and hence conflict resolution ability is still being investigated, for example by Andrea Reyes Ramirez using Ang et al.'s CQS and Kenneth Thomas and Ralph Kilmann's Conflict Mode Instrument, which portrays conflict resolution in terms of five strategies – competing, collaborating, accommodating, avoiding and compromising – reflecting assertiveness/unassertiveness and cooperativeness/uncooperativeness.[187]

So, the argument is, success as a global leader requires cultural intelligence. Perhaps this is what he meant by 'superior talent' nearly 500 years ago, when Niccolò Machiavelli asserted:

> ... when a prince acquires the sovereignty of a country differing from his own both in language, manners, and intellectual organization, great difficulties can arise; and in order to maintain the possession of it, good fortune must unite with superior talent.[188]

But if Machiavelli meant superior *political or physical* talent, then this raises moral issues, which we now address in the context of intelligence.

Moral Intelligence

Moral intelligence is 'the ability to differentiate right from wrong as defined by universal principles', those beliefs about human conduct that are common to all cultures around the world, according to Doug Lennick and Fred Kiel.[189] It is our 'mental capacity to determine how universal human principles should be applied to our values, goals, and actions'. Lennick and Kiel's research for their model of moral intelligence comprised an extensive literature review of morality and 'moral leadership', followed by in-depth interviews with 31 CEOs and 47 other senior executives in the United States. They identified four aspects of moral intelligence:

* *Integrity.* Acting consistently with one's principles, values and beliefs.[190]
* *Responsibility.* A willingness to accept accountability for the consequences of one's actions and choices and admit one's mistakes and failures.[191]
* *Compassion.* Actively caring about others.[192]
* *Forgiveness.* Letting go of one's own and others' mistakes.[193]

By 'universal', Lennick and Kiel refer to *all* people, regardless of their gender, ethnicity, religious belief or location. Research by Donald Brown and Richard Kinnier and colleagues has suggested that universal moral principles include empathy, responsibility and reciprocity – the 'Golden Rule': 'Do unto others as you would have them do unto you'[194] – and its counterpart (the 'Silver Rule'): 'Do not do to others what you would not like to be done to you.' Lennick and Kiel add respect and caring for others as universal to worldwide monotheistic religions.[195] And while emotional intelligence is free of moral values, moral intelligence concerns doing the 'right' thing in a moral sense. In doing so, Marc Hauser says, morally intelligent leaders will use a 'moral compass', the seeds for which are innate and these germinate through nurturing in childhood.[196]

Michele Borba, a consultant and educator, defines moral intelligence similarly as 'the capacity to understand right from wrong'.[197] She suggests that moral intelligence consist of seven 'essential virtues':

* *Empathy* – identifying with and feeling other people's concerns.
* *Conscience* – knowing the right and decent way to act and acting in that way.
* *Self-control* – regulating one's thoughts and actions to stop any adverse pressures from within or outside.
* *Respect* – showing others that they are valued by treating them in a courteous and considerate way.
* *Kindness* – demonstrating concern about the welfare and feelings of others.
* *Tolerance* – recognizing the dignity and rights of everybody, even those whose beliefs and behaviours we disagree with.
* *Fairness* – choosing to be open-minded and to act in a just and fair way.

Lennick and Kiel have given us a new perspective on values-based leadership and morality, and one that has great utility in these times of moral questioning of the way business is done. It is too early, however, to judge the validity of their model, or Borba's, and more research in this field is highly desirable. Nevertheless, Lennick and Kiel show how truly great business leaders never sacrifice moral integrity for financial goals and 'doing the right thing' produces the best companies and the best results.

What can we say of leaders who are perceived to be effective but bad? For example, Osama bin Laden may have had a strong value system of his own and just possibly some admirable beliefs, and he could 'walk the talk'. However, his leadership behaviour seriously violated the universal moral principles of compassion, empathy, reciprocity, and respect and caring for other people: he was willing to kill innocent people, including members of his own faith, in order to enact his other values and beliefs.

Spiritual Intelligence

Human beings have an animating need for meaning, value and a sense of worth in what they do.[198] This animating need concerns the *why* of life and work. Spiritual intelligence is displayed by understanding and responding to this need.

Management philosopher Charles Handy says that people need a purpose in life that gives them 'energy for the journey'.[199] And Danah Zohar argues that managers have not only avoided recognizing emotion at work, but also lost their sense of purpose and their 'spirituality'.[200] The German philosopher Nietzsche said: 'He who has a *why* to live can bear with almost any *how*.'[201]

Studies and surveys in the United States and UK, however, have suggested that more managers are seeking meaning in their work other than creating material wealth, associated with personal values, spiritual beliefs, or the need for personal fulfilment.[202] It is well known that material wealth does not correlate with happiness.[203] Effective leaders create 'shared meaning':[204] shared values and a shared vision and purpose that are based on them. Leaders who lead with spiritual intelligence are exercising 'spiritual leadership', which Leigh Kibby and Charmine Härtel call 'noetic' leadership after the Greek word *noös*, 'spirit'.[205] Louis Fry defines spiritual leadership as:

> ... creating a vision wherein organization members experience a sense of calling in that their life has meaning and makes a difference [and] establishing a social/organizational culture based on altruistic love whereby leaders and followers have genuine care, concern, and appreciation for both self and others, thereby producing a sense of membership and feel understood and appreciated.[206]

Using spiritual intelligence, Danah Zohar and Ian Marshall say, can move people from a state of acting from lower motivations – fear, greed, anger and self-assertion – to acting from higher motivations – exploration, cooperation, power-within, mastery and higher service.[207] This is reminiscent of transformational leadership.

Danah Zohar and Ian Marshall also argue that there is enough collective evidence from psychology, neurology, anthropology and cognitive science to show us there is a form of intelligence that they call 'spiritual intelligence' (SQ).[208] SQ is uniquely human and, the authors argue, the most fundamental intelligence. SQ is what we use to develop our longing and capacity for meaning, vision and value. It allows us to dream and to strive. It also underlies the things we believe in, and the role our beliefs and values play in the actions that we take and the way we shape our lives. It is what we use to develop our longing and capacity for meaning, vision and value. It allows us to dream and to strive. It underlies the things we believe in, and the role our beliefs and values play in the actions that we take and the way we shape our lives.

In an attempt to propose a theoretical conceptualization of spirituality and, based on this, a spirituality scale, Caroline Liu and Peter Robertson surveyed 2,230 people and found three inter-correlated but distinct constituent factors: an interconnection with human beings, an interconnection with nature and all living things, and an interconnection with a higher power.[209] They argue that 'the notion of spirituality incorporates and transcends religiousness'.

Spiritual leadership encompasses 'sense making' or 'meaning making'.[210] Interpreting the environmental complexities – the threats and opportunities of the organization's external environment and the strengths and weaknesses of its internal environment – requires the cognitive skills discussed earlier in this chapter. Leadership from the social-constructivist or constitutive viewpoint concerns providing meaning and value to followers by displaying behaviour and articulating messages that reflect the needs and wishes of others who have it in their gift to confer the status of leadership.

How does SQ relate to emotional intelligence? Danah Zohar and Ian Marshall contrast it with EQ:

> ... my emotional intelligence allows me to judge what situation I am in and then to behave appropriately within it ... But my spiritual intelligence allows me to ask if I want to be in this particular situation in the first place. Would I rather change the situation, creating a better one?[211]

Theodore Zeldin, from his conversations with business leaders and MBAs, believes that the majority of them are not primarily interested in making money. He says:

> They need money of course, but there is a deep desire to do something more useful with their lives. Our business leaders are prisoners of the system that they have inherited, entangled in bureaucratic cobwebs from which they cannot escape. Corporations were invented 100 years ago: they are no longer suitable for our aspirations today. We have to rethink how we want to organise business and what we want to replace corporations with.[212]

These ideas about meaning and value are supported by research findings by Laura Nash and Howard Stevenson. From their studies of successful professionals, top executives attending Harvard Business School programmes, HBS alumni, and members of the Young Presidents' Organization, they concluded that there are four 'irreducible components of enduring success' that people will pursue and enjoy:

✳ Achievement – accomplishments that compare favourably against similar goals that others have striven for.
✳ Significance – the feeling of having made a positive impact on people one cares about.
✳ Legacy – establishing one's values or accomplishments in a way that helps others to find future success.[213]
✳ Happiness – feelings of pleasure or contentment about life.

Mihaly Csikszentmihalyi points out that material wealth does not correlate with happiness.[214] Martin Seligman, a leading researcher into happiness and former president of the American Psychological Association, regards the sensual pleasures (often associated with material wealth) – 'the pleasant life' – as the lowest level of happiness, bettered by 'the good life' – enjoying doing something we are good at – and the highest level, the most lasting form of happiness, 'the meaningful life' – that comes from doing something one believes in, that has meaning and value.[215] John Ruskin, the nineteenth-century English art and social critic, essayist and reformer, understood this:

> Now in order that people may be happy in their work, these three things are needed: They must be fit for it: They must not do too much of it: And they must have a sense of success in it ...[216]

Mike Emmott says that the search for meaning at work includes job satisfaction and commitment but also extends to 'a sense of the wider purpose in doing the work'.[217] A Roffey Park survey found that managers were seeking different kinds of meaning in their work: associated for some with personal values and ideals, for others with spiritual beliefs or personal fulfilment.[218] And Norman Bowie writes:

> **Meaningful work is work that is freely entered into, that allows the worker to exercise their autonomy and independence; that enables the worker to develop their rational capacities; that provides a wage sufficient for physical welfare; that supports the moral development of employees and that is not paternalistic in the sense of interfering with the worker's conception of how they wish to obtain happiness.[219]**

Neal Chalofsky suggests that meaningful work – work that expresses our inner being – depends on several factors, among them:

※ Knowing one's purpose in life and how work fits into that purpose.
※ Having a positive belief about one's ability to achieve that purpose and pursuing the opportunity to do so through work.
※ Empowerment – autonomy and control over one's environment.
※ Recognizing and developing one's potential through learning.
※ The nature of work itself.[220]

Spiritual leadership takes followers beyond self-interest. It is associated with integrity, independence and justice, says Gilbert Fairholm.[221] He suggests that the foundation for spiritual leadership is morality, stewardship and community. Spiritual leadership is about identifying and affirming shared core values, beliefs and ethics, a shared vision and a shared purpose that have meaning for everybody, meaningful work, empowering people, and stewardship – holding the community's, and indeed the world's, resources in trust. Spiritual leadership is about creating Aristotle's *ethos*.

Louis Fry's model of spiritual leadership comprises vision, 'altruistic love' (values), and 'hope and faith' (effort or motivation).[222] Vision, he says, provides a broad appeal to key stakeholders, defines the destination and the journey (the strategy), reflects high ideals, encourages hope and faith, and establishes a standard of excellence. Altruistic love concerns the values of forgiveness, kindness, integrity, empathy and compassion, honesty, patience, courage, trust and loyalty, and humility. Hope and faith provide endurance, perseverance, stretch goals, the desire to do what it takes, and the expectation of a reward or victory.

According to some writers, the concept of spiritual leadership tends to be focused more on the characteristics and behaviour of the individual leader rather than on the relationship between leader and followers, their situation, or the leadership process. Douglas Hicks suggests that 'the concept of spirituality is more disparate and contested than the current leadership literature acknowledges'.[223] Ron Cacioppe says:

> **The meaning of the term 'spirituality' is often misunderstood and can have negative connotations for many people. Spirituality is often seen in the same context as organized religion, with particular beliefs, moral rules and traditions.[224]**

However, spirituality involves looking inward, he says, in contrast to organized religion, which has an external focus. Spirituality is therefore 'accessible' to everybody, whether they are religious or not.

Ian Mitroff and Elizabeth Denton report that most managers they surveyed or interviewed in the United States are positive towards spirituality but negative towards religion.[225] Douglas Hicks believes that 'The opposition between spirituality and religion creates a problem for leadership scholars who acknowledge that the "whole person" comes to work.'[226] Hicks believes the distinction between spirituality and religion is not tenable. He argues that effective leadership is not about promoting 'a single spiritual framework but ... [about creating a] culture in which leaders and followers can respectfully negotiate religious and spiritual diversity' – a culture of 'respectful pluralism' (an example of individualized consideration). The Dalai Lama for one, however, is very clear about the difference between spirituality and religion:

> **Religion I take to be concerned with faith in the claims of one faith tradition or another, an aspect of which is the acceptance of some form of heaven or nirvana. Connected with this are religious teachings or dogma, ritual prayer, and so on. Spirituality I take to be concerned with those qualities of the human spirit – such as love and compassion, patience, tolerance, forgiveness, contentment, a sense of responsibility, a sense of harmony – which bring happiness to both self and others.[227]**

Danah Zohar and Ian Marshall say that 'Self-awareness is one of the highest criteria of high spiritual intelligence but one of the lowest priorities of our ... culture.'[228] Danah Zohar and Jacquie Drake say that leaders with high SQ behave in characteristic ways that are not 'God-given' but can be developed.[229] They say that such leaders are:

※ Flexible – receptive to suggestions, surprises and change, and able to cope with ambiguity.
※ Self-aware – reflective and critical of themselves.
※ Led by their personal vision, sense of purpose and values.
※ Able to cope with and learn from failure and suffering and to turn the lessons learned into wisdom.
※ Holistic – focused on the whole person and the whole situation.
※ Welcoming of diversity.
※ Independent and willing to take a stand on issues.
※ Questioning, particularly in respect of reasons for actions, decisions and events.
※ Able to reframe situations using new perspectives and creating new options.
※ Spontaneous – in tune with the moment and unafraid of responding or initiating action.

Spiritual leadership is about creating meaning and value for people, in their work life, family life or community life. Zohar and Marshall suggest that a high-SQ leader is likely to be a servant leader: '... bringing higher vision and value to others and showing them how to use it ... a person who inspires others'.[230] Spiritual intelligence does not merely reflect existing values: it leads to new values.

Zohar and Marshall point out that spiritual intelligence is the result of the integration and unification of activity in the cognitive and emotional domains of the brain – 'a dialogue between reason and emotion, between mind and body' – that gives meaning to our existence.[231] While science, including psychology, has not explicitly addressed spiritual intelligence, Zohar and Marshall point out that much of the evidence for it has resulted from neurological, psychological and anthropological studies.[232] As in the field of leadership, there are several streams of research that have scarcely yet converged:

1. The existence of a 'God spot' in the brain – a spiritual centre in the temporal lobes which, in scans using positron emission tomography, lights up whenever subjects are exposed to spiritual or religious topics.[233]
2. The existence of a neural process in the brain that is devoted to unifying and giving meaning to our experience.[234] Serial neural connections are the basis of IQ; haphazard interconnections among huge neuron bundles are the basis for emotional intelligence; and synchronous neural oscillations suggest the basis of spiritual intelligence.
3. Language as a uniquely human, symbolic activity that evolved in parallel with the development of the brain's frontal lobes and enables meaning and symbolic imagination.[235]

Viktor Frankl suggests that our search for meaning is also our primary source of motivation.[236] Zohar and Marshall give many examples that support this notion.[237] The spiritually intelligent leader, Frances Hesselbein argues, will provide 'a consistent focus on mission ... a clear sense of direction and the opportunity to find meaning in ... work'.[238] Warren Bennis and Robert Thomas also share this view: they argue that effective leaders create shared meaning.[239] Meaning, whether to do with work or life in general, is captured in the goal – the vision – and the values that have meaning for people and thereby motivate and inspire them. Meaning has 'meta-value', Manfred Kets de Vries and Elizabeth Florent-Treacy point out:

> When people see their jobs as transcending their own personal needs (by improving the quality of life for others, for example, or by contributing to society) ... the impact can be extremely powerful.[240]

They cite as an example the pharmaceutical industry, in which the preservation and improvement of human life through the development of new medicines provide this meta-value. This is a source of motivation and inspiration, beyond making a lot of money. They argue that effective leadership entails meeting human motivational needs: effective leaders will 'pay attention to individuals' desire for *identity*; their sense of usefulness or *meaning* in life; and their feeling of *attachment* or human connectedness'.[241] It is when there is an alignment between employees' motivation and organizational values, they maintain, that people's subjective experiences and actions become meaningful.[242]

The Roffey Park report says that it is employees rather than employers who are leading the trend towards greater spirituality, perhaps because employers find the subject too vague and also perhaps, according to consultant Geraldine Brown, because of its association with weird cultism.[243] Jon Watkins quotes Richard Cree of the Institute of Directors as saying that:

> The issue of spirituality is not the kind of thing companies should be getting involved in ... It has to come from the employees ... there are still ... a lot of people that are not convinced by it.[244]

Spirituality may yet be merely another management fad.[245] On the other hand, Simon Burton, a training manager with the pub chain Greene King, believes that spirituality is linked closely to inspirational leadership and empowerment – giving employees auton-omy, giving them the room to be creative and make mistakes, and building trust between employees and the employer.[246] Burton says that inspirational leadership models use 'all the words … associated with spirituality'. 'Spirituality' in the business or work context, however, is perhaps an unfortunate word, like 'counselling' and 'empowerment': it pro-vokes an adverse emotional reaction in some 'hard-nosed' senior executives. Moreover, 'spiritual leadership' or 'spiritual management' itself has become perhaps a rather cynical business, with leaders cast as engineers of the human soul[247] and charged with providing 'meaning' in employees' lives far beyond their normal work tasks or responsibilities.[248]

Dennis Tourish and Naheed Tourish argue that the workplace spirituality move-ment 'promotes constricting cultural and behavioural norms and thus seeks to rein-force the power of leaders at the expense of autonomy for their followers'.[249] They add that the spirituality literature is 'replete with paradoxes' that may be irresolvable. Concepts and definitions of spirituality range from the religious to the secular humanist. Business leaders' values are assumed to be 'unitarist rather than sectional'. Moreover, Tourish and Tourish argue:

Influence is conceived in unidirectional terms: it flows from 'spiritual' and powerful leaders to more or less compliant followers, deemed to be in need of enlightenment, rather than vice versa.

A concept of spirituality to do with meaning, purpose and value in what we do, how-ever, is relevant to intrinsic motivation and to leadership. Inspiration comes from leadership that provides meaning, purpose and value, and, Jill Graham says, this is more powerful than charisma alone, which may lack a basis in values and therefore may not protect followers from immoral action.[250] And Zohar and Marshall argue for a new form of capitalism, 'spiritual capital', that is based on spiritual intelligence and the higher motivations we associate with transformational leadership.[251] There is a danger here that spirituality is being treated in the same way that some practitioners (and even scholars) have treated 'quality circles' and 'corporate social responsibility', among other such practices, namely merely as a means by which to help managers and leaders to achieve *their* goals and enrich their own pockets.

Behavioural Intelligence and the Practical Interplay and Expression of Multiple Intelligences in Leadership

Leaders may be able to discern and understand the need for particular behaviour, but they may not necessarily be able to *act* in that way. Behavioural intelligence is the ability to plan and *do* things, reflecting a composite of several forms of intelligence. Examples from Howard Gardner's model that were outlined at the beginning of this chapter are kinaes-thetic intelligence – the ability to use the body in skilful and complicated ways, involving a sense of timing, coordination of movement and the use of the hands, and important in engaging people by the body-language aspects of public speaking and oratory; the ability to use language to express and understand complex meaning (linguistic intelligence); the ability to manage oneself, one's thoughts and feelings (intrapersonal intelligence); and the ability to interact effectively (interpersonal intelligence).[252]

Behavioural intelligence is evident, for example, in the flexible use of different leadership styles – being directive, consultative, participative or delegative – according to the needs of different situations. Behavioural intelligence also underlies what Gerry Randell calls the 'micro-skills' of leadership: the ways leaders structure their interactions with followers and others – the physical acts of questioning, active listening (paraphrasing meaning and reflecting feelings) and, of course, the use of body language.[253]

To complicate matters, these various forms of intelligence interact in complex ways.[254] For example, how many of us struggle in managing our time effectively? Effective time management requires not only cognitive intelligence in prioritizing tasks and deciding what to do and how to do it, but also spiritual intelligence in deciding the meaning and value of these tasks in the first place, moral intelligence in assessing and deciding the 'rightness' of the tasks, emotional intelligence in using self-discipline and self-control in the face of anticipated boredom, fatigue, unpleasantness, etc., and behavioural skills in actually acting. It is no wonder that time management is difficult for many people. Another example here is writing. Albert Joseph, the American writing skills guru, says, 'You cannot write clearly [a behavioural skill] unless you have thought it out clearly [a cognitive skill].'[255] The same applies to speaking.

Concentrating on the separate intelligences of leadership in a mutually exclusive way inevitably leads to a failure to understand the interaction among the cognitive processes, emotions and volitional action (behavioural skills) in leadership. Emotions and moods interact with cognition.[256] For example, anxiety and sadness will adversely affect our attention to stimuli and our information recall.[257] Affective–cognitive consistency is a significant moderator of the relationship between job satisfaction and job performance: the greater the consistency, the stronger the relationship between job performance and job satisfaction.[258]

Martha Nussbaum suggests that emotions are ways in which human beings direct their attention to objects and that they cannot be separated from perception or cognition.[259] Mary Warnock argues likewise:

> [Jean-Paul] Sartre ... was convinced ... that one cannot separate the emotions from the intellect, that the emotions have objects (they are intentional) and that loving or hating or feeling disgust for an object is a way of perceiving that is bound up in all our understanding and knowledge of the world, giving intelligibility to that world.[260]

Nussbaum argues that compassion is socially useful provided it is informed by reason. Emotional intelligence may *enable* the intellect: once the contagion of negative emotion is dissipated or controlled, the rational, analytical mind can function more effectively. On the other hand the intellect benefits from positive emotion; indeed the synergy of reason and emotion is the fount of human achievement. Charles Rennie Mackintosh, the iconic Scottish architect, designer and artist, in contrast to Nussbaum, with a converse message, puts it this way:

> Reason informed by emotion ... expressed in beauty ... elevated by earnestness ... lightened by humour ... [that is] the ideal that should guide all artists.[261]

Malcolm Higgs and Victor Dulewicz suggest the need for a balance between the rational (cognitive) and emotional in achieving results.[262] The cognitive aspects of leadership, they say, comprise corporate business plans that are cascaded down the organization into individuals' goals or objectives; the emotional aspects comprise motives, feelings and behaviour that are associated with vision and values, and, I would add, purpose or mission.

The interaction between thinking, feeling and behaviour is complicated. Using functional magnetic resonance imaging, Jeremy Gray and colleagues found that activity in the lateral prefrontal cortex of subjects' brains as they were carrying out verbal and non-verbal tasks under conditions of emotional arousal and non-arousal was influenced by the combination of emotion and cognitive activity but not by either one alone.[263] They also found that pleasant emotions heralded a better performance on verbal tasks but a worse performance on non-verbal (visual) tasks. And the reverse was true for negative or anxious moods: anxious subjects did better on visual tasks and worse on verbal tasks.

Cognitive resource theory suggests that there are several moderators of the association between intelligence and leadership that concern emotion, for example the supportiveness of followers, leader stress and leadership style.[264] The theory also suggests that stress experienced by a leader moderates the relationship between intelligence and leadership effectiveness because of the negative emotions associated with a fear of failure, doubts about self-efficacy, and anxiety regarding evaluation.[265] Timothy Judge and colleagues, in their meta-analysis of studies of intelligence and leadership, did indeed find that intelligence and leadership were more strongly related when leader stress was lower.[266] Cognitive resource theory also predicts that leaders need to be directive in their leadership style if followers or subordinates are to benefit from their superior cognitive intelligence, which shows itself in better strategies and decisions. Again, Judge and colleagues found support for the moderating effect of directive behaviour in the relationship between intelligence and leadership.

According to Catherine Cassell and Kevin Daniels, 'The process of strategic management is essentially a rich social and cognitive process.'[267] Strategic analysis, they say, entails the analysis and selection of strategic options by management teams 'on the basis of incomplete and ambiguous data', often through 'intense debate and negotiations over … months or even years', influenced by 'the vested interests of stakeholder groups'. Cognitive, emotional, social, spiritual and even cultural processes are involved in the associated judgement and decision processes. And cognitive, emotional and social processes are involved in handling the consequences of strategic decisions, for example downsizing as a result of restructuring.

The relationship between thinking, emotion and behaviour is captured in the Leaderplex model of Robert Hooijberg and colleagues.[268] This model proposes that behavioural complexity is informed by the cognitive and social (and I would add emotional) complexity of the leader. And cognitive complexity, social or emotional intelligence and behavioural complexity are suggested by Kimberley Boal and Robert Hooijberg to have a positive association with absorptive capacity, the capacity to change and 'managerial wisdom'.[269] However, there appears to be no significant direct relationship between social or emotional intelligence and cognitive intelligence.[270]

Moreover, Boal and Hooijberg argue that a clear vision and charisma are moderators in this relationship: they strengthen it.[271]

Boal and Hooijberg also argue that cognitive intelligence, social intelligence and emotional intelligence are particularly important at the highest levels in organizations.[272] Top-level leaders who display higher levels of cognitive and social or emotional intelligence and behavioural complexity will anticipate environmental changes, for example deregulation, they will see trends more quickly, and they will start to reformulate their organizations' strategies ahead of the competition. Visioning and strategy development will usually take place in a group environment, except perhaps in some owner-managed small enterprises.[273] The dynamics need to be understood: for example, individuals may behave in a way that is cognitively dissonant in order to maintain membership of the group.

While little research has been carried out on political behaviour, political skill has been argued as an important behavioural competency in leadership.[274] This skill is defined by Gerald Ferris and colleagues as:

> **An interpersonal style construct that combines social perceptiveness or astuteness with the capacity to adjust one's behavior to different and changing situational demands in a manner that inspires trust, confidence, and genuineness, and effectively influences and controls the responses of others.[275]**

Political skill enables leaders to network and to influence and control people and situations.

Leadership is both an art and a science. It is an art in terms of the imitative or imaginative skills needed to 'achieve form, function and meaning'.[276] An example is the skills with which effective leaders create understanding and arouse positive emotions through language and speech. It is a science in terms of the systematic cognitive processes and formulated knowledge that effective leaders use in the 'forming and testing of ideas'[277] and associated practices. An example is the systematic scanning of the environment, analysis and interpretation of the findings in relation to existing knowledge, and decision making about the strategy to be employed. In conclusion, we can be confident in stating that effective leadership requires multiple intelligences and efficient and productive interaction among them. They are the focus of attention in assessing and developing effective leadership and effective leaders, and it is to this that we now turn.

Further Reading

Karl Albrecht (2006), *Social Intelligence: The New Science of Success*. Hoboken, NJ: Jossey-Bass.

Robert Cooper and Ayman Sawaf (1997), *Executive EQ*. London: Orion Business.

Viktor E. Frankl (1984), *Man's Search for Meaning*, Third Edition. New York: Simon & Schuster.

Howard Gardner (1993), *Frames of Mind: The Theory of Multiple Intelligences*. New York: Basic Books.

Daniel Goleman (1995), *Emotional Intelligence*. New York: Bantam Books.

Daniel Goleman (2006), *Social Intelligence: The New Science of Human Relationships*. New York: Bantam Books.

Charles Handy (1997), *The Hungry Spirit: Beyond Capitalism – A Quest for Purpose in the Modern World*. London: Hutchinson.

Marc D. Hauser (2006), *Moral Minds: How Nature Designed our Universal Sense of Right and Wrong*. New York: HarperCollins.

Malcolm Higgs and Victor Dulewicz (2002), *Making Sense of Emotional Intelligence*, Second Edition. London: ASE.

Doug Lennick and Fred Kiel (2008), *Moral Intelligence*. Upper Saddle River, NJ: Pearson Education.

Russ S. Moxley (2000), *Leadership and Spirit*. San Francisco, CA: Jossey-Bass.

Martha C. Nussbaum (2001), *Upheavals of Thought: The Intelligence of Emotions*. Cambridge: Cambridge University Press.

R.E. Riggio, S.E. Murphy and F.J. Pirozzolo, Editors (2001), *Multiple Intelligences and Leadership*. Mahwah, NJ: Erlbaum.

Robert J. Sternberg (1996), *Successful Intelligence*. New York: Simon & Schuster.

David C. Thomas and Kerr Inkson (2009), *Cultural Intelligence: Living and Working Globally*. San Francisco, CA: Berrett-Koehler.

Danah Zohar and Ian Marshall (2001), *Spiritual Intelligence: The Ultimate Intelligence*. London: Bloomsbury Publishing.

Danah Zohar and Ian Marshall (2004), *Spiritual Capital: Wealth We Can Live By*. San Francisco, CA: Berrett-Koehler.

Discussion Questions

1. Is there really only one form of intelligence – cognitive intelligence or general intelligence – that subsumes behaviour that is concerned with the emotional, social, cultural, moral and spiritual aspects of human life?
2. How important is cognitive intelligence in leadership in relation to the other kinds of intelligence?
3. In what way and to what extent do emotional, social, cultural, moral and spiritual intelligences interact with one another in the context of leadership?
4. Is 'behavioural intelligence' really a form of intelligence in its own right or is it the behavioural expression of the interplay among other forms of intelligence?
5. How can leaders use their range of intelligences to resolve issues to do with (a) disgruntled or uncommitted employees, (b) executive greed, (c) intolerance of people with a different religious faith, (d) the globalization of business, and (e) the pursuit of happiness?

11 The Assessment and Development of Leadership

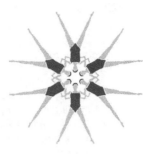

It is not a matter of whether leaders are born or made. They are born and made.[1]

Jay Conger

OVERVIEW

- Are leaders 'born' or 'made'? This question has dominated the debate about leadership development ever since the ancient Greeks. However, there is now a common view that, while there may be genetic effects, leadership can be developed and that this process starts early in life.
- Competency models are a common basis for leadership development. Leadership competencies concern the knowledge, skills and personal characteristics that are associated with effective leadership. There are several well-known generic leadership competency models, but organization-specific ones can also be developed using a variety of methods. A case study of a leadership competency model in the Royal Navy is provided.
- There are many issues concerning the ways that leadership potential is assessed and leadership development is carried out. These issues are discussed, and effective solutions are explored. Examples of good assessment practice include the use of leadership assessment centres and diagnostic leadership questionnaires, which is illustrated with a case example. Good leadership development practice entails a coherent, intelligent, integrated and comprehensive strategy linked to the organization's vision, purpose and core values.
- Leadership development programmes can be effective when they are focused on specific leadership behaviour, they are based on feedback, practice and application by using a variety of methods, and there is a desire and an opportunity to exercise, develop and use effective leadership behaviour. Leadership education and development in universities, and especially in business schools, are seriously wanting.
- The chapter explores how leaders develop, including the importance of early influences in life, and the multiple activities and processes that are involved.
- There are several barriers to both leadership and leadership development. Most barriers are internal to the individual but some are due to the organizational culture or politics or a lack of time to undertake leadership development activities. Internal barriers include low self-esteem, a lack of self-confidence, a fear of failure, shame or social disapproval, cognitive constriction (thinking 'inside the box'), and the

(Continued)

(Continued)

adverse consequences of stress. These barriers can be removed or reduced by the use of psychological principles and experiential learning methods that are illustrated with a case example.

- Self-awareness as a leader is the necessary basis for effective leadership development: leadership development begins with learning to know and control oneself first to enable self-confidence to grow. There are several other principles to be followed as well as other considerations in designing leadership development programmes (e.g. the nature of the environmental and organizational contexts) that are also discussed.
- Leadership development programmes tend to focus only on one specific or limited aspect of leadership often using one specific and limited model and sometimes one particular method. There are, however, a variety of learning and development methods that serve different purposes, and these are discussed. There are also several 'triggers' or catalysts, both planned and opportunistic, in the development of leadership. We discuss the principles that guide the effective design of leadership programmes, and examples are provided.
- There are many examples and studies of leadership development programmes with positive validated or well-documented results. We can learn and develop leadership.

Are Leaders 'Born' or 'Made'?

This question has dominated debates about leadership development ever since Plato raised the question, the historian and army general Xenophon argued that leadership could be developed, and Aristotle claimed that men were destined from the moment of birth to either rule or be ruled. William Shakespeare, like leadership scholar Jay Conger, agreed with everybody (including me): 'Some [men] are born great, some achieve greatness, and some have greatness thrust upon them' – they are born *and* made.[2]

We now know there are genetic influences on personality, for example DRD4 (chromosome 11) on novelty seeking behaviour[3] and 5-HTTLPR (the serotonin transporter gene) on neuroticism.[4] Most twin studies have demonstrated moderate to large genetic contributions to most personality dimensions,[5] on average around 40 per cent.[6]

Leadership is similarly heritable, according to research by Andrew Johnson and colleagues.[7] Their monozygotic and dizygotic twin studies found most aspects of leadership style to have a primarily genetic origin. They found that a higher-order factor resembling transformational leadership demonstrated greater genetic determination (58 per cent) than did a higher-order factor resembling transactional leadership (48 per cent). They also found substantial genetic covariance, suggesting a large overlap of genes influencing leadership behaviour. Richard Arvey and colleagues, studying some 400 sets of male twins, both identical and fraternal, found that 30 per cent of leadership role occupancy could be explained by genetics,[8] a finding that concurred with one by Ronald Riggio, that leadership is 'one third born, two thirds made'.[9]

In later research by Johnson and colleagues, transactional leadership showed a significant negative genetic correlation with conscientiousness and extraversion (two personality factors in the 'Big Five' personality model) and a significant positive genetic correlation with disagreeableness.[10] Transformational leadership on the other hand showed a significant positive genetic correlation with conscientiousness, extraversion and openness to experience. They suggested it was likely that the same gene(s) predisposing an individual to select a transactional leadership style would also predispose(s) an individual to be unconscientious, introverted and disagreeable.

One problem in the debate is the meaning of 'innate'. Is it that there is a 'leadership' gene that predetermines a desire or aptitude for exercising leadership behaviour? Or is 'leadership' something that is acquired (or not) early in life and cannot be developed later, for example by the time one starts work? The latter interpretation is not 'innate' – the term means 'inborn' – yet it is often used in this way in the debate.

David Norburn, former dean of Imperial College Management School in London, provocatively takes a more 'born rather than made' stance:

> [Leadership] is basically genetic – but it can be encouraged. The teacher (the bellows) can accelerate the embryonic leader (the spark) to burst forth (the crackling fire). The result? (Hopefully) paradigm busters, full of spirit and empathy. Those with no sign of spark – lower-quartile MBAs, perhaps – join investment banks and become androids.[11]

... and make huge amounts of money!

Another academic, Nigel Nicholson, former deputy dean at London Business School, is even less equivocal:

> The big lie sold to us by much of the management literature is the myth that any man or woman can be turned into a leader, given the right developmental intervention ... The new science of behavior genetics is steadily accumulating evidence about how much of individual character, style, and competence is inborn. As every parent with more than one child knows, each is born different and stays different.[12]

Nicholson does admit to some 'reworking' of our traits – including the motivation to lead – during childhood and by radical change in adulthood, but also believes that by the 20s these are largely fixed. This does not augur well for the leadership development industry – at least not after one's 20s.

Most scholars, however, would agree that there is still enormous scope for changing our leadership behaviour. Susan Greenfield says that genes 'make things possible' but much may happen between them and behaviour and feelings – nurture may 'trump' nature.[13] In other words, genes are necessary but not sufficient. And Lord Robert Winston says that we are not merely the product of our genes: environment has a huge impact, but in a mysterious way.[14]

In recent research (2009), Carl Senior and colleagues at Aston University and the Institute of Psychiatry in the UK and the University of Pittsburgh in the United States found that people with a dopamine-based gene display significantly greater transformational leadership (in their responses in the Multifactor Leadership

Questionnaire) than those who do not possess it.[15] They also found that a specific version of the dopamine gene – the inefficient version – is linked to low scores of two
core elements of transformational leadership: intellectual stimulation and idealized
influence (charisma). Cognitive neuroscience is playing an increasingly important
part in leadership research using traditional brain scanning techniques such as magnetic resonance imaging as well as biological techniques such as genotyping, twin
studies and the study of developmental stability.

   Developing leadership potential is a combination of the accidental, the incidental
and the planned. All of us have the potential to improve our leadership effectiveness,
some more than others for various reasons. As Amin Rajan says:

> **Some may not possess enough skills or emotional strength. Some may do so, but lack
> the necessary motivation. Some may have the ability and will, but lack the necessary
> opportunities.[16]**

The key question about leadership development is not about *whether* leadership can
be developed, but about *how* and *how much*. For example, can leadership be *taught*?
All of us have learned most of what we know and can do through experience. And this
experience has very largely come from 'real life' rather than the classroom, a point
pithily made by Oscar Wilde: 'nothing that is worth knowing can be taught'![17] But
opinions about whether leadership can be 'taught' vary, with a tendency towards
agreeing that, while little if anything can be taught, it can be learned. For example,
Hilarie Owen says:

> **Leadership cannot be taught as a list of skills. Nor can it be bolted on to management
> development, as leadership is totally different to management and requires different think-
> ing. Leadership potential is already in the individual and therefore requires recognition,
> development, growth and practice. A week's training course will not achieve this – it
> requires much more.[18]**

Even Nigel Nicholson admits to this: leadership behaviour can be 'moderated' – 'but
not transformed' – by training people who are not naturally gifted leaders in key
behaviours and habits that are associated with effective leadership. But Preston
Bottger and Jean-Louis Barsoux at IMD believe that the 'born or made?' question is a
bad question because it cannot yield a satisfactory answer.[19] They say:

> **The most significant leadership question is not 'born or made?' The important questions
> are: what are your current assets and what are you willing to do – or to sacrifice – to attain
> leadership at the highest level you can?**

We start with the notion of 'competence' as a leader, with a case example from the
Royal Navy. We then discuss the widespread need for improvement both in the
assessment of leadership development needs, with an example, and in how such needs
are addressed. Next we consider how leaders develop, succeed and survive, the barriers
to their development, and how these may be overcome, with a case example from the
Leadership Trust. Then we discuss the need and guidelines for a leadership development
strategy, the requirements for effective leadership development programmes and

studies of their effectiveness. We conclude with a case study of leadership development in the Gulf region, which brings up inter-cultural issues, and an exercise in personal analysis and planning for leadership development.

Leadership Competence[20]

Behavioural competencies are a popular method for predicting leadership success.[21] Richard Boyatzis defines competencies as attributes of the individual that are 'causally related to effective or superior performance in a job'.[22] And Bernard Bass says:

> When traits are requirements for doing something, they are called 'competencies'. Traits of leadership are competencies. They are needed if someone is to emerge, succeed or be effective as leader.[23]

Leadership Competency Models: Arguments For and Against

Competency models are the rationalist approach to leadership development and are used by a majority of companies in the private sector.[24] They are also spreading throughout the public sector.[25] They have their origins in the work of David McClelland and the McBer management consultancy company in the 1970s. Definitions of competencies vary in their focus but will typically refer to the knowledge, skills and personal behaviours and characteristics that are associated with achieving corporate objectives. Competency models are either generic or single-job specific, customized from specific 'building block' competencies.[26] They have been criticized for being too complicated and conceptual and focused on the present or the past rather than the future[27] and for being divorced from the situation or context[28], thereby setting minimal standards of leadership rather than standards of excellence.[29] In the UK's National Health Service, they have also been said to reinforce individualistic, 'heroic' approaches.[30]

Criticism in five areas by Richard Bolden and Jonathan Gosling, however, challenges the notion of using competencies for leadership: reductionism, universalism, traditionalism, behaviourism and functionalism.[31] In *reducing* skills to a few potentially non-representative traits and applying them to roles *universally*, they say, the essence of leadership is lost. And basing the competencies on best practice represents only the past (*traditional*) requirements for leadership. A focus on measurable *behaviour* neglects more subtle attributes such as values and beliefs. And finally, *functional* attempts to train managers to 'do' competencies rather than understand them erode the concept further.

The reductionist argument is that jobs involving high levels of uncertainty, unpredictability and discretion are not catered for by the competency approach because of its simplistic, atomistic fragmentation of work roles that is far removed from reality.[32] For example, Bolden and Gosling point out that competencies refer to things *done* by leaders, thereby obscuring the things that *happen* to leaders, such as 'dependent adulation or envious sabotage'.[33] However, this criticism overlooks the counterclaim that behaviours such as handling uncertainty, unpredictability, adulation and hostility and displaying discretion may themselves be expressed as competencies. What behaviours cannot be expressed in this way?

The universalist argument challenges the assumption that competencies are equally applicable to managers in all kinds of organizations and situations – for example, all sizes, hierarchical levels, industries, cultures and challenges. This is perhaps a stronger challenge to generic competencies, but it must be appreciated that applicability has different levels: the more specific the competency definition is, the more (or less) applicable it is to any given job or role. Generic models have their place: the weight behind recent research, Bernard Bass says, suggests that competencies are generic, that is *universal*.[34] And Richard Boyatzis and colleagues argue:

> ... there are a set of competencies that have been shown to cause or predict outstanding manager or leader performance. Regardless of author or study, they tend to include abilities from three clusters: (1) cognitive or intellectual ability such as systems thinking; (2) self management or intrapersonal abilities, such as adaptability; and (3) relationship management or interpersonal abilities, such as networking.[35]

Kok-Yee Ng and colleagues explored how global leaders would translate their international experience into useful learning when enhancing their global leadership effectiveness.[36] They suggested that cultural intelligence influenced experiential learning during international assignments and that it was a key reason why some global leaders would succeed and others fail. This is one of the forms of intelligence, along with the cognitive, emotional, spiritual, moral and behavioural forms, that I would argue underlie effective leadership.

The traditionalist argument criticizes the focus on what *has been* or *currently is* effective as a competency – so-called 'best practice' – rather than what is or may be needed in the future – a good argument in view of the trends in technology and globalization.[37] Yet again, however, this need not necessarily be the case: competencies can be determined on the basis of what will or may be needed in future. Scenario planning, which we discussed in Chapter 7, is an example of this.

The behaviourist argument against competencies criticizes the omission of less measurable attributes such as values, beliefs and relationships.[38] This argument hinges on the ability to identify such attributes and link them to effectiveness in behaviour as meaningful competencies. Why should this not be possible, indeed necessary? The behaviourism argument means that competencies measure leadership ability to influence followers rather than the social knowledge of *how* and *when* to use it.[39] However, competencies do measure the important social skills of the leader[40] and these *can* be tested.[41]

The functionalist argument criticizes standards and competencies as a limited and mechanistic approach that is the basis for *training* as opposed to *education* and *development*. While training is associated with providing and improving the skills and techniques that are involved in performing tasks, education and development are concerned with providing knowledge and cognitive ability.[42] This is fair comment, but this does not entail dismissing the use of competencies in training for leadership. Indeed it implies that leadership development is much more than 'training' and the acquisition of skills, as we demonstrate in this chapter.

This rationalist approach to competencies, which Bolden and Gosling criticize, is the traditional and dominant one.[43] In view of the foregoing criticisms, they offer, among alternative approaches, the 'interpretivist' approach. Contrary to the traditional rationalist approach, the interpretivist approach posits an inextricable link between the worker and the work: competencies are the meaning that work takes on for workers.[44] Competencies are therefore 'socially defined' rather than objective entities to be acquired.

More criticism of the rationalist approach centres on its conceptual vagueness[45] and definition: 'There is such confusion and debate concerning the concept of competence that it is impossible to identify or impute a coherent theory.'[46] Nevertheless, competencies, however determined, certainly have their place in leadership and leadership development. The foregoing criticisms of traditional competencies lose their force when one considers how competencies can help us to understand leadership and provide effective leadership development activities and programmes:

⁕ Competencies need to be defined carefully, for example those concerned with handling uncertainty, unpredictability and discretion.
⁕ The purpose of defining and using competencies must be clear: are generic competencies or sets of competencies appropriate and valid for purpose or do competencies need to be highly specific to their purpose, use and situation?

Development of Leadership Competency Models

Leadership competency models can be derived by several methods, including job analysis,[47] critical incident technique,[48] repertory grid techniques based on personal construct theory,[49] and the development of behaviourally anchored rating scales.[50]

A comprehensive set of management and leadership competencies in the UK is provided by the *2008 National Occupational Standards for Management and Leadership* published by the Chartered Management Institute.[51] One of the models that the UK accrediting agency Investors in People uses, *The Leadership and Management Model*, is based on the four principles of commitment, planning, action and evaluation in relation to management and leadership.[52]

The *EFQM Excellence Model 2010* is a well-regarded competency model from the European Foundation for Quality Management that regards leadership as an 'enabler'.[53] This is what an organization does and how it does it in determining 'results' – what the organization achieves:

> **Excellent organisations have leaders who shape the future and make it happen, acting as role models for its values and ethics and inspiring trust at all times. They are flexible, enabling the organisation to anticipate and react in a timely manner to ensure the ongoing success of the organisation.**

In her work in the UK on assessing, selecting and developing political leaders with Members of Parliament from all three main parties, Jo Silvester found similarities across the parties in their competency frameworks, as might be expected for a common role.[54] Table 11.1 shows the results for two of the main parties that in 2010 together formed the coalition government. Silvester also found subtle differences, however, that reflected their different situations and, more importantly, their values.

An example of a competency model comes from the Royal Navy. Its competency framework is based on the work of Mike Young and Vic Dulewicz.[55] SHL's *Occupational Personality Questionnaire* and Dulewicz and Higgs's *Leadership Dimensions*

Table 11.1 Competencies and Example Indicators for UK MPs (copyright The British Psychological Society 2010. Reproduced with kind permission)

Conservatives	Liberal Democrats
Communication Skills Articulate and fluent when addressing an audience	Communication Skills Communicates clearly, passionately and with conviction when using different forms of media
Intellectual Skills Quickly processes, understands and learns large amounts of information	Strategic Thinking and Judgement Understands the strategic relevance of information and makes links between national-level and local-level issues
Relating to People Approachable, inspires confidence and trust in others	Representing People Demonstrates tolerance in actively representing people of all backgrounds, ages, ethnicity and interests
Leading and Motivating Communicates a clear vision and persuades others to follow them	Leadership Builds trust, confidence and enthusiasm among supporters
Resilience and Drive Demonstrates stamina and persistence in overcoming resistance	Resilience Has the courage to make and defend unpopular decisions
Conviction Seeks opportunities to present views and persuades others to adopt their ideas	Values in Action Promotes beliefs and key messages through their own actions

Questionnaire were used with a sample of 251 navy officers and ratings to define a cluster of essential competencies. As we shall see in the following case study, the competency framework has been developed specifically for sea command. While the work of Young and Dulewicz addressed most of the criticisms of the competency approach outlined by Richard Bolden and Jonathan Gosling,[56] whether the competencies identified relate validly and sufficiently to *future* behavioural needs and demands and whether such needs and demands are validly and sufficiently understood are questions yet to be answered, given the changes in the way command is being exercised.[57]

CASE STUDY: LEADERSHIP POTENTIAL ASSESSMENT AND DEVELOPMENT FOR SEA COMMAND IN THE ROYAL NAVY[58]

(Continued)

The assessment, development and selection processes for sea command are those that have the most direct bearing on the Royal Navy's operational effectiveness, the morale of its people and its reputation. In 2009 the United Kingdom's Royal Navy introduced a trial to improve the way in which the personal attributes required for success in surface ship command were defined for development purposes and assessed by the Sea Appointment Selection Board (SASB).

These procedures and the associated Command Competency Framework (CCF) are intended to inform subject officers seeking an SASB recommendation and those who have responsibility for subordinate development and as reporting officers. The CCF provides information on the detailed criteria against which the selection for sea command will be based as well as a means of developing personal strengths and weaknesses, for example under the tutelage of reporting officers or coaches and mentors. While this CCF trial concerns suitability only for surface ship command at this stage and has yet to be fully adopted, its applicability across submarine, aviation and military command is under consideration. Feedback on possible improvements therefore will be welcome.

Development of the Command Competency Framework

Pivotal to the CCF are those competencies considered critical for command. In order to develop a comprehensive list of attributes inputs from three sources were collated: current policy and guidance, RN command, leadership and management literature, and interviews with subject-matter experts that included the Commander-in-Chief Fleet and Second Sea Lord.

The review of current policy and guidance highlighted the following factors:

- *Warfare skills*. War fighting expertise and the ability to fight the ship.
- *Judgement/decisiveness*. The ability to judge situations and to take decisive action.
- *Leadership*. The ability to motivate others.
- *Courage and values*. Having the moral courage to take action and the self-management to be aware, manage and develop oneself.

A similarly comprehensive analysis of the command, leadership and management literature highlighted the following command attributes:

- *Sets a clear vision*. Focuses direction towards achieving a clear goal.
- *Inspires motivation*. Motivates through enthusiasm and manages expectations; the way in which the individual communicates.
- *Individual consideration*. Shows individual awareness to maximize talent and motivation in others.
- *Self awareness and development*. Demons trates awareness of self and others and actively seeks further development.
- *Takes responsibility*. The courage to take decisions and to take responsibility for them.
- *Intelligence and adaptability*.

Finally interviews were conducted with a selection of subject-matter experts during which a further five factors relevant to successful and unsuccessful command were agreed:

- *Professional expertise*. Professional expertise obtained through operational seagoing experience and training.

(Continued)

(Continued)

- *Judgement.* Appropriately judging a situation in line with the operational demands and operational aims.
- *Personal effectiveness.* The ability to direct effort towards the goal.
- *People skills.* Eliciting the motivation and support of the ship's company.
- *Motivation.* The enduring motivation to achieve the operational goal and management of self to maintain operational focus.

The findings from all three sources were thematically analysed. From this work, five key overarching competencies were identified, each with four supporting competency indicators, as shown below.

WARFARE SKILLS
The professional skills to successfully fight their ship
- Warfare knowledge
- Platform knowledge
- Seamanship and navigation
- Wider professional knowledge

CONCEPTUALIZE
To get and share the picture of what needs to be done
- Judgement
- Risk taking
- Vision
- Innovation

CREATE SUCCESS
Deliver results
- Drive
- Resilience
- Self-awareness
- Focus

ALIGN
Focus controllable assets by converting plans into action
- Moral courage
- Direction
- Empowerment
- Subordinate development

INTERACT
Work with and through other people
- Make most of individuals
- Communication up
- Communication down
- Inspire

Figure 11.1 Royal Navy Sea Command Competencies and Competency Indicators

This model was then tabulated and, for each indicator, examples of positive and development behaviours were articulated. These lists of behavioural descriptions were not exhaustive but simply provided clarity on the definition of each competency indicator. It is intended that the CCF will have utility in support of the following functions:

- *Reporting Officer Guide.* As a competency template against which reporting officers will comment on an individual's suitability for command, thereby leading to improved evidence-based reporting in the Officers' Joint Appraisal Report (OJAR) process.
- It is essential that phraseology is not simply lifted from the behavioural descriptions. Honesty of reporting against the subject officer's performance will ensure an objective definition of an individual's potential for command as well as maintaining the credibility and utility of the CCF.

(Continued)

(Continued)

- The CCF is to be used immediately to inform the OJAR process for those seeking SASB selection. There is likelihood that an individual will not have had the benefit of this Guide to inform an OJAR being submitted for the 2010 round and to mitigate this position SASB members will be directed to consider their selections with this in mind.
- *Personal Development Tool.* For individual officers the CCF will inform their appreciation of the required command competencies against which they could judge their own strengths and weaknesses. The tool also has utility in the appraisal process and could potentially provide career management collateral.
- *SASB Reference Tool.* As a statement of required command competencies, the CCF will be used to inform the SASB deliberations.

As ever feedback will be invaluable and comments should be forwarded through the Career Management organization.

Surface Ship Command Competency Framework

The surface ship Command Competency Framework (CCF) outlines the five competencies identified as critical to success in Command. These are warfare skills and four command leadership and management skills: conceptualize, align, interact and create success. For each competence, the four indicators are listed with positive and developmental examples of behaviour (see Table 11.3). When assessing potential for command, you should consider your observations of the subject officer's behaviour against the positive and developmental behaviours. Specifically you should consider a recommendation based on the observations of behaviour as outlined in the table immediately below:

Table 11.2 Behavioural Criteria for Command Recommendation in Royal Navy Sea Command

Observation of behaviour	Recommendation for command	Equates to OJAR
Demonstrates clear and consistent evidence of positive behaviours for all competencies.	Strong recommendation for command	Exceptional
Sound evidence of behaviour mostly in line with positive behaviour examples for all competencies.	Good recommendation for command	High
Demonstrates partial evidence of behaviour in line with positive behaviour examples for most competencies.	Shows some potential for command	Yes
Evidence of behaviour mostly in line with development examples for some competencies	Requires substantial development for command	Developing
Evidence of behaviour consistently in line with development examples for most competencies.	Not recommended for command	No

(Continued)

(Continued)

Table 11.3   Examples of Positive and Development Behaviours for Competency
Indicators in Royal Navy Sea Command

Indicator	Positive Behaviours	Development Behaviours
Competency 1 – Warfare Skills		
Warfare knowledge	• Effective warfare knowledge and skill demonstrating appropriate environmental and situational awareness. • Optimal use of resources used in response to threat.	• Warfare strategy lacks appropriate environmental and situational awareness. • Resources used not appropriate for threat.
Platform knowledge	• Demonstrates effective knowledge of current platform. • Demonstrates interest in acquiring knowledge of platform functions.	• Lack of effective knowledge of platform demonstrated. • Limited interest in acquiring platform knowledge.
Seamanship and navigation	• Effective application of seamanship and navigational skills in full range of circumstances. • Demonstrates appropriate awareness of operating environment for task.	• Application of seamanship and navigational skills not demonstrated. • Awareness of operating environment not appropriately considered for the task.
Wider professional awareness	• Awareness of wider RN strategic focus. • Awareness of HQ and MOD functions relevant to operations.	• Limited awareness of wider RN strategic focus. • Limited awareness of HQ and MOD functions relevant to operations.
Competency 2 – Conceptualize		
Judgement	• Effectively judges situations using all relevant available information when making decisions. • Confidently uses intuition to inform decision making.	• Decisions are made using only some of the information available. • Does not display confidence in using intuition to guide decisions when full information is not available.
Risk taking	• Takes balanced risks in decision making, thinking beyond SOPs and instruction.	• Works solely in accordance with SOPs and instruction.
Vision	• Sets a clear vision and sense of purpose overall. • Considers long-term requirements.	• Instruction and decisions are based solely on immediate task.
Innovation	• Demonstrates creativeness. Is innovative in problem solving.	• Uses only standard instructions and policy for problem solving. Reliance on direction.

(Continued)

(Continued)

Indicator	Positive Behaviours	Development Behaviours
Competency 3 – Align		
Moral courage	• Makes decisions and takes action that is in accordance with the long-term and/or overall success that may be unpopular or to the detriment of individual or short-term success. • Takes responsibility for decisions made by self or team.	• Decision making is focused on short-term benefit to meet immediate needs. • Decisions made benefit individual over team. • Ultimate accountability (blame) for actions left with subordinates/other parties
Direction	• Is decisive and consistent in decision making. Makes decisions consistently over time.	• Direction provided is not clearly understood. • Direction is inconsistent or not always timely.
Empowerment	• Delegates responsibility to lowest level, trusting subordinates to carry out work as required. • Provides encouragement and feedback when delegating.	• Tasks are completed by self rather than delegated. • Subordinate work is overly controlled. • Subordinate support (encouragement/feedback) not provided following delegation of task.
Subordinate development	• Provides opportunities for individual development. • Coaches and mentors subordinates and/or peers.	• Encouragement not provided for development. • No time provided for subordinate development.
Competency 4 – Interact		
Understand your people	• Makes use of individual's skills and talents when delegating tasks or gathering information. • Is aware of individual motivations and utilizes them to encourage individual task performance.	• Delegates tasks and gathers information without utilizing individual's skills and talents. • Individuals' motivations are not considered resulting in de-motivation.
Subordinate communications	• Interacts effectively with subordinates. • Is open and honest in communication. Listens and responds to subordinate input.	• Required information is not passed down to subordinates. • Subordinates are not provided with the opportunity to give their input. • Subordinate input is not valued.
Chain of command communications	• Communicates with chain of command openly and honestly. • Seeks advice when relevant and responds to advice given.	• Rarely communicates with chain of command. • Does not seek or ignores advice when required.

(Continued)

(Continued)

Indicator	Positive Behaviours	Development Behaviours
Inspire	• Positively motivates people. Shows belief and encouragement of individual and team's ability to achieve goals. • Demonstrates respect and fairness to individuals. • Demonstrates integrity and a positive example; 'Leads from the front.'	• Personnel are not actively motivated. • Confidence in individual and team ability not demonstrated. • Bullying or fear of humiliation used to motivate personnel. • Own example set is not to highest professional standards.
	Competency 5 – Create Success	
Drive	• Demonstrates determination, commitment and enthusiasm to achieve goal.	• Motivation towards goal is not demonstrated. • Goals are not completed or given up on easily.
Resilience	• Remains calm under pressure and maintains mental and physical courage. • Displays mental and physical endurance and stamina.	• Fragile or struggles under pressure. • Unable to maintain mental and physical endurance over long periods.
Self-awareness	• Demonstrates awareness of impact of self on others. • Plays to strength and mitigates weaknesses. • Seeks feedback and actively works on self development.	• Unaware of impact of self on others, and is unaware of own strengths and weaknesses. • Does not actively work to develop own skills. Does not seek feedback on performance.
Focus	• Focus on team and/or achievement of goal and organization success above self.	• Action focused on self and enhancing self confidence rather than goal. • Over confidence in ability often displayed.

Case Discussion Questions

1. How useful is the Royal Navy's competency approach to assessing leadership potential and effectiveness?
2. To what extent do you think the Royal Navy's model rebuts criticisms of the competency approach?
3. Assuming the competency approach is acceptable in principle, how valid was the CCF development process? In what way(s), if any, could it have been more so?
4. On the basis of your knowledge of competency theory, assessment, selection and promotion methods, and the assessment and development of leadership potential, what feedback on possible improvements to the CCF would you give to the Chief of Staff (Personnel) at Navy Command Headquarters?
5. What do you think are the leadership challenges for the Royal Navy as it faces the future?

The Need for Improvement in the Assessment and Development of Leadership

People Management magazine reports a 2010 study, by leadership development consultancy Leadaculture, of leadership development initiatives with senior HR professionals in the public and private sectors in the UK. The findings were unsurprising:[59]

* Evidence of a comprehensive leadership development strategy was rare.
* Leadership development usually consisted of a number of isolated events and initiatives that did not constitute an ongoing, coherent development strategy.
* The focus tended to be on individuals or small groups of either high-potential staff, senior executives or newly appointed managers.
* Leadership learning tended to be based on generalized leadership theory rather than focused on what the organization required to meet its own unique challenges.

Yet two years earlier, according to a survey by DDI and The Economist Intelligence Unit, '55% of CEOs and senior leaders (globally) expected business performance to suffer in the near future due to a lack of leadership capability'.[60] Tacy Byham and Bill Byham of DDI believe that very few – less than 10 per cent – of those who take part in leadership development programmes actually *do* anything to develop themselves.[61] They attribute this to several reasons:

* Lack of awareness or acceptance of strengths and weaknesses.
* Lack of consideration of the importance of their development to the organization.
* Poor or inappropriate leadership development activities.
* Poor development plans that do not provide opportunities to apply new skills and knowledge.
* An inadequate emphasis on monitoring and measuring development progress and achievement.

Ruth Spellman, then chief executive of the UK's Chartered Management Institute (CMI), criticized the dearth of British top-level leaders in British companies.[62] One reason for this, she suggested, was a lack of aspiration (e.g. to be a CEO). Another was the relative lack of investment in developing managers compared with other European nations – €1,625 per person, which was less than half of what was spent in Germany, with only Romania spending less of the seven nations studied.

A survey by a consortium of four UK top team development providers found a 'sharp contrast between top teams that are investing in their individual and collective development and those whose attention to their own development is more often than not perfunctory, haphazard and uncoordinated'.[63] This was the case despite the fact that a high performance in business is strongly associated with the top team's attitudes to developing themselves and their people and their practices in doing so. Typical comments from respondents were: 'Development issues are not a subject [for discussion] in my company' and 'Development is not seen as a priority – operational issues come first.' This shocking self-indictment of top leadership teams must surely be a top priority for attention before leadership development can be taken seriously.

Debra Humphris and her colleagues in the Health Care Innovation Unit and the School of Management at the University of Southampton in the UK investigated the perceived impact and return on investment of a leadership development programme in the healthcare sector (the National Health Service (NHS)).[64] They discovered several issues that needed addressing for leadership development to be established as a worthwhile activity:

* Assessment of individual and organizational needs before a programme is carried out poorly or not at all, resulting in fuzzy decisions about who should participate and why.
* Little support is provided during or after the programme to aid transfer of learning to the job.
* The focus of leadership development in the NHS is leadership by the individual rather than leadership as a social process.
* There is a lack of understanding of criteria for assessing impact or measuring return on investment in leadership development.

A lack of leadership development for politicians is also a big issue in the UK because politicians in the UK are appointed to head and lead government ministries and departments without having had experience of such a role or any training for it, according to a report by the Institute for Government.[65] The report says: 'One of the most remarkable features of the UK government is the way that our political leaders are catapulted into extremely senior roles and responsibilities overnight [after a general election], and yet receive almost no personal support or development.' One former Cabinet minister was reported as saying: 'The largest thing I'd run before this was my constituency office of four people – now I have a department of tens of thousands and a budget of billions.' This inadequacy must surely take its toll in the quality and effectiveness of the services that government delivers, though who pays for it and whether every politician is to be trained are two key issues.

The following analysis, by Jo Owen, is a light-hearted assessment of the three main party leaders in the May 2010 UK general election.

CASE STUDY: A LEADERSHIP TEST FOR GORDON BROWN, DAVID CAMERON AND NICK CLEGG[66]

(Continued)

Here are five questions which the Prime Ministerial candidates must answer to pass the leadership interview. They probe the five qualities which followers most want from their leaders, based on the original research I did for *How to Lead*.

I have assigned each leader stars out of five for each question. Gordon Brown suffers because he has a track record; David Cameron and Nick Clegg suffer because they do not have a track record. I was lucky enough to interview Clegg for an afternoon, so he benefits or suffers accordingly.

As you test Brown, Cameron and Clegg with these questions, you might also test your boss on the same questions, and even test yourself.

Do you have a vision? Simply: 'this is where we are, this is where we are going and this is how we will get there'.

Brown: ** (out of five): He has talked greatly about vision, but after two years in office I still do not know what the vision is beyond 'trust me with the economy'.
Cameron: ** Clearly wants to detoxify the Tory brand and has made a start, although we will see how far voters actually believe his vision.
Clegg: ** His vision is invisible in the media, although his staff were very clear about where he would stand when confronted with unexpected issues.

Can you motivate people?

Brown: * Apparently motivates people by throwing things and shouting at them. Not quite best practice for most managers today.
Cameron: ** Not clear that he is carrying the rest of the party with him: they seem be tagging along to get power while appearing to disagree with much of what he has to say on climate change and tax.
Clegg: ** Again, suffers from media invisibility: you can't motivate people if no one knows you exist. But in private, he is outstanding. Not sure that counts though.

Are you good in a crisis?

Brown: *** Brown claims to have saved the world, which is overblown. But having led us into recession from 11 Downing Street, he has led us out again from number 10. Would your boss approve if you only solved crises you had created?
Cameron: ** Largely untested, but has shown some bottle in disciplining some of the dinosaurs in his party who got uppity about expenses and policy matters.
Clegg: *** Completely untested, which is where most leaders start out. But like any good leader he has a good team: Vince Cable might have scored five stars alone, Clegg gets one star alone but gets three for the team effort.

Are you decisive?

Brown: * Do not forget the election that never was two years ago. Brown has a reputation for never being around when there is bad news. He will only apologise for things he has not done (like slavery).
Cameron: ** No real evidence to give him a high score or a low score, so he gets a slightly mean two stars.
Clegg: ** see Cameron.

(Continued)

(Continued)

Are you honest and trustworthy?

Brown: * Has been caught making too many statistical errors recently and has the misfortune that after thirteen years in power all those half promises tend to be remembered and count against you (we will have a vote on Lisbon; we will not introduce tuition fees; we will not raise income tax). One star is the likely fate of all incumbents in this instance, eventually.

Cameron: ** Has failed to own up to how the budget will be managed, where the pain will be. And has had his dodgy moments with statistics. But at least he has said that there will be pain.

Clegg: *** Has not been caught with dodgy statistics (one of the benefits of being ignored, perhaps) and has tried to be slightly clearer about where the pain will be.

Final scores out of 25: Brown 8; Cameron 10; Clegg: 12.

The obvious conclusion is that we need to look for another leader, but I am not sure we will find them within the Scottish Nationalists, Greens, UKIP or BNP.

Equally, you can conclude that obscurity helps: the more you put a leader under the microscope, the more their flaws become apparent. What would happen if you and your boss were subject to the same relentless scrutiny by the media year after year? Few of us would come out looking good.

Following the May 2010 general election, which the Conservative Party won but without an overall majority, Gordon Brown resigned as both prime minister and leader of the Labour Party, to be replaced by Ed Miliband in September 2010, and the Conservative and Liberal Democrat Parties formed a coalition government with David Cameron as prime minister and Nick Clegg as deputy prime minister.

Leadership development suffers from several methodological and practical problems. Terry Gillen suggests that the key problems are the following:[67]

1. The criteria for effective leadership that form the basis for leadership development programmes may not be valid. Such criteria reflect only self-reports or analyses of so-called role models such as Ernest Shackleton, Jack Welch and Sven-Goran Eriksson rather than what followers seek in their leaders.
2. Managers often feel compelled to demote leadership in favour of meeting short-term demands for high performance, particularly by 'doing more themselves and managing processes rather than leading people'.
3. What is 'taught' in such programmes contradicts what apparently successful managers ('the more senior ones') do, evidenced by the frequent comment that 'it's my manager who ought to be here'; yet human beings tend to imitate those who are perceived as 'successful'.
4. The clash between the espoused values and the actual behaviour of managers, for example customer satisfaction versus tight cost control, discourages implementation of learning.
5. Programme methodologies, such as outdoor activities and using 'videos of Kenneth Branagh as Henry V' reciting 'Once more unto the breach ...', may be inappropriate for their purpose: their practical relevance – the transferability of learning – may be questionable.

The Leadership Trust in the UK has pioneered leadership development within the context of accredited business and management education by introducing an MBA programme with a specialism in Leadership Studies in collaboration with the University of Strathclyde Business School. The aim is to respond to the needs of senior managers and directors and their organizations of the future, a unique attempt to create an integrated leadership development programme. This programme combines the standard core curriculum of the Strathclyde MBA with a 'taught' course in leadership (focused on students' learning *about* leadership), experiential learning courses at the Leadership Trust (focused on developing self-awareness, emotional intelligence and leadership skills), and a leadership project (focused on the application of leadership theory and practice). The aim is to produce graduates, typically already middle-level and senior managers and on average 40 years old, who are not only knowledgeable and skilled in business and management but also effective leaders.

It has been claimed that 'conventional leadership training strategies are not enough to transform individuals into leaders' and that 'character' should be reinstated in leadership development.[68] And Warren Bennis has observed, 'Leadership courses can only teach skills. They can't teach character or vision and indeed they don't even try.'[69] How can personal integrity, trust and credibility be 'taught'? This issue has been the basis of criticism of business schools for 'training technicians'[70] and for turning out 'highly skilled barbarians'.[71] Yet not enough has changed, according to Nitin Nohria and Rakesh Khurana: they question why top business schools espouse mission statements that promise to 'educate the leaders of the future' while they fail to give leadership its intellectual due.[72]

Leadership education in business schools comes in for criticism by Dennis Tourish and colleagues. On the basis of a survey of 21 leading business schools – mainly in the United States but including three in the UK – they allege that business schools promote the notion of transformational leaders as heroic, charismatic visionaries who are well above the heads and hearts of those ordinary competent managers over whom they exercise influence and control.[73] They also allege that business schools believe their MBA programmes can make their students into such leaders.[74] Tourish and colleagues suggest that hubris and narcissism are likely to result.

The programmes that Tourish and colleagues studied also, they say, teach agency theory, namely self-interest as the dominant influence on human behaviour, with the aim of profit maximization.[75] So we have a 'marriage of inconvenience' between transformational leadership and agency theory in business school teaching that, for example, leads to the teaching of the pursuit of common interest alongside the need to assume the dominance of self-interest. Tourish and colleagues put forward five useful suggestions for improving the teaching of leadership:

✳ Recognize that leadership is a phenomenon that is co-constructed by leaders and followers, including attributional biases.
✳ Include a more critical evaluation of leadership practice that avoids the depicting of some 'successful' leaders as unarguable heroic paragons of virtue (such as Jack Welch, former CEO of General Electric).
✳ Re-balance the notions of leadership and followership.

⁕ Focus more on the benefits of frank and open communication between leaders and followers.

⁕ Consider more deeply the limitations of agency theory.[76]

Eric Jean Garcia also investigated the scope and purpose of business school lecturers' teaching in the field of leadership in MBA programmes. He found that the majority of the lecturers were disinclined to consider leadership beyond serving business ends, namely serving people and society more widely.[77] This does not augur well for improvements among MBA graduates in attitudes towards social responsibility. C.K. Prahalad, the distinguished management thinker who died in April 2010, always ended his MBA and executive education courses by sharing his perspective on how his course members could – and should – become responsible managers, exhorting them to 'strive to achieve success with responsibility.'[78] His message never changed in 33 years.

Assessment of Leadership Potential and Development Needs

Leadership potential and development needs are commonly assessed by assessment centres and diagnostic questionnaires. Assessment centres, a process, not a place, are a primary means of objectively assessing leadership potential and development needs, while diagnostic questionnaires are also used to identify leadership development needs.

Assessment Centres

Leadership assessment centres are developed and run in much the same way as general management assessment centres. Job descriptions, specifications of core competencies and behaviourally anchored rating scales for the competencies are produced. These are either customized – researched and developed in-house to address organization-specific needs – or generic models produced by academic researchers or consultancy firms that have carried out their own research and produced their own leadership models.[79] Appropriate psychometric tests, including generic leadership questionnaires such as MLQ and TLQ, are used. Simulation exercises such as role plays, (formally) leadership group exercises, and in-box and in-basket exercises are developed. All exercises need to be relevant, realistic and challenging. There are many examples of both general leadership assessment centres and, as case studies, leadership assessment centres that were customized for an organization's specific needs.[80]

The process typically entails a small group of assessees, say eight or nine, taking part in psychometric assessment, individual presentations, one-to-one interviews and the various exercises listed above. Assessors are trained in observation, recording, data integration and evaluation processes and skills. They may be senior members of the organization or professional assessors from consultancy firms or elsewhere, or a mixture of both. Assessment reports are then produced that will typically describe individual assessees' leadership strengths, limitations, development needs and potential. The assessment centre process may occupy between two and five days and be managed by an administrator and the appropriate support staff. The outcomes will typically include decisions about appointments, including promotions, and both individual and general leadership development plans.

Results in terms of their psychometric reliability and validity can be very good. Phillip Lowry describes how inter-rater reliability coefficients typically exceeded a satisfactory 0.80 and reached over 0.95 in the leadership assessment centres he had completed in the public sector.[81] Jo Silvester found a significant relationship among Conservative Party candidates for election between their performance in an assessment centre and their performance in the 2005 general election.[82]

Research by Tasha Eurich and colleagues in the United States revealed that some 93 per cent of *Fortune 500* organizations using assessment centres followed the *Guidelines and Ethical Considerations for Assessment Center Operations* produced by the International Task Force on Assessment Centers in 2000[83] (superseded by a new edition in 2008).[84] These guidelines cover professional practice with respect to job analysis and competency modelling; assessment centre development, technology, dimensions (assessment criteria), exercises (including simulations) and evaluation; assessor characteristics and training; behaviour recording and scoring; data integration; organizational assessment centre policy (including validation, assessment centre purpose and cross-cultural operations); and assessees' rights.

Diagnostic Leadership Questionnaires

Diagnostic questionnaires take the form of proprietary psychometric personality questionnaires and either proprietary or customized questionnaires based on one or more particular model(s) of leadership or set of leadership competencies. Both methods typically use both web-based and paper formats and some use 360° assessment.

An example of a proprietary questionnaire is the *Leadership Audit*, which was developed by the Research Centre for Leadership Studies at the Leadership Trust. The *Leadership Audit* draws on an earlier version of the leadership model[85] described in this book and includes related management activities and specific leadership-related areas that relate to the leadership development work of the Leadership Trust. Information about the *Leadership Audit* is provided below as a case example.

CASE EXAMPLE: THE *LEADERSHIP AUDIT*[86]

What is the *Leadership Audit*?

The *Leadership Audit* is the Leadership Trust's proprietary web-based instrument for diagnosing the leadership strengths and development needs of managers and identifying leadership issues in an organization. This diagnosis is used by Leadership Trust consultants as a basis for designing and delivering a customized leadership development programme or an OD (organization development) or team development programme.

The *Leadership Audit* is based on established models of leadership[87] and 360° assessment. It is a questionnaire comprising 79 items, typically taking 20–30 minutes to complete electronically. An individual is rated on each item on a five-point scale (0–4) on the extent to which the item applies to him or her, with a provision for 'I don't know' and 'Not applicable':

(Continued)

(Continued)

- 0 – Not at all.
- 1 – To a small extent.
- 2 – To a moderate extent.
- 3 – To a great extent.
- 4 – To a very great extent.
- 5 – I don't know.
- 6 – Not applicable.

A five-point rating scale is generally regarded as the optimal scale.[88]

The 79 items are categorized into 12 leadership and leadership-related factors:

1. Vision and mission.
2. Strategy.
3. Empowerment of others.
4. Motivation and inspiration of others.
5. Communication with others.
6. Emotional intelligence.
7. Team leadership.
8. Coaching and mentoring others.
9. Management (planning, organising, use of personal resources, monitoring progress, reviewing performance, and time management).
10. Problem solving and decision making.
11. Organizational change.
12. Leadership effectiveness and satisfaction.

Appendix 1 provides definitions of the 12 factors and a sample of the 79 self-assessment questionnaire items categorized by the respective factors and numbered according to their sequence in the questionnaire. Appendix 2 (not shown) likewise provides a sample of the questionnaire items in the 'Assessment by Other' questionnaire, which is used by the manager's own manager(s), peers, direct reports, and external contacts in rating the manager.

360° Assessment and Feedback

360° assessment is a process whereby individuals are assessed by themselves and their peers or co-workers, managers, direct reports and any external contacts that they interact with regularly (e.g. customers, clients and suppliers). That is why it is called '360°' – full circle: it looks at how individuals are perceived by all those around them, including themselves.

This method of assessment is the fairest, most comprehensive and therefore most valid way of assessing people.[89] Everybody who assesses an individual has a unique perception of him or her. Such perceptions reflect what assessors expect, or give importance to, in their working relationships and interaction with individuals. For example, an individual's manager may emphasize certain behaviours or characteristics and de-emphasize others, while a different picture may be the case for direct reports who expect or value different behaviours or characteristics.

It should be noted, however, that corporate culture (and national culture in non-UK work) should be carefully considered in recommending and using 360° assessment.

(Continued)

(Continued)

In some corporate and national cultures 360° assessment may not be familiar to people and, even if it is, it may be fraught with difficulties in relation to existing values, customs and practices. Expert advice should be sought when confronting this issue.

Nevertheless, when feedback is given on the basis of 360° assessment it is a powerful development tool, serving as a mirror to help individuals see themselves as others see them. Self-awareness is positively associated with managerial and leadership effectiveness: research has shown that more effective leaders are more aware of their competencies, personal characteristics, strengths and limitations than less effective leaders.[90]

Statistical Reliability of the *Leadership Audit*

The *Leadership Audit* questionnaire has been checked for statistical reliability, that is consistency of responses by respondents. The overall test–retest reliability is 0.81 for the Self-Assessment version, on which the 'Assessment by Other' version is based. This value exceeds the value of 0.70 that is conventionally regarded as acceptable.[91]

Using the *Leadership Audit* to Diagnose Organizational Leadership Development Needs

One key purpose of the *Leadership Audit* is to diagnose a client organization's leadership development needs as the basis for the Trust to design a customized leadership development or OD programme.

The *Leadership Audit* provides an overall picture of an organization's current collective leadership behaviour, strengths, shortcomings and development needs and any leadership issues arising. A graphic report is provided for the organization and explained to the client by our consultants (see anonymous samples available from the Trust's Research Centre). This feedback process itself can provide additional rich data for the diagnosis. Specific group or team reports may also be provided for an additional fee, depending on the objectives of the audit.

The diagnosis is normally used to set objectives for a leadership development, team development or OD programme for the organization and to formulate the programme objectives, content and methodology. Using the *Leadership Audit,* the diagnostic process is reliable, comprehensive and practical. It ensures that a programme, which may comprise one or more courses, seminars, workshops and other learning and development events, addresses specific real needs in the organization.

When the *Leadership Audit* is used for diagnostic purposes, either the whole population of managers or a representative sample of them at all levels in the organization takes part in completing the questionnaire. Such a sample may be drawn from a particular organizational level or from particular levels, from functional, operational or other groupings, or representatively from the whole population (known as a stratified random sample), depending on the purpose and scope of the diagnosis, the size of the organization, cost considerations and client requirements. When the purpose of the 360° assessment is a diagnosis of leadership development, team development and OD needs at the corporate level, feedback

(Continued)

(Continued)

is usually not provided to participating individuals as it is not relevant to them personally.

Using the *Leadership Audit* to Provide Individual Feedback for Personal Leadership Development

Another use of the *Leadership Audit* is to produce reports on individuals that are used to inform their personal leadership development, for example setting specific learning and development objectives in connection with their attendance on a leadership development programme run by the Trust. The process entails individual feedback to them by trained facilitators/coaches.

The *Leadership Audit* can provide a 'snapshot' of the current leadership behaviour, strengths and development needs of individual managers or prospective managers in an organization, with subsequent personal feedback to them. This feedback may provide useful input to a personal development planning and review process in an organization.

An individual profile – a '360° Feedback Report' – is provided to each manager and it is explained and interpreted in terms of its meaning and implications for his or her personal leadership development. The feedback may provide specific objectives for personal learning and development in connection with the manager's attendance on a leadership development or team development or an OD programme. *This feedback should not be used by a client organization to appraise the manager's work performance or to make decisions about promotion: the process is designed exclusively for learning and development.* The Leadership Trust provides training and detailed professional guidelines for facilitators/coaches in conducting one-to-one feedback sessions.

Other Uses of the *Leadership Audit*

Programme Evaluation. The *Leadership Audit* can also be used to evaluate the effectiveness of a programme conducted by the Trust. In this case the instrument must be administered to participants both before and after the programme. If those participants have already completed the *Leadership Audit* during the diagnostic phase, then they need only complete the questionnaire again after attending the programme. Ideally the *Leadership Audit* should also be administered twice (at the same time) to a 'control group' of comparable individuals who do not attend the programme. This increases the validity of the data on the difference that the programme makes. As with diagnosis, feedback is not usually provided to participating individuals when the purpose of the 360° assessment is programme evaluation.

Leadership Research. The *Leadership Audit* can also be used as a research tool, for example to investigate factors that may influence leadership behaviour and effectiveness in organizations or teams or to compare organizations either generally or in the same industry for benchmarking purposes. Appendix 3 (not shown) provides demographic information that may be collected when the *Leadership Audit* is administered for research purposes, depending on the purpose of the research.

(Continued)

(Continued)

Norms for the *Leadership Audit*

Norm tables are available that will enable a Leadership Trust consultant or a client organization's trained staff to compare an individual's ratings with ratings of other individuals in the general population (the norm group) and use this in the feedback process. This means that one can assess how high or low one individual rates compared with others in the norm group. The norm group is the population of individuals in a given category – self, peers, manager(s), direct reports or external reports – who have previously completed the *Leadership Audit* questionnaire for an individual.

The norm tables are based on ratings for 362 managers (respondents) in 33 organizations in the public and private sectors in the UK. Norms are provided for self-ratings, composite ratings by others, ratings by managers, ratings by second managers, peer ratings, ratings by direct reports, ratings by external contacts, and composite overall ratings.

Customized norms may also be produced by the Leadership Trust for a client organization. These customized norms permit comparisons to be made among departments, divisions, locations, levels, etc., within the client organization as well as benchmarking the organization overall against other organizations either in the same sector or generally across all sectors.

Appendix 1: Factor Definitions and Sample Questionnaire Items[92] (Self-assessment Version)[93]

Vision and mission: has clarity and belief in the vision and mission of the organization.

1. I believe in my organization's stated vision for the future.
9. I have a clear vision for the future for my part of the organization.

Strategy: is involved in and clear about the organization's business strategies and displays either a preference or flexibility in focusing on the 'big picture' or on detail.

2. I have a clear set of business strategies for my part of the organization.
19. I move easily between seeing the big picture and seeing the detail in work situations.

Empowerment: empowers his or her team by taking risks in delegating important tasks or responsibilities to them, allowing them to manage themselves and treating mistakes and failure as opportunities to learn.

4. I do not *manage* my team: they manage themselves.
54. I am prepared to take risks in delegating important tasks or responsibilities to my team members.

Motivation and inspiration: motivates or inspires him/herself and team members by ensuring that work has meaning and value for them, using inspirational language, displaying passion, and using challenge, recognition and reward.

6. I inspire my team in the way I talk to them.
7. I give my team members challenging tasks and responsibilities that match their competencies.
8. I use the promise of financial rewards (e.g. salary increase or bonus) as a way of motivating my team members.

(Continued)

(Continued)

26. I inspire my team members by pointing out the contribution they make.
32. I get my team members to do things they had never imagined or believed they could do.
60. I make sure my team members can fulfil their personal needs or aspirations through their work.

How Leaders Develop, Succeed and Survive

The Route to the Top[94]

Many are called but few are chosen. Those who are chosen to become a CEO and have done so will have made a winding, dynamic journey requiring learning, purposefulness, resilience and serendipity along the way. So what is the formula for making it to the top – and staying there?

On her way home after a Leadership and Management course at a leadership development organization, the Leadership Trust, a post-experience graduate student studying for the MBA in Leadership Studies had a conversation with the taxi driver that quickly offered her the subject of her MBA project and dissertation.[95] The driver had been managing director of a large construction company and then a pharmaceutical company. He had been head-hunted for his first CEO position at the age of 27 years and had had a successful career – until he lost his wife, his home and then his job. At the age of forty-something he was now driving a taxi while deciding what to do. This was the stimulus for her research. How do people make it to the top? Who they are? How do they stay there? And why do they fail?

In her study of six high-profile CEOs (Virgin Group's Richard Branson, GE's Jack Welch, Apple's Steve Jobs, Warnaco Group's Linda Wachner, Carly Fiorina at Hewlett-Packard and Philip Burgeieres at Weatherford International), three of whom continued to be successful in that role and three of whom had failed after initial success, the student found no clear association between success and personality traits.[96] Indeed Andrew Davidson et al.'s research covering 1,000 CEOs showed how there was a huge variety of personalities, backgrounds and styles of decision making that could be associated with making it to the top.[97]

Whether particular personality traits are important to being effective as a leader is a matter of much controversy among psychologists and commentators on leadership. On the one hand Peter Drucker says they do not exist.[98] On the other hand Barbara Kellerman says they help us to understand why people behave the way they do: '… whether a leader has or lacks a particular trait is likely to tell us a fair amount about how and why good, or bad, leadership was exercised'.[99] In any case, as Smiths Group's CEO Philip Bowman says, 'There's no one-size-fits-all chief executive.'[100]

Cognitive competencies – conceptual thinking, critical thinking, analytical intelligence, imagination and creativity – are common to successful CEOs but are 'threshold' qualities: they are necessary but not sufficient. And research by Gareth Edwards and myself found that transformational leadership was displayed more at the top levels of organizations and that transactional leadership was least effective there.[101]

It has also been found by other researchers that, while the presence of a particular personality trait does not necessarily lead to failure, the ability to 'manage' it *is* critical.[102]

For example, the more enduringly successful top leaders display more of Daniel Goleman's 'social competencies' as well as his 'personal competencies'[103] – particularly adaptability, according to the student's findings.[104] Adaptability in terms of the CEO's ability to repress certain personality traits and to develop new ones is suggested by Charles Farkas and Suzy Wetlaufer as improving the chances of success.[105]

A prerequisite of adaptability is self-awareness. In the words of Manfred Kets de Vries, a noted psychologist and leadership scholar at INSEAD, 'Self-knowledge is the first step toward emotional intelligence … it's also the first step toward leadership effectiveness.'[106] Enhancing self-awareness, with its positive consequences of self-control and self-confidence, is fundamental to the Leadership Trust's leadership development philosophy and practice. Jeffrey Sonnenfeld and Andrew Ward suggest that self-belief and persistence are most important factors in the face of adversity.[107] As an example, they quote former US president Jimmy Carter, who had been rejected as the nation's leader but went on to gain great acclaim as a tireless peace campaigner for the United Nations.

How do executives make it to the top? Morgan W. McCall Jr, at the University of Southern California and formerly at the Center for Creative Leadership in the United States, suggests that, to the extent it is learned (perhaps 50–70 per cent), leadership is learned from experience.[108] And, he says, certain experiences matter more than others:

* Early work experiences.
* Short-term assignments.
* Major line assignments.
* Other people (very good and very bad bosses or superiors).
* Hardships of various kinds.
* Miscellaneous events such as training programmes.

Warren Bennis and Robert Thomas speak of 'crucibles' of leadership: experiences, often unexpected and traumatic, always intense, that will cause leaders to stop in their tracks and question who they are and what really matters.[109] Crucibles shape their leadership style and abilities. Abraham Zaleznik called this being 'twice-born': such leaders have had a traumatic experience during their life – a 'second birth'.[110] Such experiences lead to the skills, desire and resilience to conquer adversity and emerge stronger.

Most if not all of us will experience setbacks as we pursue our careers. Leadership development is a non-linear pathway and a dynamic process, involving twists and turns, accidents and dead ends along the way, second attempts after failure, and serendipity. Says Morgan McCall: 'Failure to develop new strengths or to deal with weaknesses can result in derailment.'[111] This failure in turn may be the consequence of their personality traits that CEOs are not aware of or, even if they are, are not consciously managed – negative traits such as arrogance, volatility, excessive caution, habitual distrust, aloofness and perfectionism.[112]

Leaders fail, argues Adrian Furnham, for three main interrelated reasons: poor selection, paradoxical derailers and 'too much of a good thing'.[113] Poor selection usually takes the form of identifying the essential or desirable knowledge, skills and attitudes (competencies) and then looking for evidence of them in the candidates. The traditional model is that candidates are rejected if they do not have sufficient of the essential or desirable competencies. Furnham argues, however, that it is also important to identify those factors that will disqualify candidates, for example impulsivity, arrogance or volatility, which in practice is a rarer approach.[114] He says:

> **The consequences [of not doing so] are often that leaders with potential derailers sail through ... some of their derailers may actually assist them in the selection process.[115]**

However, there is no perfectively linear relationship between a competency and effectiveness. Indeed it may, like cognitive intelligence in some situations, be curvilinear, even ∩-shaped.[116] As Furnham says, 'Too much of a good thing becomes a bad thing', such as being too vigilant, too tough or too hardworking.[117] This may often be situationally determined: different situations will require different competencies or the same competencies but to different extents. Furnham warns: 'By always selecting in and never selecting out, organizations continue to make themselves vulnerable to appointing yet another elephant in the board room.'[118]

In the final analysis CEO tenure can be seen as a life cycle. Initial learning is rapid, usually making a positive impact on the organization. But eventually CEOs will grow stale, lose touch with the external environment and perform less well.[119] We can see this not only in business but also in politics, government and other areas as well. Apart from obvious reasons such as physical health and resilience, a fuller explanation must include derailers such as negative personality traits that have not been addressed. But there is no one generic explanation, no one formula for making it to the top and staying there. And the seeds are often sown early in life.

Early Influences on Leadership

The Jesuits have a saying, 'Give me a boy until he is seven and I will give you back the man.'[120] Those of us engaged in leadership development might be inspired by this: 'Give me a manager until ... and I will give you back the leader.'

Manfred Kets de Vries and Elizabeth Florent-Treacy describe how early-childhood and family influences shape character generally and leadership potential in particular.[121] The early years of a person's development are well established as a formative period. It is therefore not surprising that research carried out for the global HR consultancy DDI reinforced the link between early leadership experience and business leadership in adulthood.[122] Seventy per cent of over 100 business leaders interviewed had been school prefects, 50 per cent had been sports team captains, 30 per cent head or deputy head boy or girl, and nearly 90 per cent had held at least two leadership positions at school, with 40 per cent holding three.

Lyndon Rego and colleagues at the Center for Creative Leadership point out that many schools and community organizations in the United States have recognized and acted on the need to develop leadership skills early in life.[123] They cite examples of the YMCA, Boy Scouts and Girl Scouts, Outward Bound, Rotary, the Kiwanis and schools around the world and how they illustrate the potential of young people to develop leadership skills and how leadership development can enhance student achievement. And the role of childhood experience in developing emotional literacy, important for effective leadership, is now well recognized, with programmes in British primary schools under way.[124]

Nancy Adler suggests that a powerful early influence on future leadership behaviour is to be found in the personal stories of those emotionally close to us.[125] She also suggests that participants in leadership development programmes can be helped to recollect personal stories that will support their desired leadership behaviour. She says:

> Each of us has a personal story embedded in a cultural and family history that has shaped us as individuals and has given us our unique and highly personal combination of values, inspiration, and courage – our humanity – that we draw on in our day-to-day and larger leadership efforts. The more clearly we understand the roots of our identity and humanity, the more able we will be to use our strengths and core values to achieve the vision we have for ourselves and the world around us.

Multiple Activities and Processes in Leadership Development

In a research report for the UK government, John Burgoyne and colleagues make the point that there is no one formula for leadership development:

> There is no single form of management and leadership capability that enhances performance in the same way in all situations. And there is no single way in which management and leadership development creates this capability. Rather, there are many different forms of management and leadership development that can generate many different forms of management and leadership capability; in turn this can increase performance in different ways.[126]

Amin Rajan reports a survey of CEOs on their favoured leadership development methods.[127] In rank order of importance, these are:

1. Coaching by the CEO.
2. Learning from peers.
3. Experience.
4. Skills training.

And a survey of some 300 senior managers in the UK manufacturing sector by the Manufacturing Foundation and The Leadership Trust Foundation revealed, in order of frequency, the following 10 key 'triggers' or catalysts of leadership development:

1. Significant leadership challenge at an early age.
2. Positive role models.
3. Being 'thrown in at the deep end'.
4. Mentoring, coaching and consultant relationships.
5. Experiential leadership development courses.
6. Negative role models.
7. MBA and professional qualifications.
8. International or multicultural exposure.
9. Voluntary and community work.
10. Team sports.[128]

Triggers of leadership development appear to be both planned, for example experiential leadership development courses, and opportunistic, for example encounters with other leaders.[129] And a mix of learning methods also appears to be crucial to leadership development in manufacturing:

> For most [managers], the learning [is] derived from a powerful mix of learning from doing (work-based learning); learning from books or courses (ideas and concepts) and learning from people (social interaction).[130]

In an online survey on global leadership development issues and practices, international assignments were the most used practices to develop global leaders, followed by experience in managing global functional or process teams.[131] This survey also found that participating in global task forces to address specific organization problems or opportunities was the predominant best practice for developing global leaders with the capabilities that their organization needed. Peter Lorange argues that business schools need to refine their approaches to developing global leaders: creating a 'global meeting place', face-to-face or virtual; providing opportunities for experimentation; encouraging learning from failure; juxtaposing new business models with cherished traditional ones; and avoiding 'silo' cultures and encouraging single global 'families'.[132] Global leadership, one might say, has its own unique culture.

Sarah Watson describes how shared leadership can be an effective means of improving the leadership of those individuals involved through learning from one another.[133] Greater emphasis therefore could be placed on peer networking within and across organizations. The drawbacks, however, are that networking is time-consuming, and those involved need to have the ability to engage in a reflective process.

Self-development plays an important part in leadership development, for example volunteering to experience situations from which to expand one's repertoire of leadership behaviours.[134] Such approaches are known as 'experiential learning' and will sometimes include the use of outdoor activities. Organizations that use these in the UK include the Leadership Trust, Outward Bound, the Brathay Trust, and the Royal Military Academy at Sandhurst. Underlying outdoor learning in leadership development is the theory that leadership techniques under conditions of physical stress can be successfully applied to the high-pressure office, according to Rick Chattell:

> It is all about inspiration: inspiring yourself and others to succeed, if necessary against the odds. In business, as in other areas, there are usually obstacles to overcome such as lack of resources or time. Inspiration can be the secret to winning through.[135]

Outdoor leadership development sometimes goes even further in presenting daunting challenges, not least physical. For example, the Wharton School in the United States offers its MBA students and participants in executive education programmes several leadership development ventures: a three-week journey to the Mount Everest area, reaching over 18,000 feet above sea level, and visits to Ecuador, the Marine Corps base in Quantico, Virginia, and the site of the disastrous 1949 fire in Montana. Michael Useem believes such escapades help participants to understand what it takes to be a leader.[136] Such an approach in leadership development is underscored in management consultant Hugh Aldous's view:

> Leadership development is fundamentally about experience that tests individuals in hostile or difficult situations. It is about creating an environment in which ordinary people can have unusual experiences.[137]

Such 'unusual' experiences provide the vehicle for truly knowing oneself: we all have vast, hidden and unused potential which most of us will underestimate, acting in effect as leaders without formal subordinates.[138] But 'most would-be leaders are crushed by their early mistakes and, to spare future embarrassment, resolve never to lead again', says James O'Toole.[139] Real leaders, he says, 'learn from their failed efforts, shrug off the embarrassment, and seek out the opportunity to apply what they have learned'. And Bennis says:

> Far too often we look to psychobiography, not role, to explain human behaviour ... the roles we play in the course of our lives have more to do with our successes or failures than our personal histories.[140]

Furnham sees three factors conspiring against the 'learn-from-experience' model:

* The desire by would-be leaders to learn 'faster, cheaper and better', through short-cuts, than experience allows.
* Resistance by HR professionals who see learning from experience as undermining their control of leadership development programmes.
* The perception of experience as a test rather than a learning opportunity.[141]

His helpful conclusions are that 'leadership potential and talent should be defined as the ability to learn from experience' and 'every move, promotion or challenge should be assessed for what it can teach a manager'. Gerry Randell believes that leadership *can* be developed through experience, but only if:

* It is desired: a person must be motivated to be a leader and to develop the necessary leadership skills.
* It is focused on specific leadership behaviour.
* Leadership skills are practised and feedback is received either in real-life or in training situations.[142]

In a study of 15 'exemplary' Chinese CEOs in top-ranking enterprises in China, Cheng Zhu at the Center for Creative Leadership discovered a major contribution to their success:

> I found that the secret to the leaders' success lies not simply in their courage to endure a large dose of pain and stress during crucible events but also in their ability to reinterpret challenges and regain a balanced sense of which changes to embrace and which to resist.[143]

She points out that the Chinese word for 'business' – *sheng yi* – has two characters: *sheng* as a verb for 'generate' or 'produce' and *yi* for 'meaning, ideas or intentions'.[144] The successful Chinese CEOs she studied would invent new meanings through a constant reframing and self-transformation; this was a key process in their leadership development.

Adrian Furnham suggests that there is now a consensus among both academics and leaders themselves on what shapes successful leaders – across different companies, sectors and countries – namely six 'powerful learning experiences'.[145] He sums them up this way:

1. Early work experience, which reveals likes, dislikes, interests, abilities and talents.
2. The influence of other people, usually immediate bosses, who are positive or negative role models.
3. Short-term assignments, such as projects, which provide opportunities for new experiences and learning.
4. The first big assignment (seen as particularly important by top-level leaders) – the first promotion or a foreign posting – where the stakes are high.
5. Hardships, which provide learning, for example about coping in a crisis, the value of loyal staff, how to distinguish between needs and wants, and the virtues of stoicism and resilience. A novel approach to assessing how well people who are or will be in leadership positions will handle a crisis or emergency is the use of a flight simulation exercise in which an emergency occurs.[146]
6. Formal management and leadership development, such as 360° feedback and coaching.

Barriers to Leadership Development

The survey of leaders in the manufacturing sector in the UK by the Manufacturing Foundation and The Leadership Trust Foundation found that just over half of them experienced barriers to leadership development during their careers, mostly due to themselves but also due to organizational culture or politics and a lack of time to undertake leadership development activities.[147]

One study investigated the circumstances in which a transformational leadership development programme produced the intended changes in participants' leadership behaviour.[148] Whether it did so appeared to depend on whether the participants were aware of the need to change and had a plan to do so. A further consideration was how constrained participants were in changing their behaviour by the culture of their organization, their own boss and colleagues, and the particular tasks they were performing. Time pressures inhibited the implementation of leadership development plans for some 25 per cent of participants.

One of the barriers to transfer of learning is emotional, yet the traditional cognitive approach has ignored this.[149] Ben Franklin, undoubtedly a leader himself, said, 'How few there are who have the courage enough to own their own faults, or resolution enough to mend them.'[150] A useful starting point in leadership development, therefore, is to understand what stops people – managers – from becoming effective leaders. Once we know the psychological barriers to effective leadership and effective leadership development, we can use psychological techniques to overcome them and develop the cognitive, emotional and behavioural skills needed. Leadership development begins with learning to know and control oneself first – an essential element of emotional intelligence. Then, and only then, by building self-confidence and developing emotional intelligence, can we lead and enable others. For example, would you expect people to trust you if you did not trust yourself?

Norman Dixon describes the psychological barriers to effective leadership and leadership development:[151]

- Low self-esteem – which leads to depression and a lack of motivation. Self-esteem is a powerful motivator.
- A lack of self-confidence – as a result of not coming to terms with oneself, which in turn leads to lack of confidence in other people. Howard Hass points out, based on analysis of 150 business leaders, that most people lack the self-confidence to practise and develop leadership [152] And a KPMG Management Consulting survey revealed the insecurity and lack of self-confidence of UK managers, particularly in their communication skills and ability to motivate people.[153]
- Fear of failure, shame or social disapproval – adults fear failure, whereas, Struan Robertson says, 'children keep trying to walk until they can'.[154]
- Cognitive constriction – thinking 'inside the box' and over-rationalization, leading to 'paralysis by analysis'.
- The adverse consequences of stress – cognitive, managerial and physical.

These psychological barriers mean that many natural talents are *impaired* rather than improved by training. They can be removed in leadership development programmes through experiential learning in teams.

CASE EXAMPLE: OVERCOMING BARRIERS TO LEADERSHIP DEVELOPMENT AT THE LEADERSHIP TRUST

The process at the Leadership Trust involves generating or surfacing anxiety by imposing challenging tasks in work-related leadership projects such as a business simulation and physical activities which include rock climbing, scuba diving or caving and field projects. Anxiety is extinguished by enabling participants to discover their personal strengths. The focus is on handling aggression, resolving conflict, reviewing individual and team performance, and establishing effective working relationships. The tasks and activities comprise defining and solving problems, establishing objectives, planning, organizing team and physical resources, and implementing team action. Competition among teams is fostered but without the risk of ego damage, and group dynamics among participants are facilitated. An underlying rationale for programme activities is presented for a cognitive and emotional buy-in to the process.

(Continued)

(Continued)

Dixon describes the psychological techniques and processes that are used in this process:[155]

- Desensitization
  The gradual overcoming of fear and anxiety by equally gradual increases in difficulty of the tasks and activities, with the surmounting of each hazard being reinforced by approval and an increment in personal satisfaction.
- Reinforcement theory
  Emphasis on reward and recognition for effort and progress, not results, rather than punishment and blame, to bring about desired changes in behaviour, feelings and attitudes. Activity and task reviews are conducted in a positive, friendly, non-recriminatory and democratic way to build self-esteem.
- Psychoanalytical re-enactment
  Review of what was done and what (if anything) went wrong in projects and physical activities, with facilitation but minimal interference from the tutor, who primarily asks open questions of the team. This is a process of self-discovery.
- Acquisition of social skills
  Focuses mainly on trust and honesty and uses a questionnaire-based tool called *Spectrum* that assesses the degree of control versus nurturing. The rationale is that self-esteem leads to honesty, and honesty leads to trust. In addition, in developing social skills, humour is used liberally. Humour is a way of managing our emotions.[156] Adrian Furnham says:

  [Humour] can generate a sense of group solidarity and belongingness ... and help individuals cope with threatening experiences ... [it is] an excellent defence mechanism and a means of coping with difficulties ... it makes things funny and therefore tolerable. For many, it can be a coping strategy.[157]

  Humour thus discharges hostility to negative feedback in building self-awareness and consequently self-esteem.

- Group dynamics theory
  Teams are formed of up to nine members, each with its own identity, facilities and resources. They work and eat together, and they compete with one another. Team members develop cohesiveness through mutual helping, protection, support and friendships.

The outcome is increased self-awareness, followed in turn by increased self-control, self-confidence and self-realization as a leader.[158] The Leadership Trust's leadership self-development model that underpins this process is shown in Figure 11.2.

Self-awareness develops through examining how one reacts to situations and why one does so in those ways. Self-control is thereby enabled. Self-confidence results from knowing that one has the mechanisms for coping with situations. Self-realization occurs when one maximizes one's strengths, controls one's weaknesses, and stands up for one's values. The ultimate consequence is self-respect.

(Continued)

(Continued)

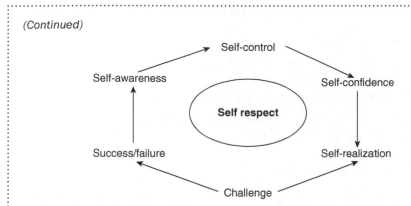

Figure 11.2 The Leadership Trust's Leadership Self-development Model (reproduced with kind permission)

The results that the Leadership Trust has achieved through this process are remarkable, according to the feedback received.[159] Norman Dixon in an evaluation of this approach reports that:

> Unless I've been duped by an astonishing illusion ... [the programme is] ... one of the best applications of sound psychological principles I [have] ever witnessed. Where else could one find sleek business-men, past their prime, emerging all the better from a course of treatment that threatens, but never quite succeeds in, the breakage of every bone in one's body, the permanent wrecking of one's reproductive capabilities and the destroying of every illusion one might have about being a tough, virile, macho jungle fighter with a tank-like ego? If there are such places, I know them not.[160]

Leadership Development Strategy

The Center for Creative Leadership in the United States reports in a 2009 White Paper that very few organizations have an explicit leadership strategy.[161] 'Is it any wonder,' CCL muses, 'that without one CEOs find that they don't have the leadership talent they require? Part of a leadership strategy is a *leadership development* strategy.'[162] A leadership development strategy should cover the assessment and development of leaders in line with the vision, mission, values and business strategies of the organization.

Having addressed the psychological barriers to effective leadership and leadership development and how they can be overcome by enhancing emotional intelligence, let us now consider how leadership development must also address these other aspects of effective leadership.

Newly appointed executives and managers in leadership positions need to be socialized into the corporate culture and the leadership culture in the organization. In addition to 'socialization' this is also known as 'induction' or, more recently, 'on-boarding'. Two further aspects of leadership development, prior to the many and varied activities that constitute leadership development programmes, are individual, team and organizational assessments and development plans that are based on them.

Leadership development action has two key requirements:

1. Accurate, predictive information about:
    - ※ who has potential to succeed in leadership roles
    - ※ how to develop leaders efficiently
    - ※ where to deploy these leaders when they are ready.
2. Commitment to and accountability for leadership development (a) at the organization level and (b) by the individual leader.[163]

Ed Kur and Richard Bunning say that:

> **Most leadership development programmes focus only on a part of leadership. For example, executive programmes often deal with strategic and/or visionary aspects of leadership, what we call 'macro-leadership', without addressing the skills associated with leading individuals or small groups. Other programmes ... focus on leading teams but fail to address leadership of individuals or of total organizations. Still others, especially those for first-line supervisors and technical leaders, emphasize one-to-one or microleadership.[164]**

The *Leadership Development: Best Practice Guide for Organizations* promotes three strategic principles for leadership development:

1. Leadership development must be driven from the top: if the CEO is not intimately involved and committed to it, it is not worth starting.
2. Leadership development supports and drives the business: if it is not core to an organization's strategy, it will not happen.
3. A leadership model must be culturally attuned: it must reflect the culture of the organization.[165]

Fast-track leadership development programmes for high-potential candidates for senior and top leadership positions may lead to disaffection and alienation among other employees who would also benefit from leadership development, suggests Paul Daley.[166] Fast-track programmes reflect over-investment in a few individuals to the detriment of the organization as a whole, says Arvinder Dhesi of the financial services and insurance group, Aviva.[167] They reflect an emphasis on the increasingly outdated 'heroic' model of leadership, where leadership is invested in only one or a few leaders.

Leadership development consultancy, Leadaculture, suggests several strategic areas that a comprehensive leadership development strategy should address:[168]

1. Strategic vision and purpose.[169]
2. Strategy.[170]
3. Top-level sponsorship.
4. A supportive organizational structure, culture and processes.
5. Thorough planning.
6. Clear leadership roles.
7. Aligned personal objectives.

8. Selection/assignment.
9. Ongoing training and development.
10. Evaluation.

Underlying any effective leadership development strategy are criteria for success in target positions and a performance management process. Byham and Byham recommend five practices in such a strategy:

1. Help participants to understand and accept their leadership strengths and weaknesses. This information typically comes from 360° (multi-rater) assessment and feedback, assessment centres, behaviour-based interviews, and personality questionnaires.
2. Make sure that participants' leadership development objectives are related to enhancing current job performance as well as equipping them for more challenging roles so that their managers are more likely to support the process.
3. Choose the most relevant leadership development activities, reflecting individual participants' learning styles – for example, experimenting, reflecting, thinking or doing – emphasizing learning from experience on the job but including opportunities to learn from others and formal training sessions.
4. Make sure that participants, in consultation with their managers, complete a development analysis and planning form (see an example at the end of this chapter).
5. Make sure that participants are set measurable development goals and their progress is monitored and reviewed.

Ron Cacioppe's useful comprehensive model for designing leadership development proposes seven stages:

1. Articulate strategic issues, objectives and competencies.
2. Set the objectives for development.
3. Identify appropriate methods.
4. Select providers and design the specific learning programme.
5. Evaluate programme delivery and effectiveness.
6. Integrate the leadership development programme with management and human resource systems.
7. Assess the overall value of the programme, broad objectives and programme philosophy.[171]

The key assumption underpinning much leadership development practice is that there exists a 'one best way' of training and developing leaders.[172] This assumption reflects the attention given by leadership researchers, including myself, to seeking a single model of leadership that has a universal application across all cultures and contexts.[173]

It is likely, however, that contextual factors – political, economic, social, technological, environmental/ecological and legal – do influence both concepts of leadership and leadership development practices. For example, Lyman Porter and Grace McLaughlin identified seven specific contextual factors that influenced leadership behaviour:

* An organization's culture and climate.
* The goals and purpose of the organization.
* The characteristics of people in the organization.
* Types of organizational processes.
* Organizational structure.
* Time effects such as organizational life cycle and the duration of leadership effects.
* The current state of the organization, for example crisis or stability.[174]

Nicholas Clarke and colleagues conducted interviews at leadership development providers in 10 sectors in the UK: the police service, healthcare, social care, local government, higher education, the third (voluntary) sector, the Anglican Church ministry, risk management/safety, telecommunications and cultural industries.[175] Their findings revealed variations among them in how they conceptualized leadership – for example, transformational/transactional, heroic (leader-centric) and servant leadership – and how the practices they used in their leadership development programmes reflected this. They found that these practices varied across the 10 different business sectors along eight dimensions that related to differences in strategy, products and the concepts of leadership. As a result of their important work, Clarke and colleagues advocated a contingency approach to designing leadership development programmes.

It is an exciting possibility that one day we will have both a universal, generic model of leadership within which there is an agreed definition of what leadership is as well as identified contingencies that, among other benefits, will enable leadership development programmes to be tailored to needs in precise and accurate ways. Indeed the possibility that one can construct an over-arching model of leadership within which there are contingencies and variations is the assumption in this book. One may perhaps see a parallel here with the relationship between general intelligence (known by psychologists as 'g') and specific intelligences that constitute models of multiple intelligences such as the one this book describes.

Designing Leadership Development Programmes

General Requirements for Leadership Development Programmes

Leadership development must also focus on environmental and organizational contexts. A conceptual framework that relates the use of power and influence to contextual conditions is necessary to understand the connections between action and context in terms of the range of discretion and the feasibility of action options.[176] Michael Porter's work on the economic and competitive characteristics of firms and nations[177] is also helpful, as is an understanding of decision making in organizations.[178]

Basic and applied research can and should inform practice. But whether leadership research is useful to leadership development, Chester Schriesheim argues, is dubious. He says that the 'misfit between the complexity of research and the limited ability of managers to use complex information on a daily basis' is a fundamental problem and that leadership development should focus on methods of skill-based training, building confidence, and replacing habitual behaviours with a broader repertoire of responses.[179] Thomas Lenz says:

> ... leadership is assumed to be largely comprised of learned behaviors – some proportion of these involve higher-order cognitive abilities, while others involve interpersonal and other related types of skills (e.g. verbal and written communication).[180]

Roya Ayman argues that a comprehensive leadership development programme has the following learning opportunities that reflect a variety of individuals' learning styles:

⚹ Cognitive learning – information and knowledge about leadership.
⚹ Insight through diverse experiences – reading case studies.
⚹ Opportunity for self-reflection and increasing self-awareness through personal feedback.
⚹ Real leadership experiences through the practical opportunity to lead.[181]

These characteristics, he suggests, reflect the Kolb learning cycle:[182]

⚹ Concrete experience (CE).
⚹ Reflective observation (RO).
⚹ Abstract conceptualization (AC).
⚹ Active experimentation (AE).

The associated learning styles are:

⚹ Accommodating (CE/AE – 'doing and feeling').
⚹ Converging (AC/AE – 'doing and thinking').
⚹ Assimilating (AC/RO – 'watching and thinking').
⚹ Diverging (CE/RO – 'feeling and watching').

Peter Honey and Alan Mumford's very similar model of learning styles, with more immediately meaningful terms, is:

⚹ Activist (= accommodating).
⚹ Reflector (= diverging).
⚹ Theorist (= assimilating).
⚹ Pragmatist (= converging).[183]

Lenz maintains: 'An overarching conception of leadership may provide a conceptual framework for relating [leadership skills] subject matter taught rather than independently in a variety of courses and training experiences.'[184] The model of six core themes and practices proposed in this book provides such a conceptual framework.

The Need for Feedback and Self-awareness in Leadership Development

Essential to any performance improvement and development process are feedback and follow-up. Peter Drucker says 'a person can perform only from strength. One cannot build performance on weaknesses' and that discovering one's strengths requires feedback analysis.[185] Drucker kept a record of his decisions and actions and what he expected would happen, and after some nine to twelve months he compared the results against his expectations. This approach was very revealing. It was nothing new, having previously been used by John Calvin and Ignatius Loyola, who founded the dominant Calvinist Church and the Jesuit order respectively. This approach, Drucker says, enables one to concentrate on using strengths and on improving them as well as discovering one's intellectual arrogance.

Feedback analysis also gives information on how one performs. For example, people are either readers or listeners. Not knowing which of the two one is can greatly reduce effectiveness, as it did, Drucker says, for former US presidents Dwight D. Eisenhower and Lyndon B. Johnson. Another example is learning style, which I mentioned earlier. He quotes Churchill as doing badly at school because there was only one way of learning, which did not suit him: by listening and reading, rather than by writing – his preferred way. Drucker also quotes a chief executive who learns by talking to his senior group for two or three hours. Other aspects of how one performs best concern oneself in relation to other people – some people learn best alone, others in groups; some as subordinates; some as advisers rather than decision makers; some under stress.

Henry Wadsworth Longfellow, the American poet, said: 'We judge ourselves by what we feel capable of doing, while others judge us by what we have done already.'[186] The importance of self-awareness as part of emotional intelligence in leadership was discussed in Chapter 10. A major contribution to enhancing self-awareness as a basis for personal development as an effective leader has come from 360° feedback.[187]

In 360° feedback, a profile of the manager's leadership behaviour in terms of strengths and development needs is synthesized from feedback from the manager's boss, peers and subordinates as well as from him- or herself. The rationale for this approach is that managers' bosses, who traditionally are the sole source of information about managers' leadership development needs, mostly see only 'upward' leadership behaviour by them, whereas leadership behaviour is exercised with peers, subordinates and clients or customers. As Beverly Alimo-Metcalfe points out

Aspects of a manager's behaviour that are deemed to be important by a boss are very different from those regarded as important by subordinates. Bosses tend to focus on technical managerial skills, such as decision making and problem solving. Subordinates are more concerned with interpersonal skills, sensitivity, empowerment and visionary leadership.[188]

It can be argued that neither a complete picture of leadership development needs nor a personal development action plan can be gained without comprehensive feedback. However, a study of organizational leaders participating in a transformational leadership development programme and their subordinates found that training and feedback each had a positive effect on the participants' transformational leadership behaviour, though incorporating both did not enhance it.[189] This suggests that training and feedback may be interchangeable approaches to leadership development. On the other hand, there is good evidence that effective leaders have a more realistic self-image than less effective leaders.[190] Upward feedback can result in a sustained change over a long time.[191] However, upward feedback may be limited to the extent to which a manager or leader meets subordinates' needs and therefore might fail to account for actual performance or achievement as a whole.[192]

While there is strong evidence for the value of 360° feedback in leadership development, factors other than the process and its content also make a difference, for example the organization's culture – its development orientation and the involvement of the leader's own team in the feedback process.[193]

The use of 360° feedback in leadership development has produced positive results, for example in the Royal Bank of Canada, where it has helped managers to become less focused on 'oppositional' power behaviour and instead to use more effective humanistic, coaching and achievement-oriented leadership styles.[194] The leadership development programme for a manufacturing company in the UK, run by the Leadership Trust and employing 360° feedback, 'revolutionised' the culture of the organization in breaking down communication barriers, according to Morice Mendoza.[195]

But not all authorities are believers in 360° feedback. For example, Edgar Schein says it is 'inappropriate'.[196] Managers may be 'too fragile' to accept negative feedback from their subordinates, and in this case managers may benefit more from 'real-time' objections during meetings and discussions based on their subordinates' 'reading' of them.

The Need for a Transfer of Learning in Leadership Development

The failures in applying what has been learned – in what psychologists call the transfer of learning – characterize all 'training', including leadership development. The requirements for effective transfer of learning are well known. Follow-up of training is necessary – on what has been learned, what has been applied, the difficulties in applying what has been learned, the lack of inclination to apply it, and the further help that is needed.

This follow-up can take many forms: checks on whether participants are working on their application objectives, feedback instruments to measure behavioural change and measures of the impact on the group and the organization.[197] These methods can motivate participants to focus on the application of learning, enhance the development process through the additional feedback, validate the process by identifying the specific impacts of the process, and gain the support of participants' managers, a key influence in transfer of learning.

Failing to apply what has been learned can also be due to the intrinsic nature of the leadership 'training' that most organizations carry out and also to the organization's structure, culture and rigid processes which do not allow people to be 'leaders', according to Hilarie Owen.[198] Her central thesis is that organizations in their present state do not encourage people to find their leadership potential or use it. She explains how organizations can transform themselves to become places where the potential of existing leaders and would-be leaders can be expressed – where leadership can be 'unleashed'.

Leadership Development Activities and Processes

Case studies. Case studies are detailed investigations of an individual, group or organization that contain background, contextual and historical information and the detail on one or more aspects of leadership. Case studies require participants to make sense of complex problems or situations using appropriate theories, identify the implications, and make recommendations for action or answer specific questions about leadership in the case study.

Film has a part to play in leadership development as a kind of enhanced case study, although, as Margie Nicholson of the International Leadership Association says, few film-makers set out to create films specifically about leadership.[199] In three particularly suitable films that she analyses – *The September Issue, Rock the Bells* and *The Hobart Shakespeareans* – she extracts three leadership themes: leaders setting high goals, leaders taking risks and making difficult decisions, and leaders facing personal attacks and challenges. Francis Beckett describes how London Business School has used the 1957 Henry Fonda film *Twelve Angry Men*, about a jury in a murder case, to discuss how to use influence rather than authority and create a 'boardroom presence'.[200] And the University of Bradford School of Management used the 1949 Gregory Peck film *Twelve O'Clock High*, in which a US bomber leader is replaced for being too accommodating to his men and his successor has them carrying out dangerous missions and soon finds out how much he cares about them.

Case studies, according to Henry Mintzberg and Joseph Lampel, are often seen as artificial ways of learning management, especially leadership.[201] They can only teach *about* management or leadership, and 'taught' courses, especially on leadership, also tend to receive a very critical press. For example, John Rink says:

> I've just been on a six-week leadership course at Harvard. It raised my awareness about things that I had not thought of. But the problem is it didn't give me [as managing partner] the soft skills that are crucial in managing this place [Allen & Overy].[202]

Skill practice through role play. Role play in leadership development also meets with mixed responses. In the absence of other feedback, it allows a manager to display leadership skills and to learn how to improve them. However, John Hunt argues:

> Unfortunately, the fact that these role-plays [occur] in front of other participants in a ferociously well lit CCTV studio [can] be inhibiting. For that minority of senior executives who are extraverts, this challenge to their thespian leanings can produce Oscar-winning performances. As luck has it, most senior executives are introverts. Role-playing [terrifies] them ... As for stimulating post-course development, it often [has] the opposite effect.[203]

Hunt believes that 360° feedback has reduced much of this anxiety, especially where role play requires participants to play themselves and not to act. And when combined with 360° feedback, he says, role plays can produce dramatic improvements.

E-learning. E-learning, or the use of web-based learning, can make a contribution to leadership development:

... as long as the technology builds on the established principles of adult learning: learn by doing; learn from others; learn ideas that are relevant and practical; learn from experimentation and reflection; and learn over time, not in one event.[204]

Mentoring. Coaching and mentoring are examples of leadership one-to-one. 'Mentor' comes from Greek mythology and refers to one who inspires and helps a person in resolving difficulties and in personal development. The usefulness of mentoring – and a dismissal of role playing as a leadership development practice – is evident in the following remark by a company chairman:

> Having the opportunity to have a risk-free conversation with a trusted third party has been enormously helpful. You can bring out your doubts and anxieties without seeming to look weak or silly ... the mentors I had helped me to be 'me'. That has helped because I am my own worst critic and I am also terrible at role playing, which still passes for leadership development in many organisations. In this age of sound-bite leadership, it is important to harbour self-doubts and discuss them ... leaders must never take themselves too seriously.[205]

Leadership projects and assignments. Leadership projects are gaining popularity as part of leadership development. Participants carry out a project focused on applying leadership theory and practice, individually or in teams, which is expected to deliver measurable business results for the organization. For example, Vodafone's 'Global Leadership Model',[206] aimed at leadership development for its most senior positions, comprises several elements, including a succession of assignments and projects:

* One-year experiences in a 'senior assignment position' in the 'home' function in the home country, in the home function in another country, in another function in the home country, and in general management.
* Business improvement projects.
* Participation in an MBA programme.
* Individual tailored experiences.
* Sponsorship and mentoring by a board member and country and functional mentors.
* Employee communication through presentations, team briefings, e-mail, intranet sites, focus groups, conferences and an International Employee Communications Forum.

The use of the arts in leadership development. In addition to film (which we discussed in the section on case studies), the arts – music, poetry, literature and theatre – have been used increasingly in leadership development in recent years.

Music played a part in the Henley and London Business School courses, where Ben Zander, conductor of the Boston Symphony Orchestra, talked about a conductor's contribution to the orchestra. Poetry is also used in leadership development. The poet David Whyte, who also worked as a management consultant, uses poetry in his 'creative leadership' development programmes to inspire participants to inspire their people.[207] He used parts of the Anglo-Saxon epic *Beowulf* as a powerful metaphor to initiate the change process at Boeing. He also uses the poem *Tramps* by Robert Frost to stimulate reflection among the consultants he advises on the leader as communicator and motivator.

At the new Globe theatre in Southwark, London, Richard Olivier has led the trend in applying theatre in leadership development by using the learning process he calls *mythodrama* in partnership with Cranfield School of Management. Mythodrama combines theatre techniques with mythology, psychology and the techniques of organizational development.[208] For example, in leadership development programmes for business leaders, he asks participants to bring a short poem, play or speech that they have found to be inspirational.[209] The common theme that emerges in whether the audience is inspired is the use of imagery and how much speakers themselves are inspired. Mythodrama entails imagining and invoking characters that participants want to play – behaviours they want to display – and 'acting them in', a form of role-playing. Olivier says that using these images opens up previously unimagined possibilities. It is 'literally "rehearsing" new ways of being'. Rehearsal – involving experimentation – is essential, he says, just as footballers and actors will warm up before a performance.

Another technique Olivier uses is to examine the leadership behaviour of Shakespeare's King Henry V in inspiring an undisciplined mob to follow him into battle against the French.[210] Key learning points are Henry's mission – to gain the territory he covets and how he overcomes his setbacks through his inspirational language. Role-playing is used, as in conventional management and leadership development programmes, but utilizing Shakespeare brings imagination and creativity to the learning process – it adds the essential emotional aspect to the process and helps develop emotional intelligence. Olivier compares Henry V's journey from his misspent youth to the battlefield of Agincourt and beyond with the challenges faced by all leaders. He uses Jungian psychology to explore the 'roles and characters we can inhabit as leaders at work' and how Henry exemplifies effective leaders adapting their behaviour to changing situations.

Olivier also uses *Julius Caesar* to illustrate emotional and political intelligence in leadership, showing how Caesar lacked insight into people's motives. And *The Winter's Tale* enables participants to explore change and regeneration in organizational life. Robert Nurden describes how this helped a director with NatWest 'move from seeing business solutions in terms of black and white to one with shades of grey'.[211] Shakespeare undoubtedly was an unwittingly insightful writer about leadership.

Unsurprisingly, opinion about using theatre in leadership development, however, is mixed. Francis Beckett quotes David Norburn of Imperial College Management School in London, for example, as strongly against it on the ground that business schools need to provide rigorous and relevant training.[212] However, Beckett also quotes Robert Owen of the Association of MBAs (AMBA)[213] as supporting the use of theatre but only for teaching presentation skills and Patricia Hodgins of the London Business School as saying that 'the heart of creativity is about intuition … Using arts, music and theatre helps us to find that.' Richard Olivier believes that arts-based leadership development, a rapid growth area in the late 1990s, can help people to be more creative, flexible and adaptable – perhaps the greatest challenge of the twenty-first century.[214]

Dialogue with leaders as teachers. Many organizations fail to appreciate their intrinsic leadership development resources: their own leaders. Many great leaders are great teachers, for example Jesus Christ, Mahatma Gandhi and Martin Luther King Jr, who transformed their followers into leaders themselves.[215] Management consultant Stephen Yearout says: 'Today's leaders need to be adept at making decision makers, not making decisions.'[216] An example of empowerment through teaching is the approach of Kevin Newman, who set up the very successful First Direct, the telephone banking company, ranked in *The Sunday Times* 2002 survey of the 100 best UK companies to work for.[217] When asked about how he took important decisions, Newman said:

I avoid taking decisions as much as possible. As chief executive, my job is to teach other people how to make the decisions.[218]

The idea of the leader as teacher has gained much popularity. Carole Barnett and Noel Tichy believe that top leaders need to take personal responsibility for developing other leaders in the organization and to energize them to be teachers.[219] In fact this is one of the most important tasks facing a leader.[220] CEOs identify having a manager as a role model early in their career as a major contribution to their development as a leader.[221] And successful organizations – such as General Electric, Hewlett-Packard, the US Navy Seals and Intel – have used their leaders to develop their leaders by sharing their experience in creative and 'teachable' ways.[222] This extends to the participation in leadership development programmes of CEOs themselves as 'Leader-teachers' who are credible and in companies like GE, PepsiCo and Shell.[223] The key prerequisites for an effective dialogue with leaders as teachers are:

* Using respected individuals who can articulate their own views well and facilitate a group discussion.
* Using a learning environment that fits the leader-teacher's own style and personality.
* Using clarity and organizing what is to be imparted.[224]

The University of Chicago Graduate School of Business has a programme for leaders that recognizes the importance of the leader-teacher in building collaborative enterprises where information is co-created and shared.[225] Using senior and chief executives as leader-teachers has several benefits to themselves, their organizations and those participating in leadership development programmes: it reinforces new ideas and directions, the thinking behind them and the behaviours required; it enables them to test the reality of their ideas; and it provides frameworks for decisions by managers.[226]

Learning methods in leadership development are many and varied. In addition to those we have briefly discussed, these include 'action learning',[227] the martial arts[228] and transcendental meditation.[229]

The Effectiveness of Leadership Development Programmes

There are many examples of leadership development programmes with positive validated or well-documented results. For example, Bass and Avolio's Full Range Leadership programme focuses on developing transformational leadership, for which many positive results have been reported.[230] And a small-scale study by Julian Barling and colleagues showed that training in transformational leadership in a Canadian bank had a positive impact on subordinates' perceptions of leaders' leadership behaviour, particularly individualized consideration, intellectual stimulation and charisma, subordinates' own organizational commitment, and the financial performance of branches.[231] Other studies have shown that leadership development can also have a positive impact on firm performance as measured by financial and market outcomes.[232]

Ed Kur and Richard Bunning's leadership development process in Pilkington Glass, British Aerospace, Greenall Whitley, SmithKline Beecham (now GlaxoSmithKline) and Motorola yielded, among other outcomes, cost savings and revenue improvements, a successful project implementation and enhanced project leadership competence and credibility in the participants.[233] And a report on the DfEE Leadership Development Programme for Serving Headteachers produced significant improvements in both organizational climate and pupils' performance.[234]

An Institute of Management survey on leadership in the UK revealed a correlation between effective leadership development in organizations and perceptions of the quality of leadership in them. Fifty-seven per cent rated the quality of leadership highly in organizations that develop leadership potential effectively, consistently and fairly compared with 21 per cent in other organizations.[235] Favoured leadership development methods comprise *in situ* activities focused on working relationships, formal mentoring, action learning, and 360° feedback. Traditional classroom-based programmes have little sustained impact on leadership development.[236] Sabine Hotho and Martin Dowling say that context and participant differences impact on the effectiveness of leadership development programmes, which may often be too didactic, emphasizing input over interaction.[237]

Research by DDI found a strong relationship between the perceived quality of leadership development programmes and the financial measures of revenue growth, profitability and market share as well as non-financial measures such as customer satisfaction, retention and employee engagement.[238] Other research by DDI found that leadership development delivered positive changes valued at US$500,000 to $1 million.

The classic study supporting the effectiveness of management training and leadership development programmes is that of Michael Burke and Russell Day in which they carried out a meta-analysis of 70 studies between 1951 and 1982.[239] Doris Collins and Elwood Holton carried out another meta-analysis of 83 studies of the effectiveness of leadership development programmes between 1982 and 2001. They found clear evidence of the effectiveness of such programmes in terms of leadership knowledge and skill provided that a prior analysis was conducted to ensure that the appropriate development was offered to the appropriate persons.[240] The survey by the Manufacturing Foundation and The Leadership Trust Foundation found that leadership development was believed to impact strongly in both 'hard' respects – productivity, quality, delivery performance and reduced overhead costs – and 'soft' respects, for example staff motivation and morale.[241]

Research studies show beyond doubt that *managers can learn to lead* through training.[242] But, like leadership itself, leadership development is a *process*, not an event. It takes place in a variety of situations, including job assignments, relationships, experiencing hardship, and other activities unrelated to work.[243] Leadership development, however, depends for its success on the readiness for development of both the individual *and* the organization. Without such readiness, the effectiveness of leadership development is seriously at risk. Such readiness therefore has to be diagnosed prior to designing or launching any leadership development programme. Of course, the lack of such readiness may itself be the focus of leadership development.

William Gentry and Jennifer Martineau of the Center for Creative Leadership in the United States suggest using hierarchical linear modelling as a multi-level method to assess change in leadership behaviour over time during a leadership development programme.[244] But Collins and Holton recommend that organizations should evaluate the return on their investment in leadership development.[245] Bruce Avolio and colleagues describe how to estimate this.[246] Using various guiding assumptions, scenarios, periods of intervention and levels of management participating in the leadership development programme, they found the return on investment in leadership development to range from a low negative value to over 200 per cent. There is no doubt that leadership development programmes in organizations are most effective when linked with their strategies and long-term scenario planning, according to Lawrena Colombo and John Verderese at PricewaterhouseCoopers.[247]

Can leadership be taught? The conclusion is 'yes', but only at the intellectual or cognitive level. *Knowing* what to do and how to do it is necessary but not sufficient. *Wanting to do it* entails 'it' making sense both cognitively and spiritually, and there are considerable emotional factors involved too. And *doing it* – using the cognitive and behavioural skills of leadership – can be learned only by actually doing it – with feedback, application and practice. We can *'learn'* leadership.

CASE STUDY: LEADERSHIP DEVELOPMENT IN THE GULF REGION[248]

A leadership development consultancy assignment was carried out for a government-owned oil company, Gulf State Oil (GSO), in the Gulf region. The lead consultant (Robert), a part-time academic and leadership development consultant based in the UK, was assisted and supported by a locally-based consultant (John), who was director of consultancy for the locally-owned Center for Management Consultancy (CMC), which provided management consultancy services in the same country. John, an Irish citizen, who until a few months previously had lived in Australia for thirty-five years, was to be the manager and coordinator of the assignment. CMC had won a tender for this assignment and several other associated assignments but felt it lacked the necessary expertise for this one.

Robert was approached through a third-party recommendation. The initial briefing of him by CMC by telephone and e-mail stated that the assignment was to be the development and delivery of a leadership development programme for up to 150 managers in GSO. A brief needs analysis had already been carried out by John and a British lecturer at a local college, Stephen, involving interviews with a few key executives, and this was provided to Robert. The key findings were as follows:

(Continued)

(Continued)

- A lack of clarity for responsibilities and goals.
- A 'silo mentality'.
- Reluctance by managers to take decisions, deferring to senior managers or doing nothing.
- A lack of accountability across all departments.
- A lack of leadership and supervisory skills.
- Poor teamwork.
- Poor communication skills.
- A culture of blame in some departments.

GSO decided to address leadership and accountability – aiming to 'foster a climate of accountability within the organization', with a two-day workshop to be developed and 'pre-piloted' within a month, a 'pilot workshop' run within two months, and then full roll-out with two workshops per month over the next 8–10 months. GSO envisaged a format including case examples, movie clips and a 'toolkit' – a managers' manual supplementing the workshop material and presentations.

Robert agreed, after negotiations with CMC by telephone and e-mail, to take on the assignment on this basis and travelled to the Gulf five days later for a two-day meeting with John and his colleagues (including Stephen) at CMC to plan and start the development phase. The pre-pilot workshop with senior managers was scheduled for five weeks later.

Another CMC consultant, Abdul, a local national, sourced culturally useful material for the workshop on leadership and accountability. However, shortly afterwards he was transferred by CMC to another pressing assignment. And at the same time, while Stephen was scheduled to shadow Robert and support John as a facilitator in the leadership workshops, he was dropped, at the request of GSO, because he was regarded as 'too didactic'.

The key contact in GSO was Chandra, Senior Training & Development Manager, who had been liaising with John. He suggested using lessons from Shackleton's expedition to the Antarctic in 1915. John and Robert acquired some books about Shackleton as an effective leader. Chandra also suggested some useful books relating to accountability. As a result of the planning session, Robert drew up a brief on who was going provide what, decisions and actions needing to be taken and by whom, and a basic structure, content and methodology for the workshop.

Chandra continued to contribute ideas and suggestions but he was starting to express some impatience and strong preferences, even directives. A great deal of potential material was located and reviewed. Under pressure to produce the toolkit, Robert and John informed Chandra that it could not be produced until the content of the workshop was finalized. This phase produced material for the pre-pilot workshop comprising presentation slides, a performance and accountability culture assessment questionnaire and scoring system, case studies, group exercises, and an action planning process (see Appendix 1 for the workshop outline).

In the pre-pilot workshop, however, several cases and exercises were not carried out as intended but instead were discussed by the participants and workshop leaders for their suitability. Attendance was much smaller than expected, which was a common phenomenon in the company according to Chandra. Feedback from the pre-pilot workshop participants was reviewed and Robert and John made improvements for the pilot workshop planned for the following month.

(Continued)

(Continued)

By this time John and Robert were feeling that the emphasis for the workshop was shifting exclusively to accountability. Meanwhile a script (from a local corporate movie producer) for a proposed GSO company movie was reviewed and John and Robert made some minor suggestions. The movie was altered after feedback from GSO to the movie producer. However, at the last minute the film was pulled on the instruction of the CEO, who was unhappy with it and had asked for it to be re-made. Two role-play exercises were developed, together with (pre-existing) related filmed behaviour models made by Robert, for agreeing accountabilities and performance expectations and for confronting performance problems. Chandra requested material for review as quickly as possible.

Chandra also made several more suggestions by e-mail that Robert and John felt were unsuitable, including one for including performance and career review and another for a new workshop outline. However, one suggestion, the use of RAMs (responsibility assignment matrices – borrowed from project management methodology), was included. A few days before the pilot workshop Chandra requested the use of non-standard, localized clip-art and a new PowerPoint template, all of which Robert and John had to incorporate hurriedly.

At about the same time, Chandra's manager, Bader, Head of Education, Training & Development, e-mailed him, John and Robert to express unhappiness about progress and instructing them to 'kindly expedite the outstanding issues'. John and Robert now sought approval or suggestions from Chandra concerning the programme content, tools and techniques (including the role-play exercises) and duly incorporated these following his approval. The pilot workshop was held as planned but, as for the pre-pilot, attendance was much smaller than expected.

Immediately after the pilot workshop, John and Robert carried out a review and planned what needed to be done. Chandra e-mailed to say that 'some progress' had been made but 'we have not yet developed the full confidence to go ahead with the first [roll-out] workshop' and that the workshop so far was 'entirely based on telling rather than facilitating'. He also requested a 'more professional' DVD to be sourced and used.

Development work continued, taking Chandra's input into account, but now proceeded more slowly owing to Robert's prior work commitments in the UK. Then suddenly, on a Thursday, Chandra e-mailed Robert in the UK asking for the workshop outline, timetable and materials to meet a request by the CEO for a briefing by himself and Bader three days later – on the following Sunday. Neither Robert nor John could comply in the time available.

Work now started on producing the toolkit and a draft was submitted. Chandra insisted on editing the draft, but errors and poor presentation resulted. Chandra informed John and Robert that the CEO had decided to abandon using the company movie and that he would introduce the workshops in person.

Robert had received no feedback from GSO by nine days before the scheduled date of the first roll-out workshop so he requested it from John. He received this the next day, with full approval of the toolkit and workshop material and methodology. However, just before the workshop Chandra e-mailed John, with copies to Robert and his (Chandra's) manager, Bader, saying: 'Gentle reminder. Since the coming workshop will be attended by some senior managers in [the company], let us ensure that the agreements from the pre-pilot are applied with care. The attached notes [from Robert and John to Chandra] may serve as a good reminder for all of us to take care.' A further

(Continued)

(Continued)

e-mail from Chandra said: 'We also need to remind Robert that lecture sessions should not be more than 20 per cent of the workshop ...' Chandra also requested that no copies of the PowerPoint presentation slides – only the (draft) toolkit – be distributed to participants.

Development work and costs were now well beyond what had been anticipated. Robert suggested to John that savings could be made by having a local consultant carry out the training workshops that were to be rolled out. In fact he was not relishing the prospect of the roll-out being led by himself. CMC shelved this idea at this point.

The first two roll-out workshops were then held (see Appendix 2 for the workshop outline). The CEO did not attend either workshop owing to 'unavailability'; instead, Bader introduced them. In the first workshop Robert showed only one filmed behaviour model (demonstrating how to confront performance problems), which was to be used as a prelude to the role-play exercise but which on the day was abandoned. In the second workshop the toolkit was distributed and the second filmed behaviour model was replaced by a live role play performed by John and Robert. This was well received by the participants.

Ratings by participants in the first roll-out workshop on a 1 (low) to 5 (high) scale were all in the 4.0–4.8 range, with facilitation and support averaging 4.4 and quality and level of interaction, 4.5. The second roll-out workshop was also a success despite the now customary low turnout. A full roll-out now appeared to be appropriate and planning for this started. It was interesting to observe that participants generally much preferred a discussion of issues and ideas to skill practice and coaching. A month after the second roll-out workshop it was agreed that Robert would not continue to lead the workshops, which would be conducted by a local consultant who had still to be sourced.

Outlines for the pre-pilot workshop and the second roll-out workshop (at Appendixes 1 and 2) show how the programme developed from the pre-pilot workshop to the roll-out workshop as a result of feedback, the consultation process and development work.

Appendix 1 – Pre-Pilot Workshop Programme

Purpose of the Workshop

To enhance overall leadership effectiveness and accountability in GSO by addressing:

- What is 'performance excellence'?
- Management versus leadership: what are they?
- The challenges and responsibilities of participants' management and leadership roles.
- GSO's core values: reality or aspiration?
- Communication, cooperation and collaboration across the organization.
- The meaning and realities of accountability.
- Empowerment as managers and leaders.
- Leadership and learning from mistakes and failure.
- Performance excellence through accountability and leadership.

(Continued)

(Continued)

Objectives of the Workshop

At the end of the workshop, participants will ...

- Understand and accept their roles and responsibilities as managers and leaders.
- Have the knowledge and motivation – even inspiration – to develop themselves in these roles.
- Understand and embrace the ways in which they are accountable.
- Understand how failure and mistakes in a learning culture free of blame can lead to success.
- Be willing and able to operate as team players and serve the interests of the organization as a whole.
- Share the values that inform the vision, direction and purpose of the organization.
- Have the ability and desire to develop, empower and inspire their staff.

Methodology

- Interactive presentations.
- Case studies, examples and incidents (oil-industry related as far as possible).
- Small-group work in groups of five or six people.
- Small-group exercises/discussions and reports.
- Movie clips of role models and scenarios.
- Practical toolkit (prescriptions, guides on questions to ask and areas to consider, 'dos and don'ts', checklists, etc.) to be developed after the pre-pilot workshop based on feedback.

Timetable

Day one

07:00   * Introduction: what is 'performance excellence'?
        * Workshop objectives.
        * DVD presentation and commentary: leadership lessons from Shackleton.
        * Small group exercise and reports on a performance excellence scenario.
08:30   Break.
09:00   * Presentation on management versus leadership.
10:30   Break.
11:00   * Presentation on corporate culture and GSO's values: reality or aspiration?
        * Small group exercise, reports and review.
        * Examples of dilemmas and challenges in GSO.
12:30   Prayer break.
13:00   * Communicating and working together: small group exercise, reports and review on encouraging communication, cooperation and collaboration across the organization.
14:30   Lunch and end of Day One.

(Continued)

(Continued)

Day two

07:00   * Presentation on the meaning and realities of accountability.
        * Small group exercise, reports and review on a mini-case.
08:30   Break.
09:00   * Presentation on empowerment, risk and trust.
        * Small group exercise, reports and review: empowering people.
10:30   Break.
11:00   * Presentation on leadership and values (learning from failure).
        * Individual exercise on achieving performance excellence: leadership   and accountability.
12:30   Prayer break.
13:00   * Small group exercise and reports on individual exercise on achieving   performance excellence and plenary session review.
        * Workshop review, conclusion and evaluation.
14:30   End of session and lunch.

Appendix 2 – Second Roll-Out Workshop Programme

Purpose of the Workshop

To enhance accountability, leadership and performance in GSO.

Objectives of the Workshop

At the end of the workshop, you will ...

* Understand the expectations of you as a GSO leader with regard to responsibility and accountability.
* Understand the defining attributes of effective company leaders and aspire to them.
* Be able to recognize and measure accountable behaviour and performance.
* Be able to confront and resolve performance problems.
* Be able to resolve complex issues of accountability and a blame culture at work.
* Be able to reinforce a new culture of performance, learning and accountability in teams.
* Be able to implement effective leadership at work.

Methodology

* Interactive presentations.
* Individual and group exercises, case discussions, group reports and plenary discussions.
* Movie/filmed illustrations.
* The GSO workshop toolkit.

(Continued)

(Continued)

Timetable

Day one

07:00   Registration and coffee.
07:30   Introduction to the Workshop.
         – Welcome and address by the CEO: The GSO company vision.
         – Introduction and expectations of staff and participants.
         – What is 'performance excellence'?
         – The GSO workshop purpose, objectives and methodology.
         – The GSO workshop toolkit.
         – Assessment exercise: performance and accountability in GSO.
09:00   Tea break.
09:30   The Meaning and Realities of Accountability.
         – Assessment exercise: analysis and conclusions.
         – Movie presentation: 'Accountability that works'.
         – The nature of accountability.
         – Group exercise: accountability cases.
         – Group reports and plenary discussion.
11:00   Break.
11:15   Shackleton's Expedition to the Antarctic: Lessons in Leadership and
         Accountability.
         – The Shackleton story.
         – Group exercise: Shackleton's leadership and accountability.
         – Group reports and plenary discussion.
         – Lessons on leadership and accountability from Shackleton.
12:30   Prayer break.
13:00   The Accountable Leader.
         – Leadership as an accountability.
         – Five key themes of effective leadership and lessons for accountability.
         – Group exercise: leadership and the GSO vision.
         – Group reports and plenary discussion.
14:30   Lunch and end of Day One.

Day two

07:30   Agreeing Accountabilities and Performance Expectations.
         – Review of Day One.
         – Key elements of accountability.
         – Assigning responsibility and accountability: The RASCI tool [a form of RAM].
         – Agreeing accountabilities and performance expectations: discussion steps.
08:30   Tea break.
09:00   Leadership, Accountability and Learning from Mistakes and Failure.
         – Empowerment and opportunity.
         – How mistakes and failure can lead to success.

(Continued)

(Continued)

	– Creating a learning culture.
	– Group exercise: learning from mistakes and failure.
	– Group reports and plenary discussion.
10:30	Break.
11:00	Confronting Performance Problems and Recognizing Progress and Achievement.
	– Progress reviews and feedback.
	– GSO policy on corrective guidance.
	– Coaching and counselling in confronting performance problems.
	– Documenting progress and feedback.
	– Key interpersonal skills in confronting performance problems.
	– Active listening.
	– Discussion steps in confronting performance problems.
	– Filmed behaviour model: confronting performance problems.
	– Group exercise: behaviour model analysis.
	– Group reports and plenary discussion.
	– Recognizing and reinforcing progress and achievement.
12:30	Prayer break.
13:00	Action Planning: Achieving Performance Excellence through Accountability and Leadership.
	– Attributes of an effective GSO leader.
	– Action planning: individual and group exercises.
	– Group reports and plenary discussion.
	– Workshop review.
14:30	End of workshop and lunch.

Case Discussion Questions

1. Comment on the quality and use of the leadership development needs diagnosis in the case.
2. Comment on the design, evolution and delivery of the leadership development programme from a cross-cultural perspective and with reference to cultural intelligence.
3. What lessons for effective leadership development in multicultural and cross-cultural settings can be drawn from this case?

 Further Reading

Paul Aitken and Malcolm Higgs (2010), *Developing Change Leaders: The Principles and Practices of Change Leadership Development*. Oxford: Butterworth–Heinemann.

Elaine Biech (2010), *The ASTD Leadership Handbook*. Alexandria, VA: American Society for Training & Development and San Francisco, CA: Berrett-Koehler. Chapters 2–16, 29–30.

Jay A. Conger and Beth Benjamin (1999), *Building Leaders: How Successful Companies Develop the Next Generation*. San Francisco, CA: Jossey-Bass.

Gareth Edwards, Paul K. Winter and Jan Bailey (2002), *Leadership in Management*. Ross-on-Wye: The Leadership Trust Foundation.

Kelly M. Hannum, Jennifer W. Martineau and Claire Reinelt, Editors (2007), *The Handbook of Leadership Development Evaluation*. San Francisco, CA: Jossey-Bass.

Kim James and John Burgoyne (2001), *Leadership Development: Best Practice Guide for Organisations*. London: Council for Excellence in Management and Leadership.

Steve Kempster (2009), *How Managers Have Learnt to Lead*. Basingstoke, Hampshire: Palgrave Macmillan.

Cynthia D. McCauley and Ellen Van Velsor, Editors (2004), *The Center for Creative Leadership Handbook of Leadership Development*, Second Edition. San Francisco, CA: Jossey-Bass.

Hilarie Owen (2001), *Unleashing Leaders: Developing Organizations for Leaders*. Chichester: John Wiley & Sons.

William J. Rothwell and H.C. Kazanas (1999), *Building In-House Leadership and Management Development Programs: Their Creation, Management, and Continuous Improvement*. Westport, CT: Quorum Books.

John J. Sosik and Don I. Jung (2009), *Full Range Leadership Development: Pathways for People, Profit and Planet*. New York and London: Psychology Press.

Peter Ward (1997), *360-degree Feedback*. London: Institute of Personnel and Development.

Peter L. Wright and David S. Taylor (1994), *Improving Leadership Performance: Interpersonal Skills for Effective Leadership*. London: Prentice Hall.

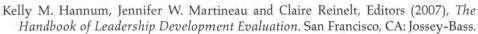 ## Discussion Questions

1. Are leaders 'born' or 'made'?
2. Is leadership competence different from leadership competencies?
3. In addition to assessment centres and leadership questionnaires, what other ways are there of assessing leadership potential?
4. How can the barriers to leadership development be removed or reduced?
5. Why is self-awareness the necessary basis for leadership development?
6. Leadership can best be learned on the job – by practising it. Discuss.
7. What events or processes have triggered or catalysed your own leadership development?
8. Can leadership be 'taught'?

EXERCISE: LEADERSHIP DEVELOPMENT: PERSONAL ANALYSIS AND PLANNING

Using the knowledge about leadership and leadership development and information you have about yourself, identify below what you consider to be your *three key strengths* and *three key development needs*. Then decide what *leadership development activities* might best enable you to capitalize on your strengths and those that might best enable you to meet your development needs.

(Continued)

(Continued)

Key strengths

1. _____

2. _____

3. _____

Key development needs

1. _____

2. _____

3. _____

Leadership development activities

1. _____

2. _____

3. _____

4. _____

5. _____

6. _____

12   Leadership Brand: Sustaining Leadership Excellence

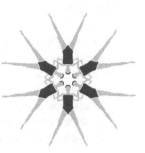

With a strong wind, even turkeys can fly. But on winds of change, only eagles will soar.[1]

OVERVIEW

- Leadership brand is the collective leadership capacity of an organization and the sum total of leadership behaviour across all organizational functions and all hierarchical levels.
- Leadership brand is a distinctive form of leadership that is effective and successful and that engages stakeholders, especially employees.
- Leadership brand requires a leadership strategy including leadership assessment and development.
- Our model of six core leadership themes and practices – vision, purpose, values, strategy, empowerment and engagement – should serve as a useful template for assessing, developing and sustaining the collective leadership capacity of the organization.
- One day every company's annual report might include the organization's leadership philosophy and practice – its leadership brand.

What is 'Leadership Brand'?

The collective leadership capacity of an organization is the sum total of leadership behaviour across all organizational functions and all hierarchical levels. When this is strong, we may say the organization has a strong *leadership brand.*

According to the consultant B.J. Cunningham, 'a brand is a promise': the highest expression of who the organization is and a statement of its business philosophy and strategic intentions – it is about being distinct.[2] Brands are a way to distinguish and market a product or service. For example, the Virgin brand is about fun, innovation and great value.[3] Dave Ulrich and colleagues point out that 'General Electric leaders are known for their ability to deliver financial results by working hard and engaging their employees ... and Intel leaders identify and respond to sudden market shifts and encourage strategic debate'.[4] Brands are a way to build customer commitment to the company, not just to its individual products.

Leadership brand, therefore, is a way to build employee commitment to the company. Brand loyalty, in the case of leadership, is employee engagement and commitment. Ulrich and colleagues say:

> Leadership brand occurs when leaders at every level are clear about which results are most important, develop a consistent approach to delivering these results, and build attributes that support [their] achievement ...[5]

Dave Ulrich and Norm Smallwood suggest that leadership brand is characterized by leadership attributes – the knowledge and skills that reflect how leaders behave – and results.[6] Attributes such as speed of innovation are related to results such as being first in the market. Leadership becomes a brand because of the distinctive link between attributes and results in a given firm: leadership brand = leadership attributes × results.[7]

Leadership brand is not merely the result of 'cascading' leadership, in which strong leaders empower other leaders throughout the organization. This is dependent, Bruce Pasternack and colleagues point out, on the personality and support of whoever the top leader is at any given time.[8] Leaders throughout the organization will behave more like owners and entrepreneurs, assuming responsibility and taking the initiative. But it is the collective actions of both formal and informal leaders in the organization that will determine a leadership culture that in turn may be perceived as a leadership brand. Indeed Barry Gibbons, former CEO of Burger King, says that 'leadership and ... branding have almost seamlessly merged into one'.[9]

A Strategy for Leadership Branding

Leadership brand is a characteristic of organizations rather than individuals and therefore requires, as we discussed in Chapter 11, a leadership strategy.[10] Our discussion of leadership and strategy in Chapter 7 hopefully provided insights into the concept and practice of strategy. In the same way as business strategies, a leadership strategy aims to close the gap between the current situation and the desired situation (vision, purpose and values of the organization). The Center for Creative Leadership provides a useful guide to what should be specified in a leadership strategy:

✳ The number and level of leaders required over the given period, say five to ten years.
✳ The characteristics in terms of demographics, internal or external sourcing, knowledge and skills (competencies) that individual leaders by function, level or location will need.
✳ The collective capabilities that leaders will need (when working collaboratively).
✳ The leadership culture (dependence, independence or interdependence among leaders), shared values, leadership style(s) and leadership practices.[11]

Our model of six core leadership themes and practices – vision, purpose, values, strategy, empowerment and engagement – should serve as a useful template for assessing, developing and sustaining the collective leadership capacity of the organization.

My review of several hundred companies' annual reports discovered the following:

✳ They always contain financial results, revenue data and organizational develop-ments and innovations.

✳ They usually contain strategy and mission statements or statements of their core purpose and often the cliché 'people are our most important asset'.

✳ Sometimes they include the organization's core values and how employees are empowered (e.g. through extensive training).

✳ Rarely is there any appealing vision for the future – only 'confidence' in it (what-ever 'it' is) – or anything about how motivated or inspired the workforce is (which is perhaps dangerous territory).

One of the best annual reports is that of Novartis AG, the Swiss pharmaceutical com-pany.[12] Its 2010 annual report communicated and emphasized the leadership of the com-pany and its corporate values, thereby reinforcing the feeling among employees that their work was meaningful.[13] One day *every company's* annual report might indeed include the organization's leadership philosophy and practice – its leadership 'brand'.

Concluding Remarks

The spirit of the Edinburgh International Festival, one of the world's greatest annual celebrations of the arts in the UK, was captured in its slogan: 'Engage the mind, touch the heart, *feed the soul.*'[14] This could well be our leadership slogan too.

The festival's brochure says: 'Challenging, moving, entertaining, profound – live performance can take you on a journey of discovery.'

So too can the study and practice of leadership. Enjoy the journey, and soar with the eagles!

Endnotes

1 Michel de Montaigne (1533–1592), *Essais*, III, xii. Ed. Maurice Rat (1958).

Chapter 1

1 Reprinted with kind permission from Scott Adams (1999), Introduction, *Don't Step in the Leadership*, Boxtree, London, page 7. Copyright © 1999 United Feature Syndicate Inc. Scott Adams is the creator of *Dilbert*, the satirical comic cartoon strip.

2 Based in part on an unpublished paper by myself for The Leadership Trust Foundation, used with kind permission.

3 C.M. Alcantara (1999), Of leadership and management. *New Straits Times*, Malaysia, September 18, 4.

4 Walter A. Friedman (2010), Leadership and history. In Nitin Nohria and Rakesh Khurana, Editors, *Handbook of Leadership Theory and Practice*. Boston, MA: Harvard Business Press, 292.

5 British Academy of Management (2008), *Newsletter*, March, 6.

6 Janine Waclawski (2001), The real world: Abraham, Martin, and John: where have all the great leaders gone? *The Industrial-Organizational Psychologist*, 38 (1), January, 70–73.

7 John Roulet (2009), Abolishing the myths of leadership. *Management-Issues*, 30 October. Downloaded on 9 December 2009 at http://www.management-issues. com/2009/10/30/opinion/abolishing-the-myths-of-leadership.asp?

8 Joel Kurtzman (2010), *Common Purpose: How Great Leaders Get Organizations to Achieve the Extraordinary*. San Francisco, CA: Jossey-Bass, xi.

9 Robert W. Terry (1993), *Authentic Leadership: Courage in Action*. San Francisco, CA: Jossey-Bass, 11.

10 Robert J. Sternberg and Victor Vroom (2002), Theoretical letters: the person versus the situation in leadership. *Leadership Quarterly*, 13, 301–323.

11 From Lewis Carroll (1871), *Through the Looking Glass, and What Alice Found There*. London: Puffin Classics, New Edition, 2003, 87.

12 Bruce E. Winston and Kathleen Patterson (2006), An integrative definition of leadership. *International Journal of Leadership Studies*, 1 (2), 6–66.

13 Mats Alvesson and Stefan Sveningsson (2003), The great disappearance act: difficulties in doing leadership. *Leadership Quarterly*, 14, 359–381.

14 Simon Kelly (2008), Leadership: a categorical mistake? *Human Relations*, 61 (6), 763–782.

15 Louis R. Pondy (1978), Leadership is a language game. In M.W. McCall Jr and M.M. Lombardo, Editors, *Leadership: Where Else Can We Go?* Durham, NC: Duke University Press, 87–99.

16 Investors in People UK (2007), *Leadership and Management*. London: IIP, 18.

17 Manfred Kets de Vries, quoted by M. Higgs and V. Dulewicz (2002), *Making Sense of Emotional Intelligence*, Second Edition. London: ASE, 103-104.

18 Warren Bennis, quoted by Simon London (2002), The geezer with lessons for geeks. *Financial Times*, September 17, 8.

19 Gary Yukl (2002), *Leadership in Organizations*, Fifth Edition. Upper Saddle River, NJ: Prentice Hall, 61.

20 Keith Grint (2000), *The Arts of Leadership*. Oxford: Oxford University Press, 10, 13.

21 Catherine Soanes and Angus Stevenson, Editors (2004), *Concise Oxford Dictionary*, Eleventh Edition. Oxford: Oxford University Press, 747.

22 David Collinson and Keith Grint (2005), Editorial: The Leadership Agenda. *Leadership*, 1 (1), February, 5–9.

23 Carly Chynoweth (2011), Directors slip out of the loop. *The Sunday Times*, Appointments, 16 January, 2.

24 The year the United States with UK backing went to war in Iraq.

25 Robert Harris (2003), *Pompeii*. London: Hutchinson, 5.

26 Donald G. Krause (1997), *The Way of the Leader*. London: Nicholas Brealey, 8.

27 Mauro F. Guillén (2010), Classical sociological processes to the study of leadership. In Nitin Nohria and Rakesh Khurana, Editors, *Handbook of Leadership Theory and Practice*. Boston, MA: Harvard Business Press, 235.

28 James MacGregor Burns (1978), *Leadership*. New York: Harper & Row, 3.

29 B.V. Moore (1927), The May Conference on leadership. *Personnel Journal*, 6, 124 (now called *Workforce* magazine).

30 Donald G. Krause (1997), *The Way of the Leader*. London: Nicholas Brealey, 3.

31 Jay Lorsch (2010), A contingency theory of leadership. In Nitin Nohria and Rakesh Khurana, Editors, *Handbook of Leadership Theory and Practice*. Boston, MA: Harvard Business Press, 414.

32 Gareth Edwards, Jan Bailey and Paul Winter (2002), *Leadership in Management*. Ross-on-Wye, Herefordshire: The Leadership Trust Foundation.

33 James MacGregor Burns (1978), *Leadership*. New York: Harper & Row.

34 Joseph S. Nye, Jr (2010), Power and leadership. In Nitin Nohria and Rakesh Khurana, Editors, *Handbook of Leadership Theory and Practice*. Boston, MA: Harvard Business Press, 306.

35 Nannerl O. Keohane (2010), *Thinking about Leadership*. Princeton, NJ: Princeton University Press, 23.

36 Charles Handy (2006), *Myself and Other More Important Matters*. London: William Heinemann.

37 EFQM (2000), *Assessing for Excellence: A Practical Guide for Self Assessment*. Brussels: European Foundation for Quality Management.

38　T.F. Hoad, Editor (1988), *The Concise Oxford Dictionary of English Etymology.* Oxford: Oxford University Press.

39　Manfred Kets de Vries and Elizabeth Florent-Treacy (1999), *AuthentiZiotic Organizations: Global Leadership from A to Z.* Working Paper 99/62/ENT, INSEAD, Fontainebleau, France, 5.

40　Catherine Soanes and Angus Stephenson, Editors (2004), *Concise Oxford Dictionary,* Eleventh Edition. Oxford: Oxford University Press, 725.

41　Catherine Soanes and Angus Stephenson, Editors (2004), *Concise Oxford Dictionary,* Eleventh Edition. Oxford: Oxford University Press, 729.

42　Catherine Soanes and Angus Stephenson, Editors (2004), *Concise Oxford Dictionary,* Eleventh Edition. Oxford: Oxford University Press, 1615.

43　Joanne B. Ciulla (1999), The importance of leadership in shaping business values. *Long Range Planning,* 32 (2), 166–172.

44　Barbara Kellerman (2004), *Bad Leadership: What It Is, How It Happens, Why It Matters.* Boston, MA: Harvard Business School Press.

45　Birgit Schyns and Tiffany Hansbrough, Editors (2010), *When Leadership Goes Wrong: Destructive Leadership, Mistakes, and Ethical Failures.* Charlotte, NC: Information Age Publishing.

46　Barbara Kellerman (2004), Leadership: warts and all. *Harvard Business Review,* January, 40–45.

47　Rosabeth Moss Kanter (2010), Leadership tips from Tony Hayward (or not). *Harvard Business Review,* http://blogs.hbr.org/kanter/2010/07/leadership-tips-from-tony-hayw.html

48　Jean Lipman-Blumen (2005), *The Allure of Toxic Leaders.* New York: Oxford University Press.

49　Michael Maccoby (2004), The power of transference. *Harvard Business Review,* 82 (9), September, 77–85.

50　Manfred Kets de Vries and Elizabeth Florent-Treacy (1999), *AuthentiZiotic Organizations: Global Leadership from A to Z.* Working Paper 99/62/ENT, INSEAD, Fontainebleau, France, 26.

51　Robert Ardrey (1970), *The Social Contract.* London: Collins.

52　Stephen R. Covey (1992), *Principle-centered Leadership.* London: Simon & Schuster, 101.

53　Joseph S. Nye, Jr (2010), Power and leadership. In Nitin Nohria and Rakesh Khurana, Editors, *Handbook of Leadership Theory and Practice.* Boston, MA: Harvard Business Press, 311.

54　Stephen Fineman (2003), *Understanding Emotion at Work.* London: SAGE Publications, 76.

55　Robert E. Kelley (1992), *The Power of Followership.* New York: Doubleday.

56　James MacGregor Burns (1978), *Leadership.* New York: Harper & Row, 116.

57　MaST leadership development courses at RMA Sandhurst, quoted by David White (2000), Sandhurst style builds teamwork. *The Sunday Telegraph,* October 8.

58　Performance Improvement Unit (2001), *Strengthening Leadership in the Public Sector.* Research study by the PIY, Cabinet Office, UK Government, www.cabinet-office.gov.uk/innovation/leadershipreport, D11.

59　R. Kelley (1992), *The Power of Followership.* New York: Doubleday Currency; I. Chaleff (1995), *The Courageous Follower.* San Francisco, CA: Berrett-Koehler.

60 Jonathan Swift (1667–1745), *Gulliver's Travels*. Norwalk, CT: The Easton Press, 1976, 298–299.

61 Jeremy Paxman (2002), *The Political Animal: An Anatomy*. London: Penguin/ Michael Joseph, 241.

62 Jeremy Paxman (2002), *The Political Animal: An Anatomy*. London: Penguin/ Michael Joseph, 280, quoting James Margach (1979), *The Anatomy of Power: An Enquiry into the Personality of Leadership*. London: W.H. Allen.

63 Jeremy Paxman (2002), *The Political Animal: An Anatomy*. London: Penguin/ Michael Joseph, Chapter 10.

64 Jeremy Paxman (2002), *The Political Animal: An Anatomy*. London: Penguin/ Michael Joseph, 266.

65 Oren Harari (2002), *The Leadership Secrets of Colin Powell*. New York: McGraw-Hill.

66 R. Kelley (1992), *The Power of Followership*. New York: Doubleday Currency.

67 Quoted by Joel Kurtzman (2010), *Common Purpose: How Great Leaders Get Organizations to Achieve the Extraordinary*. San Francisco, CA: Jossey-Bass, 143.

68 Strategy for the next decade is stated in *Going Local – Fresh Tracks Down Old Roads: Our Strategy for the Next Decade*, The National Trust, 2010. Downloaded from http:// www.nationaltrust.org.uk/main/w-trust/w-thecharity.htm on 6 February 2011.

69 *Durham University Strategy 2010–2020*. Reproduced by kind permission. Accessed at http://www.dur.ac.uk/resources/about/strategy/Finalfullstrategydocument.pdf on 9 November 2010.

70 *Eleventh National Development Plan 2011–2015*, Office of the National Economic and Social Development Board, Government of Thailand, 26 October 2010. Downloaded from http://www.nesdb.go.th/ on 17 March 2011.

71 *Eleventh National Development Plan 2011–2015*, Office of the National Economic and Social Development Board, Government of Thailand, 26 October 2010. Downloaded from http://www.nesdb.go.th/ on 17 March 2011.

72 William W. George (2001), *Keynote Address*, Academy of Management Annual Conference, Washington, DC, August. In *Academy of Management Executive*, 15(4), 39–47.

73 Marcus Buckingham (2005), What great managers do. *Harvard Business Review*, March, 70–79.

74 R.J. House and R.N. Aditya (1997), The social scientific study of leadership: *quo vadis? Journal of Management*, 23 (3), 409–465.

75 Warren Bennis and Bert Nanus (1985), *On Leaders: Strategies for Taking Charge*. New York: Harper & Row, 21.

76 Preston C. Bottger (2000), *Leaders as implementers of strategy*. Unpublished paper. Lausanne: IMD.

77 Quoted in Geraldine Abrahams (2001), Leading lights. *The Herald*, Appointments section, Glasgow, 20 March, 26.

78 P. Gronn (2003), Leadership: who needs it? *School Leadership and Management*, 23 (3), 267–290.

79 The Industrial Society, www.indsoc.co.uk/cforl, 15 January 2001.

80 Stanley A. Deetz, Sarah J. Tracy and Jennifer Lyn Simpson (2000), *Leading Organizations through Transition*. Thousand Oaks, CA: SAGE Publications, 49.

81 Quoted by John Adair (1989), *Great Leaders*. Guildford: The Talbot Adair Press, 217–220.

82 Amin Rajan (2000), *Does Management Development Fail to Produce Leaders?* Tonbridge, Kent: Centre for Research in Employment & Technology in Europe.

83 Warren Bennis (1989), *On Becoming a Leader*. Reading, MA: Addison-Wesley, 45.

84 J.P. Kotter (1990), What leaders really do. *Harvard Business Review*, May–June, 156–167; J.P. Kotter (1990), *A Force for Change: How Leadership Differs from Management*. New York: Free Press.

85 Mitch McCrimmon (2010), Management upgraded. *Management Issues*, www.management-issues.com, 26 February.

86 Mitch McCrimmon (2010), Management upgraded. *Management Issues*, www.management-issues.com, 26 February.

87 Warner W. Burke (1986), Leadership as empowering others. In S. Srivasta and Associates, Editors, *Executive Power: How Executives Influence People and Organizations*. San Francisco, CA: Jossey-Bass, 68.

88 Stephen R. Covey (1992), *Principle-centered Leadership*. London: Simon & Schuster, 248.

89 John Nicholls (1994), The 'heart, head and hands' of transforming leadership. *Leadership and Organization Development Journal*, 15 (6), 8–15.

90 Bernard M. Bass (1985), *Leadership and Performance Beyond Expectations*. New York: Free Press, viii.

91 G. Robinson (1999), Leadership vs management. *British Journal of Administrative Management*, January/February, 20–21.

92 J.M. Kouzes and B.Z. Posner (1995), *The Leadership Challenge: How to Keep Getting Extraordinary Things Done in Organizations*. San Francisco, CA: Jossey-Bass, 52.

92 Quoted by Warren Bennis and Burt Nanus (1985), *Leaders: The Strategies for Taking Charge*. New York: Harper & Row, 22.

94 Paola Hjelt (2003), The world's most admired companies 2003. *Fortune*, March 3, 24–33.

95 Dominic O'Connell (2007), America's forthright captain of industry. *The Sunday Times*, 3.11, 17 June.

96 Adrian Furnham (2010), Why we're not all doomed with Captain Mainwaring. Appointments, *The Sunday Times*, 14 March, 2.

97 Adrian Furnham (2010), Why we're not all doomed with Captain Mainwaring. Appointments, *The Sunday Times*, 14 March, 2.

98 Julian Birkinshaw (2010), An experiment in reinvention, *People Management*, 15 July, 22–24; Julian Birkinshaw (2010), *Reinventing Management: Smarter Choices for Getting Work Done*. San Francisco, CA: Jossey-Bass.

99 Based in part on Roger Gill (2008), Déjà vu: how the ghosts of changes past return to haunt us. *LT Focus*, April. Used with kind permission of the Leadership Trust.

100 Ovid (43BC–AD17), Pythagoras's teachings: the eternal flux, Book XV: 176–198, *Metamorphoses*.

101 Courtesy of Ian C. Buchanan, former chairman of Booz & Co, Asia Pacific, Sydney.

102 Rosabeth Moss Kanter (1983), *The Change Masters*. London: Allen & Unwin.

103 Bernard M. Bass (1985), *Leadership and Performance Beyond Expectations*. New York: Free Press.

104 Warren Bennis (1999), Recreating the company. *Executive Excellence*, September, 5–6.

105 Sir Michael Edwardes, quoted by Walter Goldsmith and Berry Ritchie (1987), *The New Elite*. London: Weidenfeld & Nicolson.

106 Philip Sadler (1998), *Management Consultancy: A Handbook of Best Practice*. London: Kogan Page.

107 Milan Kubr, Editor (2005), *Management Consulting: A Guide to the Profession*, Fourth Edition. Geneva: International Labour Office, 2002. Re-published by permission in 2005 by Bookwell, New Delhi, India, 90–91.

108 James O'Toole (1995), *Leading Change: Overcoming the Ideology of Comfort and the Tyranny of Custom*. San Francisco, CA: Jossey-Bass, 11.

109 James O'Toole (1995), *Leading Change: Overcoming the Ideology of Comfort and the Tyranny of Custom*. San Francisco, CA: Jossey-Bass, 12.

110 James O'Toole (1995), *Leading Change: Overcoming the Ideology of Comfort and the Tyranny of Custom*. San Francisco, CA: Jossey-Bass, 15.

111 Niccolò Machiavelli (1532), *The Prince*. Translated from the Italian by Hill Thompson (1980). Norwalk, CT: Easton Press, 55.

112 Andrew Mayo (2002), Forever change. *Training Journal*, June, 40.

113 Charlton Ogburn, Jr (1957), Merrill's marauders: the truth about an incredible adventure. *Harper's Magazine*, January.

114 Reported by Prashant Bordia, Simon Restubog, Nerina Jinnieson and Bernd Irmer in 'Haunted by the past: effects of poor change management history on employee attitudes and turnover' in the Winter 2008 issue of the *Newsletter* of the Organization Development and Change Division of the Academy of Management (USA), pages 5–6.

115 S.L. Robinson (1996), Trust and breach of psychological contract. *Administrative Science Quarterly*, 41, 574–599; J.P. Wanous, A.E. Reichers and J.T. Austin (2000), Cynicism about organizational change: measurement, antecedents, and correlates. *Group & Organization Management*, 25, 132–153.

116 C. Cammann, M. Fichman, D. Jenkins and J. Klesh (1983), Assessing the attitudes and perceptions of organizational members, in S. Seashore, E. Lawler, P. Mirvis and C. Cammann, Editors (1983), *Assessing Organizational Change: A Guide to Methods, Measures, and Practices*. New York: John Wiley & Sans, 71–138 Y. Fried, R. Tiegs, T. Naughton and B. Ashforth (1996), Managers' reactions to corporate acquisition: a test of an integrative model. *Journal of Organizational Behavior*, 17, 401–427; C. Wanberg and J. Banas (2000), Predictors and outcomes of openness to changes in reorganizing Workplace. *Journal of Applied Psychology*, 85, 132–142.

117 The State of Tennessee v. John Thomas Scopes, 21 July, 1925. Often misattributed to Charles Darwin (1809–1882).

118 Elisabeth Kübler-Ross (1969), *On Death and Dying*. New York: Macmillan.

119 John Mulligan and Paul Barber (2001), The client-consultant relationship. In Philip Sadler, Editor *Management Consultancy: A Handbook of Best Practice*, Second Edition. London: Kogan Page, 83.

120 Kurt Lewin (1948), Group decision and social change: readings in psychology. In Gertrud Weiss Lewin, Editor, *Resolving Social Conflicts, Selected Papers on Group Dynamics (1935–1946)*. New York: Harper.

121 Conclusions from the Inaugural Annual Conference, 'Leadership Development: The Challenges Ahead', The Leadership Trust Foundation, Ross-on-Wye, 2–3 February, 1998.

122 John P. Kotter (1995), *The New Rules: How to Succeed in Today's Post-Corporate World*. New York: Free Press, 21.

123 Chris Argyris (2000), *Flawed Advice and the Management Trap: How Managers Can Know When They're Getting Good Advice and When They're Not*. Oxford: Oxford University Press.

124 Ben Worthen (2011), H-P's CEO discusses his new job. *The Wall Street Journal*, Friday–Sunday, February 18–20, 19.

125 Malcolm Higgs and Deborah Rowland (2003), *Is Change Changing? An Examination of Approaches to Change and Its Leadership*. Paper presented at the Second Annual International Conference on Leadership Research, 'Studying Leadership', Lancaster University Management School, Lancaster, 15–16 December.

126 Livia Markoczy (2001), Consensus formation during strategic change. *Strategic Management Journal*, 22, 1013–1031.

127 Alvin Toffler (1971), *Future Shock*. London: Pan Books, 439–440.

128 Warren Bennis (2000), *Managing the Dream: Reflections on Leadership and Change*. New York: Perseus Publishing, xvi.

129 Raymond Caldwell (2003), Change leaders and change managers: different or complementary? *Leadership & Organization Development Journal*, 24 (5), 285–293.

130 Rosabeth Moss Kanter (1991), *World Leadership Survey: The Boundaries of Business*. Boston, MA: Harvard Business School Press.

131 Roger Gill (2003), Change management – or change leadership? *Journal of Change Management*, 3 (4), 307–318.

132 Alan Hooper and John Potter (2000), *Intelligent Leadership*. London: Random House, 5.

133 Alan Hooper and John Potter (2000), *Intelligent Leadership*. London: Random House, 10; Alan Hooper and John Potter (1997), *The Business of Leadership: Adding Lasting Value to Your Organization*. Aldershot, Hampshire: Ashgate, 2.

134 Ronald A. Heifetz and Donald L. Laurie (1997), The work of leadership. *Harvard Business Review*, January–February, 75 (1), 124–134.

135 Manfred Kets de Vries (2001), *The Leadership Mystique*. London: Pearson Education, 61.

136 Peter Drucker (2001), *The Next Society: a survey of the near future*. Insert-section, *The Economist*, 361 (8246), 3–9 November.

137 AMA (1994), *Survey on Change Management*. New York: American Management Association.

138 With thanks for this to Joyce S. Osland (2008), Leading global change. In M.E. Mendenhall, J.S. Osland, A. Bird, G.R. Oddou and M.L. Maznevski, Editors, *Global Leadership: Research, Practice, and Development*. Abingdon, Oxford and New York: Routledge.

139 Sun Tzu (c. 544–496 BC), *The Art of War*. Translation, Introduction and Commentary by Roger T. Ames, Preface by Rupert Smith. London: The Folio Society, 2007.

140 Rosabeth Moss Kanter (2003), Leadership and the psychology of turnarounds. *Harvard Business Review*, June; Rosabeth Moss Kanter (2003b), Inspire people to turn round your business. *Financial Times*, 25 August, 11.

141 Nikos Mourkogiannis (2006), *Purpose: The Starting Point of Great Companies*. New York: Palgrave Macmillan, 149.

142 Rosabeth Moss Kanter (2003), Leadership and the psychology of turnarounds. *Harvard Business Review*, June, 81 (6), 58–67.

143 METO (2000), *Management and Leadership in the Changing Economy*. The Management and Enterprise National Training Organisation, Project Report, 1 March, 27.

144 Douglas McGregor (1960), *The Human Side of Enterprise*. London: McGraw-Hill.

145 Sir Anthony Cleaver (2001), Foreword. In CEML (2001), *Excellent Managers and Leaders: Meeting the Need*. London: Council for Excellence in Management and Leadership. Sir Anthony is chairman of the CEML and chairman of AEA Technology plc.

146 CEML (2001), *Excellent Managers and Leaders: Meeting the Need*. London: Council for Excellence in Management and Leadership, 15.

147 Carly Chynoweth (2010), Win over staff and profit will follow. *The Sunday Times*, Appointments, 24 October, 4; Top-Consultant (2010), http://www.consultant-news.com/printArticle.aspx?id=7280, 14 October 2010; Kenexa (2010), *Exploring Leadership and Managerial Effectiveness*, 2010 WorkTrends research report. Wayne, PA: Kenexa Research Institute.

148 Bill George (2010), The new 21st century leaders. *Harvard Business Review, Guest Edition*, May 5.

149 Joel M. Podolny, Rakesh Khurana and Marya L. Besharov (2010), Revisiting the meaning of leadership. In Nitin Nohria and Rakesh Khurana, Editors, *Handbook of Leadership Theory and Practice*. Boston, MA: Harvard Business Press, Chapter 3, 65–105.

150 J. Richard Hackman (2010), What is this thing called leadership? In Nitin Nohria and Rakesh Khurana, Editors, *Handbook of Leadership Theory and Practice*. Boston, MA: Harvard Business Press, Chapter 4, 107–116.

151 Nitin Nohria and Rakesh Khurana, Editors (2010), Advancing leadership theory and practice. In Nitin Nohria and Rakesh Khurana, Editors, *Handbook of Leadership Theory and Practice*. Boston, MA: Harvard Business Press, 10–14.

152 James O'Toole, Jay Galbraith and Edward E. Lawler, III (2002), When two (or more) heads are better than one: the promise and pitfalls of shared leadership. *California Management Review*, Summer, 44 (4), 65–83.

153　Alan Berkeley Thomas (1988), Does leadership make a difference to organizational performance? *Administrative Science Quarterly*, 33, 388–400.

154　Noam Wasserman, Bharat Anand and Nitin Nohria (2010), When does leadership matter? In Nitin Nohria and Rakesh Khurana, Editors, *Handbook of Leadership Theory and Practice*. Boston, MA: Harvard Business Press, Chapter 2, 27–63.

155　Bruce Pasternack, Thomas D. Williams and Paul F. Anderson (2001), Beyond the cult of the CEO: building institutional leadership. *Strategy and Business*, 1st quarter, 1–12.

156　Richard S. Wellins and Patterson S. Weaver Jr (2003), From C-level to see-level leadership. *Training & Development*, September, 58–65.

157　Keith Grint, quoted by Roger Eglin (2003), Why business is no place for yes men. *The Sunday Times*, 8 September, 7.6.

158　Henry Kissinger in an interview with Romesh Ratnesar reported in *Time* magazine, 31 December 2007–7 January, 2008, 63.

159　Bruce Pasternack, Thomas D. Williams and Paul F. Anderson (2001), Beyond the cult of the CEO: building institutional leadership. *Strategy and Business*, 1st quarter, 1–12.

160　Dennis Tourish, Russell Craig and Joel Amernic (2010), Transformational leadership education and agency perspectives in business school pedagogy: a marriage of inconvenience? *British Journal of Management*, 21, S40–S59.

161　David Collinson (2008), Editorial introduction. *Distributed and Shared Leadership, Volume 8*. CEL/LSIS Leadership Research Programme, Centre for Excellence in Leadership, Lancaster University Management School, March.

162　James O'Toole (2001), When leadership is an organizational trait. In W. Bennis, G.M. Spreitzer and T.G. Cummings, Editors, *The Future of Leadership*. San Francisco, CA: Jossey-Bass; Bruce Pasternack, Thomas D. Williams and Paul F. Anderson (2001), Beyond the cult of the CEO: building institutional leadership. *Strategy and Business*, 1st quarter, 1–12.

163　Wilfred H. Drath (2001), The third way: a new source of leadership. *Leadership in Action*, 21 (2), May/June, 7–11; Wilfred H. Drath (2001b), *The Deep Blue Sea: Rethinking the Source of Leadership*. San Francisco, CA: Jossey-Bass.

164　Alan Berkeley Thomas (1988), Does leadership make a difference to organizational performance? *Administrative Science Quarterly*, 33, 388–400.

165　Wilfred H. Drath (2001), The third way: a new source of leadership. *Leadership in Action*, 21 (2), May/June, 7–11; Wilfred H. Drath (2001b), *The Deep Blue Sea: Rethinking the Source of Leadership*. San Francisco, CA: Jossey-Bass.

166　Keith Grint, quoted by Roger Eglin (2003), Why business is no place for yes men. *The Sunday Times*, September 8, 7.6.

167　Bruce Pasternack, Thomas D. Williams and Paul F. Anderson (2001), Beyond the cult of the CEO: building institutional leadership. *Strategy and Business*, 1st quarter, 1–12.

168　*The Economist* (2002), Fallen idols. May 4, 11.

169　Stefan Stern (2010), A new leadership blueprint. *Management Today*, October, 38–41.

170　Stefan Stern (2010), A new leadership blueprint. *Management Today*, October, 38–41.

171 Bruce Pasternack, Thomas D. Williams and Paul F. Anderson (2001), Beyond the cult of the CEO: building institutional leadership. *Strategy and Business*, 1st quarter, 1–12.

172 Susan V. Lawrence (2002), Daring to raise a taboo topic. *Far Eastern Economic Review*, September 12, 37.

173 Bruce Pasternack, Thomas D. Williams and Paul F. Anderson (2001), Beyond the cult of the CEO: building institutional leadership. *Strategy and Business*, 1st quarter, 1–12.

174 Bruce Pasternack, Thomas D. Williams and Paul F. Anderson (2001), Beyond the cult of the CEO: building institutional leadership. *Strategy and Business*, 1st quarter, 1–12.

175 R.J. House and R.N. Aditja (1997), The social scientific study of leadership: *quo vadis? Journal of Management*, 23 (3), 409–473.

176 David A. Heenan and Warren Bennis (1999), *Co-leaders: The Power of Great Partnership*. New York: John Wiley & Sons.

177 P. Troiano (1999), Sharing the throne. *Management Review*, 88 (2), 39–43.

178 D. Sally (2002), Co-leadership: lessons from republican Rome. *California Management Review*, 44 (4), 84–99.

179 The Manufacturing Foundation (2003), *Innovation Essentials*. Birmingham, August.

180 Micael D. Kocolowski (2010), Shared leadership: is it time for a change? *Emerging Leadership Journeys*, 3 (1), 22–32.

181 Quoted by Sharon Shinn (2003), The leader within us. *BizEd* magazine, American Association for the Advancement of Collegiate Schools of Business, November/December, 30–35.

182 Bruce Pasternack, Thomas D. Williams and Paul F. Anderson (2001), Beyond the cult of the CEO: building institutional leadership. *Strategy and Business*, 1st Quarter, 1–12.

183 James O'Toole (2001), When leadership is an organizational trait. In W. Bennis, G.M. Spreitzer and T.G. Cummings, Editors, *The Future of Leadership*. San Francisco, CA: Jossey-Bass.

184 James O'Toole, Jay Galbraith and Edward E. Lawler, III (2002), When two (or more) heads are better than one: the promise and pitfalls of shared leadership. *California Management Review*, 44 (4), Summer, 65–83.

185 Marianne Döös and Lena Wilhelmson (2003), Work processes of shared leadership. Paper presented at the Annual Conference of the British Academy of Management, Harrogate, 15–17 September.

186 Paul Staman, reported from an interview with writer Joe Tye; see http://www.joetye.com

187 Jay B. Carson, Paul E. Tesluk and Jennifer A. Marrone (2007), Shared leadership in teams: an investigation of antecedent conditions and performance. *Academy of Management Journal*, 50 (5), 1217–1234.

188 The Times (2010), Lessons unlearnt. Leading article, *The Times*, Saturday July 17, 2.

189 Philip Selznick (1957), *Leadership in Administration*. Evanston, IL: Row Peterson.

190 Jeff Gold and Alma Harris (2003), *Leading in Schools: Studying Distribution*. Paper presented at the Second Annual International Conference on Leadership Research, 'Studying Leadership', Lancaster University Management School, Lancaster, 15–16 December.

191 Peter Gronn (2002), Distributed leadership as a unit of analysis. *Leadership Quarterly*, 13 (4), 423–451.

192 James O'Toole (2001), When leadership is an organizational trait. In W. Bennis, G.M. Spreitzer and T. G. Cummings, Editors, *The Future of Leadership*. San Francisco, CA: Jossey-Bass.

193 James O'Toole, Jay Galbraith and Edward E. Lawler, III (2002), When two (or more) heads are better than one: the promise and pitfalls of shared leadership. *California Management Review*, 44 (4), Summer, 65–83.

194 Michael E. Brown and Denny A. Goia (2002), Making things click: distributive leadership in an online division of an offline organization. *Leadership Quarterly*, 13 (4), 392–419.

195 Peter Gronn (2002), Distributed leadership as a unit of analysis. *Leadership Quarterly*, 13 (4), 423–451.

196 Keith Grint (2010), The sacred in leadership: separation, sacrifice and silence. *Organization Studies*, 31, 89–107.

197 Reported by John Gill (2008), Distributed leadership model gives 'illusion' of consultation. *Times Higher Education*, 22 May, 7.

198 Bruce Pasternack, Thomas D. Williams and Paul F. Anderson (2001), Beyond the cult of the CEO: building institutional leadership. *Strategy and Business*, 1st quarter, 1–12.

199 Bruce Pasternack, senior vice president and managing partner at Booz, Allen & Hamilton, quoted by Sharon O'Shea (2000), The changing composition of leadership. *Financial Executive*, 16 (4), 35.

200 Interview of Mary Curnock Cook with Andrew Lynch (2011), It's not only the leaders who lead. *The Sunday Times*, Leading Edge, Appointments, 3 April, 4.

201 Philip Sadler (1997), *Leadership*. London: Kogan Page, 12.

202 Robert W. Fuller (2001), A new look at hierarchy. *Leader to Leader*, Summer, 6–12.

203 Robert W. Fuller (2001), A new look at hierarchy. *Leader to Leader*, Summer, 6–12.

204 Frances Hesselbein, quoted by Sharon Shinn (2003), The leader within us. *BizEd* magazine, American Association of Collegiate Schools of Business, November/December, 30–35.

205 D. Scott DeRue and Susan J. Ashford (2010), Who will lead and who will follow? A social process of leadership identity construction in organizations. *Academy of Management Review*, 35 (4), 627–647.

206 D. Scott DeRue and Susan J. Ashford (2010), Who will lead and who will follow? A social process of leadership identity construction in organizations. *Academy of Management Review*, 35 (4), 627–647.

207 D. Scott DeRue and Susan J. Ashford (2010), Who will lead and who will follow? A social process of leadership identity construction in organizations. *Academy of Management Review*, 35 (4), 627–647.

208 E.P. Hollander (1993), Legitimacy, power, and influence: a perspective on relational features of leadership. In M.M. Chemers and R. Ayman, Editors, *Leadership Theory and Research: Perspectives and Directions*, San Diego, CA: Academic Press, 29–48. David Collinson (2006), Rethinking followership: a poststructuralist analysis of follower identities. *Leadership Quarterly*, 17, 179–189; M. Van Vugt, R. Hogan and R.B. Kaiser (2008), Leadership, followership, and evolution: some lessons from the past. *American Psychologist*, 63, 182–196.

209 I make sure they don't fall off a cliff. Leading Edge, Appointments, *The Sunday Times*, March 28, 2010, 4.

210 D. Scott DeRue and Susan J. Ashford (2010), Who will lead and who will follow? A social process of leadership identity construction in organizations. *Academy of Management Review*, 35 (4), 627–647.

211 Bernard M. Bass (1954), The leaderless group discussion. *Psychological Bulletin*, 51, 465–492.

212 Philip Selznick (1957), *Leadership in Administration*. Evanston, IL: Row Peterson.

213 Robert G. Lord and Karen J. Maher (1991), *Leadership and Information Processing*. London: Routledge, 97.

214 Amatai Etzioni (1961), *A Comparative Analysis of Complex Organizations*. New York: Free Press.

215 Richard S. Wellins and Patterson S. Weaver Jr (2003), From C-level to see-level leadership. *Training & Development*, September, 58–65.

216 D. Katz. and R.L. Kahn (1978), *The Social Psychology of Organizations*. New York: John Wiley & Sons

217 S. Finkelstein and D.C. Hambrick (1996), *Strategic Leadership: Top Executives and Their Effects on Organizations*. Minneapolis, MN: West.

218 Stephen J. Zaccaro and Richard J. Klimoski (2001), The nature of organizational leadership: an introduction. In Stephen J. Zaccaro and Richard J. Klimoski, Editors, *The Nature of Organizational Leadership*. San Francisco, CA: Jossey-Bass, 12.

219 Peter Drucker (2001), The Next Society: a survey of the near future. Insert-section, *The Economist*, 361 (8246), 3–9 November.

220 Dave Ulrich, Norm Smallwood and Jack Zenger (2000), Building your leadership brand. *Leader to Leader*, 15, Winter, 40–46.

221 We discuss this further in the final chapter (Chapter 12).

222 See Chapter 9 for a discussion on leadership and employee engagement.

Chapter 2

1 Lynn R. Offermann, Paul J. Hanges and David V. Day (2001), Leaders, followers, and values: progress and prospects for theory and research. *Leadership Quarterly*, 12 (2), 129–131.

2 Adrian Furnham (2010), *Why Leaders Fail: The Psychology of Management Derailment*. Paper presented at the Leadership Forum, The Leadership Trust Foundation, Ross-on-Wye, 2 March.

3 Francesca Cunningham (2001), Interview with Henry Mintzberg. *Business Voice*, June, 49–52

4 Alison Eadie (2001), Leadership looking for a 21st century direction. *The Sunday Telegraph*, 10 June.

5 Ram Charan and Jerry Useem (2002), Why companies fail. *Fortune*, 27 May, 36–44.

6 Richard S. Tedlow (2010), *Denial: Why Business Leaders Fail to Look Facts in the Face – and What to Do About It.* New York: Portfolio (Penguin Group).

7 Sydney Finkelstein (2003a), How do you spot the signs of disaster? *Financial Times*, 6 August, 11; Sydney Finkelstein (2003b), *Why Smart Executives Fail and What You Can Learn from Their Mistakes.* New York: Portfolio.

8 Ram Charan and Jerry Useem (2002), Why companies fail. *Fortune*, 27 May, 36–44.

9 Stephen Aris (2002), Weinstock: I wanted to string up Simpson. *The Sunday Times*, 28 July, 3.8.

10 Ram Charan and Jerry Useem (2002), Why companies fail. *Fortune*, 27 May, 36–44.

11 Roger Eglin (2001), No more Mr Nice Guy as times get tough. *The Sunday Times*, 4 March.

12 Warren Bennis and James O'Toole (2000), Don't hire the wrong CEO. *Harvard Business Review*, May–June, 171–176.

13 Warren Bennis and James O'Toole (2000), Don't hire the wrong CEO. *Harvard Business Review*, 78 (3): 171–176.

14 W.F. Cascio and S. Shurygailo (2003), E-leadership and virtual teams. *Organizational Dynamics*, 31 (4), 363–376.

15 B.A.S. Koene, L.W. Vogelaar and J.L. Soeters (2002), Leadership effects on organizational climate and financial performance: local leadership effect in chain organizations. *Leadership Quarterly*, 13, 193–215.

16 L.S. Csoka (1998), *Bridging the Leadership Gap.* New York: Conference Board.

17 Susan MacDonald (1999), A crisis in leadership. *The Times*, First Executive, 12 November, 2.

18 Roger Eglin (2002), Wanted: real leaders who can be trusted. *The Sunday Times*, 28 July, 7.4.

19 Leadership – from the followers' perspective. *Professional Manager*, 11 (1), January 2002, 2; UK leaders fail to win hearts and minds (but they do if they try), http://www.inst-mgt.org.uk/press/hearts.htm, Institute of Management, 4 December, 2001; Institute of Management (2001), *Leadership: The Challenge for All?* Report by DEMOS in association with the Council for Excellence in Management and Leadership, London: Chartered Management Institute; Christine Hayhurst (2002), The power to inspire. *Peak Performance*, Spring, 7–11.

20 Institute of Management (2001), *Leadership: The Challenge for All?* Report by DEMOS in association with the Council for Excellence in Management and Leadership. London: Chartered Management Institute.

21 Mary Chapman, director-general of the Chartered Institute of Management, quoted by Jane Simms (2002), Is Britain being led astray? *Director*, January, 48–51.

22 A survey by Development Dimensions International, reported by Roger Eglin (2004), A third of Britons are bored at work. *The Sunday Times*, 7 March, 7.6.

23 Adèle Collins (2004), Where they lead we will follow. *The Sunday Times 100 Best Companies to Work For 2004*, 7 March, 8.

24 Conference Board (2002), *Developing Business Leaders for 2010*. New York: The Conference Board.

25 Quoted by Roger Eglin (2002), Wanted: real leaders who can be trusted. *The Sunday Times*, 28 July, 7.4.

26 Robert McHenry, chairman of OPP, quoted by Roger Eglin (2002), Wanted: real leaders who can be trusted. *The Sunday Times*, 28 July, 7.4.

27 The Manufacturing Foundation (2003), *Innovation Essentials*. Birmingham, August.

28 Scott Spreier and Dawn Sherman (2003), Staying ahead of the curve. *Fortune*, 3 March, 35–37.

29 Quoted by Warren Bennis (1998), *The Leadership Challenge: Generating Intellectual Capital*. The Brathay Conference: 'The Leadership Odyssey', Windermere, 14–15 May.

30 *The Sunday Times 100 Best Companies to Work For*, 24 March, 2002.

31 *The Sunday Times 100 Best Companies to Work For*, 24 March, 2002, 19.

32 *The Sunday Times 100 Best Companies to Work For 2004*, 7 March, 14.

33 *The Sunday Times 100 Best Companies to Work For 2004*, 7 March, 14.

34 Adèle Collins (2004), Where they lead we will follow. *The Sunday Times 100 Best Companies to Work For 2004*, 7 March, 8.

35 *The Sunday Times 100 Best Companies to Work For 2005*, 6 March, 4–5, 16.

36 Alastair McCall (2007), The Sunday Times 100 Best Companies to Work For 2007. *The Sunday Times*, 11 March.

37 Alastair McCall (2004), Inspired all the way to the top. *The Sunday Times 100 Best Companies to Work For 2004*, 7 March, 5.

38 Alastair McCall (2004), Inspired all the way to the top. *The Sunday Times 100 Best Companies to Work For 2004*, 7 March 4.

39 James C. Collins and Jerry I. Porras (1996), *Built to Last: Successful Habits of Visionary Companies*. London: HarperBusiness.

40 David V. Day and Robert G. Lord (1988), Executive leadership and organizational performance: suggestions for a new theory and methodology. *Journal of Management*, 14, 453–464.

41 R. Thomas Lenz (1993), Strategic management and organizational learning: a meta-theory of executive leadership. In J. Hendry, G. Johnson and J. Newton, Editors, *Strategic Thinking: Leadership and the Management of Change*. Chichester: John Wiley & Sons, 171.

42 *The Sunday Times 100 Best Companies to Work For*, 24 March, 2002, 46.

43 Quoted by Warren Bennis (1998), *The Leadership Challenge: Generating Intellectual Capital*. The Brathay Conference: 'The Leadership Odyssey', Windermere, 14–15 May.

44 Quoted by Roger Gill (2001), Does executive education really improve business performance? *The Independent on Sunday*, 16 December.

45 CEML (2002), *Managers and Leaders: Raising Our Game*. London: Council for Excellence in Management and Leadership.

46 Sue Law (2002), Getting the measure of leadership. *Professional Manager*, July, 26–28.

47 Fred I. Greenstein (2004), *The Presidential Difference: Leadership Style from FDR to George W. Bush*. Princeton, NJ: Princeton University Press.

48 Joseph Nye, Jr (2008), *The Powers to Lead*. New York: Oxford University Press.

49 Joseph Masciulli, Mikhail A. Molchanov and W. Andy Knight, Editors (2009), Preface. *The Ashgate Research Companion to Political Leadership*. Farnham, Surrey: Ashgate Publishing, xv–xvi.

50 Joseph Masciulli, Mikhail A. Molchanov and W. Andy Knight, Editors (2009), Preface. *The Ashgate Research Companion to Political Leadership*. Farnham, Surrey: Ashgate Publishing, xv–xvi.

51 Mark Stier (1997), The whole truth and nothing but the truth? Deception and the educative ideal of politics. In Laura Duham Kaplan and Lawrence W. Bove, Editors, *Philosophical Perspectives on Power and Domination*. Amsterdam: Rodopi, 115–132.

52 Joseph Masciulli, Mikhail A. Molchanov and W. Andy Knight, Editors (2009), Preface. *The Ashgate Research Companion to Political Leadership*. Farnham, Surrey: Ashgate Publishing, xv–xvi.

53 Dennis Kavanagh (1990), *British Politics: Continuities and Change*, Second Edition. Oxford: Oxford University Press, 63–65.

54 Anthony Seldon, with Lewis Baston (1997), *Major: A Political Life*. London: Weidenfeld & Nicolson.

55 Kevin Theakston (2003), Political skills and context in prime ministerial leadership in Britain. In Erwin C. Hargrove and John E. Owens, Editors, *Leadership in Context*. Lanham, MD: Rowman & Littlefield Publishers, 108–109.

56 Peter Riddell (2001), Blair as prime minister. In Anthony Seldon, Editor, *The Blair Effect*. London: Little, Brown, 35, 38.

57 Robert Elgie (1995), *Political Leadership in Liberal Democracies*. Basingstoke: Macmillan.

58 Stanley Cloud (1996), *Nixon*. New York: Harper & Row.

59 Doris Kearns Goodwin (1998), Lessons of presidential leadership. *Leader to Leader*, 9, 23–30.

60 Tony Blair (2010), A call to greatness. *Time*, 13 September, 34–37.

61 Steven J. Rubenzer and Tom R. Faschingbauer (2004), *Personality, Character & Leadership in the White House: Psychologists Assess the Presidents*. Washington, DC: Brassey's.

62 Steven J. Rubenzer, quoted by Sadie F. Dingfelder (2004), A presidential personality. *Monitor on Psychology*, American Psychological Association, November, 26–28.

63 Anthony Giddens (2000), *Runaway World: How Globalization Is Reshaping Our Lives*. New York: Routledge.

64 Jeremy Paxman (2002), *The Political Animal: An Anatomy*. London: Penguin/ Michael Joseph, 282–290.

65 Mark Goyder (2001), Learn to lead, not manage. *The Sunday Times,* 18 November 8, 7.9.

66 Based in part on Roger Gill (2009), Leadership in the public and private sectors: is it different? *LT Focus,* Summer. Used with kind permission of The Leadership Trust Foundation.

67 Reported by Kevin Theakston (1999), *Leadership in Whitehall.* Basingstoke: Macmillan, 252.

68 Paul Joyce (2003), Leading change in the public sector. *Strategy Magazine,* 1, 11–13.

69 Norman Bettison (2010), I'm not worth £213,000. This wage bill is mad. *The Times,* 12 April, 21.

70 John Philpott, *People Management,* online blog, 30 November 2009, http://www.peoplemanagement.co.uk/pm/sections/blogs

71 Public sector productivity fell, John Philpott says, by 3.2% between 1997 and 2007, despite rapid growth in public spending, according to the Office for National Statistics, http://www.statistics.gov.uk/CCI/nscl.asp?ID=7176

72 For example, some very clear recommendations in the report, *Strengthening Leadership in the Public Sector: A Research Study by the PIU* (Performance & Innovation Unit, Cabinet Office, 2001) and leadership development initiatives and programmes in a wide range of government sectors and the National School of Government.

73 Roger Gill (2009), Leadership in public services and the private sector: a comparison and the implications for handling crises and emergencies. *International Journal of Leadership in Public Services,* 5 (4), 20–26.

74 Richard Donkin (2004), Private versus public sector leadership. *Donkin on Work – Leadership,* www.RichardDonkin.com, November.

75 D. Osborne and T. Gaebler (1992), *Reinventing Government: How the Entrepreneurial Spirit is Transforming the Public Sector from Schoolhouse to State House, City to Pentagon.* Reading, MA: Addison-Wesley; H.G. Frederickson (1996), Comparing the reinventing government movement with the new public administration. *Public Administration Review,* 56 (3), 263–270.

76 E. Braverman, A. De Smet and B. Schaninger (2009), Improving worker performance in the US government. *McKinsey Quarterly,* November.

77 Roger Gill (2004), The leadership challenge in the public sector. *LT Focus,* September.

78 Michael Bristow and Martin Clarke (n.d.), General Management Development Group, Cranfield School of Management. www.cranfield.ac.uk/som/gmdp

79 C.P. Schofield, V. Holton, M. Pegg, D. Sweeney and J. Rizzello (2008), *Leadership and Management Issues in the UK Public Sector.* Berkhamsted: Ashridge and Ascot: National School of Government.

80 Quoted by S. Lister (2009), Working to develop a healthier NHS. *The Times,* 3 April, 62.

81 Thomas H. Lee (2010), Turning doctors into leaders. Monthly Update, *Harvard Business Review,* April; Thomas H. Lee and James J. Mongan (2009), *Chaos and Organization in Health Care.* Cambridge, MA: MIT Press.

82   Nick Rodrigues and Jamie McGinnes (2010), Together for the good of the UK. In Alastair McCall, Editor, *The Sunday Times 75 Best Places to Work in the Public Sector 2010.* London: The Sunday Times, 14 March, 4–5. The survey reports responses from 45,000 employees in over 200 organizations.

83   Norman Bettison (2010), I'm not worth £213,000. This wage bill is mad. *The Times,* 12 April, 21.

84   Nick Rodrigues and Jamie McGinnes (2010), Together for the good of the UK. In Alastair McCall, Editor, *The Sunday Times 75 Best Places to Work in the Public Sector 2010.* London: The Sunday Times, 14 March, 4–5.

85   Nick Rodrigues and Jamie McGinnes (2010), Together for the good of the UK. In Alastair McCall, Editor, *The Sunday Times 75 Best Places to Work in the Public Sector 2010.* London: The Sunday Times, 14 March, 4–5.

86   Mansour Javidan and David Waldman (2003), Exploring charismatic leadership in the public sector: measurement and consequences. *Public Administration Review,* 63 (2), 229–242.

87   Jamaica Information Service (2009), More transformational leadership needed in public sector – Senator Nelson. *Caribseek,* March 19.

88   Jon Howell and Bruce Avolio (1993), Transformational leadership, transactional leadership, locus of control, and support for innovation: key predictors of consolidated business-unit performance. *Journal of Applied Psychology,* 78 (6), 891–902.

89   Badrinarayan Pawar and Kenneth K. Eastman (1997), The nature and implications of contextual influences on transformational leadership: a conceptual examination. *Academy of Management Review,* 22 (1), 80–109; Jay Conger (1999), Charismatic and transformational leadership in organizations: an insider's perspective on these developing streams of research. *Leadership Quarterly,* 10 (2), 145–179.

90   David A. Waldman and Francis Yammarino (1999), CEO charismatic leadership: levels-of-management and levels-of-analysis effects. *Academy of Management Review,* 24 (2), 266–285; David A. Waldman, Gabriel G. Ramirez, Robert J. House and Phanish Puranam (2001), Does leadership matter? CEO leadership and profitability under conditions of perceived environmental uncertainty. *Academy of Management Journal,* 44 (1), 134–144.

91   Michael Bristow and Martin Clarke (n.d.), General Management Development Group, Cranfield School of Management, www.cranfield.ac.uk/som/gmdp

92   Mansour Javidan and David A. Waldman (2003), Exploring charismatic leadership in the public sector: measurement and consequences. *Public Administration Review,* 63 (2), 229–242.

93   Carina Paine Schofield (2008), Key challenges facing public sector leaders. *360° The Ashridge Journal,* Autumn, 1–6.

94   P. Kenmore (2009), Public sector leadership – a time bomb waiting to go off. *People Torque,* HayGroup, April, 2.

95   John Alban-Metcalfe and Beverly Alimo-Metcalfe (2009), Engaging leadership part one: competencies are like Brighton Pier. *International Journal of Leadership in Public Services,* 5 (1), 10–18.

96 Catherine Soanes and Angus Stevenson, Editors (2004), *Concise Oxford English Dictionary*, Eleventh Edition. Oxford: Oxford University Press, 88.

97 C.P. Schofield, V. Holton, M. Pegg, D. Sweeney and J. Rizzello (2008), *Leadership and Management Issues in the UK Public Sector*. Berkhamsted: Ashridge and Ascot: National School of Government.

98 Frank Blackler (2006), Chief executives and the modernization of the English National Health Service. *Leadership*, 2 (1), 5–30.

99 Michael Bichard (2010), In my opinion. *Management Today*, April, 10.

100 Michael Bichard (2010), In my opinion. *Management Today*, April, 10.

101 Based in part on Roger Gill (2006), Leadership in UK higher education institutions. *LT Focus*, December. Used with kind permission of The Leadership Trust Foundation.

102 Sharon Turnbull and Gareth Edwards (2005), Leadership development for organizational change in a new UK university. *Advances in Human Resource Development*, 7 (3), August, 396–413; *LT Focus*, 11 (4), March 2006.

103 Ian McNay and Jennifer Bone (2006), *Higher Education and the Human Good*, quoted by Phil Baty (2006), Academia has sold out, 72% believe. *The Times Higher Education Supplement*, 27 October, 1, 7.

104 Robin Middlehurst (1993), *Leading Academics*. Buckingham: SRHE and Open University Press.

105 The Research Assessment Exercise (RAE) has been the government's system for assessing the quality of research publications in higher education institutions that determines the funding that they receive. It is being replaced for implementation in 2014 by the Research Excellence Framework (REF).

106 Sir Ivor Crewe (2005), *President's Speech*. Developing Leadership in Higher Education Conference, Universities UK, 10 February.

107 Sir Ivor Crewe (2005), *President's Speech*. Developing Leadership in Higher Education Conference, Universities UK, 10 February.

108 Sir Ivor Crewe (2005), *President's Speech*. Developing Leadership in Higher Education Conference, Universities UK, 10 February.

109 Boris Johnson, quoted by Phil Baty (2006), Academia has sold out, 72% believe. *The Times Higher Education Supplement*, 27 October, 1.

110 Ian McNay and Jennifer Bone (2006), *Higher Education and the Human Good*, quoted by Phil Baty (2006), Academia has sold out, 72% believe. *The Times Higher Education Supplement*, 27 October, 1.

111 Reported by Simon Baker (2010), Spirit of the money age leads academy to mislay its values. *Times Higher Education*, 2 September.

112 Laissez-faire leadership is a concept that is part of the Full Range Leadership model discussed in the Chapter 3 on leadership theory.

113 Roger Lindsay (2010), 'Followership' is the thing. Letter to the Editor, *Times Higher Education*, 19 August, 29.

114 Robin Middlehurst (1993), *Leading Academics*. Buckingham: SRHE and Open University Press; M. Shattock (2003), *Managing Successful Universities*. Buckingham: SRHE and Open University Press.

115 C.P. Snow (1959), *The Two Cultures.* The 1959 Rede Lecture. Cambridge: Cambridge University Press.

116 Nikos Mourkogiannis (2006), *Purpose – The Starting Point of Great Companies.* Basingstoke: Palgrave Macmillan; Roger Gill (2006), *Theory and Practice of Leadership.* London: SAGE Publications, Chapter 4.

117 B.R. Clark (2004), *Sustaining Change in Universities.* Maidenhead: SRHE and Open University Press.

118 P. Ramsden (1998), *Learning to Lead in Higher Education.* London: Routledge.

119 Georgy Petrov (2006), Leadership in higher education. In Richard Bolden Editor, *Leadership Development in Context.* Leadership South West Research Report 3, University of Exeter Centre for Leadership Studies, 37.

120 Georgy Petrov (2006), Leadership in higher education. In Richard Bolden Editor, *Leadership Development in Context.* Leadership South West Research Report 3, University of Exeter Centre for Leadership Studies, 37.

121 Based in part on Roger Gill (2009), Leadership in the private and public sectors: is it different? *LT Focus,* Summer. Used with kind permission of The Leadership Trust Foundation.

122 Thomas J. Tierney (2006), *Understanding the Nonprofit Sector's Leadership Deficit.* Special Supplement, The Bridgespan Group, Inc., Boston, MA.

123 Carly Chynoweth (2009), Warm hearts must be ruled by cool heads. Social Entrepreneur Awards supplement, *The Sunday Times,* 21 June.

124 Roger Gill (2009), Leadership in the public and private sectors: is it different? *LT Focus,* Summer.

125 M.S. Hall (1994), Core competencies for effective nonprofit managers. *Leadership IS,* 7–15.

126 Thomas J. Tierney (2006), *Understanding the Nonprofit Sector's Leadership Deficit.* Special Supplement, The Bridgespan Group, Inc., Boston, MA.

127 J. Carl and G. Stokes (1991), Ordinary people, extraordinary organizations. *Nonprofit World,* 9 (6), 21–26.

128 Bernard M. Bass (2008), *The Bass Handbook of Leadership: Theory, Research, & Managerial Applications.* New York: Free Press, 638–640.

129 Bernard M. Bass and Ronald E. Riggio (2006), *Transformational Leadership,* Second Edition. Mahwah, NJ: Lawrence Erlbaum, 94–95.

130 Senay Boztas (2009), The Sunday Times 100 Best Small Companies to Work For 2009. *The Sunday Times,* 1 March.

131 The Sunday Times 100 Best Companies to Work For 2009. *The Sunday Times,* 1 March.

132 Roger Gill (2008), Sustaining creativity and innovation: the role of leadership. *LT Focus,* Summer.

133 K. Jaskyte (2004), Transformational leadership, organizational culture, and innovativeness in nonprofit organizations. *Nonprofit Management & Leadership,* 15 (2), 153–168.

134 *Looking after Leaders – Leadership Development for Leaders in the Health and Social Care Sector,* reported by Emma Maier (2008), Healthcare charities 'need more leadership support'. *Third Sector Online,* 17 March.

135 Angela Smith, the then UK Government's Third Sector Minister, speaking at the Third Sector Excellence Awards at the Grosvenor House Hotel in London on 24 September 2009.

136 Godfrey Smith (2000), A Battle of Britain hero we forgot. *The Sunday Times,* September 10.

137 Joseph Masciulli, Mikhail A. Molchanov and W. Andy Knight (2009), Political leadership in context. In Joseph Masciulli, Mikhail A. Molchanov and W. Andy Knight, Editors, *The Ashgate Research Companion to Political Leadership.* Farnham, Surrey: Ashgate Publishing, Chapter 1, 5.

138 Cf. Jürgen Habermas (1971), *Knowledge and Human Interests.* Boston, MA: Beacon.

139 Joseph Masciulli, Mikhail A. Molchanov and W. Andy Knight (2009), Political leadership in context. In Joseph Masciulli, Mikhail A. Molchanov and W. Andy Knight, Editors, *The Ashgate Research Companion to Political Leadership.* Farnham, Surrey: Ashgate Publishing, Chapter 1, 5.

140 Norman Dixon (1976), *On the Psychology of Military Incompetence.* London: Jonathan Cape.

141 Baron Antoine Henri de Jomini (1838), *Précis de l'Art de la Guerre: Des Principales Combinaisons de la Stratégie, de la Grande Tactique et de la Politique Militaire.* Brussels: Meline, Cans et Copagnie, 1838. English translations: Baron de Jomini, trans. Major O.F. Winship and Lieut. E.E. McLean (1854), *The Art of War.* New York: G.P. Putnam; Baron de Jomini, trans. Capt. G.H. Mendell and Lieut. W.P. Craighill (1862), *The Art of War.* Philadelphia, PA: J.B. Lippincott; reprinted, Westport, CT: Greenwood Press, 1971; reprinted, with a new introduction by Charles Messenger, London: Greenhill Books, 1992.

142 Douglas MacArthur (1964), *Reminiscences.* New York: McGraw-Hill.

143 Royal Navy (2004), *British Maritime Doctrine,* Third Edition. Norwich: Her Majesty's Stationery Office, 105.

144 W. Wallace (2005), Network enabled battle command. *Military Review,* May–June, 2–5.

145 David S. Alberts and Mark E. Nissen (2009), Toward harmonizing command and control with organization and management theory. *The International C2 Journal,* 3 (2), 1–59.

146 C. Burns, D. Bryant and B. Chalmers (2005), Boundary, purpose and values in work-domain models: models of naval command and control. *Man and Cybernetics,* 35 (5), 603–616.

147 David S. Alberts (2007), Agility, focus, and convergence: the future of command and control. *The International C2 Journal,* 1 (1), 1–30.

148 U.S. Army (1999), *U.S. Army Vision Statement,* 7. Available at www.army.mil/vision/Documents/The %20–Army%20Vision.pdf

149 U.S. Army (1990), *Field Manual 22–100, Army Leadership.* Washington, DC: US Government Printing Office, para. 2.6.

150 Leonard Wong, Paul Bliese and Dennis McGurk (2003), Military leadership: a context specific review. *Leadership Quarterly,* 14, 657–692.

151 Donald J. Campbell, Sean T. Hannah and Michael D. Matthews (2010), Leadership in military and other dangerous contexts: introduction to the Special Topic Issue. *Military Psychology,* 22, S1–S14.

152 Donald J. Campbell, Sean T. Hannah and Michael D. Matthews (2010), Leadership in military and other dangerous contexts: introduction to the Special Topic Issue. *Military Psychology*, 22, S1–S14.

153 Francis J. Yammarino, Michael D. Mumford, Mary Shane Connelly and Shelley D. Dionne (2010), Leadership and team dynamics for dangerous military contexts. *Military Psychology*, 22, S15–S41.

154 Benjamin E, Baran and Cliff W. Scott (2010), Organizing ambiguity: a grounded theory of leadership and sense-making within dangerous contexts. *Military Psychology*, 22, S42–S69.

155 Benjamin E. Baran and Cliff W. Scott (2010), Organizing ambiguity: a grounded theory of leadership and sense-making within dangerous contexts. *Military Psychology*, 22, S42–S69.

156 Donald J. Campbell, Sean T. Hannah and Michael D. Matthews (2010), Leadership in military and other dangerous contexts: introduction to the Special Topic Issue. *Military Psychology*, 22, S1–S14.

157 Patrick J. Sweeney (2010), Do soldiers reevaluate trust in their leaders prior to combat operations? *Military Psychology*, 22, S70–S88.

158 Kelly Fisher, Katherine Hutchings and James C. Sarros (2010), The 'bright' and 'shadow' aspects of in-extremis leadership. *Military Psychology*, 22, S89–S116.

159 Olav K. Olsen, Jarle Eid and Gerry Larsson (2010), Leadership and ethical justice behavior in a high moral intensity operational context. *Military Psychology*, 22, S137–S156.

160 Kelly Fisher, Katherine Hutchings and James C. Sarros (2010), The 'bright' and 'shadow' aspects of in-extremis leadership. *Military Psychology*, 22, S89–S116.

161 Leonard Wong, Paul Bliese and Dennis McGurk (2003), Military leadership: a context specific review. *Leadership Quarterly*, 14, 657–692.

162 Leonard Wong, Paul Bliese and Dennis McGurk (2003), Military leadership: a context specific review. *Leadership Quarterly*, 14, 657–692.

163 John Lockard (2010), A military view of leadership in the private sector. In Elaine Biech, Editor, *The ASTD Leadership Handbook*. Alexandria, VA: ASTD Press and San Francisco, CA: Berrett-Koehler, Chapter 31, 428–429.

164 John Adair (1973), *Action-Centred Leadership*. New York: McGraw-Hill.

165 Greg McMahon (2007), Functional leadership in Australia: the story. In Jonathan Gosling, Peter Case and Morgen Witzel, Editors, *John Adair: Fundamentals of Leadership*. Basingstoke: Palgrave Macmillan, 163–188.

166 Sir Brian Burridge (2007), Action-centred leadership in the Royal Air Force: final landing or new horizon? In Jonathan Gosling, Peter Case and Morgen Witzel, Editors, *John Adair: Fundamentals of Leadership*. Basingstoke: Palgrave Macmillan, 107.

Chapter 3

1 Nitin Nohria and Rakesh Khurana (2010), Advancing leadership theory and practice. In Nitin Nohria and Rakesh Khurana, Editors, *Handbook of Leadership Theory and Practice*. Boston, MA: Harvard Business Press, 12.

2 Quoted by Zöe Perkins (2010), Six lessons in leadership. *Imperial Matters,* Spring, 14–17.

3 Ted Honderich, Editor (2005), *The Oxford Companion to Philosophy,* Second Edition. Oxford: Oxford University Press, 131.

4 Mary Ann Glynn and Rich DeJordy (2010), Leadership through an organization behaviour lens. In Nitin Nohria and Rakesh Khurana, Editors, *Handbook of Leadership Theory and Practice.* Boston, MA: Harvard Business Press, Chapter 5

5 Mary Ann Glynn and Rich DeJordy (2010), Leadership through an organization behaviour lens. In Nitin Nohria and Rakesh Khurana, Editors, *Handbook of Leadership Theory and Practice.* Boston, MA: Harvard Business Press, Chapter 5.

6 Euripides (480–406 BC), *The Suppliant Women,* Trans. Frank William Jones, *Euripides IV,* ed. David Grene and Richmond Lattimore. Chicago: University of Chicago Press, 1958.

7 Sun Tzu (c. 500BC), *The Art of War,* translated by Roger T. Ames (1993). London: The Folio Society, 2007, 77.

8 D.A. Van Sters and R.H.G. Field (1990), The evolution of leadership theory. *Journal of Organizational Change Management,* 3 (3), 29–45.

9 L.L. Bernard (1926), *An Introduction to Social Psychology.* New York: Holt.

10 Ralph M. Stogdill (1974), *Handbook of Leadership: A Survey of the Literature.* New York: Free Press.

11 Mauro F. Guillén (2010), Classical sociological approaches to the study of leadership. In Nitin Nohria and Rakesh Khurana, Editors, *Handbook of Leadership Theory and Practice.* Boston, MA: Harvard Business Press, 235.

12 R. Whittington (1993), Social structures and strategic leadership. In J. Hendry, G. Johnson and J. Newton, Editors, *Strategic Thinking: Leadership and the Management of Change.* Chichester: John Wiley & Sons.

13 Reported in 'Public sector – not as good looking as the private sector'. Society daily, www.guardian.co.uk, 24 March 2010.

14 James MacGregor Burns (1978), *Leadership.* New York: Harper & Row, 880.

15 W.B. Yeats (1892), *The Countess Cathleen,* Scene 5.

16 John P. Kotter (1990), *A Force for Change: How Leadership Differs from Management.* New York: Free Press, 106.

17 Timothy A. Judge, Amy E. Colbert and Remus Ilies (2004), Intelligence and leadership: a quantitative review and test of theoretical propositions. *Journal of Applied Psychology,* 89 (3), 542–552.

18 Research by Dean K. Simonton reported by Sadie F. Dingfelder (2004), A presidential personality. *Monitor on Psychology,* American Psychological Association, November, 26–28.

19 C. Levicki (1998), *The Leadership Gene: The Genetic Code for a Life-long Leadership Career.* London: Financial Times Management, 98–99.

20 Roger Gill (1982), A trainability concept for management potential and an empirical study of its relationship with intelligence for two managerial skills. *Journal of Occupational Psychology,* 55 (2), 139–147; Roger Gill (1980), *Intelligence and Trainability in Managerial Prioritizing and Decision-making: An Empirical Investigation.* Paper presented at the British Psychological Society Annual London Conference, London, December.

21 Bernard M. Bass (1990), *Bass and Stogdill's Handbook of Leadership: Theory, Research and Managerial Applications*, Third Edition. New York: Free Press.
22 Research by Dean K. Simonton reported by Sadie F. Dingfelder (2004), A presidential personality. *Monitor on Psychology*, American Psychological Association, November, 26–28.
23 Peter G. Northouse (2010), *Leadership: Theory and Practice*, Fifth Edition. Thousand Oaks, CA: SAGE Publications, 19–22.
24 T.A. Judge, J.E. Bono, R. Ilies and M.W. Gerhardt (2002), Personality and leadership: a qualitative and quantitative review. *Journal of Applied Psychology*, 87, 765–780.
25 Ram Charan and Geoffrey Colvin (1999), Why CEOs fail. *Fortune*, 21, 68–75.
26 Randall S. Peterson, D. Brent Smith, Paul V. Martorana and Pamela D. Owens (2003), The impact of chief executive officer personality on top management team dynamics: one mechanism by which leadership affects organizational performance. *Journal of Applied Psychology*, 88 (5), 795–808.
27 B.J. Avolio, B.M. Bass and D.I. Jung (1999), Re-examining the components of transformational and transactional leadership using the Multifactor Leadership Questionnaire. *Journal of Occupational and Organizational Psychology*, 72, 441–462.
28 Joyce E. Bono and Timothy A. Judge (2004), Personality and transformational and transactional leadership: a meta-analysis. *Journal of Applied Psychology*, 89 (5), 901–910.
29 J.M. Digman (1990), Personality structure: emergence of the five-factor model. *Annual Review of Psychology*, 41, 417–440.
30 Sydney Finkelstein, Charles Harvey and Thomas Lawton (2007), *Breakout Strategy: Meeting the Challenge of Double-Digit Growth*. New York: McGraw-Hill, 297–326.
31 Knowledge@Wharton (2010), Effective leaders: why extraverts are not always the most successful bosses. *Knowledge@Wharton*, 14 (11–12). Downloaded from http://knowledge.wharton.upenn.edu/article.cfm?articleid=2638
32 Andrew M. Johnson, Philip A. Vernon, Julie A. Harris and Kerry L. Jang (2004), A behaviour genetic investigation of the relationship between leadership and personality. *Twin Research*, 7, 27–32.
33 James C. Collins (2001), *Good to Great: Why Some Companies Make the Leap – and Others Don't*. New York: HarperBusiness.
34 Adrian Furnham (2010), *Why Leaders Fail: The Psychology of Management Derailment*. Paper presented at a Leadership Forum, The Leadership Trust Foundation, Ross-on-Wye, 2 March.
35 Lew Perren and John Burgoyne (2002), *Management and Leadership Abilities: An Analysis of Texts, Testimony and Practice*. London: Council for Excellence in Management and Leadership.
36 Nitin Nohria and Rakesh Khurana (2010), Advancing leadership theory and practice. In Nitin Nohria and Rakesh Khurana, Editors, *Handbook of Leadership Theory and Practice*. Boston, MA: Harvard Business Press, 15.
37 Mike Pedler, John Burgoyne and Tom Boydell (2004), *A Manager's Guide to Leadership*. Maidenhead, Berkshire: McGraw-Hill.

38 Leon Festinger (1957), *A Theory of Cognitive Dissonance*. Evanston, IL: Row, Peterson.

39 Norman Dixon (1976), *On the Psychology of Military Incompetence*. London: Jonathan Cape.

40 Adrian Furnham (2010), *Why Leaders Fail: The Psychology of Management Derailment*. Paper presented at a Leadership Forum, The Leadership Trust Foundation, Ross-on-Wye, 2 March.

41 Richard Bolden and Jonathan Gosling (2004), *Leadership and Management Competencies: Lessons from the National Occupational Standards*. Paper presented at the SAM/IFSAM VIIth World Congress: Management in a World of Diversity and Change. 5–7 July, Göteborg, Sweden.

42 Adrian Furnham (2010), *Why Leaders Fail: The Psychology of Management Derailment*. Paper presented at the Leadership Forum, The Leadership Trust Foundation, Ross-on-Wye, 2 March.

43 Quoted by Tom Marshall (1991), *Understanding Leadership*. Tonbridge, Kent: Sovereign World, 19.

44 M.A. Hogg (2001), A social identity theory of leadership. *Personality and Social Psychology Review*, 5, 184–200.

45 W.H. Whyte (1943), *Street Corner Society*. Chicago: University of Chicago Press.

46 R.J. House and R.R. Mitchell (1974), Path-goal theory of leadership. *Journal of Contemporary Business*, 3 (4), 81–98.

47 G. Graen (1976), Role-making processes within complex organizations. In M.D. Dunnette, Editor, *Handbook of Industrial and Organizational Psychology*. Chicago: Rand McNally.

48 Alexandre Auguste Ledru-Rollin (1807–1874), quoted in E. de Mirecourt, *Histoire Contemporaine*, no. 79, Ledru-Rollin, 1857.

49 Robert Greenleaf (1977), *Servant Leadership*. New York: Paulist Press.

50 John Adair (1989), *Great Leaders*. Guildford: The Talbot Adair Press, 39.

51 *1 Corinthians*, 9, 19, The Bible.

52 Tim Cross (1998), *Christian Leadership*. Speech at Welbeck College, London, 5 July.

53 Quoted by Gregory G. Dess and Joseph C. Picken (2000), Changing roles: leadership in the 21st century. *Organizational Dynamics*, 28, 3, 18–34.

54 Quoted in *Annual Report 1998*, Center for Effective Organizations, Marshall School of Business, University of Southern California, Los Angeles, 13.

55 Anat Arkin (2004), Serve the servants. *People Management*, 23 December, 30–33.

56 Quoted by John Monks (2000), *Engaging the Work Force during Change*, The National Leadership Conference. MCI-METO, Royal Military Academy, Sandhurst, 24 May.

57 Tom Marshall (1991), *Understanding Leadership*. Tonbridge, Kent: Sovereign World, 67.

58 Robert Greenleaf (1977), *Servant Leadership*. New York: Paulist Press.

59 Robert Greenleaf, quoted by Richard Bolden (2004), *What is Leadership?* Research Report, Leadership South West, Centre for Leadership Studies, University of Exeter, 67.

60   Robert Greenleaf (1977), *Servant Leadership*. New York: Paulist Press, 23.
61   Danah Zohar and Ian Marshall (2001), *Spiritual Intelligence: The Ultimate Intelligence*. London: Bloomsbury Publishing, 33.
62   Danah Zohar and Ian Marshall (2001), *Spiritual Intelligence: The Ultimate Intelligence*. London: Bloomsbury Publishing, 262–263.
63   Mitch McCrimmon (2010), Why servant leadership is a bad idea. *Management-Issues*, 16 August, http://www.management-issues.com/2010/8/16/opinion/why-servant-leadership-is-a-bad-idea.asp?
64   Eric Berne (1964), *Games People Play*. New York: Grove Press.
65   D. Katz, N. Maccoby and N.C. Morse (1950), *Productivity, Supervision and Morale in an Office Situation*. Ann Arbor, MI: University of Michigan Institute for Social Research; D. Katz, N. Maccoby, G. Gurin and L. Floor (1951), *Productivity, Supervision and Morale Among Railroad Workers*. Ann Arbor, MI: University of Michigan Institute for Social Research.
66   E.A. Fleishman (1953), The description of supervisory behavior. *Journal of Applied Psychology*, 37 (1–6), 1953; A.W. Haplin and B.J. Winer (1957), A factorial study of leader behavior descriptions. In R.M. Stogdill and A.E. Coons, Editors, *Leader Behavior: Its Description and Measurement*. Columbus, OH: Bureau of Business Research, Ohio State University; E.A. Fleishman and E.F. Harris (1962), Patterns of leadership behavior related to employee grievances and turnover. *Personnel Psychology*, 15 (1), 43–56.
67   F.E. Fiedler and R.J. House (1988), Leadership theory and research: a report of progress. In C.L. Cooper and I.T. Robertson, Editors, *International Review of Industrial and Organizational Psychology*. Chichester: John Wiley & Sons.
68   Rensis Likert (1961), *New Patterns of Management*. New York: McGraw-Hill.
69   R. Tannenbaum and W.H. Schmidt (1968), How to choose a leadership pattern. *Harvard Business Review*, 36, 95–101.
70   Norman Dixon (1985), Why lefties make the best leaders. *Personnel Management*, November, 36–39.
71   Robert R. Blake and Jane S. Mouton (1964), *The Managerial Grid*. Houston, TX: Gulf; Robert R. Blake and Jane S. Mouton (1978), *The New Managerial Grid*. Houston, TX: Gulf.
72   Robert R. Blake and Anne Adams McCanse (1991), *Leadership Dilemmas – Grid Solutions*. Houston, TX: Gulf.
73   B. Alimo-Metcalfe (1996), The feedback revolution. *Health Service Journal*, June 13, 26–28.
74   Based on B.M. Bass and E.R. Valenzi (1974), Contingent aspects of effective management styles. In J.G. Hunt and L.L. Larson, Editors, *Contingency Approaches to Leadership*. Carbondale, IL: Southern Illinois University Press; B.M. Bass, E.R. Valenzi, D.L. Farrow and R.J. Solomon (1975), Management styles associated with organizational, task, personal, and interpersonal contingencies. *Journal of Applied Psychology*, 60 (6), 720–729; Bernard M. Bass (1976), A systems survey research feedback for management and organizational development. *Journal of Applied Behavioral Science*, 12 (2), 215–229.
75   See the beginning of Chapter 1.

76 Noam Chomsky (1999), *Profit over People: Neoliberalism and Global Order*. New York: Seven Stories Press, 53; Zani Dannhauser (2007), *The Relationship between Servant Leadership, Follower Trust, Team Commitment and Unit Effectiveness*, unpublished doctoral thesis, Stellenbosch University, South Africa.

77 Claus Møller (1994), Employeeship: the necessary prerequisite for empowerment. *Empowerment in Organizations*, 2 (2), 4–13; Stefan Tengblad (2003), *What is Employeeship?* Paper presented at the 17th Nordic Conference on Business Studies, Reykjavik, Iceland; Stefan Tengblad (2003), *Den myndige medarbetaren – Strategier för ett konstruktivt medarbetarskap*. Kristianstad, Sweden: Liber AB; S. Tengblad, F. Hällsten, F.C. Ackerman and J. Velten (2007), *Medarbetarskap.Från ord till Handling! [Employeeship: from Words to Action!]* Malmö, Sweden: Liber.

78 John Adair (1973), *Action-Centred Leadership*. New York: McGraw-Hill, viii.

79 Jonathan Gosling (2005), *John Adair: A Lifetime's Contribution to Leadership Studies*. Speech at the Lifetime Contribution Award Ceremony, Hewitt Associates, London, 23 February.

80 John Adair (1973), *Action-Centred Leadership*. New York: McGraw-Hill; John Adair (1983), *Effective Leadership: A Self-Development Manual*. Aldershot: Gower; John Adair (1984), *The Skills of Leadership*. Aldershot: Gower.

81 John Adair (1989), *Great Leaders*. Guildford: The Talbot Adair Press, 61.

82 David C. McClelland (1988), *Human Motivation*. Cambridge: Cambridge University Press.

83 John Adair (1973), *Action-Centred Leadership*. New York: McGraw-Hill, 59–68.

84 Roger Gill (2005), *Extending Action-Centred Leadership: 'Task' as Vision, Mission and Strategy and the Place of Values*. Paper presented at The John Adair International Colloquium and Festschrift, St George's House, Windsor, 5–6 September.

85 Arthur K. Yeung and Douglas A. Ready (1995), Developing leadership capabilities of global corporations. *Human Resource Management*, 34 (4), 529–547.

86 Marian Iszatt White (n.d.), *Explicating John Adair's Action Centred Leadership: Case Study 1*. Lancaster: Centre for Excellence in Leadership.

87 Keith Grint (2007), Foreword. In Jonathan Gosling, Peter Case and Morgen Witzel, Editors, *John Adair: Fundamentals of Leadership*. Basingstoke: Palgrave Macmillan, xi.

88 John Adair (2007), The forward view. In Jonathan Gosling, Peter Case and Morgen Witzel, Editors, *John Adair: Fundamentals of Leadership*. Basingstoke: Palgrave Macmillan, Chapter 12, 212.

89 R. Whipp and A. Pettigrew (1993), Leading change and the management of competition. In J. Hendry, G. Johnson and J. Newton, Editors, *Strategic Thinking: Leadership and the Management of Change*. Chichester: John Wiley & Sons, 205.

90 A.K. Korman (1966), 'Consideration', 'initiating structure,' and organizational criteria – a review. *Personnel Psychology*, 19, 349–361; S. Kerr, C.A. Schriesheim, C.J. Murphy and R.M. Stogdill (1974), Towards a contingency theory of leadership based upon the consideration and initiating structure literature. *Organizational Behavior and Human Performance*, 12, 62–82; C.A. Schriesheim

and C.J. Murphy (1976), Relationships between leader behavior and subordinate satisfaction and performance: a test of some situational moderators. *Journal of Applied Psychology,* 61, 634–641; R. Katz (1977), The influence of group conflict on leadership effectiveness. *Organizational Behavior and Human Performance,* 20, 265–286; J.F. Schriesheim (1980), The social context of leader-subordinate relations: an investigation of the effects of group cohesiveness. *Journal of Applied Psychology,* 65, 183–194.

91 Stephem J. Zaccaro and Richard J. Klimoski (2001), The nature of organizational leadership: an introduction. In Stephem J. Zaccaro and Richard J. Klimoski, Editors, *The Nature of Organizational Leadership: Understanding the Performance Imperatives Confronting Today's Leaders.* San Francisco, CA: Jossey-Bass, 16.

92 R. Goffee and G. Jones (2000), Why should anyone be led by you? *Harvard Business Review,* September–October, 78 (5), 62–70.

93 Helge Hoel, Lars Glasø, Jørn Hetland, Cary L. Cooper and Ståle Einarsen (2009), Leadership styles as predictors of self-reported and observed workplace bullying. *British Journal of Management,* 21 (2), 453–468.

94 A.K. Korman (1966), 'Consideration', 'initiating structure,' and organizational criteria – a review. *Personnel Psychology,* 19, 349–361; L.L. Larson, J.G. Hunt and R.N. Osborn (1976), The great hi-hi leader behavior myth: a lesson from Occam's razor. *Academy of Management Journal,* 19, 628–641; P.C. Nystrom (1978), Managers and the hi-hi leader myth. *Academy of Management Journal,* 21, 324–331.

95 C.N. Greene (1975), The reciprocal nature of influence between leader and subordinate. *Journal of Applied Psychology,* 60, 187–193.

96 C.A. Schriesheim and S. Kerr (1977), Theories and methods of leadership: a critical appraisal of current and future directions. In J.G. Hunt and L.L. Larsen, Editors, *Leadership: The Cutting Edge.* Carbondale, IL: Southern Illinois University Press, 9–45; Alan Bryman (1992), *Charisma and Leadership in Organizations.* London: SAGE Publications, 8–9.

97 Alan Bryman (1992), *Charisma and Leadership in Organizations.* London: SAGE Publications, 10–11.

98 Timothy A. Judge, Ronald F. Piccolo and Remus Ilies (2004), The forgotten ones? The validity of consideration and initiating structure in leadership research. *Journal of Applied Psychology,* 89 (1), 36–51.

99 Peter L. Wright and David S. Taylor (2000), *The Interpersonal Skills of Leadership: Behavioural Aspects.* Bradford: University of Bradford School of Management; Gerry Randell (2008), The core of leadership. *Business Leadership Review,* V: III; Gerry Randell (1998), *The 'Micro-Skills' Approach to Leadership Development.* Paper presented to The Leadership Trust Foundation Inaugural Conference on 'Leadership Development: 'The Challenges Ahead', The Leadership Trust Foundation, Ross-on-Wye, February 2–3; Peter L. Wright and David S. Taylor (1994), *Improving Leadership Performance: Interpersonal Skills for Effective Leadership.* London: Prentice Hall.

100 Roger Gill and David Taylor (1976), Training managers to handle discipline and grievance interviews. *Journal of European Training,* 5, 217–117; C.W. Allinson

(1977), Training in performance appraisal interviewing: an evaluation study. *Journal of Management Studies*, 14, 179–191; David S. Taylor and Peter L. Wright (1977), Training auditors in interviewing skills. *Journal of European Industrial Training*, 1, 8–16; David S. Taylor and Peter L. Wright (1982), Influencing work performance: the development of diagnostic skills. *Journal of Management Development*, 1, 44–50; B.M. Alban-Metcalfe (1982), *Micro-skills of leadership*, unpublished PhD thesis, University of Bradford; Catherine T. Bailey and David Butcher (1983), Interpersonal skills training 1: the nature of skill acquisition and its implications for training design and management. *Management Education and Development*, 14, 106–112; Peter L. Wright and David S. Taylor (1984), *Improving Leadership Performance*. London: Prentice Hall; B.M. Alban-Metcalfe and P.L. Wright (1986), Social skills training for managers. In C. Hollin and P. Trower, Editors, *Handbook of Social Skills Training, Volume 1: Applications across the Lifespan*. Oxford: Pergamon; Peter L. Wright and David S. Taylor (1994), *Improving Leadership Performance: Interpersonal Skills for Effective Leadership*, Second Edition. London: Prentice Hall; Gerry Randell (1998), *The 'Micro-Skills' Approach to Leadership Development*. Paper presented to The Leadership Trust Foundation Inaugural Conference on 'Leadership Development: 'The Challenges Ahead', The Leadership Trust Foundation, Ross-on-Wye, February 2–3; Gerry Randell (2008), The core of leadership. *Business Leadership Review*, V: III.

101 F. Dansereau, G. Graen and W.J. Haga (1975), A vertical dyad linkage approach to leadership within formal organizations: a longitudinal investigation of the role making process. *Organizational Behavior and Human Performance*, 14, 46–78; G. Graen (1976), Role-making processes within complex organizations. In M.D. Dunnette, Editors, *Handbook of Industrial and Organizational Psychology*. Chicago, IL: Rand McNally, 1201–1245; G. Graen, J. Cashman, S. Ginsburgh and W. Schiesmann (1977), Effects of linking-pin quality upon the quality of working life of lower participants: a longitudinal investigation of the managerial understructure. *Administrative Science Quarterly*, 22, 491–504.

102 E.L. Stech (2004), Psychodynamic approach. In P.G. Northouse, Editor, *Leadership: Theory and Practice*, Third Edition. London: SAGE Publications.

103 B. Karlgren (1950), *The Book of Documents*. Stockholm: Museum of Far Eastern Antiquities.

104 R.C. Liden and G. Graen (1980), Generalizability of the vertical dyad linkage model of leadership. *Academy of Management Journal*, 23, 451–465.

105 Douglas J. Brown and Robert G. Lord (2001), Leadership and perceiver cognition: moving beyond first order constructs. In M. London, Editor, *How People Evaluate Others in Organizations*. Mahwah, NJ: Lawrence Erlbaum Associates, 181–202.

106 Peter G. Northouse (2010), *Leadership: Theory and Practice*, Fifth Edition. Thousand Oaks, CA: SAGE Publications, 156.

107 Peter G. Northouse (2010), *Leadership: Theory and Practice*, Fifth Edition. Thousand Oaks, CA: SAGE Publications, 156–157.

108 M.G. Evans (1970), The effects of supervisory behavior on the path-goal relationship. *Organizational Behavior and Human Performance*, 5, 277–298; R.J. House (1973), A path-goal theory of leadership effectiveness. In E.A. Fleishman

and J.G. Hunt, Editors, *Current Developments in the Study of Leadership*, Carbondale, IL: Southern Illinois University Press; R.J. House and T.R. Mitchell (1974), Path-goal theory of leadership. *Journal of Contemporary Business*, 3, 81–97.

109 Alan Bryman (1992), *Charisma and Leadership in Organizations*. London: SAGE Publications, 13–20.

110 Alan Bryman (1992), *Charisma and Leadership in Organizations*. London: SAGE Publications, 20.

111 Will Durant (1885–1981), American writer and philosopher. Quoted by Perry M. Rogers (2003), *Aspects of Western Civilization: Volume II, Problems and Sources in History*, Fifth Edition. Upper Saddle River, NJ: Pearson Education, 419.

112 B.M. Bass, E.R. Valenzi, D.L. Farrow and R.J. Solomon (1975), Management styles associated with organizational, task, personal, and interpersonal contingencies. *Journal of Applied Psychology*, 60 (6), 720–729.

113 Philip Hodgson and Randall White (2001), Leadership – the ne(x)t generation. *Directions: The Ashridge Journal*, Summer, 18–22.

114 B. Karlgren (1970), *Glosses on the Book of Documents*. Stockholm: Museum of Far Eastern Antiquities.

115 F.E. Fiedler (1969), Leadership – a new model. In C.A. Gibb (Editor), *Leadership*. Harmondsworth, Middlesex: Penguin, 230–241.

116 Peter L. Wright (1996), *Managerial Leadership*. London: Routledge.

117 Leader-Match concept. In Peter L. Wright (1996), *Managerial Leadership*. London: Routledge, 88–89.

118 Alan Bryman (1992), *Charisma and Leadership in Organizations*. London: SAGE Publications, 20.

119 P. Hersey and K.H. Blanchard (1969), The life cycle theory of leadership. *Training and Development Journal*, 23 (5), 26–34; P. Hersey and K.H. Blanchard (1993), *Management of Organizational Behavior: Utilizing Human Resources*, Sixth Edition. Englewood Cliffs, NJ: Prentice Hall.

120 W.J. Reddin (1970a), The tri-dimensional grid. *The Canadian Personnel and Industrial Relations Journal*, January, 13–20; W.J. Reddin (1970b), *Managerial Effectiveness*. New York: McGraw-Hill. W.J. Reddin (1987), *How To Make Your Management Style More Effective*. Maidenhead: McGraw-Hill.

121 Stephen J. Zaccaro and Richard J. Klimoski (2001), The nature of organizational leadership: an introduction. In Stephem J. Zaccaro and Richard J. Klimoski, Editors, *The Nature of Organizational Leadership: Understanding the Performance Imperatives Confronting Today's Leaders*. San Francisco, CA: Jossey-Bass.

122 Nigel Nicholson (2001), Gene politics and the natural selection of leaders. *Leader to Leader*, 20, 46–52.

123 E.A. Fleishman, M.D. Mumford, S.J. Zaccaro, K.Y. Levin, A.L. Korotkin and M.B. Hein (1991), Taxonomic efforts in the description of leader behavior: a synthesis and functional interpretation. *Leadership Quarterly*, 2, 245–287.

124 Robert Goffee and Gareth Jones (2000), Why should anyone be led by you? *Harvard Business Review*, September–October, 63–70.

125 Joanne B. Ciulla (1999), The importance of leadership in shaping business values. *Long Range Planning*, 32 (2), 166–172.

126 Alan Bryman (1992), *Charisma and Leadership in Organizations.* London: SAGE Publications, 20–21.

127 J.V. Downton (1973), *Rebel Leadership: Commitment and Charisma in the Revolutionary Process.* New York: Free Press.

128 James MacGregor Burns (1978), *Leadership.* New York: Harper & Row.

129 James MacGregor Burns (1978), *Leadership.* New York: Harper & Row, 20.

130 Joanne B. Ciulla (1999), The importance of leadership in shaping business values. *Long Range Planning,* 32 (2),166–172.

131 R.N. Kanungo and M. Mendonca (1996), *Ethical Dimensions in Leadership.* Beverly Hills, CA: SAGE Publications.

132 Micha Popper and Ofra Mayseless (2003), Back to basics: applying a parenting perspective to transformational leadership. *Leadership Quarterly,* 14, 41–65.

133 Abraham Maslow (1987), *Motivation and Personality,* Third Edition. New York: Harper & Row.

134 J.M. Hays and C.Y. Kim (2008), *Renaissance Leadership: Transforming Leadership for the 21st Century. Part 1: The New Leadership.* The Australian National University School of Management, Marketing, and International Business Working Paper Series. ISSN: 1833–6558.

135 Bernard M. Bass (1985), *Leadership and Performance Beyond Expectations.* New York: Free Press; Bernard M. Bass (1990), From transactional to transformational leadership: learning to share the vision. *Organizational Dynamics,* 18, 19–31; Bernard M. Bass and Bruce J. Avolio (1994), Introduction. In Bernard M. Bass and Bruce J. Avolio, Editors, *Improving Organizational Effectiveness through Transformational Leadership.* Thousand Oaks, CA: SAGE Publications.

136 Roger Gill (1997), *The Leadership Styles of Transactional and Transformational Leaders.* Working paper LT-RG-97–1, Ross-on-Wye: The Leadership Trust Foundation.

137 Merethe Schanke Aasland, Anders Skogstad, Guy Notelaers, Morten Birkeland Nielsen and Ståle Einarsen (2009), The prevalence of destructive leadership behaviour. *British Journal of Management,* 21 (2), 438–452.

138 Bernard M. Bass (1990), From transactional to transformational leadership: learning to share the vision. *Organizational Dynamics,* 18, 19–31.

139 Roger Gill (1997), *The Leadership Styles of Transactional and Transformational Leaders.* Working paper LT-RG-97–1, Ross-on-Wye: The Leadership Trust Foundation.

140 Gerry Randell (2008), The core of leadership. *Business Leadership Review,* V: III; Gerry Randell (1998), *The 'Micro-Skills' Approach to Leadership Development.* Paper presented to The Leadership Trust Foundation Inaugural Conference on 'Leadership Development: 'The Challenges Ahead', The Leadership Trust Foundation, Ross-on-Wye, February 2–3; Peter L. Wright and David S. Taylor (1994), *Improving Leadership Performance: Interpersonal Skills for Effective Leadership.* London: Prentice Hall.

141 Bernard M. Bass (1985), *Leadership and Performance Beyond Expectations.* New York: Free Press.

142 Bruce J. Avolio and Bernard M. Bass (1990), *Basic Workshop in Full Range Leadership Development.* Binghamton, NY: Bass, Avolio and Associates; Rebecca Hazell (1997), *Heroes: Great Men through the Ages.* New York: Abbeville Press Publishers, 8–12.

143 Attributed to Oliver Wendell Holmes, Jr (1841–1935).

144 E. Kelloway and J. Barling (2000), What have we learned about developing transformational leaders? *Leadership and Organizational Development Journal*, 22 (5), 221–229.

145 Bernard M. Bass (1985), *Leadership and Performance Beyond Expectations.* New York: Free Press, 4.

146 Paul 'Bear' Bryant, quoted in http://coachlikeapro.tripod.com

147 Bernard M. Bass (1997), *The Ethics of Transformational Leadership.* Kellogg Leadership Studies Program: Transformational Leadership, Working Papers. College Park, MD: Academy of Leadership Press.

148 Roger Gill (1997), *The Leadership Styles of Transactional and Transformational Leaders,* Working paper LT-RG-97–1, Ross-on-Wye: The Leadership Trust Foundation.

149 Thomas J. Peters and Robert H. Waterman (1982), *In Search of Excellence: Lessons. from America's Best-Run Companies.* New York: Harper & Row.

150 Abraham Sagie, Nurit Zaidman, Yair Amichal-Hamburger, Dov Te'eni and David G. Schwartz (2002), An empirical assessment of the loose-tight leadership model: quantitative and qualitative analyses. *Journal of Organizational Behaviour,* 23, 303–320.

151 Bruce J. Avolio and Bernard M. Bass (1995), Individual consideration viewed at multiple levels of analysis: a multi-level framework for examining the diffusion of transformational leadership. *Leadership Quarterly,* 6, 199–218.

152 Deanne N. Den Hartog, Robert J. House, Paul J. Hanges, S. Antonio Ruiz-Quintanilla, Peter W. Dorfman *et al.* (1999), Culture specific and cross-culturally generalizable implict leadership theories: are attributes of charismatic/transformational leadership universally endorsed? *Leadership Quarterly,* 10 (2), 219–256.

153 Bernard M. Bass and Bruce J. Avolio (1997), *Revised Manual for the Multifactor Leadership Questionnaire.* Palo Alto, CA: Mind Garden.

154 Gareth Edwards and Roger Gill (2003a), *Hierarchical Level as a Moderator of Leadership Behaviour: A 360–degree Investigation.* Paper presented at the Annual Occupational Psychology Conference, British Psychological Society, Bournemouth, 8–10 January; Gareth Edwards and Roger Gill (2003), *An Investigation of the 'Full Range Leadership' Model at Different Hierarchical Levels of an Organisation Using Multiple Ratings.* Paper presented at the Annual Conference of the British Academy of Management, Harrogate, September 15–17; Gareth Edwards (2005), *Transformational and Transactional Leadership Behaviour of Managers at Different Levels of an Organization's Hierarchy,* unpublished PhD thesis, University of Strathclyde; Gareth Edwards and Roger Gill (2009), *Leadership across Hierarchical Levels in Organisations: Developing a Framework based on Transformational, Transactional and Laissez-Faire Behaviours.* Working Paper, Ross-on-Wye: The Leadership Trust Foundation; Gareth Edwards and Roger Gill (2012), Transformational leadership across hierarchical levels in UK manufacturing organizations. *Leadership & Organization Development Journal* (In press).

155 B.M. Bass, D.A. Waldman, B.J. Avolio and M. Bebb (1987), Transformational leadership and the falling dominoes effect. *Group and Organization Studies*, 12, 73–87; Titus Oshagbemi and Roger Gill (2004), Differences in leadership styles and behaviour across hierarchical levels in UK organizations. *Leadership & Organization Development Journal*, 25 (1), 93–106.

156 K.B. Lowe, K.G. Kroeck and N. Sivasubramaniam (1996), Effectiveness correlates of transformational and transactional leadership. *Leadership Quarterly*, 7, 385–425.

157 Titus Oshagbemi and Roger Gill (2004), Differences in leadership styles and behaviour across hierarchical levels in UK organisations. *Leadership & Organization Development Journal*, 25 (1), 93–106.

158 Stephen J. Zaccaro and Richard J. Klimoski (2001), The Nature of Organizational Leadership: An Introduction. In Stephen J. Zaccaro and Richard J. Klimoski, Editors, *The Nature of Organizational Leadership*. San Francisco, CA: Jossey-Bass.

159 Bernard M. Bass (1997), *The Ethics of Transformational Leadership*. Kellogg Leadership Studies Program: Transformational Leadership, Working Papers, College Park, MD: Academy of Leadership Press; Bernard M. Bass and Bruce J. Avolio (1997), *Full Range Leadership Development: Manual for the Multifactor Leadership Questionnaire*. Redwood City, CA: Mind Garden, 93–94.

160 J.M. Howell and R.I. House (1993), *Socialized and Personalized Charisma*. London, Ontario: University of Western Ontario, Western Business School.

161 Timothy A. Judge and Ronald F. Piccolo (2004), Transformational and transactional leadership: a meta-analytic test of their relative validity. *Journal of Applied Psychology*, 89 (5), 755–768.

162 Bernard M. Bass (1997), Does the transactional-transformational leadership paradigm transcend organizational and national boundaries? *American Psychologist*, 52, 130–139.

163 D.N. Den Hartog, J.J. Van Muijen and P.L. Koopman (1997), Transactional versus transformational leadership: an observational field study, *Journal of Occupational and Organizational Psychology*, 70, 19–34; Timothy R. Hinkin and J. Bruce Tracey (1999), The relevance of charisma for transformational leadership in stable organizations. *Journal of Organizational Change Management*, 12 (2), 105–119.

164 P. Bycio, R. Hackett and J.S. Allen (1995), Further assessment of Bass's (1985) conceptualization of transactional and transformational leadership, *Journal of Applied Psychology*, 80, 468–478; S.A. Carless (1998), Assessing the discriminant validity of transformational leader behaviour as measured by the MLQ, *Journal of Occupational and Organizational Psychology*, 71, 353–358.

165 Bruce J. Avolio, Bernard M. Bass and Dong I. Jung (1999), Re-examining the components of transformational and transactional leadership using the Multifactor Leadership Questionnaire. *Journal of Occupational and Organizational Psychology*, 72, 441–462.

166 Stanley A. Deetz, Sarah J. Tracy and Jennifer Lyn Simpson (2000), *Leading Organizations through Transition*. Thousand Oaks, California: SAGE Publications, 49.

167 A. Bryman (1996), Leadership in organizations. In S.R. Clegg, C. Hardy and W.R. Nord, Editors, *Handbook of Organizational Studies*. London: SAGE Publications, 276–292.

168 Bernard M. Bass (1997), Does the transactional-transformational leadership paradigm transcend organizational and national boundaries? *American Psychologist*, 52, 130–139.

169 Gareth Edwards and Roger Gill (2003), *Hierarchical Level as a Moderator of Leadership Behaviour: A 360–degree Investigation*. Paper presented at the Annual Occupational Psychology Conference, British Psychological Society, Bournemouth, 8–10 January; Gareth Edwards and Roger Gill (2003), *An Investigation of the 'Full Range Leadership' Model at Different Hierarchical Levels of an Organisation Using Multiple Ratings*. Paper presented at the Annual Conference of the British Academy of Management, Harrogate, September 15–17; Titus Oshagbemi and Roger Gill (2004), Differences in leadership styles and behaviour across hierarchical levels in UK organisations. *Leadership & Organization Development Journal*, 25 (1), 93–106.

170 S.J. Zaccaro and R.J. Klimoski, Editors (2001), *The Nature of Organizational Leadership: Understanding the Performance Imperatives Confronting Today's Leaders*. San Francisco, CA: Jossey-Bass.

171 John Antonakis (2001), *Construct Validation of the Full-Range Leadership Model Using Independent Data Sets*. Paper presented at the *Festschrift* for Bernard M. Bass, State University of New York at Binghamton, May 31–June 1.

172 K.B. Lowe, K.G. Kroeck and N. Sivasubramaniam (1996), Effectiveness correlates of transformational and transactional leadership. *Leadership Quarterly*, 7, 385–425.

173 Gareth Edwards and Roger Gill (2003), *Hierarchical Level as a Moderator of Leadership Behaviour: A 360-degree Investigation*. Paper presented at the Annual Occupational Psychology Conference, British Psychological Society, Bournemouth, 8–10 January.

174 Philip Sadler (1997), *Leadership*. London: Kogan Page, 45.

175 Alan Bryman (1992), *Charisma and Leadership in Organizations*. London: SAGE Publications, 97.

176 Manfred Kets de Vries and Elizabeth Florent-Treacy (1999), *AuthentiZiotic Organizations: Global Leadership from A to Z*. Working Paper 99/62/ENT, INSEAD, Fontainebleau, France, 7–8.

177 Beverly Alimo-Metcalfe and Robert J. Alban-Metcalfe (2001), The development of a new Transformational Leadership Questionnaire. *Journal of Occupational and Organizational Psychology*, 74, 1–27.

178 B. Shamir (1995), Social distance and charisma: theoretical notes and an exploratory study. *Leadership Quarterly*, 6, 19–47.

179 Beverly Alimo-Metcalfe and Robert J. Alban-Metcalfe (2001), The development of a new Transformational Leadership Questionnaire. *Journal of Occupational and Organizational Psychology*, 74, 1–27.

180 John Alban-Metcalfe and Beverly Alimo-Metcalfe (2007). Development of a private sector version of the (Engaging) Transformational Leadership Questionnaire.

Leadership & Organizational Development Journal, 28, 104–121; John Dobby, Jane Anscombe and Rachel Tuffin (2004), *Police Leadership: Expectations and Impact*. London: Home Office Online Report 20/04.

181 Beverly Alimo-Metcalfe, John Alban-Metcalfe, Chiara Samele, Margaret Bradley and Jeevi Mariathasan (2007), *The Impact of Leadership Factors in Implementing Change in Complex Health and Social Care Environments*. Research project supported by NHS Grant SDO/22/2002.

182 R.K. Greenleaf (1977), *Servant Leadership: A Journey into the Nature of Legitimate Power and Greatness*. New York: Paulist Press.

183 Beverly Alimo-Metcalfe and John Alban-Metcalfe (2002), *Leadership: Time to Debunk the Myths*. Cabinet Office report. Leeds: Leadership Research and Development, 3.

184 A.H. Maslow (1954), *Motivation and Personality*. New York: Harper.

185 Andrew Kelly (2008), *Was Burns Right? Leadership and Power in the Knowledge Economy*, unpublished PhD thesis, University of Strathclyde.

186 Malcolm Higgs and Vic Dulewicz (2002), *Making Sense of Emotional Intelligence*, Second Edition. London: ASE, 113–117.

187 N.M. Tichy and M.A. Devanna (1986), *The Transformational Leader*. New York: John Wiley & Sons.

188 A.E. Rafferty and M.A. Griffin (2004), Dimensions of transformational leadership: conceptual and empirical extensions. *Leadership Quarterly*, 15, 329–354.

189 Marshall Sashkin (1988), The visionary leader. In J.A. Conger and R.N. Kanungo, Editors, *Charismatic Leadership: The Elusive Factor in Organizational Effectiveness*. San Francisco, CA: Jossey-Bass.

190 Marshall Sashkin (1992), Strategic leadership competencies: what are they? How do they operate? What can be done to develop them? In R.L. Phillips and J.G. Hunt, Editors, *Leadership: A Multiorganizational-level Perspective*. New York: Quorum Books; M. Sashkin and W.E. Rosenbach (1998), A new vision of leadership. In W.E. Rosenbach and R.L. Taylor, Editors, *Contemporary Issues in Leadership*, Fourth Edition. Boulder, CO: Westview Press.

191 S. Streufert and R.W. Swezey (1986), *Complexity, Managers, and Organizations*. Orlando, FL: Academic Press.

192 Bernard M. Bass (1992), Assessing the charismatic leader. In M. Syrett and C. Hogg, Editors, *Frontiers of Leadership*. Oxford: Blackwell.

193 Francis J. Flynn and Barry M. Staw (2004), Lend me your wallets: the effect of charismatic leadership on external support for an organization. *Strategic Management Journal*, 25, 309–330.

194 David A. Waldman, Gabriel G. Ramírez, Robert J. House and Phanish Puranam (2001), Does leadership matter? CEO leadership attributes and profitability under conditions of perceived environmental uncertainty. *Academy of Management Journal*, 44 (1), 134–143.

195 Max Weber (1864–1920), *Wirtschaft und Gesellschaft*, 1925 (G. Roth and C. Wittich, Editors, *Economy and Society*, 3 Volumes. New York: Bedminster, 1968).

196 R.J. House (1977), A 1976 theory of charismatic leadership. In J.G. Hunt and L.L. Larson, Editors, *Leadership: The Cutting Edge*. Carbondale, IL: Southern Illinois University Press, 189–207; J.A. Conger and R.N. Kanungo (1987), Toward a behavioral theory of charismatic leadership in organizational settings. *Academy of Management Review*, 12, 637–647; B. Shamir, R.J. House and M.B. Arthur (1993), The motivational effects of charismatic leadership: a self-concept based theory. *Organization Science*, 4, 577–594.

197 Mark G. Ehrhart and Katherine J. Klein (2001), Predicting followers' preferences for charismatic leadership: the influence of follower values and personality. *Leadership Quarterly*, 12 (2), 153–179.

198 Joanne B. Ciulla (1999), The importance of leadership in shaping business values. *Long Range Planning*, 32 (2), 166–172.

199 Gayle Avery (2004), *Understanding Leadership*. London: SAGE Publications, 19.

200 Gayle Avery (2004), *Understanding Leadership*. London: SAGE Publications, 29–30.

201 Joanna Barsh, Josephine Mogelof and Caroline Webb (2010), How centered leaders achieve extraordinary results. *McKinsey Quarterly*, October.

202 Martin Seligman (2004), *Authentic Happiness: Using the New Positive Psychology to Realize Your Potential for Lasting Fulfillment*. New York: Free Press; Ron Kaniel, Cade Massey and David T. Robinson (2010), *The Importance of Being an Optimist: Evidence from Labor Markets*. NBER Working Paper No. 16328. Cambridge, MA: National Bureau of Economic Research.

203 Michael A. Cohn, Barbara L. Frederickson, Stephanie L. Brown, Joseph A. Mikels and Anne M. Conway (2009), Happiness unpacked: positive emotions increase life satisfaction by building resilience. *Emotion*, 9 (3), 361–368.

204 McKinsey and Company (2010), The value of centered leadership. *McKinsey Quarterly*, October.

205 P. Gronn (1995), Greatness revisited: the current obsession with transformational leadership. *Leading and Managing*, 1 (1), 14–27; P. Gronn (2002), Distributed leadership as a unit of analysis. *Leadership Quarterly*, 13 (4), 423–451.

206 Gary Yukl (1999), An evaluation of the conceptual weaknesses in transformational and charismatic leadership theories. *Leadership Quarterly*, 10 (2), 285–305; Peter Gronn (1999), Substituting for leadership: the neglected role of the leadership couple. *Leadership Quarterly*, 10 (1), 41–62.

207 J.G. Hunt (1999), Transformational/charismatic leadership's transformation of the field: an historical essay. *Leadership Quarterly*, 10 (2), 129–144.

208 B.A.S. Koene, L.W. Vogelaar and J.L. Soeters (2002), Leadership effects on organizational climate and financial performance: local leadership effect in chain organizations. *Leadership Quarterly*, 13, 193–215.

209 Brian Leavy and David Wilson (1994), *Strategy and Leadership*. London: Routledge, 161–162.

210 Sir Peter Parker, chairman of Mitsubishi Electric Europe BV, quoted by Amin Rajan (2000), *Does Management Development Fail to Produce Leaders?* Tonbridge, Kent: Centre for Research in Employment & Technology in Europe.

211 Michael D. Mumford and Judy R. Van Dorn (2001), The leadership of pragmatism: reconsidering Franklin in the age of charisma. *Leadership Quarterly*, 12, 279–309.

212 Michael D. Mumford and Judy R. Van Dorn (2001), The leadership of pragmatism: reconsidering Franklin in the age of charisma. *Leadership Quarterly*, 12,
279–309.

213 D.C. Nice (1998), The warrior model of leadership: classic perspectives and contemporary relevance. *Leadership Quarterly*, 9 (3), 321–332.

214 Gerry Johnson and Kevan Scholes (2002), *Exploring Corporate Strategy*, Sixth Edition.
Harlow, Essex: Pearson Education, 38.

215 Gerry Johnson and Kevan Scholes (2002), *Exploring Corporate Strategy*, Sixth Edition.
Harlow, Essex: Pearson Education, 65.

216 Philip Stiles (2001), The impact of the board on strategy: an empirical investigation. *Journal of Management Studies*, 38 (5), 627–650.

217 S.L. Brown and K.M. Eisenhardt (1998), *Competing on the Edge*. Boston, MA:
Harvard Business School Press.

218 Beverley Mobbs (2004), *Linking the Balanced Scorecard to the [EFQM]
Excellence Model*. Paper presented at the 'Quest for Excellence' Conference,
Quality Award Secretariat and Department of Economic Development, Dubai,
UAE, and the British Quality Foundation, Dubai, UAE, March 15.

219 Katherine Beatty and Laura Quinn (2002), Strategic command: taking the long
view for organizational success. *Leadership in Action*, 22 (2), May/June, 3–7.

220 D. Hambrick and P. Mason (1984), Upper echelons: the organization as a reflection of its top managers. *Academy of Management Review*, 9, 193–206.

221 P. Johnson, K. Daniels and A. Huff (2001), Sensemaking leadership and mental
models. In Stephen J. Zaccaro and Richard J. Klimoski, Editors, *The Nature of
Organizational Leadership: Understanding the Performance Imperatives
Confronting Today's Leaders*. San Francisco, CA: Jossey-Bass.

222 Michael A. Hitt, R. Duane Ireland and Robert E. Hoskisson (1995), *Strategic
Management: Competitiveness and Globalization*. Minneapolis/St Paul, MN: West.

223 Abdalla Hagen, Semere Haile and Mahmoud Yousef (2003), CEOs' perceptions
of strategic flexibility and its impact on organizational performance: empirical
investigation. *Research Journal of the Olu Olu Institute Academy International
Congress*, 1 (1).

224 Katherine Beatty and Laura Quinn (2002), Strategic command: taking the long
view for organizational success. *Leadership in Action*, 22 (2), May/June, 3–7.

225 John J. Sosik and Don I. Jung (2009), *Full Range Leadership Development:
Pathways for People, Profit and Planet*. New York and London: Psychology
Press, 324.

226 Bruce Nixon (2002), Responding positively to the big issues. *Professional
Consultancy*, 4, April, 24–26.

227 Mark van Vugt and Anjana Ahuja (2010), *Selected: Why Some People Lead, Why
Others Follow, and Why It Matters*. London: Profile Books.

228 Mark van Vugt and Anjana Ahuja (2010), *Selected: Why Some People Lead, Why
Others Follow, and Why It Matters*. London: Profile Books, 5.

229 Mark van Vugt and Anjana Ahuja (2010), *Selected: Why Some People Lead, Why
Others Follow, and Why It Matters*. London: Profile Books, 6.

230 Mark Van Vugt (2006), Evolutionary origins of leadership and followership.
Personality and Social Psychology Review, 10 (4), 354–371.

231　Jelmer W. Eerkens, Kevin J. Vaughn and John Kantner (2009), Introduction: the evolution of leadership. Santa Fe, NM: School for Advanced Research Press, 5.

232　Jelmer W. Eerkens, Kevin J. Vaughn and John Kantner (2009), Introduction: the evolution of leadership. Santa Fe, NM: School for Advanced Research Press, 7–8.

233　Mark Van Vugt (2006), Evolutionary origins of leadership and followership. *Personality and Social Psychology Review*, 10 (4), 354–371.

234　Mark Van Vugt, Robert Hogan and Robert B. Kaiser (2008), Leadership, followership, and evolution. *American Psychologist*, 63 (3), 182–196.

235　Nikolaas Tinbergen (1963), On the aims and methods in ethology. *Zeitschrift für Tierpsychology*, 20, 410–433.

236　Mark Van Vugt, Robert Hogan and Robert B. Kaiser (2008), Leadership, followership, and evolution. *American Psychologist*, 63 (3), 182–196.

237　Glynis M. Breakwell (2011), The origins of speciousness. Review of Mark van Vugt and Anjana Ahuja (2010), *Selected: Why Some People Lead, Why Others Follow, and Why It Matters* (London: Profile Books). *Times Higher Education*, 20 January, 54.

238　Gary Yukl (1989), Managerial leadership: a review of theory and research. *Journal of Management*, 15 (2), 251–289.

239　Leigh Kibby and Charmine Härtel (2003), *Noetic Leadership: Leadership Skills that Manage the Existential Dilemma.* Paper presented at the Annual Conference of the British Academy of Management, Harrogate, 15–17 September.

240　The Industrial Society, www.indsoc.co.uk/cforl, 15 January 2001.

241　Brian Leavy and David Wilson (1994), *Strategy and Leadership.* London: Routledge, 1.

242　Joseph C. Rost (1993), Leadership development in the new millennium. *Journal of Leadership Studies*, November, 91–110.

243　R. Whipp and A. Pettigrew (1993), Leading change and the management of competition. In J. Hendry, G. Johnson and J. Newton, Editors, *Strategic Thinking: Leadership and the Management of Change.* Chichester: John Wiley & Sons, 207.

244　Beverly Alimo-Metcalfe and Robert J. Alban-Metcalfe (2001), The development of a new Transformational Leadership Questionnaire. *Journal of Occupational and Organizational Psychology*, 74, 1–27.

245　Bruce J. Avolio (2001), in a speech at the Bernard M. Bass Festschrift, Binghamton University, 31 May–1 June.

246　Peter L. Wright (1996), *Managerial Leadership.* London: Routledge.

247　M.W. Katzko (2002), The rhetoric of psychological research and the problem of unification in psychology. *American Psychologist*, 57, 262–270.

248　Peter Gronn (1995), *A Realistic View of Leadership.* Paper presented at the ELO-AusAsia online conference on Educational Leadership for the New Millennium, http://elo.eddirect.com; Peter Gronn (1995b), Greatness re-visited: the current obsession with transformational leadership. *Leading and Managing,* 1 (1), 14–27.

249　Gayle Avery (2004), *Understanding Leadership.* London: SAGE Publications, 146–149.

250 Bruce J. Avolio, Fred O. Walumbwa and Todd J. Weber (2009), Leadership: current theories, research, and future directions. In Susan T. Fiske, Daniel L. Schacter and Robert Sternberg, Editors, *Annual Review of Psychology, Volume 60*. Palo Alto, CA: Annual Reviews, 421–449.

251 James MacGregor Burns (2001), in a teleconference at the Bernard M. Bass Festschrift, Binghamton University, New York, 31 May–1 June.

252 Katherine Mangan (2002), Leading the way in leadership: the unending quest of the discipline's founding father, James MacGregor Burns. *The Chronicle of Higher Education*, 31 May, 1.

253 Roseanne J. Foti and John B. Miner (2003), Theoretical letters. Individual differences and organizational forms in the leadership process. *Leadership Quarterly*, 14, 83–112.

254 Edwin A. Locke (1997), The motivation to work: what we know. In M. Maehr and P. Pintrich, Editors, *Advances in Motivation and Achievement, Volume 10*. Greenwich, CT: JAI Press, 375–412.

255 F. Schmidt (1992), What do data really mean? Research findings, meta-analysis, and cumulative knowledge in psychology. *American Psychologist*, 47, 1171–1181.

256 F. Schmidt, J. Hunter and A. Outerbridge (1986), The impact of job experience and ability on job knowledge, work sample performance, and supervisory ratings of job performance. *Journal of Applied Psychology*, 71, 432–439.

257 Roger Gill (2006), *Theory and Practice of Leadership*. London: SAGE Publications.

258 Robert Kreitner and Angelo Kinicki (1998), *Organizational Behavior*, Fourth Edition. Boston, MA: Irwin/McGraw-Hill,

259 Arthur K. Yeung and Douglas A. Ready (1995), Developing leadership capabilities of global corporations. *Human Resource Management*, 34 (4), 529.

260 With an average turnover of £87 million, average turnover per employee of £138,000, and a 13% return on capital employed.

261 The Manufacturing Foundation (2003), *Innovation Essentials*. Birmingham, August.

262 R. Levering and M. Moskowitz (1993), *The 100 Best Companies to Work For in America*. New York: Currency/Doubleday.

263 M. Lipton (1996), Demystifying the development of an organizational vision. *Sloan Management Review*, 37 (June), 83–92.

264 William W. George (2001), *Keynote Address*, Academy of Management Annual Conference, Washington, DC, August. In *Academy of Management Executive*, 15 (4), 39–47.

265 Patrick Bolton, Markus K. Brunnermeier and Laura Veldkamp (2010), Economists' perspectives on leadership. In Nitin Nohria and Rakesh Khurana, Editors, *Handbook of Leadership Theory and Practice*. Boston, MA: Harvard Business Press, Chapter 9.

266 John P. Kotter (1990), What leaders really do. *Harvard Business Review*, May–June, 156–167.

267 J.P. Kotter and J.L. Hesketh (1992), *Corporate Culture and Performance*. New York: Free Press.

268 James Kouzes and Barry Z. Posner (1995), *The Leadership Challenge*. San Francisco, CA: Jossey-Bass.

269 Bruce E. Winston and Kathleen Patterson (2006), An integrative definition of leadership. *International Journal of Leadership Studies*, 1 (2), 6–66.

270 W.W. Burke and G.H. Litwin (1989), A causal model of organizational performance. In J.W. Pfeiffer, Editor, *The 1989 Annual: Developing Human Resources*. San Diego, CA: University Associates; W.W. Burke and G.H. Litwin (1992), A causal model of organizational performance. *Journal of Management*, 18 (3), 523–545.

271 Frederick W. Cannon (2004), *Leadership and Culture as Determinants of Organisational Climate: An Exploration of Perceptions in a European Division of a Global Financial Services Firm*, unpublished DBA thesis, Henley Management College and Brunel University.

272 Stephen J. Zaccaro and Deanna J. Banks (2001), Leadership, vision, and organizational effectiveness. In Stephen J. Zaccaro and Richard J. Klimoski, Editors, *The Nature of Organizational Leadership: Understanding the Performance Imperatives Confronting Today's Leaders*. San Francisco, CA: Jossey-Bass, 181.

273 Stephen J. Zaccaro and Richard J. Klimoski (2001), The nature of organizational leadership: an introduction. In Stephen J. Zaccaro and Richard J. Klimoski, Editors, *The Nature of Organizational Leadership: Understanding the Performance Imperatives Confronting Today's Leaders*. San Francisco, CA: Jossey-Bass, 6–7.

274 P. Lawrence and J. Lorsch (1967), *Organization and Environment*. Boston, MA: Harvard Business School Division of Research; J.D. Thompson (1967), *Organizations in Action*. New York: McGraw-Hill; M.S. Wortman (1982), Strategic management and changing leader-follower roles. *Journal of Applied Behavioral Science*, 18, 371–282; L.J. Bourgeois, III (1985), Strategic goals, perceived uncertainty, and economic performance in volatile environments. *Academy of Management Journal*, 28, 548–573.

275 Cynthia A. Montgomery (2008), Putting leadership back into strategy. *Harvard Business Review*, January 2008.

276 Michael Porter (1996), What is strategy? *Harvard Business Review*, 74 (6), November–December, 61–78.

277 Robert E. Staub (1996), *The Heart of Leadership: 12 Practices of Courageous Leaders*. Provo, UT: Executive Excellence Publications.

278 Arthur K. Yeung and Douglas A. Ready (1995), Developing leadership capabilities of global corporations: a comparative study of eight nations. *Human Resource Management Journal*, 34 (4), 529–548.

279 Ellen F. Goldman and Andrea Casey (2010), Building a culture that encourages strategic thinking. *Journal of Leadership & Organizational Studies*, 17 (2), 119–128; Georgia Sorensen (2010), Leadership beyond the battlefield. *The Public Manager*, Winter, 5–7.

280 Bill George (2010), The new 21st century leaders. *Harvard Business Review, Guest Edition*, 5 May.

281 See the Preface to this book.

Chapter 4

1   M. Sashkin (1986), The visionary leader. *Training and Development Journal*, 40 (5), 58–61.

2   Stephen R. Covey (1992), *Principle-centered Leadership*. London: Simon & Schuster, 96.

3   James M. Kouzes and Barry Z. Posner (1991), *The Leadership Challenge*. San Francisco, CA: Jossey-Bass, 135.

4   Sydney Finkelstein, Charles Harvey and Thomas Lawton (2007), *Breakout Strategy: Meeting the Challenge of Double-Digit Growth*. New York: McGraw-Hill, 145–146, 156–164.

5   Chartered Management Institute (2003), *Leading Change in the Public Sector: Making the Difference*, reported in *Professional Manager*, July, 6.

6   Quoted by Mark Zupan (2010), An economic perspective on leadership. In Nitin Nohria and Rakesh Khurana, Editors, *Handbook of Leadership Theory and Practice*. Boston, MA: Harvard Business Press, 269.

7   Catherine Soanes and Angus Stevenson, Editors (2004), *The Concise Oxford English Dictionary*, Eleventh Edition. Oxford: Oxford University Press, 1615.

8   Stephen J. Zaccaro and Deanna J. Banks (2001), Leadership, vision, and organizational effectiveness. In Stephen J. Zaccaro and Richard J. Klimoski, Editors, *The Nature of Organizational Leadership: Understanding the Performance Imperatives Confronting Today's Leaders*. San Francisco, CA: Jossey-Bass, 184–185.

9   McDonald's Corporate Webpage (2000), November. Website: http://www.mcdonalds.com/corporate/investor/about/vision/index.html

10 John P. Kotter (1990), *A Force for Change: How Leadership Differs from Management*. New York: Free Press.

11 J.A. Conger and R.N. Kanungo (1987), Toward a behavioral theory of charismatic leadership in organizational settings. *Academy of Management Review*, 12, 637–647.

12 B. Shamir, R.J. House and M. Arthur (1993), The motivational effects of charismatic leadership: a self-concept based theory. *Organization Science*, 4, 577–594; S.A. Kirkpatrick and E.A. Locke (1996), Direct and indirect effects of three core charismatic leadership components on performance and attitudes. *Journal of Applied Psychology*, 81, 36–51.

13 B. Shamir, R.J. House and M. Arthur (1993), The motivational effects of charismatic leadership: a self-concept based theory. *Organization Science*, 4, 577–594.

14 Jill M. Strange and Michael D. Mumford (2002), The origins of vision: charismatic versus ideological leadership. *Leadership Quarterly*, 13, 343–377.

15 Stanley A. Deetz, Sarah J. Tracy and Jennifer L. Simpson (2000), *Leading Organizations through Transition*. Thousand Oaks, CA: SAGE Publications, 73.

16 John P. Kotter (1990), *A Force for Change: How Leadership Differs from Management*. New York Free Press; J. Kelly (1993), *Facts against Fictions of Executive Behavior: A Critical Analysis of What Managers Do*. Westport, CT: Quorum Books.

17   T.O. Jacobs and E. Jaques (1990), Military executive leadership. In K.E. Clark and M.B. Clark, Editors, *Measures of Leadership*. Greensboro, NC: Center for Creative Leadership; T.O. Jacobs and E. Jaques (1991), Executive leadership. In R. Gal and A.D. Manglesdorf, Editors, *Handbook of Military Psychology*. New York: John Wiley & Sons; Stephen J. Zaccaro (1996), *Models and Theories of Executive Leadership: A Conceptual/Empirical Review and Integration*. Alexandria, VA: U.S. Army Research Institute for the Behavioral and Social Sciences.

18   Management Today (2002), *Sheer Inspiration: The UK's 100 Most Visionary Companies*. London: Management Today.

19   General Electric's annual report (1990), quoted by Stuart Crainer (1996), Bridging the gap between noble aspirations and reality. *Professional Manager*, July, 7.

20   *Durham University Strategy 2010–2020*. Accessed on 9 November 2010 at http://www.dur.ac.uk/resources/about/strategy/Finalfullstrategydocument.pdf. Reproduced with kind permission.

21   Stewart D. Friedman (2001), Leadership DNA: the Ford Motor story. *Training & Development*, March, 23–29.

22   *Concept for Nigeria's Vision 2020*. The Presidency, Government of Nigeria, NV2020/NSC (2008) 02.

23   John Harvey-Jones (1988), *Making It Happen*. London: HarperCollins, 18–19; John P. Kotter (1995), Leading change: why transformation efforts fail. *Harvard Business Review*, March–April; Andrew Kakabadse (2001), What is vision? *Sheer Inspiration: The UK's 100 Most Visionary Companies*. London: Management Today, 4–5.

24   Stuart Cross (2010), In the dark: leadership lessons from the UK election. *BNET*, May 4. Retrieved from http://blogs.bnet.co.uk.

25   Laura Frith, in an interview with Hashi Syedain (2007), Reed's psychological MD. *World Business*, January–February, 73.

26   Kees Van der Heijden (1993), Strategic vision at work: discussing strategic vision in management teams. In J. Hendry, G. Johnson and J. Newton, Editors, *Strategic Thinking: Leadership and the Management of Change*. Chichester: John Wiley & Sons, 142.

27   Sir Ronnie Flanagan (2000), *Leadership during Cultural and Institutional Change*. Paper presented at the National Leadership Conference, MCI-METO, The Royal Military Academy, Sandhurst, 24 May. Sir Ronnie was then Chief Constable, Royal Ulster Constabulary (which was shortly afterwards replaced by the Police Service of Northern Ireland), and later Chief Inspector of Constabulary of the UK (excluding Scotland).

28   Warren Bennis (2010), Leadership competencies. *Leadership Excellence*, February, 20.

29   Quoted by Ruth Tait (1996), The attributes of leadership. *Leadership & Organization Development Journal*, 17 (1), 27–31.

30   Thomas J. Peters (1987), *Thriving on Chaos*. New York: HarperCollins.

31   J. Robert Baum, Edwin A. Locke and Shelley A. Kirkpatrick (1998), A longitudinal study of the relation of vision and vision communication to venture growth in entrepreneurial firms. *Journal of Applied Psychology*, 83 (1), 43–54.

32 J.J. Hater and B.M. Bass (1988), Supervisors' evaluations and subordinates' perceptions of transformational leadership. *Journal of Applied Psychology*, 73, 695–702; P.M. Podsakoff, S.B. MacKenzie, R.H. Moorman and R. Fetter (1990), Transformational leader behaviors and their effects on followers' trust in leader, satisfaction, and organizational citizenship behavior. *Leadership Quarterly*, 1, 107–142; F.J. Yammarino, W.D. Spangler and B.M. Bass (1993), Transformational leadership and performance. *Leadership Quarterly*, 4, 81–102; J.M. Howell and B.J. Avolio (1993), Transformational leadership, transactional leadership, locus of control, and support for innovation: key predictors of business unit performance. *Journal of Applied Psychology*, 78, 891–902.

33 Paul C. Nutt and Robert W. Backoff (1997), Crafting vision. *Journal of Management Inquiry*, 6, 308–328.

34 Bert Nanus (1992), *Visionary Leadership*. San Francisco, CA: Jossey-Bass.

35 Lindsay Levin (2000), *Transforming our business through people*. Paper presented at the Third Annual Leadership Conference, 'The Head and Heart of Leadership', The Leadership Trust Foundation, Ross-on-Wye, September 6–7.

36 Kees Van der Heijden (1993), Strategic vision at work: discussing strategic vision in management teams. In J. Hendry, G. Johnson and J. Newton, Editors, *Strategic Thinking: Leadership and the Management of Change*. Chichester: John Wiley & Sons, 137–150.

37 Stephen J. Zaccaro and Deanna J. Banks (2001), Leadership, vision, and organizational effectiveness. In Stephen J. Zaccaro and Richard J. Klimoski, Editors, *The Nature of Organizational Leadership: Understanding the Performance Imperatives Confronting Today's Leaders*. San Francisco, CA: Jossey-Bass, 188.

38 Boas Shamir (1995), Social distance and charisma: theoretical notes and an exploratory study. *Leadership Quarterly*, 6, 19–47.

39 P.M. Senge (1990), *The Fifth Discipline: The Art and Practice of the Learning Organization*. New York: Doubleday.

40 James C. Collins and Jerry I. Porras (1996a), *Built to Last: Successful Habits of Visionary Companies*, London: HarperBusiness; James C. Collins and Jerry I. Porras (1996b), Building your company's vision. *Harvard Business Review*, September–October.

41 James C. Collins and Jerry I. Porras (1996b), Building your company's vision. *Harvard Business Review*, September–October.

42 Ira M. Levin (2000), Vision revisited: telling the story of the future. *Journal of Applied Behavioral Science*, 36 (1), 91–107.

43 John P. Kotter (1997), Leading by vision and strategy. *Executive Excellence*, October, 15–16.

44 John P. Kotter (1988), *The Leadership Factor*. New York: Free Press.

45 Patricia Seybold, quoted by R.F. Maruca (2000), State of the new economy. *Fast Company*, September, 105.

46 Stanley A. Deetz, Sarah J. Tracy and Jennifer L. Simpson (2000), *Leading Organizations through Transition*. Thousand Oaks, CA: SAGE Publications, 53.

47 Gregory G. Dess and Joseph C. Picken (2000), Changing roles: leadership in the 21st century. *Organizational Dynamics*, 28 (3), 18–34.

48 David Butcher and Mike Meldrum (2001), Defy gravity. *People Management*, 28 June, 40–44.

49 Sally Lansdell (2002), *The Vision Thing*. Oxford: Capstone Publishing, 43.

50 The Guardian (2000), Briefcase: Watch out for: Rentokil Initial. *Guardian*, May 17.

51 Hay Group, *Top Teams – Why Some Work and Some Don't*. Reported by Alison Maitland (2001), Solitary geniuses need not apply. *Financial Times*, 14 November, 17.

52 John Kotter, quoted by Carly Chynoweth (2010), Win their hearts if you want success. *The Sunday Times*, Appointments, 17 October, 4; John Kotter and Lorne Whitehead (2010), *Buy-In: Saving Your Good Idea from Getting Shot Down*. Boston, MA: Harvard Business School Press.

53 John Middleton and Bob Gorzynski (2002), *Strategy Express*. Oxford: Capstone Publishing, 105.

54 Peter Senge (1990), *The Fifth Discipline*. New York: Doubleday.

55 John P. Kotter (1997), Leading by vision and strategy. *Executive Excellence*, October, 15–16.

56 Kees Van der Heijden (1993), Strategic vision at work: discussing strategic vision in management teams. In J. Hendry, G. Johnson and J. Newton (Editors), *Strategic Thinking: Leadership and the Management of Change*, Chichester: John Wiley & Sons, 137–150.

57 Kees Van der Heijden (1993), Strategic vision at work: discussing strategic vision in management teams. In J. Hendry, G. Johnson and J. Newton, Editors, *Strategic Thinking: Leadership and the Management of Change*. Chichester: John Wiley & Sons, 137–139.

58 P. Senge, C. Roberts, R.B. Ross, B.J. Smith and A. Kleiner (1994), *The Fifth Discipline Fieldbook: Strategies and Tools for Building a Learning Organization*. London: Nicholas Brealey Publishing.

59 James M. Kouzes and Barry Z. Posner (1991), *The Leadership Challenge*. San Francisco, CA: Jossey-Bass, 124.

60 Robert K. Greenleaf (1991), *The Servant as Leader*. Indianapolis, IL: The Robert K. Greenleaf Center.

61 Sal F. Marino (1999), Where there is no visionary, companies falter. *Industry Week*, March 15.

62 John Middleton and Bob Gorzynski (2002), *Strategy Express*. Oxford: Capstone Publishing, 106.

63 David Whyte (1997), *The House of Belonging*. Langley, WA: Many Rivers Press.

64 Jo Owen (2002), Alexander the reasonable? *Daily Telegraph*, 7 July.

65 E.H. Schein (1991), The role of the founder in the creation of organizational culture. In P.J. Frost, L.F. Moore, M.R. Louis, C. Lundberg and J. Martin, Editors, *Organizational Culture*. London: SAGE Publications.

66 Kees Van der Heijden (1993), Strategic vision at work: discussing strategic vision in management teams. In J. Hendry, G. Johnson and J. Newton, Editors, *Strategic Thinking: Leadership and the Management of Change*. Chichester: John Wiley & Sons, 137–139.

67 Andrew Kakabadse (2001), What is vision? *Sheer Inspiration: The UK's 100 Most Visionary Companies*. London: Management Today, 4–5.

68 Kees Van Der Heijden (1993), Strategic vision at work: discussing strategic vision in management teams. In J. Hendry, G. Johnson and J. Newton, Editors, *Strategic Thinking: Leadership and the Management of Change*. Chichester: John Wiley & Sons, 140.

69 J.A. Conger (1989), *The Charismatic Leader: Behind the Mystique of Exceptional Leadership*. San Francisco, CA: Jossey-Bass.

70 Charles Handy (1992), The language of leadership. In M. Syrett and C. Hogg, Editors, *Frontiers of Leadership*. Oxford: Blackwell.

71 John Harvey-Jones (1988), *Making It Happen*. London: HarperCollins, 26.

72 John Harvey-Jones (1988), *Making It Happen*. London: HarperCollins, 97.

73 Kees Van der Heijden (1993), Strategic vision at work: discussing strategic vision in management teams. In J. Hendry, G. Johnson and J. Newton, Editors, *Strategic Thinking: Leadership and the Management of Change*. Chichester: John Wiley & Sons, 146.

74 Kees Van der Heijden (1993), Strategic vision at work: discussing strategic vision in management teams. In J. Hendry, G. Johnson and J. Newton, Editors, *Strategic Thinking: Leadership and the Management of Change*. Chichester: John Wiley & Sons, 149.

75 D. Keith Denton (2001), Mission statements miss the point. *Leadership & Organization Development Journal*, 22 (7), 309–314.

76 Sydney Finkelstein, Charles Harvey and Thomas Lawton (2007), *Breakout Strategy: Meeting the Challenge of Double-Digit Growth*. New York: McGraw-Hill, 172–174.

77 Stephen J. Zaccaro and Deanna J. Banks (2001), Leadership, vision, and organizational effectiveness. In Stephen J. Zaccaro and Richard J. Klimoski, Editors, *The Nature of Organizational Leadership: Understanding the Performance Imperatives Confronting Today's Leaders*. San Francisco, CA: Jossey-Bass, 190–191.

78 S.R. Robbins and R.B. Duncan (1988), The role of the CEO and top management in the creation and implementation of strategic vision. In D.C. Hambrick, Editor, *The Executive Effect: Concepts and Methods for Studying Top Managers*. Greenwich, CT: JAI Press, 229.

79 Stephen J. Zaccaro and Deanna J. Banks (2001), Leadership, vision, and organizational effectiveness. In Stephen J. Zaccaro and Richard J. Klimoski, Editors, *The Nature of Organizational Leadership: Understanding the Performance Imperatives Confronting Today's Leaders*. San Francisco, CA: Jossey-Bass, 192.

80 Andrew J. Dubrin (2001), *Leadership: Research Findings, Practice and Skills*, Third Edition. Boston, MA: Houghton Mifflin.

81 Warren Bennis and Bert Nanus (1985), *Leaders: Strategies for Taking Charge*. New York: Harper & Row.

82 James M. Kouzes and Barry Z. Posner (1987), *The Leadership Challenge*. San Francisco, CA: Jossey-Bass.

83 Richard Allen (1995), On a clear day you can have a vision. *Leadership & Organization Development Journal*, 16, 39–45.

84 Thomas S. Bateman, Hugh O'Neill and Amy Kenworthy-U'Ren (2002), A hierarchical taxonomy of top managers' goals. *Journal of Applied Psychology*, 87 (6), 1134–1148.

85 Monica McCaffrey and Larry Reynolds (2003), Small group, big impact: how to facilitate a vision workshop. *Training Journal*, March, 18–21.

86 Warren Bennis and Bert Nanus (1985), *Leaders: Strategies for Taking Charge*. New York: Harper & Row; N.M. Tichy and M.A. Devanna (1990), *The Transformational Leader: The Key to Global Competitiveness*, Second Edition. New York: John Wiley & Sons; John P. Kotter (1990), *A Force for Change: How Leadership Differs from Management*. New York: Free Press; S.A. Kirkpatrick and E.A. Locke (1991), Leadership: do traits matter? *The Executive*, 5, 48–60; John P. Kotter (1996), *Leading Change*. Boston, MA: Harvard Business School Press.

87 Gareth P. Edwards (2000), *In Search of the Holy Grail: Leadership in Management*. Working Paper, Ross-on-Wye: The Leadership Trust Foundation.

88 Andrew Kakabadse and Nana Kakabadse (1996), *Essence of Leadership*. London: International Thomson Business Press.

89 Quoted by Margaret Coles (1998), Vision is key to good leadership. *The Sunday Times*, 18 October, 7.20.

90 Gregory G. Dess and Joseph C. Picken (2000), Changing roles: leadership in the 21st century. *Organizational Dynamics*, 28 (3), 18–34.

91 Robert J. House (1995), Leadership in the twenty-first century: a spectacular inquiry. In A. Howard, Editor, *The Changing Nature of Work*. San Francisco, CA: Jossey-Bass, 411–450.

92 Richard Olivier (2001), *Inspirational Leadership: Henry V and the Muse of Fire*. London: The Industrial Society, 34.

93 Richard Olivier (2001), *Inspirational Leadership: Henry V and the Muse of Fire*. London: The Industrial Society, 34–35.

94 Sally Lansdell (2002), *The Vision Thing*. Oxford: Capstone Publishing, 45–47.

95 Beverly Kaye and Betsy Jacobson (1999), True tales and tall tales: the power of organizational storytelling. *Training & Development*, March, 45–50.

96 Michael Lissack and Johan Roos (2000), *The Next Common Sense*. London: Nicholas Brealey Publishing, 143–153.

97 Quoted by T. O'Brien (2001), A storyteller for our time. www.SiliconValley.com, 4 February.

98 Tara Jones (2010), What's your vision? *Leadership Excellence*, 27 (3), March, 6–7.

99 John P. Kotter (2007), Leading change – why transformational efforts fail. *Harvard Business Review*, January, 96–103. (First published in 1995.)

100 Stephen J. Zaccaro and Deanna J. Banks (2001), Leadership, vision, and organizational effectiveness. In Stephen J. Zaccaro and Richard J. Klimoski, Editors, *The Nature of Organizational Leadership: Understanding the Performance Imperatives Confronting Today's Leaders*. San Francisco, CA: Jossey-Bass, 192–193.

101 James MacGregor Burns (1978), *Leadership*. New York: HarperCollins, 97.

102 J. Robert Baum, Edwin A. Locke and Shelley A. Kirkpatrick (1998), A longitudinal study of vision and vision communication to venture growth in entrepreneurial firms. *Journal of Applied Psychology*, 83, 43–54.

103 Robert J. House and Boas Shamir (1993), Towards an integration of transformational, charismatic, and visionary theories. In M.M. Chemers and R. Ayman, Editors, *Leadership Theory and Research: Perspectives and Directions*. Orlando, FL: Academic Press.

104 Robert J. House (1977), A 1976 theory of charismatic leadership. In J.G. Hunt and L.L. Larson, Editors, *Leadership: The Cutting Edge*. Carbondale, IL: Southern Illinois University Press; D. Eden (1984), Self-fulfilling prophecy as a management tool: harnessing Pygmalion. *Academy of Management Review*, 12, 76–90; D. Eden (1990), *Pygmalion in Management: Productivity as a Self-fulfilling Prophecy*. San Francisco, CA: New Lexington Press.

105 John Kotter (1996), *Leading Change*. Boston, MA: Harvard Business School Press.

106 Sally Lansdell (2002), *The Vision Thing*. Oxford: Capstone Publishing, 40.

107 James M. Kouzes and Barry Z. Posner (1991), *The Leadership Challenge*. San Francisco, CA: Jossey-Bass, 124.

108 Tom Marshall (1991), *Understanding Leadership*. Tonbridge, Kent: Sovereign World, 35.

109 Tom Marshall (1991), *Understanding Leadership*. Tonbridge, Kent: Sovereign World, 40.

110 Stanley A. Deetz, Sarah J. Tracy and Jennifer L. Simpson (2000), *Leading Organizations through Transition*. Thousand Oaks, CA: SAGE Publications, 49.

111 Thomas J. Peters and Nancy Austin (1985), *A Passion for Excellence*. New York: Random House, 284.

112 Stanley A. Deetz, Sarah J. Tracy and Jennifer L. Simpson (2000), *Leading Organizations through Transition*. Thousand Oaks, CA: SAGE Publications, 73.

113 J.M. Howell and P.J. Frost (1989), A laboratory study of charismatic leadership. *Organizational Behavior and Human Decision Processes*, 43, 243–269; B. Shamir, M. Arthur and R.J. House (1994), The rhetoric of charismatic leadership: a theoretical extension, a case study, and implications for research. *Leadership Quarterly*, 5, 25–42; D.N. Den Hartog and R.M. Verburg (1997), Charisma and rhetoric: communicative techniques of international business leaders. *Leadership Quarterly*, 8, 355–391.

114 J.M. Howell and P.J. Frost (1989), A laboratory study of charismatic leadership. *Organizational Behavior and Human Decision Processes*, 43, 243–269; S.J. Holladay and W.T. Coombs (1994), Speaking of visions and visions being spoken: an exploration of the effects of content and delivery on perceptions of leader charisma. *Management Communication Quarterly*, 8, 165–189; R. Awamleh and W. Gardner (1999), Perceptions of leader charisma and effectiveness: the effects of vision content, delivery, and organizational performance. *Leadership Quarterly*, 10 (3), 345–373.

115 Michael Frese, Susanne Beimel and Sandra Schoenborn (2003), Action training for charismatic leadership: two evaluations of studies of a commercial training module on inspirational communication of a vision. *Personnel Psychology*, 56, 671–697.

116 Roger Eglin (2001), Preaching fails to convert workforce. *The Sunday Times*, 11 March.

117 Lin Grensing-Pophal (2000), Follow me. *HR Magazine*, 45 (2), February, 36–41.
118 J. A. Byrne (1998), How Jack Welch runs GE. *Business Week*, 8 June.
119 Sally Lansdell (2002), *The Vision Thing*. Oxford: Capstone Publishing, 52–68.
120 Peter M. Senge (1990), *The Fifth Discipline: The Art and Practice of the Learning Organization*. New York: Doubleday, 225.
121 *Vision for the Future*, The University of Manchester. Downloaded from http://www.manchester.ac.uk/aboutus/facts/vision/ on 21 April 2011.
122 James Champy and Nitin Nohria (2000), *The Arc of Ambition*. Chichester: John Wiley & Sons, 1.
123 Richard Olivier (2001), *Inspirational Leadership: Henry V and the Muse of Fire*. London: The Industrial Society, 12–13.
124 Warren Bennis (1989), *On Becoming a Leader*. Reading, MA: Addison-Wesley.
125 Roman Herzog (1997), Germany's future: moving into the 21st century. Speech at the opening of the Hotel Adlon on 26 April. Herzog was then the federal president of Germany. Published in Lessons from the Past, Visions for the Future, American Institute for Contemporary German Studies, The Johns Hopkins University, *German Issues*, 18, 85–98.
126 Stanley A. Deetz, Sarah J. Tracy and Jennifer L. Simpson (2000), *Leading Organizations through Transition*. Thousand Oaks, CA: SAGE Publications, 52.
127 Bert Nanus (1992), *Visionary Leadership: Creating a Compelling Sense of Direction for Your Organization*. San Francisco, CA: Jossey-Bass, 25–26.
128 *Annual Report & Accounts 2000*, Domino's Pizza UK & IRL plc.
129 Beverley Mobbs (2004), *Linking the Balanced Scorecard to the [EFQM] Excellence Model*. Paper presented at the 'Quest for Excellence' Conference, Quality Award Secretariat and Department of Economic Development, Dubai, UAE, and the British Quality Foundation, Dubai, UAE, March 15.
130 Louis Andre, United States Defence Intelligence Agency, in a personal communication to and quoted by James M. Simon, Jr (2001), *Crucified on a Cross of Goldwater–Nichols*. Paper presented at a Seminar on Intelligence, Command, and Control, Program on Information Resources Policy, Harvard University and the Center for Information Policy Research, Cambridge, Massachusetts, July.
131 I am grateful to Dr Günther Dobrauz, a University of Strathclyde MBA student in 2007 in Zurich, Switzerland, for some of these examples.
132 Bain and Company's 8th Annual Management Tools Survey, quoted by Darrell K. Rigby (2001), Management tools 2001. *Forum*, European Foundation for Management Development, December, 24–26.
133 The Leadership Trust (2002), *Senior Management Attitude Survey*. Ross-on-Wye: The Leadership Trust Foundation.
134 Bert Nanus (1992), *Visionary Leadership*. San Francisco, CA: Jossey-Bass.
135 S. Kirkpatrick and E.A. Locke (1996), Direct and indirect effects of three core charismatic leadership components on performance and attitudes. *Journal of Applied Psychology*, 81, 36–51; K.B. Lowe, K.G. Koreck and N. Sivasubramaniam (1996), Effectiveness correlates of transformational and transactional leadership: a meta-analytic review of the MLQ literature. *Leadership Quarterly*, 7, 385–425.

136 D.N. Den Hartog, R.J. House, P.J. Hanges, S.A. Quintanilla, P.U. Dorfman et al. (1999), Culture specific and cross-culturally generalizable implict leadership theories: are the attributes of charismatic/transformational leadership universally endorsed? *Leadership Quarterly*, 10, 219–256.

137 K.W. Parry and S.B. Proctor-Thompson (2001), *Validation of the Social Process of Leadership Scale (SPL)*. Paper presented at the *Festschrift* for Dr Bernard M. Bass, State University of New York at Binghamton, New York, June; J.J. Sosik, S.S. Kahai and B.J. Avolio (1999), Leadership style, anonymity, and creativity in group decision support systems: the mediating role of optimal flow. *Journal of Creative Behavior*, 33, 227–256.

138 Dave O'Connell, Karl Hickerson and Arun Pillutla (2011), Organizational visioning: an integrative review. *Group & Organization Management*, 36, 103–125.

139 Danny Miller and John O'Whitney (1999), Beyond strategy: configuration as a pillar of competitive advantage. *Business Horizons*, 42 (3), May–June, 5–17.

140 Mark Lipton (1996), Demystifying the development of an organizational vision. *Sloan Management Review*, 37 (June), 83–92.

141 *Wall Street Journal* (1993), 4 October.

142 James M. Kouzes and Barry Z. Posner (1991), *The Leadership Challenge*. San Francisco, CA: Jossey-Bass, 124.

143 Joseph H. Boyett and Jimmie T. Boyett (1996), *Beyond Workplace 2000*. New York: Plume.

144 R.N. Kanungo and J.A. Conger (1992), Charisma: exploring new dimensions of leadership behavior. *Psychology and Developing Societies*, 4, 21–38.

145 Stephen J. Zaccaro and Deanna J. Banks (2001), Leadership, vision, and organizational effectiveness. In Stephen J. Zaccaro and Richard J. Klimoski, Editors, *The Nature of Organizational Leadership: Understanding the Performance Imperatives Confronting Today's Leaders*. San Francisco, CA: Jossey-Bass, 196–197.

146 C.M. Fiol, D. Harris and R.J. House (1999), Charismatic leadership: strategies for effecting social change. *Leadership Quarterly*, 10, 440–482.

147 Korn/Ferry (1989), *Reinventing the CEO*. New York: Korn/Ferry International and Columbia Business School.

148 J.W. Thompson (1992), Corporate leadership in the 21st Century. In J. Renesch, Editor, *New Traditions in Business*. San Francisco, CA: Berrett-Koehler.

149 Philip Stiles (2001), The impact of the board on strategy: an empirical investigation. *Journal of Management Studies*, 38 (5), 627–650.

150 Peter Drucker (1966), *The Effective Executive*. New York: HarperBusiness (revised edition, 2002).

151 Joseph Jaworski (1996), *Synchronicity: The Inner Path of Leadership*. San Francisco, CA: Berrett-Koehler.

152 Larry Reynolds (2000), What is leadership? *Training Journal*, November, 26–27.

153 James C. Collins and Jerry I. Porras (1994), *Built To Last: Successful Habits of Visionary Companies*. New York: HarperCollins.

154 W. Glenn Rowe (2001), Creating wealth in organizations: the role of strategic leadership. *Academy of Management Executive*, 15 (1), 81–94.

155 Stephen Rush and Martin Wilcox (2001), Visionary leadership: a talk with Jay Conger. *Leadership in Action*, 21 (2), 19–22.
156 James Champy and Nitin Nohria (2000), *The Arc of Ambition*. Chichester: John Wiley & Sons, 31.
157 Kees Van Der Heijden (1993), Strategic Vision at Work: Discussing Strategic Vision in Management Teams. In J. Hendry, G. Johnson and J. Newton, Editors, *Strategic Thinking: Leadership and the Management of Change.* Chichester: John Wiley & Sons.
158 Alan Bryman (1992), *Charisma and Leadership in Organizations.* London: SAGE Publications, 168.
159 Robert J. House and Jane M. Howell (1992), Personality and charismatic leadership. *Leadership Quarterly,* 3, 81–108.
160 J.M. Strange and Michael D. Mumford (2002), The origins of vision: charismatic versus ideological leadership. *Leadership Quarterly,* 13, 343–377.
161 M.D. Mumford and J.M. Strange (2002), Vision and mental models: the case of charismatic and ideological leadership. In Bruce J. Avolio and Francis J. Yammarino, Editors, *Charismatic and Transformational Leadership: The Road Ahead.* New York: JAI Elsevier.
162 J.A. O'Connor, M.D. Mumford, T.C. Clifton, T.E. Gessner and M.S. Connelly (1995), Charismatic leaders and destructiveness: a historiometric study. *Leadership Quarterly,* 6, 529–555.
163 Colin Wilson (1963), *The Outsider.* London: Pan Books, 222.
164 W. Glenn Rowe (2001), Creating wealth in organizations: the role of strategic leadership. *Academy of Management Executive,* 15 (1), 81–94.
165 R. Evans (1997), Follow the leader. *Report on Business,* November, 56–63; L.T. Hosmer (1982), The importance of strategic leadership. *Journal of Business Strategy,* 3 (2), Fall, 47–57; L. Sooklal (1991), The leader as a broker of dreams. *Human Relations,* 44 (8), 833–856; A. Zaleznik (1990), The leadership gap. *The Academy of Management Executive,* 4 (1), 7–22.
166 Colin Wilson (1963), *The Outsider.* London: Pan Books, 225.
167 Colin Wilson (1963), *The Outsider.* London: Pan Books, 227.
168 Colin Wilson (1963), *The Outsider.* London: Pan Books, 254.
169 Colin Wilson (1963), *The Outsider.* London: Pan Books, 260.
170 Tom Marshall (1991), *Understanding Leadership.* Tonbridge, Kent: Sovereign World, 30.
171 Robert Craven (1998), Let's take it from the top. *Independent on Sunday,* Smart Moves, 15 February, 2.
172 James C. Collins and Jerry I. Porras (1994), *Built to Last: Successful Habits of Visionary Companies.* New York: HarperBusiness.
173 James C. Collins (1996), Aligning action and values. *Leader to Leader,* 1, Summer, 19–24.
174 With updating amendments, reproduced with kind permission from *Sheer Inspiration: The UK's 100 Most Visionary Companies.* London: Management Today, 2001, 20–22.
175 Yahoo (2007), Sagentia. Accessed at http://uk.finance.yahoo.com/q?s=SGA.L on 4 May 2007.

176 London Stock Exchange (2011), Sagentia. Accessed at http://www.lse.co.uk/ SharePrice.asp?shareprice=SAG on 8 March 2011.

177 James C. Collins and Jerry I. Porras (1995), The ultimate vision. *Across the Board*, January.

Chapter 5

1 Roger Fisher (2006), Foreword. In Nikos Mourkogiannis (2006), *Purpose: The Starting Point of Great Companies*. New York: Palgrave Macmillan, xiv.

2 Thucydides (c. 460–c. 395 BC), *The Peloponnesian War*. Trans. Steven Lattimore (1998). Indianapolis, IN: Hackett Publishing.

3 Nikos Mourkogiannis (2006), *Purpose: The Starting Point of Great Companies*. New York: Palgrave Macmillan, 16.

4 Nikos Mourkogiannis (2006), *Purpose: The Starting Point of Great Companies*. New York: Palgrave Macmillan, 43.

5 Nikos Mourkogiannis (2006), *Purpose: The Starting Point of Great Companies*. New York: Palgrave Macmillan, 19–20, 57–107.

6 Joel Kurtzman (2010), *Common Purpose: How Great Leaders Get Organizations to Achieve the Extraordinary*. San Francisco, CA: Jossey-Bass, xxii.

7 Joel Kurtzman (2010), *Common Purpose: How Great Leaders Get Organizations to Achieve the Extraordinary*. San Francisco, CA: Jossey-Bass, 50.

8 Joel Kurtzman (2010), *Common Purpose: How Great Leaders Get Organizations to Achieve the Extraordinary*. San Francisco, CA: Jossey-Bass, xxi.

9 Roger Fisher (2006), Foreword. In Nikos Mourkogiannis (2006), *Purpose: The Starting Point of Great Companies*. New York: Palgrave Macmillan, xiv.

10 Bill Quirke (2002), Managers must convey the big picture. *Professional Management*, May, 24–25.

11 We discuss spiritual intelligence in leadership in a later chapter.

12 Marshall Goldsmith (2010), Foreword. In Joel Kurtzman, *Common Purpose: How Great Leaders Get Organizations to Achieve the Extraordinary*. San Francisco, CA: Jossey-Bass, ix–x.

13 Hillary Rodham Clinton (2011), Way to lead. In *The World in 2011*. London: The Economist, 76.

14 Joel Kurtzman (2010), *Common Purpose: How Great Leaders Get Organizations to Achieve the Extraordinary*. San Francisco, CA: Jossey-Bass, xii.

15 Catherine Soanes and Angus Stevenson, Editors (2004), *The Concise Oxford English Dictionary*, Eleventh Edition. Oxford: Oxford University Press, 1615.

16 Catherine Soanes and Angus Stevenson, Editors (2004), *The Concise Oxford English Dictionary*, Eleventh Edition. Oxford: Oxford University Press, 1167.

17 Nikos Mourkogiannis (2006), *Purpose: The Starting Point of Great Companies*. New York: Palgrave Macmillan, 53.

18 Elizabeth W. Gordon (2007), Vision-mission-purpose: what does it all mean? Downloaded from http://EzineArticles.com/?expert=Elizabeth_W._Gordon on 9 March 2011. Originally published on 13 February 2007.

19 CIPD (2011), *Sustainable Organisation Performance: What Really Makes the Difference?* Final Report. London: Chartered Institute of Personnel and Development, 3.

20 Stephen Covey, reported by Michael Skapinker (2002), Straight from the stick. *Financial Times,* 2 May, 13.

21 Richard Scase (2004), Are mission statements a waste of space? *Business Voice,* February, 22.

22 Benjamin Disraeli (1872), in a speech at a banquet of the National Union of Conservative and Constitutional Associations, Crystal Palace, London, 24 June 1872. In T.E. Kebbel, Editor (1882), *Selected Speeches of the Right Honourable the Earl of Beaconsfield, Volume 2.* London: Longmans, 535.

23 Joel Kurtzman (2010), *Common Purpose: How Great Leaders Get Organizations to Achieve the Extraordinary.* San Francisco, CA: Jossey-Bass, xii.

24 Marshall Goldsmith (2008), Mission control: align purpose and goals. *Leadership Excellence,* June, 13–14.

25 CIPD (2011), *Sustainable Organisation Performance: What Really Makes the Difference?* Final Report. London: Chartered Institute of Personnel and Development, 18.

26 CIPD (2011), *Sustainable Organisation Performance: What Really Makes the Difference?* Final Report. London: Chartered Institute of Personnel and Development, 19.

27 CIPD (2011), *Sustainable Organisation Performance: What Really Makes the Difference?* Final Report. London: Chartered Institute of Personnel and Development, 20.

28 CIPD (2011), *Sustainable Organisation Performance: What Really Makes the Difference?* Final Report. London: Chartered Institute of Personnel and Development, 20.

29 Leopold Vansina (1999), Leadership in strategic business unit management. *European Journal of Work and Organizational Psychology,* 8 (1), 87–108; Leopold S. Vansina (1988), The general manager and organisational leadership. In M. Lambrechts, Editor, *Corporate Revival: Managing into the Nineties.* Leuven, Belgium: University Press.

30 Richard Scase (2004), Are mission statements a waste of space? *Business Voice,* February, 22.

31 Joel Kurtzman (2010), *Common Purpose: How Great Leaders Get Organizations to Achieve the Extraordinary.* San Francisco, CA: Jossey-Bass, 131–132.

32 Michael Raynor (1998), That vision thing: do we need it? *Long Range Planning,* 31 (3), 368–376.

33 F. O'Brien and M. Meadows (2000), Corporate visioning: a survey of UK practice. *Journal of the Operational Research Society,* 51, 36–44.

34 Alex Miller and Gregory G. Dess (1996), *Strategic Management,* Second Edition. New York: McGraw-Hill, 9–10.

35 Stanley A. Deetz, Sarah J. Tracy and Jennifer L. Simpson (2000), *Leading Organizations through Transition.* Thousand Oaks, CA: SAGE Publications, 51.

36 D. Keith Denton (2001), Mission statements miss the point. *Leadership & Organization Development Journal,* 22 (7), 309–314.

37 Performance Improvement Unit (2001), *Strengthening Leadership in the Public Sector*. Research study by the PIY, Cabinet Office, UK Government, www.cabinet-office.gov.uk/innovation/leadershipreport, 5.26.

38 Transforming Travel, *Annual Review 2002*, FirstGroup plc.

39 Quoted by Rhymer Rigby (1998), Mission statements. *Management Today*, March.

40 Rhymer Rigby (1998), Mission statements. *Management Today*, March.

41 *Annual Report/Form 10–K*, Perot Systems Corporation, 2001.

42 James P. Walsh (2010), *President's Message: Co-creating Our Future – The 2008–2010 Strategic Planning Task Force*. Academy of Management, July.

43 Fred R. David (1989), How companies define their mission. *Long Range Planning*, 22 (1), 90–97; John A. Pearce (1982), The company mission as a strategic tool. *Sloan Management Review*, Spring, 15–24.

44 Michael Raynor (1998), That vision thing: do we need it? *Long Range Planning*, 31 (3), 368–376.

45 James C. Collins and Jerry I. Porras (1991), Organizational vision and visionary organizations. *California Management Review*, 34 (1), 30–52.

46 J. Vogt (1994), Demystifying the mission statement. *Nonprofit World*, 12, 29–32.

47 R.D. Ireland and M.A Hitt (1992), Mission statements: importance, challenge, and recommendations for development. *Business Horizons*, May–June, 34–42.

48 S. Cummings and J. Davies (1994), Mission, vision, fusion. *Long Range Planning*, 27 (6), 147–150.

49 Michael Raynor (1998), That vision thing: do we need it? *Long Range Planning*, 31 (3), 368–376.

50 Stephen R. Covey (1989), Universal mission statement. *Executive Excellence*, March, 7–9.

51 Michael Raynor (1998), That vision thing: do we need it? *Long Range Planning*, 31 (3), 368–376.

52 Richard Olivier (2001), *Inspirational Leadership: Henry V and the Muse of Fire*. London: The Industrial Society, 46–47.

53 *Annual Review and Summary Financial Statement 2001*, Tesco PLC.

54 *Annual Review and Summary Financial Statement 2003*, Marks & Spencer Group p.l.c.

55 Downloaded from the website http://www.co-operative.coop/corporate/aboutus/ourvisionandaims/ on 13 January 2011.

56 A cooperative is 'an autonomous association of persons united voluntarily to meet their economic, social and cultural needs and aspirations through a jointly-owned and democratically controlled enterprise' (The International Co-operative Alliance Statement on the Co-operative Identity, Manchester, 1995).

57 Stephen R. Covey (1992), *Principle-centered Leadership*. London: Simon & Schuster, 296.

58 G.A. Yukl (1994), *Leadership in Organizations*, Third Edition. Englewood Cliffs, NJ: Prentice Hall, 362.

59 Quoted by Rhymer Rigby (1998), Mission statements. *Management Today*, March.

60   Michael Raynor (1998), That vision thing: do we need it? *Long Range Planning,* 31 (3), 368–376.

61   Sally Lansdell (2002), *The Vision Thing.* Oxford: Capstone Publishing, 3.

62   Scott Adams (1997), *The Dilbert Principle.* London: Boxtree, 36.

63   Nikos Mourkogiannis (2006), *Purpose: The Starting Point of Great Companies.* New York: Palgrave Macmillan, 175–179.

64   Gail T. Fairhurst and Robert A. Sarr (1996), *The Art of Framing.* San Francisco, CA: Jossey-Bass.

65   Quoted by Gregory G. Dess and Joseph C. Picken (2000), Changing roles: leadership in the 21st century. *Organizational Dynamics,* 28 (3), 18–34.

66   Downloaded from http://www.nationaltrust.org.uk/main/w-trust/w-thecharity.htm on 6th February 2011.

67   Nikos Mourkogiannis (2006), *Purpose: The Starting Point of Great Companies.* New York: Palgrave Macmillan, 16–17.

68   Nikos Mourkogiannis (2006), *Purpose: The Starting Point of Great Companies.* New York: Palgrave Macmillan, 30.

69   Nikos Mourkogiannis (2006), *Purpose: The Starting Point of Great Companies.* New York: Palgrave Macmillan, 32.

70   Nikos Mourkogiannis (2006), *Purpose: The Starting Point of Great Companies.* New York: Palgrave Macmillan, 34.

71   Nikos Mourkogiannis (2006), *Purpose: The Starting Point of Great Companies.* New York: Palgrave Macmillan, 36.

72   Nikos Mourkogiannis (2006), *Purpose: The Starting Point of Great Companies.* New York: Palgrave Macmillan, 38–40.

73   Nikos Mourkogiannis (2006), *Purpose: The Starting Point of Great Companies.* New York: Palgrave Macmillan, 53.

74   *Annual Review 2000,* Lloyds TSB Group.

75   Iain Mangham (2004), Leadership and integrity. In John Storey, Editor, *Leadership in Organizations: Current Issues and Key Trends.* London: Routledge, 53.

76   James C. Collins and Jerry I. Porras (1996), Building your company's vision. *Harvard Business Review,* September–October.

77   Sharon Turnbull (2010), A leadership ethic of responsibility and conviction. *LTFocus,* Summer, 2–3.

78   Quoted from an interview of Peter Drucker with Tony Jackson (1999), Reflections of a knowledge worker. *Financial Times,* 27 April, 14.

79   Peter Doyle (1996), The loss from profits. *Financial Times,* October 25.

80   William W. George (2001), *Keynote Address,* Academy of Management Annual Conference, Washington, DC, August. In *Academy of Management Executive,* 15 (4), 39–47.

81   William W. George (2001), *Keynote Address,* Academy of Management Annual Conference, Washington, DC, August. In *Academy of Management Executive,* 15 (4), 39–47.

82   Stephen Aris (2002), Weinstock: I wanted to string up Simpson. *The Sunday Times,* 28 July, 8.

83 William W. George (2001), *Keynote Address,* Academy of Management Annual Conference, Washington, DC, August. In *Academy of Management Executive,* 15 (4), 39–47.

84 Gregory G. Dess and Joseph C. Picken (2000), Changing roles: leadership in the 21st century. *Organizational Dynamics,* 28 (3), 18–34.

85 Richard R. Ellsworth (2002), *Leading with Purpose: The New Corporate Realities.* Stanford, CA: Stanford Business Books, xi.

86 Scott A. Snook (2003), Review of Richard R. Ellsworth (2002), *Leading with Purpose: The New Corporate Realities.* Stanford, CA: Stanford Business Books. *Academy of Management Review,* October, 675–677.

87 RSA (1995), *Tomorrow's Company Inquiry.* London: Gower.

88 *Annual Review and Summary Financial Statement 2002,* Barclays PLC.

89 CIPD (2009), *Shared Purpose and Sustainable Organisation Performance,* Research Insight. London: Chartered Institute of Personnel and Development, October, 4.

90 Oscar Wilde (1892), Lord Darlington, Act III, *Lady Windermere's Fan.*

91 John Kay (2010), The cash comes second. Appointments, *The Sunday Times,* 28 March, 6; John Kay (2010), *Obliquity.* London: Profile Books. Also see a discussion of this issue in the next chapter in relation to corporate values and culture and the case of Goldman Sachs.

92 Chris Hohn, chairman of The Children's Investment Fund, in Nikos Mourkogiannis (2006), *Purpose: The Starting Point of Great Companies.* New York: Palgrave Macmillan, i.

93 John J. Sosik and Don I. Jung (2009), *Full Range Leadership Development: Pathways for People, Profit and Planet.* New York and London: Psychology Press, 324.

94 John J. Sosik and Don I. Jung (2009), *Full Range Leadership Development: Pathways for People, Profit and Planet.* New York and London: Psychology Press, 324.

95 Ian Buckingham (2009), Wanted: truly sustainable 'performance cultures'. *People Management,* 14 December. Downloaded from http://www.peoplemanagement. co.uk/pm/sections/your-say/blogs/specialists/ian-buckingham.htm?page=3. Accessed 07 September 2011.

96 John Elkington (1998), *Cannibals with Forks: The Triple Bottom Line of 21st Century Business.* New York: Capstone Publishing.

97 John J. Sosik and Don I. Jung (2009), *Full Range Leadership Development: Pathways for People, Profit and Planet.* New York and London: Psychology Press, 333.

98 The Economist (2010), Shareholders v stakeholders: a new idolatry. *The Economist,* April 24, 65–66.

99 Nikos Mourkogiannis (2006), *Purpose: The Starting Point of Great Companies.* New York: Palgrave Macmillan, 46–47.

100 Michael C. Jensen and William H. Meckling (1976), Theory of the firm: managerial behaviour, agency costs and ownership structure. *Journal of Financial Economics,* 3 (4), 305–360.

101 Milton Friedman (1970). The social responsibility of business is to increase its profits. *New York Times Magazine,* 32ff.

102 The Economist (2010), Shareholders v stakeholders: a new idolatry. *The Economist,* April 24, 65–66.

103 Roger Martin (2010), The age of customer capitalism. *Harvard Business Review,* January–February.

104 Bill George (2010), The new 21st century leaders. *Harvard Business Review,* Guest Edition, May 5.

105 Michael E. Porter and Mark R. Kramer (2007), Strategy and society: the link between competitive advantage and corporate social responsibility. *Harvard Business Review,* 84 (12), 78–92; Michael E. Porter and Mark R. Kramer (2011), The big idea: creating shared value. *Harvard Business Review,* 89 (1), 62–77; Schumpeter (2011), Oh, Mr Porter, *The Economist,* 12 March, 78.

106 William Clay Ford, Jr (2000), *Corporate Citizenship Report.* Ford Motor Company.

107 Kim Kanaga and Sonya Prestridge (2002), The right start: a team's first meeting is key. *Leadership in Action,* 22 (2), May/June, 14–17.

108 Fran Ackermann and Colin Eden (2005), *The Practice of Making Strategy.* London: SAGE Publications.

109 Nikos Mourkogiannis (2006), *Purpose: The Starting Point of Great Companies.* New York: Palgrave Macmillan, 20–21.

110 CIPD (2009), *Shared Purpose and Sustainable Organisation Performance,* Research Insight. London: Chartered Institute of Personnel and Development, October, 4.

111 Chris K. Bart and J.C. Tabone (1998), Mission statement rationales and organizational alignment in the not-for-profit heath care sector. *Health Care Management Review,* 23 (4), 54–70.

112 Paul Joyce and Adrian Woods (2001), *Strategic Management: A Fresh Approach to Developing Skills, Knowledge and Creativity.* London: Kogan Page, 69–71.

113 Sanjay T. Menon (2001), Employee empowerment: an integrative psychological approach. *Applied Psychology: An International Review,* 50 (1), 153–180.

114 Owen Hughes (2003), Making vision a reality. *Charity Times,* 10 (1), January, 43.

115 Milton Moskowitz and Robert Levering (2003), Where are the best workplaces? *Best Workplaces 2003,* Special Report, *Financial Times,* March 28, 3.

116 C. William Pollard (2000), Mission as an organizing principle. *Leader to Leader,* 16, Spring, 17–21.

117 Nikos Mourkogiannis (2006), *Purpose: The Starting Point of Great Companies.* New York: Palgrave Macmillan, 6–7.

118 Nikos Mourkogiannis (2006), *Purpose: The Starting Point of Great Companies.* New York: Palgrave Macmillan, 21–22.

119 CIPD (2009), *Shared Purpose and Sustainable Organisation Performance,* Research Insight. London: Chartered Institute of Personnel and Development, October, 3.

120 CIPD (2009), *Shared Purpose and Sustainable Organisation Performance,* Research Insight. London: Chartered Institute of Personnel and Development, October, 5.

121 CIPD (2009), *Shared Purpose and Sustainable Organisation Performance,* Research Insight. London: Chartered Institute of Personnel and Development, October, 3.

122 Stephen Bevan, Marc Cowling, Louise Horner, Nick Isles and Natalie Turner (2005), *Cracking the Performance Code,* research report. London: The Work Foundation; F. Buytendijk (2006), The five keys to building a high-performance organisation. *Business Performance Management,* February, 24–30.

123 Richard E. Ellsworth (2002), *Leading with Purpose: The New Corporate Realities.* Stanford, CA: Stanford University Press.

124 CIPD (2010), *Shared Purpose: The Golden Thread?* Survey Report. London: Chartered Institute of Personnel and Development.

125 CIPD (2011), *Sustainable Organisation Performance: What Really Makes the Difference?* Final Report. London: Chartered Institute of Personnel and Development, 4.

126 Nikos Mourkogiannis (2006), *Purpose: The Starting Point of Great Companies.* New York: Palgrave Macmillan, 54.

127 CIPD (2011), *Sustainable Organisation Performance: What Really Makes the Difference?* Final Report. London: Chartered Institute of Personnel and Development, 4.

128 CIPD (2011), *Sustainable Organisation Performance: What Really Makes the Difference?* Final Report. London: Chartered Institute of Personnel and Development, 17.

129 CIPD (2009), *Shared Purpose and Sustainable Organisation Performance,* Research Insight. London: Chartered Institute of Personnel and Development, October, 4.

130 Dr Reto Francioni, CEO and chairman of the Executive Board of Deutsche Borse, in Nikos Mourkogiannis (2006), *Purpose: The Starting Point of Great Companies.* New York: Palgrave Macmillan, ii.

131 Richard Scase (2004), Are mission statements a waste of space? *Business Voice,* February, 22.

132 From *Shared Purpose and Sustainable Organisation Performance,* Research Insight. London. Chartered Institute of Personnel and Development, October 2009, http://www.cipd.co.uk/subjects/corpstrtgy/_shared_purpose_organisation_ performance.htm. Used with the permission of the publisher, the Chartered Institute of Personnel and Development, London (www.cipd.co.uk).

133 These questions have been set by the author. They do not appear in the original research article published by the CIPD.

134 W.K. Shooter (2010), Charity salaries. Letter to the Editor, *The Times,* Monday 19 July, 23; Philip Circus (2010), Charity donations and pension plans. Letter to the Editor, *The Times,* Tuesday 20 July, 25.

135 Barrie Behenna (2010), Going swimmingly. Letter to the Editor, *The Times,* Wednesday 21 July, 23; R. Warnock (2010), Model charity. Letter to the Editor, *The Times,* Thursday 22 July, 25.

Chapter 6

1 Catherine Soanes and Angus Stevenson, Editors (2004), *The Concise Oxford English Dictionary,* Eleventh Edition. Oxford: Oxford University Press, 1597.

2 R. Roe and P. Ester (1999), Values and work: empirical findings and theoretical perspectives. *Applied Psychology: An International Review,* 48, 1–21; S.H. Schwartz (1992), Universals in the content and structure of values: theoretical advances and empirical tests in 20 countries. In M.P. Zanna, Editor, *Advances in Experimental Social Psychology, Volume 25.* San Diego, CA: Academic Press, 2.

3 B.M. Meglino and E.C. Ravlin (1998), Individual values in organizations: concepts, controversies, and research. *Journal of Management,* 24, 351–389.

4 Jo Silvester (2010), What makes a good politician? *The Psychologist,* 23 (5), 394–397.

5 StrategicRISK (2010), *Newsletter* accessed on 1 July 2010 at http://www.strategicrisk.co.uk/story.asp?sectionacode=23&storycode-385174&c=2, 23 June.

6 Niall Ferguson (2010), To do 'God's work', bankers need morals. *Telegraph.co.uk,* 5 July. Accessed on 7 July 2010 at http://www.telegraph.co.uk/finance/newsbysector/banksandfinance/7871781/To-do-God's-work-bankers-need-morals.

7 Barry Morgan (2011), MBA oath provides an ethical foundation. *FT.com,* 7 February.

8 Sandra J. Sucher (2007), *The Moral Leader: Challenges, Tools and Insights.* New York: Routledge.

9 Doug Lennick and Fred Kiel (2008), *Moral Intelligence.* Upper Saddle River, NJ: Pearson Education.

10 James C. Sarros and Joseph C. Santora (2001), Leaders and values: a cross-cultural study. *Leadership & Organization Development Journal,* 22 (5), 243–248.

11 Nick Turner, Julian Barling, Olga Epitropaki, Vicky Butcher and Caroline Milner (2002), Transformational leadership and moral reasoning. *Journal of Applied Psychology,* 87 (2), 304–311.

12 James O'Toole (1995), *Leading Change: Overcoming the Ideology of Comfort and the Tyranny of Custom.* San Francisco, CA: Jossey-Bass, 9.

13 R.N. Kanungo and M. Mendonca (1996), *Ethical Dimensions in Leadership.* Beverly Hills, CA: SAGE Publications, 46.

14 Micha Popper and Ofra Mayseless (2003), Back to basics: applying a parenting perspective to transformational leadership. *Leadership Quarterly,* 14, 41–65.

15 Ian Buckingham (2010), MBAs lead the way to a more ethical future. *People Management,* 9 December, 14.

16 Stephen R. Covey (1992), *Principle-centered Leadership.* London: Simon & Schuster, 19.

17 Stephen R. Covey (1992), *Principle-centered Leadership.* London: Simon & Schuster, 19.

18 Sharon Turnbull (2001), Corporate ideology – meanings and contradictions for middle managers. *British Journal of Management,* 12, 231–242.

19 CIPD (2010), *Shared Purpose: The Golden Thread?* Survey Report. London: Chartered Institute of Personnel and Development.

20 Quoted by Steve Yearout, Gerry Miles and Richard H. Koonce (2001), Multi-level visioning. *Training & Development,* March, 31–39.

21 Peter F. Drucker (1999), *Management Challenges for the 21st Century.* New York: HarperCollins, 177.

22 Quoted by Rebecca Hoar (2004), Work with meaning. *Management Today,* May, 44–53.

23 Patrick M. Lencioni (2002), Make your values mean something. *Harvard Business Review,* 80, 7, July, 113–117.

24 Mark Goyder (1999), Value and values: lessons for Tomorrow's Company. *Long Range Planning,* 32, 2, 217–224.

25 Quoted by Peter Wickens (1999), Values added. *People Management,* 5 (10), 20 May, 33–38.

26 Google (2009), *Code of Conduct.* Google Investor Relations, April 8. Downloaded from www.investor.google.com/conduct.html on 20 April 2011.

27 Sally Stewart and Gabriel Donleavy (1995), *Whose Business Values?* Hong Kong: Hong Kong University Press.

28 Simon Webley (1999), Sources of corporate values. *Long Range Planning,* 32 (2), 173–178.

29 For example, the *Code of Professional Management Practice* published by the Chartered Management Institute, Corby, July 2002.

30 *Principles for Business.* Caux Round Table, The Hague, 1996.

31 *An Interfaith Declaration: A Code of Ethics on International Business for Christians, Muslims and Jews.* London, 1994 (reproduced in *Business Ethics – A European Review,* 5 (1), 55–57, 1996).

32 Lilach Sagiv and Shalom H. Schwartz (2007), Cultural values in organisations: insights for Europe. *European Journal of International Management,* 1 (3), 176–190.

33 Simon Webley (1992), *Business Ethics and Company Codes.* London: Institute of Business Ethics.

34 William E. Loges and Rushworth M. Kidder (1997), *Global Values, Moral Boundaries. A Pilot Survey.* Camden, ME: The Institute for Global Ethics.

35 Based on Section Two: Values, *Durham University Strategy 2010–2010,* Durham University, UK. Used with kind permission.

36 Downloaded from http://www.nationaltrust.org.uk/main/w-trust/w-thecharity.htm on 6 February 2011.

37 John Clemens (1986), A lesson from 431 BC. *Fortune,* 13 October, 161, 164.

38 J. Pfeffer (1981), Management as a symbolic action. In L.L. Cummings and B.M. Staw, Editors, *Research in Organizational Behavior, Volume 3.* Greenwich, CT: JAI Press, 1–52; S. Albert and D. Whetten (1985), Organizational identity. In L.L. Cummings and B.M. Staw, Editors, *Research in Organizational Behavior, Volume 7.* Greenwich, CT: JAI Press, 263–295.

39 S. Albert and D. Whetten (1985), Organizational identity. In L.L. Cummings and B.M. Staw, Editors, *Research in Organizational Behavior, Volume 7.* Greenwich, CT: JAI Press, 263–295.

40 Laurence D. Ackerman (2000), *Identity is Destiny: Leadership and the Roots of Value Creation.* San Francisco, CA: Berrett-Koehler.

41 Stephen R. Covey (1992), *Principle-centered Leadership.* London: Simon & Schuster.

42 J.A. Chatman (1991), Matching people and organizations: selection and socialization in public accounting firms. *Administrative Science Quarterly,* 36, 459–484.

43 K.A. Jehn, C. Chadwick and S.M.B. Thatcher (1997), To agree or not to agree: the effects of value congruence, individual demographic dissimilarity, and conflict on workgroup outcomes. *International Journal of Conflict*, 8, 287–305.

44 Mark A. Tannenbaum (2003), Organizational values and leadership. *The Public Manager*, 32 (2), 19–20.

45 G.G. Gordon and N. DiTomaso (1992), Predicting corporate performance from organizational culture. *Journal of Management Studies*, 29, 783–798.

46 Anne Nicotera and Donald Cushman (1992), Organizational ethics: a within-organization view. *Journal of Applied Communication Research*, 20, 437–463.

47 Peter F. Drucker (1999), Managing oneself. *Harvard Business Review*, March–April, 65–74.

48 D.I. Jung and B.J. Avolio (2000), Opening the black box: an empirical investigation of the mediating effects of trust and value congruence on transformational and transactional leadership. *Journal of Organizational Behaviour*, 21, 949–964.

49 Stephen R. Covey (1992), *Principle-centered Leadership*. London: Simon & Schuster, 102.

50 C. Horn (2001), Leading by example. *Personnel Today*, 12 June.

51 Terry L. Price (2003), The ethics of authentic transformational leadership. *Leadership Quarterly*, 14, 67–81.

52 Miranda Kennett (2004), First-class coach. *Management Today*, January, 72.

53 Richard Reeves (2006), When lying is acceptable. *Management Today*, May, 29.

54 Bernard Williams (2004), *Truth and Truthfulness: An Essay in Genealogy, New Edition*. Princeton, NJ: Princeton University Press.

55 Richard Olivier (2001), *Inspirational Leadership: Henry V and the Muse of Fire*. London: The Industrial Society, 138.

56 Richard Reeves (2006), When lying is acceptable. *Management Today*, May, 29.

57 Reported by Hashi Syeddain (2010), In whom we trust. *People Management*, 28 January, 24–26.

58 Stephen Covey (1989), *The Seven Habits of Highly Effective People*. New York: Fireside, 195.

59 Warren Bennis and Joan Goldsmith (1997), *Learning to Lead*. London: Nicholas Brealey Publishing, 145.

60 Sun Tzu (*The Art of War*) and Confucius (*Analects*).

61 Tony L. Simons (1999), Behavioral integrity as a critical ingredient for transformational leadership. *Journal of Organizational Change Management*, 12 (2), 89–104.

62 Stephen R. Covey (1992), *Principle-centered Leadership*. London: Simon & Schuster, 168.

63 Adrian Furnham (2010), The managers who leave their integrity at the door. *The Sunday Times*, Appointments, 24 October, 2.

64 Adrian Furnham (2010), The managers who leave their integrity at the door. *The Sunday Times*, Appointments, 24 October, 2.

65 Quoted by A. Brown (1995), *Organisational Culture*. London: Pitman, 15.

66 Alan Hooper and John Potter (2000), *Intelligent Leadership*. London: Random House, 7.

67 Bachman (1963), in Robert Bartels, Editor, *Ethics in Business*. Columbus, OH: Bureau of Business Research, College of Commerce and Administration, Ohio State University, 116.

68 W.B. Yeats (1895), The Countess Cathleen, act 3. *Poems*.

69 William W. George (2001), *Keynote Address*, Academy of Management Annual Conference, Washington, DC, August. In *Academy of Management Executive*, 15 (4), 39–47.

70 Adrian Furnham (2001), Industry needs more captains courageous. *Financial Times*, September 5, 13.

71 Based in part on Roger Gill (2010), Trust, trustworthiness and leadership. *LT Focus*, Spring. Used with kind permission of The Leadership Trust Foundation.

72 Nick Rodrigues (2010), Making it all work for staff has its rewards. *The Sunday Times 100 Best Companies to Work For*. London: The Sunday Times, 7 March, 10.

73 Anthony Seldon (2009), *Trust: How We Lost It and How To Get It Back*. London: Biteback, ix–xv.

74 Penny Tamkin, Gemma Pearson, Wendy Hirsh and Susie Constable (2010), *Exceeding Expectation: The Principles of Outstanding Leadership*. London: The Work Foundation, January, 86.

75 Catherine Soanes and Angus Stevenson, Editors (2004), *Concise Oxford English Dictionary*, Eleventh Edition. Oxford: Oxford University Press, 1549.

76 Penny Tamkin, Gemma Pearson, Wendy Hirsh and Susie Constable (2010), *Exceeding Expectation: The Principles of Outstanding Leadership*. London: The Work Foundation, January.

77 Penny Tamkin, Gemma Pearson, Wendy Hirsh and Susie Constable (2010), *Exceeding Expectation: The Principles of Outstanding Leadership*. London: The Work Foundation, January, 15.

78 Casey Wilson (2009), Trust: the critical factor in leadership. *The Public Manager*, Spring, 48–52.

79 Reported by Hashi Syeddain (2010), In whom we trust. *People Management*, 28 January, 24–26.

80 CIPD (2010), *Quarterly Survey Report: Employee Outlook. Emerging from the Downturn?* London: Chartered Institute of Personnel and Development, Winter (January).

81 CIPD (2010), *Building Productive Public Sector Workplaces. Part One: Improving People Management*. London: Chartered Institute of Personnel and Development, January, 3.

82 CIPD (2010), *Building Productive Public Sector Workplaces. Overview. Delivering More with Less: The People Management Challenge*. London: Chartered Institute of Personnel and Development, January, 4.

83 Brian Amble (2010), Business leaders need to build trust. *Management Issues*, 29 January.

84 *13th Annual Global CEO Survey: Setting a Smarter Course for Growth* (2010), London: PricewaterhouseCoopers, January, 20.

85 Annette Sinclair, Jo Hennessy, Jonny Gifford and Dilip Boury (2010), *The Management Agenda 2010*. Horsham: Roffey Park Institute.

86 R.C. Mayer, J.H. Davis and F.D. Schoorman (1995), An integrative model of organizational trust. *Academy of Management Review,* 20, 709–734.

87 A. Chaudhuri and L. Gangadharan (2007), An experimental analysis of trust and trustworthiness, *Southern Economic Journal,* 73, 959–985; J.H. Dyer and W. Chu (2003), The role of trustworthiness in reducing transaction costs and improving performance: empirical evidence from the United States, Japan, and Korea. *Organization Science,* 14, 57–68.

88 Roger C. Mayer and James H. Davis (1999), The effect of the performance appraisal system on trust for management: a field quasi-experiment. *Journal of Applied Psychology,* 84 (1), February, 123–136.

89 Reported by Hashi Syeddain (2010), In whom we trust. *People Management,* 28 January, 24–26.

90 Reported by Hashi Syeddain (2010), In whom we trust. *People Management,* 28 January, 24–26.

91 Pamela Shockley-Zalabak, Sherwyn Morreale and Michael Z. Hackman (2010), Build high trust. *Leadership Excellence,* July, 19; Pamela Shockley-Zalabak, Sherwyn Morreale and Michael Z. Hackman (2010), *Building the High-Trust Organization: Strategies for Supporting Five Key Dimensions of Trust.* San Francisco, CA: Jossey-Bass.

92 Bagehot (2011), A plague on their House. *The Economist,* 1 January, 21.

93 Institute of Leadership & Management (2010), *Index of Leadership Trust 2010.* London: ILM.

94 Eric Uslaner (2002), *The Moral Foundations of Trust.* Cambridge: Cambridge University Press.

95 Marek Kohn (2008), *Trust: Self-Interest and the Common Good.* Oxford: Oxford University Press, 133.

96 Anthony Seldon (2009), *Trust: How We Lost It and How To Get It Back.* London: Biteback, Preface and ix–xv.

97 Based in part on Roger Gill (2008), Do leaders' values affect their firms' performance? *LT Focus,* Winter. Used with kind permission of The Leadership Trust Foundation.

98 Alastair McCall (2007), The Sunday Times 100 Best Companies to Work For 2007. *The Sunday Times,* 11 March. 5.

99 Quoted by Lt.-Col. L. Urwick of management consultants Urwick, Orr & Partners Limited in an address to Production Conference organized by the Ministry of Production at the Royal Technical College, Glasgow, on 5 September 1944.

100 Carolyn B. Aiken and Scott P. Keller (2007), The CEO's role in leading transformation. *The McKinsey Quarterly,* February.

101 Victoria Winkler at the CIPD, quoted by Rod Newing (2007), Leaders must set the best example. *FT Report – Professional Development 2007,* FT.com, November 12.

102 John Drysdale, quoted by Rod Newing (2007), Leaders must set the best example. *FT Report – Professional Development 2007,* FT.com, November 12.

103 K.R. Andrews (1971), *The Concept of Corporate Strategy,* Homewood, IL: Irwin; J.R. Kimberley (1979), Issues in the creation of organizations. *Academy of Management Journal,* 22, 437–457; D. Miller, M.F.R. Kets De Vries and

J.-M. Toulouse (1982), Top executive locus of control and its relationship to strategy-making, structure, and environment. *Academy of Management Journal*, 25, 237–253; D. Miller and J.-M. Toulouse (1986), Chief executive personality and corporate strategy and structure in small firms. *Management Science*, 32, 1389–1409; D. Miller and C. Dröge (1986), Psychological and traditional determinants of structure. *Administrative Science Quarterly*, 31, 539–560.

104 Yan Ling, Hao Zhao and Robert A, Baron (2007), Influence of founder-CEOs' personal values on firm performance: moderating effects of firm age and size. *Journal of Management*, 33 (5), 673–696.

105 N.C. Churchill and V.L. Lewis (1983), The five stages of small business growth. *Harvard Business Review*, 61 (3), 30–50; H.R. Dodge, S. Fullerton and J.E. Robbins (1994), Stage of the organizational life cycle and competition as mediators of problem perception for small businesses. *Strategic Management Journal*, 15, 121–135.

106 S.I. Mohan-Neill (1995), The influence of firm's age and size on its environmental scanning activities. *Journal of Small Business Management*, 33, 10–21; N. Jayaraman, A. Khorana, E. Nelling and J. Covin (2000), CEO founder status and firm financial performance. *Strategic Management Journal*, 21, 1215–1224.

107 Yan Ling, Hao Zhao and Robert A. Baron (2007), Influence of founder-CEOs' personal values on firm performance: moderating effects of firm age and size. *Journal of Management*, 33 (5), 673–696.

108 M.H. Morris and D.L. Davis (1994), Fostering corporate entrepreneurship: cross-cultural comparisons of the importance of individualism versus collectivism. *Journal of International Business Studies*, 25, 65–89.

109 D. Hambrick and G. Brandon (1988), Executive values. In D. Hambrick, Editor, *The Executive Effect: Concepts and Methods for Studying Top Managers*. Greenwich, CT: JAI Press, 3–34; C.M. Ford and D.A. Gioia (2000), Factors influencing creativity in the domain of managerial decision making. *Journal of Management*, 26, 705–732.

110 D. Hambrick and G. Brandon (1988), Executive values. In D. Hambrick, Editor, *The Executive Effect: Concepts and Methods for Studying Top Managers*. Greenwich, CT: JAI Press, 3–34.

111 M.H. Morris, R.A. Avila and J. Allen (1993), Individualism and the modern corporation: implications for innovation and entrepreneurship. *Journal of Management*, 19, 595–612; A. Lipparini and M. Sobrero (1994), The glue and the pieces: entrepreneurship and innovation in small firm networks. *Journal of Business Venturing*, 9, 125–140; S. Shane and S. Venkataraman (2000), The promise of entrepreneurship as a field of research. *Academy of Management Review*, 25, 217–226.

112 James O'Toole (1995), *Leading Change: Overcoming the Ideology of Comfort and the Tyranny of Custom*. San Francisco, CA: Jossey-Bass, xiii.

113 James O'Toole (1995), *Leading Change: Overcoming the Ideology of Comfort and the Tyranny of Custom*. San Francisco, CA: Jossey-Bass, xiii.

114 Robert Howard (1990), Values make the company: an interview with Robert Haas. *Harvard Business Review*, September–October.

115 E. Ogbonna and L.C. Harris (2001), The founder's legacy: hangover or inheritance? *British Journal of Management*, 12, 13–31.

116 John W. Gardner (1990), *On Leadership*. New York: Free Press, 191.

117 Adam Faruk (2002a), Corporate responsibility: beyond niceness. *The Ashridge Journal*, Summer, 28–31; Adam Faruk (2002b), *Ashridge Corporate Responsibility Survey*. Ashridge: Ashridge Management College.

118 James O'Toole (1995), *Leading Change: Overcoming the Ideology of Comfort and the Tyranny of Custom*. San Francisco, CA: Jossey-Bass, 258–261.

119 Ian Davis (2003), Learning to grow again. *The Economist: The World in 2004*.

120 Arthur Sharplin (1985), *Strategic Management*. New York: McGraw-Hill, 69.

121 Li-Fang Chou, An-Chih Wang, Ting-Yu Wang, Min-Ping Huang and Bor-Shiuan Cheng (2008), Shared work values and team member effectiveness: the mediation of trustfulness and trustworthiness. *Human Relations*, 61 (12), 1713–1742.

122 Peter Wickens (1999a), Values added. *People Management*, 5 (10), 20 May, 33–38; Peter Wickens (1999b), *Energise Your Enterprise*. Basingstoke: Macmillan.

123 Patrick M. Lencioni (2002), Make your values mean something. *Harvard Business Review*, 80 (7), July, 113–117.

124 Stanley A. Deetz, Sarah J. Tracy and Jennifer L. Simpson (2000), *Leading Organizations through Transition*. Thousand Oaks, CA: SAGE Publications, 76.

125 Diane J. Coutu (2002), The anxiety of learning: the HBR interview [with Edgar H, Schein]. *Harvard Business Review*, March, 100–106.

126 James Brockett (2010), New values framework used as basis for three-year engagement strategy. *People Management Online*, 22 March, http://www.peoplemanagement.co.uk/pm/articles/2010/03.

127 A.C. Grayling (2004), What is the good life? Richer not happier: a 21st-century search for the good life. Debate on 11 February 2004 at the Royal Society of Arts, London. *RSA Journal*, July, 36–39.

128 A.P. Brief, J. Dietz, R.R. Cohen, S.D. Pugh and J.B. Vaslow (2000), Just doing business: modern racism and obedience to authority as explanations for employment discrimination. *Organization Behavior and Human Decision Processes*, 81, 72–97.

129 Marshall Schminke, Deborah Wells, Joseph Peyrefitte and Terrence C. Sebora (2002), Leadership and ethics in work groups. *Group & Organization Management*, 27 (2), 272–293.

130 Marcus W. Dickson, D. Brent Smith, Michael W. Grojean and Mark Ehrhart (2001), An organizational climate regarding ethics: the outcome of leader values and the practices that reflect them. *Leadership Quarterly*, 12 (2), 197–217.

131 Philippe de Woot, quoted by Loredana Oliva (2004), Ethics edges on to courses. *Financial Times*, February 16, 11.

132 Terry L. Price (2003), The ethics of authentic transformational leadership. *Leadership Quarterly*, 14, 67–81.

133 Milton Friedman (1962), *Capitalism and Freedom*. Chicago: Chicago University Press, studies, 133.

134 Geoffrey Colvin (2001), Should companies care? *Fortune*, June 11, 26.

135 Roger Gill (2006), *Theory and Practice of Leadership*. London: SAGE Publications, 167–170.

136 Based in part on Roger Gill (2007), The best companies to work for have exemplary leadership. *LT Focus*, July. Used with kind permission of The Leadership Trust Foundation.

137 N.M. Tichy and S. Sherman (1994), *Control Your Own Destiny or Someone Else Will*. New York: Harper Business; F. Fukuyama (1995), *Trust: The Social Values and the Creation of Prosperity*. London: Hamish Hamilton.

138 Thomas J. Peters and Robert H. Waterman (1982), *In Search of Excellence: Lessons from America's Best-Run Companies*. New York: Harper & Row.

139 Manfred Kets de Vries (2000), Beyond Sloan: trust is at the core of corporate values. Mastering Management, *Financial Times*, October 2.

140 Alastair McCall (2007), The Sunday Times 100 Best Companies to Work For 2007. *The Sunday Times*, March 11.

141 Roger Gill (2006), *Theory and Practice of Leadership*. London: SAGE Publications, 146–152.

142 Alastair McCall (2007), The Sunday Times 100 Best Companies to Work For 2007. *The Sunday Times*, 11 March, 5.

143 Alastair McCall (2007), The Sunday Times 100 Best Companies to Work For 2007. *The Sunday Times*, 11 March, 5.

144 Alastair McCall, Editor (2011), The Sunday Times 100 Best Companies to Work For 2011. *The Sunday Times*, 6 March, 20.

145 John Housego, quoted by Alastair McCall (2007), The Sunday Times 100 Best Companies to Work For 2007. *The Sunday Times*, 11 March, 4.

146 Ranked first as the best company to work for in the UK in the big-company category in the 2007 survey and ranked second in the 2010 and 2011 surveys.

147 Pete Bradon, quoted by Alastair McCall (2007), The Sunday Times 100 Best Companies to Work For 2007. *The Sunday Times*, 11 March, 4.

148 Alastair McCall (2007), The Sunday Times 100 Best Companies to Work For 2007. *The Sunday Times*, 11 March, 5.

149 Nick Rodrigues (2007), The Sunday Times 100 Best Companies to Work For 2007. *The Sunday Times*, 11 March, 12.

150 Richard Caseby (2007), The Sunday Times 100 Best Companies to Work For 2007. *The Sunday Times*, 11 March, 4.

151 Jonathan Austin, quoted by Alastair McCall (2007), The Sunday Times 100 Best Companies to Work For 2007. *The Sunday Times*, 11 March, 4.

152 Based in part on Roger Gill (2010), Leading with responsibility and conviction. *LT Focus*, Summer. Used with kind permission of The Leadership Trust Foundation.

153 Roger Gill (2007), The buck stops here – with the leader. *LT Focus*, Autumn.

154 Catherine Soanes and Angus Stephenson, Editors (2004), *Concise Oxford English Dictionary*, Eleventh Edition. Oxford: Oxford University Press, 313.

155 Jo Silvester (2010), What makes a good politician? *The Psychologist*, 23 (5), 394–397.

156 Roger Gill (2007), The buck stops here – with the leader. *LT Focus*, Autumn.

157 Eileen M. Rogers (2009), Optimism or positivity: it's the leader's edge in tough times. *Leadership Excellence*, May, 19.

158 Warren Bennis, quoted by Eileen M. Rogers (2009), Optimism or positivity: it's the leader's edge in tough times, *Leadership Excellence*, May, 19.

159 Carol Harlow and Richard Rawlings (1992), *Pressure through Law*. London: Routledge, 291.

160 P. Lassman and R. Speirs, Editors/Translators (1994), *Weber: Political Writings*. Cambridge: Cambridge University Press.

161 Robert L. Joss (2009), *Leadership is Responsibility, Not Power*. Valedictory speech as Dean of Stanford Graduate School of Business, May.

162 C.K. Prahalad (2010), The responsible manager. *Harvard Business Review*, January/February.

163 Roy J. Eidelson and Judy I. Eidelson (2003), Dangerous ideas: five beliefs that propel groups towards conflict. *American Psychologist*, 58 (3), 182–192.

164 Martha Maznevski and Joe DiStefano (n.d.), *The Impact of Culture on Work*, unpublished paper, Lausanne, Switzerland: IMD; adapted from H.W. Lane, J.J. DiStefano and M.L. Maznevski (2000), *International Management Behavior*, Fourth Edition. Cambridge, MA: Blackwell.

165 Linda Smircich and Marta Calás (1987), Organizational culture: a critical assessment. In F. Jablin, L. Putnam, K. Roberts and L. Porter, Editors, *Handbook of Organizational Communication*. Newbury Park, CA: SAGE Publications, 228–263.

166 Andrew Leigh and Michael Maynard (2000), Making sense of culture. *Training Journal*, December, 26–29.

167 Harry C. Triandis (1996), The psychological measurement of cultural syndromes. *American Psychologist*, 51, 407–415.

168 Work Systems Associates (1996), *The Courage to Change*. Lexington, MA: Work Systems Associates/Linkage Incorporated, 22.

169 Edgar H. Schein (1992), *Organizational Culture and Leadership*, Second Edition. San Francisco, CA: Jossey-Bass, 2.

170 Gideon Kunda and Stephen Barley (1988), *Designing Devotion: Corporate Cultures and Ideologies of Workplace Control*. Paper presented at the 83rd Annual Meeting of the American Sociological Association, San Francisco, CA, August.

171 Jennifer A. Chatman and Sandra Eunyoung Cha (2003), Leading by leveraging culture. *California Management Review*, 45 (4), Summer, 20–34.

172 Stanley A. Deetz, Sarah J. Tracy and Jennifer L. Simpson (2000), *Leading Organizations through Transition*. Thousand Oaks, CA: SAGE Publications, 7.

173 William Ouchi (1981), *Theory Z*. Reading, MA: Addison-Wesley.

174 Michiyo Nakamoto (2001), Sparing the pheasants that cry out. Japanese Management, Part 1. *Financial Times*, March 14.

175 T.J. Hennessy, Jr (1998), 'Reinventing government': does leadership make the difference? *Public Administration Review*, 58, 522–531.

176 Bernard M. Bass (1985), *Leadership and Performance beyond Expectations*. New York: Free Press.

177 Edgar H. Schein (2004), *Organizational Culture and Leadership*, Third Edition. San Francisco, CA: Jossey-Bass.

178 Terrence Deal and Allan Kennedy (1982), *Corporate Cultures: The Rites and Rituals of Corporate Life*. Reading, MA: Addison-Wesley.

179 Tom Peters and Robert Waterman (1982), *In Search of Excellence*. New York: Harper & Row.

180 Emmanuel Ogbonna and Lloyd Harris (1998), Organizational culture: it's not what you think ... *Journal of General Management*, 23 (3), 35–48.

181 W.W. Burke and G.H. Litwin (1989), A causal model of organizational performance. In J. W. Pfeiffer, Editor, *The 1989 Annual: Developing Human Resources*. San Diego, CA: University Associates, 16.

182 Emmanuel Ogbonna and Lloyd Harris (1998), Organizational culture: it's not what you think... *Journal of General Management*, 23 (3), 35–48.

183 Geert Hofstede (1998), Identifying organizational subcultures: an empirical investigation. *Journal of Management Studies*, 35 (1), 1–12.

184 Edgar H. Schein (2004), *Organizational Culture and Leadership*, Third Edition. San Francisco, CA: Jossey-Bass, 12–13.

185 Karen Legge, quoted by D. Buchanan and A. Huczinski (1997), *Organizational Behaviour: An Introductory Text*, Third Edition. London: Prentice Hall.

186 Stanley A. Deetz, Sarah J. Tracy and Jennifer L. Simpson (2000), *Leading Organizations through Transition*. Thousand Oaks, CA: SAGE Publications, 11.

187 N.M. Ashkanasy, C. Wilderom and M.F. Peterson, Editors (2000), *Handbook of Organizational Culture and Climate*. Thousand Oaks, CA: SAGE Publications.

188 J.M. Beyer and D. Nino (2001), Culture as a source, expression, and reinforcer of emotions in organizations. In R. Payne and C.L. Cooper, Editors, *Emotions at Work*. New York: John Wiley & Sons, 173–197.

189 E.H. Schein (1990), Organizational culture. *American Psychologist*, 45 (2), 109–119.

190 S. Fineman (2001), Emotions and organizational control. In R. Payne and C. L. Cooper, Editors, *Emotions at Work*. New York: John Wiley & Sons, 214–239

191 D. Tourish and A. Pinnington (2002), Transformational leadership, corporate cultism and the spirituality paradigm: an unholy trinity in the workplace. *Human Relations*, 55, 147–172.

192 Dennis Tourish and Ashly Pinnington (2002), Transformational leadership, corporate cultism and the spirituality paradigm: an unholy trinity in the workplace. *Human Relations*, 55, 147–172.

193 C.E.J. Härtel and Y. Fujimoto (2000), Diversity is not the problem: openness to perceived dissimilarity is. *Journal of the Australian and New Zealand Academy of Management*, 5, 14–27.

194 I. Janis (1982), *Victims of Groupthink: A Psychological Study of Foreign Policy Decisions and Fiasco*, Second Edition. Boston, MA: Houghton Mifflin.

195 S. Milgram (1963), Behavioral study of obedience. *Journal of Abnormal and Social Psychology*, 67, 371–378.

196 Martha Maznevski and Joe DiStefano (n.d.), *The Impact of Culture on Work*, unpublished paper, Lausanne, Switzerland: IMD; adapted from H.W. Lane, J.J. DiStefano and M.L. Maznevski (2000), *International Management Behavior*, Fourth Edition. Cambridge, MA: Blackwell.

197 Stanley A. Deetz, Sarah J. Tracy and Jennifer L. Simpson (2000), *Leading Organizations through Transition*. Thousand Oaks, CA: SAGE Publications, 31.

198 Adam Zuckerman (2002), Strong corporate cultures and firm performance: are there tradeoffs? *Academy of Management Executive*, November, 158–160.

199 John Micklethwait and Adrian Wooldridge (2000), *A Future Perfect: The Challenge and Promise of Globalization*. New York: Crown Business.

200 Emmanuel Ogbonna and Lloyd C. Harris (2000), Leadership style, organizational culture and performance: empirical evidence from UK companies. *International Journal of Human Resource Management*, 11 (4), 766–788.

201 J.B. Sorensen (2002), The strength of corporate culture and the reliability of firm performance. *Administrative Science Quarterly*, 47 (1), 70–91.

202 Stephen Ackroyd and Philip Crowdy (1990), Can culture be managed? *Personnel Review*, 19 (5), 3–13.

203 Stanley A. Deetz, Sarah J. Tracy and Jennifer L. Simpson (2000), *Leading Organizations through Transition*. Thousand Oaks, CA: SAGE Publications, 33.

204 J. Cooper and J. Hartley (1991), Reconsidering the case for organisational commitment. *Human Resource Management Journal*, 3, Spring, 18–32.

205 Stanley A. Deetz, Sarah J. Tracy and Jennifer L. Simpson (2000), *Leading Organizations through Transition*. Thousand Oaks, CA: SAGE Publications, 32.

206 John P. Kotter and James L. Heskett (1992), *Corporate Culture and Performance*. New York: Free Press.

207 James C. Collins and Jerry L. Porras (1995), *Built to Last: Successful Habits of Visionary Companies*. London: Century Business Books, 83.

208 David A. Buchanan and Andrzej Huczyinski (1997), *Organizational Behaviour: An Introductory Text*, Third Edition. London: Prentice Hall, 530.

209 *Annual Report/Form 10–K*, Perot Systems Corporation, 2001.

210 Stanley A. Deetz, Sarah J. Tracy and Jennifer L. Simpson (2000), *Leading Organizations through Transition*. Thousand Oaks, CA: SAGE Publications, 162–163.

211 Richard Dawkins (1998), *Unweaving the Rainbow*. New York: Penguin.

212 Susan Blakemore (1999), *The Meme Machine*. New York: Oxford University Press, 6.

213 Richard Hooker, Editor (1993), *Manoeuvre Warfare: An Anthology*. Novato: Presidio Press, 27–28.

214 Stanley A. Deetz, Sarah J. Tracy and Jennifer L. Simpson (2000), *Leading Organizations through Transition*. Thousand Oaks, CA: SAGE Publications, 21.

215 Amin Rajan (2000), *How Can Leaders Achieve Successful Culture Change?* Tonbridge, Kent: Centre for Research in Employment & Technology in Europe.

216 Aya Fukushige and David P. Spicer (2007), Leadership preferences in Japan: an exploratory study. *Leadership and Organization Development Journal*, 28 (6), 508–530.

217 Roger Gill (2001), Leadership sans frontières. *City to City*, 12, September/October, 32–33.

218 Tom Cannon (2000), *Leadership in the New Economy*. Paper presented at The National Leadership Conference, MCI-METO, The Royal Military Academy, Sandhurst, 24 May.

219 Hayat Kabasakal and Ali Dastmalchian (2001), Introduction to the special issue on leadership and culture in the Middle East. *Applied Psychology: An International Review,* 50 (4), 479–488.

220 M. Haire, E. Ghiselli and L. Porter (1966), *Managerial Thinking: An International Study.* New York: John Wiley & Sons.

221 Bernard M. Bass (1997), Does the transactional-transformational leadership paradigm transcend organizational and national boundaries? *American Psychologist,* 52, 130–139.

222 *The Economist* (2001), The voters give Koizumi a chance. Will the LDP? 4 August, 21–23.

223 John Adair (1989), *Great Leaders.* Guildford: The Talbot Adair Press, 55.

224 PA Consulting Group (1996), *Leading into the Millennium.* London: PA Consulting Group.

225 Garry Griffiths (1999), *The Cross-cultural Chessboard at BT.* Paper presented at the Second Annual Conference of The Leadership Trust Foundation on 'Leadership sans Frontiéres', Ross-on-Wye, February 1–2.

226 Roger Gill (1997), *Cross-cultural Similarities and Differences in Leadership Styles and Behaviour: A Comparison between UK and Southeast Asian Managers.* Working Paper no. LT-RG-97–6, Ross-on-Wye: The Leadership Trust Foundation.

227 Hayat Kabasakal and Ali Dastmalchian (2001), Introduction to the special issue on leadership and culture in the Middle East. *Applied Psychology: An International Review,* 50 (4), 479–488.

228 Mansour Javidan and Ali Dastmalchian (2003), Culture and leadership in Iran: the land of individual achievers, strong family ties, and powerful elite. *Academy of Management Executive,* 17 (4), November, 127–142.

229 Roger Gill (1997), *Cross-cultural Similarities and Differences in Leadership Styles and Behaviour: A Comparison between UK and Southeast Asian Managers.* Working Paper no. LT-RG-97–6, Ross-on-Wye: The Leadership Trust Foundation.

230 Uma D. Jogulu (2010), Culturally-linked leadership styles. *Leadership & Organization Development Journal,* 31 (8), 705–719.

231 Geert Hofstede (1984), *Culture's Consequences.* Thousand Oaks, CA: SAGE Publications; Geert Hofstede (1994), *Values Survey Module 1994 Manual,* University of Limburg, Maastricht, The Netherlands.

232 P. Dorfman (2004), International and cross-cultural research. In B.J. Punnett and O. Shenkar, Editors, *Handbook for International Management Research.* Ann Arbor, MI: University of Michigan Press, 265–355.

233 D. Carl, V. Gupta and M. Javidan (2004), Power distance. In R. House, P. Hanges, M. Javidan, P. Dorfman and V. Gupta, Editors, *Culture, Leadership, and Organizations: The GLOBE Study of 62 Societies.* Thousand Oaks, CA: SAGE Publications, 513–563; P. Dorfman, P. Hanges and F. Brodbeck (2004), Leadership and culture variations: the identification of culturally endorsed leadership profiles. In R. House, P. Hanges, M. Javidan, P. Dorfman and V. Gupta, Editors, *Culture, Leadership, and Organizations: The GLOBE Study of 62 Societies.* Thousand Oaks, CA: SAGE Publications, 669–719.

234 Maarten van Beek (2000), *People Oriented Makes a Difference: A Comparative Study of Dutch, British, American, Swedish, Italian and French Organizational Leaders*, unpublished Master's thesis, Leiden University, The Netherlands.

235 Peter B. Smith (1999), *Similarities and Differences in Leadership Across Cultures: A 43–Nation Study*. Paper presented at the Second Annual Conference of The Leadership Trust Foundation on 'Leadership sans Frontiéres', Ross-on-Wye, February 1–2.

236 S. Arzu Wasti (2003), The influence of cultural values on antecedents of organisational commitment: an individual-level analysis. *Applied Psychology: An International Review*, 52 (4), 533–554.

237 Mahathir Mohamad (1997), *New Straits Times*, Malaysia, 4 September.

238 Fons Trompenaars (2000), *Cultural Diversity within the Head and Heart of Leadership*. Paper presented at the Third Annual Conference, 'The Head and Heart of Leadership', The Leadership Trust Foundation, Ross-on-Wye, 6–7 September.

239 Sally Lansdell (2002), *The Vision Thing*. Oxford: Capstone Publishing, 33.

240 Robert House, Mansour Javidan and Peter W. Dorfman (2001), Project GLOBE: an introduction. *Applied Psychology: An International Review*, 50 (4), 489–505; R.J. House, P.J. Hanges, S.A. Ruiz-Quintanilla, P.W. Dorfman, M. Javidan, M. Dickson, V. Gupta and GLOBE (1999), Cultural influences on leadership and organizations. *Advances in Global Leadership*, 1, 171–233, Stamford, CN: JAI Press; Robert J. House, Paul J. Hanges, Mansour Javidan, Peter W. Dorfman and Vipin Gupta, Editors (2004), *Culture, Leadership, and Organizations: The GLOBE Study of 62 Societies*. Thousand Oaks, CA: SAGE Publications; Mansour Javidan and Ali Dastmalchian (2009), Managerial implications of the GLOBE project: a study of 62 societies. *Asia Pacific Journal of Human Resources*, 47 (1), 41–58; Mansour Javidan, Peter W. Dorfman, Jon Paul Howell and Paul J. Hanges (2010), Leadership and cultural context. In Nitin Nohria and Rakesh Khurana, Editors, *Handbook of Leadership Theory and Practice*. Boston, MA: Harvard Business Press, Chapter 13.

241 Mansour Javidan, Peter W. Dorfman, Jon Paul Howell and Paul J. Hanges (2010), Leadership and cultural context. In Nitin Nohria and Rakesh Khurana, Editors, *Handbook of Leadership Theory and Practice*. Boston, MA: Harvard Business Press, Chapter 13, 344.

242 Mansour Javidan, Peter W. Dorfman, Jon Paul Howell and Paul J. Hanges (2010), Leadership and cultural context. In Nitin Nohria and Rakesh Khurana, Editors, *Handbook of Leadership Theory and Practice*. Boston, MA: Harvard Business Press, Chapter 13, 345–346.

243 Mansour Javidan, Peter W. Dorfman, Jon Paul Howell and Paul J. Hanges (2010), Leadership and cultural context. In Nitin Nohria and Rakesh Khurana, Editors, *Handbook of Leadership Theory and Practice*. Boston, MA: Harvard Business Press, Chapter 13, 347.

244 Felix C. Brodbeck et al. (2000), Cultural variation of leadership prototypes across 22 European countries. *Journal of Occupational and Organizational Psychology*, 73, 1–29.

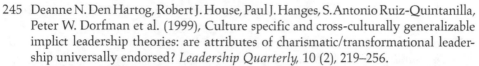

245 Deanne N. Den Hartog, Robert J. House, Paul J. Hanges, S. Antonio Ruiz-Quintanilla, Peter W. Dorfman et al. (1999), Culture specific and cross-culturally generalizable implict leadership theories: are attributes of charismatic/transformational leadership universally endorsed? *Leadership Quarterly*, 10 (2), 219–256.

246 Jagdeep S. Chhokar, Felix C. Brodbeck and Robert J. House (2007), *Culture and Leadership Across the World: The GLOBE Book of In-Depth Studies of 25 Societies*. Hove, East Sussex: Psychology Press.

247 Hayat Kabasakal and Ali Dastmalchian (2001), Introduction to the special issue on leadership and culture in the Middle East. *Applied Psychology: An International Review*, 50 (4), 479–488.

248 Ilmihal (1999), Divantas Publications. Istanbul: Medya Ofset.

249 H. Kabasakal and M. Bodur (1998), *Leadership, Values and Institutions: the Case of Turkey*, Research Papers, Bogaziçi University, Istanbul, Turkey; Ikhlas A. Abdalla and Moudi A. Al-Homoud (2001), Exploring the implicit leadership theory in the Arabian Gulf states. *Applied Psychology: An International Review*, 50 (4), 506–531; Ali Dastmalcian, Mansour Javidan and Kamran Alam (2001), Effective leadership and culture in Iran: an empirical study. *Applied Psychology: An International Review*, 50 (4), 532–558; Selda Fikret Pasa, Hayat Kabasakal and Muzaffer Bodur (2001), Society, organisations, and leadership in Turkey. *Applied Psychology: An International Review*, 50 (4), 559–589.

250 Felix Brodbeck, Michael Frese and Mansour Javidan (2002), Leadership made in Germany: low on compassion, high on performance. *Academy of Management Executive*, 16 (1), 16–29.

251 Mansour Javidan, Peter W. Dorfman, Jon Paul Howell and Paul J. Hanges (2010), Leadership and cultural context. In Nitin Nohria and Rakesh Khurana, Editors, *Handbook of Leadership Theory and Practice*. Boston, MA: Harvard Business Press, 336–337.

252 Mansour Javidan, Peter W. Dorfman, Jon Paul Howell and Paul J. Hanges (2010), Leadership and cultural context. In Nitin Nohria and Rakesh Khurana, Editors, *Handbook of Leadership Theory and Practice*. Boston, MA: Harvard Business Press, 346–372.

253 Mansour Javidan, Peter W. Dorfman, Jon Paul Howell and Paul J. Hanges (2010), Leadership and cultural context. In Nitin Nohria and Rakesh Khurana, Editors, *Handbook of Leadership Theory and Practice*. Boston, MA: Harvard Business Press, 369–371.

254 Mansour Javidan, Peter W. Dorfman, Jon Paul Howell and Paul J. Hanges (2010), Leadership and cultural context. In Nitin Nohria and Rakesh Khurana, Editors, *Handbook of Leadership Theory and Practice*. Boston, MA: Harvard Business Press, 369–371.

255 Mansour Javidan, Peter W. Dorfman, Jon Paul Howell and Paul J. Hanges (2010), Leadership and cultural context. In Nitin Nohria and Rakesh Khurana, Editors, *Handbook of Leadership Theory and Practice*. Boston, MA: Harvard Business Press, 369–371; S. Beechler and M. Javidan (2007), Leading with a global mindset. In M. Javidan, M.A. Hitt and R.M. Steers (Editors), *Advances in International Management, Volume 19, the Global Mindset*. Oxford: Elsevier, 131–170.

256 The Sunday Times 100 Best Companies to Work For 2007. *The Sunday Times*, 11 March.
257 Zoe Thomas (2007), The Sunday Times 100 Best Companies to Work For 2007. *The Sunday Times*, 11 March, 10.
258 The Times (2010), Crock of gold. Leading article, *The Times*, Saturday 17 July, 2.
259 The Times (2010), Crock of gold. Leading article, *The Times*, Saturday 17 July, 2.
260 Sathnam Sanghera (2010), How Goldman Sachs lost its glitter. *The Times*, Wednesday 21 July, 43.
261 Sathnam Sanghera (2010), How Goldman Sachs lost its glitter. *The Times*, Wednesday 21 July, 43.
262 The Times (2010), Crock of gold. Leading article, *The Times*, Saturday 17 July, 2.

Chapter 7

1 Stephen Aris (2002), Weinstock: I wanted to string up Simpson. *The Sunday Times*, 28 July, 3.8; Stephen Aris (1998), *Arnold Weinstock and the Making of GEC*. London: Aurum Press.
 2 Stephen Aris (2002), Weinstock: I wanted to string up Simpson. *The Sunday Times*, 28 July, 3.8; Stephen Aris (1998), *Arnold Weinstock and the Making of GEC*. London: Aurum Press.
 3 R. Evered (1980), *So What Is Strategy?* Working Paper, Naval Postgraduate School, Monterey, CA; J.B. Quinn (1980), *Strategies for Change: Logical Incrementalism*. Homewood, IL: Richard D. Irwin; H. Mintzberg and J.B. Quinn (1996), *The Strategy Process: Concepts, Contexts, Cases*, Third Edition. Upper Saddle River, NJ: Prentice Hall.
 4 Donald C. Hambrick and James W. Fredrickson (2001), Are you sure you have a strategy? *Academy of Management Executive*, 15 (4), 48–59.
 5 John Middleton and Bob Gorzynski (2002), *Strategy Express*. Oxford: Capstone Publishing, 14.
 6 Alfred D. Chandler (1962), *Strategy and Structure: Chapters in the History of the Industrial Enterprise*. Cambridge, MA: MIT Press.
 7 *The Economist* (1997), Making strategy. 1 March, 81.
 8 Moshe Farjoun (2002), Towards an organic perspective on strategy. *Strategic Management Journal*, 23, 561–594.
 9 J.B. Quinn (1980), *Strategies for Change: Logical Incrementalism*. Homewood, IL: Richard D. Irwin.
 10 Moshe Farjoun (2002), Towards an organic perspective on strategy. *Strategic Management Journal*, 23, 561–594.
 11 J. Pfeffer and G.R. Salancik (1978), *The External Control of Organizations*. New York: Harper & Row; L.J. Bourgeois (1984), Strategic management and determinism. *Academy of Management Review*, 9 (4), 586–596; H. Itami and T.W. Roehl (1987), *Mobilizing Invisible Assets*. Cambridge, MA: Harvard University Press; M.E. Porter (1991), Towards a dynamic theory of strategy. *Strategic Management Journal*, Winter Special Issue, 12, 95–117.

12 Moshe Farjoun (2002), Towards an organic perspective on strategy. *Strategic Management Journal,* 23, 561–594.

13 David Grayson and Adrian Hodges (2004), *Corporate Social Opportunity!* Sheffield: Greenleaf Publishing, 157.

14 Moshe Farjoun (2002), Towards an organic perspective on strategy. *Strategic Management Journal,* 23, 561–594.

15 Christopher Bartlett and Sumantra Ghoshal (1989), *Managing across Borders: The Transnational Solution.* London: Century Business.

16 Loren Gary (2001), Strategy as process. *Burning Questions 2001, Harvard Management Update,* July, 8.

17 Orit Gadiesh, chairman of Bain & Company, management consultants, quoted by Loren Gary (2001), Strategy as process. *Burning Questions 2001, Harvard Management Update,* July, 8.

18 Orit Gadiesh and James Gilbert (2001), Transforming corner-office strategy into frontline action. *Harvard Business Review,* 79 (5), May, 72–79.

19 David Grayson and Adrian Hodges (2004), *Corporate Social Opportunity!* Sheffield: Greenleaf Publishing.

20 Igor Ansoff (1962), *Corporate Strategy: an Analytic Approach to Business Policy for Growth and Expansion.* New York: McGraw-Hill.

21 Herbert A. Simon (1957), *Administrative Behavior: A Study of Decision-Making Processes in Administrative Organization,* Second Edition. New York: Macmillan.

22 David G. Hoopes, Tammy L. Madsen and Gordon Walker (2003), Guest editors' introduction to the special issue: why is there a resource-based view? Toward a theory of competitive heterogeneity. *Strategic Management Journal,* 24, 889–902.

23 John Kay (1996), Happy combination. *Financial Times,* 25 October 25, 18

24 John Kay (1996), Happy combination. *Financial Times,* 25 October, 18.

25 Andrew M. Pettigrew and Richard Whipp (1993), *Managing Change for Competitive Success.* Oxford: Blackwell, 201.

26 John Middleton and Bob Gorzynski (2002), *Strategy Express.* Oxford: Capstone Publishing, 3.

27 John Middleton and Bob Gorzynski (2002), *Strategy Express.* Oxford: Capstone Publishing, 3.

28 Gary Hamel and C.K. Prahalad (1994), *Competing for the Future: Breakthrough Strategies for Seizing Control of your Industry and Creating the Markets of Tomorrow.* Boston, MA: Harvard Business School Press.

29 Leopold Vansina (1999), Leadership in strategic business unit management. *European Journal of Work and Organizational Psychology,* 8 (1), 87–108.

30 John P. Kotter, quoted by Bill Finnie and Marilyn Norris (1997), On leading change: a conversation with John P. Kotter. *Strategy and Leadership,* 25 (1), 18.

31 Neil Ferrier, Editor (1965), *Churchill: The Man of the Century.* London: Purnell, 6.

32 Stephen R. Covey (1992), *Principle-centered Leadership.* London: Simon & Schuster, 166–167.

33 Leonard D. Goodstein (2010), Strategic planning: a leadership imperative. In Elaine Biech, Editor, *The ASTD Leadership Handbook*. Alexandria, VA, ASTD Press and San Francisco, CA: Berrett-Koehler, Chapter 4, 45–46.

34 Quoted by C. Marlena Fiol and Edward J. O'Connor (2002), *Future Planning + Present Mindfulness = Strategic Foresight*. Paper presented at the International Conference on 'Probing the Future: Developing Organizational Foresight in the Knowledge Economy', University of Strathclyde Graduate School of Business, Glasgow, 11–13 July.

35 Quoted by Katherine Beatty and Laura Quinn (2002), Strategic command: taking the long view for organizational success. *Leadership in Action*, 22, 2, May/June, 3–7.

36 James Champy and Nitin Nohria (2000), *The Arc of Ambition*. Chichester: John Wiley & Sons, 12.

37 J.A. Pearce. III (1981), An executive-level perspective on the strategic management process. *California Management Review*, 24, 39–48; L.J. Bourgeois, III (1984), Strategic management aand determinism. *Academy of Management Review*, 9, 586–596; L.J. Bourgeois, III (1985), Strategic goals, perceived uncertainty, and economic performance in volatile environments. *Academy of Management Journal*, 28, 548–573; M.A. Hitt and B.B. Tyler (1991), Strategic decision models: integrating different perspectives. *Strategic Management Journal*, 12, 327–351.

38 J.E. Dutton, L. Fahey and V.K. Narayanan (1983), Understanding strategic issue diagnosis. *Strategic Management Journal*, 14, 307–323; J.E. Dutton and S. Jackson (1987), Categorizing strategic issues: links to organizational action. *Academy of Management Review*, 12 (1), 76–90; J.E. Dutton, E.J. Walton and E.C. Abrahamson (1989), Important dimensions of strategic issues: separating the wheat from the chaff. *Journal of Management Studies*, 26, 379–396.

39 L. Festinger (1957), *A Theory of Cognitive Dissonance*. Stanford, CA: Stanford University Press.

40 S.T. Fiske and S.E. Taylor (1991), *Social Cognition*. New York: McGraw-Hill.

41 G.N. Johnson (1987), *Strategic Change and the Management Process*. Oxford: Basil Blackwell.

42 Gerry Johnson and Kevan Scholes (2002), *Exploring Corporate Strategy*, Sixth Edition. Harlow, Essex: Pearson Education, 550.

43 John Adair, quoted by Jane Simms (2002), Is Britain being led astray? *Director*, January, 48–51.

44 *Full Disclosure 2002* study, Shelley Taylor & Associates, reported by Andrew Parker (2003), Study criticises companies for poor reports. *Financial Times*, 6 February, 27.

45 Christine Y. Chen (2002), The world's most admired companies 2002. *Fortune*, 4 March, 26–32.

46 S.J. Nadin, C.M. Cassell and M.T. Older (1998), *The Change Management Needs of South Yorkshire SMEs: A Needs Analysis*. Sheffield: IWP.

47 Darrell K. Rigby (2001), Management Tools 2001. *Forum*, European Foundation for Management Development, December, 24–26.

48 Reported by Ben Willmott (2003), Documenting HR strategies is essential to people and profits. *Personnel Today*, 7 January.

49 Michael C. Mankins and Richard Steele (2005), Turning great strategy into great performance. *Harvard Business Review*, 83 (7/8), July–August, 64–72.

50 Michael Diamond (2002), Academic leadership: turning vision into reality. *Forum*, European Foundation for Management Education, April, 14–18.

51 V. Kasturi Rangan (2004), Lofty missions, down-to-earth plans. *Harvard Business Review*, March, 112–119.

52 W. Chan Kim and Renée Mauborgne (2003), Think for yourself – stop copying a rival. *Financial Times*, August 11, 9.

53 Michael Porter (1980), *Competitive Strategy: Techniques for Analyzing Industries and Competitors*. New York: Free Press.

54 Michael Porter (1980), *Competitive Strategy*. New York: Free Press.

55 John Middleton and Bob Gorzynski (2002), *Strategy Express*. Oxford: Capstone Publishing, 17.

56 W. Chan Kim and Renée Mauborgne (2003), Think for yourself – stop copying a rival. *Financial Times*, August 11, 9.

57 Gary Hamel and C.K. Prahalad (1994), *Competing for the Future*. Boston, MA: Harvard Business School Press.

58 Gary Hamel (2001), *Leading the Revolution*. New York: McGraw-Hill.

59 Christopher A. Bartlett and Sumantra Ghoshal (1994), Changing the role of top management beyond strategy to purpose. *Harvard Business Review*, November–December; Christopher A. Bartlett and Sumantra Ghoshal (1995), Changing the role of top management beyond structure to processes. *Harvard Business Review*, January–February; Christopher A. Bartlett and Sumantra Ghoshal (1995), Changing the role of top management beyond systems to people. *Harvard Business Review*, May–June; Christopher A. Bartlett and Sumantra Ghoshal (1998), *The Individualized Corporation*. London: Heinemann.

60 See Chapter 1 and Warren Bennis and Burt Nanus (1985), *Leaders: The Strategies for Taking Charge*. New York: Harper & Row, 22.

61 Robert S. Kaplan and David P. Norton (2001), *The Strategy-Focused Organization: How Balanced Scorecard Companies Thrive in the New Business Environment*. Boston, MA: Harvard Business School Press.

62 Leonard D. Goodstein (2010), Strategic planning: a leadership imperative. In Elaine Biech, Editor, *The ASTD Leadership Handbook*. Alexandria, VA: ASTD Press and San Francisco, CA: Berrett-Koehler, Chapter 4, 43.

63 Leonard D. Goodstein (2010), Strategic planning: a leadership imperative. In Elaine Biech, Editor, *The ASTD Leadership Handbook*. Alexandria, VA: ASTD Press and San Francisco, CA: Berrett-Koehler, Chapter 4, 44.

64 Leonard D. Goodstein (2010), Strategic planning: a leadership imperative. In Elaine Biech, Editor, *The ASTD Leadership Handbook*. Alexandria, VA: ASTD Press and San Francisco, CA: Berrett-Koehler, Chapter 4, 43, 45–46.

65 Leonard D. Goodstein (2010), Strategic planning: a leadership imperative. in Elaine Biech, Editor, *The ASTD Leadership Handbook*. Alexandria, VA: ASTD Press and San Francisco, CA: Berrett-Koehler, Chapter 4, 44.[C7Q2].

66 Michael Porter (1997), Creating tomorrow's advantages. In R. Gibson, Editor, *Rethinking the Future*. London: Nicholas Brealey, 54.

67 Bill Cockburn (2000), *Leadership During Change.* Paper presented at The National Leadership Conference, 'Leaders and Managers: Fit for the Future, The Royal Military Academy, Sandhurst, 24 May. (Cockburn was BT's CEO.)

68 Strategy for the next decade is stated in *Going Local – Fresh Tracks Down Old Roads: Our Strategy for the Next Decade,* The National Trust, 2010. Downloaded from http://www.nationaltrust.org.uk/main/w-trust/w-thecharity.htm on 6 February 2011.

69 *Durham University Strategy 2010–2020.* Reproduced by kind permission. Accessed at http://www.dur.ac.uk/resources/about/strategy/Finalfullstrategydocument.pdf on 9 November 2010.

70 *Eleventh National Development Plan 2011–2015,* Office of the National Economic and Social Development Board, Government of Thailand, 26 October 2010. Downloaded from http://www.nesdb.go.th/ on 17 March 2011.

71 *Eleventh National Development Plan 2011–2015,* Office of the National Economic and Social Development Board, Government of Thailand, 26 October 2010. Downloaded from http://www.nesdb.go.th/ on 17 March 2011.

72 William W. George (2001), *Keynote Address,* Academy of Management Annual Conference, Washington, DC, August. In *Academy of Management Executive,* 15 (4), 39–47.

73 McKinsey & Company (2011), Creating more value with corporate strategy. McKinsey Global Survey results. *McKinsey Quarterly,* downloaded from http://e.mckinseyquarterly.com/11497b51blayfousubkh3iqaaaaaaatxj54ucgpj2s yyaaaaa on 25 January 2011.

74 Colin Eden (1993), Strategy development and implementation: cognitive mapping for Group Support. In J. Hendry, G. Johnson and J. Newton, Editors, *Strategic Thinking: Leadership and the Management of Change.* Chichester: John Wiley & Sons, 118.

75 Management Today (2001), *Sheer Inspiration: The UK's 100 Most Visionary Companies.* London: Management Today, 22–23.

76 The Manufacturing Foundation (2003), *Innovation Essentials.* Birmingham, August.

77 James A. Champy (1997), Preparing for organizational change. In Frances Hesselbein, Marshall Goldsmith and Richard Beckhard, Editors, *The Organization of the Future.* San Francisco, CA: Jossey-Bass.

78 Kees Van der Heijden (1996), *Scenarios: The Art of Strategic Conversation.* Chichester: John Wiley & Sons.

79 Peter Linkow (1999), What gifted strategic thinkers do. *Training & Development,* 53 (7), 34–37.

80 Ian Johnson (2005), *Strategic Conversation: Defining, Measuring and Applying the Construct in Organisations,* unpublished PhD thesis, Griffith University, Australia.

81 Bruce Pasternack, senior vice president and managing partner at Booz, Allen & Hamilton, quoted by Sharon O'Shea (2000), The changing composition of leadership. *Financial Executive,* 16 (4), 35; Bruce Pasternack, Thomas D. Williams and Paul F. Anderson (2001), Beyond the cult of the CEO: building institutional leadership. *Strategy and Business,* 1st quarter, 1–12.

82 Gerry Johnson, Kevan Scholes and Richard Whittington (2005), *Exploring Corporate Strategy*, Seventh Edition. Harlow, Essex: Pearson Education, 41–58

83 Gerry Johnson, Kevan Scholes and Richard Whittington (2005), *Exploring Corporate Strategy*, Seventh Edition. Harlow, Essex: Pearson Education, 41–58.

84 Based on Colin Eden (1993), Strategy development and implementation: cognitive mapping for Group Support. In J. Hendry, G. Johnson and J. Newton, Editors, *Strategic Thinking: Leadership and the Management of Change.* Chichester: John Wiley & Sons, 117.

85 Donald C. Hambrick and James W. Fredrickson (2001), Are you sure you have a strategy? *Academy of Management Executive,* 15 (4), 48–59.

86 Leonard D. Goodstein (2010), Strategic planning: a leadership imperative. In Elaine Biech, Editor, *The ASTD Leadership Handbook.* Alexandria, VA: ASTD Press and San Francisco, CA: Berrett-Koehler, Chapter 4, 46–53; T.M. Nolan, L.D. Goodstein and J. Goodstein (2008), *Applied Strategic Planning: An Introduction,* Second Edition. San Francisco, CA: Pfeiffer/Wiley.

87 Phyllis Johnson, Kevin Daniels and Anne Huff (2001), Sense making, leadership and mental models. In S.J. Zaccaro and R.J. Klimoski, Editors, *The Nature of Organizational Leadership: Understanding the Performance Imperatives Confronting Today's Leaders.* San Francisco, CA: Jossey-Bass.

88 P. Corner, A.J. Kinicki and B.W. Keats (1994), Integrating organizational and individual processing perspectives on choice. *Organization Science,* 5 (3), 294–308.

89 R. Calori, G. Johnson and P. Sarnin (1994), CEOs' cognitive maps and the scope of the organization. *Strategic Management Journal,* 15 (6), 437–457.

90 Karl E. Weick (1995), *Sensemaking in Organizations.* Newbury Park, CA: SAGE Publications.

91 Christopher Bartlett (2000), Closing the strategic generation gap. *Leader to Leader,* 15, Winter, 27–32.

92 Christopher Bartlett (2000), Closing the strategic generation gap. *Leader to Leader,* 15, Winter, 27–32.

93 Kevin Daniels, Leslie De Chernatony and Gerry Johnson (1995), Validating a method for mapping managers' mental models of competitive industry structures. *Human Relations,* 47, 975–991.

94 D.A. Gioia and H. P. Sims (1986), *The Thinking Organization: Dynamics of Organizational Social Cognition.* San Francisco, CA: Jossey-Bass; A.S. Huff (1990), *Mapping Strategic Thought.* Chichester: John Wiley & Sons; M. Fiol and A.S. Huff (1992), Maps for managers: where are we? Where do we go from here? *Journal of Management Studies,* 29 (3), 267–285; A.S. Huff (1997), A current and future agenda for cognitive research in organisations. *Journal of Management Studies,* 34 (6), 947–952.

95 Phyllis Johnson, Kevin Daniels and Anne Huff (2001), Sense making, leadership and mental models. In S. Zaccaro and R. Klimoski, Editors, *The Nature of Organizational Leadership.* San Francisco, CA: Jossey-Bass.

96 Michelle A. Marks, Stephen J. Zaccaro and John E. Mathiue (2000), Performance implications of leader briefings and team-interaction training for team adaptation to novel environments. *Journal of Applied Psychology,* 85 (6), 971–986.

97   Edward de Bono, quoted by Michael Costello (2010), The thoughts that count. *People Management*, 29 July, 28–29.

98   K. Williams, S.G. Harkins and B. Latane (1979), Many hands make light the work: the causes and consequences of social loafing. *Journal of Personality and Social Psychology*, 37, 822–832.

99   Phyllis Johnson, Kevin Daniels and Anne Huff (2001), Sense making, leadership and mental models. In S. Zaccaro and R. Klimoski, Editors, *The Nature of Organizational Leadership*. San Francisco, CA: Jossey-Bass.

100 S. Hampson (1999), State of the art: personality. *The Psychologist*, 12 (6), 284–288.

101 E. Hatfield, J.T. Cacioppo and R. Rapson (1992), Primitive emotional contagion. In M.S. Clark, Editor, *Review of Personality and Social Psychology, Volume. 14: Emotion and Social Behavior*. Newbury Park, CA: SAGE Publications.

102 J.P. Walsh (1995), Managerial and organizational cognition: notes from a trip down memory lane. *Organization Science*, 6, 280–321.

103 T. Dalgleish and F.N. Watts (1990), Biases of attention and memory in disorders of anxiety and depression. *Clinical Psychology Review*, 10, 589–604; C. MacCleod (1991), Clinical anxiety and the selective encoding of threatening information. *International Review of Psychiatry*, 3, 279–292; A. Mathew (1993), Biases in processing emotional information. *The Psychologist*, 6, 493–499.

104 K. Daniels (1998), Toward integrating emotion into strategic management research: trait affect and the perception of the strategic environment. *British Journal of Management*, 9, 163–168.

105 Phyllis Johnson, Kevin Daniels and Anne Huff (2001), Sense making, leadership and mental models. In S. Zaccaro and R. Klimoski, Editors, *The Nature of Organizational Leadership*. San Francisco, CA: Jossey-Bass.

106 K. Daniels (1999), Emotion and strategic decision making. *The Psychologist*, 12, 24–28.

107 Roderick Gilkey, Rocardo Caceda and Clinton Kilts (2010), When emotional reasoning trumps IQ. *Harvard Business Review*, 88 (9), September, 27.

108 We discuss these and other forms of intelligence in the chapter on the multiple intelligences of leadership.

109 Robert Kaplan and David Norton (1992), The balanced scorecard: measures that drive performance. *Harvard Business Review*, January–February, 70–79.

110 Robert S. Kaplan and David P. Norton (2001), Using the Balanced Scorecard to create strategy-focused organizations. *Ivey Business Journal*, May/June, 12–19.

111 John J. Sosik and Don I. Jung (2009), *Full Range Leadership Development: Pathways for People, Profit and Planet*. New York and London: Psychology Press, 325–333.

112 R. Calori, G. Johnson and P. Sarnin (1994), CEOs' cognitive maps and the scope of the organization. *Strategic Management Journal*, 15 (6), 437–457.

113 Mary Coulter (2002), *Strategic Management in Action*, Second Edition. Upper Saddle River, NJ: Prentice Hall, 66.

114 Phyllis Johnson, Kevin Daniels and Anne Huff (2001), Sense making, leadership and mental models. In S. Zaccaro and R. Klimoski, Editors, *The Nature of Organizational Leadership*. San Francisco, CA: Jossey-Bass, 81–82.

115 Bruce Pasternack (2002), Yellow-light leadership. *The Asian Wall Street Journal*, September 18, A6.

116 Mike Morrison (2008), *PESTLE Analysis*. CIPD Factsheet. London: Chartered Institute of Personnel and Development.

117 Francis J. Aguilar (1967), *Scanning the Business Environment*. London: Macmillan.

118 Michael Porter (1980), *Competitive Strategy: Techniques for Analyzing Industries and Competitors*. New York: Free Press, 4.

119 W. Chan Kim and Renée Mauborgne (2002), Pursuing the holy grail of clear vision. *Financial Times*, August 6, 11.

120 P. Selznick (1957), *Leadership in Administrative Framework*. New York: Harper & Row; Mike Morrison (2008), *SWOT Analysis*, CIPD Factsheet. London: Chartered Institute of Personnel and Development.

121 J.B. Barney (1997), *Gaining and Sustaining Competitive Advantage*. Reading, MA: Addison-Wesley.

122 Morgen Witzel (2003), The search for shortcomings. *Financial Times*, 6 August, 11.

123 Gary Hamel and C.K. Prahalad (1994), *Competing for the Future*. Boston, MA: Harvard Business School Press.

124 Bruce Pasternack (2002), Yellow-light leadership. *The Asian Wall Street Journal*, 18 September A6.

125 Bruce A, Pasternack and James O'Toole (2002), *Yellow-Light Leadership: How the World's Best Companies Manage Uncertainty*. McLean, VA: Booz Allen & Hamilton.

126 Kees Van der Heijden (1996), *Scenarios: The Art of Strategic Conversation*. Chichester: John Wiley & Sons.

127 Des Dearlove (1997), Just imagine. *Human Resources*, July/August.

128 Kees Van der Heijden (1996), *Scenarios: The Art of Strategic Conversation*. Chichester: John Wiley & Sons 21.

129 Reported in *The Economist* (2001), The next big surprise, October 13–19, 76.

130 Henry Mintzberg (1978), Patterns in strategy formation. *Management Science*, 24 (9), 934–948; Henry Mintzberg (1987), Crafting strategy. *Harvard Business Review*, 65, July–August, 66–75.

131 Brian Leavy and David Wilson (1994), *Strategy and Leadership*. London: Routledge, 2; Andrew M. Pettigrew (1985), *The Awakening Giant*. Oxford: Blackwell, 1985; Andrew M. Pettigrew (1990), Longitudinal field research on change: theory and practice. *Organisational Science*, 1, 267–292.

132 Brian Leavy and David Wilson (1994), *Strategy and Leadership*. London: Routledge, 3.

133 Phyllis Johnson, Kevin Daniels and Anne Huff (2001), Sense making, leadership and mental models. In S. Zaccaro and R. Klimoski, Editors, *The Nature of Organizational Leadership*. San Francisco, CA: Jossey-Bass.

134 M.P. Sharfman and J.W. Dean (1998), The effects of context on strategic decision making processes and outcomes. In V. Papadakis and P. Barwise, Editors, *Strategic Decisions*. Boston, MA: Kluwer Academic Publishers, 179–203.

135 N. Rajagopalan, A.M.A. Rasheed and D.K. Datta (1993), Strategic decision processes: critical review and future directions. *Journal of Management*, 19 (2), 349–384.

136 A. Nahavandi and A.R. Malekzadeh (1993), Leader style in strategy and organizational performance: an integrative framework. *Journal of Management Studies*, 30 (3), 405–425; A.Y. Lewin and C.U. Stephens (1994), CEO attributes as determinants of organizational design: an integrated model. *Organization Studies*, 15 (2), 183–212.

137 A.Y. Lewin and C.U. Stephens (1994), CEO attributes as determinants of organizational design: an integrated model. *Organization Studies*, 15 (2), 183–212; J. Haleblian and S. Finkelstein (1993), Top management team size, CEO dominance, and firm performance: the moderating roles of environmental turbulence and discretion. *Academy of Management Journal*, 36 (4), 844–863.

138 Gerry Johnson (1989), Rethinking incrementalism. In D. Asch and C. Bowman, Editors, *Readings in Strategic Management*. London: Macmillan.

139 Stanley A. Deetz, Sarah J. Tracy and Jennifer Lyn Simpson (2000), *Leading Organizations through Transition*. Thousand Oaks, CA: SAGE Publications, 3.

140 J.P. Walsh, C.M. Henderson and J. Deighton (1988), Negotiated belief structures and decision performance: an empirical investigation. *Organizational Behavior and Decision Processes*, 42, 194–216.

141 A.M. Pettigrew and T. McNulty (1995), Power and influence in and around the board room. *Human Relations*, 48 (8), 845–873.

142 Henry Mintzberg (1987), Crafting strategy. *Harvard Business Review*, July–August, 66–75

143 H. Mintzberg and J.A. Waters (1985), Of strategies, deliberate and emergent. *Strategic Management Journal*, 6 (3), 257–272.

144 H. Mintzberg, B. Ahlstrand and J. Lampel (1998), *The Strategy Safari: A Guided Tour through the Wilds of Strategic Management*. New York: Free Press.

145 Thomas A. Stewart (2010), Putting strategy into practice. *Strategy+Business*, 19 April.

146 Roger L. Martin (2010), The execution trap. *Harvard Business Review*, July–August.

147 Laurence Capron and Will Mitchell (2010), Finding the right path. *Harvard Business Review*, July–August.

148 Reported by Stefan Stern (2008), Messages lost in translation. *FT.com*, 15 December.

149 Jeffrey E. Garten (2001), *The Mind of the CEO*. New York: Basic Books, 147–149.

150 John P. Kotter (2007), Leading change – why transformational efforts fail. *Harvard Business Review*, January, 96–103. (First published in 1995)

151 Robert Mittelstaedt (2003), Why don't they understand our strategy? *Financial Times*, August 20, 11.

152 *Durham University Strategy 2010–2020*. Accessed on 9 November 2010 at http://www.dur.ac.uk/about/strategy2020/faq/

153 W. Chan Kim and Renée Mauborgne (2002), Pursuing the Holy Grail of clear vision. *Financial Times*, 6 August, 11.

154 Jocelyn R. Davis (2010), Three traps that slow down strategy, accessed on 19 July 2010 at http://blogs.bnet.co,uk/sterling-performance/2010/07/19/three-traps-that-slow-down_strategy; Jocelyn R. Davis, Henry M. Frechette Jr and Edwin H. Boswell (2010), *Strategic Speed: Mobilize People, Accelerate Execution*. Boston, MA: Harvard Business School Press.

155 Colin Eden (1993), Strategy development and implementation: cognitive mapping for Group Support. In J. Hendry, G. Johnson and J. Newton, Editors, *Strategic Thinking: Leadership and the Management of Change*. Chichester: John Wiley & Sons.

156 R. Calori, G. Johnson and P. Sarnin (1994), CEOs' cognitive maps and the scope of the organization. *Strategic Management Journal*, 15 (6), 437–457.

157 T. McNulty and A. Pettigrew (1999), Strategists on the board. *Organization Studies*, 20 (1), 47–74.

158 Brian Leavy and David Wilson (1994), *Strategy and Leadership*. London: Routledge, 16–17.

159 Richard E. Byrd (1987), Corporate leadership skills: a new synthesis. *Organizational Dynamics*, 16, 34–43.

160 John Adair (1990), *Great Leaders*. Guildford: The Talbot Adair Press.

161 Alan Hooper and John Potter (2001), *Intelligent Leadership: Creating a Passion for Change*. London: Random House Business Books.

162 R. Duane Ireland and Michael A. Hitt (1999), Achieving and maintaining strategic competitiveness in the 21st century: the role of strategic leadership. *Academy of Management Executive*, 13 (1), February.

163 Francis J. Milliken and David A. Volrath (1991), Strategic decision-making tasks and group effectiveness: insights from theory and research on small group performance. *Human Relations*, 44 (2), 1229–1253.

164 Donald C. Hambrick (1989), Guest editor's introduction: putting top managers back in the strategy process. *Journal of Strategic Management*, special issue, Summer, 5–15.

165 Paul Shrivastava and Sidney A. Nachman (1989), Strategic leadership patterns. *Journal of Strategic Management*, special issue, Summer, 57–66.

166 Sydney Finkelstein, Charles Harvey and Thomas Lawton (2007), *Breakout Strategy: Meeting the Challenge of Double-Digit Growth*. New York: McGraw-Hill, 14–15.

167 Gerry Johnson and Kevan Scholes (2005), *Exploring Corporate Strategy*, Seventh Edition. Harlow, Essex: Pearson Education, 606–607.

168 James C. Collins and Jerry I. Porras (1996), Building your company's vision. *Harvard Business Review*, September–October, 74 (5), 65–77.

169 Reports in the *Guardian* on 18 May 1997 and 20 May 1997 quoted by Janice Winship (2007), *The Value of Story: The Making of Marks & Spencer, 1950–1983*. Paper presented at the CRESC (Centre for Research on Socio-Cultural Change) Annual Conference on 'Rethinking Cultural Economy', Manchester, September.

170 Luc Vandevelde (2002), speech at the *Second Annual CBI Business Summit*, 12 June, London. Reported in The CBI View: 'Strength through adversity'. *Business Voice*, July/August 2002, 16.

171 Chairman's message, *Annual Review and Summary Financial Statement 2002*, Marks & Spencer plc.

172 Jonathan Brown (2004), Luc Vandevelde, hailed as saviour of M&S, is ousted by the board. *Independent*, 10 May.

173 Stuart Rose: a life in retail. *Guardian*, Tuesday 7 July 2009.

174 http://plana.marksandspencer.com/about/the-plan, downloaded on 9 April 2010; *Our Plan A Commitments 2010–2015*, Marks & Spencer, March 2010.

175 Sir Stuart Rose (2010), *Our Plan A Commitments 2010–2015*, Marks & Spencer, March, 3.

176 http://corporate.marksandspencer.com/aboutus/Our_plan(3), downloaded on 9 April 2010.

177 Quoted by Marcus Leroux (2010), Bonuses in store for all: Rose's £80m parting gift. *The Times*, 9 April, 39.

178 Quoted by Marcus Leroux (2010), Bonuses in store for all: Rose's £80m parting gift. *The Times*, 9 April, 39.

179 Philip Dorgan, quoted by Zoe Wood (2010), Marks & Spencer on a high as Stuart Rose bows out. Guardian.co.uk, Thursday 8 April.

180 William W. George (2001), *Keynote Address*, Academy of Management Annual Conference, Washington, DC, August. In *Academy of Management Executive*, 15 (4), 39–47.

Chapter 8

1 Lao Tzu (c. 500 BC), *The Way of Lao Tzu*, Number 17.

2 R. Thomas Lenz (1993), Strategic management and organizational learning: a meta-theory of executive leadership. In J. Hendry, G. Johnson and J. Newton, Editors, *Strategic Thinking: Leadership and the Management of Change.* Chichester: John Wiley & Sons, 160.

3 R. Thomas Lenz (1993), Strategic management and organizational learning: a meta-theory of executive leadership. In J. Hendry, G. Johnson and J. Newton, Editors, *Strategic Thinking: Leadership and the Management of Change.* Chichester: John Wiley & Sons, 157.

4 R. Stengel (1994), The making of a leader. *Time* magazine, 143 (19), 6–12.

5 Mark Goyder (2001), Learn to lead, not manage. *The Sunday Times*, November 18, 7.9.

6 Catherine Soanes and Angus Stevenson, Editors (2004), *The Concise Oxford English Dictionary*, Eleventh Edition. Oxford: Oxford University Press, 468.

7 Catherine Soanes and Angus Stevenson, Editors (2004), *The Concise Oxford English Dictionary*, Eleventh Edition. Oxford: Oxford University Press, 1125.

8 Robert Heller (1997), *In Search of European Excellence*. London: HarperCollins Business.

9 Richard Olivier (2001), *Inspirational Leadership: Henry V and the Muse of Fire.* London: The Industrial Society, 37.

10 Johann Wolfgang von Goethe (1749–1832), Prelude at the theatre, *Faust*, 214–30, translated from the German by John Anster (1888). London: White and Allen.

11 St Thomas Aquinas, quoted by Sir Ronnie Flanagan (2000), *Leadership during Cultural and Institutional Change.* Paper presented at the National Leadership Conference, MCI-METO, The Royal Military Academy, Sandhurst, 24 May.

12   Francis J. Yammarino (1994), Indirect Leadership: Transformational Leadership at a Distance. In Bernard M. Bass and Bruce J. Avolio, Editors, *Improving Organizational Effectiveness through Transformational Leadership*. Thousand Oaks, CA: SAGE Publications, 45–46.

13   E.A. Locke and D.M. Schweiger (1979), Participation in decision making: one more look. In B.M. Staw, Editor, *Research in Organizational Behavior, Volume 1.* Greenwich, CT: JAI, 265–339.

14   William C. Byham (1988), *Zapp! The Lightning of Empowerment*. Pittsburgh, PA: Development Dimensions International Press.

15   D. Collins (1994), The disempowering logic of empowerment. *Empowerment in Organizations*, 2 (2), 14–21; I. Cunningham, J. Hyman and C. Baldry (1996), Empowerment: the power to do what? *Industrial Relations Journal*, 27 (2), 143–151; B. Hennestad (1998), Empowering by de-powering: towards an HR strategy for realizing the power of empowerment. *International Journal of Human Resource Management*, 9 (5), 934–953.

16   P.E. Waterson, C.W. Clegg, R. Bolden, K. Pepper, P.B. Warr and T.D. Wall (1999), The use and effectiveness of modern manufacturing practices. *International Journal of Production Research*, 37, 2271–2292.

17   D. McGregor (1960), *The Human Side of Enterprise.* New York: McGraw-Hill.

18   R. Likert (1961), *New Patterns of Management.* New York: McGraw-Hill.

19   F. Herzberg (1966), *Work and the Nature of Man.* Cleveland, OH: World Publishing.

20   J.R. Hackman and G.R. Oldham (1976), Motivation through the design of work: test of a theory. *Organizational Behavior and Human Performance*, 15, 250–279.

21   L.E. Davis and A.B. Cherns (1975), *The Quality of Working Life, Volume 1.* London: Free Press.

22   Bernard M. Bass (1985), *Leadership and Performance Beyond Expectations.* New York: Free Press

23   Sanjay T. Menon (2001), Employee empowerment: an integrative psychological approach. *Applied Psychology: An International Review*, 50 (1), 153–180.

24   Toby Wall, John L. Cordery and Chris W. Clegg (2002), Empowerment, performance and operational uncertainty. *Applied Psychology: An International Review*, 51 (1),146–169.

25   Chris Argyris (2000), *Flawed Advice and the Management Trap.* Oxford: Oxford University Press.

26   Peter K. Mills and Gerardo R. Ungson (2003), Reassessing the limits of structural empowerment: organizational constitution and trust as controls. *Academy of Management Review*, 28 (1), 143–153.

27   Jerald Greenberg and Robert A. Baron (2000), *Behavior in Organizations.* Harlow, Essex: Prentice Hall.

28   Holly R. Rudolph and Joy V. Peluchette (1993), The power gap: is sharing or accumulating power the answer? *Journal of Applied Business Research*, 9 (3), 12–20.

29   Peter K. Mills and Gerardo R. Ungson (2003), Reassessing the limits of structural empowerment: organizational constitution and trust as controls. *Academy of Management Review*, 28 (1), 143–153, after Henry Mintzberg (1979), *The Structuring of Organizations.* Englewood Cliffs, NJ: Prentice Hall.

30 Christine R. Koberg, Jason C. Senjem and Eric A. Goodman (1999), Antecedents and outcomes of empowerment. *Group & Organization Management*, 24 (1), 71–91.

31 Roy C. Herrenkohl, G. Thomas Judson and Judith A. Heffner (1999), Defining and measuring employee empowerment. *Journal of Applied Behavioral Science*, 35 (3), September, 373–389.

32 Roy C. Herrenkohl, G. Thomas Judson and Judith A. Heffner (1999), Defining and measuring employee empowerment. *Journal of Applied Behavioral Science*, 35 (3), September, 373–389.

33 Bradley Kirkman and Benson Rosen (1999), Beyond self-management: antecedents and consequences of team empowerment. *Academy of Management Journal*, 42 (1), 58–74.

34 Scott E. Seibert, Seth R. Silver and W. Alan Randolph (2004), Taking empowerment to the next level: a multiple-level model of empowerment, performance, and satisfaction. *Academy of Management Journal*, 47 (3), 332–349.

35 A. Frohman (1997), Igniting organizational change from below: the power of personal initiative. *Organizational Dynamics*, Winter, 39–53.

36 Phil Lowe (1994), Empowerment: management dilemma, leadership challenge. *Executive Development*, 7 (6), 23–24.

37 John Harvey-Jones (1988), *Making It Happen*. London: HarperCollins, 87.

38 Sanjay T. Menon (2001), Employee empowerment: an integrative psychological approach. *Applied Psychology: An International Review*, 50 (1), 153–180.

39 Sanjay T. Menon (2001), Employee empowerment: an integrative psychological approach. *Applied Psychology: An International Review*, 50 (1), 153–180.

40 Victor Vroom (1964), *Work and Motivation*. New York: John Wiley & Sons; L.W. Porter and E.E. Lawler (1968), *Managerial Attitudes and Performance*. Homewood, IL: Irwin.

41 R.E. Wood and A. Bandura (1989), Impact of conceptions of ability on self-regulatory mechanisms and complex decision making. *Journal of Personality and Social Psychology*, 56, 407–415.

42 J.A. Conger and R.N. Kanungo (1988), The empowerment process: integrating theory and practice. *Academy of Management Review*, 13, 471–482.

43 Sanjay T. Menon (2001), Employee empowerment: an integrative psychological approach. *Applied Psychology: An International Review*, 50 (1), 153–180.

44 Francis J. Yammarino (1994), Indirect leadership: transformational leadership at a distance. In Bernard M. Bass and Bruce J. Avolio, Editors, *Improving Organizational Effectiveness through Transformational Leadership*. Thousand Oaks, CA: SAGE Publications, 46.

45 J.R. Blau and R.D. Alba (1982), Empowering nets of participation. *Administrative Science Quarterly*, 27, 363–379; M. Sashkin (1984), Participative management is an ethical imperative. *Organizational Dynamics*, 12, 4–22; R.J. Burke (1986), The present and future status of stress research. *Journal of Organizational Behaviour Management*, 8, 249–267; S.J. Smits, E.R. McLean and J.R. Tanner (1993), Managing high-achieving information systems professionals. *Journal of Management Information Systems*, 9 (4), 103–120; M. Donovan (1994), The

empowerment plan. *Journal for Quality and Participation*, July/August, 12–14; B.E. Hayes (1994), How to measure empowerment. *Quality Progress*, February, 41–46; G. Labianca, B. Gray and D.J. Brass (1997), *A grounded model of organizational schema change during empowerment*. Paper presented at the National Academy of Management meeting, August 8–12, Boston, MA.

46 Rob Lebow, reported by David Creelman (2003b), *Interview: Rob Lebow on Accountability, Freedom and Responsibility*. www.HR.com, 14 November.

47 Nannerl O. Keohane (2010), *Thinking about Leadership*. Princeton, NJ: Princeton University Press, 62.

48 Roger Gill (1997), *The Leadership Styles of Transactional and Transformational Leaders*. Working Paper LT-RG-97–01, Ross-on-Wye: The Leadership Trust Foundation.

49 E.P. Hollander and L.R. Offerman (1990), Power and leadership in organizations. *American Psychologist*, February, 179–188; K.M. Bartol and D.C. Martin (1991), *Management*. New York: McGraw-Hill.

50 Anne Nederveen Pieterse, Daan van Knippenberg, Michaéla Schippers and Daan Stam (2009), Transformational and transactional leadership and innovative behaviour: the moderating role of psychological empowerment. *Journal of Organizational Behavior*, 31 (4), 609–623.

51 Micha Popper and Ofra Mayseless (2003), Back to basics: applying a parenting perspective to transformational leadership. *Leadership Quarterly*, 14, 41–65.

52 K. Blanchard, J.P. Carlos and A. Randolph (1995), *Empowerment Takes More Than a Minute*. San Francisco, CA: Berrett-Koehler; W.A. Randolph (1995), Navigating the journey to empowerment. *Organizational Dynamics*, 23 (4), 19–32.

53 Robert E. Quinn and Gretchen M. Spreitzer (1997), The road to empowerment: seven questions every leader should consider. *Organizational Dynamics*, 26 (2), 37–49.

54 Quoted in British firms lead the way in empowerment. *Management Skills & Development*, March 1998, 4–5.

55 Stephen R. Covey (1992), *Principle-centered Leadership*. London: Simon & Schuster, 190–199.

56 Karl W. Kuhnert (1994), Transforming leadership: developing people through delegation. In Bernard M. Bass and Bruce J. Avolio, Editors, *Improving Organizational Effectiveness through Transformational Leadership*. Thousand Oaks, CA: SAGE Publications, 10–25.

57 Karl W. Kuhnert (1994), Transforming leadership: developing people through delegation. In Bernard M. Bass and Bruce J. Avolio, Editors, *Improving Organizational Effectiveness through Transformational Leadership*. Thousand Oaks, CA: SAGE Publications, 13.

58 Karl W. Kuhnert (1994), Transforming leadership: developing people through delegation. In Bernard M. Bass and Bruce J. Avolio, Editors, *Improving Organizational Effectiveness through Transformational Leadership*. Thousand Oaks, CA: SAGE Publications, 18–24.

59 Phil Lowe (1994), Empowerment: management dilemma, leadership challenge. *Executive Development*, 7 (6), 23–24.

60 R. Kark, B. Shamir and G. Chen (2003), The two faces of transformational leadership: empowerment and dependency. *Journal of Applied Psychology,* 88 (2), 246–255.

61 The Joint Doctrine and Concepts Centre (2001), *British Defence Doctrine, Second Edition.* Joint Warfare Publication 0–01, 3–7.

62 Eileen C. Shapiro (2000), Managing in the cappuccino economy. Review of Chris Argyris (2000), *Flawed Advice and the Management Trap,* Oxford: Oxford University Press. *Harvard Business Review,* March–April, 177–184.

63 John Timpson (2010), *Upside Down Management: A Common Sense Guide to Better Business.* Chichester: John Wiley & Sons.

64 Robert Spector and Robert D. McCarthy (1996), *The Nordstrom Way: The Inside Story of America's #1 Customer Service Company.* Hoboken, NJ: John Wiley & Sons.

65 Vineet Nayar (2010), Back to front. *People Management,* 12 August, 26–29.

66 For information on Semco SA, access http://semco.locaweb.com.br/en/content. asp

67 Simon Caulkin (2003), Who's in charge here? No one. *Observer,* Sunday 27 April.

68 W. Alan Randolph and Edwards R. Kemery (2011), Managerial use of power bases in a model of managerial empowerment practices and employee psychological empowerment. *Journal of Leadership & Organizational Studies,* 18 (1), 95–106.

69 G.M. Spreitzer (1995), Psychological empowerment in the work place: construct definition, measurement, and validation. *Academy of Management Journal,* 38, 1442–1465.

70 J.R.P. French and B. Raven (1959), The bases of social power. In D. Cartwright (Editor), *Studies in Social Power,* Ann Arbor, MI: Institute for Social Research, 150–167.

71 Amin Rajan (2000), *How Can Leaders Achieve Successful Culture Change?* Tonbridge, Kent: Centre for Research in Employment & Technology in Europe.

72 Geert Hofstede (1994), *Cultures and Organizations: Software of the Mind,* Paperback Edition. London: HarperCollins.

73 W. Alan Randolph and Marshall Sashkin (2002), Can organizational empowerment work in multinational settings? *Academy of Management Executive,* 16 (1), 102–115.

74 K. Blanchard, J.P. Carlos and A. Randolph (1995), *Empowerment Takes More Than a Minute.* San Francisco, CA: Berrett-Koehler.

75 Chris Argyris (1998), Empowerment: the emperor's new clothes. *Harvard Business Review,* 76, 98–105.

76 Gregory G. Dess and Joseph C. Picken (2000), Changing roles: leadership in the 21st century. *Organizational Dynamics,* 28 (3), 18–34.

77 Attributed to Lord Brougham (1778–1868), Lord Chancellor 1830–34, in Antony Jay, Editor (1996), *The Oxford Dictionary of Political Quotations.* Oxford: Oxford University Press, 58.

78 David G. Myers (1993), *The Pursuit of Happiness.* London: The Aquarian Press, 130.

79 David G. Myers (1993), *The Pursuit of Happiness.* London: The Aquarian Press, 131.

80 Bill Birchard (2010), Herman Miller's design for growth. *Strategy+Business,* summer, issue 59.

81 Max De Pree (1990), *Leadership Is an Art.* New York: Bantam Doubleday Dell Publishing Group.

82 Peter B.B. Turney (1993), Beyond TQM with workforce activity-based management. *Management Accounting,* September, 28–31.

83 G.R. Bushe, S.J. Havlovic and G. Coetzer (1996), Exploring empowerment from the inside out. *Journal for Quality and Participation,* 19 (2), 36–45.

84 Leonard Greenhalgh (2001), Managers face up to the new era. Mastering Management. *Financial Times,* January 22.

85 John Seddon (1991), Attitudes and behaviour. *Management Service Quality,* May, 193–196.

86 J. Rucci, S.P. Kirn and R.T. Quinn (1998), The employee-customer-profit chain at Sears. *Harvard Business Review,* January–February.

87 N. Georgiades and R. MacDonell (1998), *Leadership for Competitive Advantage.* Chichester: John Wiley & Sons.

88 Mihaly Csikszentmihalyi and Isabella S. Csikszentmihalyi (1988), *Optimal Experience: Psychological Studies of Flow in Consciousness.* Cambridge: Cambridge University Press, 261.

89 John Kotter (1996), *Leading Change.* Cambridge, MA: Harvard Business School Press.

90 Philip Hodgson and Randall White (2001), Leadership – the ne(x)t generation. *Directions: The Ashridge Journal,* Summer, 18–22.

91 E.E. Lawler, III, S.A. Mohrman and G.E. Ledford, Jr (1992), *Employee Involvement and Total Quality Management.* San Francisco, CA: Jossey-Bass.

92 Gretchen M. Spreitzer, Suzanne C. De Janasz and Robert E. Quinn (1999), Empowered to lead: the role of psychological empowerment in leadership. *Journal of Organizational Behaviour,* 20, 511–526.

93 David G. Myers (1993), *The Pursuit of Happiness.* London: The Aquarian Press, 134.

94 Gretchen M. Spreitzer and Robert E. Quinn (1996), Empowering middle managers to be transformational leaders. *Journal of Applied Behavioral Science,* 32 (3), 237–261.

95 William James (1890), *The Principles of Psychology.* New York: Holt.

96 Sir Kenneth Wheare (1974), *On the Sin of Pride.* Quinquagesima Sermon, University of Oxford, 24 November, reprinted in *Oxford,* the journal of the Oxford Society, LII, 2, November 2000, 26–28.

97 D.J. Leach, T.D. Wall and P.R. Jackson (2003), The effect of empowerment on job knowledge: an empirical test involving operators of complex technology. *Journal of Occupational and Organizational Psychology,* 76 (1), 27–53.

98 D. Dennison (1984), Bringing corporate culture to the bottom line. *Organizational Dynamics,* 13 (2), 4–22.

99 Stanley A. Deetz, Sarah J. Tracy and Jennifer L. Simpson (2000), *Leading Organizations through Transition.* Thousand Oaks, CA: SAGE Publications, 100.

100 Chris Argyris (1998), Empowerment: the emperor's new clothes. *Harvard Business Review,* May–June, 98–105.

101 Henry J. Coleman (1996), Why employee empowerment is not just a fad. *Leadership & Organization Development Journal*, 17 (4), 28–35.
102 Chris Argyris (1998), Empowerment: the emperor's new clothes. *Harvard Business Review*, 76, 98–105.
103 Peter Wright (1996), *Managerial Leadership*. London: Routledge.
104 Toby Wall, John L. Cordery and Chris W. Clegg (2002), Empowerment, performance and operational uncertainty. *Applied Psychology: An International Review*, 51 (1), 146–169.
105 Bernard M. Bass (1998), *Transformational Leadership: Industrial, Military, and Educational Impact*. Mahwah, NJ: Lawrence Erlbaum.
106 W. Randolph (1995), Navigating the journey to empowerment. *Organizational Dynamics*, 26 (2), 19–32.
107 *The Economist* (2002e), Like herding cats. April 20, 78.
108 Adrian Wilkinson (1998), Empowerment theory and practice. *Personnel Review*, 27, 40–56.
109 A. Nevins and F.E. Hill (1954), *Ford: The Times, the Man, the Company*. New York: Charles Scribner.
110 R. Blauner (1964), *Alienation and Freedom*. Chicago: University of Chicago Press; Max Weber (1964), *The Theory of Social and Economic Organization*. New York: Free Press; Warren Bennis (1973), *Beyond Bureaucracy*. New York: McGraw-Hill.
111 Michel Crozier (1964), *The Bureaucratic Phenomenon*. Chicago: Tavistock.
112 Douglas C. Pitt, X. Yan and N. Levine (1996), Touching stones to cross the river: evolving telecommunication policy priorities in contemporary China. *Journal of Contemporary China*, 5, 347–365.
113 Tom Burns and George M. Stalker (1969), *The Management of Innovation*. London: Tavistock.
114 Bala Chakravarty and Martin Gargiulo (1998), Maintaining leadership legitimacy in the transition to new organizational forms. *Journal of Management Studies*, 35 (4), 437–456.
115 Ian McNay (2004), More than a branch of UKHE plc. *The Times Higher*, January 2, 12.
116 Stephen R. Covey (1992), *Principle-centered Leadership*. London: Simon & Schuster, 213.
117 Richard Hodgetts (1996), A conversation with Warren Bennis on leadership in the midst of downsizing. *Organizational Dynamics*, 25 (1), 79.
118 Andrew Roberts (2003), *Hitler – Military Command*. 'Secrets of Leadership' series. London: BBC2.
119 Neil Ferrier, Editor (1965), *Churchill: The Man of the Century*. London: Purnell, 6.
120 Janet Street-Porter (2000), *Radical Approaches to Leadership*. Paper presented at The National Leadership Conference, MCI-METO, The Royal Military Academy, Sandhurst, 24 May.
121 Adrian Furnham (2001), Industry needs more captains courageous. *Financial Times*, 5 September, 13.

122 Sir Ronnie Flanagan (2000), *Leadership during Cultural and Institutional Change.* Paper presented at the National Leadership Conference, MCI-METO, The Royal Military Academy, Sandhurst, 24 May.

123 P.C. Fleming (1991), Empowerment strengthens the rock. *Management Review,* 80 (12), 34–37.

124 *Financial Times* (2000), February 18.

125 Patrick Bolton, Markus K. Brunnermeier and Laura Veldkamp (2010), Economists' perspectives on leadership. In Nitin Nohria and Rakesh Khurana, Editors, *Handbook of Leadership Theory and Practice.* Boston, MA: Harvard Business Press, Chapter 9.

126 Natalia Hakimi, Daan van Knippenberg and Steffen Giessner (2010), Leader empowering behaviour: the leader's perspective. *British Journal of Management,* 21, 701–716.

127 Peter K. Mills and Gerardo R. Ungson (2003), Reassessing the limits of structural empowerment: organizational constitution and trust as controls. *Academy of Management Review,* 28 (1), 143–153.

128 M. Zald (1970), Political economy: a framework for comparative analysis. In M. Zald, Editor, *Power in Organizations.* Nashville, TN: Vanderbilt University Press.

129 G.A. Bigley and J.L. Pearce (1998), Straining for shared meaning in organizational science: problems of trust and distrust. *Academy of Management Review,* 23, 405–421.

130 J. Rotter (1980), Generalized expectancies for interpersonal trust. *Journal of Personality,* 35, 651–665.

131 M. Granovetter (1985), Economic action and social structure: the problem of embeddedness. *American Journal of Sociology,* 91, 481–510.

132 Blair H. Sheppard and Dana M. Sherman (1998), The grammars of trust: a model and general implications. *Academy of Management Review,* 23, 422–437.

133 Reported by Alison Eadie (1999), When empowerment may be bad for you. *Daily Telegraph,* July 29, A14.

134 T.K. Capozzoli (1995), Managers and leaders: a matter of cognitive difference. *Journal of Leadership Studies,* 2 (3), 20–29.

135 Robert E. Colvin (2001), *Leading from the Middle: A Challenge for Middle Managers.* Paper presented at the Bernard M. Bass Festschrift, Binghamton University, May 31–June 1.

136 T. Keighley (1993), Creating an empowered organization. *Training and Development in Australia,* December, 6–11.

137 John P. Scully (1993), A point of view: actions speak louder than buzzwords. *National Productivity Review,* Autumn, 453–456.

138 Stanley A. Deetz, Sarah J. Tracy and Jennifer L. Simpson (2000), *Leading Organizations through Transition.* Thousand Oaks, CA: SAGE Publications, 103.

139 Phil Lowe (1994), Empowerment: management dilemma, leadership challenge. *Executive Development,* 7 (6), 23–24.

140 Robert Haas, quoted by R. Howard (1992), Values make the company: an interview with Robert Haas, in Warren Bennis, Editor, *Leaders on Leaders.* Boston, MA: Harvard Business School Press, 36.

141 Chris Argyris (2000), *Flawed Advice and the Management Trap*. Oxford: Oxford University Press.

142 Eileen C. Shapiro (2000), Managing in the cappuccino economy. Review of Chris Argyris (2000), *Flawed Advice and the Management Trap*, Oxford: Oxford University Press. *Harvard Business Review*, March–April, 177–184.

143 Judith M. Bardwick (1996), Peacetime management and wartime leadership. In Frances Hesselbein, Marshall Goldsmith and Richard Beckhard, Editors, *The Leader of the Future*. San Francisco, CA: Jossey-Bass, 131–140.

144 Windle Priem, president and CEO of Korn Ferry International, and David Finegold, University of Southern California, *Strategies for the Knowledge Economy: from Rhetoric to Reality*, Korn Ferry International, reported by Margaret Coles (2000), Sharing knowledge boosts efficiency. *The Sunday Times*, 7.16, April 30.

145 Ian Windle (2001), Efficiency through knowledge. *Financial Times*, February 21.

146 Gregory G. Dess and Joseph C. Picken (2000), Changing roles: leadership in the 21st century. *Organizational Dynamics*, 28 (3), 18–34.

147 Peter M. Senge (1990), *The Fifth Discipline*. London: Century Business; M. Pedler, J. Burgoyne and T. Boydell (1991), *The Learning Company: A Strategy for Sustainable Development*. Maidenhead: McGraw-Hill.

148 PA Consulting Group (1996), *Leading into the Millennium*. London: PA Consulting Group.

149 Chris Collison, knowledge management consultant, Korn Ferry International, reported by Margaret Coles (2000), Sharing knowledge boosts efficiency. *The Sunday Times*, 7.16, April 30.

150 Joe Prochaska (2002), A new view of creativity and innovation. Letter to the Editor, *Leadership in Action*, 22 (2), May/June, 24.

151 Gary A. Steiner (1965), Introduction. In Gary A. Steiner, Editor, *The Creative Organization*. Chicago: University of Chicago Press.

152 Joe Prochaska (2002), A new view of creativity and innovation. Letter to the Editor, *Leadership in Action*, 22 (2), May/June, 24.

153 John W. Hafile (1962), *Creativity and Innovation*. New York: Reinhold.

154 Gerald Nadler and Shozo Hibino (1994), *Breakthrough Thinking: The Seven Principles of Creative Problem Solving*. Rocklin, CA: Prima Publishing.

Chapter 9

1 Theodore Zeldin (2004), What is the good life? Richer not happier: a 21st-century search for the good life. Debate on 11 February 2004 at the Royal Society of Arts, London. *RSA Journal*, July, 36–39.

2 Brian Amble (2010), CEOs misunderstand employee engagement. Management-Issues, 7 December. Downloaded from http://www.management-issues.com/2010/12/7/research/ceos-misunderstand-employee-engagement.asp?section=research&id=6102&specifier=&mode=print&is_authenticated=0&reference= on 4 January 2011.

3 The Talent Foundation (2010), *Weekly Insight*, 8 September.
4 Ruth Sutherland (2010), Employee engagement: are more firms listening to their staff, or are they just paying lip service? *Observer*, Sunday 22 August.
5 D. Macleod and N. Clarke (2009), *Engaging for Success: Enhancing Performance through Employee Engagement*. London: Department for Business, Innovation and Skills. Available at http://www.berr.gov.uk/whatwedo/employment/employee-engagement/index.html
6 Carly Chynoweth (2010), Win over staff and profit will follow. *The Sunday Times*, Appointments, 24 October, 4; Top-Consultant (2010), http://www.consultant-news.com/printArticle.aspx?id=7280, 14 October 2010; Kenexa (2010), Exploring leadership and managerial effectiveness. *2010 WorkTrends*, research report, Wayne, PA: Kenexa Research Institute.
7 Zoe Thomas (2010), Happy staff drive up profits. *The Sunday Times*, Appointments, 10 October, 5.
8 Stefan Stern (2010), Share the power. FT.com, 22 March, http://www.ft.com
9 Reported by Stefan Stern (2010), Share the power. FT.com, 22 March, http://www.ft.com
10 Reported by Stefan Stern (2010), Share the power. FT.com, 22 March http://www.ft.com
11 McKinsey & Company (2010), What successful transformations share: McKinsey Global Survey results. *McKinsey Quarterly*, March.
12 C. Truss, E. Soane, C. Edwards, K. Wisdom, A. Croll and J. Burnett (2006), *Working Life: Employee Attitudes and Engagement*. London: Chartered Institute of Personnel and Development.
13 Sandeep Kular, Mark Gatenby, Chris Rees, Emma Soane and Katie Truss (2008), *Employee Engagement: A Literature Review*. Working Paper Series no. 19, Kingston Business School, Kingston University, UK.
14 Chartered Institute of Personnel and Development (2009), *Employee Engagement*. Factsheet. London: CIPD.
15 Towers Perrin (2005), *Reconnecting with Employees: Quantifying the Value of Engaging your Workforce*. London: Towers Perrin.
16 Ivan T. Robertson and Cary L. Cooper (2010), Full engagement: the integration of employee engagement and psychological well-being. *Leadership & Organization Development Journal*, 31 (4), 324–336.
17 Annie Britton and Martin J. Shipley (2010), Bored to death? *International Journal of Epidemiology*, 39 (2), 370–371.
18 Adrian Furnham (2010), You don't need to be married to your job – just engaged. *The Sunday Times*, Appointments, 16 May, 2.
19 Ron Kaniel, Cade Massey and David T. Robinson (2010), The importance of being an optimist: evidence from labor markets. *NBER Working Paper No. 16328*. Cambridge, MA: National Bureau of Economic Research.
20 James Watson and Sarah Murray (2010), Global experience. FT.com, 22 March, http://www.ft.com
21 James Watson and Sarah Murray (2010), Global experience. FT.com, 22 March, http://www.ft.com

22 Julian Goldsmith (2010), British Gas in dispute over employee disengagement. newsletters@bnet.online.com, http://blogs.bnet.co.uk/sterling-performance/2010/03/11/british-gas-in-dispute-over-employee-disengagement

23 Carly Chynoweth (2010), So where is your evidence? *The Sunday Times*, Appointments, 21 March, 2.

24 Carly Chynoweth (2010), So where is your evidence? *The Sunday Times*, Appointments, 21 March, 2.

25 Carly Chynoweth (2010), So where is your evidence? *The Sunday Times*, Appointments, 21 March, 2.

26 Thomas A. Wright, Russell Cropanzano, Philip J. Denney and Gary L. Moline (2002), When a happy worker is a productive worker: a preliminary examination of three models. *Canadian Journal of Behavioural Science*, 34 (3), 146–150; Russell Cropanzano and Thomas A. Wright (2001), When a 'happy' worker is really a 'productive' worker: a review and further refinement of the happy-productive worker thesis. *Consulting Psychology Journal*, 53 (3), 182–199; Timothy A. Judge, Carl J. Thorensen, Joyce E. Bono and Gregory K. Patton (2001), The job satisfaction-job performance relationship: a qualitative and quantitative review. *Psychological Bulletin*, 127 (3), 376–407; Deidra J. Schleicher, John D. Watt and Gary J. Greguras (2004), Reexamining the job satisfaction-performance relationship: the complexity of attitudes. *Journal of Applied Psychology*, 89 (1), 165–177; John M. Zelenski, Steven A. Murphy and David A, Jenkins (2008), The happy-productive worker thesis revisited. *Journal of Happiness Studies*, 9 (4), 521–537.

27 Christian Jarrett (2011), National well-being and the wandering mind. *The Psychologist*, 24 (1), January, 12–13.

28 Peter Hosie, Peter Sevastos and Cary L. Cooper (2007), The 'happy productive worker thesis' and Australian managers. *Journal of Human Values*, 13 (2), 151–176.

29 Cynthia D. Fisher (2010), Happiness at work. *International Journal of Management Reviews*, 12 (4), 384–412.

30 Jon Cromby (2011), Happiness – a distraction from economic fairness. Letter to the Editor, *The Psychologist*, 24 (1), January, 2–3.

31 Steve Reicher and Alex Haslam (2011), Forum – the real world. *The Psychologist*, 24 (1), January, 9.

32 George A. Miller (1962), *Psychology:, the Science of Mental Life*. New York: Harper & Row.

33 Terence R. Mitchell (1982), Motivation: new directions for theory, research, and practice. *Academy of Management Review*, 7 (1), 80–88.

34 Rita L. Atkinson, Richard C. Atkinson and Ernest R. Hilgard (1990), *Introduction to Psychology*, Tenth Edition. San Diego, CA: Harcourt Brace Jovanovich, 361.

35 R. deCharms (1968), *Personal Causation: The Internal Affective Determinants of Behavior*. New York: Academic Press.

36 Mihaly Csikszentmihalyi, reported by David Creelman (2003), Interview: Dr Csikszentmihalyi on Flow and Leadership. www.HR.com, 31 October.

37 Richard M Ryan and Edward L. Deci (2000), Self-determination theory and the facilitation of intrinsic motivation, social development, and well-being. *American Psychologist*, 55 (1), 68–78.

38 L.W. Fry (2003), Toward a theory of spiritual leadership. *Leadership Quarterly*, 14, 693–727.
39 Teresa M. Amabile (1996), *Creativity in Context*. Boulder, CO: Westview Press.
40 Stephen R. Covey (1992), *Principle-Centered Leadership*. London: Simon & Schuster, 191–192.
41 Abraham Maslow (1970), *Motivation and Personality*. New York: Harper & Row; Abraham Maslow (1987), *Motivation and Personality*, Third Edition. New York: Harper & Row.
42 Douglas McGregor (1960), *The Human Side of Enterprise*. New York: McGraw-Hill
43 Frederick Herzberg, Bernard Mausner and Barbara Bloch Snyderman (1959), *The Motivation to Work*, Second Edition. New York: John Wiley & Sons; Frederick Herzberg (1964), The motivation-hygiene concept and problems of manpower. *Personnel Administrator*, 27, 3–7.
44 Victor Vroom (1964), *Work and Motivation*. New York: John Wiley & Sons; L.W. Porter and E.E. Lawler (1968), *Managerial Attitudes and Performance*. Homewood, IL: Irwin; Mark C. Scott (2000), *Reinspiring the Corporation: The Seven Seminal Paths to Corporate Greatness*. Chichester: John Wiley & Sons.
45 A.D. Stajkovic and F. Luthans (1998), Self-efficacy and work-related performance, a meta-analysis. *Psychological Bulletin*, 124, 240–261; A.D. Stajkovic and F. Luthans (2003), Social cognitive theory and self-efficacy: implications for motivation theory and practice. In L.W. Porter, G.A. Bigley and R.M. Steers, Editors, *Motivation and Work Behavior*, Seventh Edition. Burr Ridge, IL: Irwin/ McGraw-Hill, 126–140.
46 J.S. Adams (1965), Injustice in social exchange. In L. Berkowitz, Editor, *Advances in Experimental Social Psychology*. London: Academic Press.
47 E.A. Locke (1968), Towards a theory of task motivation and incentives. *Organizational Behavior and Human Performance*, 3, 157–189; E.A. Locke and G. Latham (1990), *A Theory of Goal Setting and Task Performance*. Englewood Cliffs, NJ: Prentice Hall; J. Austin and J. Vancouver (1996), Goal constructs in society: structure, process, and content. *Psychological Bulletin*, 120, 338–375; Robert G. Isaac, Wilfred J. Zerbe and Douglas C. Pitt (2001), Leadership and motivation: the effective application of expectancy theory. *Journal of Managerial Issues*, 13 (2), 211–226.
48 S. Livingstone (1969), Pygmalion in management. *Harvard Business Review*, 47, 81–89; R. Rosenthal and L. Jacobson (1968), *Pygmalion in the Classroom: Teacher Expectations and Pupils' Intellectual Development*. New York: Holt, Rinehart and Winston; D. Eden and A.B. Shani (1982), Pygmalion goes to boot camp: expectancy, leadership, and trainee performance. *Journal of Applied Psychology*, 67, 194–199; D. Eden and G. Ravid (1982), Pygmalion vs. self-expectancy: effects of instructor- and self-expectancy on trainee performance. *Organizational Behavior and Human Performance*, 30, 351–364; E.A. Locke, L.M. Saari, K.N. Shaw and G.P. Latham (1981), Goal setting and task performance: 1969–1980. *Psychological Bulletin*, 90, 125–152; D. Eden (1984), Self-fulfilling prophecy as a management tool: harnessing Pygmalion. *Academy of Management Review*, 9, 64–73; D.K. Goodwin (1998), Lessons of presidential leadership. *Leader to Leader*, 9, 23–30.

49 David C. McClelland (1988), *Human Motivation*. Cambridge: Cambridge University Press.

50 F. Luthans (2001), The case for positive organizational behavior. *Current Issues in Management*, 1 (1), 10–21; Kim S. Cameron, Jane E. Dutton and Robert E. Quinn, Editors (2003), *Positive Organizational Scholarship: Foundations of a New Discipline*. San Francisco, CA: Berrett-Koehler.

51 Kim Cameron, quoted from an interview with Jennifer J. Salopek (2003), Accentuate the positive. *Training & Development*, September, 19–21.

52 Kim Cameron, quoted from an interview with Jennifer J. Salopek (2003), Accentuate the positive. *Training & Development*, September, 19–21.

53 This case study appeared in 'Share the Power' by Stefan Stern, FT.com (*Financial Times*), on March 22, 2010 (http://www.ft.com) and it is reproduced with kind permission of the author and copyright holder, John Smythe of consultancy Engage for Change (http://www.engageforchange.com/make_contact.html).

54 Henry Kissinger, quoted in the *New York Times*, 19 January 1971, 12.

55 Tom Marshall (1991), *Understanding* Leadership. Tonbridge, Kent: Sovereign World, 71–73.

56 John R.P. French and Bertram H. Raven (1959), The bases of social power. In D. Cartwright and A.F. Zander, Editors, *Group Dynamics: Research and Theory*. New York: Harper & Row; J.P. French and B.H. Raven (1986), The bases of social power. In D. Cartwright and A.F. Zander, Editors, *Group Dynamics: Research and Theory*, Third Edition. New York: Harper & Row; Bertram H. Raven (1993), The bases of power: origins and recent developments. *Journal of Social Issues*, 49 (4), 227–251.

57 Robert G. Isaac, Wilfred J. Zerbe and Douglas C. Pitt (2001), Leadership and motivation: the effective application of expectancy theory. *Journal of Managerial Issues*, 13 (2), 211–226.

58 John Laughland (2000), The great dictator. *The Spectator*, 28 October, 16.

59 George Orwell (1949), *Nineteen Eighty-Four, a Novel*. London: Secker & Warburg, 3:3.

60 Stephen R. Covey (1992), *Principle-centered Leadership*. London: Simon & Schuster, 103–104.

61 R.J. House, J. Woycke and E.M. Foder (1988), Charismatic and non-charismatic leaders: differences in behavior and effectiveness. In J. A. Conger and R.N. Kanungo, Editors, *Chrismatic Leadership: The Elusive Factor in Organizational Effectiveness*. San Francisco, CA: Jossey-Bass.

62 Fiona Dent and Mike Brent (2001), Influencing: a new model. *Training Journal*, July, 14–17.

63 Irwin Stelzer (2001), Bush gets higher grades from the university of life. *The Sunday Times*, 12 August, 3.4.

64 A.J.P. Taylor (1965), *English History, 1914–1945*. New York: Oxford University Press, Chapter 1.

65 Robert Goffee and Gareth Jones (2000), Why should anyone be led by you? *Harvard Business Review*, September–October, 63–70.

66 Robin Butler (2000), The road from fruit and veg to purest iron. Review of John Campbell, *Margaret Thatcher Volume One: The Grocer's Daughter*, London: Jonathan Cape. *The Times Higher Education Supplement*, 20 October, 29.

67 Dennis Kavanagh (1990), *British Politics: Continuities and Change*, Second Edition. Oxford: Oxford University Press, 57.

68 Siri Carpenter (2001), They're positively inspiring. *Monitor on Psychology*, 32 (7), July/August, 74–76.

69 D.K. Goodwin (1998), Lessons of presidential leadership. *Leader to Leader*, 9, 23–30.

70 James M. Kouzes and Barry Z. Posner (1991), *The Leadership Challenge*. San Francisco, CA: Jossey-Bass.

71 Jean Vanhoegaerden (1999), Letting go. *Directions*, Ashridge Management College, April.

72 Quoted by Jean Vanhoegaerden (1999), Letting go. *Directions*, Ashridge Management College, April.

73 Margot Morrell and Stephanie Capparell (2001), *Shackleton's Way*. London: Nicholas Brealey.

74 Connson C. Locke and Cameron Anderson (2010), *The Downside of Looking Like a Leader: Leaders' Powerful Demeanour Stifles Follower Voice in Participative Decision-Making*. London: London School of Economics.

75 *1 Corinthians*, 8:1, The Bible.

76 Tom Marshall (1991), *Understanding Leadership*. Tonbridge, Kent: Sovereign World, 42.

77 Mike Clayton (2010), *Brilliant Influence: What the Most Influential People Know, Do and Say*. Upper Saddle River, NJ: Prentice Hall, 43, 167–176.

78 Mike Clayton (2010), *Brilliant Influence: What the Most Influential People Know, Do and Say*. Upper Saddle River, NJ: Prentice Hall, 42.

79 Joseph S. Nye, Jr (2010), Power and leadership. In Nitin Nohria and Rakesh Khurana, Editors, *Handbook of Leadership Theory and Practice*. Boston, MA: Harvard Business Press, Chapter 12.

80 Joseph S. Nye, Jr (2010), Power and leadership. In Nitin Nohria and Rakesh Khurana, Editors, *Handbook of Leadership Theory and Practice*. Boston, MA: Harvard Business Press, 305.

81 Andrew M. Coleman (2006), *A Dictionary of Psychology*, Second Edition. Oxford: Oxford University Press, 496.

82 Zoe Thomas (2007), The Sunday Times 100 Best Companies to Work For 2007, 10. *The Sunday Times*, 11 March.

83 Joseph S. Nye, Jr (2010), Power and leadership. In Nitin Nohria and Rakesh Khurana, Editors, *Handbook of Leadership Theory and Practice*. Boston, MA: Harvard Business Press, 308.

84 Reported by Thom Shaker (2003), Retiring army chief of staff warns against arrogance. *The New York Times*, 12 June, A32.

85 B.M. Bass and B.J. Avolio (1994), Introduction. In B.M. Bass and B.J. Avolio, Editors, *Improving Organizational Effectiveness through Transformational Leadership*. Thousand Oaks, CA: SAGE Publications, 3.

86 Richard Olivier (2001), *Inspirational Leadership: Henry V and the Muse of Fire.* London: The Industrial Society, 33.
87 Hamid Dabash (2000), In the absence of the face. *Social Research,* 67 (1), 127.
88 Bernard M. Bass (1992), Assessing the charismatic leader. In M. Syrett and C. Hogg, Editors, *Frontiers of Leadership,* Oxford: Blackwell.
89 O. Behling and J.M. McFillen (1996), A syncretical model of charismatic/ transformational leadership. *Group and Organizational Management,* 21 (2), 163–185.
90 L.R. Sayles (1993), *The Working Leader.* New York: Free Press; Peter F. Drucker (1992), *Managing for the Future.* Oxford: Butterworth–Heinemann.
91 George Binney and Colin Williams (1995), *Leaning into the Future: Changing the Way People Change Organisations.* London: Nicholas Brealey.
92 Michael Maccoby (2000), Narcissistic leaders: the incredible pros and the inevitable cons. *Harvard Business Review,* January–February.
93 J. Collins (2001), Level 5 leadership: the triumph of humility and fierce resolve. *Harvard Business Review,* January-February.
94 Robert Goffee and Gareth Jones (2000), Why should anyone be led by you? *Harvard Business Review,* September–October, 63–70.
95 Mahatma Gandhi, quoted by Suresh Lulla (2002), Leadership = character x competence. *Indian Management, Journal of the All-India Management Association,* June.
96 Alan Bryman (1992), *Charisma and Leadership in Organizations.* London: SAGE Publications, 30.
97 Quoted by Robert Bailey (2000), Great expectations. *Management Skills & Development,* 3 (1), 58–59.
98 Bernard M. Bass (1985), *Leadership and Performance Beyond Expectations.* New York: Free Press, 65–66.
99 Abraham Maslow (1987), *Motivation and Personality,* Third Edition. New York: Harper & Row; James MacGregor Burns (1978), *Leadership.* New York: Harper & Row.
100 Bernard M. Bass (1998), *Transformational Leadership: Industrial, Military, and Educational Impact.* Mahwah, NJ: Lawrence Erlbaum, 5.
101 Bernard M. Bass (1988), The inspirational processes of leadership. *Journal of Management Development,* 7 (5), 21–31.
102 John Roulet (2009), Abolishing the myths of leadership. management-issues, 30 October. Downloaded on 9 December 2009 at http://www.management-issues.com/2009/10/30/opinion/abolishing-the-myths-of-leadership.asp? Used by kind permission of the editor of management-issues.
103 Quoted by Simon Schama (2002), Friends, Romans, Eminem, lend me your ears. *The Sunday Times,* 21 July, 4.7.
104 Vincent Leung (2000), The making of an impressive speech. End-of-millennium Lecture, *The Millennium Journal 2000,* Robert Black College, University of Hong Kong.
105 J.M. Atkinson (1984), *Our Masters' Voices: The Language and Body Language of Politics.* London: Methuen.

106 John Robins, chief executive of Guardian Insurance Ltd, quoted by Amin Rajan (2000a), *Does Management Development Fail to Produce Leaders?* Tonbridge, Kent: Centre for Research in Employment & Technology in Europe.

107 Peter Honey (2010), What wins an election debate: style or substance? *People Management Online*, 21 April, http://www.peoplemanagement.co.uk/pm/blog-posts/2010/04/

108 Peter Honey (2010), What wins an election debate: style or substance? *People Management Online*, 21 April, http://www.peoplemanagement.co.uk/pm/blog-posts/2010/04/

109 Peggy Noonan, in What I Saw at the Revolution, quoted by Brian MacArthur, Editor (1999), *The Penguin Book of Twentieth-Century Speeches*, Second Revised Edition. London: Penguin, xxiv.

110 D.K. Goodwin (1998), Lessons of presidential leadership. *Leader to Leader*, 9, 23–30.

111 Nick Morgan (2001), The kinesthetic speaker: putting action into words. *Harvard Business Review*, April, 113–120.

112 Brian MacArthur, Editor (1999), *The Penguin Book of Twentieth-Century Speeches*, Second Revised Edition. London: Penguin, xvii.

113 Benjamin Disraeli (1878), speech at a banquet at the Riding School, Knightsbridge, London, 17 July.

114 Peggy Noonan, in What I Saw at the Revolution, quoted by Brian MacArthur, Editor (1999), *The Penguin Book of Twentieth-Century Speeches*, Second Revised Edition. London: Penguin, xvi–xvii.

115 Nick Morgan (2001), The kinesthetic speaker: putting action into words. *Harvard Business Review*, April, 113–120.

116 Jeremy Paxman (2002), *The Political Animal: An Anatomy*. London: Michael Joseph/Penguin, 151–152.

117 Francis Bacon (1561–1626), De Dignitate et Augmentis Scientarium (Of the Advancement and Proficience of Learning, or, The Partitions of Sciences, IX Books), 1, vi, 31, *Antiheta*, 6, 1, translated by Gilbert Watts (1640), Oxford: Robert Young and Edward Forrest, publishers.

118 John Adair (1989), *Great Leaders*. Guildford: The Talbot Adair Press, 44.

119 Brian MacArthur, Editor (1996), *The Penguin Book of Historic Speeches*. London: Penguin, xv.

120 Safi-ur-Rahman al-Mubarakpuri (1995), *Ar-Raheeq Al-Makhtum (The Sealed Nectar): Biography of the Noble Prophet*. Riyadh, Saudi Arabia: Maktaba Dar-us-Salam, 496–497.

121 Brian MacArthur, Editor (1999), *The Penguin Book of Twentieth-Century Speeches*, Second Revised Edition. London: Penguin, xxiv.

122 Ken Rea (2010), Leaders must act like they mean it. *The Sunday Times*, Appointments, 10 October, 4.

123 James M. Kouzes and Barry Z. Posner (1991), *The Leadership Challenge*. San Francisco, CA: Jossey-Bass.

124 Quoted by James M. Kouzes and Barry Z. Posner (1991), *The Leadership Challenge*. San Francisco: Jossey-Bass, 121.

125　William Hazlitt (1807), The Eloquence of the British Senate. In Geoffrey Keynes, Editor (1946), *Selected Essays of William Hazlitt: 1778–1830*. London: The Nonesuch Press.

126　James M. Kouzes and Barry Z. Posner (1991), *The Leadership Challenge*. San Francisco, CA: Jossey-Bass, 125.

127　Brian MacArthur, Editor (1996), *The Penguin Book of Historic Speeches*. London: Penguin, xv.

128　Philip Collins (2011), They don't make speeches like they used to. *The Times*, Thursday 20 January, 23.

129　John F. Kennedy (1961), Inaugural presidential address, 20 January. Published in *Vital Speeches*, 1 February 1961, 226–227.

130　Winston Churchill (1940), *Hansard*, 20 August, col.1166.

131　Winston Churchill (1940), *Hansard*, 4 June, col.796.

132　Brighton, 30 September 1997.

133　Brian MacArthur, Editor (1999), *The Penguin Book of Twentieth-Century Speeches*, Second Revised Edition. London: Penguin, 511–512.

134　Roy J. Eidelson and Judy I. Eidelson (2003), Dangerous ideas: five beliefs that propel groups towards conflict. *American Psychologist*, 58 (3), 182–192.

135　T.F. Homer-Dixon (1999), *Environment, Scarcity, and Violence*. Princeton, NJ: Princeton University Press.

136　P. C. Stern (1995), Why do people sacrifice for their nations? *Political Psychology*, 16, 217–235.

137　Brian MacArthur, Editor (1999), *The Penguin Book of Twentieth-Century Speeches*, Second Revised Edition. London: Penguin, xvii.

138　Brian MacArthur, Editor (1999), *The Penguin Book of Twentieth-Century Speeches*, Second Revised Edition. London: Penguin, xix-xx.

139　Norman Lebrecht (2000), The humanising of Hitler. *The Spectator*, 28 October, 60–61.

140　Nick Georgiades and Richard Macdonnell (1998), *Leadership for Competitive Advantage*. Chichester: John Wiley & Sons.

141　Jay Conger (1999), The new age of persuasion. *Leader to Leader*, Spring, 37–44.

142　Gail Fairhurst and Robert Sarr (1996), *The Art of Framing*. San Francisco, CA: Jossey-Bass.

143　Bernard M. Bass (1990), *Bass and Stogdill's Handbook of Leadership*, Third Edition. New York: Free Press, 208.

144　Jay Conger (1999), The new age of persuasion. *Leader to Leader*, Spring, 37–44

145　James M. Kouzes and Barry Z. Posner (1991), *The Leadership Challenge*. San Francisco, CA: Jossey-Bass,

146　Doris Kearns Goodwin (1998), Lessons of presidential leadership. *Leader to Leader*, 9, 23–30.

147　Nick Morgan (2001), The kinesthetic speaker: putting action into words. *Harvard Business Review*, April, 113–120.

148　D.K. Goodwin (1998), Lessons of presidential leadership. *Leader to Leader*, 9, 23–30.

149　J.W. Hunt (1998), A differential equation. *Financial Times*, 25 March, 25.

150 Vincent Leung (2000), The making of an impressive speech. End-of-millennium Lecture, *The Millennium Journal 2000*, Robert Black College, University of Hong Kong.

151 Jay Conger (1999), The new age of persuasion. *Leader to Leader*, Spring, 37–44.

152 Nick Georgiades and Richard Macdonnell (1998), *Leadership for Competitive Advantage*. Chichester: John Wiley & Sons, 111.

153 Charles M. Goldie and Richard G.E. Pinch (1991), *Communication Theory*. New York: Press Syndicate of the University of Cambridge.

154 Nick Morgan (2001), The kinesthetic speaker: putting action into words. *Harvard Business Review*, April, 113–120.

155 Quoted by Joanna Higgins (2010), The Eyes Have It: Gestures to Watch for in Leaders' Debate. BNET blogs, 15 April.

156 C.R. Rogers and H.M. Greenberg (1952), Barriers and gateways to communication. *Harvard Business Review*, republished 1 November 1991.

157 Quoted by Robert Bailey (2000), Great expectations. *Management Skills & Development*, 3 (1), 58–59.

158 Brian MacArthur, Editor (1999), *The Penguin Book of Twentieth-Century Speeches*, Second Revised Edition. London: Penguin, xxi–xxii.

159 Simon Schama (2002), Friends, Romans, Eminem, lend me your ears. *The Sunday Times*, 21 July, 4.7.

160 Howard E. Gardner, with Emma Laskin (1996), *Leading Minds: An Anatomy of Leadership*. New York: Basic Books, 60.

161 B.M. Bass (1988), The inspirational processes of leadership. *Journal of Management Development*, 7 (5), 21–31.

162 Adrian Furnham (2010), What makes leaders look as if they're fit for purpose? *The Sunday Times*, Appointments, 7 November, 2.

163 E. de Bono (1998), *Simplicity*. Harmondsworth, Middlesex: Penguin, 55.

164 Steve Richards (2010), Why did Brown make this blunder? *Independent*, 29 April.

165 Stefan Stern (2010), Should business leaders speak freely? FT.Com, 13 July.

166 Stefan Stern (2010), Should business leaders speak freely? FT.Com, 13 July.

167 Stefan Stern (2010), Should business leaders speak freely? FT.Com, 13 July.

168 C.M. Fiol, D. Harris and R.J. House (1999), Charismatic leadership: strategies for effecting social change. *Leadership Quarterly*, 10, 440–482.

169 Jay Conger (1999), The new age of persuasion. *Leader to Leader*, Spring, 37–44; Bernard M. Bass (1990), *Bass and Stogdill's Handbook of Leadership*, Third Edition. New York: Free Press, 208.

170 Nick Morgan (2001), The kinesthetic speaker: putting action into words. *Harvard Business Review*, April, 113–120.

171 Nick Morgan (2001), The kinesthetic speaker: putting action into words. *Harvard Business Review*, April, 113–120.

172 David Greatbatch and Timothy Clark (2005), *Management Speak: Why We Listen to What Management Gurus Tell Us*. Abingdon, Oxford: Routledge, 49.

173 Nick Morgan (2001), The kinesthetic speaker: putting action into words. *Harvard Business Review*, April, 113–120.

174 Ronald Reagan, speaking in West Berlin in 1987, quoted by Tony Allen-Mills (2004), Deceptive face of the man they always underestimated. *The Sunday Times*, 6 June, 1.26.

175 P.J. O'Rourke (1992), *Parliament of Whores*. London: Picador, 24.

176 Catherine Soanes and Angus Stevenson, Editors (2004), *The Concise Oxford English Dictionary*, Eleventh Edition. Oxford: Oxford University Press, 79–80.

177 Catherine Soanes and Angus Stevenson, Editors (2004), *The Concise Oxford English Dictionary*, Eleventh Edition. Oxford: Oxford University Press, 35.

178 Catherine Soanes and Angus Stevenson, Editors (2004), *The Concise Oxford English Dictionary*, Eleventh Edition. Oxford: Oxford University Press, 832.

179 Catherine Soanes and Angus Stevenson, Editors (2004), *The Concise Oxford English Dictionary*, Eleventh Edition. Oxford: Oxford University Press, 1101.

180 Catherine Soanes and Angus Stevenson, Editors (2004), *The Concise Oxford English Dictionary*, Eleventh Edition. Oxford: Oxford University Press, 497.

181 Catherine Soanes and Angus Stevenson, Editors (2004), *The Concise Oxford English Dictionary*, Eleventh Edition. Oxford: Oxford University Press, 267.

182 Catherine Soanes and Angus Stevenson, Editors (2004), *The Concise Oxford English Dictionary*, Eleventh Edition. Oxford: Oxford University Press, 479.

183 Adrian Beard (2000), *The Language of Politics*. London: Routlege.

184 Bernard M. Bass (1988), The inspirational processes of leadership. *Journal of Management Development*, 7 (5), 21–31.

185 Robert McKee (2003), Storytelling that moves people. *Harvard Business Review*, June, 51–55.

186 Talula Cartwright (2002), A question of leadership. *Leadership in Action*, 22 (2), May/June, 12.

187 James M. Kouzes and Barry Z. Posner (1991), *The Leadership Challenge*. San Francisco, CA: Jossey-Bass, 145.

188 Bernard M. Bass (1988), The inspirational processes of leadership. *Journal of Management Development*, 7 (5), 21–31.

189 Howard Gardner (1995), *Leading Minds: An Anatomy of Leadership*. New York: Basic Books, 261.

190 Tihamér von Ghyczy (2003), The fruitful flaws of strategy metaphors. *Harvard Business Review*, September, 86–94.

191 John Adair (1988), *The Action Centred Leader*. London: The Industrial Society.

192 David Greatbatch and Timothy Clark (2005), *Management Speak: Why We Listen to What Management Gurus Tell Us*. Abingdon, Oxford: Routledge, 48.

193 Jeanne E. Ormrod (1995), *Human Learning*, Second Edition. Columbus, OH: Merrill.

194 Winston Churchill, quoted by Robert A. Fitton (1997), *Leadership: Quotations from the World's Greatest Motivators*. Oxford: Westview Press.

195 Jim Gray (2010), *How Leaders Speak*. Toronto: Dundurn Press, 9.

196 Philip Collins (2011), They don't make speeches like they used to. *The Times*, Thursday 20 January, 23.

197 Matt Ridley (2010), *The Rational Optimist*. London: Harper Collins.

198 Chancellor of the Exchequer (finance minister) in the UK coalition government from 2010.

199 Philip Collins (2011), They don't make speeches like they used to. *The Times*, Thursday 20 January, 23.

200 Jim Collins (2002), Foreword. In Frances Hesselbein, *Hesselbein on Leadership*. San Francisco, CA: Jossey-Bass.

201 Walter Lippmann (1945), *New York Herald Tribune*, 14 April.

202 Chartered Management Institute (2010), Best companies creates new management engagement tool. http://www.managers.org.uk, 27 July.

203 Carly Chynoweth (2011), Keep the team in the loop. *The Sunday Times*, Appointments, 20 February, 2.

Chapter 10

1 Tom Marshall (1991), *Understanding Leadership*. Tonbridge, Kent: Sovereign World, 75.

2 Manfred Kets de Vries and Elizabeth Florent-Treacy (1999), *AuthentiZiotic Organizations: Global Leadership from A to Z*. Working Paper 99/62/ENT, INSEAD, Fontainebleau, France, 8.

3 Marshall Sashkin and Molly G. Sashkin (2003), *Leadership That Matters: The Critical Factors for Making a Difference in People's Lives and Organizations' Success*. San Francisco, CA: Berrett-Koehler.

4 D.W. Bray, R.J. Campbell and D.L. Grant (1974), *Formative Years in Business: A Long-Term AT&T Study of Managerial Lives*. New York: John Wiley & Sons; D.W. Bray (1982), The assessment center and the study of lives. *American Psychologist*, 37, 180–189; A. Howard and D.W. Bray (1988), *Managerial Lives in Transition: Advancing Age and Changing Times*. New York: Guilford Press.

5 Gilbert W. Fairholm (1996), Spiritual leadership: fulfilling whole-self needs at work. *Leadership & Organization Development Journal*, 17 (5), 11–17.

6 Constance R. Campbell (2007), On the journey towards wholeness in leadership theory. *Leadership & Organization Development Journal*, 28 (2), 137–153.

7 Dave Ulrich, Norm Smallwood and Jack Zenger (2000), Building your leadership brand. *Leader to Leader*, 15, Winter, 40–46.

8 Howard Gardner (1983), *Frames of Mind: The Theory of Multiple Intelligences*. New York: Basic Books; Howard Gardner (1993), *Multiple Intelligences: The Theory in Practice*. New York: Basic Books; Howard Gardner (1999), *Intelligence Reframed: Multiple Intelligences for the 21st Century*. New York: Basic Books.

9 H. Gardner and T. Hatch (1989), Multiple intelligences go to school: educational implications of the theory of multiple intelligences. *Educational Researcher*, 18 (8), 4–9.

10 Russell S. Moxley (2000), *Leadership and Spirit*. San Francisco, CA: Jossey-Bass.

11 Howard Gardner (1999), *Intelligence Reframed: Multiple Intelligences for the 21st Century*. New York: Basic Books, 59–66.

12 Howard Gardner (1999), *Intelligence Reframed: Multiple Intelligences for the 21st Century*. New York: Basic Books, 70–77.

13 John White (1997), *Do Howard Gardner's Multiple Intelligences Add Up?* London: Institute of Education, University of London.

14 R.E. Riggio, S.E. Murphy and F.J. Pirozzolo, Editors (2001), *Multiple Intelligences and Leadership*. Mahwah, NJ: Lawrence Erlbaum, 91.

15 Robert J. Sternberg (1985), *Beyond IQ: A Triarchic Theory of Human Intelligence*. Cambridge: Cambridge University Press, 45.

16 Robert J. Sternberg (1988), *The Triarchic Mind: A New Theory of Human Intelligence*. New York: Penguin.

17 Robert J. Sternberg (1997), *Successful Intelligence: How Practical and Creative Intelligence Determine Success in Life*. New York: Plume Books.

18 Linda Gottfredson (2003), Dissecting practical intelligence theory: its claims and its evidence. *Intelligence, 31*, 343–397.

19 Timothy A. Judge, Amy E. Colbert and Remus Ilies (2004), Intelligence and leadership: a quantitative review and test of theoretical propositions. *Journal of Applied Psychology*, 89 (3), 542–552.

20 R.G. Lord, R.J. Foti and C.L. De Vader (1984), A test of leadership categorization theory: internal structure, information processing, and leadership perceptions. *Organizational Behavior and Human Performance*. 34, 343–378.

21 Reported in Ruth Tait (1996), The attributes of leadership. *Leadership & Organization Development Journal*, 17 (1), 27–31.

22 F.E. Fiedler (2002), The curious role of cognitive resources in leadership. In R.E. Riggio, S.E. Murphy and F.J. Pirozzolo, Editors, *Multiple Intelligences and Leadership*. Mahwah, NJ: Lawrence Erlbaum, 91.

23 Reported in Ruth Tait (1996), The attributes of leadership. *Leadership & Organization Development Journal*, 17 (1), 27–31.

24 Tom Peters and Robert Waterman (1982), *In Search of Excellence*. New York: Harper & Row, 287.

25 Gerry Johnson and Kevan Scholes (2002), *Exploring Corporate Strategy*, Sixth Edition. Harlow, Essex: Pearson Education, 550.

26 Robert J. Sternberg and Victor Vroom (2002), Theoretical letters: the person versus the situation in leadership. *Leadership Quarterly*, 13, 301–323.

27 G. Fink and N.J. Holden (2007), Introduction: new contours of European international management research. *European Journal of International Management*, 1 (1), 4–13; N.J. Holden (2008), Reflections of a cross-cultural scholar: context and language in management thought. *International Journal of Cross Cultural Management*, 8 (2), 239–250; David J. Pauleen, David Rooney and Nigel J. Holden (2010), Practical wisdom and the development of cross-cultural knowledge management: a global leadership perspective. *European Journal of International Management*, 4 (4), 382–395.

28 Nigel Rees (2010), quoting the Israeli writer Uri Avnery (b. 1923). *The Quote ... Unquote Newsletter*, 19 (3), July.

29 Howard Gardner (1993), *Frames of Mind: The Theory of Multiple Intelligences*. New York: Basic Books.

30 Leopold S. Vansina (1988), The general manager and organisational leadership. In M. Lambrechts, Editor, *Corporate Revival: Managing into the Nineties*. Leuven, Belgium: University Press.

31 Tom Marshall (1991), *Understanding Leadership*. Tonbridge, Kent: Sovereign World, 10–11.

32 T.O. Jacobs and E. Jaques (1987), Leadership in complex systems. In J. Zeidner, Editor, *Human Productivity Enhancement, Volume 2*. New York: Praeger; P. Lewis and T.O. Jacobs (1992), Individual differences in strategic leadership capacity: a constructive/development view. In R.L. Phillips and J.G. Hunt, Editors, *Strategic Leadership: A Multiorganizational Perspective*. Westport, CT: Quorum Books; M. Sashkin (1988), The visionary leader. In J.A. Conger and R.N. Kanungo, Editors, *Charismatic Leadership: The Elusive Factor in Organizational Effectiveness*. San Francisco, CA: Jossey-Bass.

33 Stephen J. Zaccaro and Deanna J. Banks (2001), Leadership, vision, and organizational effectiveness. In Stephen J. Zaccaro and Richard J. Klimoski, Editors, *The Nature of Organizational Leadership: Understanding the Performance Imperatives Confronting Today's Leaders*. San Francisco, CA: Jossey-Bass, 202.

34 John Kotter (1988), *The Leadership Factor*. New York: Free Press, 29.

35 Tom Marshall (1991), *Understanding Leadership*. Tonbridge, Kent: Sovereign World, 20–21.

36 Stephen J. Zaccaro and Deanna J. Banks (2001), Leadership, vision, and organizational effectiveness. In Stephen J. Zaccaro and Richard J. Klimoski, Editors, *The Nature of Organizational Leadership: Understanding the Performance Imperatives Confronting Today's Leaders*. San Francisco, CA: Jossey-Bass.

37 J. Davidson, R. Deuser and R.J. Sternberg (1994), The role of metacognition in problem solving. In J. Metcalf and A.P. Shimamura, Editors, *Metacognition: Knowing about Knowing*. Cambridge, MA: MIT Press.

38 A.B. Dahl (1998), *Command Dysfunction: Minding the Cognitive War*. Maxwell Air Force Base, AL: Air University Press.

39 T. Owen Jacobs and Michael L. McGee (2001), Competitive advantage: conceptual imperatives for executives. In Stephen J. Zaccaro and Richard J. Klimoski, Editors, *The Nature of Organizational Leadership: Understanding the Performance Imperatives Confronting Today's Leaders*. San Francisco, CA: Jossey-Bass, 74.

40 James Moncrieff (1998), Making a difference. *Directions*, Ashridge Management College, November.

41 A.S. Huff (1990), *Mapping Strategic Thought*. Chichester: John Wiley & Sons.

42 Peter Linkow (1999), What gifted strategic thinkers do. *Training & Development*, 53 (7), July, 34–37.

43 Experts answer questionnaires in two or more rounds. After each round, a facilitator provides an anonymous summary of the experts' forecasts from the previous round as well as the reasons they provided for their judgements. Each expert is encouraged to revise his or her earlier answers in light of the replies of the others. It is expected that, during this process, the range of the answers will decrease and the group will converge towards the 'correct' answer. Finally, the process is stopped after a pre-defined criterion (e.g. number of rounds, achievement of consensus, stability of results, etc.). The mean or median scores of the final round will determine the results.

44 Eileen Shapiro (1996), *Fad Surfing in the Boardroom: Managing in the Age of Instant Answers.* Reading, MA: Addison-Wesley; Keith Grint (1997), TQM, BPR, JIT, BSCs and TLAs: managerial waves or drownings? *Management Decision,* 35 (10), 731–738.

45 Naomi J. Brookes and Michel Leseure (2003), *The Influence of Top Managers on Their Organizations: A Cognitive Perspective.* Paper presented at the Annual Conference of the British Academy of Management, Harrogate, September 15–17.

46 Philip Hodgson and Randall White (2001), Leadership – the ne(x)t generation. *Directions: The Ashridge Journal,* Summer, 18–22.

47 Michael E. Porter (1985), *Competitive Advantage: Creating and Sustaining Superior Performance.* New York: Free Press; G. Hamel and C.K. Prahalad (1994), *Competing for the Future: Breakthrough Strategies for Seizing Control of Your Industry and Creating the Markets of Tomorrow.* Cambridge, MA: Harvard Business School Press.

48 Donald G. Krause (1997), *The Way of the Leader.* London: Nicholas Brealey, 6.

49 Daniel Katz and Robert L. Kahn (1978), *The Social Psychology of Organizations.* New York: John Wiley & Sons.

50 Albert Joseph (1972), *Put It In Writing.* Cleveland, OH: Industrial Writing Institute.

51 Alice W. Heim (1968), *AH5 Group Test of High-level Intelligence.* Windsor: NFER Publishing Company.

52 Roger Gill (1982), A trainability concept for management potential and an empirical study of its relationship with intelligence for two managerial skills. *Journal of Occupational Psychology,* 55, (2), 139–147.

53 Based in part on Roger Gill (2007), The intuitive leader. *LT Focus,* March. Used with kind permission of The Leadership Trust Foundation.

54 Baroness Susan Greenfield (2003), *The Intuitive Brain – What Is Its Future?* Paper presented at the Sixth Annual Leadership Conference, 'Intuition, Leadership, Instinct', The Leadership Trust Foundation, Ross-on-Wye, September 23–24.

55 Roger Gill (2006), *Theory and Practice of Leadership.* London: SAGE Publications, 63 and 69–71.

56 Andrew M. Colman (2006), *Oxford Dictionary of Psychology,* Second Edition. Oxford: Oxford University Press, 389.

57 Erik Dane and Michael G. Pratt (2007), Exploring intuition and its role in managerial decision making, *Academy of Management Review,* 32 (1), 33–54.

58 Erik Dane and Michael G. Pratt (2007), Exploring intuition and its role in managerial decision making, *Academy of Management Review,* 32 (1), 33–54.

59 R.M. Pirsig (1974), *Zen and the Art of Motorcycle Maintenance: An Inquiry into Values.* New York: Morrow, 196.

60 S. Epstein (1990), Cognitive-experiential self-theory. In L. Pervin, Editor, *Handbook of Personality: Theory and Research.* New York: Guilford Press, 165–192; S. Epstein (1994), Integration of the cognitive and psychodynamic unconscious. *American Psychologist,* 49, 709–724; S. Epstein (2002), Cognitive-experiential self-theory of personality. In T. Millon and M.J. Lerner,

Editors, *Comprehensive Handbook of Psychology, Volume 5: Personality and Social Psychology*. Hoboken, NJ: John Wiley & Sons, 159–184.

61 Andrew M. Colman (2006), *Oxford Dictionary of Psychology*, Second Edition. Oxford: Oxford University Press, 380.

62 Andrew M. Colman (2006), *Oxford Dictionary of Psychology*, Second Edition. Oxford: Oxford University Press, 379.

63 Bruce J. Avolio and Bernard M. Bass (1990), *Basic Workshop in Full Range Leadership Development*. Binghamton, NY: Bass, Avolio and Associates; R. Hazell (1997), *Heroes: Great Men through the Ages*. New York: Abbeville Press, 8–12.

64 W.A. Agor (1986), The logic of intuition: how top executives make important decisions. *Organizational Dynamics*, 14 (3), 5–18.

65 A.M. Hayashi (2001), When to trust your gut. *Harvard Business Review*, February, 59–65.

66 N. Khatri and H.A. Ng (2000), The role of intuition in strategic decision making. *Human Relations*, 53, 57–86.

67 J. Haidt, (2001), The emotional dog and its rational tail: a social intuitionist approach to moral judgment. *Psychological Review*, 108, 814–834; K.R. Hammond, R.M. Hamm, J. Grassia and T. Pearson (1987), Direct comparison of the efficacy of intuitive and analytical cognition in expert judgment. *IEEE Transactions on Systems, Man, and Cybernetics*, 17, 753–770; T.D. Wilson and J.W. Schooler (1991), Thinking too much: introspection can reduce the quality of preferences and decisions. *Journal of Personality and Social Psychology*, 60, 181–192.

68 Geert Hofstede (2001), *Culture's Consequences*, Second Edition. Thousand Oaks, CA: SAGE Publications.

69 Erik Dane and Michael G. Pratt (2007), Exploring intuition and its role in managerial decision making. *Academy of Management Review*, 32 (1), 33–54.

70 Erik Dane and Michael G. Pratt (2007), Exploring intuition and its role in managerial decision making. *Academy of Management Review*, 32 (1), 33–54.

71 Christopher W. Allinson, Steven J. Armstrong and John Hayes (2001), The effects of cognitive style on leader-member exchange: a study of manager-subordinate dyads. *Journal of Occupational and Organizational Psychology*, 74, 201–220.

72 John Adair (1989), *Great Leaders*. Guildford: The Talbot Adair Press, 90.

73 Daniel Kahneman (2010), Strategic decisions: when can you trust your gut? An interview with Olivier Sibony and Dan Lovallo. *McKinsey Quarterly*, March.

74 Gerry Johnson and Kevan Scholes (2002), *Exploring Corporate Strategy*, Sixth Edition. Harlow, Essex: Pearson Education, 66.

75 John Adair (1989), *Great Leaders*. Guildford: The Talbot Adair Press, 89.

76 Randall P. White, Phil Hodgson and Stuart Crainer (1996), *The Future of Leadership*. Lanham, MD: Pitman Publishing.

77 Reported by Des Dearlove (1997), No substitute for bright ideas. Management Plus, *The Times*, July 3, 5.

78 Alden M. Hayashi (2001), When to trust your gut. *Harvard Business Review*, 79, 2, February, 59–65.

79 Ralph Rolls (1976), *Image and Imagination*. Nutfield, Surrey: Denholm House Press, 14.

80 William Wordsworth (1770–1850), *Daffodils*. Sir Arthur Quiller-Couch, Editor (1939), *The Oxford Book of English Verse*, Second Edition. Oxford: Oxford University Press, 621–622.

81 Ralph Rolls (1976), *Image and Imagination*. Nutfield, Surrey: Denholm House Press, 14.

82 John Adair (1989), *Great Leaders*. Guildford: The Talbot Adair Press, 93.

83 Quoted by Richard Olivier (2001), *Inspirational Leadership: Henry V and the Muse of Fire*. London: The Industrial Society, 6.

84 Susan Greenfield (2003), *The Intuitive Brain – What Is Its Future?* Paper presented at the Sixth Annual Leadership Conference, 'Intuition, Leadership, Instinct', The Leadership Trust Foundation, Ross-on-Wye, September 23–24.

85 A. Ostell (1996), Managing dysfunctional emotions in organisations. *Journal of Management Studies*, 33, 525–557.

86 Daniel Goleman, Richard Boyatzis and Annie McKee (2001), Primal leadership: the hidden driver of great performance. Breakthrough Leadership, *Harvard Business Review*, December, 43–51.

87 Steve Fineman (1996), Emotion and organizing. In S.R. Clegg, C. Hardy and W.R. Nord, Editors, *Handbook of Organization Studies*. London: SAGE Publications.

88 Guy Lubitsh and John Higgins (2001), Thinking from the heart. *Directions: The Ashridge Journal*, Summer, 32–35.

89 Peter J. Frost (2003), *Toxic Emotions at Work: How Compassionate Managers Handle Pain and Conflict*. Boston, MA: Harvard Business School Press, 13.

90 Kjell Nordstrom (2000), *Funky Business*. Harlow, Essex: Pearson Education.

91 E. Hatfield, J.T. Cacioppo and R.L. Rapson (1992), Primitive emotional contagion. In M.S. Clark, Editor, *Review of Personality and Social Psychology, Volume 14: Emotion and Social Behaviour*. Newbury Park, CA: SAGE Publications.

92 Daniel Goleman, Richard Boyatzis and Annie McKee (2001), Primal leadership: the hidden driver of great performance. Breakthrough Leadership, *Harvard Business Review*, December, 43–51.

93 Alistair Ostell (1996), Managing dysfunctional emotions in organisations. *Journal of Management Studies*, 33, 525–557.

94 Kevin Daniels, Affect and strategic decision making (1999). *The Psychologist*, 12 (1), 24–28.

95 Daniel Goleman (1998), The emotional intelligence of leaders. *Leader to Leader*, Fall, 20–26.

96 Sharon Turnbull (2003), *The Emotions of Re-constructing Leader Identities after a Leadership Development Programme*. Paper presented at the Second Annual International Conference on Leadership Research, 'Studying Leadership', Lancaster University Management School, Lancaster, 15–16 December.

97 Warren Bennis (1994), *On Becoming a Leader*, Second Edition. Reading, MA: Addison-Wesley.

98 Daniel Goleman (1997), *Beyond IQ: Developing the Leadership Competencies of Emotional Intelligence*. Paper presented at the Second International Competency Conference, London, October.

99   Brian Amble (2010), Emotionally intelligent people make better workers. *Management-Issues*, 2 November; Ernest H. O'Boyle, Jr, Ronald H. Humphrey, Jeffrey M. Pollack, Thomas H. Hawver and Paul A. Story (2010), The relation between emotional intelligence and job performance: a meta-analysis. *Journal of Organizational Behavior*, published online 29 June.

100 Benjamin Palmer, Melissa Walls, Zena Burgess and Con Stough (2001), Emotional intelligence and effective leadership. *Leadership & Organization Development Journal*, 22 (1), 5–10; Lisa Gardner and Con Stough (2002), Examining the relationship between leadership and emotional intelligence in senior level managers. *Leadership & Organization Development Journal*, 23 (2), 68–78.

101 E.L. Thorndike (1920), A constant error in psychological ratings. *Journal of Applied Psychology*, 4, 25–29; W. Williams and R. Sternberg (1988), Group intelligence: why some groups are better than others. *Intelligence*, November, 104.

102 Kimberley B. Boal and Robert Hooijberg (2001), Strategic leadership research: moving on. *Leadership Quarterly*, 11 (4), 515–549.

103 Howard Gardner (1985), *The Mind's New Science: A History of the Cognitive Revolution*. New York: Basic Books, 239.

104 Peter Salovey and John D. Mayer (1990), Emotional intelligence. *Imagination, Cognition and Personality*, 3 (3), 185–211.

105 J.D. Mayer, D.R. Caruso and P. Salovey (1999), Emotional intelligence meets traditional standards for an intelligence. *Intelligence*, 27, 267–298.

106 Howard Gardner (1993), *Frames of Mind: The Theory of Multiple Intelligences*. New York: Basic Books.

107 Robert Cooper (1997), Applying emotional intelligence in the workplace. *Training & Development*, December, 31–38; Robert Cooper and Ayman Sawaf (1997), *Executive EQ*. London: Orion Business.

108 Malcolm Higgs and Vic Dulewicz (1999), *Making Sense of Emotional Intelligence*, Windsor: NFER–Nelson; Victor Dulewicz and Malcolm Higgs (2000), Emotional intelligence: a review and evaluation study. *Journal of Managerial Psychology*, 15 (4), 341–372.

109 Robert Cooper and Ayman Sawaf (1997), *Executive EQ*. London: Orion Business.

110 Daniel Goleman (1995), *Emotional Intelligence*. New York: Bantam Books.

111 Daniel Goleman (1998), *Working with Emotional Intelligence*. London: Bloomsbury.

112 Measured in the Emotional Competency Inventory published by HayMcBer.

113 Measured in the Emotional Intelligence Questionnaire published by ASE, Windsor. Victor Dulewicz and Malcolm Higgs (2000), Emotional intelligence: a review and evaluation study. *Journal of Managerial Psychology*, 15 (4), 341–372.

114 Ernest H. O'Boyle, Jr, Ronald H. Humphrey, Jeffrey M, Pollack, Thomas H. Hawver and Paul A. Story (2010), The relation between emotional intelligence and job performance: a meta-analysis. *Journal of Organizational Behavior*, published online, 29 June, DOI: 10.1002/job.714.

115 Tim Sparrow, Buckholdt Associates, quoted by Helen Pickles (2000), I feel, therefore I am. *Business Life*, July/August, 37–41.

116 Quoted in Robert Cooper (1997), Applying emotional intelligence in the workplace. *Training & Development*, December, 31.

117 Eric Hoffer, American sociologist, quoted by Robert Cooper and Ayman Sawaf (1997), *Executive EQ*. London: Orion Business, 10.

118 Robert Burns (1759–1796), *To a Louse*. On Seeing One on a Lady's Bonnet, At Church (1786).

119 Charles Cooley (1902), *Human Nature and the Social Order*. New York: Scribners.

120 Lucy Kellaway (2003), Only an idiot asks leaders why they are so brilliant. *Financial Times*, August 25, 10.

121 Philip Massinger (1624), *The Bondman*, I, iii.

122 Allan H. Church (1997), Managerial self-awareness in high-performing individuals in organizations. *Journal of Applied Psychology*, 82 (2), 281–292; Allan H. Church and Janine Waclawski (1999), The impact of leadership style on global management practices. *Journal of Applied Social Psychology*, 29 (7), 1416–1443.

123 Bernard M. Bass and Francis J. Yammarino (1991), Congruence of self and others: leadership ratings of naval officers for understanding successful performance. *Applied Psychology: An International Review*, 40, 437–454.

124 J.J. Sosik and L.E. Magerian (1999), Understanding leader emotional intelligence and performance. *Group and Organizational Management*, 24 (3), 367–391.

125 J.J. Sosik and L.E. Magerian (1999), Understanding leader emotional intelligence and performance. *Group and Organizational Management*, 24 (3), 367–391.

126 Reported by Stuart Crainer (1999), Group leaders. *Management Skills & Development*, 2 (18), June/July, 38–40.

127 Quoted by Philip Holden (2000), *Ethics for Leaders*. Paper presented at a seminar, The Leadership Trust Foundation, Ross-on-Wye, 16 March.

128 R.J. House (1977), A 1976 theory of charismatic leadership. In J.G. Hunt and L.L. Larson, Editors, *Leadership: The Cutting Edge*. Carbondale, IL: Southern Illinois University Press; B.M. Bass (1985), *Leadership and Performance beyond Expectations*. New York: Free Press; K.B. Boal and J.M. Bryson (1988), Charismatic leadership: a phenomenological and structural approach. In J.G. Hunt, B.R. Baliga, H.P. Dachler and C.A. Schriesheim, Editors, *Emerging Leadership Vistas*. Lexington, MA: Heath; L.E. Atwater, R. Penn and L. Rucker (1991), Personal qualities of charismatic leaders. *Leadership and Organization Development Journal*, 12, 7–10; R.J. House and J.M. Howell (1992), Personality and charismatic leadership. *Leadership Quarterly*, 3, 81–108; Stephen J. Zaccaro and Deanna J. Banks (2001), Leadership, vision, and organizational effectiveness. In Stephen J. Zaccaro and Richard J. Klimoski, Editors, *The Nature of Organizational Leadership: Understanding the Performance Imperatives Confronting Today's Leaders*. San Francisco, CA: Jossey-Bass, 203

129 Jeremy Paxman (2002), *The Political Animal: An Anatomy*. London: Penguin/ Michael Joseph, 8–9, 43.

130 David Gilbert-Smith (2003), *Winning Hearts and Minds*. London: Pen Press Publishers, 10.

131 Alistair Ostell, Sian Baverstock and Peter Wright (1999), Interpersonal skills of managing emotion at work. *The Psychologist*, 12 (1), 30–34.

132 Alistair Ostell (1996), Managing dysfunctional emotions in organisations. *Journal of Management Studies*, 33, 525–557.

133 Peter F. Drucker, quoted by Robert Cooper (1998), *Emotional Intelligence: Its Value and Application in Leadership and Organisations. An Introductory Program.* The Institute of Personnel and Development, London, 2 April.

134 Simon Baron-Cohen (2011), *Zero Degrees of Empathy: A New Theory of Human Cruelty.* London: Penguin/Allen Lane.

135 Nelson Mandela (1994), *A Long Walk to Freedom.* London: Abacus.

136 Daniel Goleman, quoted by Helen Pickles (2000), I feel, therefore I am. *Business Life*, July/August, 37–41.

137 Robert J. Sternberg (1996), *Successful Intelligence.* New York: Simon & Schuster.

138 Malcolm Higgs and Vic Dulewicz (1999), *Making Sense of Emotional Intelligence.* Windsor: NFER–Nelson.

139 Victor Dulewicz and Malcolm Higgs (2000), Emotional intelligence: a review and evaluation study. *Journal of Managerial Psychology*, 15 (4), 341–372.

140 R.T. Keller (1986), Predictors of the performance of project groups in R&D organizations. *Academy of Management Journal*, 29, 715–726; R.R. McCrae and P.T. Costa (1987), Adding *Liebe* and *Arbeit*: the full five-factor model and well-being. *Personality and Social Psychology Bulletin*, 17, 227–232; M.R. Barrick and M.K. Mount (1991), The big five personality dimensions and job performance: a meta-analysis. *Personnel Psychology*, 44, 1–26; M.D. Mumford, W.A. Baughman, K.V. Threlfall, D.P. Constanza and C.E. Uhlman (1993), Personality, adaptability, and performance: performance on well-defined and ill-defined problem-solving tasks. *Human Performance*, 6, 245–285; M.D. Mumford, D.P. Comstanza, K.V. Threlfall, W.A. Baughman and R. Reiter-Palmon (1993), Personality variables and problem construction activities: an exploratory investigation. *Creativity Research Journal*, 6, 365–389.

141 N. Tichy and M.A. Devanna (1986), The transformational leader. *Training and Development Journal*, 40, 27–32; N. Tichy and MA. Devanna (1986), *Transformational Leadership.* New York: John Wiley & Sons.

142 S.J. Zaccaro, J.A. Gilbert, K.K. Thor and M.D. Mumford (1991), Leadership and social intelligence: linking social perceptiveness and behavioral flexibility to leader effectiveness. *Leadership Quarterly*, 2, 317–331; S.J. Zaccaro (1999), Social complexity and the competencies required for effective military leadership. In J.G. Hunt, G.E. Dodge and L. Wong, Editors, *Out-of-the-box Leadership: Transforming the Twenty-first Century Army and Other Top-performing Organizations.* Greenwich, CT: JAI Press.

143 Kimberley B. Boal and Robert Hooijberg (2001), Strategic leadership research: moving on. *Leadership Quarterly*, 11 (4), 515–549.

144 Alison Maitland (2001), Solitary geniuses need not apply. *Financial Times*, November 14, 17.

145 Victor Dulewicz and Malcolm Higgs (2002), *Emotional Intelligence, Motivation and Personality: A Study of Leaders and Teams in a Round-the-World Yacht Race.* Henley Working paper 0203, Henley Management College.

146 Victor Dulewicz, Malcolm Higgs and Jane Cranwell-Ward (2002), Ocean's twelve. *People Management*, 30 May, 32–35.

147 Malcolm Higgs and Vic Dulewicz (2002), *Making Sense of Emotional Intelligence*, Second Edition. London: ASE, 113–117.

148 Benjamin Palmer, Melissa Walls, Zena Burgess and Con Stough (2001), Emotional intelligence and effective leadership. *Leadership & Organization Development Journal*, 22 (1), 5–10.

149 Lisa Gardner and Con Stough (2002), Examining the relationship between leadership and emotional intelligence in senior level managers. *Leadership & Organization Development Journal*, 23 (2), 68–78.

150 Roderick Gilkey, Rocardo Caceda and Clinton Kilts (2010), When emotional reasoning trumps IQ. *Harvard Business Review*, 88 (9), September, 27.

151 Daniel Goleman, Richard Boyatzis and Annie McKee (2001), Primal leadership: the hidden driver of great performance. *Harvard Business Review*, December, 43–51.

152 E.A. Locke (2005), Why emotional intelligence is an invalid concept. *Journal of Organizational Behavior*, 26 (4), 425–431.

153 An alternative acronym for EQ.

154 E.A. Locke (2005), Why emotional intelligence is an invalid concept. *Journal of Organizational Behavior*, 26 (4), 425–431.

155 John Antonakis, Neal Ashkanasy and Marie Dasborough (2008), Does leadership need emotional intelligence? *Leadership Quarterly*, 20 (2), 247–261.

156 Hans J. Eysenck (1998), *Intelligence: A New Look*. New Brunswick, NJ: Transaction Publishers.

157 F.J. Landy (2005), Some historical and scientific issues related to research on emotional intelligence. *Journal of Organizational Behavior*, 26, 411–424.

158 K.V. Petrides, A. Furnham and N. Frederickson (2004), Emotional intelligence. *The Psychologist*, 17 (10), 574–577.

159 K.V. Petrides, A. Furnham and N. Frederickson (2004), Emotional intelligence. *The Psychologist*, 17 (10), 574–577.

160 R.M. O'Connor and I.S. Little (2003), Revisiting the predictive validity of emotional intelligence: self-report versus ability-based measures. *Personality and Individual Differences*, 35, 1893–1902.

161 John Antonakis, Neal Ashkanasy and Marie Dasborough (2008), Does leadership need emotional intelligence? *Leadership Quarterly*, 20 (2), 247–261.

162 S. Côté and C.T.H. Miners (2006), Emotional intelligence, cognitive intelligence and job performance. *Administrative Science Quarterly*, 51 (1), 1–28.

163 Organizational citizenship behaviour was measured by unauthorized absences (truancy). Low-trait-EI pupils were more likely to have been excluded from school for antisocial behaviour.

164 K.V. Petrides, N. Frederickson and A. Furnham (2004), The role of trait emotional intelligence in academic performance and deviant behaviour at school. *Personality and Individual Differences*, 36, 277–293.

165 John Antonakis, Neal Ashkanasy and Marie Dasborough (2008), Does leadership need emotional intelligence? *Leadership Quarterly*, 20 (2), 247–261.

166 John D. Mayer, Richard D. Roberts and Sigal G. Barsade (2008), Human abilities: emotional intelligence. *Annual Review of Psychology*, 59, 507–536.

167 James M. Conway and Charles E. Lance (2010), What reviewers should expect from authors regarding common method bias in organizational research. *Journal of Business Psychology*, 25, 325–334; D.H. Doty and W.H. Glick (1998), Common methods bias: does common methods variance really bias results? *Organizational Research Methods*, 1, 374–406; T.J.B. Kline, L.M. Sulsky and S. D. Rever-Moriyama (2000), Common method variance and specification errors: a practical approach to detection. *Journal of Psychology*, 134, 401–421; M.K. Lindell and D.J. Whitney (2001), Accounting for common methods variance in cross-sectional research designs. *Journal of Applied Psychology*, 86, 114–121; Philip M. Podsakoff, Scott B. MacKenzie, Jeong-Yeon Lee and Nathan P. Podsakoff (2003), Common method biases in behavioral research: a critical review of the literature and recommended remedies. *Journal of Applied Psychology*, 88 (5), 879–903.

168 Dirk Lindebaum and Susan Cartwright (2010), A critical examination of the relationship between emotional intelligence and transformational leadership. *Journal of Management Studies*, 47 (7), 1317–1342.

169 Dirk Lindebaum and Susan Cartwright (2010), A critical examination of the relationship between emotional intelligence and transformational leadership. *Journal of Management Studies*, 47 (7), 1317–1342.

170 Frank Walter, Michael S. Cole and Ronald H. Humphrey (2011), Emotional intelligence: sine qua non of leadership or folderol? *Academy of Management Perspectives*, February, 45–59.

171 E.L. Thorndike (1920), Intelligence and its use. *Harper's Magazine*, 140, 227–235.

172 F.A. Moss and T. Hunt (1927), Are you socially intelligent? *Scientific American*, 137, 108–110.

173 Philip E. Vernon (1933), Some characteristics of the good judge of personality. *Journal of Social Psychology*, 4, 42–57.

174 Karl Albrecht (2006), *Social Intelligence: The New Science of Success*. San Francisco, CA: Jossey-Bass.

175 Daniel Goleman (2006), *Social Intelligence: The New Science of Human Relationships*. New York: Bantam Books.

176 David Wechsler (1958), *The Measurement and Appraisal of Adult Intelligence*, Fourth Edition. Baltimore, MD: Williams & Wilkins, 75.

177 R.J. Schneider, P.L. Ackerman and R. Kanfer (1996), To 'act wisely in human relations': exploring the dimensions of social competence. *Personality & Individual Differences*, 21, 469–482.

178 John F. Kihlstrom and Nancy Cantor (2000), Social intelligence. In Robert J. Sternberg, Editor, *Handbook of Intelligence*, Second Edition. Cambridge: Cambridge University Press, 359–379.

179 E. Willman, K. Feldt and M. Armstrong (1997), Prototypical behaviour patterns of social intelligence: an intercultural comparison between Chinese and German subjects. *International Journal of Psychology*, 32 (5), 329–346.

180 P.C. Earley (2002), Refining interactions across cultures and organization: moving forward with cultural intelligence. *Research in Organizational Behavior*, 24, 271–299.

181 David C. Thomas and Kerr Inkson (2009), *Cultural Intelligence: Living and Working Globally*. San Francisco, CA: Berrett-Koehler, 174.

182 S. Ang, L. Van Dyne, C. Koh, K. Yee Ng, J. Templer, C. Tay and N. Chandrasekar (2007), Cultural intelligence: its measurement and effects on cultural judgment and decision making, cultural adaptation and task performance. *Management and Organization Review*, 3 (3), 335–371.

183 S. Ang, L. Van Dyne, C. Koh, K. Yee Ng, J. Templer, C. Tay and N. Chandrasekar (2007), Cultural intelligence: its measurement and effects on cultural judgment and decision making, cultural adaptation and task performance. *Management and Organization Review*, 3 (3), 335–371.

184 S. Ang, L. Van Dyne, C. Koh, K. Yee Ng, J. Templer, C. Tay and N. Chandrasekar (2007), Cultural intelligence: its measurement and effects on cultural judgment and decision making, cultural adaptation and task performance. *Management and Organization Review*, 3 (3), 335–371; R. Brislin, R. Worthley and B. MacNab (2006), Cultural intelligence: understanding behaviors that serve people's goals. *Group & Organization Management*, 31 (1), 40–55.

185 I. Alon and J.M. Higgins (2005), Global leadership success through emotional and cultural intelligences. *Business Horizons*, 48 (6), 501–512.

186 Kok-Yee Ng, Linn Van Dyne and Soon Ang (2009), From experience to experiential learning: cultural intelligence as a learning capability for global leader development. *Academy of Management Learning & Education*, 8 (4), 511–526.

187 Kenneth W. Thomas and Ralph H. Kilmann (2007), *Thomas-Kilmann Conflict Mode Instrument*. Mountain View, CA: Xicom CPP.

188 Machiavelli, N. (1532), *The Prince*. Translated from the Italian by H. Thompson (1980). Norwalk, CT: Easton Press.

189 Doug Lennick and Fred Kiel (2008), *Moral Intelligence*. Upper Saddle River, NJ: Pearson Education, xxxi.

190 Doug Lennick and Fred Kiel (2008), *Moral Intelligence*. Upper Saddle River, NJ: Pearson Education, 80.

191 Doug Lennick and Fred Kiel (2008), *Moral Intelligence*. Upper Saddle River, NJ: Pearson Education, 95.

192 Doug Lennick and Fred Kiel (2008), *Moral Intelligence*. Upper Saddle River, NJ: Pearson Education, 105–106.

193 Doug Lennick and Fred Kiel (2008), *Moral Intelligence*. Upper Saddle River, NJ: Pearson Education, 109; Richard Holloway (2002), *On Forgiveness*. Edinburgh: Canongate Books.

194 Donald E. Brown (1991), *Human Universals*. Philadelphia, PA: Temple University Press; R.T. Kinnier, J.L. Kernes and T.M. Dautheribes (2000), A short list of universal moral principles. *Counseling and Values*, 45 (1), 4–16.

195 Doug Lennick and Fred Kiel (2008), *Moral Intelligence*. Upper Saddle River, NJ: Pearson Education.

196 Marc D. Hauser (2006), *Moral Minds: How Nature Designed our Universal Sense of Right and Wrong*. New York: HarperCollins.

197 Michele Borba (2001), *Building Moral Intelligence*. San Francisco, CA: Jossey-Bass.

198 Viktor E. Frankl (1984), *Man's Search for Meaning*, Third Edition. New York: Simon & Schuster.

199 Charles Handy (1997), *The Hungry Spirit: Beyond Capitalism – A Quest for Purpose in the Modern World*. London: Hutchinson, 108.

200 Danah Zohar and Ian Marshall (2001), *Spiritual Intelligence: The Ultimate Intelligence*. London: Bloomsbury Publishing.

201 Reported by G.W. Allport (1983), Preface. In Viktor E. Frankl, *Man's Search for Meaning*. New York: Washington Square Press, 12.

202 S. Overell (2002), The search for corporate meaning. *Financial Times*, September 13, 12; N. Chalofsky (2003), Meaningful work. *Training & Development*, December, 52–58; R. Hoar (2004), Work with meaning. *Management Today*, May, 44–53; L. Nash and H. Stevenson (2004), Success that lasts. *Harvard Business Review*, February, 102–109.

203 Mikhail Csikszentmihalyi (1999), If we are so rich, why aren't we happy? *American Psychologist*, 54, 821–827; Martin Seligman (2002), *Authentic Happiness*. New York: Free Press; J. Elliott (2003), Think happy. *The Sunday Times*, November 23, 1.23.

204 Warren Bennis and R. Thomas (2002), *Geeks & Geezers: How Era, Values, and Defining Moments Shape Leaders*. Boston, MA: Harvard Business School Press.

205 Leigh Kibby and Charmine Härtel (2003), *Noetic Leadership: Leadership Skills that Manage the Existential Dilemma*. Paper presented at the Annual Conference of the British Academy of Management, Harrogate, September 15–17.

206 Louis W. Fry (2003), Toward a theory of spiritual leadership. *Leadership Quarterly*, 14, 693–727.

207 Danah Zohar and Ian Marshall (2004), *Spiritual Capital: Wealth We Can Live By*. San Francisco, CA: Berrett-Koehler.

208 Danah Zohar and Ian Marshall (2001), *Spiritual Intelligence: The Ultimate Intelligence*. London: Bloomsbury Publishing.

209 Caroline H. Liu and Peter J. Robertson (2011), Spirituality in the workplace. *Journal of Management Inquiry*, 20, 35–50.

210 K.W. Weick (1995), *Sensemaking in Organizations*. Newbury Park, CA: SAGE Publications.

211 Danah Zohar and Ian Marshall (2001), *Spiritual Intelligence: The Ultimate Intelligence*. London: Bloomsbury Publishing, 5.

212 Theodore Zeldin (2004), What is the good life? Richer not happier: a 21st-century search for the good life. Debate on 11 February 2004 at the Royal Society of Arts, London. *RSA Journal*, July, 36–39.

213 Laura Nash and Howard Stevenson (2004), Success that lasts. *Harvard Business Review*, February, 102–109.

214 Mihaly Csikszentmihalyi (1999), If we are so rich, why aren't we happy? *American Psychologist*, 54, 821–827.

215 Martin Seligman, quoted by John Elliott (2003), Think happy. *The Sunday Times*, November 23, 1.23; Martin Seligman (2002), *Authentic Happiness*. New York: Free Press.

216 John Ruskin (1819–1900), *Pre-Raphaelitism*, 1851. New York: John Wiley & Sons, 1865, 7.

217 Quoted by Stephen Overell (2002), The search for corporate meaning. *Financial Times*, September 13, 12.

218 Quoted by Rebecca Hoar (2004), Work with meaning. *Management Today*, May, 44–53.

219 Quoted by Stephen Overell (2002), The search for corporate meaning. *Financial Times*, September 13, 12; Norman Bowie (1998), A Kantian theory of meaningful work. *Journal of Business Ethics*, 17 (9–10), July, 1083–1092.

220 Neal Chalofsky (2003), Meaningful work. *Training & Development*, December, 52–58.

221 Gilbert W. Fairholm (1996), Spiritual leadership: fulfilling whole-self needs at work. *Leadership & Organization Development Journal*, 17 (5), 11–17.

222 Louis W. Fry (2003), Toward a theory of spiritual leadership. *Leadership Quarterly*, 14, 693–727.

223 Douglas A. Hicks (2002), Spiritual and religious diversity in the workplace: implications for leadership. *Leadership Quarterly*, 13, 370–396.

224 R. Cacioppe (2000), Creating spirit at work: re-visioning organization development and leadership – part 1. *Leadership & Organization Development Journal*, 21, 48–54.

225 I.I. Mitroff and E.A. Denton (1999a), *A Spiritual Audit of Corporate America: A Hard Look at Spirituality, Religion, and Values in the Workplace*. San Francisco, CA: Jossey-Bass; I.I. Mitroff and E.A. Denton (1999b), A study of spirituality in the workplace. *Sloan Management Review*, 40, 83–92.

226 Douglas A. Hicks (2002), Spiritual and religious diversity in the workplace: implications for leadership. *Leadership Quarterly*, 13, 370–396.

227 Dalai Lama XIV (1999), *Ethics for the New Millennium*. New York: Putnam, 22.

228 Danah Zohar and Ian Marshall (2001), *Spiritual Intelligence: The Ultimate Intelligence*. London: Bloomsbury Publishing, 285.

229 Danah Zohar and Jacquie Drake (2000), On the whole. *People Management*, 6 (8), 13 April, 55; Danah Zohar and Ian Marshall (2001), *Spiritual Intelligence: The Ultimate Intelligence*, London: Bloomsbury Publishing, 15.

230 Danah Zohar and Ian Marshall (2001), *Spiritual Intelligence: The Ultimate Intelligence*. London: Bloomsbury Publishing, 16.

231 Danah Zohar and Ian Marshall (2001), *Spiritual Intelligence: The Ultimate Intelligence*. London: Bloomsbury Publishing, 7.

232 Danah Zohar and Ian Marshall (2001), *Spiritual Intelligence: The Ultimate Intelligence*. London: Bloomsbury Publishing, 11–13.

233 M.A. Persinger (1996), Feelings of past lives as expected perturbations within the neurocognitive processes that generate the sense of self: contributions from limbic lability and vectorial hemisphericity. *Perceptual and Motor Skills*, 83, 3 (2), December, 1107–1121; V.S. Ramachandran and Sandra Blakeslee (1998), *Phantoms in the Brain*. London: Fourth Estate.

234 W. Singer and C.M. Gray (1995), Visual feature integration and the temporal correlation hypothesis. *Annual Review of Neuroscience*, 18, 555–586; W. Singer (1999), Striving for coherence. *Nature*, 397, 391–393, 4 February; Rodolfo Llinas and Urs Ribary (1993), Coherent 40–Hz oscillation characterizes dream state in humans. *Proceedings of the National Academy of Science, USA*, 90, 2078–2081, March.

235 Terrance Deacon (1997), *The Symbolic Species*. London: Penguin.

236 Viktor E. Frankl (1984), *Man's Search for Meaning*, Third Edition. New York: Simon & Schuster.

237 Danah Zohar and Ian Marshall (2001), *Spiritual Intelligence: The Ultimate Intelligence*. London: Bloomsbury Publishing, 19–32.

238 Frances Hesselbein (2002), *Hesselbein on Leadership*. San Francisco, CA: Jossey-Bass.

239 Warren Bennis and Robert Thomas (2002), *Geeks & Geezers: How Era, Values, and Defining Moments Shape Leaders*. Boston, MA: Harvard Business School Press.

240 Manfred Kets de Vries and Elizabeth Florent-Treacy (1999), *AuthentiZiotic Organizations: Global Leadership from A to Z*. Working Paper 99/62/ENT, INSEAD, Fontainebleau, France, 36.

241 Manfred Kets de Vries and Elizabeth Florent-Treacy (1999), *AuthentiZiotic Organizations: Global Leadership from A to Z*. Working Paper 99/62/ENT, INSEAD, Fontainebleau, France, 27.

242 Manfred Kets de Vries and Elizabeth Florent-Treacy (1999), *AuthentiZiotic Organizations: Global Leadership from A to Z*. Working Paper 99/62/ENT, INSEAD, Fontainebleau, France, 38.

243 Quoted by Jon Watkins (2003), Spiritual guidance. *People Management*, 20 February, 16–17.

244 Jon Watkins (2003), Spiritual guidance. *People Management*, 20 February, 16–17.

245 Paul Gibbons, a management consultant with PricewaterhouseCoopers, quoted by Jon Watkins (2003), Spiritual guidance. *People Management*, 20 February, 16–17.

246 Quoted by Jon Watkins (2003), Spiritual guidance. *People Management*, 20 February, 16–17.

247 E. Bell and S. Taylor (2004), 'From outward bound to inward bound': the prophetic voices and discursive practices of spiritual management development. *Human Relations*, 57, 439–466.

248 Dennis Tourish, Russell Craig and Joel Amernic (2010), Transformational leadership education and agency perspectives in business school pedagogy: a marriage of inconvenience? *British Journal of Management*, 21, S40–S59.

249 Dennis Tourish and Naheed Tourish (2010), Spirituality at work and its implications for leadership and followership: a post-structuralist perspective. *Leadership*, 6 (2), 207–224.

250 Jill W. Graham (1991), Servant-leadership in organizations: inspirational and moral. *Leadership Quarterly*, 2 (2), 105–119.

251 Danah Zohar and Ian Marshall (2004), *Spiritual Capital: Wealth We Can Live By*. San Francisco, CA: Berrett-Koehler.

252 Howard Gardner (1993), *Frames of Mind: The Theory of Multiple Intelligences*. New York: Basic Books.

253 Gerald A. Randell (1998), *The Micro-skills Approach to Leadership Development*. Paper presented to the Inaugural Conference of The Leadership Trust Foundation: 'Leadership Development: The Challenges Ahead', Ross-on-Wye, February 2–3.

254 B. Parkinson (1995), *Ideas and Realities of Emotion*. London: Routledge; J.P. Walsh (1995), Managerial and organizational cognition: notes from a trip down memory lane. *Organization Science*, 6, 280–321; P. Johnson, K. Daniels and A. Huff (2001), Sensemaking, leadership and mental models. In S.J. Zaccaro and R.J. Klimoski, Editors, *The Nature of Organizational Leadership: Understanding the Performance Imperatives Confronting Today's Leaders*. San Francisco, CA: Jossey-Bass; M.C. Nussbaum (2001), *Upheavals of Thought: The Intelligence of Emotions*. Cambridge: Cambridge University Press; J.R. Gray, T.S. Braver and M.E. Raichle (2002), *Monitor on Psychology*. American Psychological Association, 33 (6), 18.

255 Albert M. Joseph (1986), *Put It In Writing*, Third Edition. Cleveland, OH: International Writing Institute, 34.

256 B. Parkinson (1995), *Ideas and Realities of Emotion*. London: Routledge.

257 T. Dalgleish and F.N. Watts (1990), Biases of attention and memory in disorders of anxiety and depression. *Clinical Psychology Review*, 10, 589–604; C. MacCleod (1991), Clinical anxiety and the selective encoding of threatening information. *International Review of Psychiatry*, 3, 272–292; A. Mathews (1993), Biases in processing emotional information. *The Psychologist*, 6, 493–499; J.M.G. Williams, F.N. Watts, C. MacCleod and A. Mathews (1996), *Cognitive Psychology and Emotional Disorders*, Second Edition. Chichester: John Wiley & Sons.

258 Deidra J. Schleicher, John D. Watt and Gary J. Greguras (2004), Reexamining the job satisfaction-performance relationship: the complexity of attitudes. *Journal of Applied Psychology*, 89 (1), 165–177.

259 Martha C. Nussbaum (2001), *Upheavals of Thought: The Intelligence of Emotions*. Cambridge: Cambridge University Press.

260 Baroness Mary Warnock (2002), Being intelligent about love's uses. Review of Martha C. Nussbaum, *Upheavals of Thought: The Intelligence of Emotions*, Cambridge: Cambridge University Press. *The Times Higher*, August 2, 22.

261 Charles Rennie Mackintosh (1868–1928), quoted by John McKean and Colin Baxter (2000), *Charles Rennie Mackintosh: Architect, Artist, Icon*. Edinburgh: Lomond Books, 139.

262 Malcolm Higgs and Victor Dulewicz (2002), *Making Sense of Emotional Intelligence*, Second Edition. London: ASE, 141–143.

263 Jeremy R. Gray, Todd S. Braver and Marcus E. Raichle at Washington University, St Louis, Missouri, reported by the *Monitor on Psychology*, American Psychological Association, 33 (6), June 2002, 18.

264 F.E. Fiedler and J.E. Garcia (1987), *New Approaches to Effective Leadership: Cognitive Resources and Organizational Performance*. New York: John Wiley & Sons.

265 F.E. Fiedler (1986), The contribution of cognitive resources and leader behaviour to organizational performance. *Journal of Applied Social Psychology*, 16, 532–548.

266 Timothy A. Judge, Amy E. Colbert and Remus Ilies (2004), Intelligence and leadership: a quantitative review and test of theoretical propositions. *Journal of Applied Psychology*, 89 (3), 542–552.

267 Catherine Cassell and Kevin Daniels (1998), A missed opportunity? The contribution of occupational psychology to strategic management research. *The Occupational Psychologist*, August, 35, 17–21.

268 Robert Hooijberg, James G. Hunt and George E. Dodge (1997), Leadership com-
     plexity and development of the leaderplex model. *Journal of Management*, 23,
     375–408.
269 Kimberley B. Boal and Robert Hooijberg (2001), Strategic leadership research:
     moving on. *Leadership Quarterly*, 11 (4), 515–549.
270 R.J. Sternberg (1985), *Beyond IQ*. Cambridge, MA: Cambridge University Press;
     R.L. Rosnow, A.A. Skleder, M.E. Jaeger and B. Rind (1994), Intelligence and the
     epistemics of interpersonal acumen: testing some implications of Gardner's
     Theory. *Intelligence*, 19, 92–116; R.J. Sternberg, R.K. Wagner, W. Williams and
     J. Horvath (1995), Testing common sense. *American Psychologist*, 50 (11),
     912–927.
271 Kimberley B. Boal and Robert Hooijberg (2001), Strategic leadership research:
     moving on. *Leadership Quarterly*, 11 (4), 515–549.
272 Kimberley B. Boal and Robert Hooijberg (2001), Strategic leadership research:
     moving on. *Leadership Quarterly*, 11 (4), 515–549.
273 Phyllis Johnson (1998), *A Study of Cognition and Behaviour in Top Management
     Team Interaction*, unpublished PhD thesis, Cranfield University.
274 Henry Mintzberg (1983), *Power in and around Organizations*. Englewood Cliffs,
     NJ: Prentice Hall; Henry Mintzberg (1985), The organization as a political arena.
     Journal of Management Studies, 22, 133–154; P.L. Perrewé, K.L. Zellars,
     G.R. Ferris, A.M. Rossi and D.A. Ralston (2004), Neutralizing job stressors:
     political skill as an antidote to the dysfunctional consequences of role conflict
     stressors. *Academy of Management Journal*, 47, 141–152; Darren C. Treadway,
     Wayne A. Hochwarter, Gerald R. Ferris, Charles J. Kacmar, Caesar Douglas,
     Anthony P. Ammeter and M. Ronald Buckley (2004), Leader political skill and
     employee reactions. *Leadership Quarterly*, 15, 493–513.
275 G.R. Ferris, W.A. Hochwarter, C. Douglas, R. Blass, R.W. Kolodinsky and
     D.C. Treadway (2002), Social influence processes in human resources systems. In
     G.R. Ferris and J.J. Martocchio, Editors, *Research in Personnel and Human
     Resources Management, Volume 21*. Oxford: JAI Press/Elsevier Science, 65–127.
276 Charles J. Palus (1999), The art and science of leadership. *Leadership in Action*,
     19 (1), 12–13.
277 Charles J. Palus (1999), The art and science of leadership. *Leadership in Action*,
     19 (1), 12–13.

Chapter 11

1 Jay A. Conger (2004), Developing leadership capability: what's inside the black
   box? *Academy of Management Executive*, 18 (3), 136–139.
2 William Shakespeare (1564–1616), *Twelfth Night*. Malvolio, Act II, Scene V.
3 Y. Okuyama, H. Ishiguro, M. Nankai, H. Shibuya, A. Watanabe and T. Arinami
   (2000), Identification of a polymorphism in the promoter region of DRD4 associated with the human novelty seeking personality trait. *Molecular Psychiatry*,
   January, 5 (1), 64–69.

4 K.P. Lesch, D. Bengel, A. Heils, S.Z. Sabol, B.D. Greenberg, S. Petri, J. Benjamin, C.R. Müller, D.H. Hamer and D.L. Murphy (1996), Association of anxiety-related traits with a polymorphism in the serotonin transporter gene regulatory region. *Science*, 274 (5292), 1527–1531.

5 R. Plomin, J.C. DeFries and G.E. McClearn (1990), *Behavioral Genetics: A Primer*, Second Edition. Oxford: W.H. Freeman; J.C. Loehlin (1992), *Genes and Environment in Personality Development*. Newbury Park, CA: SAGE Publications.

6 John C. Loehlin (1992), *Genes and Environment in Personality Development*. Newbury Park, CA: SAGE Publications.

7 A.M. Johnson, P.A. Vernon, J.M. McCarthy, M. Molson, J.A. Harris and K.L. Jang (1998), Nature vs nurture: are leaders born or made? A behaviour genetic investigation into leadership style. *Twin Research*, 1, 216–223.

8 R.D. Arvey, M. Rotundo, W. Johnson, Z. Zhang and M. McGue (2006), The determinants of leadership role occupancy: genetic and personality factors. *Leadership Quarterly*, 17, 1–20.

9 Ronald E. Riggio (2009), Leaders – born or made? *Psychology Today*, March 18.

10 Andrew M. Johnson, Philip A. Vernon, Julie A. Harris and Kerry L. Jang (2004), A behaviour genetic investigation of the relationship between leadership and personality. *Twin Research*, 7, 27–32.

11 David Norburn (2001), quoted by *Ambassador* magazine, AMBA (Association of MBAs), March, 6.

12 Nigel Nicholson (2001), Gene politics and the natural selection of leaders. *Leader to Leader*, 20, 46–52.

13 Susan Greenfield (2003), *The Intuitive Brain – What Is Its Future?* Paper presented at the Sixth Annual Leadership Conference, 'Intuition, Leadership, Instinct', The Leadership Trust Foundation, Ross-on-Wye, September 23–24.

14 Robert Winston (2003), *Human Instinct.* Paper presented at the Sixth Annual Leadership Conference, 'Intuition, Leadership, Instinct', The Leadership Trust Foundation, Ross-on-Wye, September 23–24.

15 C. Senior, N. Lee, M. Butler, J. Powell, M. Phillips and S. Surguladze (2009), *Dopamine, Empathy and the Neurobiology of Leadership.* Poster presentation at the Annual Conference 2009 of the British Psychological Society, Brighton, 1–3 April.

16 Amin Rajan (2000a), *Does Management Development Fail to Produce Leaders?* Tonbridge, Kent: Centre for Research in Employment & Technology in Europe.

17 Oscar Wilde (1891), The critic as artist. *Intentions*, London: James R. Osgood, McIvaine & Co; also appearing in Oscar Wilde (1894), *Intentions*. New York: Dodd, Mead and Co.

18 Hilarie Owen (2001), quoted by *Ambassador* magazine, AMBA (Association of MBAs), March, 6.

19 Preston C. Bottger and Jean-Louis Barsoux (2010), *Are Leaders Born or Made? Or Is the Question Even Relevant?* Lausanne, Switzerland: IMD, March.

20 I am grateful to Lt-Cdr Matt R. Offord, RN, for his information and ideas on leadership competencies for this section.

21 R. Dainty, M. Cheng and D. Moore (2005), Competency based model for predicting construction project managers performance. *Journal of Management in Engineering*, 21 (1), 2–9; M. Touron (2009), Why a multinational company introduces a competency-based leadership model: a two theory approach. *The International Journal of Human Resource Management*, 20 (3), 606–632.

22 Richard E. Boyatzis (1982), *The Competent Manager: A Model for Effective Performance*. New York: John Wiley & Sons.

23 Bernard M. Bass (2008), *The Bass Handbook of Leadership*, Fourth Edition. New York: Free Press, 106.

24 J.A. Conger and D.A. Ready (2004), Rethinking leadership competencies. *Leader to Leader*, 32, 41–47; J.P. Briscoe and D.T. Hall (1999), Grooming and picking leaders using competency frameworks: do they work? An alternative approach and new guidelines for practice. *Organizational Dynamics*, 28 (2), 37–52.

25 Tim Mau (2009), Is public sector leadership distinct? A comparative analysis of core competencies in the senior executive service. In Jeffrey A. Raffel, Peter Leisink and Anthony E. Middlebrooks, Editors, *Public Sector Leadership: International Challenges and Perspectives*. Cheltenham: Edward Elgar, Chapter 17, 315–316; Gambhir Bhatta (2001), Enabling the cream to rise to the top: a cross-jurisdictional comparison of competencies for senior managers in the public sector. *Public Performance and Management Review*, 25 (2), 194–207.

26 R.S. Mansfield (1996), Building competency models: approaches for HR professionals. *Human Resources Management*, 35 (1), 7–18.

27 J.A. Conger and D.A. Ready (2004), Rethinking leadership competencies. *Leader to Leader*, 32, 41–47.

28 Tim Mau (2009), Is public sector leadership distinct? A comparative analysis of core competencies in the senior executive service. In Jeffrey A. Raffel, Peter Leisink and Anthony E. Middlebrooks, Editors, *Public Sector Leadership: International Challenges and Perspectives*. Cheltenham: Edward Elgar, Chapter 17, 318.

29 G.P. Hollenbeck, M.W. McCall Jr and R.F. Silzer (2006), Leadership competency models. *Leadership Quarterly*, 17, 398–413.

30 R. Bolden, M. Wood and J. Gosling (2006), Is the NHS Leadership Qualities Framework missing the wood for the trees? In A.L. Casebeer, A. Harrison and A.L. Mark, Editors, *Innovations in Health Care: A Reality Check*. Basingstoke: Palgrave Macmillan, 17–29.

31 Richard Bolden and Jonathan Gosling (2004), *Leadership and Management Competencies: Lessons from the National Occupational Standards*. Paper presented at the SAM/IFSAM VIIth World Congress: Management in a World of Diversity and Change. 5–7 July, Göteborg, Sweden; Richard Bolden and Jonathan Gosling (2006), Leadership competencies: time to change the tune? *Leadership*, 2 (2), 147–163.

32 S. Lester (1994), Management standards: a critical approach. *Competency*, 2 (1), 28–32; Irena Grugulis (1997), The consequences of competence: a critical assessment of the Management NVQ. *Personnel Review*, 26 (6), 428–444.

33 Richard Bolden and Jonathan Gosling (2004), *Leadership and Management Competencies: Lessons from the National Occupational Standards*. Paper

presented at the SAM/IFSAM VIIth World Congress: Management in a World of Diversity and Change. 5–7 July, Göteborg, Sweden.

34 Bernard M. Bass (2008), *The Bass Handbook of Leadership*, Fourth Edition. New York: Free Press, 103.

35 R. Boyatzis, E. Stubbs and S. Taylor (2002), Learning cognitive and emotional intelligence competencies through graduate management education. *Academy of Management Learning and Education*, 1 (2), 150–162.

36 Kok-Yee Ng, Linn Van Dyne and Soon Ang (2009), From experience to experiential learning: cultural intelligence as a learning capability for global leader development. *Academy of Management Learning & Education*, 8 (4), 511–526.

37 Richard Bolden and Jonathan Gosling (2004), *Leadership and Management Competencies: Lessons from the National Occupational Standards.* Paper presented at the SAM/IFSAM VIIth World Congress: Management in a World of Diversity and Change. 5–7 July, Göteborg, Sweden.

38 E. Bell, S. Taylor and R. Thorpe (2002), A step in the right direction? Investors in People and the learning organization. *British Journal of Management*, 13, 161–171.

39 M.Z. Mumford (2000), Leadership skills for a changing world: solving complex social problems. *Leadership Quarterly*, 11 (1), 11–35.

40 M.Z. Mumford (2000), Leadership skills for a changing world: solving complex social problems. *Leadership Quarterly*, 11 (1), 11–35.

41 J. Marshall-Mies, E. Fleishman, S. Zaccarro, W. Baughman and M. McGee (2000), Development and evaluation of cognitive and meta-cognitive measures for predicting leadership potential. *Leadership Quarterly*, 11 (1), 135–153.

42 M. Brundrett (2000), The question of competence: the origins, strengths and inadequacies of a leadership training paradigm. *School Leadership and Management*, 20 (3), 353–369.

43 Richard Bolden and Jonathan Gosling (2004), *Leadership and Management Competencies: Lessons from the National Occupational Standards.* Paper presented at the SAM/IFSAM VIIth World Congress: Management in a World of Diversity and Change. 5–7 July, Göteborg, Sweden.

44 Jörgen Sandberg (2000), Understanding human competence at work: an interpretative approach. *Academy of Management Journal*, 43 (1), 9–25.

45 M.S. Robinson (2007), Forecasting future competency requirements: a three-phase methodology. *Personnel Review*, 36 (1), 65–90.

46 F. Delamare Le Deist and J. Winterton (2005), What is competence? *Human Resource Development International*, 8 (1), 27–46.

47 Erich P. Prien, Leonard D. Goodstein, Jeanette Goodstein and Louis G. Gamble, Jr (2009), *A Practical Guide to Job Analysis.* San Francisco, CA: Pfeiffer/John Wiley & Sons.

48 John C. Flanagan (1954), The critical incident technique. *Psychological Bulletin*, 51 (4), 327–358.

49 R.A. Neimeyer and G.J. Neimeyer, Editors (2002), *Advances in Personal Construct Psychology.* New York: Praeger; Fay Fransella and Don Bannister (1977), *A Manual for Repertory Grid Technique.* London: Academic Press; G.A. Kelly (1955), *The Psychology of Personal Constructs, Volumes 1 and 2.* New York: Norton.

50 J.P. Campbell, M.D. Dunnette, R.D. Arvey and L.V. Hellervick (1973), The development and evaluation of behaviourally based rating scales. *Journal of Applied Psychology*, 57 (1), 15–22; Erich P. Prien, Leonard D. Goodstein, Jeanette Goodstein and Louis G. Gamble Jr (2009), *A Practical Guide to Job Analysis*. San Francisco, CA: Pfeiffer/John Wiley & Sons, Chapter 6.

51 Management Standards Centre (2008), *National Occupational Standards for Management and Leadership*. London: Chartered Management Institute.

52 IIP (2007), *Leadership and Management*. London: Investors in People UK.

53 EFQM (2010), *The EFQM Excellence Model 2010*. Brussels: European Foundation for Quality Management.

54 Jo Silvester (2010), What makes a good politician? *The Psychologist*, 23 (5), 394–397.

55 M. Young and V. Dulewicz (2003), *Design of a New Instrument to Assess Leadership Dimesions and Styles*, Henley Working Paper 0311, Henley Management College; M. Young and V. Dulewicz (2005), A model of command, leadership and management competency in the British Royal Navy. *Leadership and Organisation Development Journal*, 26 (3), 228–241; SHL (2006), SHL's assessment tool helps Royal Navy define leadership qualities. *SHL Newsletter*, February, downloaded on 21 March 2006 from http://www.shl-newsletter.com/display/?print=4334; M. Young (2006), Leadership styles, change context and leader performance in the Royal Navy. *Journal of Change Management*, 6 (4), 383–396; M. Young and V. Dulewicz (2008), Similarities and differences between leadership and management: high-performance competencies in the British Royal Navy. *British Journal of Management*, 19, 17–32; M. Young and V. Dulewicz (2009), A study into leadership and management competencies predicting superior performance in the British Royal Navy. *Journal of Management Development*, 28 (9), 794–820.

56 Richard Bolden and Jonathan Gosling (2004), *Leadership and Management Competencies: Lessons from the National Occupational Standards*, Paper presented at the SAM/IFSAM VIIth World Congress: Management in a World of Diversity and Change. 5–7 July, Göteborg, Sweden; Richard Bolden and Jonathan Gosling (2006), Leadership competencies: time to change the tune? *Leadership*, 2 (2), 147–163.

57 David S. Alberts (2007), Agility, focus, and convergence: the future of command and control. *The International C2 Journal*, 1 (1), 1–30.

58 Based on a Galaxy Briefing Note from the Chief of Staff (Personnel), United Kingdom Navy Command Headquarters, October 2009, with kind permission of the Royal Navy and the developer of the Command Competency Framework, Rachel Tate, C.Psychol, HPC Registered Occupational Psychologist, HR Research Manager – Directorate of Naval Personnel Strategy.

59 People Management (2010), Research topic: leadership development. Study notes. *People Management*, 29 July, 35.

60 DDI and Economist Intelligence Unit (2008), *Growing Global Executive Talent: High Priority, Limited Progress*. Pittsburgh, PA: Development Dimensions International and Economist Intelligence Unit.

61 Tacy M. Byham and William C. Byham (2010), Leadership development strategy. In Elaine Biech, Editor, *The ASTD Leadership Handbook*. Alexandria, VA: ASTD Press and San Francisco, CA: Berrett-Koehler, Chapter 11, 156–157.

62 Ruth Spellman (2010), Where are all the UK leaders? *People Management*, PM Online, 24 August.

63 Erik de Haan, Inge Wels, Bill Lucas, Jonathan Winter and David Clutterbuck (2010), *Development at the Top: Who Really Cares? A Survey of Executive Teams*. Ashridge: Clutterbuck Associates, Ashridge, Career Innovation, and The Talent Foundation.

64 Debra Humphris, Con Connell and Edgar Meyer (2004), *Leadership Evaluation: An Impact Evaluation of a Leadership Development Programme*. Health Care Innovation Unit and the School of Management, University of Southampton, 31 June.

65 Michelle Stevens (2010), Lack of training for new ministers is wrong, says think-tank. *People Management*, PM Online, 6 May.

66 Written by Jo Owen, a serial entrepreneur, author and business speaker, and published on 7 April 2010, by BNET UK at http://blogs.bnet.co.uk/sterling-performance/2010/04/07/a-leadership-test-for-gordon-brown,-david-cameron-and-nick-clegg. Copyright © 2010 CBS Interactive Inc. All Rights Reserved. BNET UK is a registered service mark of CBS Interactive Inc. BNET Logo is a service mark of CBS Interactive Inc. Reproduced with kind permission.

67 Terry Gillen (2003), Leadership training: how to give it practical impact. *Training Journal*, December, 16–21.

68 S.K. Chakraborty (1995), *Ethics in Management: Vedic Perspective*. Delhi: Oxford University Press.

69 Quoted by S.K. Chakraborty (1995), *Ethics in Management: Vedic Perspective*. Delhi: Oxford University Press, 155.

70 R. Thomas Lenz (1993), Strategic management and organizational learning: a meta-theory of executive leadership. In J. Hendry, G. Johnson and J. Newton, Editors, *Strategic Thinking: Leadership and the Management of Change*. Chichester: John Wiley & Sons, 173.

71 The cover story in an issue of *Newsweek* in the early 1980s.

72 Nitin Nohria and Rakesh Khurana, Editors (2010), *Handbook of Leadership Theory and Practice*. Boston, MA: Harvard Business Press.

73 Dennis Tourish, Russell Craig and Joel Amernic (2010), Transformational leadership education and agency perspectives in business school pedagogy: a marriage of inconvenience? *British Journal of Management*, 21, S40–S59.

74 Dennis Tourish, Russell Craig and Joel Amernic (2010), Transformational leadership education and agency perspectives in business school pedagogy: a marriage of inconvenience? *British Journal of Management*, 21, S40–S59.

75 Dennis Tourish, Russell Craig and Joel Amernic (2010), Transformational leadership education and agency perspectives in business school pedagogy: a marriage of inconvenience? *British Journal of Management*, 21, S40–S59.

76 Dennis Tourish, Russell Craig and Joel Amernic (2010), Transformational leadership education and agency perspectives in business school pedagogy: a marriage of inconvenience? *British Journal of Management*, 21, S40–S59.

77 Eric Jean Garcia (2010), MBA lecturers' curriculum interests in leadership. *Management Learning*, 41 (1), 21–36.

78 C.K. Prahalad (2010), The responsible manager. *Harvard Business Review*, January/February.

79 Examples include the HayGroup (www.haygroup.com) whose leadership model comprises six leadership styles; the Australian Public Service Commission's Leadership Capability Framework that covers key leadership areas (www.apsc.gov.au); and SHL Group's Corporate Leadership Model of four leadership functions (www.shl.com).

80 Some examples are The Boardroom Assessment Centre (www.theboardroomltd. co.uk).

81 Phillip E. Lowry (1995), The assessment center process: assessing leadership in the public sector. *Public Personnel Management*, 25 (4).

82 J. Silvester and C. Dykes (2007), Selecting political candidates: a longitudinal study of assessment centre performance and electoral success in the 2005 UK General Election. *Journal of Occupational and Organizational Psychology*, 80, 11–25.

83 Tasha L. Eurich, Diana E. Krause, Konstantin Cigularov and George C. Thornton III (2009), Assessment centers: current practices in the United States. *Journal of Business and Psychology*, 24 (4), 387–408.

84 International Task Force on Assessment Center Guidelines (2009), Guidelines and ethical considerations for assessment center operations. *International Journal of Selection and Asessessment*, 17 (3), 243–253.

85 Roger Gill (2006), *Theory and Practice of Leadership*. London: SAGE Publications.

86 Roger Gill and Gareth Edwards (2006), *Manual for the Leadership Audit*. Ross-on-Wye: The Leadership Trust Foundation. Extracts used with kind permission of the Leadership Trust. For further information, contact the Leadership Trust at www.leadership.org.uk

87 Including the models used in the Trust's leadership development programmes: Leadership in Management; Leadership Dynamics – Trust, Fear and Motivation; and Coaching and Mentoring – Leadership One-to-One; and relevant commonly accepted aspects of management, organizational change, leadership development and expected leadership outcomes.

88 Uma Sekaran (1992), *Research Methods for Business: A Skill-Building Approach*. New York: John Wiley & Sons.

89 T.V. Rao and Raju Rao (2005), *The Power of 360 Degree Feedback*. New Delhi: SAGE Publications; Mark R. Edwards and Ann J. Ewen (1996), *360° Feedback*. New York: AMACOM; Peter Ward (1997), *360-Degree Feedback*. London: Chartered Institute of Personnel and Development.

90 Allan H. Church (1997), Managerial self-awareness in high-performing individuals in organizations. *Journal of Applied Psychology*, 82 (2), 281–292.

91 J.C. Nunnally (1978), *Psychometric Theory*, Second Edition. New York: McGraw-Hill; R. Peterson (1994), A meta-analysis of Cronbach's coefficient alpha. *Journal of Consumer Research*, 21 (2), 381–391.

92 Numbers stated are actual item numbers in the questionnaire.

93 In questionnaire versions in which a manager is assessed by others (e.g. peers, his or her manager, etc.) questionnaire items are rephrased accordingly, e.g. 'He/She believes in the organization's stated vision for the future.'

94 Based in part on Roger Gill (2009), The journey to the top: how executives make it. *LT Focus*, Winter. Used with kind permission of The Leadership Trust Foundation.

95 Karen Hynd (2008), *The Psychology of Leadership*, unpublished MBA dissertation, University of Strathclyde.

96 The 'Big Five' personality traits described by P.T. Costa and R.R. McCrae (1985), *The NEO Personality Inventory Manual*. Odessa, FL: Psychological Assessment Resources; the 11 'derailers' described by D.L. Dotlich and P.C. Cairo (2003), *Why CEOs Fail*. San Francisco, CA: Jossey-Bass.

97 Andrew Davidson et al. (2009), *1000 CEOs: Proven Strategies for Success from the World's Smartest Executives*. London: Dorling Kindersley.

98 Frances Hesselbein, Marshall Goldsmith and Richard Beckhard, Editors (1997), *The Leader of the Future*. San Francisco, CA: Jossey-Bass, xi.

99 Barbara Kellerman (2004), *Bad Leadership*. Boston, MA: Harvard Business School Press, 19.

100 Philip Bowman, CEO, Smiths Group, quoted by Martin Baker (2009), The model of a modern chief executive. *Daily Telegraph*, 2 October, A3.

101 Gareth Edwards and Roger Gill (2003), *Hierarchical Level as a Moderator of Leadership Behaviour: A 360-degree Investigation*. Paper presented at the Annual Occupational Psychology Conference, British Psychological Society, Bournemouth, January 8–10; Gareth Edwards and Roger Gill (2003), *An Investigation of the 'Full Range Leadership' Model at Different Hierarchical Levels of an Organisation Using Multiple Ratings*. Paper presented at the Annual Conference of the British Academy of Management, Harrogate, September 15–17.

102 D.L. Dotlich and P.C. Cairo (2003), *Why CEOs Fail*. San Francisco, CA: Jossey-Bass.

103 Daniel Goleman (2000), *Working with Emotional Intelligence*. New York: Bantam.

104 Karen Hynd (2008), *The Psychology of Leadership*, unpublished MBA dissertation, University of Strathclyde.

105 Charles M. Farkas and Suzy Wetlaufer (1996), The way chief executive officers lead. *Harvard Business Review*, May–June, 74 (3), 110–122.

106 Manfred Kets de Vries (2006), *The Leadership Mystique*, Second Edition. London: Prentice Hall/Financial Times, 26.

107 Jeffrey Sonnenfeld and Andrew Ward (2007), *Firing Back: How Great Leaders Rebound after Career Disasters*. Boston, MA: Harvard Business School Press.

108 Morgan W. McCall Jr (2009), Recasting leadership development. *Industrial and Organizational Psychology: Perspectives on Science and Practice*, 3 (1).

109 Warren G. Bennis and Robert J. Thomas (2002), *Geeks and Geezers*. Boston, MA: Harvard Business School Press.

110 Abraham Zaleznik (1977), Managers and leaders: are they different? *Harvard Business Review*, May–June.

111 Morgan W. McCall, Jr (2009), Recasting leadership development. *Industrial and Organizational Psychology: Perspectives on Science and Practice*, 3 (1).

112 D.L. Dotlich and P.C. Cairo (2003), *Why CEOs Fail*. San Francisco, CA: Jossey-Bass.

113 Adrian Furnham (2010), *The Elephant in the Boardroom: The Causes of Leadership Derailment*. Basingstoke: Palgrave Macmillan, 26.

114 Adrian Furnham (2010), *The Elephant in the Boardroom: The Causes of Leadership Derailment*. Basingstoke: Palgrave Macmillan, 28.

115 Adrian Furnham (2010), *The Elephant in the Boardroom: The Causes of Leadership Derailment*. Basingstoke: Palgrave Macmillan, 28.

116 Roger Gill (1982), A trainability concept for management potential and an empirical study of its relationship with intelligence for two managerial skills. *Journal of Occupational Psychology*, 55 (2), 139–147.

117 Adrian Furnham (2010), *The Elephant in the Boardroom: The Causes of Leadership Derailment*. Basingstoke: Palgrave Macmillan, 29.

118 Adrian Furnham (2010), *The Elephant in the Boardroom: The Causes of Leadership Derailment*. Basingstoke: Palgrave Macmillan, 33.

119 A.D. Henderson, D. Miller and D.C. Hambrick (2006), How quickly do CEOs become obsolete? Industry dynamism, CEO tenure, and company performance. *Strategic Management Journal*, 27 (5), 447–460.

120 Attributed to St Francis Xavier.

121 Manfred Kets de Vries and Elizabeth Florent-Treacy (1999), *AuthentiZiotic Organizations: Global Leadership from A to Z*. Working Paper 99/62/ENT, INSEAD, Fontainebleau, France, 18–20.

122 Reported by Roger Eglin (2005), Leadership begins in the playground. *The Sunday Times*, January 9, 7.9.

123 Lyndon Rego, Steadman D. Harrison and David G. Altman (2010), Why leadership development should go to school. In Elaine Biech, Editor, *The ASTD Leadership Handbook*. Alexandria, VA: ASTD Press and San Francisco, CA: Berrett-Koehler, Chapter 29, 405–410.

124 *The Economist* (2001c), The feelgood factor. February 15, 37.

125 Nancy J. Adler (2008), I am my mother's daughter: early developmental influences on leadership. *European Journal of International Management*, 2 (1), 6–21.

126 John Burgoyne, Wendy Hirsch and Sadie Williams (2004), *The Development of Management and Leadership Capability and Its Contribution to Performance: The Evidence, the Prospects and the Research Need*, Research Report RR560, Lancaster University and the Department for Education and Skills, Executive Summary, 2. Nottingham: DfES Publications.

127 Amin Rajan (2000a). *Does Management Development Fail to Produce Leaders?* Tonbridge, Kent: Centre for Research in Employment & Technology in Europe.

128 James Bentley and Sharon Turnbull (2005), *Stimulating Leaders: Developing Manufacturing Leadership Skills*. Birmingham: Manufacturing Foundation.

129 James Bentley and Sharon Turnbull (2005), *Stimulating Leaders: Developing Manufacturing Leadership Skills*. Birmingham: Manufacturing Foundation, 15.

130 James Bentley and Sharon Turnbull (2005), *Stimulating Leaders: Developing Manufacturing Leadership Skills*. Birmingham: Manufacturing Foundation, 5.

131 Alesandra Lanto and William Mobley (1998), *Summary of Participant Interactive Voting on Global Leadership Development Issues and Practices*. The Global Leadership Development Conference, London, 19–20 November.

132 Peter Lorange (2003), Developing global leaders. *BizEd*, September/October, 24–27.

133 Sarah Watson (2008), Developing shared leadership: a hands-off approach. In David Collinson, Editor, *Distributed and Shared Leadership, Volume 8*. CEL/LSIS Leadership Research Programme, Centre for Excellence in Leadership, Lancaster University Management School, March.

134 Warren Bennis (1989), *On Becoming a Leader*. New York: Addison-Wesley.

135 Rick Chattell, sometime project manager for leadership development courses at RMA Sandhurst, quoted by David White (2000), Sandhurst style builds teamwork. *Sunday Telegraph*, October 8.

136 The Economist Global Executive (2002) High climbers. *The Economist Global Executive*, January 28.

137 Hugh Aldous, managing partner of Robson Rhodes, quoted by Amin Rajan (2000b), *How Can Companies Identify Leadership Potential?* Tonbridge, Kent: Centre for Research in Employment & Technology in Europe.

138 Simon Smith (2000), *Inner Leadership: REALise Your Self-Leading Potential*. London: Nicholas Brealey.

139 James O'Toole (2010), Donning a leader's garb. *Strategy+Business*, October 1.

140 Warren Bennis, with Patricia Ward Biederman (2010), *Still Surprised: A Memoir of Life in Leadership*. San Francisco, CA: Jossey-Bass, Chapter 1.

141 Adrian Furnham (2010), Six learning experiences that shape all top people. *The Sunday Times*, Appointments, October 10, 2.

142 Gerry Randell (1998), *The 'Micro-Skills' Approach to Leadership Development*. Paper presented to The Leadership Trust Foundation Inaugural Conference on 'Leadership Development: The Challenges Ahead'. The Leadership Trust Foundation, Ross-on-Wye, February 2–3.

143 Cheng Zhu (2010), Chinese 'sheng yi': reinterpreting challenges for leaders. In Elaine Biech, Editor, *The ASTD Leadership Handbook*. Alexandria, VA: ASTD Press and San Francisco, CA: Berrett-Koehler, Chapter 33, 444.

144 Cheng Zhu (2010), Chinese 'sheng yi': reinterpreting challenges for leaders. In Elaine Biech, Editor, *The ASTD Leadership Handbook*. Alexandria, VA: ASTD Press and San Francisco, CA: Berrett-Koehler, Chapter 33, 443.

145 Adrian Furnham (2010), Six learning experiences that shape all top people. *The Sunday Times*, Appointments, October 10, 2.

146 Carly Chynoweth (2010), Send the bosses into the cockpit. *The Sunday Times*, Appointments, 18 July, 4.

147 James Bentley and Sharon Turnbull (2005), *Stimulating Leaders: Developing Manufacturing Leadership Skills*. Birmingham: Manufacturing Foundation, 5.

148 Bruce J. Avolio and Bernard M. Bass (1998), You can drag a horse to water but you can't make it drink unless it is thirsty. *The Journal of Leadership Studies*, 5 (1), 4–17.

149 Steve Fineman (1997), Emotion and management learning. *Management Learning*, 28 (1), 13–25.

150 Quoted by Blaine McCormick (2000), *Ben Franklin's 12 Rules of Management*. Irvine, CA: Entrepreneur Press.

151 Norman Dixon (1985), Why 'lefties' make the best leaders. *Personnel Management*, November, 36–39; elaborated in Norman Dixon (1985), *The Leadership Trust: An Examination of Their Concepts and Methods*, unpublished paper, Ross-on-Wye: The Leadership Trust Foundation; and Norman Dixon (1985), *The Training of Leaders*, unpublished paper, Ross-on-Wye: The Leadership Trust Foundation. Used with kind permission of Emeritus Professor Norman Dixon.

152 Howard Hass (1992), *The Leaders Within: An Empowering Path of Self-discovery*. New York: Harper Business.

153 Reported by Michael Beckett (1999), Tomorrow's leaders filled with self-doubt. *Daily Telegraph*, August 26, 26.

154 Struan Robertson (2002), *Transformational Leadership*. Paper presented at a conference on 'The Successful Leader', Institute of Directors, London, 3 May.

155 Norman Dixon (1985a), Why 'lefties' make the best leaders. *Personnel Management*, November, 36–39; elaborated in Norman Dixon (1985b), *The Leadership Trust: An Examination of Their Concepts and Methods*, unpublished paper, Ross-on-Wye: The Leadership Trust Foundation and Norman Dixon (1985c), *The Training of Leaders*, unpublished paper, Ross-on-Wye: The Leadership Trust Foundation.

156 Mariana Funes (2000), *Laughing Matters: Live Creatively with Laughter*. Dublin: Newleaf.

157 Adrian Furnham (2001), Cut the comedy? You must be joking. *Daily Telegraph*, February 22.

158 Gareth Edwards, Paul K. Winter and Jan Bailey (2002), *Leadership in Management*. Ross-on-Wye: The Leadership Trust Foundation, 29–34.

159 Reported by Alan Berry (2001), The tide of change. *Business South West*, February, 28.

160 Norman Dixon (1985), Why 'lefties' make the best leaders. *Personnel Management*, November, 36–39; elaborated in Norman Dixon (1985), *The Leadership Trust: An Examination of Their Concepts and Methods*, unpublished paper, Ross-on-Wye: The Leadership Trust Foundation; and Norman Dixon (1985), *The Training of Leaders*, unpublished paper, Ross-on-Wye: The Leadership Trust Foundation.

161 Center for Creative Leadership (2009), *Developing a Leadership Strategy*. White Paper, Greensboro, NC: CCL.

162 Center for Creative Leadership (2009), *Developing a Leadership Strategy*. White Paper, Greensboro, NC: CCL.

163 Tacy M. Byham and William C. Byham (2010), Leadership development strategy. In Elaine Biech, Editor, *The ASTD Leadership Handbook*. Alexandria, VA: ASTD Press and San Francisco, CA: Berrett-Koehler, Chapter 11, 156.

164 Ed Kur and Richard Bunning (1996), A three-track process for executive leadership development. *Leadership & Organization Development Journal*, 17 (4), 4–12.

165 K. James and J. Burgoyne (2001), *Leadership Development: Best Practice Guide for Organisations*. London: Council for Excellence in Management and Leadership.

166 Paul Daley (2010), Workforce development or workforce disaffection? *Management-Issues*, 29 March.

167 Quoted by Paul Daley (2010), Workforce development or workforce disaffection? *Management-Issues*, 29 March.

168 People Management (2010), Research topic: leadership development. Study notes. *People Management*, 29 July, 35.

169 These relate to our discussion of leadership, vision and purpose in Chapter 4 and Chapter 5 respectively.

170 This relates to our discussion of leadership and strategy in Chapter 7.

171 Ron Cacioppe (1998a), An integrated model and approach for the design of effective leadership development programs. *Leadership & Organization Development Journal*, 19, 1, 44–53.

172 J. Edmonstone and J. Western (2002), Leadership development in health care: what do we know? *Journal of Management in Medicine*, 16, 34–47; Nicholas Clarke and Malcolm Higgs (2011), *Leadership Training and Development across Business Sectors*. Report to the University Foundation for Human Resource Development (UFHRD), School of Management, University of Southampton; Nicholas Clarke (2011), *A Multilevel Model for Evaluating Leadership Development*. Paper presented at the 12th International Conference on HRD Research and Development Across Europe, University of Gloucestershire, Cheltenham, UK.

173 Malcolm J. Higgs (2003), How can we make sense of leadership in the 21st century? *Leadership and Organizational Development Journal*, 24 (5), 273–284; R.G. Hamlin (2004), In support of universalistic models of managerial and leadership effectiveness: implications for HRD research and practice. *Human Resource Development Quarterly*, 15 (2), 189–215; F.O. Walumbwa, B.J. Avolio, W.L. Gardner, T.S. Warning and S.J. Peterson (2008), Authentic leadership: development and validation of a theory-based measure. *Journal of Management*, 34 (1), 89–126.

174 L.W. Porter and G.B. McLaughlin (2006), Leadership and the organizational context: like the weather? *Leadership Quarterly*, 17 (6), 559–576.

175 Nicholas Clarke and Malcolm Higgs (2011), *Leadership Training and Development across Business Sectors*. Report to the University Foundation for Human Resource Development (UFHRD), School of Management, University of Southampton; Nicholas Clarke (2011), *A Multilevel Model for Evaluating Leadership Development*. Paper presented at the 12th International Conference on HRD Research and Development Across Europe, University of Gloucestershire, Cheltenham, UK.

176 R. Thomas Lenz (1993), Strategic management and organizational learning: a meta-theory of executive leadership. In J. Hendry, G. Johnson and J. Newton, Editors, *Strategic Thinking: Leadership and the Management of Change*. Chichester: John Wiley & Sons, 173–177.

177 Michael Porter (1980), *Competitive Strategy*. New York: Free Press; Michael Porter (1990), *The Competitive Advantage of Nations*. New York: Free Press.

178 R. Thomas Lenz (1993), Strategic management and organizational learning: a meta-theory of executive leadership. In J. Hendry, G. Johnson and J. Newton, Editors, *Strategic Thinking: Leadership and the Management of Change.* Chichester: John Wiley & Sons, 174.

179 Chester Schriesheim (2001), *Why Leadership Research is Irrelevant for Leadership Development.* Paper presented at the Eleventh Annual Kravis-deRoulet Conference, 'The Future of Leadership Development', Claremont McKenna College, Claremont, CA, March 23–24.

180 R. Thomas Lenz (1993), Strategic management and organizational learning: a meta-theory of executive leadership. In J. Hendry, G. Johnson and J. Newton, Editors, *Strategic Thinking: Leadership and the Management of Change.* Chichester: John Wiley & Sons, 172.

181 Roya Ayman (2001), *Leadership Development in Higher Education: Present and Future.* Paper presented at the Eleventh Annual Kravis-deRoulet Conference, 'The Future of Leadership Development', Claremont McKenna College, Claremont, CA, March 23–24.

182 David A. Kolb (1985), *Experiential Learning: Experience as the Source of Learning and Development.* Harlow, Essex: Prentice Hall.

183 Peter Honey and Alan Mumford (1992), *The Manual of Learning Styles,* Third Edition. Maidenhead: Peter Honey Publications.

184 R. Thomas Lenz (1993), Strategic management and organizational learning: a meta-theory of executive leadership. In J. Hendry, G. Johnson and J. Newton, Editors, *Strategic Thinking: Leadership and the Management of Change.* Chichester: John Wiley & Sons, 175.

185 Peter Drucker (1999), Managing oneself. *Harvard Business Review,* March–April, 65–74.

186 Henry Wadsworth Longfellow (1807–1882), *Kavanagh,* Chapter 1.

187 P. Ward (1997), *360-degree Feedback.* London: Institute of Personnel and Development.

188 Beverly Alimo-Metcalfe (1996), The feedback revolution. *Health Service Journal,* 13 June, 26–28.

189 E. Kevin Holloway, Julian Baring and Jane Helleur (2000), Enhancing transformational leadership: the roles of training and feedback. *Leadership & Organization Development Journal,* 21 (3), 145–149.

190 Roger Gill (1998), *The Impact of 360-degree Feedback on Leadership Behaviour.* Paper presented at a Symposium on 'What Can Be Learned from the Analysis of 360-degree/Multirater Feedback Data and Its Applications in Organizations?' at the 2Fourth International Congress of Applied Psychology, San Francisco, CA, 9–14 August.

191 R.R. Reilly, J.W. Smither and N.L. Vasilopoulos (1996), A longitudinal study of upward feedback. *Personnel Psychology,* 49, 599–612.

192 N. Mukhopadhyay (1996), *Performance Appraisal: A Critical Analysis,* unpublished MSc dissertation, University of Strathclyde.

193 Todd J. Maurer, Deborah R.D. Mitchell and Francisco G. Berbeiti (2002), Predictors of attitudes towards a 360-degree feedback system and involvement in

post-feedback management development activity. *Journal of Occupational and Organizational Psychology,* 75 (1), March, 87–107.

194 Thane Crossley and Irene Taylor (1995), Developing competitive advantage through 360-degree feedback. *American Journal of Management Development,* 1, (1), 11–15.

195 Morice Mendoza (2000), Eye of the storm. *Human Resources,* August.

196 Diane J. Coutu (2002), The anxiety of learning: the HBR interview [with Edgar H. Schein]. *Harvard Business Review,* March, 100–106.

197 Jennifer W. Martineau and Judith L. Steed (2001), Follow-up: a valuable tool in leadership development. *Leadership in Action,* Center for Creative Leadership, 21 (1), 1–6.

198 Hilarie Owen (2001), *Unleashing Leaders: Developing Organizations for Leaders.* Chichester: John Wiley & Sons.

199 Margie Nicholson (2010), Documenting leaders in action: understanding leadership through film. *Member Connector Newsletter,* International Leadership Association, August, www.ila-org. See www.reel-leaders.org for more information.

200 Francis Beckett (1999), Creative way to better management. *Financial Times,* November 8, 16.

201 Henry Mintzberg and Joseph Lampel, quoted by Alison Eadie (2001), Class acts with MBAs are no guarantee of success as a chief executive. *Daily Telegraph,* February 22.

202 John Rink, Managing Partner of Allen & Overy, quoted by Amin Rajan (2000a), *Does Management Development Fail to Produce Leaders?* Tonbridge, Kent: Centre for Research in Employment & Technology in Europe.

203 John W. Hunt (2002), Fertile feedback. *Financial Times,* June 21.

204 Dave Ulrich and Paige Hinkson (2001), Net heads. *People Management,* 7 (2), 25 January, 32–36.

205 Amin Rajan (2000d), *What Are Mentoring and Coaching and Why Are They Central to Leadership Development?* Tonbridge, Kent: Centre for Research in Employment & Technology in Europe.

206 *Vodafone future,* Corporate Social Responsibility Report 2000–2001, Vodafone Group plc.

207 Poet David Whyte, who also works as a management consultant, quoted by Stephen Hoare (2001), Rhymes with leadership. Sunday Business, *Sunday Telegraph,* 4 March, 4.

208 Richard Olivier (2001), *Inspirational Leadership: Henry V and the Muse of Fire.* London: The Industrial Society, xxii–xxiii.

209 Robert Bailey (2000), Great expectations. *Management Skills & Development,* 3 (1), 58–59.

210 Robert Nurden (1999), Henry's lesson in leadership. *Independent on Sunday,* 23 May; Richard Olivier (2001), *Inspirational Leadership: Henry V and the Muse of Fire.* London: The Industrial Society.

211 Robert Nurden (1999), Henry's lesson in leadership. *Independent on Sunday,* 23 May.

212 Quoted by Francis Beckett (1999), Creative way to better management. *Financial Times,* November 8, 16.

213 The Association of MBAs, the UK's MBA accreditation agency.

214 Richard Olivier (2001), *Inspirational Leadership: Henry V and the Muse of Fire.* London: The Industrial Society, 5.

215 Ron Cacioppe (1998b), Leaders developing leaders: an effective way to enhance leadership development programs. *Leadership & Organization Development Journal,* 19 (4), 194–198.

216 Quoted by Sharon O'Shea (2000), The changing composition of leadership. *Financial Executive,* 16 (4), 35.

217 *The Sunday Times 100 Best Companies to Work For,* March 24, 2002.

218 Quoted by Larry Reynolds (2000), What is leadership? *Training Journal,* November, 24–27.

219 Carole K. Barnett and Noel M. Tichy (2000), How new leaders learn to take charge. *Organizational Dynamics,* 29 (1), 16–32.

220 Eli Cohen and Noel Tichy (1997), How leaders develop leaders. *Training and Development,* 51 (5), May, 58–63, 65–67, 69–73.

221 Charles J. Margerison and Andrew P. Kakabadse (1984), *How American Chief Executives Succeed,* AMA Survey Report. New York: American Management Association.

222 E. Cohen and N. Tichy (1997), How leaders develop leaders. *Training & Development,* May, 51 (5), 58–73.

223 Ron Cacioppe (1998b), Leaders developing leaders: an effective way to enhance leadership development programs. *Leadership & Organization Development Journal,* 19 (4), 194–198.

224 Paul Russell (1997), *The PepsiCo Leadership Center: How PepsiCo's Leaders Develop Leaders.* Conference Proceedings, The 2nd Annual Leadership Development Conference, Linkage, Inc., 97–138.

225 *Enhancing Leadership Performance: The Leader as Teacher,* The University of Chicago Graduate School of Business.

226 Noel Tichy (1997), *The Leadership Engine: How Winning Companies Create Leaders at all Levels.* Conference Proceedings, The 2nd Annual Leadership Development Conference, Linkage, Inc., 57–81.

227 Reginald W. Revans (1998), *ABC of Action Learning,* Third Edition. London: Lemos Crane.

228 James G. Clawson and Jonathan Doner (1996), Teaching leadership through aikido. *Journal of Management Education,* 20 (2), 182–205.

229 Harald S. Harung, Dennis P. Heaton and Charles N. Alexander (1995), A unified theory of leadership: experiences of higher states of consciousness in world-class leaders. *Leadership & Organization Development Journal,* 16 (7), 44–59.

230 Bernard M. Bass (1998), *Transformational Leadership: Industrial, Military, and Educational Impact.* Mahwah, NJ: Lawrence Erlbaum, 85–86, 99, 102–116, 171; John J. Sosik and Don I. Jung (2009), *Full Range Leadership Development: Pathways for People, Profit and Planet.* New York and London: Psychology Press.

231 Julian Barling, Tom Weber and E. Kevin Kelloway (1996), Effects of transformational leadership training on attitudinal and financial outcomes: a field experiment. *Journal of Applied Psychology,* 81 (6), 827–832.

232 Afroditi Dalakoura (2010), Examining the effects of leadership development on firm performance. *Journal of Leadership Studies*, 4 (1), 59–70.

233 Ed Kur and Richard Bunning (1996), A three-track process for executive leadership development. *Leadership & Organization Development Journal*, 17 (4), 4–12.

234 Stephen Topple (2000), *Leadership Programmes – A Sketch*. Paper presented at a Seminar on Leadership for the 21st Century, Cambridge University Local Industry Links, Wolfson College, Cambridge, 20 September.

235 Professional Manager (2002), Leadership – from the followers' perspective. *Professional Manager*, 11 (1), January, 2; IMC (2001), UK leaders fail to win hearts and minds (but they do if they try), http://www.inst-mgt.org.uk/press/hearts.htm, Institute of Management, 4 December 2001; Institute of Management (2001), *Leadership: The Challenge for All?* Report by DEMOS in association with the Council for Excellence in Management and Leadership.

236 A study in 1999 by Warren Bennis and Linkage, Inc., *Best Practices in Leadership Development*, reported in PIU (2001), *Strengthening Leadership in the Public Sector*. Research study by the Performance Improvement Unit, Cabinet Office, UK Government, www.cabinet-office.gov.uk/innovation/leadershipreport, 6.8.

237 Sabine Hotho and Martin Dowling (2010), Revisiting leadership development: the participant perspective. *Leadership & Organization Development Journal*, 31 (7), 609–629.

238 Richard S. Wellins and Patterson S. Weaver Jr (2003), From C-level to see-level leadership. *Training & Development*, September, 58–65.

239 Michael J. Burke and Russell R. Day (1986), A cumulative study of the effectiveness of management training. *Journal of Applied Psychology*, 71, 232–245.

240 Doris Collins and Elwood F. Holton III (2004), The effectiveness of managerial leadership development programs: a meta-analysis of studies from 1982 to 2001. *Human Resource Development Quarterly*, 15 (2), Summer, 217–248.

241 James Bentley and Sharon Turnbull (2005), *Stimulating Leaders: Developing Manufacturing Leadership Skills*. Birmingham: Manufacturing Foundation, 5.

242 J.A. Conger (1992), *Learning to Lead*. San Francisco, CA: Jossey-Bass.

243 C. McCauley, R. Moxley and E. Van Velsor (1998), *The Center for Creative Leadership's Handbook of Leadership Development*. San Francisco, CA: Jossey-Bass.

244 William A. Gentry and Jennifer W. Martineau (2010), Hierarchical linear modeling as an example for measuring change over time in a leadership development evaluation context. *Leadership Quarterly*, 21 (4), 645–656.

245 Doris Collins and Elwood F. Holton III (2004), The effectiveness of managerial leadership development programs: a meta-analysis of studies from 1982 to 2001. *Human Resource Development Quarterly*, 15 (2), Summer, 217–248.

246 Bruce J. Avolio, James B. Avery and David Quisenberry (2010), Estimating return on leadership development investment. *Leadership Quarterly*, 21 (4), 633–644.

247 Lawrena Colombo and John Verderse (2010), Growing tomorrow's leaders for the worlds of 2020. In Elaine Biech, Editor, *The ASTD Leadership Handbook*. Alexandria, VA: ASTD Press and San Francisco, CA: Berrett-Koehler, Chapter 30, 417–425.

248 This case study is an amended version of one published in *Management Consultancy: A Guide for Students* by David Biggs, Editor (2010), Andover: Cengage Learning EMEA, 102–108. All names have been changed to preserve anonymity.

Chapter 12

1 With acknowledgement to Charnchai Charuvastr, sometime President and CEO of Samart, Thailand, and Ian C. Buchanan, formerly Chairman, Asia Pacific, Booz & Co, management consultants, Sydney, Australia.
2 B.J. Cunningham (2002), Brand Leadership. Paper presented at a conference on 'The Successful Leader', Institute of Directors, London, 3 May.
3 Barry Gibbons (2003), in an interview with David Creelman, 'Thinking out loud with Barry Gibbons', www.HR.com
4 Dave Ulrich, Norm Smallwood and Jack Zenger (2000), Building your leadership brand. *Leader to Leader*, 15, Winter, 40–46.
5 Dave Ulrich, Norm Smallwood and Jack Zenger (2000), Building your leadership brand. *Leader to Leader*, 15, Winter, 40–46.
6 Dave Ulrich and Norm Smallwood (2000), Leadership brand in fundamental change. *Training Journal*, September, 16–18.
7 Dave Ulrich, Norm Smallwood and Jack Zenger (2000), Building your leadership brand. *Leader to Leader*, 15, Winter, 40–46
8 Bruce Pasternack, Thomas D. Williams and Paul F. Anderson (2001), Beyond the cult of the CEO: building institutional leadership. *Strategy and Business*, 1st quarter, 1–12.
9 Barry Gibbons (2003), in an interview with David Creelman, 'Thinking out loud with Barry Gibbons', www.HR.com
10 CCL (2009), *Developing a Leadership Strategy*. White Paper, Greensboro, NC: Center for Creative Leadership.
11 CCL (2009), *Developing a Leadership Strategy*. White Paper, Greensboro, NC: Center for Creative Leadership.
12 www.novartis.com/annualreport2009
13 Milton Moskowitz (2010), Clarity from Switzerland. *Strategy+Business*, 5 April.
14 Edinburgh International Festival 2003, *Festival 2003*, brochure, Edinburgh, UK.

Resources

Books

John Antonakis, Anna T. Cianciolo and Robert J. Sternberg, Editors (2004), *The Nature of Leadership*. Thousand Oaks, CA: SAGE Publications.

N.M. Ashkanasy, C. Wilderom and M.F. Peterson, Editors (2000), *Handbook of Organizational Culture and Climate*. Thousand Oaks, CA: SAGE Publications.

Alan Bryman, David Collinson, Keith Grint, Mary Uhl-Bien and Brad Jaclson (2011), *The SAGE Handbook of Leadership*. London: SAGE Publications.

Mary L. Connerley and Paul B. Pedersen (2005), *Leadership in a Diverse and Multicultural Environment: Developing Awareness, Knowledge, and Skills*. Thousand Oaks, CA: SAGE Publications.

Stanley A. Deetz, Sarah J. Tracy and Jennifer L. Simpson (2000), *Leading Organizations through Transition*. Thousand Oaks, CA: SAGE Publications.

Roger Gill (2006), *Theory and Practice of Leadership*. London: SAGE Publications.

Robert J. House, Paul J. Hanges, Mansour Javidan, Peter W. Dorfman and Vipin Gupta, Editors (2004), *Culture, Leadership, and Organizations: The GLOBE Study of 62 Societies*. Thousand Oaks, CA: SAGE Publications.

Peter G. Northouse (2010), *Leadership: Theory and Practice*, Fifth Edition. Thousand Oaks, CA: SAGE Publications.

Simon Western (2008), *Leadership: A Critical Text*. London: SAGE Publications.

Journals

Leadership Quarterly (USA)
www.elsevier.com/wps/product/cws_home/620221

Leadership (UK)
www.sagepub.co.uk/journal.aspx?pid=106128

Journal of Leadership and Organization Studies (USA)
https://www.baker.edu/departments/leadership/jls-main.cfm

Leadership and Organization Development Journal (UK)
www.emeraldinsight.com/lodj.htm

Business Leadership Review (UK)
(Association of MBAs)
www.mbaworld.com/blr

Leadership in Action (USA)
(Center for Creative Leadership)
www.ccl.org

Leadership Review (USA)
(Kravis Leadership Institute, Claremont McKenna College)
www.leadershipreview.org

Leader to Leader (USA)
(The Leader to Leader Foundation, formerly the Drucker Foundation)
http://leadertoleader.org

International Journal of Leadership Studies (USA)
(Regent University)
www.regent.edu/leadership/ijls

Leadership Advance Online (USA)
(Regent University)
www.regent.edu/acad/sls/publications/journals/leadershipadvance/home.htm

Leadership Excellence (USA)
(International Leadership Association)
www.ila-net.org

Wharton Leadership Digest (USA)
http://leadership.wharton.upenn.edu/digest/index.shtml

Leadership Centres and Websites

The Leadership Trust, UK: enquiries@leadership.org.uk; www.leadership.org.uk
Center for Creative Leadership, USA: www.ccl.org
Centre for Leadership Studies, UK, University of Exeter: www.centres.exeter.ac.uk/cls/
The International Leadership Association, USA: www.ila-net.org
The James MacGregor Burns Academy of Leadership, USA: http://www.academyo-fleadership.org/
Lancaster Leadership Centre, UK, Lancaster University Management School: www.lums.lancs.ac.uk/leadership
Wharton Center for Leadership and Change Management, USA:
http://leadership.wharton.upenn.edu/welcome/index.shtml
Network of Leadership Scholars, Academy of Management, USA: LDRNET-L@AOMLISTS.PACE.EDU

Index

Page references to Figures or Tables will be in *italics*